D1588894

R.J. Gibbs

NEW TOWNS OF THE MIDDLE AGES

Town Plantation in
England, Wales and Gascony

A.

Frontispiece.   A West Prospect of Conway Castle (1749), from an engraving by J. Boydell.

NEW TOWNS
OF THE
MIDDLE AGES

Town Plantation in
England, Wales and Gascony

MAURICE BERESFORD
Professor of Economic History in the University of Leeds

LONDON
LUTTERWORTH PRESS

First published, 1967

COPYRIGHT © 1967 MAURICE BERESFORD

Made and printed in Great Britain by
William Clowes and Sons, Limited, London and Beccles

Author's Preface

EVERY TOWN was once new, and the title of this book might seem an over-dramatic announcement of a general history of English towns. However, the words *New Town* are intended in a sense very near the familiar twentieth-century usage. In medieval Europe decisions were taken to plant towns where no settlement existed, and the results of such decisions form the subject-matter of this book. It considers the town planting activity of English kings and their subjects in England, and beyond England in Wales and south-west France.

Imperfections of documentation sometimes prevent the accurate dating of a town's foundation, and sometimes obscure the origins of a town sufficiently for it to be uncertain whether the town was preceded by a village. The three Gazetteers give full references to the documentation that has been employed in the search for New Towns, but if through ignorance some normal towns have been embraced, there is less damage than errors of demarcation normally bring, for the general economic circumstances which prompted new plantations were also those which prompted the far larger number of "organic" villages-turned-town. These ex-villages were like veteran Members of the House of Commons chosen for elevation to the Lords: but our concern here is with peers called suddenly into existence by their sovereign from virtually nowhere. Yet, when the benches are full of scarlet and ermine, and new coronets have acquired a look of familiarity and age, who—except historians—will recall the days when there was no Liverpool, no Portsmouth, no Salisbury and no Chelmsford?

v

TO

Rob, Clive, Roger, Bruce, Eric, Jeremy, Peter,
Ken, Barry, Philip, Hamish and Jim: bastidors
in the fields of England, Wales and Gascony,
1956–62

'Dark as the history of our villages may be,
the history of the boroughs is darker yet ... '
F. W. Maitland
Domesday Book and Beyond (1897), p. 172

Contents

Author's Acknowledgments

MY INTEREST in this subject was aroused, and I was seduced from agricultural history, by reading T. F. Tout's essay, *Medieval Town Planning*, while considering subjects for the anthology of air photographs which Dr. J. K. S. St. Joseph and I published in 1958. My first acknowledgments must be to these two scholars. Visits to the towns in England, Wales and Gascony were made possible by a grant from the Leverhulme Trustees, supplemented by others from the Departmental Research Funds of the University of Leeds. A grant from the University of Leeds Publications fund has assisted this book. Help in transport, mapping and photography is acknowledged in the dedication.

Particular assistance has been given by my colleague, Professor John Le Patourel, and by Dr. L. A. S. Butler, then of the Royal Commission on Historical Monuments, Wales; and by Mr. F. Noble of Knighton; Jean-Paul Trabut-Cussac has been a continual bridge with Gascony. I have also been able to draw on the knowledge of Mr. J. W. Cox, Mr. E. J. Cole, Mr. P. M. Gulland and Dr. R. E. Glasscock. Mrs. Betty Watt undertook the difficult typing of the Gazetteer, and many chapters were checked by Mr. J. E. Tozer; other checking has been done by Mr. Kenneth Gilbert. Professor H. P. R. Finberg has assisted with the proof-reading. The index is by Miss Joan Newiss, B.A., A.L.A. The errors that remain after this help and advice must, of course, be my responsibility.

The maps were drawn for me by Dr. R. E. Glasscock, Mr. M. J. Mortimore, Mr. Alan Palmer and a number of students of the Department of Geography, the University of Leeds. Acknowledgments for copyright material in Plates and Figures appear on p. x.

The University, Leeds. Summer, 1966.

Acknowledgments for Plates and Figures

Plate 1 is from P.R.O. SC11/660; plates 2 and 7 from photographs by C. L. D. Semple; plates 3 and 4 from air photographs which are the copyright of the Institut Géographique National, Paris; plate 6 is by Dr. J. K. S. St. Joseph, Air Ministry copyright; in plate 5, the Naish plan is British Museum copyright; plate 9 is by Ray Delvert, Villeneuve sur Lot, Lot et Garonne; plate 11 from a photograph by J. G. Watt; plate 12 from P.R.O. E179/242/53; plate 13 from E36/201 f. 3 by permission of the Controller of H.M. Stationery Office. Permission to reproduce is acknowledged with thanks. Plates 8 and 10 are from photographs by the author.

Figures, 1, 2, 5, 8, 10, 11–19, 22, 24–27, 31, 33, 35–36, 37, 40–41, 43–52 and 58, although specially drawn for this book, are based on Ordnance Survey maps, Crown copyright reserved. Figures 21, 34, and part of plate 5 are reproductions of portions of Ordnance Survey maps. Figures 23, 42, and 54–56 are based on air photographs which are the copyright of the Institut Géographique National, Paris. Figure 64 is from Eccles. 2/159292 m. 9d, by permission of the Controller of H.M. Stationery Office. Like transcripts and translations of material from the Public Record Office in the text of this book, this figure, with plates 12 and 13, are part of Crown copyright records.

List of Plates

xi

List of Illustrations in Text

List of Tables in Text

LIST OF TABLES IN TEXT

Abbreviations and Short Titles of Works Frequently Cited

ABBREVIATED TITLE	FULL TITLE
Albe	E. Albe, "Les Suites du Traité de Paris", *Annales du Midi*, xxiii (1911), pp. 472–491; and xxiv (1912), pp. 59–78; 218–231; and 396–410.
A.P.	A. M. E. Molinier, ed., *Correspondence Administrative d'Alphonse de Poitiers*, 2 vols. (1894–1900).
A.P.E.A.	P.-F. Fournier and P. Guébin, eds., *Enquêtes Administratives d'Alphonse de Poitiers, 1249–71* (1959).
A.P. Mission	Reference to air photographs in the national collection of the Institut Géographique: Photothèque, Avenue Pasteur, Saint-Mandé, Seine.
Arch. Camb.	*Archaeologia Cambrensis.*
Ballard	A. Ballard, *British Borough Charters, 1042–1216* (1913).
Ballard and Tait	A. Ballard and J. Tait, *British Borough Charters, 1216–1307* (1923).
Beresford and St. Joseph	M. W. Beresford and J. K. S. St. Joseph, *Medieval England: an aerial survey* (1958).
B.I.H.R.	*Bulletin of the Institute of Historical Research.*
Bull. B.C.S.	*Bulletin of the Board of Celtic Studies.*
C. (in Gascon Gazetteer headings)	Sheet and quarter-sheet reference on the *Carte de l'État Majeure*, scale 1:50,000.
C. (elsewhere)	Public Record Office, Chancery.
Cal. Chart. Rolls	*Calendar of Charter Rolls.*
Cal. Close Rolls	*Calendar of Close Rolls.*
Cal. Inq. Misc.	*Calendar of Inquisitions, Miscellaneous.*
Cal. I.P.M.	*Calendar of Inquisitions Post Mortem.*
Cal. Lib. Rolls	*Calendar of Liberate Rolls.*
Cal. Pat. Rolls	*Calendar of Patent Rolls.*
Cal. Welsh Rolls	*Calendar of Welsh Rolls.*

ABBREVIATED TITLE	FULL TITLE
Chaplais	P. Chaplais, ed., *The War of St. Sardos* (Camden Soc., 3rd ser., lxxxvii (1954)).
Clark, Cartae	G. T. Clark, *Cartae et Alia Munimenta*, 4 vols. (1885).
Cym. Rec. Ser.	*Cymmrodorion Record Series.*
Deffontaines	P. Deffontaines, *Les hommes et leurs travaux dans le pays de la Moyenne Garonne* (1932).
D.L.	Public Record Office, Duchy of Lancaster.
Dugdale Monasticon	Sir William Dugdale, *Monasticon Anglicanum*, 8 vols., ed. J. Caley, H. Ellis, and B. Bandinel (1817–30).
E.	Public Record Office, Exchequer.
Eccles.	Ecclesiastical Commission Records, formerly at Public Record Office.
Econ. Hist. Rev.	*Economic History Review.*
E.H.R.	*English Historical Review.*
E.Y.C.	*Early Yorkshire Charters*, i–iii (ed. W. Farrar, 1914–16), iv–xi (ed. C. T. Clay, 1935–63).
Ekwall	Eilert Ekwall, *The Concise Oxford Dictionary of English Place-Names* (4th ed., 1960).
Eyton	R. W. Eyton, *Antiquities of Shropshire*, 12 vols. (1854–60).
F.A.	*Feudal Aids and Assessments, 1284–1431*, 6 vols. (1899–1921).
G.C.	G. P. Cuttino, ed., *The Gascon Calendar of 1322* (Camden Soc., 3rd ser., lxx (1949)). References are normally to the document number.
Gouron	M. Gouron, *Les Chartes de Franchises de Guienne et Gascogne* (1935). References are normally to the document number.
G.R.	Grid Reference, six or eight figures, on the Carte Nationale, France; National Grid reference, six figures, Ordnance Survey.
Hist. King's Works	R. A. Brown, H. M. Colvin, and A. J. Taylor, *The History of the King's Works*, 2 vols. (1963).
J.I.	Public Record Office, Itinerant Justices.
J.R.I.C.	*Journal of the Royal Institution of Cornwall.*
K.B.	Public Record Office, King's (Queen's) Bench.
Lavedan	P. Lavedan, *L'histoire de l'Urbanisme*, 2 vols. (1926).

ABBREVIATED TITLE	FULL TITLE
Lloyd	Sir J. E. Lloyd, *A History of Wales*, 2 vols. (1911).
Lodge	E. C. Lodge, *Gascony under English Rule* (1926).
M.	Sheet reference to the Carte Michelin, scale, 1:200,000.
Mont. Coll.	*Montgomeryshire Historical Collections* (Powysland Club).
M.P. (also M.R.)	Public Record Office, Maps.
N.C.H.	*A History of Northumberland.* 14 vols. (1893–1940).
O.S.	Ordnance Survey.
Plac. Abb.	*Placitorum Abbreviatio*, ed. G. Rose and W. Illingworth (1811).
P.N.	English Place-Name Society, *The Place-Names of . . .*, followed by county name.
P.R.O.	Public Record Office, London.
P.R.S.	*Pipe Roll Society Publications.*
R.C.H.M.	Royal Commission on Historical and Ancient Monuments, England, county *Inventories*.
R.C.H.M.W.	Royal Commission on Historical Monuments, Wales, county *Inventories*.
Regesta	*Regesta Regum Anglo-Normannorum*, i (ed. H. W. C. Davies, 1913); ii (ed. C. Johnson and H. A. Cronne, 1956).
R.F.	C. Bémont, ed., *Recogniciones Feodorum in Aquitania* (1914). References are normally to the document number.
R.G.	*Rôles Gascons*. i–iii (ed. C. Bémont, 1896–1906); iv, ed. Y. Renouard (1962). References are normally to the document number.
R.H.	*Rotuli Hundredorum*, 2 vols., ed. W. Illingworth and J. Caley (1812–18).
Rot. Chart.	*Rotuli Chartarum*, ed. T. D. Hardy (1837).
Rot. Lit. Claus.	*Rotuli Litterarum Clausarum*, ed. T. D. Hardy, 2 vols. (1833–44).
Rot. Parl.	*Rotuli Parliamentorum*, ed. J. Strachey, J. Pridden, and E. Upham, 6 vols. (1832).

ABBREVIATED TITLE	FULL TITLE
S.A.C.	Sussex Archaeological Collections.
S.C.	Public Record Office: SC 6, Minister's Accounts; SC 8, Ancient Petitions; SC 11–12, Rentals and Surveys.
S.P.	Public Record Office, State Papers.
Testut	L. Testut, La Bastide de Beaumont en Périgord, 1272–1789, 2 vols. (1920).
T.L.A.S.	Transactions of the Leicestershire Archaeological Society.
Tout	T. F. Tout, "Medieval Town Planning", Bulletin of the John Rylands Library, iv (1917–18), pp. 26–58.
V.C.H.	Victoria History of the County of . . .
Vigié	A. Vigié, "Les bastides du Périgord et les rôles gascons", Bull. Soc. Hist. et Arch. du Périgord, xlvii (1920), pp. 143–154.
Weinbaum	M. Weinbaum, British Borough Charters, 1307–1660 (1943).
Y.A.J.	Yorkshire Archaeological Journal.
Y.A.S.R.S.	Yorkshire Archaeological Society Record Series.
Y.I.	Yorkshire Inquisitions (Y.A.S.R.S., vols. xii, xxiii, xxxi, xxxvii (1892–1906)).

INTRODUCTION

In these two chapters the main subject-matter of the book is introduced by taking three men who were brought together in a unique Parliamentary meeting at Harwich in 1297: a king of England and two merchants. One merchant was associated with the building of New Winchelsea, the other with the planted towns (or bastides) of Edward I's territory in south-western France. The king himself, the convenor of the little Parliament of town-planners, is seen as an active founder of new towns in England, Wales and Gascony.

CHAPTER ONE

An Assembly of Notables

Now men are drawn together upon sundry causes and occasions thereunto them moving, some by Authority, some by Force, some by Pleasure, and some by Profit that proceedeth of it."

> G. Botero, *Of the Greatness of Cities,*
> trans. R. Peterson (1606), p. 1.

I

WE begin near the end of the story, at Harwich in January 1297, and with three notables, Edward I of England; Sir Henry le Waleys of London and Bordeaux; and Thomas Alard of New Winchelsea. The king summoned le Waleys, Alard and other prominent townsmen of England to a *colloquium,* a conference to advise him on a subject which is the theme of this book: how best to lay out the streets, buildings and defences of a newly-created medieval town, and how best to devise its form of government. All three notables, the king and the two merchants, were well versed in these problems, and the colloquium came late in their careers as town-planners, and—indeed—late in the history of medieval town plantation. Yet it was a unique occasion. Representatives of towns had been called to confer with Edward I on particular matters, such as the new duty on wool in 1275, but never before and never afterwards did a king issue a summons for a Parliament on the single issue of town plantation.

During the autumn Parliament of 1296, held at Bury St. Edmunds, there had been a tentative move to gather advisors when twenty-four English towns were ordered

> to elect men from among your wisest and ablest who know best how to devise, order and array a new town to the greatest profit of Ourselves and of merchants.[1]

These men were separate from the representatives of boroughs in the

[1] F. Palgrave, ed., *Parliamentary Writs,* i (1827), p. 48.

Commons.[2] The Bury Parliament was stormy, and there is no record of what business the "wisest and ablest" were able to do. Just after the end of this Parliament a fresh set of letters was sent out by the king, and this time not to selected towns but to selected men, called by name from London and twenty other English towns: among them were Alard and le Waleys. The group was ordered to come to the king, wherever he happened to be, and the agendum was more specific than for the Bury meeting: it was to set out a new town at Berwick on Tweed, lately burned and damaged in the war with Scotland.[3]

The colloquium met at Harwich, and a smaller working-party was then assigned the task of going north and executing the project.[4] Its course was far from smooth: the expert from Stamford had to be excused attendance at the last minute, and the men from Lincoln and Grantham had to be replaced by others, only to find that the Grantham substitute was deaf and ineligible.[5] No details of the discussion have survived, but in 1302 Edward issued a charter of liberties to the new community on the border.

A new lay-out, fortifications and constitution for Berwick were necessary in 1297 because of the events of the previous year. In March 1296 Edward had stormed and sacked old Berwick and in April the king of Scotland had surrendered there. In August among the ruins, Edward, back from Scone with the coronation stone, held a great Parliament to receive homage and oaths of loyalty from the Estates of Scotland. It now remained to rebuild Berwick in the image of those towns which Edward had planted along the coast of north Wales earlier in the reign after his conquest of Wales. Like Flint, Conway, Carnarvon and the others, the new Berwick was to serve the needs of peace and war. It was to be a border garrison designed to keep the peace but it was also to rise as a port and market-town. As in north Wales, the conqueror hoped that the conquered would come to accept his rule by appreciating the opportunity afforded them in the market place where they could dispose of their agricultural produce and buy what the ships brought in from outside; at the same time he hoped that a smoothly organised market would ease the problem of supplies for feeding and clothing the garrison.

[2] R. R. Sharpe, ed., *Cal. of Letter Books . . . of the City of London: Letter Book 'C'* (1901), p. 25.
[3] Palgrave, *op. cit.*, p. 49.
[4] *Ibid.*, p. 51.
[5] *Ibid.*, p. 52.

There is no rental of new Berwick from the years of its refoundation, so that the lay-out of houses cannot be known as Edward's new Winchelsea can be known. There is only the evidence of the street-plan and the remains of the castle and walls. Originally the castle and town were linked by one set of walls. This unity of town and castle can still be seen at Carnarvon and Conway. At Berwick the railway has destroyed a good deal of the castle, and much of Edward I's town-walls had been absorbed earlier into the elaborate Tudor refortifications. These defences enclosed an area smaller than Edward's new Berwick, so that some lengths of the old walls, with a tower, stand high and dry on the golf-course; while the smaller circuit of Tudor walls has caused some of the medieval streets in the western quarter of the town to be amputated, leaving streets of full width that end abruptly at the wall-face.[6]

II

The members of the Harwich colloquium came from twenty different English towns and cities. Most of these towns were not plantations by origin, but had developed organically from villages or were on the site of former Roman towns. Two of the twenty towns were plantations, although one of them—Newcastle on Tyne—was more than 200 years old and, despite its name, the circumstances of its birth were probably not well known. The other, New Winchelsea, was a very recent plantation in which the king had shown personal interest, and Thomas Alard was its leading merchant.

By 1297 there were more than 120 planted towns in existence in England, some large and some small, and they were not ignored when the king needed counsel.[7] Nine of them were among the 114 towns that sent Members to the full Parliament of 1295, and ten of these plantations were represented in the full Parliament of 1297. For the colloquium the king wished to draw on the experience of all types of town, seeking to build at Berwick not a novel form of town but one which imitated the best and most successful towns in the kingdom, no matter what their origin. The king sought to draw on the experience of townsmen from places like Northampton, Lincoln, Stamford, Bristol, Leicester, Southampton and Yarmouth. There were four Londoners, one of them le Waleys; two men from the old Saxon

[6] *Hist. King's Works*, ii, pp. 563–571. For full title of this and other works frequently cited in short form in the foot-notes and Gazetteer, see pp. xvii-xx.
[7] M. McKisack, *The Parliamentary Representation of English Boroughs during the Middle Ages* (1932), pp. 1–23.

5

capital, Winchester; and three from the northern capital, York. They were men from well-established towns, and as men of business they might be expected to have plenty of experience of what was needed to make a town almost anew, and to make it (in the king's words) "to the greatest profit of Ourselves and of merchants".

Two of the notables, however, could claim a more direct experience of town plantation, although only one of them was actually living in a newly-planted town. These were Henry le Waleys and Thomas Alard, and for that reason they were set at the beginning of this chapter. Alard was a leading citizen of a town, New Winchelsea, which had been planted in Edward I's lifetime. Its streets and houses and its parish church were less than ten years old and its walls and gates were still unfinished when Thomas Alard left them to join the king and others at Harwich. As a later chapter will show, New Winchelsea has the best documented and the best preserved plan of all the medieval plantations on this side of the Channel, and it is possible to show exactly where Alard and other members of his family took up their building plots in the new town. Thomas Alard, since his story takes us to Winchelsea and to the details of a characteristic town plan, leads straight to an important part of the subject.

Sir Henry le Waleys personifies another important aspect of the subject: the plantation of towns by the English and by English kings in the territories outside England. In 1297 le Waleys was the most distinguished member of the largest mercantile community in the kingdom.[8] For many years he had been an alderman of the City of London; in 1273–74, 1281–84 and 1298–99 he was Lord Mayor. He was a trusted administrator and diplomat in Edward's service: in 1274 he had been one of the representatives of the City of London called to met Edward in Paris on the eve of his return to England to be crowned. He was experienced in the proper equipment of a city. In 1274 as Mayor he had greeted Edward I's return by sweeping away the victuallers' stalls that cluttered Cheap. In his next mayoralty (1281–84) he built a new victuals market, a new prison, a conduit, and a new weighbridge for corn, and designed a new housing project near St. Paul's. In the environment of a very old town he displayed the mentality of a planner of new towns, and in 1281 he had been one of those commissioned to work on the planning of New Winchelsea.

[8] *Dict. Nat. Biog.*, lix (1899), pp. 35–37; G. A. Williams, *Medieval London* (1963), pp. 333–335.

When Edward's summons to the town planning Parliament of 1297 reached him, le Waleys was freshly returned from a mission to Gascony on the king's behalf. He was equally at home there, for his private fortune had been made in the wine trade, the great economic link between England and its remaining possessions in France. He, if anyone, would be able to recommend how new Berwick could be made "of profit to merchants" living there or coming there to trade. Indeed, he backed his judgement by taking up building plots; he erected houses for himself in the new town and had a private quay.

The towns planted in England and by English kings in Gascony will often be described and discussed together in the chapters that follow: the subject gains if the two aspects, French and English, are considered comparatively. This community of interest is personified by le Waleys, moving with equal familiarity in the streets of London or Bordeaux, for he had the unique distinction of having been Mayor of Bordeaux in 1275, the year after being Lord Mayor of London. Bordeaux, like London, was no new town, but the Gascon countryside to the east and south, along the Dordogne and Garonne, proved in le Waleys' lifetime to be the most fertile soil in Europe for the plantation of new towns, only surpassed by the gargantuan German colonisation in the newly cultivated lands of the eastern frontiers.

Between 1263 and 1297 more than seventy new towns had been planted in that part of south-west France which owed allegiance to Henry III of England and his son Edward. Across the local frontiers—sometimes contested—even more new towns were planted in the same period in that part of the south-west which called itself French. It was in the market places of these Gascon towns that the wine of the countryside was collected for the first stages of its long journey to customers in England and north-west Europe. Down the Lot, the Garonne, the Dordogne and their smaller tributaries went the river-barges bringing the wines to the ships which awaited them at the great riverside quay at Bordeaux. It was in this trade that le Waleys shared, and it was this trade which made a wine merchant equally at home in Bordeaux or London. By coincidence, his own birthplace was Striguil (Chepstow), itself a Norman plantation on the Welsh border.

III

The king himself, taking counsel at Harwich in 1297, was no amateur in the business of town plantation. His full achievements in England,

Wales and Gascony will be set out in subsequent chapters, but the principal themes can be anticipated here by considering some of the other occasions when he, Thomas Alard and Henry le Waleys had been involved together as *bastidors*, the builders of new towns.[9] Within a morning's ride of Bordeaux, le Waleys could reach six Gascon towns that were newly planted. Within a day's ride were another dozen. In the woods a few miles from the south-west gate of Bordeaux was the town of Camparian, a site which has now gone back again to woodland but where Edward I stayed two nights in June 1287. Nearby was the town of Baa, named after Edward's chancellor, Robert Burnell, bishop of Bath (a Latin form of which was *Ba*'). Along the banks of the Gironde estuary, passed by the wine-ships on their way from Bordeaux to the open sea, were the towns of Cussac and Burgus Reginae, the latter named after an English queen. In the triangle of country between the Garonne and the Dordogne the nearest plantation to Bordeaux was Sauveterre de Guienne, a town whose foundation in 1281 involved Edward in a swirl of petitions and litigation sponsored by those older towns who thought there was no room for another newcomer. In 1316 Edward I's son, Edward II, was to assist in the foundation of another town nearby: Créon, sometimes called in the documents *bastida inter dua maria*, the "two seas" being the Dordogne and the Garonne.

The Gascon word *bastide* was the usual term for the planted town in south-western France, and in its Latin form *bastida* occurs in almost every foundation charter. Sometimes, as at La Bastide d'Armagnac and La Bastide Chalosse, the term was used in naming the new town. In England the word was not employed and there was no equivalent which had such universal use. *Novus burgus* and *nova villa* are fairly commonly found in foundation charters and contemporary documents; Newton and Newtown recur as town names: but there was no single English word which was the equivalent of *bastide* or *novus burgus*. "Bastide" will be employed with reference to foundations in France, and "new town" or "planted town" for foundations in England and Wales.

The word *bastide* derived originally from a southern form of a verb meaning "to build", the same word which in modern French has

---

[9] For documentary and bibliographical references to places mentioned in the text without foot-notes see the entries (under counties and Departments) in the English, Welsh and Gascon gazetteers, Chapters 15–17. The main facts about Edward I derive from *Dict. Nat. Biog.*, xvii (1889), pp. 14–38, and J.-P. Trabut-Cussac, *B.I.H.R.*, xxv (1952), pp. 160–203.

become *bâtir*. The new towns were constructions: agglomerations of man-made features such as houses, streets, shops, market places, churches, gates and walls. These constructions and the characteristic shape which they possessed in a bastide will be described in the chapters which follow. The historical interest of these constructions, however, is much wider than the interest of well-fashioned buildings and calculated town-plans, for the constructions had a social and economic purpose which will have to be examined.

It will be shown that the economic benefits resulting from the creation of a bastide were enjoyed by more than one man or a small group: but—with qualifications—the territorial lord on whose land the town had been planted would normally expect an increase in revenue. It was in this connection that le Waleys became involved in the history of town plantation in Gascony and it may have been this experience on which Edward wished to draw when he summoned him to the conference of 1297. Le Waleys' knowledge of bastides in general could have arisen naturally from the central position of Bordeaux and from the important role that the new towns played in the wine trade: but his knowledge of bastides in particular arose from his own private investments.

It was often convenient for the territorial lord of a medieval town to farm out the collection of rents, taxes and tolls to someone who would undertake the detailed effort of collection. The farmer of the revenues paid the lord a fixed sum negotiated in advance and recouped himself by what he could raise from the townspeople above this amount. For a king there was the convenience of a fixed and certain revenue with none of the troubles of collection. For a merchant the farm of the revenue could be a profitable investment, and it was by this route that le Waleys became involved with the revenues of royal bastides in Gascony.

In July 1284 Edward I was at Carnarvon in North Wales busy about the work of planning the castle and the new town which was being built there. Among the letters and grants which issued from the royal secretariat that month was one appointing le Waleys as farmer of the revenues of six Gascon bastides in return for an annual payment of £170 sterling for the next ten years.[10] The six towns were Beaulieu, Beaumont du Perigord, Fonroque, La Bastide Villefranche (Monestier), Lalinde and Molières. Lalinde had been founded in 1267 and Beau-

---

[10] *R.G.*, ii, pp. 225–226.

mont du Périgord was the first Gascon bastide of Edward I's reign, chartered in 1272. La Bastide Villefranche, Fonroque and Beaulieu had only just been founded and Molières may not yet have been completed in 1284.

The six were unequal in size, population and value and they occupied very different geographical situations. Lalinde was on the Dordogne alongside an important weir and bridge while the others were up in the hills to the south and west. Only Lalinde and Beaumont still preserve any vigorous commercial life; Molières is badly decayed and the site of Villefranche is little more than a hamlet; the site of Beaulieu has left no visible trace.

The five bastides where remains are to be seen have each their own variation on the theme of rectangularity, a characteristic alinement of streets and building plots which will be described in later chapters. In a slightly modified form it had been imposed on Carnarvon and Conway by Edward I, while at Flint the whole town plan might well be that of some bastide on the Dordogne or Garonne instead of by the sands of Dee. The plan of the rebuilt Berwick discussed at the conferences of 1297 has some rectangular features but the town is far from geometrical in design. It is possible that more of old Berwick survived the siege of 1296 than the chroniclers' descriptions would allow, and the town of 1297 may not have been built *de novo*.

The most rectilinear of the English towns with which Edward I had been concerned was Winchelsea, an even more thorough excursion into the geometrical than Flint. Had Thomas Alard ever seen le Waleys discuss revenues from Beaumont du Périgord and sketch out its shape with a finger on the table-top, he could well have mistaken it for his own native town of Winchelsea.

The foundation of Beaumont du Périgord in November 1272 dates from the first month of Edward I's reign, but the king cannot be credited with any personal part in its foundation since he had not yet arrived back in France from the Near East: the work was directed by his seneschal, Luke de Thenney. It was to de Thenney that in 1274 Edward gave full powers "to erect towns or bastides in the king's name" wherever in Gascony the seneschal saw fit; but when Edward later returned to Gascony he took part personally in the foundation of other Gascon towns and in the course of his journeys stayed at some of them. Documents survive from his visits to Libourne, Villeréal, and Ste. Foy la Grande.

Only a year before the capture of Berwick he had founded Beaumaris in Anglesey, the last of a succession of new towns along the coast of north Wales. Two years before Beaumaris he had been personally concerned with the extension of the Humber port of Wyke and its transformation into the town of Kingston upon Hull. Before his accession in 1272 he had fought in Gascony and had administered the country on his father's behalf; with his mother he had joined in founding bastides there; and after the news of his father's death reached him on crusade he had paused and spent nearly two busy years on the affairs of Gascony before coming home leisurely to be crowned.

IV

Edward I, *rex et bastidor*, is sometimes said to have learned the art of town plantation during his journeys overseas, from the sight of Mediterranean and near-eastern cities visited while on crusade, and from his part in the foundation of Gascon bastides. The close relation between towns planted in Britain and Gascony is emphasised in subsequent chapters of this book, but it is important to realise that town plantation was not an alien idea introduced into England in the intellectual baggage-train of a king back from crusade or of Edward's kinsmen from Savoy, Castile and Provence. English kings had been bastidors before the word bastide was known in England, and our beginning, the town-planning conferences of 1296–97, comes very near the end of a long royal tradition of town plantation.

The tradition of English town plantation was in fact almost as old as the English themselves. This book is mainly concerned with the towns which were founded after 1066, but, as Chapter 11 will show, there is a good deal of indirect evidence to suggest that several of the towns already well established in 1066 had their streets laid out in the deliberate drawingboard manner of a Winchelsea or a Lalinde, and had been in their day the New Towns of the Anglo-Saxons. Even if Edward had not learned from seeing these towns as he moved around his kingdom, he would have been familiar with such Norman plantations as New Windsor, Ludlow and Richmond (Yorks). From Henry III he could have learned how Henry's father, King John, had founded Liverpool or how his uncle, Richard I, had founded Portsmouth on the Solent and Petit Andelys on the Seine under the walls of Château Gaillard: and at Harwich, had he made enquiries, he could have learned that the very town where the town-planners met in 1297 was itself a plantation of his father's reign.

Soon after the committee of experts had moved up to Berwick the king went to a town where the rectilinearity of streets and house plots bore witness to another plantation of his father's reign: in February 1297 Edward moved from East Anglia over to Salisbury, there to meet a full Parliament. The new cathedral of the bishop's new city had been completed and consecrated in Edward's life-time, and there would have been citizens to cheer him in the streets who remembered when it was first founded. From Old Sarum, by the pillaged ruins of the Norman cathedral, the king could have looked down to the new city in the meadows and wondered at the audacious transplantation.

Bury St. Edmund's, where the autumn Parliament of 1296 had been held and where the first abortive colloquium had gathered, was yet another town whose parallel streets crossed other streets at right angles. Domesday Book itself describes the occasion of their building and reckoned 342 houses planted over the corn fields in the twenty years since the Norman Conquest.

Bury, with its shrine of the martyr king, Edmund, was a town that Edward I always held in great affection. While on crusade in 1271 he vowed to make a pilgrimage to the shrine of St. Edmund, should he be spared to return home. Two years were to pass between his father's death and Edward's arrival in England, but in the spring following the coronation he took Queen Eleanor with him on solemn pilgrimage to Bury.

Eleanor of Castile had been in Gascony during 1254–55, and had assisted in founding bastides: one Gascon town, *Burgus Reginae*, was named in her honour (1287–88). She had also been with Edward in Gascony in the period between his accession and his coronation. She was not with her husband at Bury in 1296, for she had died in 1290, but Bury and his dead queen were closely associated in Edward's mind, and in 1292 he took his son and daughters to celebrate the feast of St. Edmund at Bury.

Even the funeral journey of the queen's cortège in 1290 leads us back to planted towns. The mourning king ordered stone crosses to be erected in the villages and towns where the coffin had rested overnight on its journey from Lincolnshire to Westminster. Two of the Eleanor crosses were set up in New Towns: one night the cortège rested at

Stony Stratford on the Watling Street; and the next evening at Dunstable.

There was hardly a main road radiating from London where a traveller in the late thirteenth century did not pass through at least one planted town before he had gone 50 miles from the capital. From Chelmsford through Royston, Baldock, Dunstable, Wokingham, Maidenhead and Reigate they ringed London. It is their proliferation in the provinces that gives economic significance to the New Towns of the medieval period, and they were as well known to those who followed the merchant profession of Thomas Alard and Henry le Waleys as to itinerant kings and their courts. Three of Edward's plantations, two Welsh and one Gascon—Carnarvon, Conway and Libourne—were well enough known to appear among the towns on the famous Hereford world map of c. 1290.

Being so numerous, it is not surprising that planted towns figured among the places where kings assembled armies—Liverpool and Portsmouth; where their notables assembled for Parliaments—Bury St. Edmunds and Salisbury; and where the muffled tread of Queen Eleanor's cortège was heard at Stony Stratford and Dunstable.

CHAPTER TWO

An Array of Towns

"I am far from thinking that any one history should be told of
all our boroughs."

> F. W. Maitland, *Township and Borough*
> (1898), p. 36.

THE duties of Edward I's twenty-four town-planners were
described in his writ by three verbs: they were to devise, order
and array a new town. The devising would select and procure
the site; the ordering would organise the recruitment of townsmen
and furnish them with privileges and legal security; the arraying would
give the new town the physical accoutrements appropriate for its role.
The final purpose, as expressed in the same writ, was "the greatest
profit of Ourselves and merchants".

Four later chapters of this book will be devoted to a general account
of the methods employed in the foundation of towns and of the profits
that were expected to accrue. The whole period between the Norman
Conquest and the early seventeenth century will be considered, and
evidence will be taken from England, Wales and Gascony. In advance
of these generalities and their necessarily wide sweep of time, this
second chapter of the Introduction confines itself to a few specific acts of
town plantation that were associated with one or other of the three
notables, Edward I, Thomas Alard and Henry le Waleys.

I

Edward I and Thomas Alard: New Winchelsea

Edward I and Thomas Alard were concerned together about the
affairs of Old and New Winchelsea on several occasions, and in two
royal commissions to order the business of the new town the name of le
Waleys also appears. Old Winchelsea was a flourishing Channel port
and valuable enough for Henry III to have taken possession of it in 1247
by a compulsory exchange with its owner, the Norman abbey of

14

Fécamp. The town was held for a time by the rebellious barons in 1266, and Edward had then besieged and punished the town. When he next visited the town, a decade later, it was for the purpose of defending the town, this time against the violence of the waves and the fickleness of the currents.[1]

The whole Sussex coast was suffering, but the length from Hastings to the estuary of the Brede in particular. There were heavy losses of houses in Old Winchelsea in 1250 and 1252, and in 1262 the sea reached the market place. In 1271 Henry III gave land to endow a fund for repair of the quay on the south side of the churchyard, and in that year a great deal of the parish church fell. Money was spent on sea walls in 1273, and in the year of Edward I's visit of inspection 5,000 square feet of land were given to the townsmen for a new quay and further sea defences.[2]

Edward I's plan for the salvation of the town was more radical, being nothing less than the removal of the town to a new site. This plan, this devising, was too radical for the burgesses, who displayed the same optimism as King Canute's courtiers in their attitude to the rising waters. It was in the king's interests that a Cinque Port should not be lost, and as lord of the town he did not wish to see its revenues washed away with the quays. From 1272 to 1273 the tolls of the port fell from £87 to £33, never to recover, and the surviving lists of duties paid week-by-week[3] carry the story of the decline through to 1275. The storms that drove away the rearguard of townsmen into consent were those of February 1287, when the river Rother was forced into a new course and the town of Broomhill, lying between Winchelsea and Rye, was completely drowned.

The site that Edward chose for New Winchelsea was very similar to that of nearby Rye. It was a hill-top site, high enough never to be submerged unless Noah's flood should come again. The Brede flowed past the cliffs on the east of the site, and on the Strand, a narrow shelf between the Brede and the north cliff, there was room for a harbour, a quay and warehouses. The king obtained the site by exchanging lands with the owners, the lord and lady of Iham.

The dominant form that gives order and pattern to the arraying of

---

[1] Except where indicated, this section is based on W. D. Cooper, *The History of Winchelsea* (1850), with Stephens's plan of 1763 as its frontispiece; and on *V.C.H. Sussex*, ix, pp. 62–75.
[2] *Cal. Chart. Rolls*, ii, p. 177; *Cal. Close Rolls, 1272–9*, p. 50; *Cal. Pat. Rolls, 1272–81*, p. 151.
[3] *Cal. Pat. Rolls, 1247–58*, p. 39; *Cal. Fine Rolls, 1272–1300*, pp. 79, 97, 161, 183 and 200; E372/123 m. 21; SC6/1031/19–21. Cp. SC6/1031/26 and E352/98 m. 32d.

New Winchelsea is the rectangle. The *placeae*, the plots for houses and gardens, are rectangular; the streets intersect at right angles and divide the hill-top into rectangles called *Insulae* (Islands): within these Islands lay the Plots (Fig. 1). The whole array of the town, covering the hill-top, being a sum of rectangles, was itself as nearly a rectangle as Nature would allow. The straight line is not commonly found in natural features on the surface of the English countryside, and the hill-top of Iham was neither perfectly level nor bounded by straight edges. On the outer edges of the outer Islands, therefore, there were irregularly shaped spaces that sometimes gave room for a house and sometimes for a piece of grazing ground. The cliff sides themselves were too steep on the north to afford any utility, but on the east, south and west the sloping grounds had grazing value: they appear as *subpendentes montis* in the rental of the town.

After the decay of New Winchelsea, but long before the inquisitiveness of modern historians and geographers, the rectilinear street-pattern impressed strangers. The author of a report to the Privy Council in 1570 described the decayed haven, and then wrote of the town:[4]

> the most excellent proporcion thereof: being devyded in to xxxix quarters the most part square, with streats very large and broad, all strayght as the same wear layd with a line.

There is no specific evidence for the use of a line to lay out the hill-top at New Winchelsea but rope was certainly bought for this purpose by Edward I's officials elsewhere. The frequency of the rectangle is easily explicable by its practicability. It was the simplest way of drawing the main lines of the town—its streets—and then dividing and subdividing into the smallest units, the building plots. It made the calculation of areas simple, and the first rental of New Winchelsea, made in 1292, has an orderliness that transmits to parchment something of the marshalled order of the new houses and streets on the hill-top. The rental (illustrated in Plate I) divides the town first by its east–west streets, which it numbers off in military fashion, *Prima Strata, Secunda Strata, Tertia Strata*, like the streets of New York. The rectangles bounded by the street it numbers off as Quarters, *Quarteria*, making the thirty-nine that the survey of 1570 noted, and the same thirty-nine that appear in Charles Stephen's *Map of the Ancient Town of Winchelsea*, drawn in 1763. Within the Quarters the tenants are

4 SP12/75/70.

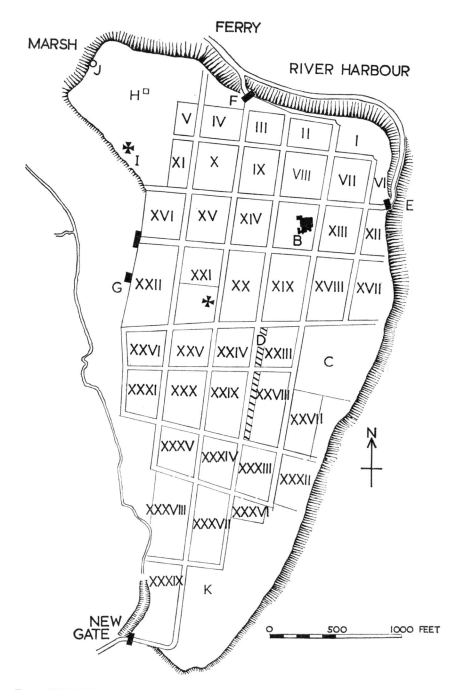

FIG. 1. NEW WINCHELSEA, Sussex. Chequers (*insulæ*) numbered in the rental of 1292. For Chequer VIII and key to letters *A–F* see Fig. 2 and p. 19.   *G*: pre-existing house in Iham; *H*: windmill; *I*: St Leonard's church, Iham; *J*: wells; *K*: King's Green.

named, and each plot has its area stated in *virgae* (rods, poles or perches), 160 *virgae* making an acre. The rent paid is the final item in the line. At the end of each Quarter the area and the rents are summed.[5]

The name of Thomas Alard appears in three different Quarters of the rental as well as at the Strand Quay, and the name Alard many times. The Alard family were among the patricians of Old Winchelsea and their family tombs were moved from old St. Thomas's up to the new church. Brothers, uncles, sons and nephews of Thomas Alard took up building plots, and the repetition of some Alard names in the southern Quarters, away from the fashionable and commercial Quarters, suggests that they took up land as an investment as well as for occupation.

Thomas Alard's own house lay in Quarter Eight, between Second Street and the church. Other Alards will also be seen in the rental for this Quarter, which (in translation) is as follows:

SECOND STREET

In the Eighth Quarter

	virgae	*rent due*
Henry Yve	$12\frac{1}{2}$	$3\frac{1}{4}$d.
Petronilla Clobbere	$12\frac{1}{2}$	3d.
Alice widow of Robert Gerveys	$12\frac{1}{2}$	$3\frac{1}{4}$d.
Nicholas Alard	10	$2\frac{1}{2}$d.
Gervase Alard junior	45	$11\frac{1}{4}$d.
Nicholas Alard	51	$12\frac{3}{4}$d.
Reginald Alard senior	74	$18\frac{1}{2}$d.
Gervase Alard senior	$66\frac{1}{2}$	$16\frac{1}{2}$d.
Thomas Alard	$47\frac{1}{2}$	12d.
William Seman	20	5d.
William Mot of Hastings	$12\frac{1}{2}$	3d.
Adam Pistor (Baker)	$13\frac{3}{4}$	$3\frac{1}{2}$d.

Total of land of this Quarter: $2\frac{1}{4}$ acres $17\frac{3}{4}$ virgae. Sum of pence: 6s. 9d. (actually 7s. $10\frac{1}{2}$d.).

(The *virga* measured 1/160 part of an acre, or $30\frac{1}{4}$ square yards: that is the area of a square, each side of which was $5\frac{1}{2}$ yards, the square pole of the arithmetic books.)

To locate the Quarters and streets in modern Winchelsea presents no

[5] SC11/673 and 674.

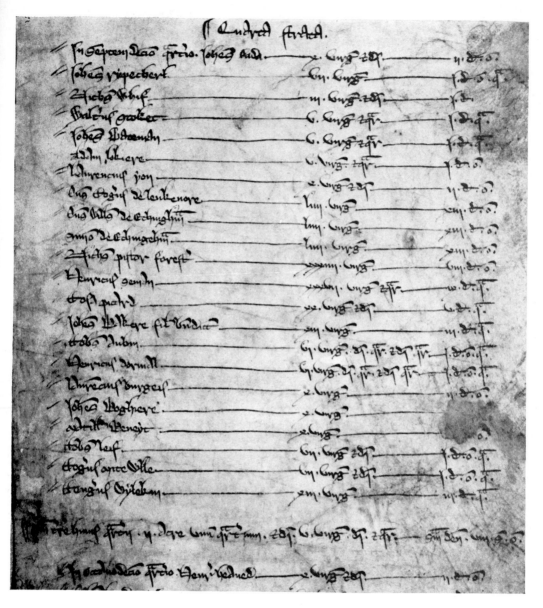

Plate 1. NEW WINCHELSEA, 1292. Part of the town rental, giving the occupants of each plot in Quarter XVII with the heading, Fourth Street, *Quarta Strata*. For the location of this Quarter see Fig. 1. (*Excerpt from P.R.O., SC11/660*).

difficulties. The traditional numbering continued, as we have seen, until the map of 1763, since when there has been very little change in the topography of the town (Fig. 1). Thanks to the researches of Mr. W. McL. Homan it is also possible to assign the building plots to their appropriate part of each Quarter, using the measurements given in the rental.[6] Fig. 2 indicates the neighbourhood of Thomas Alard's house. Quarter Eight is marked A and numbered plots correspond to the order of the rental. Thomas Alard's plot is the ninth, on the north-west corner of the Quarter. The Alards' plots, numbered four to nine, took in all the western half of the Quarter. At the end of Third Street was the gate (E) leading down to the Town Quay at the Strand, and occupying a whole Quarter between Thirteen and Fourteen was St. Thomas's church (B). F indicates the site of St. Giles's church, D the Monday Market Place and C the site of the Grey Friary.

The burgesses of Old Winchelsea clung to their old town until the spring of 1287, and no formal transfer of land from the owners of Iham to the king, and from the king to the burgesses of New Winchelsea, took place until later that year, although the first commission of survey had been appointed in November 1280, and the laying out of building plots had been assigned to another commission in 1281. (It was this commission which brought Henry le Waleys to the hill of Iham.)

> You shall plan and give directions for streets and lanes, and assign places suitable for a market and for two churches.[7]

These new churches were to replace St. Thomas's and St. Giles's in the old town. As much of the new town as possible was to be like the old: the townsmen were guaranteed the same liberties in the new town as kings of England had granted to the old.

Meanwhile the value of the old town was falling. In 1249 the royal revenue arising within it from fees and tolls had been farmed out for £86 13s. 4d. In 1267–68 the actual receipts were only a little lower than this, and in 1268–69 and 1271–72 were in excess: but they fell off in 1272–73 and 1274–5. In 1278 the bid accepted for farming and revenue was only £42; in 1282 it was £33 6s. 8d.; and in 1283 it was £26 13s. 4d. Indeed, the farmers of the revenues had begun to default in 1281. The sum contracted for 1283 was still in arrears in 1291—

[6] W. McL. Homan, "The Founding of New Winchelsea", *Sussex Arch. Coll.*, lxxxviii (1949), pp. 22–41; a more conventional account is G. E. Chambers, "The French Bastides and the Town Plan of New Winchelsea", *Arch. Journ.*, xciv (1938), pp. 177 sqq.
[7] *Cal. Pat. Rolls, 1272–81*, p. 414; *Cal. Pat. Rolls, 1281–92*, pp. 3, 58 and 81; SC11/660, 661 and 674; SC12/15/59–60.

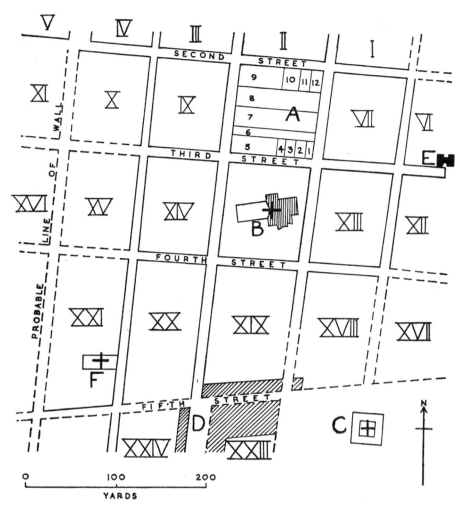

FIG. 2. NEW WINCHELSEA. Central chequers with the church, *B*, and the building plots within Quarter VIII, including that of Thomas Alard. For other reference letters see p. 19.

after the old town had been totally abandoned—and the annual Exchequer accounts continued hopefully to record the debt for the next seventeen years.[8]

[8] H. Playford, ed., *Rotulorum Originalium Abbreviatio*, i (1805), pp. 30, 40, 45 and 48; E372/ 134 m. 7; E372/154 m. 5.

The king had obtained 150 acres for the new town but not all this was available for building plots. Some was required for streets, the market place, the two churches and the cemetery, and 12 acres, the King's Green, were left open in the south-east corner of the town. The remainder, useless for building upon, consisted of parcels of waste on the cliff edge and on the cliff slopes, as well as irregularly-shaped pieces of land between the straight edges of the *placeae* and the town ditch.

The first rent-roll, from which the topography of the town is known, was drawn up in the autumn of 1292 by the Mayor, twenty-four *jurats* and the Lord Treasurer. The rents stated were not actually collected that year, for the king had granted all newcomers seven years free of rent as an encouragement. The rental is divided by the Streets, of which there were eight, and subdivided by the Quarters. In the broadest part of the hill it was possible to fit in six Quarters but south of Fifth Street the number is one less, and south of Seventh Street diminishes to four, three and one. The Quarters occupied by St. Thomas's church and by the friary were not included in the numeration, as Table II.1 shows.

TABLE II.I

NEW WINCHELSEA: SCHEME OF STREET AND QUARTER ENUMERATION, 1292

		Prima Strata			
V	IV	III	II	I	
		Secunda Strata			
XI	X	IX	VIII	VII	VI
		Tertia Strata			
XVI	XV	XIV	Church	XIII	XII
		Quarta Strata			
XXII	XXI*	XX	XIX	XVIII	XVII
		Quinta Strata			
XXVI	XXV	XXIV	XXIII†	Friary	
		Sexta Strata			
XXXI	XXX	XXIX	XXVIII†	XXVII	
		Septima Strata			
	XXXV	XXXIV	XXXIII	XXXII	
		Octava Strata			
	XXXVIII	XXXVII	XXXVI		
	XXXIX				
		Gate			

* Quarter XXI was partly occupied by the church of St. Giles: the area available for building was reduced from 2½ acres to 1⅛ acre.

† The Market Place was set in the street at the west of Quarters XXIII and XXVIII.

TABLE II.2

NEW WINCHELSEA, 1292: AREA OF EACH QUARTER (IN ACRES) WITH NUMBER OF BUILDING PLOTS OR HOUSES IN EACH

Qr.	Ac.	Ho.	Qr.	Ac.	Ho.	Qr.	Ac.	Ho.	Qr.	Ac.	Ho.	Qr.	Ac.	Ho.	Qr.	Ac.	Ho.
V	$1\frac{1}{8}$	20	IV	$2\frac{3}{8}$	10	III	$1\frac{3}{8}$	16	II	$1\frac{5}{8}$	29	I	1	24	—	—	—
XI	$1\frac{1}{2}$	18	X	$2\frac{5}{8}$	29	IX	$2\frac{1}{4}$	17	VIII	$2\frac{3}{8}$	12	VII	$2\frac{1}{4}$	22	VI	$\frac{3}{8}$	9
XVI	$3\frac{1}{2}$	24	XV	$2\frac{1}{2}$	25	XIV	$2\frac{1}{4}$	21	Church	$2\frac{1}{4}$	0	XIII	$2\frac{1}{4}$	26	XII	$1\frac{1}{4}$	9
XXII	$3\frac{1}{2}$	20	XXI	$1\frac{1}{8}$	15	XX	$3\frac{1}{2}$	20	XIX	$3\frac{3}{4}$	19	XVIII	$3\frac{3}{8}$	38	XVII	$2\frac{3}{8}$	22
XXVI	2	12	XXV	$2\frac{1}{8}$	19	XXIV	$1\frac{7}{8}$	16	XXIII	1	17	Friary		0	—	—	—
XXXI	1	7	XXX	$2\frac{1}{8}$	22	XXIX	$2\frac{1}{8}$	33	XXVIII	$3\frac{3}{8}$	42	XXVII	$2\frac{1}{2}$	12	—	—	—
—	—	—	XXXV	$1\frac{3}{20}$	5	XXXIV	$1\frac{1}{4}$	11	XXXIII	$1\frac{1}{4}$	25	XXXII	2	5	—	—	—
—	—	—	XXXVIII	$3\frac{3}{4}$	16	XXXVII	$3\frac{1}{4}$	22	XXXVI	$1\frac{1}{8}$	4	—	—	—	—	—	—
—	—	—	XXXIX	$3\frac{1}{2}$	3	—			—			—			—	—	—

Notes on Quarters:

I–V	The area of these is curtailed by the north cliff.
VI	Area curtailed by east cliff.
VII–XI	Normal size.
XII	Curtailed by east cliff.
XIII	Included the rectory.
XIV–XV	Normal.
XVI	Including one complete acre held by Gervase Alard.
XVII	Slightly curtailed by east cliff.
XVIII–XX	Normal.
XXI	The whole Quarter was about the same size as XX but it contained St. Giles's church; one of the fifteen houses was the rectory.
XXIII	Curtailed by the Market on the west side of the Quarter in the widened street.
XXVII	The Mayor of that year (1292) lived in this Quarter.
XXVIII	Curtailed by the Market on the west side of the Quarter in the widened street.
XXXI	Curtailed by the narrowing of the hill-top in the south-west corner.
XXXIV	Included the House of St. John.
XXXVI	Curtailed by the narrowing of the hill-top and the King's Green to the east.
XXXIX	Two of the three houses were those of St. Bartholomew and Holy Cross.

Subpendentes

On the north side of the hill, on the land next to the salt marshes, were seventy-nine holdings making up just under 4 acres.

All areas in the Table are rounded to the nearest eighth acre. The rental of 1292 gives acres down to quarter poles.

Judging from the alinement of the modern streets and lanes, the "north–south" streets of New Winchelsea were set out parallel to each other. The "east–west" streets named Second, Third, Fourth and Seventh are within degrees of being at right angles to them, as is the eastern part of First Street (now North Street). Too little remains of the other "east–west" streets to be certain of their course, but there may have been an unusually large space between Fourth and Fifth Street. Seventh and Eight Streets seem to be parallel to First, Second, Third and Fourth Streets: but Fifth and Sixth Streets, which bounded the Market Place, may have been set at another angle.

The land left between the streets for building was therefore not exactly rectilinear nor divided into equal areas. The size of each Quarter is shown in the Table opposite, together with the number of houses in it. As the subdivisions of Thomas Alard's Quarter VIII show (Fig. 2), the larger holdings ran right through from street to street while others had shorter garths behind their house. In Quarter VIII the through-plots were some 300 feet long, but the seven smaller plots had to be fitted into the ends of two other holdings and were only 80 feet long.

Some of the differences in size were due to physical irregularities on the hill-top, but there were marked differences also in density of plots and in rents per acre. Table II.3 shows the densities of the various Quarters schematically. It will be seen that there are marked concentrations near the entrance from the harbour (Strand Gate) which lay just east of Quarter VI. Quarter I and those Quarters along First Street gained from this proximity to the shore. A second concentration is visible near the Market Place (M) which lay in the street between Quarters XXIII/XXIV and XXVIII/XXIX. In view of the concentration of Houses in Quarter XXXIII it is difficult to accept Mr. Homan's contention that there was a gate between Quarters XXVIII and XXIX putting Seventh Street at the edge of the town; it would also be unlikely that Eighth Street would have had that name if it had been outside the wall.

The significant extra-mural tenements were those *subpendentes*, lying on the slope below the north cliff and adjoining the quay or strand. Here there were seventy-nine holdings crowded into just 4 acres, equalling the density of Quarter XXXIII by the Market and, as Mr. Homan shows, the principal citizens of Winchelsea had *subpendentes*

23

TABLE II.3

DENSITY OF BUILDING PLOTS PER ACRE IN QUARTERS
OF NEW WINCHELSEA, 1292

Quarter					
V 16	IV 4	III 12	II 16	I 24	
XI 12	X 11	IX 8	VIII 4	VII 8	VI 24
XVI 7	XV 10	XIV 9	Church —	XIII 12	XII 7
XXII 6	XXI 8+CH	XX 6	XIX 4	XVIII 11	XVII 9
XXVI 6	XXV 8	XXIV 8	XXIII M 17	Friary	
XXXI 7	XXX 9	XXIX 16	XXVIII M 12	XXVII 5	
	XXXV 4	XXXIV 8	XXXIII 20	XXXII 2½	
	XXXVIII 4	XXXVII 7	XXXVI 3		
	XXXIX 1				

holdings in addition to their houses within the walls. Nine of the Alard family, for example, were to be found there.

The rents paid for the building plots were arrived at by sharing out the sum of £14 11s. 5¾d. This odd amount was the annual value of the agricultural land (with one house) within Iham manor that Edward had granted to the commonalty of New Winchelsea for their town. The "rental" of 1292 is actually a sworn valuation of this land followed by detailed assessments of the rent of each *placea*—716 in all—and the seventy-nine *subpendentes* plots. There is no sign of any standard rent per acre in these assessments and they would seem to be a realistic valuation of their worth to their new tenants.

The highest-rented Quarter was XXIII, on the east of the Market Place, probably made more valuable by the stalls that could be set out in front of the houses or shops: here 81d. per acre was paid; almost as valuable was Quarter VI next to the Strand Gate, the houses or shops first to be spied by the stranger-merchant entering the town from the harbour: here 75d. per acre was paid. In Quarter XXXIV, to the south-west of the Market Place, 69d. per acre was paid. In the plot partly occupied by St. Giles's church (XXI) 64d. per acre was paid for lay houses. No other Quarters were in the same range: the next step down is to Quarters I, XXVII, XXVIII, XXIX and XXXIII (neighbours, it will be noted, of the most valuable Quarters): rents here lay between 48d. and 56d. per acre.

The most valuable building land was not necessarily that which was most crowded with tenants. Table II.4 sets out the most valuable Quarters in the first column and the densities of these Quarters in the next. Quarter XXIII had the most valued land and was the second densest, while Quarter VI, the second most valued, was the most densely settled; but other valuable sites such as Quarters XXIV, XXVII and XXVIII were valuable but lightly settled, rather like some exclusive suburb of a modern town. The Mayor of 1292 lived in Quarter XXVII, and Gervase Alard senior held land there.

TABLE II.4

NEW WINCHELSEA, 1292: DENSITY OF PLOTS IN MOST
VALUABLE QUARTERS

Quarter	pence per acre rent	houses per acre
XXIII	81	17
VI	75	24
XXXIV	69	8
XXI	64	8 and church of St. Giles
XXVII	56	5
XXIX	52	16
XXXIII	52	20
I	49	24
XXVIII	48	12

New Winchelsea, like Old, was to be a community of merchants, and their working-places were warehouses (at the Quay and in cellars beneath the new houses) but especially the Market Place. With such a generous provision of Quarters for the church and monastic houses it is surprising that, as Fig. 2 shows, the space allowed for the Market Place was so meagre. A roadway south of St. Thomas's was widened by some 40 feet along the west side of Quarters XXIII and XXVIII but no complete Quarter seems to have been allocated. The open area shown as the *Monday Market* on the plan of 1763 comprised the whole of what had been Quarters XXIII and XXVIII in 1292 when seventeen and forty-two houses stood upon them. There can have been nothing like the complete Quarter so commonly left for a market place in the Welsh and Gascon towns contemporary with New Winchelsea.

What else was necessary in the devising and arraying of a new seaport town? The Town Quay was laid out at the foot of the north cliff, and the fishermen landed their catch there and paid duty as in Old Winchelsea. In the five years 1299–1304 the tolls of fish formed about one third of the royal revenue from the town.[9] In the year 1299–1300 the royal income from the town was:

	£	s.	d.
Rents of building plots	14	11	$5\frac{3}{4}$
Tolls of markets and fairs	7	0	0
Customs of fish	13	8	0
Fines and other profits of justice	9	4	0
Toll of the weigh-beam		12	0
Miscellaneous new rents	1	19	$6\frac{1}{4}$
Total	£46	15	0

On the hill-top the new townsmen needed water, and four more wells were provided to augment the existing two wells on Fécamp land near St. Leonard's church. In 1293–94 the king built a bridge *subtus villam*,[10] probably on the road that came in through the south gate, while others were meantime building on their plots, and vacant plots were finding tenants: by 1298–99 the rent roll[11] was augmented by £2 11s. $6\frac{3}{4}$d. The Grey Friars built their friary in the space allocated to them, equivalent in area to two whole Quarters. (Its ruins were still standing in 1850 and are illustrated in Cooper's *History of Winchelsea*.) The Black Friars came in 1318, being given building space on the King's Green, the open space south of Quarters XXXII and XXXVI. In 1358 they moved to a site (later *Chestnut Field*) in Quarter XV.[12]

The two churches of Old Winchelsea were dedicated to St. Thomas and St. Giles. These two churches were shown on the Counter-seal of the town, and its inscription invoked the two saints. St. Thomas's church was rebuilt in the new town in the central position, with a whole Quarter to itself; St. Giles's occupied the southern half of Quarter

9 SC6/1031/26 and E352/98 m. 32d.
10 SC6/1031/25.
11 SC6/1031/26.
12 The sites of the Friaries appear in Camb. Univ. Air Photograph Coll. AAM 42–3 (ex. inf. Dr. J. K. S. St. Joseph).

XXI. St. Leonard's, Iham, was already in existence at the north-west corner of the hill but outside the town site. St. Leonard's bounds were regularly beaten each Rogationtide until 1747 to distinguish its parish from the town: the site of the church is now occupied by a windmill mound, but the plan of 1763 shows its churchyard as well as that of St. Giles's. St. Giles's church was destroyed by lightning in 1413 and not rebuilt.

Although now much smaller in extent than in the early fourteenth century and although bereft of all sea-borne commerce, New Winchelsea has shared enough in the general rebuilding of the post-medieval centuries to have very little of its merchant houses remaining above ground. It is probable that excavation would yield house-foundations in all the thirty Quarters that are now grass-grown; and perhaps more: for there are vaulted cellars remaining under many houses in the northern Quarters, and Stephens's plan of 1763 marked with a cross the *crypts* then visible in the Quarters west and south of the church. These were described in 1570 as[13]

> maney costly vaults, arched and sett forthe with pyllers of Caene stone, as meant to have houses built over them meet for famous merchants.

The author of this survey was reporting to Elizabeth's Privy Council on the possibility of reviving the haven and bringing back "famous merchants" to the town. There were only sixty households left in the town in 1575, and in 1603 there were only 180 communicants. Defoe and John Wesley came to New Winchelsea in the eighteenth century and each chose the same simile: it was a Poor Skeleton of a Town.

What had killed it? In 1343, six years before the Black Death, there were sixty empty building plots in the town as well as thirty-four holdings *subpendentes*. The years following the plagues were dark:[14] there were French raids in 1359, 1360 and 1377. In 1380 the Pipewell Gate and the nave of St. Thomas's church were destroyed. Edward III's rent-roll was well below that of his grandfather. In 1364 rent-relief had to be granted to 358 townsmen; in 1367 to 288; and in 1370 to 377.

The death of Winchelsea as a port came finally not with plague or invasion but through the fickleness of the waters. As any modern map shows, the sea has retreated far from the foot of Winchelsea cliff, and the whole estuary is silted up and marshy. The stone-vaulted cellars

[13] SP12/75/70; see *Med. Archaeol.*, viii (1964) pp. 268–69 for a recent description.
[14] See references in Gazetteer, *sub loco*.

under the grass fields, the truncated church of St. Thomas and the buried church of St. Giles, the Town Gates and the fragments of walls: these are the anatomical details of the Skeleton of Thomas Alard's New Winchelsea.

II

Henry le Waleys and Six Gascon Towns

Edward I was duke in Gascony as well as king in England, and his father had endowed him with the rule of Gascony when he married Eleanor of Castile in 1254. The six towns to be briefly considered

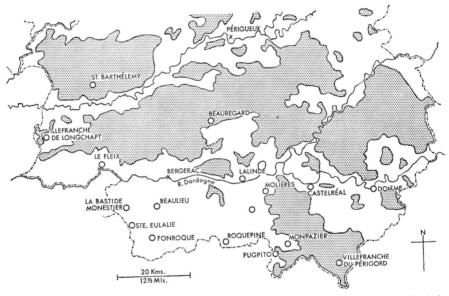

FIG. 3. ENGLISH BASTIDES IN PÉRIGORD. Circles indicate bastides. The shaded area is that of surviving woodland in 1961.

were founded between 1267 and 1284. Edward was in Gascony for less than four years of this period, and the foundations were executed for him by his seneschals. One town to be considered, Lalinde, was named after one of these royal officials, Jean de la Linde. We shall not, therefore, find Edward at the foundation of these six towns as we find him at New Winchelsea or at the new towns of north Wales, although he did on occasions visit his Gascon towns while they were being set out. There is a record in the royal accounts[15] of eight shillingsworth of drinks provided for the men of the new town of Baa near Bordeaux when the king-duke visited it in March 1287.

The connection of Henry le Waleys with these six towns was financial, as a revenue-farmer. Kings always welcomed those monied men who were prepared to pay an annual fixed sum to them, and then be recouped over the period when the tax or revenues were collected. The money which le Waleys had for investment came principally from the Anglo-Gascon wine trade. Like Edward, le Waleys was at home in Gascony as in England, in Bordeaux as in London, the town of his other mayoralty. The six bastides whose revenues he took to farm lay in the north of Gascony, within Périgord (or the modern Department of Dordogne) between the rivers Dropt and Dordogne. They lay near the political frontier and also near an economic frontier, for although southern Périgord is as fertile as parts of the Garonne valley, its northern half merges into the hills, woods and heath of the Limousin.

One of the six bastides whose revenues were farmed by le Waleys was *Molières*, founded in 1284 just before the farm was negotiated. Its foundation had helped to colonise and pacify the local countryside:[16]

in which before that time many thefts, robberies and murders were committed. Pilgrims, clergy and other men were frequently slain.

Today Molières is no more than a village, but at its centre are the plain remains of a market place, and one arcaded shop (*cornière*) remains as pathetic reminder of the commercial privileges that Edward I's charter once bestowed upon the town. The streets of the village are wide and straight, and laid out in the rectilinear pattern already encountered at New Winchelsea. The church is of almost cathedral dimensions, with an enormous bell-tower out of which weeds and a trailing briar incongruously flower. Behind padlocked railings are the substantial remains of a castle or fortified house.

Although the economic bases of Gascon towns differed from those of New Winchelsea and the Welsh sea-board—depending so largely on the production and export of wine—the basic needs of the new townsmen, as expressed in the physical framework of living provided for them, appear to have been very similar. Indeed, the formal chequer plan is even more prevalent in Gascony than in the contemporary planta-

[15] E36/201 f. 55.   [16] *Vigié*, p. 144.

tions of Wales and England. Within this grid, the essential units of the building plots and interstreet chequers were marshalled much as we have seen them in the plan of New Winchelsea; we see the same provision of a complete chequer for the town church; the same allocation of a central chequer for the market place; the same prevalence of right-angles in the town plan.[17]

Lalinde, founded in 1267, was the oldest of the six bastides which le Waleys took to farm. It has a complete rectilinear grid, the long axis running east and west, parallel to the bank of the river Dordogne. The improvement of the river here was a service for which Bertrand de Panissals claimed credit in 1303. The church at Lalinde, unlike that at Molières, stands exterior to the town, rather like that of St. Leonard's, Iham, at New Winchelsea. There may have been a riverside church before Jean de la Linde laid out the site for his master, and a document of 1293 shows the rector of this church among those whose land was taken for the new town, or bastide. The coming together of partners, who provided the land for the king-duke to found a town upon, was a frequent occurrence in thirteenth-century Gascony. The duke was not lavishly endowed with demesnes in Périgord, and in a partnership agreement (*paréage*) he gave the blessing of his sovereign authority and his protection while his partner or partners gave the land. The revenues were usually shared, and a town's coat of arms was often made up of the intermingled arms of the king-duke and the partners.

Beaumont du Périgord, also taken to farm by le Waleys, was founded for Edward by his seneschal, Luke de Thenney, while the king was on his way back from Sicily and the Crusade in the year of his father's death (1272). When the townspeople asked Edward, thirty years later, whether he would permit (and perhaps finance) the building of town walls, they proudly claimed that theirs was the premier bastide of Périgord:[18]

la premiere de totes les autres bastides de notre seigneur le Roi en Peregorz.

The claim was moral rather than historic, for Lalinde was five years older, but Beaumont would have good reasons for making the claim today. Lalinde's riverside site cannot compare with the hill-top of

---

[17] A general account of the political and economic context of the Gascon bastides is given in Chapter 13; detailed references appear in the individual entries in the Gazetteer, Chapter 17. See also E. C. Lodge, *Gascony Under English Rule* (1926), and F. M. Powicke, *The Thirteenth Century* (1953), ch. 7.

[18] SC8/7383; also PRO/7/154.

Beaumont, *bellus mons*; Lalinde has been demoralised by the passage of a main road through it, and Beaumont has preserved more of its buildings from rebuilding; and in addition to the charm of its situation and the magnificence of its church, Beaumont may boast of the 1,116 pages of the astonishing book in which Testut, professor of anatomy at Lyon, celebrated the history and topography of pre-Revolutionary Beaumont. On the page facing the title appears a list of Testut's medical works, including a treatise on the human anatomy. To his study of Beaumont he brought the technique of minute dissection but added warmth and affection for his birthplace that would have been out of place in the anatomy schools. Hardly any English town, let alone a planted one, has received treatment on this scale. Each street and building of the medieval town is minutely described and illustrated by line-drawings and plans. There survives no rental or survey such as we have used to reconstruct Alard's Winchelsea: but one can still see a good deal more of the original buildings of Beaumont, and the minute study of these together with the evidence from archives and verbal tradition enabled Testut to recreate the original *bastida de bello monte*.

The four parties to the *paréage* for Beaumont were the seigneur of Biron, the prior of St. Avit-Senieur, the abbot of Cadouin and the king of England's seneschal. The abbot later disputed the title of the prior, claiming that the site of the town was clearly in his own jurisdiction since it lay within the parish of Belpech (a Romanesque church that still stands in the fields north of the town). Another preliminary to the creation of the town is evidenced by an agreement of 1272 between the abbot, the prior and two other seigneurs enabling Beaumont to be made an independent parish and a parish church erected in it.

The plan (Fig. 4) shows that the town was basically rectilinear again, but (like Winchelsea) conceding a little to the shape of the hill-back upon which it was placed: the chequers north of the market place, and the streets surrounding them, are out of line by a few degrees with those on the south. Two main streets, 25 feet wide, form the axis of the town, running north and south, and the market place is set between these. Two narrower streets, parallel to these, complete the north–south part of the grid, and the walls follow the gardens behind these streets. On the shorter side of the rectangle there is no major road through from gate to gate, but within the town there are the remains of eight transversal roads, none wider than 10 feet, the whole making

31

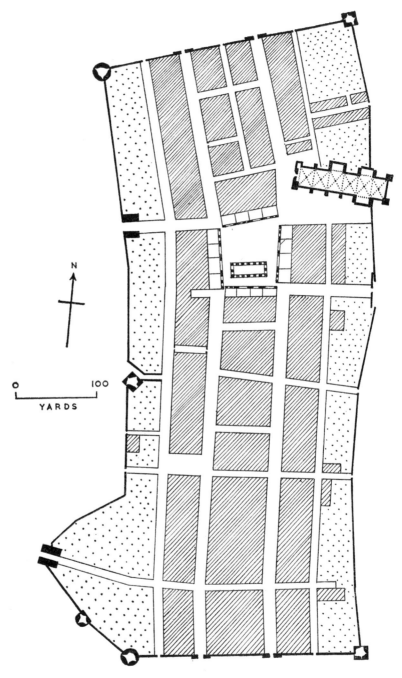

Fig. 4. BEAUMONT DU PÉRIGORD.   Plan of streets, chequers, walls, market-place and church (after *Testut*); see also Plate 2.

twenty-three chequers of various sizes. There were six principal gates, four on the major axis and two on the western side leading to the fields: the eastern walls stood on the top of a steep slope and there was no original road needing access on this flank. The town is 1,115 feet long and 450 feet wide, making an area roughly equal to that of its neighbours Lalinde, Villeréal, Castillonès and Montflanquin. Only the greater bastides such as Libourne and Villeneuve sur Lot overtower it: Monpazier, a neighbour whose geometrical regularity has often been reproduced in books on town planning, is a little larger.

Many of the house-plots, the *placeae*, still bear all or part of the original structures of the late thirteenth century; most others, even after new building, retain the dimensions of the original building units. These commonly had a frontage of from 20 to 27 feet and a depth of about twice these dimensions. One often encounters the *androyne* or gulley, a narrow passage between houses, hardly the width of a man, serving both as a boundary and as a drain for the water dripping from the roofs that almost meet above it.

The principal *Place*, now the Place Publique, stood near the church. The two roads from the north gates, the two from the south gates and one from the main west gate lead directly into its corners. In 1289 Edward ordered a market hall to be built; it stood on the south side of the Square but was demolished in 1864. The Square was lined by four arcaded shops on each side. The line of the principal roads ran straight through these arcades. Plate 2 shows this Square on market day, looking from one of these arcades (*cornières*) across to the fortified tower of the church. On this western side of the market place there are two shops with *cornières* that are clearly original. At the south-west of the Square is the *Cornière Perraudin* with two large arches for the passage of traffic along the main road and two smaller arches giving on to the square; adjoining it on the north is the *Cornière Coste* with its two arches for the main road and a single (but equally large) arch giving access to the square. It was through this arch that the photograph in Plate 2 was taken; it will be seen that the shops on the north side of the Square have been rebuilt in the eighteenth century. In this remodelling of 1776 the thirteenth-century *cornière* arches were replaced by arches with circular tops; and in the course of road widening and rebuilding, nine of the sixteen *cornières* have completely disappeared, but it is clear from old photographs reproduced by Testut that the Square was originally surrounded on all sides by these arcades and that traffic could have

33

access from the Main Street only by entering the arcades and then turning at a right angle through an arch into the Square. At Monpazier, built thirteen years later, the inconvenience of this knight's move must have become apparent, for the corners of the Square were opened up by cutting a way through and supporting the upper stories of the houses by corbels.

To defend the town, four corner towers may have been built by Edward I, but the building of the gates and the wall that surrounded the town was delayed until after 1320: such tardiness in providing a new town with stone defences has been already encountered at Winchelsea and it occurred elsewhere in Gascony. The implication, as M. Trabut-Cussac has argued, is that defences were not an essential part of the equipment of bastides, and military strength not a principal motive in their foundation. It also says something of the state of the royal purse.

Beaumont was no Conway nor a Flint. It had no castle associated with it, and for the first half century of its life it had no stone walls even in turbulent years of Anglo-French relations, and Beaumont was not far from the frontier. It was the church itself that became the place of refuge for the townsmen, shown by the great crenellated towers (of which the south-western can be seen in Plate 2) and by the fortified west doorway. The church was even provided with a staircase down to a well so that the townspeople and animals gathered within it could withstand a siege.

Of the origins of the bastide of *Fonroque* virtually nothing is known before the document by which Edward farmed its revenues to le Waleys in 1284. Its rectangular plan proclaims its origin (and is reproduced in *Lavedan*, Fig. 168) but its original character has been drowned by the passage of the Route Nationale. *La Bastide Monestier* and *Beaulieu* were less successful foundations. The site of Beaulieu may have been in Pertus parish but not even the earthworks of a decayed town can be seen today. La Bastide Monestier had forty-three houses a century after its foundation but today it is very small indeed: there is a central grass square and a decayed grid-pattern of streets and lanes rather like the dilapidated Francheville in the Isle of Wight (Fig. 53). On the south-east of this square is a small parish church which is remarkably English in its appearance, and one surviving *cornière* where the arcade is used as an open garage by the farm that it abuts. However unsuccessful they later turned out to be, it must have been worth while for

34

Plate 2. BEAUMONT DU PÉRIGORD. Market place and church seen through a *cornière*.

le Waleys to take these two bastides at farm with the other four. They do demonstrate, however, that there was no automatic prescription for a new town to be successful. Royal patronage or foundation by a royal official was not in itself enough and could not shelter a bastide from the vagaries of economic chance nor from the mischances of destruction in war.

III

Edward I and Ten Welsh Towns

The group of towns which Edward I planted in north Wales was thoroughly Edwardian. All were set on territory that Edward himself had re-won or conquered for the English Crown for the first time. The king visited their sites to assist in the planning, lived in several of them while building was in progress, and visited them all. His eldest son was born in one of these towns, Carnarvon, and from it was proclaimed Prince of Wales in 1301; the prince's nurse was rewarded with a burgage plot. The Welsh towns also influenced the king's political relations with his English subjects, for the cost absorbed very considerable revenues and added to the friction over taxation.[19]

The economic context of these Welsh towns will be examined more closely in Chapter 12 but their important economic role may not appear at first glance. Their castles and walls are still such striking monuments to Edward's energy that it is easy to consider the towns merely as appendages to the castles, the town walls a further ring of defences for the castles. Yet these towns, at first glance so much the result of war and the fear of war, were designed to house civilians as well as garrisons, merchants as well as camp followers, Welshmen as well as Englishmen. If the stone walls and turrets were part of a plan to overawe the native Welsh, then the market places were designed to woo them to more pacific pursuits. The civilians in the Welsh towns, traders, and part-time traders, and part-time farmers, were as much concerned with making and dealing as the inhabitants of any bastide. The physical framework of a new Welsh town does not emerge, therefore, as very different from New Winchelsea or those that we have

[19] A general account of town building in Wales will be found in Chapter 12, and individual references in the Gazetteer, Chapter 16. See also J. E. Lloyd, *A History of Wales*, 2 vols. (1911); W. Rees, *An Historical Atlas of Medieval Wales* (1959); J. G. Edwards, "Edward I's Castle Building in Wales", *Proc. British Acad.*, xxxii (1946), pp. 15–81; A. J. Taylor in E. M. Jope, ed., *Studies in Building History* (1961), pp. 104–133; *Hist. King's Works*, esp. ch. 6; C. Schillaber, "Edward I, Builder of Towns", *Speculum*, xxii (1947), pp. 297–309, has no original material on this subject.

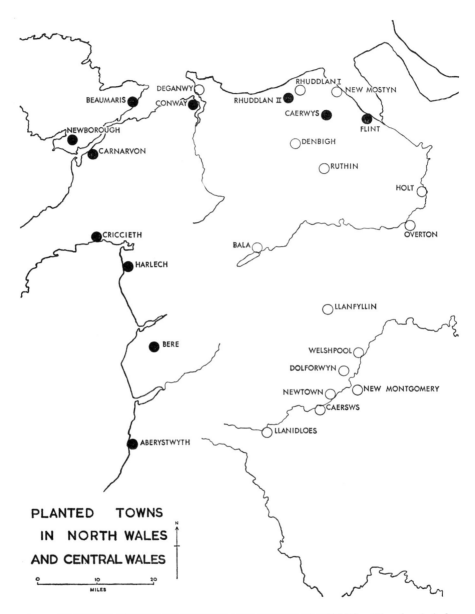

DEGANWY

BEAUMARIS
CONWAY

RHUDDLAN I
RHUDDLAN II
NEW MOSTYN

CAERWYS
FLINT

NEWBOROUGH
CARNARVON

DENBIGH

RUTHIN

HOLT

CRICCIETH

BALA

OVERTON

HARLECH

LLANFYLLIN

BERE

WELSHPOOL
DOLFORWYN

NEWTOWN
NEW MONTGOMERY
CAERSWS

LLANIDLOES

ABERYSTWYTH

PLANTED TOWNS
IN NORTH WALES
AND CENTRAL WALES

N

0   10   20
MILES

FIG. 5. PLANTED TOWNS IN NORTH AND CENTRAL WALES. The closed circles distinguish the Edwardian plantations.

examined in Périgord, and we meet the familiar straight streets, chequers, rectangular *placeae*; and market places that are true squares.

Nine of the ten Edwardian towns in Wales were completed before the town-planning colloquium of 1297, and the tenth, Beaumaris, had been under way since April 1295. Their political context is war: three (Flint, Rhuddlan and Aberystwyth) followed the end of the war of 1277; five (Conway, Carnarvon, Harlech, Criccieth and Bere) followed the fall of Llewelyn in 1282; and Beaumaris (with Newborough) was created after the Welsh rising of 1294; only the tenth, Caerwys, seems to have been a purely commercial plantation. The ten towns stretch down the coast and coastal plain of Wales from Flint in the Dee estuary to Aberystwyth, halfway down Cardigan Bay.

Rhuddlan, the first to be considered, approached New Winchelsea in conception, for Edward's town was really a New Rhuddlan. There was already an Old Rhuddlan, the site of Saxon and Norman plantations, but Edward deliberately moved both castle and town. The *burh* of Clwdmouth mentioned in 921 was probably located here, and c. 1073 the earl of Chester built the 60-foot high motte, *Twthill,* which can still be seen. This castle, and a church, market, mills and fisheries, are recorded in Domesday Book together with eighteen burgesses and a mint in the earl's "new borough". Two hundred years afterwards Edward created his own *novus burgus.* The process can be followed in the surviving account rolls for the wages of masons and others who were brought to north Wales to construct the massive public works.

The king himself arrived at Rhuddlan in August 1277 and remained there or nearby until November. Building work on the castle is recorded from September, and just over £3,000 was spent by March 1279; the work on the defences of the town and castle then went ahead side by side: between March 1279 and November 1280 £4,216 was spent on the castle and £1,025 was spent on the town, while in the next eighteen months another £250 was spent *de claustura ville* at the same time as the final expenditure (rather smaller than this amount) on the castle works. The river was also led into a tidal canal, *fossa maris,* dug by dykers from the Fens. Burgages were being laid out in 1278 near the castle and were actually being constructed in March 1279, just when the accounts show the expenditure on the town beginning. Professor J. G. Edwards has shown that the principal expenditure was on the wages of ditch-diggers and carpenters, so that (like Flint) Rhuddlan's defences were earth banks, a ditch and a wooden palisade,

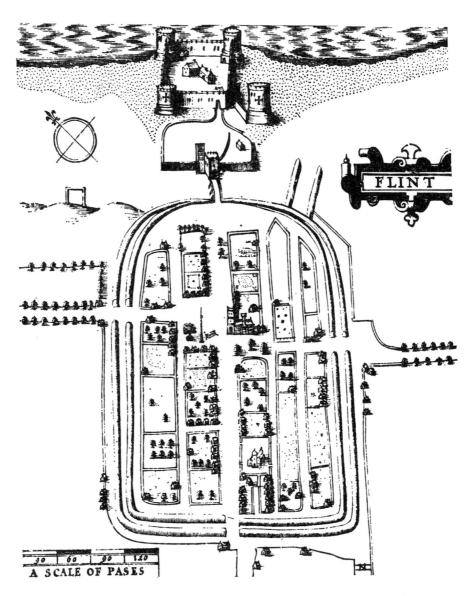

FLINT

A SCALE OF PASES

FIG. 6. FLINT IN 1610. By John Speed.

not stone walls. The carpenters may also have been at work on the burgages themselves. The charter of liberties to encourage the new burgesses had been issued the previous November,[20] identical with those of Flint, Conway and Carnarvon, and it was the privileges of Rhuddlan "down to every comma" (*in puncto ad punctum*) that in 1303 the townsmen of Newborough (Anglesey) requested for themselves. The borough privileges were those of Hereford, and the rents the standard shilling a year. Anyone coming to take up a *placea* was welcome.

There were still vacancies for newcomers in July 1279, and in November 1280 the fee farm of £40 due to the king from the town was remitted for seven years since the burgesses were "making their town, building it and improving it".[21] Early in the fourteenth century a full year's rent from the town was £36 14s. 1d.[22]

Edward also had hopes of dignifying his new town with a cathedral by moving the see of St. Asaph, offering the Pope the costs of the removal; but what had been possible in his father's time, when the cathedral of Old Sarum was moved to New Salisbury, did not prove feasible for Edward in North Wales.[23]

The town of *Flint* resembles Rhuddlan in being integrated with a castle, but there was no pre-existing town or village. The site seems to have been decided by the presence of a firm rock alongside the sands of Dee, halfway between Chester and Rhuddlan, within the territory of two of the many vills in Northop parish. The purity of the bastide plan, firmly rectangular with a chequer for the new town church and another for the market, is now partially obscured by the railway, the railway station and the Holyhead road, but Speed's plan of 1610 shows the town very much as Edward I made it. Its name is also bastide-like, a nickname christening like its near-contemporary, Larroque (Gers) in Gascony. The natural shelf of sandstone gave the town its name: *le flynt and y fflint*. In royal letters dating from the end of 1277 the place is sometimes called *le Caillou* or *le Chaylou* but the Norman-French form did not survive here.[24]

[20] *Cal. Welsh Rolls*, p. 289.
[21] *Ibid.*, p. 188; see also pp. 165, 178 and 201; and *Cal. Pat. Rolls, 1278–81*, p. 259.
[22] R. Stewart-Brown, ed., *Cheshire in the Pipe Rolls* (Lancs. and Chesh. Rec. Soc., xcii (1938)), p. 150; and *Accounts of the Chamberlains of the County of Chester (ibid.*, lix (1910)), p. 20; A. Jones, ed., *Flintshire Ministers' Accounts* (Flints. Hist. Soc. Publcs., iii (1912–13).
[23] J. G. Edwards, ed., *Cal. of Ancient Correspondence Concerning Wales* (1935), p. 264; see also A. J. Taylor, *Rhuddlan Castle* (1957).
[24] See A. J. Taylor in E. M. Jope, ed., *op. cit.*, p. 129, fn. 3, for a dissenting opinion: that "Flint" was a code-word for the military campaign.

The castle could be provisioned by water at high tide and there was no need of any artificial watercourse like that at Rhuddlan. The castle-rock had marshes to the north and west while to the south the ground soon began to rise to foothills. The town was fitted in (as Fig. 6 shows) outside the south gate of the castle with the shorter side of the grid alongside the moat. The task of Flint was to hold the coastal road from Chester into north Wales and to guard the Dee estuary. The building of castle and town began in July 1277 and lasted four and a half years; within a year of completion came the rebellion of prince Llewelyn and his brother, and both Flint and Rhuddlan were temporarily lost.

Since Flint and Rhuddlan were the first of Edward's great castle-towns in Britain, it is natural to look for French and Gascon models; in 1277 it was only three years since he had been in Gascony. The defences of Aigues Mortes, that great Mediterranean bastide, have been suggested as the model for the donjon tower of the castle. Aigues Mortes was not in Gascony, of course, but it had been Edward's departure port for the Crusade in 1270: yet the Gascon towns that Edward visited in 1273–74 may equally well have been prototypes for Flint, if Edward had not already sufficient inspiration from his predecessors' plantations in mid- and south Wales, or from civil settlements such as New Salisbury, then only half a century old.

Edward does not seem to have envisaged any stone defences for Flint. A ditch, a bank and a wooden palisade sufficed as they did at Rhuddlan and as they probably did at New Salisbury. Ditches and banks succumb more easily than stone walls to levelling by later generations, but the position of ditch and rampart can still be seen influencing the levels in the south and south-west parts of Flint, especially between Mount Street (the outer street of the grid) and Earl Street where gardens fall away incongruously from the level of the street and the houses.

One interpretation of the documentary evidence is that these town defences did not have priority in the plan of work. The castle masons began work in July 1277, but it is March 1281 before the accounts show expenditure on ditch-diggers and carpenters *de claustura ville*, and the largest sums, in total only 3% of the £7,000 spent at Flint, date only from 1284–86. Rhuddlan town defences, it will be recalled, had cost £1,300. (Professor J. G. Edwards, however, suggests that the cost of early work on the town defences is concealed in the general building accounts, where large numbers of ditch-diggers—1,806 in one week of August 1277—are shown at work. In this view, the work in 1284–86 appears as repairs of damage after David's attack in March 1282).

In the summer of 1277 Edward was concerned with the planning, not only of these two towns to hold the country between Chester and the Conway river, but with a third town, *Aberystwyth*, far away at the northern end of Cardiganshire. Edward himself was preoccupied and detained by events near Chester and Rhuddlan but the *Welsh Brut y Tywysogion* chronicles that[25]

> Edmund, the king's brother, accompanied by an army, came to Llanbadarn on 25 July, 1277 and began the building of the castle.

As at Rhuddlan, a position was chosen that supplanted existing castles further down the river. The obvious advantage of the new site was that (like Flint—and Rhuddlan after the canal) it lay open to access from the sea.

One of the paradoxes of Aberystwyth is that it does not stand at the mouth of the Ystwyth at all, but at that of the Rheidol. Initially the town was simply called "the borough of Llanbadarn" after the name of the older village within whose territory it was sited and where the parish church stood. Thus in the tax list[26] of 1292 the names of the burgesses appear under the heading *burgenses de Lampaden de castro regis*. The name "Aberystwyth" is a transfer of name from one of the older up-river castles, which did stand on the Ystwyth, to the new castle; and thence from the new castle to the new town.

The town's charter was granted in December 1277, giving the burgesses the right to wall their town; to have a gild merchant; to have all the privileges of Henry III's borough of New Montgomery; and to have two fairs and a weekly market. A survey of 1279 describes the town as walled with stone and measuring 1,500 feet by 1,420 feet. Burgesses were already in residence by March 1278. Property holders in Llanbadarn were compensated for the loss of land by being given other land at Nantbran in Perfedd. There is a rental of 1280, and from 1298–1304 other accounts show that there were reckoned to be 140 to 147 burgages in the town each paying their shilling a year rent; in 1308 there were 157. The town wall was under way in 1280–81, when £200 was spent

---

[25] J. Williams Ab Ithel, ed., *Brut y Tywysogion* (Rolls Series, 1860), sub anno.
[26] E179/242/48.

on it: the total for town and castle was £3,888, about half that for Flint and less than half that for Rhuddlan.[27]

Conway, Carnarvon and Harlech date from 1283 after the fall of Llewelyn had opened up the western part of north Wales beyond the river Conway, which had previously formed the frontier of English Wales. The towns of Conway and Carnarvon were to guard the Menai Straits and the passage to Anglesey; and Harlech, the coastal road south down the shore of Cardigan Bay to where Aberystwyth already stood, though damaged in the war. A fourth town, Bere, near Towyn, would have joined this chain had it succeeded: but it did not.[28]

In March 1283 Edward himself came west from Rhuddlan to stay at the mouth of the Conway and supervise the work. The creation of his borough at *Conway* involved an even more difficult problem than at Rhuddlan. It was not a question of transferring a town to an empty site but of building a town on a site already occupied by a Cistercian monastery. The chronicle[29] of the abbey of Aberconway says:

> King Edward, wanting to hold Wales more firmly, moved the Cistercian abbey of Aberconway that was built at the entrance to Snowdonia, and he made a castle and town there. He gave the monks another site, however, at Maenan and contributed generously to the new buildings.

The amount of compensation was £427, and the new works at Conway—erected at speed in five building seasons (1283–87)—cost at least £14,000, and probably more. The abbey buildings formed a temporary headquarters for the royal household but they were scheduled for early demolition. What Edward obtained, apart from the abbey site and any building stone that was re-used, was a church for his burgesses, who simply took over the abbey church for their parish church.

The Cistercian rule, ordering solitude, usually ensured that there were neither Cistercian houses in towns nor any towns planted immediately at the gates of Cistercian houses. It is surprising, therefore, to find that the valuation of the abbey site at the take-over included "the abbot's borough". May it be that these burgages were in fact located across the river in the town of Deganwy? This town (whose

---

[27] E142/5; *Cal. Welsh Rolls*, p. 166; SC6/1158/1; E372/125; E372/146; SC6/1218/1, 6 and 10; G. E. Evans, *Aberystwyth and Its Court Leet* (1902), for plan of walls.

[28] A fully documented account of the boroughs of Snowdonia is given in E. A. Lewis, *The Medieval Boroughs of Snowdonia* (1912); see also the county volumes of the Royal Comm. on Hist. Monuments, Wales.

[29] H. Ellis, ed., *The Register of the Abbey of Aberconway* (Camden Soc., xxxix (1847)), p. 13.

origins are described in the Gazetteer, pp. 546–47) had passed several times from English hands to Welsh and back, but in 1277 had become English by the treaty of Aberconway. It may be significant that the Conway rental of 1305–06, long after Edward's town was built, was divided into three parts: "Conway"; "under the wall of Conway towards the water" and "in Deganwy (*Ganneu*)"; and that in this rental the nineteen houses in Deganwy (*Gannough*) were called *placeae*. If the abbot's burgages were not in Deganwy, then they must be placed outside the abbey precinct, probably at the river-side where the important ferry from Deganwy landed.[30]

It was not possible to make Conway completely rectangular: the curve of a small stream, the Afon Gyffin, forced the southern wall to follow suit, and the necessity of welding the abbey church into the street-plan made it necessary to distort some of the right angles of the chequers. The castle and all the medieval buildings within the town have been described and illustrated in two recent publications with detailed plans, and there is no need to say more here. The castle and the town walls with its gates and twenty-one towers are still well preserved, and although the interior of the town lacks the medieval atmosphere of its Gascon contemporaries, the distant prospect (see frontispiece) is most pleasing.

In the first surviving rental[31] (c. 1295) there were 112 burgage plots occupied and Henry le Waleys would have been pleased to know that one of these was occupied by a merchant of Bordeaux.[32] A document of 1305 accounts for 121¾ burgages.[33] A fuller rental of 1305–06, divided into six sections, that may be streets or chequers, lists 109 burgesses.[34] The two figures are not incompatible, for it was common for the wealthier burgesses of a town to possess more than one burgage: the 112 burgages of the 1295 document were held by only ninety-nine burgesses. In 1305–06 there were twelve temporary shops in the market place, and two butcher's stalls; fifteen buildings were rented outside the walls at the ferry landing.

While these burgages were being planned at Conway in the summer of 1283, operations at *Carnarvon* were begun. The site for the castle

---

[30] SC6/1170/2–5; J. Griffiths, "Documents relating to the Early History of Conway", *Trans. Caern. Hist. Soc.*, viii (1947), pp. 5–19.
[31] SC12/17/87.
[32] *Cal. Pat. Rolls, 1292–1301*, p. 156; there were also Gascon volunteers with Edward's army in the Welsh campaigns.
[33] SC6/1170/5.
[34] SC12/17/88.

and town was a level shelf alongside the sea, with a castle-quay almost ready-made. As at Llanvaes, Nevin and Towyn (see p. 574 below) there was a Welsh commercial centre already at Carnarvon by the water side, based on the *maenor* of the Welsh princes and the Norman motte nearby. The princes' revenues included customs duties paid at the port and the profits of justice in the "borough court". It should surprise no one (except those brought up in the old historical traditions of wild Welsh tribesmen) to find Welsh princes learning the same lessons as the English: that trade was both useful and profitable, and that selected places could shelter commercial and artisan elements alongside agriculturalists.

Indeed, in the spring of 1273 when Edward was in Gascony, prince Llewelyn had aroused the anger of the English council of regents by founding a Welsh bastide in the Severn valley at Dolforwyn. They dispatched the prior of Wenlock with instructions to deliver a strong letter of protest personally to the prince:[35]

We forbid you to erect *de novo* a borough or town or market.

Llewelyn replied that he was sure Edward himself would never have written so harshly and with such lack of understanding. But the councillors acted: the castle-works were besieged and taken by the English, and any burgages that had been erected in the bailey were destroyed for ever.

The Welsh settlement at Carnarvon was overwhelmed by the works of the new castle and town, although the Norman motte was left standing in the outer bailey of the new castle. Its moat was deepened and extended, and houses that obstructed the line chosen for the new town-ditch were swept away. The rectangular grid of streets of houses in Edward's town shows that no concessions were made to existing streets or houses.[36]

The main construction took place between 1283 and 1287, although the present form of the castle dates from after 1294 when the defences were strengthened following the Welsh rising, and almost as much was spent between 1295 and 1301 as between 1284 and 1287. The town wall cost at least £3,500 out of a total (again minimal) of £12,000. Carnarvon and Conway, with their circuit of town walls built as

[35] *Cal. Close Rolls, 1272–9*, p. 51; J. G. Edwards, ed., *Littere Wallie* (1940), pp. 23–24; *Cal. of Anc. Corresp. concerning Wales* (1935), p. 86.
[36] See the plans and photographs in Royal Comm. Hist. Mons. Wales, *Caernarvonshire II* (1960), pp. 115–158.

strongly as the castle itself, were the most expensive of the Edwardian projects studied in this chapter. Together they account for about one-third of all Edward's expenditure on towns and castles in north Wales up to 1301 when he transferred Wales to the rule of his eldest son.

Modern Carnarvon has its market place and shopping streets outside the medieval walls, and the suburban sprawl prevents an adequate appreciation of the unity of the castle and the walled town: perhaps the best view is from the sea or from the fields on the opposite side of the river (see endpapers).

The walled town is made up of three streets running north-south and the High Street that runs across them from the East Gate on the land-ward side to the West Gate by the quay. The best modern plan of the town, showing the imprint of the original burgage plots, each 60 feet by eight, is the 1:5,000 Ordnance Survey plan of 1887. The narrow neck of land between the rivers Seiont and Cadnant restricted the area available for burgages: there were fifty-nine in 1298 and sixty-three in 1309. The town church was the garrison chapel of St. Mary, attached to a corner-tower of the town walls by taking over a burgage plot. The mother church was at Llanbeblig, up on the hill outside the town. A semi-legible entry in a rental of 1298 suggests that the burgesses had stalls outside the walls on market days, finding that in peace-time the walls tended to cabin and confine their commercial spirit.[37]

At *Harlech*, work on the castle also began in June 1283, and Edward was there himself in September. There was an older castle, Welsh in origin, but probably no Welsh town. The centre of Welsh settlement was the *maenor* of Estingwern which was demolished at the conquest, the houses destroyed and the mill and lands rented to the new burgesses in the same way as those of old Carnarvon.[38] On these lands, men of Harlech boasted to Edward II that they had produced enough butter, meat and cheese to save themselves and the garrison from starvation during Madoc's rebellion of 1294.

Harlech was a small borough and there is no evidence that it was intended to have a walled borough linked to the castle, although Speed's plan of 1610 has a suggestion of a wall on one side of the town. In 1312 only 29¾ burgages were recorded,[39] and there is no more evidence of a grid plan than at Criccieth. The houses simply cluster round the castle-

[37] SC/12/17/86, printed in *Bull. B.C.S.*, ix (1938), pp. 238 241, along with the extent of 1284.
[38] SC6/1231/10.
[39] Lewis, *op. cit.*, p. 66.

gate, and the steepness of the slope is such that anything more formal would have been difficult. In 1294–95 the population of the town was forty-four and the garrison numbered forty-two;[40] in 1292 there were twelve taxpayers assessed at 52s. 7d. in all.[41] The town was planted in the narrow coastal parish of Llandanwg and had no church of its own; St. Tanwg's church is now abandoned in the sands at the foot of the

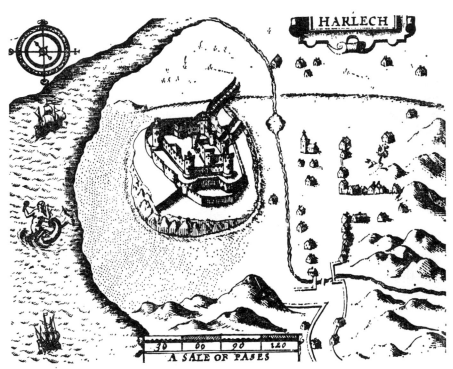

FIG. 7. HARLECH IN 1610. By John Speed.

castle cliff. The sea once came to the foot of Harlech castle, but, as at Winchelsea, the sea gate leads now only to grass, sand dunes and the pleasures of a golf course. Small as the borough was, its charter of November 1284 gave its settlers the full privileges of the city of Hereford. Nor was the castle cheap: it cost at least £8,000 between 1283 and 1292, in the same class as the whole work at Flint or Rhuddlan, and in a busy

[40] *Bull. B.C.S.*, viii (1937), pp. 149–150.
[41] E179/242/53 m. 2d.

season there were on the average 900 workmen employed on it, almost as many as the comparable average for Conway and Carnarvon.

Closest to Harlech geographically and in origin is the little borough of *Criccieth* on the Nevin peninsula. (The little town of Nevin, like Pwllheli and Towyn, was already in existence as a small Welsh town with municipal institutions granted by Welsh princes.) There was a castle of the Welsh princes at the site of Criccieth, but no borough before Edward's charter of November 1284, issued on the same day as that of Harlech. The burgages at Criccieth were the same size as those at Carnarvon but the whole scale of the town was different. By 1308 there were twenty-three burgages,[42] and only twenty-five in the mid-century.[43] In a garrison list of 1295 the civilian population consisted of eight burgesses, thirteen women and nine boys.[44] There are no signs of town walls today, but the older houses are loosely grouped around what may once have been the market place.[45]

A third borough of Snowdonia received its charter on the same day as Pwllheli and Harlech: the virtually forgotten town of *Bere*. The site of Bere castle is now emerging from the excavations conducted by the Inspectorate of Ancient Monuments on a rocky site near the south-west slopes of Cader Idris at the end of the Afon Cader, where there can have been little hope for a centre of civil commerce.

Nevertheless Edward visited here in May, July and November 1284 and on November 22 issued from Cardigan a charter similar in terms to those for Harlech, Carnarvon and Conway, conferring on the burgesses of Bere the privileges of Hereford. E. A. Lewis wrote:

Bere has no history beyond its charter and may be dismissed here,

but his own thirty-two-line footnote shows that this was too modest a judgement.[46]

It is known that the hill-top site had been fortified in the time of the Welsh princes and lost to David in 1283. Edward must have hoped that the site could be strengthened by new works and the addition of a civil settlement. The settlers came: the names of three mayors are known, the last in 1293, the year when the last constable of the castle was appointed. In 1298 this constable was pardoned the arrears that he owed the Crown, and the town then disappears from the public records. In 1292 a tax list[47] carries the names of sixteen taxpayers

[42] SC6/1170/6.   [43] SC6/1173/1.   [44] E101/5/18.
[45] R.C.H.M.W., *Caernarvonshire II* (1960), pp. 57–65.
[46] Lewis, *op. cit.*, p. 36.   [47] E179/242/53 m. 2 see Plate 12.

under the rubrick *Bere,* with a total of 76s. 11¾d.   They cannot be the taxpayers of the old Welsh settlement of Llanfihangel-y-Pennant that is nearby, for that community appears elsewhere in the roll with thirteen taxpayers.   The total paid at Bere may be compared with Harlech's 52s. 7d., although one man, William Dann, contributed almost a third of the sum from Bere.   Some of the names in the Bere list are certainly Welsh.

Where was the borough?   The slopes are almost as steep as at Harlech, but Harlech certainly had a small borough by its gate.   It is possible that the burgesses of Bere shared the outer bailey of the castle as did burgesses in some of the smaller boroughs of mid-Wales.   The slopes west of the castle are still covered with wood and scrub, and official excavations have not extended to that area.

Six years after the foundation of Bere and Harlech there appeared a royal borough at the eastern end of north Wales not far from Flint and Rhuddlan, where our narrative began.   This borough, *Caerwys,* was given the privileges of Conway and until 1672 was an assize town. Although now only a village, it has the full rectilinear form characteristic of the planted town.   Yet it was no walled town like Conway and its position has no defensive strength at all.   In Gascon terms it would have been reckoned a mere *bastide de commerce.*

Its relation to any preceding Welsh settlement in the locality is unclear.   It is possible that the borough was laid out alongside the church of an older settlement; there was a vill of Caerwys in 1242[48] and in 1244 the church of Caerwys was chosen by the Pope to be the meeting place of the two Welsh abbots appointed to judge whether David had concluded his treaty with Henry III under duress or not. Nearby at Maes y Mynan there was a house of the Welsh princes, and *Tref Edwyn* (sometimes identified as the original village of Caerwys) was one of the places claimed by the men of the border district of Englefield as a seat of justice.

The Wheeler valley, which seems to have determined the Welsh and English interest in this site, now carries the railway and a direct road from Chester to Denbigh.   The importance of the route may have made it worthwhile planting a second borough so near to Flint, and within thirteen years.   Other foundations had also come to the area: Ruthin was founded by Reginald de Gray in 1282; Denbigh, a private foundation of the earl of Lincoln, received its charter by 1290; and in 1292

48 *Cal. Chart. Rolls,* i, p. 272.

48

Overton received its charter. Holt was also founded in the last decade of the century, and there is a rather mysterious settlement of New Mostyn recorded in 1292, only 6 miles from Flint.

The last two Edwardian plantations to be considered were laid out in Anglesey on the shores of the Menai Straits. The first and largest project, of which the second was a delayed consequence, was begun at *Beaumaris* in 1295. It was on the scale of Carnarvon and Conway in expenditure—about £9,000 was spent up to 1301—and it envisaged a walled town alongside the castle, with access to the sea. The average number of men employed on the site in the spring and summer of 1295 was no less than 3,000 at a time when the repairs at Carnarvon were absorbing at least another 600.

Beaumaris, like Flint, was set among marshes, and the Norman-French name, *Beau Mareys* (*beau marais*) testified to something attractive in the site. For Edward, who had visited the area in 1283, the real beauty of the marshy site was its commanding position on the Menai Straits guarding the crossing into Anglesey. Carnarvon was just over the water: its foundation had followed the defeat of the Welsh in 1283, and after it had shown itself vulnerable to capture in 1294, Edward decided that a second barrier to disturbance would be worthwhile. Beaumaris castle was an elaborate concentric fortification with eight towers in the inner ring and twelve in the outer, a third ring being provided by a moat.

The town charter was granted at the end of the second building season on the castle in November 1296. It was modelled on Conway. The borough of Beaumaris involved Edward again in the necessity of moving an existing community: not a monastery as at Conway, nor a Norman borough as at Rhuddlan, but a small commercial town that had been developed by the Welsh princes on one of their principal demesne vills (*maerdref*) at Llanvaes;[49] St. Katherine's, its church, is still standing about a mile from Beaumaris. It was evidently thought that the traffic would not bear two towns within sight of each other, and the inhabitants of Llanvaes were transported 12 miles to another corner of the island and housed in yet another town, Newborough. Not all the inhabitants wanted to go. The doctor and more than thirty others were fined for unreasonable delay,[50] and seven years elapsed before Newborough received its own charter (see below).

[49] C145/79/12; *Hist. King's Works*, p. 402; *R.C.H.M. Wales, Anglesey* (1937), pp. 3–16.
[50] E101/109/2.

Its rent roll was arranged to be that of Llanvaes exactly to the farthing.

In 1298, with the castle still far from complete, there were 140 burgages in Beaumaris,[51] and in 1305 there were 132¼.[52] For the first ten years the new burgesses were encouraged by being rent free.[53] Their plots were 80 feet by 60 feet, and lay within the usual chequers and grid of streets. The new church of St. Mary was in the north-west quadrant of the town, which was walled. Short lengths of wall still remain, but the town has now spread beyond the north and west gates.

While the English burgesses were settling in at Beaumaris, the dispossessed Welsh of Llanvaes were having difficulties at *Newborough*. They had been given part of the royal demesne of Rhosfair,[54] and for some years there were Welsh bondmen of Rhosfair still living alongside them, lowering the dignity of the place as a town. In 1305 the burgesses petitioned for the bondmen to be moved and offered to take over the bond lands and compensate the king for any loss of rent.[55] They obtained their wish to have the bond lands, but some bondmen remained at Hendre Rossir, and if this is the farm now called Hendref (G.R. 422655), some stones of the boundary between borough and bond are still visible (O.S. 2½ inch map: 431655 to 434657). The townsmen of Newborough were very sensitive about status: it was they, it will be recalled, who were not satisfied that their charter proclaimed that their borough had all the privileges of Rhuddlan; they wanted these setting out *in puncto ad punctum*.

The town is now only a plain village with vestigial burgage plots along a straight east-west road. The plots do not seem to go as far as the isolated church which may be a remnant of Rhosfair; Hendref Farm is its nearest neighbour. The whole place is dismal on all but the sunniest days, and the western part of the parish has been inundated with sand, an encroachment that was already diminishing the king's rents in 1333.

Yet, disgruntled as the townsmen of Newborough were in 1305, they cannot have imagined that theirs was nearly the last borough that their conquerors would plant in medieval Wales. The chronology of medi-

[51] SC12/17/86.
[52] SC11/767.
[53] SC6/1211/2.
[54] SC11/768–9; E372/176; E352/94 m. 22d.
[55] H. Ellis, ed., *Record of Caernarvon* (1838), pp. 218 and 222–223.

eval town plantation, to be studied in detail in a later chapter, is quite unambiguous: the active decades in Gascony and Wales from 1270 to 1300 were very near the end of the story, and the town planners called together by Edward I in 1296 and 1297 were in fact meeting to practise what was soon (in England and Wales) to become a dead art.   Plantation of towns ceased for nearly 300 years, and when it was revived by James I and the London Companies it was for the soil of Ulster[56] not England.   When economic circumstances next encouraged new towns in England the bastidors were not kings but men like the Lowthers who created the port of Whitehaven; the promoters of eighteenth-century watering-places; and the factory-owners who built towns at their gate much as kings and barons had once built towns at theirs.

[56] G. Camblin, *The Town in Ulster* (1951), pp. 17–46; D. A. Chart, ed., *Londonderry and the London Companies* (1928).

PART ONE

THE ENDOWMENT OF NEW TOWNS

Each of these five chapters bears the name of a planted town, and each name indicates a different quality which the founder of the town wished to emphasise. Chapter 3 shows how landowners of all types could benefit from town plantation, and how the king himself was in a unique position to benefit. The four following chapters deal with the various provisions that recruits to a new town might expect to find; some at the charge of the founder and some at the charge of the first inhabitants.

CHAPTER THREE

Novum Forum: or, The Profit from a New Town

Quandam novam villam disponere et ordinare ad maius commodum nostri et mercatorum ibidem accedentium et aliorum quos ibidem habitare contigerit et morari.

Edward I's writ of September 24, 1296
(*Parliamentary Writs*, i, p. 49).

I

THE significance of a planted town is quite misunderstood if it is viewed in isolation from contemporary urban growth that took other forms. Many of the economic forces that encouraged seigneurs to plant new towns were also prompting them to transform existing villages into boroughs. "Organic" towns of this sort are found in all counties, intermingled with New Towns, and a seigneur who followed one course of profit was likely to follow the other as well. Thus, a bishop of Lincoln created New Thame and New Sleaford, but at Biggleswade the episcopal borough was made by promoting a village. A bishop of Bath planted Radeclive in an isolated position on the banks of the Axe, but the episcopal borough of Chard was the extension of an existing village. When the abbots of Burton-on-Trent wanted to make a borough at Burton itself, they added burghal areas to the old village, but at Abbots Bromley they simply enfranchised the village.[1] The borough of Higham Ferrers was created by a similar enfranchisement, but the Ferrers town of Newborough in Needwood Forest was created *de novo*. Successive kings of England planted towns on their demesnes, but no king was thereby prevented from following the more formal course of granting a charter to one of his villages. The real significance

---

[1] Documentary references for the planted towns will be found in the Gazetteers; the organic town references are: Biggleswade, *V.C.H. Beds.*, ii, p. 212; Abbots Bromley, *Ballard and Tait*, p. 44; Chard, *ibid.*, p. 3; Burton-on-Trent, *ibid.*, p. 50; *Ballard*, pp. 42–43; *Dugdale Monasticon*, iii, p. 48.

of the planted towns is that they were additional to a great movement of "organic" town development, and that the economy of the period between the Norman Conquest and the late thirteenth century had room for towns of both types, promoted villages and new plantations.[2]

The conjunction of old and new was as marked on the coasts of England as in the inland counties. By the end of the thirteenth century, a ship bringing wine from Gascony, and meeting a sudden gale that drove it towards a port of refuge, could find itself in places like Yarmouth (I.O.W.), Lymington and Portsmouth, none of which was much more than a century old. If he chose to land at New Winchelsea instead of one of the older Cinque Ports, the captain would see a church still in its scaffolding, and the town's walls incomplete. River shipping making its way down the Humber might begin at the wharves of old York and be heading for the old port of Grimsby, but on the way it passed the new towns of Airmyn, Hedon, Hull and Ravenserodd. If the river barges went upstream from York to the limits of the navigation of the Ouse they found themselves at the new borough of Boroughbridge; if they went up the Aire they would reach Maurice Paynel's new borough of Leeds laid out by the Aire bridge; or near the head of the Idle they would find the wharves of new Bawtry.

The simultaneous development of promoted villages (like the borough of Higham Ferrers) and planted towns (like the Ferrers borough of Newborough) was no accident. It relates to a contemporary economic situation that must be briefly stated. Brevity is possible since two chapters in the *Cambridge Economic History of Europe* have recently expounded the general character of medieval urbanism (and kindly devoted a few lines to the plantation of New Towns).[3] Professor Carus-Wilson has a brilliant essay on the connection between towns and trade,[4] and the general principles no longer need elaborate reiteration.

The towns were specialised centres of making and dealing. The successful foundation of so many towns would not have been possible without increased skills in the arts and crafts of the workshop and the counter, but towns also profited from the increase of rural populations all over Europe. The extra hands and mouths were potential producers

[2] Higham was enfranchised by William de Ferrers in 1251 (*Cal. Ch. Rolls*, i, p. 372); M. W. Beresford, *History on the Ground* (1957), ch. 6.

[3] *Camb. Econ. Hist. of Europe*, iii, ed. M. M. Postan, E. E. Rich and E. Miller (1963), chs. i and iv; the bastide reference is at the foot of p. 300.

[4] "Towns and Trade", in A. L. Poole, ed., *Medieval England* (1958), i, pp. 209–263.

of food and the raw materials on which a town fed, and they were potential customers in its market place and fairs. From them a town could recruit its newcomers, and if the population of other countries was also rising, then the towns that were ports stood to gain further from international trade.

It might be thought that a more numerous peasantry, equipped with poor agricultural techniques and vulnerable to disease and starvation in years of bad harvests, would have nothing to spare for the town market place. In fact, two powerful forces worked against the likelihood of total rural self-sufficiency. In the first place, it was the lords and not the peasants who controlled the product of the demesnes, and food could go to market while peasants went hungry. The first call on the energies of the majority of the peasantry was enjoyed by their seigneurs, who were not slow to be educated in the advantage of taking surpluses to market, once their own household needs had been met.

Yet town markets were not merely places where conscripted villeins carted the demesne products that they would rather have eaten themselves. The advantages of local specialisation, even to peasants, were apparent whenever good harvest years came and they, too, were in a position to take some of their own surplus to market; or whenever they had an opportunity to exercise any latent skill as part-time (even unofficial) craftsmen and dealers. In England local geographical features change significantly within quite short distances, and this fact laid the elementary basis for local specialisation on production of those crops or animals for which the area was best suited. Pastoral districts then needed to buy cereals from elsewhere, as did miners, quarrymen and salters. It is true that fear of starvation in a year of poor harvests set a limit on local specialisation, and there had to be arable husbandry in what would today seem very unlikely parts of England: but fear could only limit and not prevent local specialisation.

The lessons of specialisation did not need book-learning before they were appreciated. The eye and the purse were great educators. The lessons were quickly learned by the lords of great estates whose scattered territories enabled them to organise local specialisation within the estate, and the lessons were learned by part-time traders and artisans of the village. For such men the petty profits of their part-time labours demonstrated the real advantage that would come if they could be free from all agricultural ties. Thus, whoever they were, those learning the lessons could see how the development of towns met their need. In towns, as the next chapter will particularise, the professional merchants and craftsmen were better placed than elsewhere in the kingdom; and most obviously so in the towns that were also ports. It was in towns also, as the later pages of this chapter will show, that the seigneurs saw the produce from their rural acres finding more eager and more able buyers than in the existing small markets of the countryside.

Urban and rural economic expansion had reciprocal and beneficial action upon each other. The artisans in towns could not have existed without a supply of raw materials from the forests, the quarries, the mines and the grazing herds of the countryside; while the metal-workers, wood-workers, masons, tanners and weavers needed more food than a town's fields could supply. In turn, the town craftsmen produced goods that tempted lords and peasants alike to increase their agricultural production, to bring the surplus to market and to use it to purchase these town-made goods. Whatever conflicts of interest there were between seigneurs and townsmen, the towns were a great educator of landowners in the facts of life, especially the lesson that a rural estate organised to produce for the market was one route to achieve whatever was desired in the way of new fashions: armour, horses, weapons, apparel, manor houses, churches, castles and crusading expeditions; and if a lord's appetite outran achievement—as it often did—then it was in towns, too, that landowners found the moneylenders.

The planted towns, like the other towns, rode on the wave of rising production and population in the rural areas in the two centuries following the Norman Conquest. In Gascony the planted town was sometimes named in documents as *bastida seu nova populacio*, and in Spain the planted town was *nova poblacio*. It was this prolonged rise in European population that made it possible for the new towns to be populated without depopulating their neighbours. On the best accepted estimates, the population of England, that was perhaps $1\frac{1}{4}$ million in 1086, multiplied threefold in the next 250 years, the very period when town plantation was in progress.[5] In some rural areas it is very likely that the rate of increase was more than threefold.[6] Where could the extra hands find work and the extra mouths be fed?

[5] J. C. Russell, *British Medieval Population* (1948), p. 246.
[6] J. B. Harley, "Population Trends and Agricultural Development", *Econ. Hist. Rev.*, 2nd ser. xi (1958), pp. 8–18; H. E. Hallam, *The New Lands of Elloe* (1954); the connection of the fenland colonisation and the growth of Lynn is set out by Prof. Carus-Wilson in *Med. Archaeol.*, vi–vii (1962–63), pp. 187–201.

Colonisation did not reach its high-water mark before the late thirteenth century, and until that date there was room for new populations in the countryside, especially near the margins of cultivation. The expanding old-established towns were able to provide some employment, but new towns that had to be peopled very quickly were contributing uniquely to the absorption of surplus population. The oligarchic structure of the older towns gave less encouragement to newcomers than did the new towns, and each new town was a place of refuge to newcomers before it settled down in its turn to assert the characteristic rights of the Insider against the Outsider: but the door had been open for a while; and new doors were being opened all the time.

Increased demand for craftsmen and traders produced some increase in the numbers of such specialists even within villages, just as many organised markets and fairs were established in country places that laid no claim at all to being towns. But, before 1350, there were powerful reasons why such specialists might be expected to proliferate fastest within communities that were different from villages: that is, which had the distinctive status of a borough.

In a village the low incomes of the peasants, free or bond, set an upper limit to the sales that any craftsmen, however skilled, could hope to make. The incomes and tastes of the peasantry also set a limit to the sales that any trader could make, however cunning he was in laying out a good bargain. Only when a local feast-day brought people together from more than one village was there much chance that anything like a fair could develop, but one-day-a-year opportunities were not very encouraging to specialisation.

From the seigneur's side it always paid to have a few villagers with developed manual skills, especially those who could mend a plough, shoe a horse or repair a mill-wheel. But from 1150 to about 1350 the main value of a village labour-force to a seigneur was demonstrated when he had it working on his demesne. By showing how profitable it was to produce a surplus for the market, the very success of towns made seigneurs more aggressive in exacting the maximum effort from their rural labour-force. The villeins were conscripts on the lord's demesnes. Town air bred free, as the saying went; but the villeins who were still bound to the soil were able to breathe very little of it. As far as they were concerned, the heady air that their lord breathed in the towns merely aroused his appetite for more and more demesne produce:

59

and for them the result was heavier labour services and heavier manorial burdens.[7]

Thus, the self-interest of the seigneur forms the central theme for this chapter. It illustrates the various hopes of profit, direct and indirect, that the founder of a town might entertain and it shows what gains actually accrued to particular founders.

II

New Berwick, in the words of Edward I's writ to the colloquium of town planners, was to be laid out

> for the greater profit of Ourselves and of merchants coming to dwell there, and of others who happen to reside there.

We must now anatomise the "profit" that founders expected from their plantations. "Ourselves" in Edward I's writ was the royal "We", but a king's profits from being lord of a borough were paralleled in the account rolls of those of his subjects who had become lords of boroughs. For brevity, the whole class of borough lords will be called seigneurs, whether barons, petty manorial lords, abbots or bishops, and the important economic interest that the king uniquely enjoyed as sovereign will not be treated until the general interest of landowners has been demonstrated. In England it was not essential for the king to give permission before a seigneur made a borough on his own land, although it might be politic to seek a royal charter. Similarly, a seigneur did not have to enrol his borough charter at the royal Chancery, although the habit of so doing grew with the passage of time. Under these influences the royal and seigneurial boroughs grew closer together in economic character and constitutional form, especially since baronial boroughs could fall to the Crown by escheat, and royal boroughs could be mediatised to others: Newcastle under Lyme passed to the earl of Lancaster from the Crown in 1265, but returned to the Crown later when the duchy of Lancaster estates became vested in the Crown.

A seigneur's simplest hope was that a new town would augment his rent-roll. More revenue was always welcome, especially when warfare, buildings, armour and weapons became increasingly elaborate and

[7] M. M. Postan, "The Chronology of Labour Services", *Trans. Royal Hist. Soc.*, 4th ser. xx (1937), pp. 169–194.

expensive as the skills of masons and metal-workers increased, and as merchants displayed the tempting produce of foreign craftsmen.

The traditional revenues from an estate were taken in the form of agricultural goods and the personal services of the tenantry; although, if we follow Professor Postan's chronology of labour services, we see that the seigneurs learned a lesson from falling prices and a reduced population in the decades following the Norman Conquest. If land was temporarily at a discount through wasted holdings, then food was cheap to buy in the market, and, since man-power as well as villages had been devastated in the Conquest, all labour would be more expensive. In these circumstances the seigneurs learned the lesson of commutation and took cash instead of goods, rent instead of services. The extent of local recovery by 1086 is indicated in Domesday Book, but within half a century the civil war of the Anarchy brought destruction again to the towns and countryside, and it is not until after 1154, as Chapter 11 shows, that real vigour in English town plantation becomes apparent. Nevertheless, even in a period inimical to massive expansion of population and settlement, there were attractions in founding a new town if there was some local opportunity. Periods of warfare and conquest followed by rebellions were particularly conducive to frontier- and garrison-towns, as the Norman settlement of Wales and the Marches so strikingly shows. Other aspects of a new ruler and his immigrant followers favoured new urban settlement: in some towns it took the form of a "French borough" set alongside the English, and in others (such as Pontefract, Ludlow and Richmond, Yorks.) it took the form of a new castle-town. On the north bank of the Tyne a town arose with the name of Newcastle, and on the south bank of the Thames opposite Eton the royal palace was moved from a meadowside site to a defensible cliff, and created a New Windsor.

The post-Conquest period could not have been devoid of new commercial opportunities, even among disorder, for the early foundations at Boston and Lynn show that successful Norman town plantation did not depend only on the protection of a great castle; and by 1125 St. Ives and St. Neots were teaching the same lessons.

Whatever local dislocations and contractions had accompanied the Conquest and the Anarchy, there is little doubt that, from the mid-twelfth century, population expanded steadily, culminating in the great land-hunger of the late thirteenth century. This land-hunger put a strong bargaining weapon into the hands of all who possessed land, besieged by the land-hungry. Seigneurs were able to re-assert their claims to demesne labour, but they did not abandon the market-economy and take up primitive barter as a way of disposing of the surplus produce from their demesnes: this little piggy still went to market. Seigneurs encouraged the multiplication of markets and towns with one hand, while with the other they bound the majority of their villeins firmly to the soil.

Educated by the successful town plantations of the king and the great seigneurs, it was possible for others to learn the lesson that a piece of barren land could breed precious metal for its owner. If a few acres of land by a river bank were lost to agriculture, the rent-roll was diminished: but the new burgage rents could be more than compensatory. There is not much local evidence for the value of arable land per acre in the early twelfth century but it was certainly nothing like the shilling a year that became the conventional burgage rent, and a burgage occupied only a fraction of an acre. In order to make room for the houses and streets of Ludlow, New Windsor, Boston and Lynn it was not good agricultural land that was sacrificed. In 1100 Shropshire and Windsor Forest were far from having every acre under the plough, while in the Fens the great colonising movement that Dr. Hallam has described was only just beginning. Yet the bishops of Norwich found that the demand for building sites at Lynn was so great that by 1135 a second town had been laid out alongside the first on the banks of the Ouse. To have all these rents in exchange for a few acres of waste land invites a simile that the bishops who were lords of Lynn would have understood: it was manna from Heaven.

For a short while the smile of Heaven warmed the lords of Holderness even more generously. A sandbank at the mouth of the Humber began to expand in size and provided foothold large enough for the borough of Ravenserodd. In the decade beginning 1260 it yielded £6 a year; in 1270, £12; in 1271, £26; in 1287, £39; in 1281, £48; and in 1307, £68. This was pure gain, for not an inch of soil had been lost to agricultural production.

Even though the returning pressure of thirteenth-century population had enhanced the value of arable acres, the gap between the burgage rent and the agricultural value of the plot remained. The lords had no need to fear the increase in population. It was the ultimate source of recruits for their towns; it increased the cultivation of new lands and brought more goods into their market places; it made the villeins more hungry for land, and it increased the lord's bargaining power over his villeins.

With the increase in the number of market centres, the lord of a town had an interest in the prosperity of market places that went beyond the rent of his burgage plots.   In the first instance he was the recipient of all the tolls paid by those outsiders who used the market.   Every town had a grant of a market (and usually a fair) that derived from the lord of the town or from the Crown's grant to the lord.   Markets also gave the lord of the town further rents from the booths and stalls that were set up in the market place itself.   It is not accidental that the early accounts for the bishop of Winchester's boroughs refer indifferently to *Novus Burgus* and *Novum Forum*, nor that one planted town on the border of Suffolk and Cambridge still proclaims that it was a Newmarket. The purpose of the lord of Oswestry's bailiff when he admitted tenants to the burgages was stated plainly in the charter to be

ad emendationem mercati mei

just as when the bishop of Lincoln allowed a hundred-yard frontage to be built in New Thame market place it was

ut redditus suus accresceret.

When the abbot of Eynsham sacrificed a few acres of Eynsham fields to lay out the *Novus Burgus* of 1215 the charter was equally frank about the economic purpose:

pro utilitate et promocione domus nostrae.[8]

The goods chosen for tolls in the new towns do not seem to have differed from those in the organic boroughs, and the rates stated in charters and customals show no unique levels.   The Gascon bastides sometimes have a few exotic items that rarely came to English or Welsh market-stalls, but the basic commodities of exchange between town and country appear in all the lists.   Since typical tolls are tabulated and classified in the digests of borough charters made by Ballard and Tait there is no purpose in repetition here.

The surviving account rolls of the lords of planted towns do not usually detail the commodities that paid tolls, and many accounts do not separate the tolls of markets from the tolls of fairs.   Single refer-

---

[8] Oswestry: *Ballard*, p. 81; New Thame: *R.H.* ii, p. 30; Eynsham: H. E. Salter, ed., *The Cartulary of the Abbey of Eynsham* (Oxford Hist. Soc., xlix and li), i (1907), no. 44a; and ii (1908), p. xli.

ences occur to tolls such as might be found in any organic borough: passagium, pontagium, cheminagium, cariagium, keelagium, kaiagium, picagium and stallagium. For a few years a chance survival of documents affords details of the ships that came to unload at the quays of New Winchelsea, and for other years there are weekly totals of tolls paid, showing the ebb and flow through the seasons and storms of the last decade of the thirteenth century.

The full burden of tolls on inter-urban trade was in practice mitigated by the widespread exemption that all seigneurs granted their burgesses, making them free of tolls in all the boroughs of that seigneur. The exemptions granted throughout the kingdom by the king, the greatest of seigneurs, were the most valuable, and the charter given by the Empress Matilda to the new town of Devizes declared:

> I grant to my burgesses of Devizes that in consideration of their service to me they shall be quit of toll, passage and lastage (i.e. loading duty) in all my land and in the seaports.[9]

The men of Hythe had freedom that extended into Normandy, and Portsmouth at its foundation in 1194 received from Richard I this grant:

> to be quit and free of toll and pontage and stallage both by land by sea wherever they may come in all our land.[10]

Trade within a town was not "free" in the modern sense. The burgesses did not pay the tolls that outsiders had to pay when they came to sell goods at fairs and markets, but there were restrictions on the quality of goods sold, strict regulations concerning the hours of sale and the cornering of scarce commodities, and public supervision of the accuracy of weights and measures. Townsmen were as frail as outsiders when temptation beckoned, and the lord of the town gained financially since the fines levied in the courts of market and borough cases went to him (unless granted away in the foundation charter). Major breaches of the assizes of measures brought offenders before the king's judges, and the fines into the king's pocket. The first documentation that has survived for some Cornish and Devon boroughs is an appearance on the Assize Roll: the rules for the sale of wine and cloth had been broken.[11] Justice, went the saying, is a great Profit.

---

[9] *Ballard*, p. 181.
[10] *Ibid.*, pp. 171 and 182.
[11] J.I. 1/174 mm. 27d. 38d., and 1/175 m. 41, the latter case concerning a merchant from a Cornish plantation, Tregoney; cloth offences in J.I. 1/775 m. 23 and 1/778 m. 53 (Hants.).

III

Table III.1 sets out the components of seigneurial revenue for a group of towns in different parts of England and Wales. It shows that the burgage rents were sometimes the principal element in the revenue that had come with the plantation (Chipping Sodbury, Cowbridge, Petersfield), but in other towns the market revenues outweighed the burgage rents (Llanidloes, Chepstow, Newport (Salop.), Monmouth). In 1293 Llanidloes had only sixty-six burgages but its markets, fairs and courts brought its lord the equivalent of 252 burgage shillings. Chepstow had 308 burgages but in 1308 the other revenues exceeded the burgage rents. Clearly, a prosperous catchment area for the trade of a market and fair was as important an item in the success of a town as the ability of the seigneur to recruit burgesses. In south Wales in particular there was a category of burgess whose name indicates that he was not permanently resident in the town. He was the burgess *de vento*, the man of the wind, who thought it worth while having a stake in the new town but whose other interests—rural or urban—kept him on the move from place to place. In the town rentals and accounts these burgesses are usually enumerated separately from the residents.

The absolute amounts that a seigneur drew from the revenues of a planted town may not appear to be very significant. It is more useful to view these revenues in perspective, either in relation to a seigneur's revenues from his organic boroughs or to his revenues from the parent manor.

Table III.2 shows the values of the boroughs on the estates of five families, taken from inquisitions *post mortem* dating between 1245 and 1339. When the number of burgages is stated in the document the first column gives this figure; the bracketed figures derive from other near-contemporary documents.[12]

The most extensive borough-owners in the Table were the earls of Hertford and Gloucester with twenty-one English boroughs, three in Monmouth and seven in Wales. Twelve of these can be claimed as plantations, and all but one of the twelve contained more than 100 burgages. The size of the Welsh boroughs is particularly impressive. The nine organic towns made the earls £234 better off than if they had not urbanised their rural manors; and the twelve plantations rewarded

---

[12] Burgage rents from a large sample of boroughs are given in M. de W. Hemmeon, *Burgage Tenure in Medieval England* (1914), pp. 67–70.

TABLE III.I

COMPONENTS OF REVENUE FROM PLANTED TOWNS

Place	Year	Burgage and other rents (£ s. d.)	Tolls of markets and fairs (£ s. d.)	Profits of justice (£ s. d.)	Other items (£ s. d.)	Sources
WELSHPOOL	1293	12 15 7	12 0 0	2 0 0	6 0 0	C133/64/16
LLANIDLOES	1293	2 19 2	11 6 0	1 6 8	1 6 0	C133/64/16
HENLEY IN ARDEN	1296	7 18 10	4 0 0	2 18 8		C133/76/4
CHIPPING SODBURY	1296	9 11 7	2 0 0	1 0 0	17 4	C133/77/3
	1363	9 18 0	1 6 8	1 10 0		C135/177/2
COWBRIDGE	1296	11 12 0	3 3 4	1 0 0		C133/77/3
CHEPSTOW	1307	15 8 4	20 0 0		25 12 8	C133/127
PETERSFIELD	1307	7 1 6	2 10 0	5 0		C133/129
	1314–15	6 14 10½	13 4	13 4		C134/42
NOSS MAYO	1309	4 16 2		4 0		C134/16/9
LLANDOVERY	1316–17	3 18 0	4 13 4	2 0 0		C134/56/3
NEWPORT (Salop)	1316–17	4 1 0	7 6 0	5 13 0		C134/56/3
HAVERFORD WEST	1324	18 0 7½	3 0 0			C134/83
	1326	4 1 2½	3 0	2 0 0		C134/99
NEW RADNOR	1335	10 0 0	10 0 0	1 4 0		C135/45/21
COWBRIDGE	1349	7 11 0	2 10 0	6 13 4	8 0 0	C135/105
NEATH	1349	7 9 10½	1 6 8	2 0 0	2 0 0	C135/105
STOCKBRIDGE	1361	5 6 3	1 0 0	2 13 0		C135/160/5
MONMOUTH	1361	6 13 0	25 0 0	15 0 0	15 0 0	C135/161
	1362	7 13 0	25 6 8	15 0 0		C135/169/3
KIDWELLY	1362	15 0 0	3 6 8	30 0 0		C135/169/3
ABERGAVENNY	1368	10 0 0	4 5 0			C135/200

TABLE III.2

BURGAGES AND REVENUES OF PLANTED AND ORGANIC TOWNS OF SEIGNEURS, 1245–1339

(Planted Boroughs in Italics)

A. EARLS OF HERTFORD AND GLOUCESTER 1262–1314; CLARE, 1329–39

County	Borough	Burgages		Revenue £ s. d.	
BUCKS.	Marlowe	—		—	(1262, 1314)
DORSET	Cranborne	45	(1314)	1 2 6	(1306–07)
	Wareham	—		36 2 7¾	(1329–30)
	Weymouth	[260]		20 12 9	(1329–30)
ESSEX	Great Bardfield	—		9 10 10	(1329–30)
GLOUCS.	Campden, Chipping*	—		1 13 6	(1295)
	Fairford	68	(1306–07)	5 3 0	(1306–07)
	Gloucester	—		—	(1262)
	Sodbury, Chipping	176	(1306–07)	12 11 7	(1295)
	Tewkesbury	148⅚	(1306–07)	7 8 10	(1306–07)
	Thornbury	119	(1314)	8 0 0	(1295)
HANTS.	*Petersfield*	—		9 16 10	(1306–07)
HERTS.	Standon	—		11 8 7½	(1262)
KENT	Bletchingley	—		8 13 0	(1262)
	Brasted	—		5 7 4	(1314)
	Tonbridge	—		4 2 4	(1295)
NORTHANTS.	Rothwell	—		31 5 3½	(1262)
OXON.	Burford	—		14 6	(1314)
SUFFOLK	Clare	—		15 16 9½	(1262)
	Sudbury	—		32 5 10	(1329–30)
WILTS.	Bedwyn	—		—	(1314)
MONMOUTH	*Newport*	275	(1314)	13 15 0	(1314)
	Trellech	271	(1306–07)	27 2 0	(1329–30)
	Usk	300	(1306–07)	52 7 6½	(1329–30)
GLAMORGAN	Caerleon	—		55 3 9	(1338–39)
	Caerphilly	80[+ 116]	(1295)	4 15 0	(1314)
	Cardiff	423	(1306–07)	21 3 0	(1306–07)
	Cowbridge	276¾	(1306–07)	19 18 9	(1306–07)
	Kenfig	142	(1306–07)	7 2 0	(1306–07)
	Neath	128	(1306–07)	3 4 0	(1306–07)
	Llantrissant	226	(1314)	12 3 8	(1314)

Sources: 1262: C132/27/5
1295: C133/77/3
1306–07: C133/128–130
1314: C134/42
1329–30: SC11/799
1338–39: SC11/801

Note: Chipping Campden (Glos.) may on some counts be reckoned a plantation: see Gazetteer.

TABLE III.2—(cont.)

County	Borough	Burgages	Revenue £ s. d.
B. BALDWIN, EARL OF DEVON, 1245			
DEVON	Honiton	—	5 15 4
	Plympton	—	24 2 2
	Tiverton	—	5 4 11
	Source: C132/3/10		
C. HUGH DE COURTENAY, 1292			
DEVON	Chulmleigh	83	2 15 2
	Colyford	111	5 4 5
	Newton Poppleford	55½	3 2 0½
	Okehampton	140	8 15 5
	Source: C133/62/7		
D. OWEN DE LA POLE, 1293			
MONTGOM.	Llanidloes	[66]	16 11 10
	Welshpool	[225]	32 15 7
	Source: C133/64/16		
E. AYMER, EARL OF PEMBROKE, 1327			
HERTS.	Hertford	—	—
LINCS.	Gainsborough	—	—
PEMBROKE	Haverford West	[360]	21 0 7½
	Pembroke	220[227½]	—
	Tenby	220[267]	—
	Source: C134/83–5		
F. WILLIAM MARTIN, 1326			
DEVON	Barnstaple	156	
	Bow	34	9 1 2½
	Combe Martin	82	11 17 2
	Ford, North	68	11 17 2
	Holsworthy	19	6 5 10
	Ilfracombe	52	—
	Molton, South	160	—
	Torrington	43	—
	Totnes, Little	58	—
PEMBROKE	Newport	[46?]	16 6 8
	Source: C134/99; figures in brackets from Table IX.2.		

them with a further £205 for not being content with their organic towns. The increment is significant: 88%.

Even where detailed account rolls are wanting, the standard shilling burgage rent that prevailed almost everywhere enables a minimal assessment to be made of the increment from planted towns. Table IX.2 gives the number of burgages that graced the rent-rolls of the king and his barons in the towns of Wales, and the burgage shillings were only the beginning of the profit from these towns, as is shown when documents are explicit about the components of the other urban revenues. Thus, besides Beaumaris's 154¼ burgages, the king could expect £7 or £8 from the ferry, markets, fairs and courts of the town. Besides the sixty-three burgage rents in Carnarvon he could expect £11 from the ancillary revenues. At Aberystwyth in 1301–02 the perquisites of court at £6 14s. 4d. were almost as valuable as the burgage rents of £7.[13]

Another useful comparison is between the income from a borough and the income from the manor in which it had been planted. The surviving accounts underestimate the value of the manor to the lord, for the figures of clear profit at which the manorial accountant arrived were in fact simply the cash surplus of the enterprise. If the manorial enterprise provided corn, cheese, butter, meat, eggs, timber, or stone for its lord's needs there would be no transfer of cash to be accounted for. It would be important to make some estimate of these values, were not the ratios already so consistently in favour of the manor, in favour of the mother against the child.

Thus the small borough of Downton, planted by the bishop of Winchester c. 1208, brought increasing burgage rents as the town was peopled, until a maximum revenue was soon reached, of about £10 a year. The clear revenue of the rural manor of Downton was reckoned by the accountant as £140 in 1208–09 and a little greater in 1232–33 and 1274–75. About the same ratio can be observed at another Winchester borough, that of Hindon in Knoyle manor. Hindon town was worth about £10 a year to the bishop once the recruiting period was over, but the rural manor of Knoyle was worth about £100 clear. New Alresford, the most valuable of the bishop's plantations, was worth about £20 in the mid-thirteenth century when Old Alresford provided the bishop with a cash revenue five times greater. The bishop of Lincoln then drew from his manor of Old Thame about six times the yield of the seventy-six burgages in New Thame. The new towns were valuable increments to revenues from traditional manorial sources, and even small increments are welcome to those who have more expenditure in mind, but we must keep them in proportion. Increments from organic towns, it may be added, show the same feature: a useful addition to manorial revenues, but not a high proportionate

[13] SC6/1211/2 and 1218/1.

increase. In 1262 the organic borough made from the village of Clare was assessed at one-seventh of the value of the rural manor.[14]

The beauty of the burghal increment, from the seigneur's point of view, was the relatively small effort required to obtain it. The manor of Clare had a value of £113 in the early fourteenth century when the four plantations that remained to Elizabeth de Burgh (Weymouth, Usk, Trellech and Denbigh) brought her £207. To obtain the £113, between 550 and 660 acres had to be sown each year; sheep tended and pastured so as to yield 300 fleeces; tenants for surplus pasture had to be found; and between 3,000 and 4,000 villein works organised and supervised. To obtain £16 from Clare borough, there was only the effort of rent-collecting (£4), organising the court (£6 revenue) and collecting the single sum of £6 for which the market and fair tolls were then being farmed. The £10 that the bishops of Winchester gained from the creation of Hindon may not seem great alongside the £67 that the manor yielded in 1264–65 or the £100 in 1274–75, but to obtain the manorial income a demesne of between 387 and 453 acres had to be cultivated and the labour-force organised or hired; a flock of sheep never less than 1,000 and sometimes 3,000 strong had to be cared for; smaller herds of other animals were maintained, and the produce in grain, animals, food and industrial raw materials had to be gathered, sometimes processed, and then sent to market.[15]

The maintenance and renewal of the manorial equipment was a direct charge of the seigneur, and all reeves' accounts show this sort of expenditure: but the initial capital equipment of a town was not necessarily at the lord's charge, and if he had not provided the market hall, the quays, the walls and the other buildings described below (pp. 142–78) he had no responsibility for maintenance and renewal. What he had sacrificed was the produce or rent from a small area of land on which the burgages had been laid out. If the land lay on common pasture near the edge of a parish or alongside some marshland creeks, then the sacrifice was not very demanding on the founder. The reeve of the earl of Cornwall in Tybeste manor recorded a loss of pasture *propter burgum*. Six shillings rent had been sacrificed, but the same membrane

[14] Winchester episcopal plantations: data from M. W. Beresford, "The Six New Towns of the Bishops of Winchester", *Med. Archaeol.*, ii (1959), pp. 187–215, based on Pipe Rolls, formerly P.R.O. Eccles, 2/159270B et sqq., now at County Record Office, Winchester; Thame: Queen's College, Oxford, Ms. 366, transcript kindly loaned by M. W. Barley; Clare: C132/27/5.

[15] SC11/799 and 801; George Holmes, *The Estates of the Higher Nobility in Fourteenth Century England* (1957), pp. 142–143.

carries the record of thirty burgages in this borough, Grampound, their total being five times the value of the sacrifice.[16]

The continuous series of accounts from the bishop of Winchester's manors also makes it possible to measure some of the sacrifices made for the land on which to develop a new borough. In the late fourteenth century the reeves of Overton were still absolving themselves from the annual obligation to return 36s. from sixteen separate pieces of land *tractae in burgum*. This was the most lavish sacrifice in any of the bishop's six plantations, perhaps because of the siting of the new town on the main road that ran through the fields of old Overton village. At Newtown (I.O.W.) the reeve was similarly exonerated in 1254–55 from 20s. rent *in defectu terrae de Stretleya tractae in burgum*. At Hindon the sacrifice made for the town site was 6s. 11¾d., the rent of a croft and 1½ virgates of land "taken into the borough". The tenants of this croft, Ada and Roger *de Hinedon*, must have been living in an isolated farm on the hill from which they (and the new town) took their name. At Downton the value of *iii terrae tractae in burgum* was 6s. or, if we wish to be as accurate as the bishop's reeves, it was six shillings and twelve hens. The non-arrival of these hens on the traditional day was carefully noted in the *Instaurum* (stock) part of the account; the plantation of Newtown (I.O.W.) had robbed the lord of 40 eggs a year, and the site of Overton cost him 72 hens a year.

Instead of hens and eggs the bishop now had burgesses, rents, tolls and perquisites of court. The four sacrifices detailed above total £3 8s. 11¾d. Yet the clear revenues from these four towns in the mid-thirteenth century was £33 14s. 3½d., or nearly ten times the value of the land sacrificed.

The first years of a town's life would show receipts climbing as the burgage plots began to fill with houses. The 19 burgages of the first year's account for Downton were 30 in the second year, 72 five years later and 89 after five years more. At Overton (Hants.) there were 22 burgages in 1218–19, 26½ in 1219–20, 32½ in 1220–21, 36 in 1223–24, 38 in 1225–26, and 40 in 1223–24. At Newtown (Hants.) there were 67 in 1218–19, 69 in 1219–20 and 75 in 1220–21.

If some of these newcomers were villeins permitted to leave one of the founder's manors, then he could also gain revenue by selling the right to emigrate from the demesne. The accounts for Downton in 1210–11

---

[16] L. M. Midgley, *Ministers' Accounts of the Earldom of Cornwall 1296–7* (Camden Soc. 3rd ser. lxvii (1945)), p. 235.

included a payment from one Odo of three shillings *ut possit remanere in foro*, and in 1211–12, when a payment of more than twice this amount was made by another villein, the verb employed by the reeve changed from *posse* to *audere*, emphasising the permission that had been given:

una marca de Helya Bel ut audeat remanere in foro.

It is possible that the large sums paid at Tybeste in 1296–97

pro carta domini Comitis de libertate habenda

came from villeins who were anxious to move the short distance that separated their homes from the new borough of Grampound which had been planted by the earl of Cornwall within the bounds of their parish.[17]

Migration was a two-way traffic, and strong competition might at any time produce vacant holdings. "Decay of rent" is a not uncommon entry in the reeve's account, even when towns were quite newly founded, and while newcomers were still arriving to take up other plots in the same town.

There were other reasons why revenues from a town's burgages, courts and tolls should fluctuate from year to year, for there was no law of man or nature to arrange that the same fines would be levied in the borough court each year, nor that exactly the same goods would come to pay toll in the markets and fairs. The revenues from the royal town of Kingston on Hull in the years 1293–1305, when it was well established, fluctuated as follows:[18]

	£	s.	d.		£	s.	d.
1293–94	115	10	8	1299–1300	118	7	4½
1294–95	112	19	10	1300–01	120	5	4
1295–96	111	17	11	1301–02	119	14	11½
1296–97	122	1	4½	1302–03	121	12	0½
1297–98	115	10	9½	1303–04	130	9	7½
1298–99	117	8	9½	1304–05	143	8	6½

Whenever there was serious misfortune—a fine or an armed attack— the *decasus redditus* entries proliferated, and after warfare on the borders in Wales or Gascony the decrease in rents was substantial and might last some years. It was harder to rebuild town houses than the flimsier village houses, and it took more seasons to restore confidence and bring traders back into residence than it did to re-sow the burned fields of

[17] *Loc. cit.* in fn. 16.
[18] E372/152B mm. 1–34; SC11/743.

some ravaged village. When the earl of Gloucester's estates were surveyed after his death in 1295 there were 80 burgages destroyed by burning in Caerphilly, 102 in Trellech, 180 in Usk and 190 in Newport (Mon.). When his widow's estates were surveyed after her death in 1306 there were still burned buildings in Caerphilly and Llantrissant, and in 1314, on Gilbert de Clare's death, there were still 29 burgages empty in Llantrissant.[19]

There was little a seigneur could do in these circumstances to extract the old rents, and the burgesses might in any case have died in the attack on the town, but the smaller fluctuations between good and bad trading years could be insured against if the town contracted to pay a fixed annual sum to the seigneur instead of his collecting the rents, tolls and court fees. The seigneur had won certainty of revenue and he no longer had the trouble of collection; the town would fix the sum (the fee farm) at a rate that gave it a profit; and the town gained some independence once the lord's officials ceased to have daily interest in the petty revenues of the town.

Thus the Pipe Roll shows that the new borough of Portsmouth first paid a fee farm of £16 4s. 8d., and Liverpool in 1229 paid a fee farm of £10, the first of four annual payments. Revision of the fee farm was possible when the contractual period ran out. The fee farm of Portsmouth was raised in 1229 by £2, and the fee farm of New Winchelsea was fixed in 1288 at the same sum as the fee farm of Old Winchelsea, as some compensation to the burgesses for the losses they had sustained in Old Winchelsea.[20]

The accounts for Gascony show that the king farmed most of the town revenues there. Henry le Waleys, we have seen, farmed six of the Périgord bastides for ten years beginning in 1284 at £170 sterling per annum. In the year 1311–12 Edward II received the following farms from the bastides of the Agenais:[21]

	£ s. d.		£ s. d.
Monclar	25 0 0	Nicole	15 17 6
La Parade	28 15 0	St Julien de Colorbisse	44 15 0

[19] C133/77/3. Warfare also brought destruction to Gascon towns: see Chapter 13.
[20] Portsmouth: *Ballard and Tait*, p. 308; Liverpool: *ibid.*, p. 309; New Winchelsea: *ibid.*, p. 321.
[21] E101/164/1 mm. 5r.–6r. The sums here are expressed in £ *bord.* and an approximate sterling equivalent can be obtained by dividing by five.

	£	s.	d.		£	s.	d.
Castelnaud and				Montréal	143	15	0
St. Pastour	6	5	0	Lamontjoie	4	7	6
Villeneuve	37	10	0	Larroque-			
Lagruère	37	10	0	Fourcès	7	15	5
Damazan	83	5	0	Marmande	250	0	0
Miramont	38	2	6	Valence-			
				d'Agen	34	7	6

In England, the following examples of fee farms are taken from charters of planted towns:[22]

		£	s.	d.
Richmond (Yorks.)	1137–45	29	0	0
	1268	40	0	0
Pontefract	1194	200	0	0
Appleby	1200	sum not stated		
Newcastle on Tyne	1201	60	0	0
New Montgomery	1228–29	40	0	0
Liverpool	1229	10	0	0
Plympton Erle	1242	24	2	2
Newcastle under Lyme	1251	sum not stated		
Clitheroe	1272–91	6	13	4
Newport (I.O.W.)	1262–93	18	2	2 (rents)
Brecon	1277–82	86	13	4
		12	0	0 (mills, tolls and customs)

The revenues of additional towns also made it easier for a seigneur to live beyond his income. On the one hand was the chance that some of the townsmen would accumulate enough wealth (even after taxes and tolls) to have some available for putting out on loan. Rich townsmen had less appetite than lords for extravagances of castle-building and crusading, and a burgess might consider even a low rate of interest a good bargain if it won the seigneur's goodwill and some other concessions. Collectively, as a corporation or as a guild merchant, the richer townsmen had it in their power to be even more obliging to their lord.

The town revenues also strengthened the seigneur's power to borrow.

[22] *Ballard*, pp. 220–232.

The future revenues were acceptable as a pledge, especially if there was a contract for a fee-farm, and although the main evidence for borrowing on the anticipation of urban revenues comes from that great seigneur, the king, the principles apply equally to the more slender credit of the lesser landowners.

IV

It would not need exceptional insight for a seigneur to notice that the establishment of a town had repercussions on his income far beyond the bounds of the borough. A proportion, albeit an unknown proportion, of the revenues from his manors must be attributed to the impact of towns on the rural economies. The towns, after all, were sited on or near the seigneur's other estates. His demesnes produced food and raw materials for the market, and if the towns engendered any increase in demand, his demesnes would share in the benefits. The planted towns were particularly likely to increase the demand for food, since many of them had no agricultural land beyond their walls. The land immediately surrounding them already belonged to the fields or commons of an older settlement and the burgesses could claim no part of them. The organic towns, being promoted villages, already had their fields and were not so dependant on food grown elsewhere.

The more the town flourished, the greater the demand for food. It was not merely more mouths: as the incomes of townsmen rose they could afford more food; and as their workshops became busier they needed more raw materials from the countryside. The basic raw materials of the town craftsmen were country-bred: wool from the country sheep, hides from the country cattle, wood and charcoal from the forests, stone from the quarries, metals and ores from the rural mines. These rural products came to town markets and augmented the tolls of the markets: but some of them had come from the demesnes of the seigneur who was lord of the town, and their sale had augmented his income once already.

Yet there was an important difference between the increase in a lord's income that came from the sale of more demesne produce and an increase that came from the successful plantation of yet another town. In order to obtain any extra demesne produce, the lord (or his stewards) had to jerk into faster action the whole apparatus of villein services (for in the period of greatest urban expansion, after 1150, production by

75

conscripted villein labour was normal in the manors of the English low-lands). When village populations were small it had been possible to increase the demesne (and its product) by taking in assarted land, but as the thirteenth century progressed, the ploughs came nearer and nearer to the margins of cultivation and England began to look like a fair field over-full of folk. Attempts to wrench a greater product from the soil came up against the dumb resistance of the peasantry and the harsh fact of diminishing marginal returns. Compared with these wrestling matches, how effortless it must have seemed to be able to increase one's income by using seigneurial authority to say, "Let there be a town."

It was a relatively effortless gain of this sort that the earl of Pem-broke praised when (between 1189 and 1219) he confirmed the grants of ten librates of field-land at Weston (Herts.) that an ancestor had made to the Templars fifty years earlier:

> *predictam terram multum emendaverunt per sua purchacia et per magnas libertates quod dominus rex eis dedit.*

Like the Profitable Servant, they had invested their ten talents wisely; they had laid out the borough of Baldock on the edge of the fields.[23]

The indirect gain that arose by the colonisation of a town's hinter-land was most apparent when the town was set in under-developed territory. There were towns in Gascony and Wales that could claim that there was no flourishing agricultural hinterland until they came to develop it, but the most extensive association of new towns with rural colonisation is seen outside the area of English plantations. In the twelfth and thirteenth centuries the expanding frontiers of Germanic settlement were peopling eastern Europe with fields, villages and towns in one great operation of colonisation and conquest.[24]

The same thing happened west of the Rhine in earlier centuries. There is a charter of 957 given by the abbot of St. Mihiel: it records that peasants have taken a block of land near Verdun in order to bring it under cultivation and then to live upon it; in the middle of the territory the abbot preserved land for a market hall and a market place, and

---

[23] *Dugdale Monasticon*, vi, p. 820.

[24] There is a large literature on Germanic colonisation and town-plantation: see the bibliographies in *Camb. Econ. Hist. Europe*, i–iii; also P. Francastel, ed., *Les Origines des Villes Polonaises* (Paris, 1960); H. Planitz, *Die Deutsche Stadt im Mittelalter* (Graz-Köln, 1954), with bibliography and many plans; E. Keyser, *Städtegrundungen und Städtegebau in N-W Deutschland im Mittelalter* (Remagen, 1958), with volume of plans.

four streets were to be laid out and named.[25]   It is significant that in Spain the name given to a seigneur who planted towns was *el poblador*, the populator, and that in Gascon documents the word bastide was often glossed as *bastida sive nova populacio*.

The affinity between colonising villages and new towns is indicated elsewhere in France by the indifferent use of the place-names *Sauveterre* and *Villeneuve* for new colonising settlements, whether urban or village; and sometimes the very name of a colonists' village in the tenth or eleventh centuries reads like the name of a thirteenth-century bastide. A contemporary account of the creation of a forest village (c. 1063) runs:

> cutting down trees and burning them, they made fruitful and fertile the land formerly waste and uncultivated.   They then added a church and other useful things and called the place Charleville (*villa Caroli*).[26]

When extensive marshlands were being reclaimed in the twelfth and thirteenth centuries there were all the preconditions for the accompanying development of new towns.   Marshland reclamation, an act of innovation, brought population to areas that were unlikely to have their own towns already; the reclamation usually produced very fertile soils capable of sustaining dense rural populations and offering large surpluses to markets; and if the sea and river channels were deep enough to afford access to shipping, there was a good chance of the marshland town taking on the functions of a port.

The most extensive areas of reclamation in this period were along the coast of the Low Countries, and in this period arose many towns of modern Holland and the coast of Belgium.[27]   In England the areas of marshland reclamation were less extensive, and towns serving the marshland lay at the junction with the upland and were able to fill their market place with products of both the marshland and the upland agronomies.   Lynn, New Sleaford, Boston, New Romney and New Winchelsea were towns of this kind and the truly isolated marshland town is rare in England.   Rye may be one such, but even the distance here from dry land is very small compared with the islands of reclamation in the Low Countries or with the isolation of Aigues Mortes in the Camargue marshes.   It will be seen, on the other hand, that the un-

[25] E. Sackur, *Die Cluniacenser*, i (Halle, 1892), p. 382.
[26] J. Flach, *Les Origines de l'ancienne France*, ii (Paris, 1893), p. 156.
[27] References to printed works on the towns planted in other European countries are given in Appendix IV, pp. 652–55, below.

7

colonised marshlands of the Landes coast in Fig. 62 were completely devoid of medieval towns, organic or planted. This remained the most barren area in Gascony, indeed in medieval France: for neither the Alps of Savoy nor the mountains of the Massif Central could show so many continuous square miles devoid of settlement.

After the fens of Lincolnshire and the marshes of Romney the greatest area of marshland colonisation in medieval England was in Holderness between the Yorkshire Wolds and the sea. The two principal agents of colonisation were the lords of the seignory, the earls of Aumale, and the monks of Meaux abbey. The earls were also the agents of three new towns: of Skipsea (*sc.* "the isle of the ships") at the northern edge of the marshland; of Hedon on a small tributary of the Humber; and of Ravenserodd near Spurn Point. The monks of Meaux founded Wyke, the forerunner of Kingston on Hull. Their position on or near the Humber estuary involved these latter towns with the traffic of the sea and with the traffic of the great rivers that flowed into the Humber from Yorkshire and the Midlands. Yet they were also towns that looked into their hinterland: to the wool of the Wolds; to the products of the unreclaimed marsh; and to an increasing proportion of farm produce from the reclaimed acres of Holderness itself.

The economy of the coastal marshes was strengthened by the development of the industry of salt-extraction. The industry itself did not produce a town, for it demanded space for its salt-pans and salt-houses, and fuel to evaporate the brine: a good deal of smoke resulted. It was an industry that had to wade in the marsh, and townsmen generally liked to keep their feet, and the feet of their houses, dry. The type of town that salt production encouraged was a port for transhipment since the customers were scattered all over England and beyond. New Lymington is the plantation whose records are most explicit about its connection with salt. The salterns just outside the town greatly augmented the revenues of the seigneur by the salt that they gave him for sale and by the tolls that were levied upon the marketing and shipping of the salt by others.

Whatever the local product, a new town could aid the colonisation of its hinterland in two ways. It would stimulate production by offering a market for the fruits of the soil—its commonest function; or it could itself participate in the extension of cultivation.

In the first case the town would not be likely to have extensive field-land of its own. Chapter 7 shows that the characteristic boundary of a new town coincided with its walls, and the adjoining fields continued to belong to the village whose parish had been invaded by the new town, and to be tilled from the village rather than from the town. Yet a small number of planted towns did have extensive fields of their own, together with rights over common pasture and surrounding woodland. These are symptoms of towns that had invaded no one's territory; of towns whose inhabitants were conducting all the local reclamation, being set where there were as yet no villages and fields.

Of the areas studied in this book it is Gascony that shows most examples of this direct role in colonisation. For reasons discussed in Chapter 13, Gascony had greater areas of uncleared forest than England at the very moment when the market was showing itself able to absorb more and more Gascon wine. The newcomers to towns like Monpazier, that still stand ringed by extensive forests, were each given a unit area of land for clearing, a process assisted by the need for timber in the construction of the town. Rectilinear divisions, such as sometimes appear in the fields surrounding bastides, probably arose from this type of allocation.

In north Wales the garrison towns needed as much grain, meat and dairy produce as possible, and there were usually fields and commons available for the burgesses. In 1298 five out of every six burgesses in Carnarvon held some agricultural land, and newcomers to Criccieth were promised 60 acres apiece. In 1305 Beaumaris had more than 1,000 acres of arable, more than 100 acres of meadow, and more than 50 acres in underwood, pasture and turbary.[28]

The rapid multiplication of small towns in Devon and Cornwall was connected with colonisation of a different sort: the invasion of the moorland by family farmsteads and small villages; and the exploitation of the mineral veins.[29] The best evidence for towns developing in an area where forests were being cleared in England comes from Staffordshire, where the medieval colonisation was still remembered in the mid-sixteenth century. In 1558 the surveyor William Humberston was commissioned to describe for Queen Elizabeth I the Honour of Tutbury, a considerable estate that she held in her right as duke of Lancaster. The estate had come to the house of Lancaster (in rather discreditable circumstances) after the defeat of Robert de Ferrers, earl of Derby, and it was the borough-making activity of successive earls of

---

[28] E. A. Lewis, *Medieval Boroughs of Snowdonia* (1912), pp. 46–51.
[29] W. G. Hoskins, *Devon* (1954), chs. iv–vii.

Derby between the Norman Conquest and the forfeiture of 1266 that caught the surveyor's attention. Success in Humberston's profession depended on reading documents as well as measuring fields and sizing up the value of an acre, but the preface to Humberston's survey of Tutbury must rather have surprised his superiors. It was an essay in historical geography or economic history rather than in the land economics of the day.[30]

From the vantage point of the alabaster rock where Tutbury castle stands, Humberston was able to look north over the Dove to Derbyshire and south across Needwood into Staffordshire. He praised the Derbyshire part of the estate and then turned to the Needwood view:

> on the other side of the Ryver in the Countie of Stafford for the most parte all woodland but now by men's industrye converted into tyllage and pasture.

He credited the successive Ferrers lords with the encouragement of woodland clearance and the development of tillage; this piece of historical knowledge almost certainly came from the duchy records, possibly from the charters of Tutbury Priory, for Humberston quite gratuitously reports:

> I find in the auncient recordes of the Castle that in anno thirteen of William the fyrst was Tutbury Priory founded;

and the charters to the Priory do show the lords of Tutbury giving the Priory a share in the increased income that came from the improved lands.[31]

But for our present purpose the significant connection drawn by Humberston was between the agricultural history of the Honour and the three boroughs—two organic and one planted—that the earls had founded within a few miles of each other as part of the exploitation of colonised land.

> Then begann they to devise to increase their possessions with people to defend themselves and their countrye in tyme of warr, and to make the Honour more populous and statelie erected three burroughes within six myles of the Castle, One at Tutburye, One other at Agardsley called Newburghe and One other at Uttoxeter . . . and to make men more

[30] B.M. Harl. Ms. 71 ff. 6 sqq.; part is quoted in S. Shaw, *History and Antiquities of Staffs.*, i (1798), p. 44; the B.M. volume is part of a series, the remainder of which are in the Public Record Office: *cp.* DL42/109.
[31] *The Cartulary of Tutbury Priory*, ed. A. Saltman (Wm. Salt Soc. 4th ser., iv (1962)), pp. 7, 63 and 65.

desirous to plant ther habytacions in those places procured for them
marketts and ffayres and graunted to the burgesses dyvers lyberties of
common of pasture, panage and estover in the forest of Neadwood.

In all, 410 burgages were created: 182 at Tutbury, 101 at Newborough
and 127 at Uttoxeter.   At Abbots Bromley, also in Needwood Forest
and not far from Newborough, the monks of Burton abbey promoted a
village to a borough in 1222, while at Burton on Trent itself they added
four successive burghal extensions to the original village nucleus.

Tutbury was converted from a village to a borough soon after the
Norman Conquest; "Agardsley called Newburghe" was a plantation;
Uttoxeter was an organic borough, promoted from a village in 1251
in the same year that the earl of Derby enfranchised his village of
Higham Ferrers in Northamptonshire, two years before he made a
borough of Bolton (Lancs.), and six years before his borough of Chorley
(Lancs.).   The planted boroughs flourished in the same soil and had
the same patrons as the organic.

The peopling of Needwood, to which Humberston looked back, had
been motivated by more than a zeal for larger rent rolls.   In Humberston's words,

> the lords made these provisions for hospitality that the greatest burden of
> ther ordinary howsehould should bee without charge or trouble, and
> directed themselves to be served by these poore villaines.

How were charge and trouble to the seigneur's household lessened by
the creation of a town?   Colonisation increased the local food supply,
and new markets brought that supply within reach and eye of the seigneur.   In a period when transport was poor and expensive there was
always the chance of local shortage of provisions, even when harvests
were generally good.   In the years of bad harvests, which came
irregularly but inexorably, starvation was widespread not only through
poverty but through inability to obtain supplies.   When a bad harvest
was suspected there was little enthusiasm for a corn-growing area to send
the usual amounts of grain to market.   It preferred to hoard them for
its own use (or in the hope of starvation prices to come).   A seigneur
with a large household to maintain would be vitally interested in the
working of the markets in country towns, and his interest extended
beyond food to other products of the countryside.   This interest is seen
at its greatest in the permanent problem of provisioning the royal
household, and in the powers that the officers of the household were

given to commandeer supplies and fix maximum prices for their purchases.

The creation of a new town on a seigneur's lands gave the surrounding countryside an additional market, and the founder was often able to claim in the new market place something like the compulsory powers that the royal household claimed nationally. When the bishop of Norwich was at Lynn he could claim to have first call on the grain that was brought to market, and the charter of Hartlepool (1230) acknowledged the same right of pre-emption.[32] The lord of a castle had a similar interest in acquiring food for the garrison and stores against a siege, especially (as in north Wales) where the natives might be sympathetic to the enemy.

There is a revealing clause in a memorandum of April 1282 setting out action to be taken to encourage the building programme of Edward I in north Wales. As might be expected, the officials were to organise the import of carpenters, diggers and building workers; they were to organise the collection and carriage of food—salt, meat, live oxen, cows and pigs, wheat, oats and barley—but the bishop, whom the king appointed as organiser, was to address a mass meeting of other essential elements in the peopling of a town, the merchants foreign and English. By giving a guarantee against loss, they were to be tempted to risk the long journey to Chester and north Wales:

> *Item de mercatoribus indigenis et alienigenis quod quamvis eis videtur grave venire ad partes Cestriae propter longum cursum, quod episcopus eis convocatis dicat eis ex parte Regis quod audacter ibidem accedant cum suis mercandisis et Rex refundet eis dampnum quod sustinuerint pro suo cursu ibidem faciendo.*[33]

No documentary record of a payment from the king or his agent, the bishop, has survived, and it is therefore impossible to know what losses merchants claimed on account of their journey to Cheshire and the wild north-west. Merchants certainly came, and their names occur among the early rentals of the new towns.

The prospects for merchants were strengthened by banning trade in the major commodities of Wales ("oxen, cows, horses and other wares") from all other places except the new towns of Conway, Beaumaris, Newborough, Carnarvon, Harlech and Bala.[34]

[32] *Ballard*, p. 256; *Ballard and Tait*, p. 298.
[33] B.M. Cott. Ms. Vit. CX f. 162v., cited by A. J. Taylor in E. M. Jope, ed., *Studies in Building History* (1961), p. 112.
[34] *Ballard and Tait*, p. 245.

The foundation of Wavermouth by Edward I was intended to create a port for adequate provisioning of the fleets operating off the Cumberland coast against the Scots. The haste was fatal, for the chosen site was washed away in a storm; a second site at Skinburgh, chartered in 1301, was no more fortunate but its charter made a recruiting speech to merchants much like that made in north Wales twenty years earlier:

> all merchants both native and alien, so long as they are in friendship and peace with us and wish to come to the borough with their goods and wares by land or by water, may freely come and remain there and do business and return thence without hindrance, provided that they exercise lawful trades and pay the customs due in our realm.[35]

Here, the twin interests of "Ourselves and merchants" were served by the single act of creating a victualling port in the Solway. The earlier towns in mid- and south Wales were also outposts of colonisation as well as military penetration. They are described by Professor Rees in these words:

> the castle, the manor and the borough represented the essentially foreign elements in the lordship. These were to be found usually in the more lowland parts which, as the area of foreign settlement, formed the *Englishry*. Here the lord would grant estates to his knightly followers . . . the remainder of the lordship, usually the more hilly parts, and commonly known as the *Welshry*, continued to be held by the Welsh living their own mode of life;[36]

although one suspects that the description underestimates the influence of the castle market-town on the economic life within the Welshry.

The name Sauveté (*Sauveterre, Salvitas,* etc.) given to a community in newly colonised land highlights the element of security that a compact settlement might provide even when the *sauvetés* were no more than villages. Uncolonised forest was a place of refuge for the outlaws and a natural cover for the activities of thieves and brigands. Merchants and peaceable citizens journeying along country roads could not avoid passing woodland, and where there was much uncleared woodland, there was potential danger for miles at a time. At one stroke, colonisation diminished woodland and provided places of refuge.[37]

---

[35] *Ibid.,* p. 274.
[36] W. Rees, *An Historical Atlas of Wales* (1959), p. 28.
[37] The sauvetés of south-western France appear very much as half-way steps to bastides: in 1203 King John granted a charter (*Gouron* no. 37) authorising the archbishop of Bordeaux to create *sauvetés* or *populationes* on his estates, including the right to fortify. The foundation of another, St. Nicholas de la Grave, in 1135 is described by Prof. Higounet as "*un veritable*

The English statute of Winchester (1285) began with a statement that

> every day robbery, homicide and arson are committed more frequently than used to be the case;

it continued with an order for sterner police measures in town and villages; and then concluded with an order to cut down woodland that screened robbers:

> it is commanded that highways from one trading town to another shall be enlarged wherever there are woods, hedges or ditches; so that there shall be neither ditches, underbrush nor bushes for two hundred feet on the one side and two hundred feet on the other where men can hide with evil intent; this statute shall not apply to oaks nor to any great trees so long as they are cleared underneath.[38]

Perhaps because the Gascon forests were extensive, or perhaps because Gascony was more lawless than England, the bastides afford more evidence than the English plantations that their founders looked upon them as an insurance against local disorder. It has been shown in the last chapter that Molières was founded in an unruly district that did not scruple to murder even priests and foreigners, and the same arguments were used in a petition of 1305 when Arnaud–Loup of Estibeaux asked the king-duke to join him in pacifying the local countryside by planting a bastide in the forest at Ozourt.[39] He hopefully estimated that two thousand inhabitants would be eager to come and dwell in it. The word for these men was *poblantiz*, (*populationes*, colonists).

The charter of Bala in 1324 emphasised the same feature: there were notorious groups of wrong-doers and thieves at a place called Penthlyn and the justiciar was pleased to approve the establishment of a merchant town.[40] The same reasons appear in a Lincolnshire plantation of 1345. New Eagle was to be sited half way along the Foss Way between Lincoln and Newark, a stretch of road completely devoid of villages from the gates of Lincoln to as far as the gates of Newark, exactly one

paréage", and this *sauveté*, like many others, had a regular grid plan (C. Higounet, "Les Sauvetés de Moissac", *Annales du Midi*, lxxv (1964), pp. 505–512). There is a model account of a sauveté near Bordeaux in J. Flach, *op. cit.* in fn. 26 above, pp. 177–186. See also P. Ourliac, *Annales*, iv (1949), pp. 268–277.

[38] *Statutes of the Realm*, i, p. 97.
[39] SC8/2943 and 14543.
[40] Lewis, *op. cit.*, in fn. 28 above, p. 283.

of those roads envisaged in the Statute of Winchester. The preamble to the charter of the new town recalled these facts: there have been felonies and robberies on the Foss Way; the reason is the long open stretch without any vill; the prior of the hospital of St. John of Jerusalem at Eagle has requested that he may build and settle men on his ground in a place called Swinderby Moor hard by the way of Foss; the king therefore licences a chapel of the Holy Trinity, and authorises the creation of a town and houses about it, with building-plots ready for men willing to settle there for the entertainment of travellers on the road; a weekly market and two fairs a year are granted.[41]

V

Peace and good order apart, the king's interest in new towns exceeded that of any single one of his subjects, for the size and scattered character of the royal demesnes enabled him to profit from every kind of plantation. There were royal manors where castles were built, and with the castle a town; there were royal hunting lodges with their appendant towns; there were places where ports were created for the embarkment of royal fleets; there were the great highways along which overland trade moved, and these highways passed through royal estates, over bridges and fords, to river-ports and to estuarine ferries, each offering an opportunity for an urban promotion.

Yet kings of England were more than grand seigneurs; they were sovereigns; and with sovereignty came revenues from towns that were not planted on royal demesnes. For example, it came to be accepted that new markets and fairs, wherever held, needed a royal charter: and his subjects paid the sovereign for his grant. Seigneurs who were creating organic boroughs or planting towns could enfranchise their villeins by private charter, but it became increasingly common for seignorial boroughs to be backed by a royal charter confirming the liberties: for this charter, payment was made to the king, and after the accession of a new sovereign it was often thought prudent to ask (and to pay) for a renewal of the charter. Thus Henry II issued charters confirming his grandfather's grants to Pembroke and Newport (Salop.), while Henry III and Edward I re-issued or renewed the charters of twenty-four planted towns, not all of them royal. (Seigneurs also

---

[41] *Cal. Chart. Rolls*, v, p. 40.

profited from re-issues: between 1137 and 1145 count Alan of Brittany re-issued the charters of his father and uncle to Richmond (Yorks.), and between 1145 and 1175 his son, Conan, confirmed the charters of all three ancestors; in 1248 the burgesses of Poole paid their lord £46 13s. 4d. to have their fifty-year-old borough charter confirmed.)[42]

The sovereign also found himself lord of planted towns by inheritance, escheat and forfeiture.[43] The assimilation to the Crown of the lands of the Duchy of Lancaster and the Earldom of Cornwall brought revenues to the royal Exchequer from burgages that had been planted and from markets and fairs in *novi burgi*, as well as providing further territory on which yet more towns might be projected. In Wales there were planted towns of Marcher lords which became royal after their lords had raised unsuccessful rebellions and, as the next Chapter will show, the king was able to use his authority to force the owners of sites to sell or exchange them with him if he wished to develop a town upon them. In Gascony it was his ducal authority that enabled him to share in the partnerships or *paréages*, setting up bastides on the lands of others, and it was by inheritance that an English king obtained the Agenais and the bastides already planted in that territory. As Table IV.1 shows, the king-duke had by 1320 made himself the greatest of bastidors.

Successful war could also bring additions of territory on which towns were already planted or where towns might be projected. Edward I's colloquium of town planners was occasioned by the capture of Berwick, and the sites for his great array of towns in north Wales were the product of military conquest. The English plantations in Ireland were also on land won by the sword, and although the net result of the Hundred Years War was the total loss of Gascon bastides, the period did see one acquisition: Calais, captured in 1347. It is very probable that Calais originated as a plantation in the coastal marshes, like its neighbours, Dunkirk and Nieuport:

> Edward III took possession of one of the most strongly defended localities in Northern France. The town was regularly built in the form of a

[42] *Ballard*, p. 16; *Ballard and Tait*, p. 339.
[43] Edward I acquired the Humber towns of Hedon and Ravenserodd by escheat from the countess of Aumale, Isabella de Fortibus; he purchased a third Humber plantation from the monks of Meaux, and enlarged it into Kingston on Hull. In the Isle of Wight he acquired Newport from Isabella, and Newtown from the bishops of Winchester under pressure (*Reg. Johannis de Pontissara*, ed. C. Deedes (Cant. and York Soc. xxx (1924)), pp. 411, 421, 423 and 434).

parallelogram, with a central market-place. Round it were the walls and towers erected early in the thirteenth century by the Capetian Count of Boulogne. . . .

Mints, like war, became accepted as a royal monopoly, and the establishment of a mint in a new town brought revenues to the king. The extension of royal justice was also a widening source of profit: once a practical system of itinerant judges was established, the profits of justice came to the king not only from the courts at Westminster but from the provincial assizes.

It has already been argued that the plantation of a new town was likely to increase the value of all estates in its vicinity through its encouragement to produce for its markets. The wide distribution of the royal estates gave the king good hope of secondary, windfall gains of this kind, but there was an increasingly profitable royal estate in another sense, the Estate of the Kingdom. As sovereign, the king had the power to tax and, as this power widened and deepened, the king became shareholder in the prosperity of all town communities, and by the early fourteenth century he was able through customs duties to tax merchants in the course of their business, and through direct taxes on personal property he was able to tax other forms of urban wealth. The total tax paid by the laity of the planted towns in 1334 was almost equal to that paid by London (p. 92, below).

Long before these sophisticated techniques of taxation enabled the king to share in the wealth of burgesses, he had been able to tax his towns by extending to them the feudal principle that tenants aided their lord on well-defined occasions of extra expenditure, especially in war. The Pipe Roll of 1130 shows the old Danegeld being superseded by round sums, called borough *aids*, that may have been introduced by Henry I. Under Henry II these sums did not become conventionalised, and in the continuous series of Pipe Rolls that begins in 1159 each collection of a *tallage* from the borough communities reveals different sums and a different ranking order.[44]

None of the planted boroughs is recorded as paying Danegeld aids to Henry I, but if all Henry II's tallages are totalled, Newcastle on Tyne ranked fourteenth; if Scarborough and Orford were truly planted towns, there were three members of that class in the first thirty-five. During the reign of Henry II Bridgnorth and Newcastle under Lyme

[44] The borough aids are tabulated in C. Stephenson, *Borough and Town* (1933), pp. 222-225.

first appear among the tallaged towns.   In the Aid of 1177 the payments were:

	£ s. d.		£ s. d.
Newcastle on Tyne	36 13 4	Bridgnorth	13 6 8
Scarborough	13 6 8	Newcastle	
Orford	10 0 0	under Lyme	1 13 4

The £75 0s. 0d. yielded by these five towns was equal to the yield from single county towns such as Exeter, Bedford or Norwich.

In 1227 Henry III announced that he intended to proceed overseas to recover what John had lost, and for that purpose ordered a general tallage.   John's new town of Liverpool was at that time only twenty years old but the investment was beginning to pay off.   Its tallage was £7 14s. 4d. when the older towns of Lancaster and Preston paid £8 15s. 4d. and £10 0s. 6d. respectively.[45]

There were also opportunities for seigneurs to levy tallage on their towns whenever the king tallaged his own demesne.   The charter of Poole declared in 1248:

> when the king, whoever he may be, takes tallage from his cities or boroughs, according to the custom of his cities and boroughs, it shall be lawful for me and my heirs to take tallage from the said burgesses of Poole.[46]

The tallage was sometimes resisted by burgesses, as at New Salisbury in 1306, when the burgesses declared that if the price of their charter of liberties was the payment of tallage to the bishop they would rather tear up their charter.[47]   In 1280 a local jury reporting on the decline in the value of the town of Hedon, a plantation on the Humber, said:

> the men of Hedon are straitened and poor; many of them wish to move away on account of being tallaged; they have near them two other good towns, Ravenserodd and Hull, which have good harbours and grow day by day; and if they go there they can dwell without paying tallage.[48]

Ravenserodd and Hull, it will be noted, were also plantations.

It was only in 1275 that the king successfully asserted his right to a regular tax levied on foreign trade.

[45] *Lancashire Lay Subsidies*, ed. J. A. C. Vincent (Lancs. and Cheshire Rec. Soc., xxvii (1893)), pp. 106–107.
[46] *Ballard and Tait*, p. 116.
[47] *Ibid.*, pp. 116 and 325–326.
[48] *Y.I.*, i, p. 216.

In 1275 there came to an end the long era of virtual free trade which England had enjoyed from time immemorial. Local tolls, indeed, there had been but many were exempted therefrom; national customs, rarely imposed and fleeting in duration, had hitherto been negligible.[49]

One of these fleeting occasions had been in 1203 when John collected a tax of one-fifteenth of the value of imports and exports. The Pipe Roll of 1203–04 recorded substantial payments from seven planted towns (£2,024) that made up 40% of the total paid by London and the coastal ports, from Newcastle down to Fowey.[50]

	£	s.	d.
Newcastle on Tyne	158	5	11
Hedon	60	8	4
Hull (Wyke)	344	14	4½
Boston	780	15	3
Lynn	651	11	11
New Shoreham	20	14	9
Saltash	7	4	8

But since these occasions were intermittent it cannot be said that English kings were enthused to create new seaport towns purely by their interest in customs revenue. In ordinary years, local tolls and petty customs were all that Henry III could expect from royal ports like Liverpool and Portsmouth, and individuals and members of merchant communities enjoyed widespread exemption from such tolls. The real value to a king of a Liverpool or a Portsmouth lay in its fee-farm and its strategic services as a place of assembly for fleets and the embarkation of troops.

Though the ability of English kings to take a significant share in the revenues from foreign trade is limited to the period after 1275, there had already developed a form of internal taxation that enabled them to claim a fraction of personal property from their wealthier subjects, irrespective of whether they were royal tenants. Urban wealth could thus be tapped which the older feudal dues and taxes based on the land-geld had not touched. These personal taxes began with the tithes raised for the crusade of 1188, and there were occasional levies under Richard I and John. There were four levies under Henry III (1225, 1232, 1237 and 1269) but nine in the reign of Edward I, seven of these after 1289. As with modern income tax, townsmen with small wealth

[49] E. M. Carus-Wilson and O. Coleman, *England's Export Trade, 1275–1347* (1963), p. 1.
[50] *P.R.S.*, n.s. x (1940), p. 218.

were not called upon to pay, but a community with successful merchants and traders would have a long list of townsmen's names sent in to the Exchequer by the assessors, each name being followed by a valuation of personal movable property.   A fixed fraction of this valuation was due in taxation.

There was a characteristic of these taxes on personal property that enhanced the value of a borough to the king.   Burgesses paid greater fractions of their assessed personal wealth than men in rural vills.   This higher rate applied to all places recognised as "boroughs", whether on the king's own demesne or on the lands of seigneurs.   In 1296 the two fractions were an eleventh from the ordinary rural vills and a seventh from the boroughs.   The status of a place thus became relevant to the king's capacity to share in the wealth of its inhabitants.   Thus, the large vill of Wooler (Northumberland) was not reckoned a borough, and Adam the Dyer, living there, was assessed at £12 12s. od.   Of this valuation he had to pay one-eleventh part.   In the borough of Newcastle on Tyne, Thomas de Tindal, bailiff, customs collector and importer of wine and cloth, was assessed at approximately the same as Adam of Wooler but the king was able to take one-seventh.   Towns offered such opportunities to accumulate wealth, compared with a village, that single rich burgesses were worth as much to the king as many villages.

The richest man in St. John's parish, Newcastle on Tyne, was assessed on £31 10s. and therefore paid in tax £4 10s.   In the country-side immediately west of the city (Tyne and Wansbeck Ward) the average vill was paying £1 4s. 10d.   The richest man in the whole of Newcastle, Sampson the cutler of St. Nicholas parish, was assessed on £53 3s. 4d. and paid £7 11s. 10d.   To the Exchequer collectors the name of Sampson was equivalent to more than six vills.[51]   O brave new world that had such people in it!

The benefit of having boroughs to tax can also be illustrated from the records of the tax paid in Sussex that same year.[52]   The ancient borough of Lewes paid £10 17s. 9¾d.; the town of New Shoreham paid £19 17s. 9¾d.; the mother village of Old Shoreham paid £6 6s. 0¾d. The small plantation of Midhurst was worth £2 11s. 11¾d., and Edward took £6 17s. 11d. from the burgesses of Battle.   William I had given

---

[51] F. Bradshaw, "The Lay Subsidy Roll of 1296", *Arch. Aeliana*, 3rd ser. xiii (1936), pp. 186–302.

[52] *The Three Earliest Subsidies for the County of Sussex*, ed. W. Hudson (Sussex Rec. Soc., x (1909)), pp. 3–105.

the abbey a circle of land 3 miles in diameter, and the first benefits from the town planted at the abbey gate had all accrued to the monks in the form of urban rents, but now Edward I was reaping where William I had sown.   Similarly, Edward's predecessors had given away land to endow Dunstable Priory; the priory then founded a town on the Watling Street outside its gate, and although it was the abbey alone that profited from the rents of the burgages in Dunstable, Edward I was able to tax the wealth of the burgesses.

The detailed assessment for 1297 has survived: £22 0s. 11½d. was collected from Dunstable towards the cost of Edward's expedition in Flanders.   The anatomy of the town's economy is laid bare by the assessments.   Apart from substantial quantities of farm animals and cereals—52 bushels of corn per taxpayer—the following goods were assessed: tiles and lime; skins; tanning stock; felt; meat; skinners' stocks; fish; grease and tallow; fruit; wood and charcoal; spices; iron; leather; cloth; poulterer's stock; malt; and the contents of a tannery. Of Robert Brian, senior, the taxors recorded

he has nothing except in merchandise:

but the value of that merchandise—£5—was equivalent to 30 quarters of wheat or 20 cows or 16 horses or 100 sheep.   The goods of John Duraunt, corn and wool merchant, were valued for tax at £20 16s. 8d., twice the value of all the oxen on the demesnes of the earl of Cornwall's well-stocked manor of Sundon, nearby.[53]

In 1332 the Warwickshire tax assessments show that the plantations of Henley and Stratford contributed eighty-two names to the tax-list; the document is torn and partly indecipherable so that the individual amounts paid by these eighty-two burgesses are not shown.   The total was just over £19, a little more than for the intra- and extra-mural parishes of Warwick itself.   The two plantations were worth a county-town in terms of tax.[54]   In the collection of 1296 the four planted towns of Newcastle on Tyne, Ludlow, Portsmouth and Lynn paid £200 in tax; this was as much as the whole county of Westmorland, and two-thirds of the amount paid by the citizens of London.

In 1334 (and subsequent years) the direct assessment of individuals' property was abandoned in favour of an assessment of the total wealth of a village or town.   The records of these assessments are virtually

[53] *The Taxation of 1297*, ed. A. T. Gaydon (Beds. Hist. Rec. Soc., xxxix (1959)), pp. 90–96.
[54] *The Lay Subsidy Roll for Warwickshire of 6 Edward III*, ed. W. F. Carter (Dugdale Soc. Publns., vi (1926)), pp. 2–6.

complete and they have been used in Chapter 9 to compare the achievements of different plantations, and to compare the plantations with the organic towns.

The total contribution of all the plantations in 1334 may be estimated at a sum between £605 and £625. Measured in terms of tax paid, the plantations were then giving the king almost an extra London (£733) or an extra town that was compounded of York, Bristol, Lincoln, Shrewsbury and Great Yarmouth (£581). Few wars could hope to capture such prizes.

It was therefore in the period between 1275 and the eve of the Black Death that the planted towns were at their peak of usefulness in providing tax revenues. Additional to the tenths granted by the boroughs after 1334, were the new customs revenues from alien merchants that were first levied in 1303, and, after 1347, a general export duty on cloth; in Gascony the thriving wine trade was augmenting the royal customs levied at Bordeaux and Bayonne.

VI

How were the profitable lessons of town plantation learned? The lessons were so simple and so visible that a seigneur would have had to be exceptionally dim-witted not to have learned them, and even dim-witted seigneurs had astute wives and stewards to educate them. In Normandy the lesson was well known before William and his barons sailed for England. In England itself there were Anglo-Saxon boroughs to observe. Across the channel new towns were being created in the Low Countries, and when England became part of the Angevin Empire there were town-builders from the Pyrenees to the Cheviots who were related to each other by blood, who had estates in all parts of the Empire and whom administration and war led into ceaseless travel. North of the Cheviots the Scottish barons were also planting their towns, and the Norman Conquest of Ireland enabled the Anglo-Norman baronial families to begin all over again. Warfare took English kings and their barons among the towns of Normandy and Maine and eventually among the planted towns of French seigneurs in Gascony. The Crusaders took kings and their followers to Aigues Mortes, the great four-square embarkation port that the king of France had planted at the mouth of the Rhône.

Within England the court followed the king on the ceaseless itineraries set in train by sport, war and the pursuit of domestic politics. From such social habits came the new royal residence at New Windsor and the hunting-lodge near Woodstock: with each, a New Town. Indeed, a night's sojourn in a town planted by an ancestor was a painless way for any king to learn the advantages of being a bastidor. Henry I was often at New Windsor and Dunstable. From his palace at Clarendon, Henry III could look down on the bishop of Salisbury's works at New Sarum; and in the year after the foundation of Liverpool King John was in company with the bishop of Winchester at the episcopal manor houses of Downton and Knoyle: did the bishop learn from the king, for he was soon to plant towns in both these manors? or had the bishop, born in Poitou, kept his eyes open while soldiering with Richard I, the founder of at least three *villeneuves* in France?

Edward I was educated in the ways of bastides when he served his father in Gascony, and during his itineraries in England he is known to have stayed in New Windsor, New Thame, New Woodstock, Battle, Baldock, Dunstable, Royston, New Salisbury, Newmarket, Newcastle on Tyne, Boston, St. Ives (Hunts.), Morpeth, Portsmouth, New Winchelsea, Tickhill, Kingston on Hull and New Sleaford: all were plantations. In addition he spent a good deal of time in his own plantations in north Wales and in Gascon bastides founded by his father, his mother or himself.

Mr. A. J. Taylor's researches have shown that the expertise on which Edward I was able to draw derived not only from Gascony but from the county of Savoy, a region that is now divided between France, Switzerland and Italy.[55] In the early thirteenth century it comprised the northern valleys of the French Alps (now Haute Savoie) and, on the Italian side, the upper valley of the Po. By the end of the thirteenth century the territories of Chablais and Vaud had extended the duchy to the shores of Lake Geneva. There was a family connection between the counts of Savoy and the kings of England: Count Peter was the uncle of Henry III's queen, and before he succeeded to the county in 1263 he spent a good deal of time in England and became earl of Richmond. His predecessor, Count Amadeus, had acknowledged that part of his ancestral property in Savoy was a fief held of Henry III. This curious and unhistorical statement was part of a diplomatic war that was then involving the Pope and the Holy Roman Emperor, but in 1273 Count Philip also did homage to Edward I for these lands.

[55] A. J. Taylor, "Some Notes on the Savoyards in North Wales, 1277–1300", *Genava*, n.s. xi (1963), pp. 289–315; id., "Castle-building in Wales", in E. M. Jope, ed., *Studies in Building History* (1961), pp. 104–133; and *Hist. King's Works*, i (1963), pp. 293–408.

The Savoy connection brought Savoyards to the English court, and among them were architects and military engineers who were engaged on works for the kings of England as well as in their native Savoy. In Savoy these works included fortified towns such as Henry III and Edward I were building in Wales. St. Georges d'Espéranche (Isère) was founded between 1250 and 1256 by Philip of Savoy, then archbishop of Lyon:

> the formal foundation of St. Georges as a characteristic thirteenth century *ville neuve,*

as Mr. Taylor described it; and in a document of 1262 St. Georges was explicitly called *villa nova.*[56] The house of Savoy had planted others. Count Thomas was a creator of new towns *par excellence.* He founded Villeneuve outside the walls of his castle of Chillon in 1214, and attempted another new town at Villafranca in the Aosta valley.[57] These towns were on key routes across the Alps from France and southern Germany; (like the Welsh towns) they had military and economic purposes. A Swiss historian described Villeneuve thus:

> *Le comte de Savoie a besoin des hommes pour la garde du château de Chillon. Il y attire les gens de la région par l'attrait du commerce á un passage très important, par des franchises très libérales et leur assure á eux-mêmes la sécurité en entourant l'agglomeration de remparts.*[58]

This is almost the very language of Edward I's appeal to merchants to take up residence in his towns in north Wales (p. 82 above), and it was in north Wales that the Savoyard "Master James of St. George" (*sc.* d'Espéranche) was employed as master of the king's works during the quarter century (1277 to 1298) of Edward's great programme of castles and walled towns. Mr. Taylor has shown that Master James had worked at St. Georges and at the count's bastide of Yverdon on Lake Neuchâtel before coming to the service of Edward I. It was while staying in St. Georges in 1273 that Edward had taken the count of Savoy's homage, and during the visit he may have noted Master James's skill. Master James entered Edward's service by the spring of 1278, and Mr. Taylor declares that

[56] A. J. Taylor, "The Castle of St. Georges d'Espéranche", *Antiq. Journ.*, xxxiii (1953), pp. 33–47.

[57] C. W. Previté-Orton, *The House of Savoy* (1912), p. 447.

[58] M. Godet, H. Türler and V. Attinger, *Dictionnaire Historique de la Suisse* (Neuchâtel, (1921–34), vii, p. 133.

he must be credited with the basic design of all the great Edwardian castles in Wales, including Caernarvon. In the winter of 1287 he was summoned to join the king in Gascony where he may have remained until the court returned to England in 1289. In 1298 the Scottish war gave him a new sphere of activity in the king's service;

and for the last ten years of his life Master James's principal works were on Scottish defences.

There were lesser masters from Savoy who acted as Master James's assistants in Wales, including another of St. Georges, Master Giles, who was active in the building of Aberystwyth; Philip the Carpenter (also of St. Georges) who worked at Flint; Stephen the Painter; John Francis and William Seyssel, no doubt a native of Seyssel in Savoy; Gillot de Chalons (Isère) built one of the towers of Rhuddlan Castle and later took up $3\frac{1}{4}$ burgage plots in Conway; Adam Boynard, another Savoyard, was a burgess of Harlech and its bailiff in 1292–93; Albert de Menz, who dressed stone and made chimneys in Harlech castle, came from the Valais. It is not surprising that Mr. Taylor has been able to show striking architectural parallels between military works and the town walls in Savoy and those of the same period in north Wales.[59]

VII

English landowners of every degree seem to have shared the royal enthusiasm for town-making. The inquisitions *post mortem* on the estates of the Crown's own tenants-in-chief give the impression that everyone was either a bastidor or a blood relative of one. Some of these multi-borough seigneurs have already been encountered in Table III.2 but the list could be easily extended. Bishops were equally infected. Winchester is the see with the best-documented plantations but by 1300 the sees of Salisbury, Bath, Lincoln, Worcester, Norwich, Chichester, Exeter, Durham and St. David's could all boast planted towns on their demesnes. No archbishop, it is true, has yet been found planting a town, unless the mysterious project at Brough on Humber was a plantation: had Edward I succeeded in installing Robert Burnell at Canterbury instead of at Bath, he might have had a truly

---

[59] Jean de Grilly, so active as a creator of bastides for Edward I in Gascony, was also a Savoyard (*R.G.*, iii, pp. xxxiii–xlvii).

urban metropolitan. The *Dictionary of National Biography* writes of the Bishop that

> to make his native village of Acton Burnell a flourishing town (was an object) constantly pursued by him for nearly thirty years.

That particular ambition was not very successful, but Burnell did have a Gascon bastide named in honour of his see (*Baa*, Gironde), and he was deeply involved in Edward's plantation of towns in 1278 and from 1286–89; in 1282–83 he was with the king among the plantations of Wales and his native border; he was a witness to the charter of Flint, and he was at Swainston when Edward I went to take over Newtown, I.O.W., from the bishop of Winchester.

There was also a handful of royal officials who could claim to be bastidors, especially the seneschals in Gascony. Some of these were known in Britain. Luke de Thenney, seneschal of Gascony from 1272 to 1278, was active in the creation of many bastides and in 1282 he appeared among the towns of north Wales, campaigning for Edward I. John de Hastings, second baron Bergavenny, was the king's lieutenant in Aquitaine from 1302 to 1305 and seneschal of Aquitaine for Edward's son until his death in 1313. Like Burnell, he had a bastide named after him, and his son married into the family of de Leybourne, after whom Libourne had been named.

This brief review of inter-connected bastidors ends with a minor and rather pathetic figure. Apart from the great seneschals whose name appeared on membrane after membrane of the Gascon Rolls and in *paréage* after *paréage* as the king's agents, there were the lesser men— most of them now unidentifiable—who were engaged in negotiating the purchase of the land, marking out the ground, providing public works and proclaiming the opportunities that awaited any newcomer to the bastides: *locatores*, they sometimes styled themselves.

One such agent was Bertrand Panissals, at one time lieutenant for Jean de Grilly (Edward I's seneschal) in the countryside between the rivers Dropt and Dordogne. In 1303 he was taken prisoner by the French, lost his property but survived to petition the king after the war for some assistance in view of services that he enumerated.[60] He had procured, he claimed, the castle of Puyguilhem and its dependant territories in 1265, and on the land of Bajanès he had built the bastide of Roquepine in 1283. In the same district he had built Molières for

[60] *Vigié*, pp. 143–144.

the king (1278–84) near the abbey of Cadouin. He also claimed Monpazier (1285) as his. After three years' work on these bastides he had been set to improve the Dordogne at Lalinde (an earlier bastide, founded in 1267). Under contract he had built a great dam, and alongside it two four-wheel water-mills. Was not all this work worth a reward? he asked; and in the asking, his petition employed four words that echo the quotation with which this chapter began, and summarise its argument: was it not profit and honour—*magnum commodum et honorem*—that the king had enjoyed from the work of his servant who had planted three bastides and improved a fourth?

CHAPTER FOUR

Beau Lieu: or, The Choice of Site

"And this was the tyme, and this was the manner of the new Townes begeninge and building, where nowe it standeth... and this place in many deeds for the space of one age after was written *Novus Burgus*, the newe burrowe Towne."

J. Smyth, *Lives of the Berkeleys,*
(ed. J. Maclean, 1883), i, p. 118.

THE new Berwick which Edward I planned in 1297 was not to profit the king alone: if the planners succeeded in the task that Edward set them, Berwick was to be "profitable to its merchants and to others who would come and dwell there in the future". Indeed it was only by the activity of its inhabitants that the king—or the lord of any other new town—could expect any profit for himself from the venture. Once a town was founded, its fortunes depended mainly on the vigour of the townsmen, and after the initial endowment a founder could take up the role of a sleeping partner. Edward I, like Richard I before him, impressed contemporaries by throwing off his coat and helping to move earth for the ditches of a newly arrayed town, but this was only a symbol of involvement, a dramatic gesture. He had no intention of making his home in Berwick on Tweed, and no lord of a new town had any intention of setting up as a merchant or craftsman.

But in the initial endowment of a new town the founder's role was real and earnest, and from an adequate endowment the future fortunes of the plantation flowed. "Endowment" here embraces the site itself, the physical equipment of the town's buildings, and the legal privileges conferred on its inhabitants. The planners were thus to "devise and array" a new Berwick. In Berwick, as in all plantations, some endowments depended on the gift of the founder; but there were also gifts of nature; and there were benefits that came from aspects of contemporary economic and political life that were external to the town: some endowments brought a founder some financial sacrifice, and others cost him very little. This chapter is concerned with the endowments that

98

the founders thought necessary in the devising and arraying of their new towns.

I

The acquisition of the site was usually the least troublesome problem, for whether king, seigneur, bishop or abbot, a founder was certain to possess demesnes: these did not have to be extensive, for a town did not occupy many acres, and many petty boroughs in the south-west of England were founded by men who were lords of only a few manors. Yet any founder's choice of site was necessarily restricted to his own demesnes. There was no equivalent of the modern speculator riding the countryside to spy out a good site and then acquire it for development as a town. The developers were the territorial landowners themselves.

The king, as the greatest landowner, and having no one to ask for permission, had the greatest facility and the greatest choice of site. Table IV.1 shows that English kings founded one-third of the new towns in Wales, and a slightly greater proportion in Gascony. In England, one plantation in eight was royal. Thus, by 1300, the king owned more plantations than any single one of his subjects. In Gascony the king-duke had a further opportunity to develop towns on sites that did not lie on his demesnes. The instrument was the partnership or *paréage*. A local landowner was taken into partnership: he provided a site, and the royal patron endowed the town with liberties and promised it his protection. The revenues from the town were divided among the partners, usually in equal shares.

An obsolescent English word *parceners* (those sharing the rights of a common) has the same root as the Gascon word *paréage*; and *parseners* actually occurs in the *paréage* for the foundation of the bastide of Ste. Eulalie in 1265 when thirteen landowners with property near the castle of Puyguilhem agreed to co-operate with Henry III, his queen and his son

a far una bastida clausa en marcadil fora lo casted de Pugh Guillem.[1]

Table IV.1 shows that nearly half the foundations in English Gascony were by *paréage*, and three-quarters of these *paréages* involved the English king.

The practice extended beyond English Gascony: it was much used by

[1] *R.F.*, 472.

TABLE IV. I

THE FOUNDERS OF TOWNS: ENGLAND

Kings alone	21	(12%)
Seigneurs alone	77	(45%)
Bishops alone	25	(15%)
Abbots alone	31	(18%)
Unknown	18	(10%)
Total	172	

THE FOUNDERS OF TOWNS: WALES

Kings alone	29	(35%)
Seigneurs alone	39	(46%)
Bishops alone	6	(7%)
Native princes alone	5	(6%)
Unknown	5	(6%)
Total	84	

THE FOUNDERS OF TOWNS: GASCONY

Without Paréages	French kings alone	3	(2%)
	Count of Toulouse alone	8	(7%)
	English kings alone	48	(39%)
	Seigneurs alone	4	(3%)
		63	(51%)
By Paréages	French kings + seigneurs	1	(1%)
	+ abbots or priors	3	(2%)
	Count of Toulouse + seigneurs	2	(1%)
	+ bishop	1	(1%)
	+ abbots or priors	7	(6%)
	English kings + seigneurs	26	(21%)
	+ bishops	2	(1%)
	+ abbots or priors	12	(10%)
	Seigneurs + abbots or priors	2	(1%)
		56	(44%)
Not Known:		5	(4%)
Total		124	

Alphonse de Poitiers in founding his bastides in the decade before 1265. Professor Higounet has shown that between 1252 and 1325 there were forty-four *paréages* for bastides in the Garonne basin.[2] It was an

[2] C. Higounet, "Cisterciens et Bastides", *Le Moyen Age*, lvi (1950), pp. 69–84; see also id., "La Frange Orientale des Bastides", *Annales du Midi*, lxi (1948–49), pp. 359–367; *Le Comté de Comminges* (Toulouse, 1949), i, pp. 170–176 and ii, pp. 416–418.

effective way for the royal power to make itself felt in areas dominated by local seigneurs and for draining some revenue to the crown. In the area studied by Higounet the preponderance of *paréages* was between the count of Toulouse (acting on his own behalf or for the French king) and abbots of Cistercian houses, particularly those that had outlying granges with territory that was well placed for urban development. One plantation, Villeneuve du Paréage (Ariège), preserves in its name the circumstances of its origin.

Table IV.1 shows that in English Gascony a seigneur's main hope of promoting a bastide lay in a contract of *paréage*. Of the 124 bastides in this area, only four were the work of seigneurs alone. Most of the sixty-three bastides without *paréages* were founded by the king-duke, or by the king of France or by the count of Toulouse.[3] For Gascon abbots and bishops the position was the same: if they wished to plant towns, they needed the approval and partnership of the king or of the seneschals acting in his name.

In Gascony there was a ceremony during the establishment of a new town that emphasised the role of the territorial lord in providing the site and also demonstrated the approval and patronage of the king-duke. It was usual to erect a pole (in Gascon, *pal* or *pau*) at the centre of the place where the streets and burgage plots had been marked out, and on the pole there flew a flag bearing the emblems of the founders.

The procedure is particularised in the document giving Edward II's formal approval to the foundation of Toulouzette in 1321. William of Toulouse, after whom the town was named, was the king's seneschal in the Landes, and he performed the ceremonies: he dug a hole, erected the *pal* and made it firm; he declared that any who wished to live in the town should come and build their houses and receive the same liberties as the bastide of Geaune en Tursan (then three years old); he confirmed the articles of the privileges in the name of God, the Holy Virgin and all the saints; he handed over the letters patent that bore the seals of the king-duke and his seneschal. The formalities were complete.[4]

At the French bastide of St. Sardos (see pp. 239) the same type of flag-staff became the unhappy occasion of war between France and England in October 1323. The resentment of the lord of Montpezat, a local anglophile, caused him to raid the place on the eve of the

---

[3] Table IV.1 shows that the king-duke was able to found forty-eight bastides on his own initiative: the *paréages* enabled him to be a partner in forty more.

[4] *Gouron*, 1988.

proclamation and to hang the royal herald from the pole in place of the French flag.[5]

In England and Wales the formal type of partnership agreement is not often found. The nearest approach that has been noted is at Knutsford (Cheshire) where a deed of c. 1293 divided the tolls of the market and fair equally between Sir Richard Massey of Tatton and his under-tenant, William de Tabley. William had instituted burgages at Knutsford, probably on former arable land, since each of the 19 burgage plots was stated to contain $2\frac{1}{2}$ selions. But it is not certain that the division of tolls arose from a premeditated partnership: the deed can be construed as the reaction of an overlord, aggrieved that his under-tenant has broken the statute of alienations and therefore anxious to protect himself against his own overlord, the king.

The absence of *paréages* in England and Wales meant that if the king did wish to develop a town on land outside his demesne it was necessary to persuade the owner or tenant-in-chief to enter into an exchange. New Winchelsea, we have seen, was built on land obtained in this way. There were good precedents: Richard I, when count of Poitou, had obtained the site for St. Rémy de la Haye in 1184 by exchanging lands with the abbot of Maillezais who had a grange at the foot of the river cliff on which Richard wished to place his castle and town. Thirteen years later, Richard, now king of England, wished to build another castle—Château Gaillard—on another river-cliff; and to obtain the site for the accompanying town of Petit Andelys he again had to exchange lands with the church, this time with the archbishop of Rouen to whom he gave Boulogne. Edward I obtained the site for Aberystwyth castle and town in 1277 by giving its owners some land at Nantbran in Perfedd. When he wanted land for a Newtown in Purbeck in 1286 he had to purchase the site from the local seigneur, Robert de Muchegros.

It was difficult to resist these requests for exchange, as the monks of Meaux found when Edward I cast covetous eyes on the small town of Wyke on Hull that they had developed at the junction of the Hull and Humber rivers. After the exchange they complained bitterly that the land they had obtained in exchange was worth only two-thirds of its official valuation. Edward's negotiations with another Cistercian house, Aberconway, gave less cause for complaint. The chapter-

---

[5] Statements made in this Chapter are based on evidence for individual places described in the three Gazetteers, Chapters 15–17, where full references are given. References are not repeated in foot-notes, except for quotations.

general of the Order at Citeaux was consulted, and approval was given for an exchange of lands, provided that revenues were not diminished and the Pope did not object. The transfer was bolder than those involving granges and manors, for the king wanted the site of the abbey itself for development as a walled town. In June 1284 Edward announced that the Order's approval had been given, and in October a new site at Maenan was granted to the abbey by charter. The king paid £40 as immediate compensation for loss of revenues during the first year of transfer, followed by a lump sum payment of £386 13s. 4d. These payments were not the end of the king's costs: the Maenan site itself did not belong to the king, and it in turn had to be paid for by grants of royal lands worth £18 2s. 8d. a year.

Wyke on Hull was not the only plantation that Edward I coveted. There was a small port in the north-west of the Isle of Wight that had been planted in 1256 by the Bishop of Winchester as Newtown, or Francheville. By 1284, when Edward sought to acquire the town, it had 77½ burgages on its rent roll. The territory of a bishop was not so easy for the king to acquire as the lands of a delinquent baron or an heirless tenant. Bishoprics did not become extinct, and normally the only share of profits that a king could expect to have in an episcopal town was during the vacancy of a see when, like other income from the bishop's temporalities, the town revenues were collected by the Exchequer. Yet Edward obtained Newtown.

In the bishop's account roll for 1283–84, the last in which Newtown appears, there is an ominous item among the expenses: the cost of making an extent and survey of the manor. In June 1284, two years after his appointment, bishop Pontissara paid a fine of £2,000 to enter upon his temporalities: but Swainston, the manor in which Newtown had been planted, was significantly omitted from the list. All that the bishop retained here was the advowson of the village church. Edward himself came to inspect Newtown in October 1285 and stayed for nine days at the former episcopal manor house. From there he issued a charter confirming the municipal liberties of Francheville. The king had obtained Naboth's vineyard.

If exchange or purchase was impossible, then the king's only hope was that the tenant's line would become extinct or that some misdemeanour would give an opportunity for confiscating the land. When Isabella de Fortibus died without an heir, Edward I was able to acquire a valuable group of Aumale boroughs, including two Humber ports, Hedon and

Ravenserodd, and the principal town of the Isle of Wight, Newport. When the earldom of Cornwall and the duchy of Lancaster became attached to the Crown estate, another fine crop of boroughs was effortlessly gathered. Similarly, the return of the Agenais to the king-duke (under circumstances described in Chapter 13) brought Edward I a group of bastides founded by the counts of Toulouse.

II

George Unwin once observed that three things were necessary for the success of any medieval town: a social force, a legal title and a geographical potential. The first of these blessings was hardly the founder's to bestow. The vigour of their social institutions was more the concern of the townsmen than of their lord. Intelligence, acumen and commercial sense came from experience and self-education, not from any endowment that lay in the founder's gift. His contribution lay in the other two directions: in procuring a sound and generous legal title, and in selecting a good geographical position. Inadequacies in the town's charter and errors in legal title could be corrected afterwards, but the choice of site was an almost irrevocable decision.[6] Streets, houses and public buildings did not transplant easily, and the story of Old Winchelsea has shown that the townsmen were reluctant to move, even when the waves were battering them. In the whole of Europe there are few parallels to the successful migration from Old Salisbury to the present site of New Salisbury.

The actual provision of a site, as we have seen in the previous chapter, was rarely a great sacrifice. At the most, the founder gave up a few acres of open-field land and a few shillings a year rent. More frequently the site of the town was on uncultivated land. Much more valuable to the future of the town than this petty sacrifice was the founder's skill or good fortune in the selection of the site.

Planted towns were built on the lands of seigneurs who had rejected the simpler alternative of urbanising a site that a village community already occupied. The bastidors were like kings who rejected the heir presumptive in order to show favour to some upstart. Put in these terms, it might seem that a town could arise anywhere on the demesnes

---

[6] A *paréage* for Corneillas (G. P. Cuttino, ed., *Le Livre d'Agenais: Bodley Ms. 917* (Toulouse, 1951), p. 24) described an earlier agreement as unsatisfactory "*propter loci ipsius strictitudinem paucitatem seu etiam raritatem*".

at the lord's whim: but planting a town was different from planting a hedge. A hedge might grow anywhere, but a town's fortunes were not independent of its geographical position. As the failed towns of Chapter 10 show, it was one thing to proclaim a new town and another to people it.

The livelihood of villagers depended entirely on the fertility of the soil but the livelihood of the townsmen came only when the town attracted a regular concourse of people. There were strict limits on the number of people whom coercion could bring. A founder might coerce the villeins of his own estates to desert a traditional market-place in favour of his new town, but the very strangers and outsiders whose attendance was essential for the prosperity of a new foundation were not to be coerced. They could come and go as they pleased in all market places in the kingdom, and nothing but the lure of good bargains and their own self-interest would lead them to abandon old habits. They were not indifferent to the endowments that competing towns possessed.

The emphasis upon siting in the pages that follow is not the product of faith in crude geographical determinism. The great individuality of town sites is apparent from the descriptions in the Gazetteers, and some sites were the triumph of optimism over harsh physical obstacles. Conversely, the study of the failures in Chapter 10 shows that towns with text-book situations could end with grass growing in their market places. Yet looking back after the event, we can see that certain types of site were highly favoured by the conditions of their time, and these types and conditions must now be examined.

The deliberate plantation of a town indicates that local villages lacked some ingredient that the founder thought necessary for success. It would have been so much easier for him to utilise an existing village in the way that William de Ferrers, fifth earl of Derby, created the borough of Higham Ferrers in 1251: simply giving burgess status to ninety villagers of Higham. It was possible to make a town out of a village at Higham because the village already lay on the main road from London to Leicester and Derby, the present A6. Had the earl's Northamptonshire villages all lain off the main road, he would have been forced to plant a new town. This is not a hypothetical surmise: a little further north, where the same main road crossed the Welland near the Leicestershire border, a new town was created at Market Harborough even though there was a flourishing village a little off the course of the main road at Great Bowden. The burgage plots were laid out over the selions of *Hauerberga*, "the hill where the oats grow".

The plans in Figs. 8–10 illustrate the range of choice when a burghal community was added to a rural settlement. In the first case, Olney (Bucks.), there was already a large village in 1086, and the knot of winding streets north and west of the riverside church have the characteristic sprawl of a slowly developing rural settlement. The first record so far known for a borough of Olney dates from 1237, but since the manor was divided among a number of legatees in 1237 it is likely that the borough was granted in the time of an earl of Chester who died in 1232; in 1301 fifty-six burgages existed. The distinct contrast between the settlement near the church and the part north of the market place does not need emphasis: a straight street instead of winding streets; plots of burgage character; and a neat envelope to the northern area formed by the parallel back streets, East Street and West Street. The triangular market place lies at the junction of the two areas, and since market places were usually at or near the church gate, it is likely that the market place in its present site belongs to the borough rather than to the village.

The contiguity of old and new settlements at Olney deprives it of a claim to be a true planted town, for its founder was clearly satisfied with the site of the village but wished to extend it. Harewood (Yorks.), shown in Fig. 9, crosses the shadowy boundary between an organic borough and a planted town, while South Zeal (Devon), shown in Fig. 10, is quite clearly a separate as well as an additional creature. Much of the former village of Harewood has been eroded by the making of the park that surrounds Harewood House, but the isolated position of the church within the parkland indicates how far the original village must have stretched across the northern part of the plan, which is based on a late seventeenth-century plan; more of the village has since been replaced by woodland. The borough, in the south-east corner of the plan, is a quite different matter. Its only street, the broad open space, was also its market place, and the Ordnance Survey marks the site of a market cross at the west end. The medieval castle on the extreme north further emphasises that the original centre of gravity of the village lay away from the market place.

South Zeal is separate in name and position from its parent, South Tawton. More than half a mile separates the two, and there is the same contrast between the twisting streets of the village and the

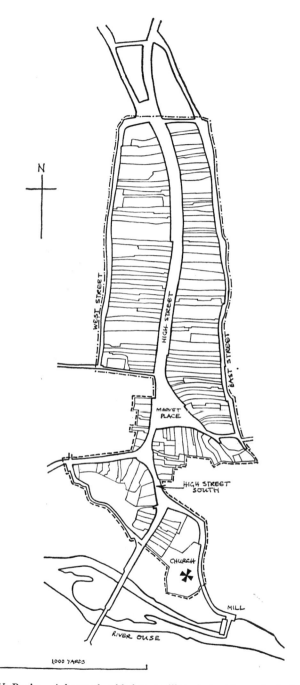

N

WEST STREET

HIGH STREET

EAST STREET

MARKET PLACE

HIGH STREET SOUTH

CHURCH

MILL

RIVER OUSE

1,000 YARDS

Fig. 8. OLNEY, Bucks.   A borough added to a village but with no physical separation.

straight line and set-square limits of the burgage area, focused upon the main road.

Sometimes the same seigneur can be detected choosing at one time one solution, and at another time the other. Thus, the bishops of Winchester, founders of six new towns, were not so wedded to novelty for its own sake that all their boroughs had to be plantations. On

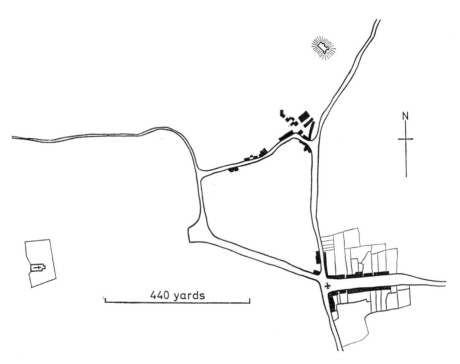

Fig. 9. HAREWOOD, Yorks., W.R. A borough placed near a village, but separate. Detail from plan c. 1690, Harewood Estate MSS., Leeds City Library, Archives Department. The village may once have extended as far as the church, extreme left. The castle is top right.

their manors of Witney and Farnham there were villages that they were perfectly happy to transform into boroughs. Yet at Downton (Wilts.) where the village was large, and where the bishops had a fortified manor house or castle, the village site was patently rejected as the centre for new development: for the borough site was a few hundred yards away, and on the other bank of the Avon.

A similar rejection can be seen at Alresford (Hants.) where the bishop rejected the village that is now known as Old Alresford, and chose instead an open space in the south of the parish, and within the village fields. There they laid out Alresford *Forum*, New Alresford (Fig. 11). In this case there is no doubt where the magnet lay: in 1200 the Alre

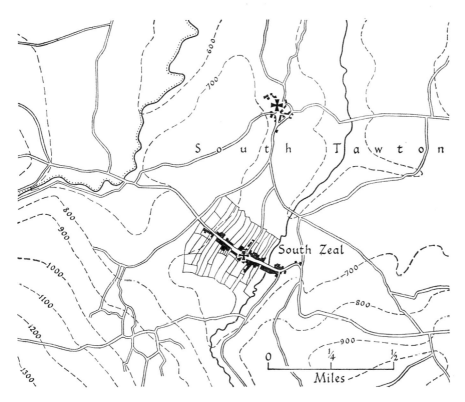

FIG. 10. SOUTH ZEAL, Devon. A planted borough more than a half-mile from the parent village, South Tawton, but set on a main road.

river had been canalised, and an artificial pool at the head of the navigation kept the canal supplied with water. Old Alresford village did not lie on the waterway, which terminated near the main London road. A narrow road across the great dam of the canal pool led to the bishop's village, but between the canal and the London road a broad market place was laid out on more level ground. The burgages were set on three sides of the *Forum*, the London road made the fourth, and a church was built, closing the gap. From the canal wharves and through the New Market came the carts and horses that had collected the goods from the barges, and through the Market came the traffic from the hinterland that was going to the canal, and thence to Winchester and Southampton and the sea.

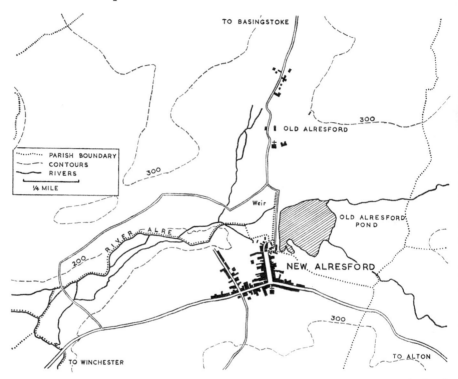

FIG. 11. NEW ALRESFORD, Hants. A plantation by a bishop of Winchester at the head of the Alre canal but a half-mile from the parent village of Old Alresford.

These rejections of existing settlements in favour of new projects draw attention to one of the qualities that any successful site needed: access to traffic and human concourse. It was this quality which led to towns outside castle-gates and to towns alongside ferries and bridges. The chain of causation thus leads back to other decisions to build or construct. The most fruitful period of town plantation will be one when general economic conditions permit and encourage the building of new bridges; when foreign trade offers a livelihood for the inhabitants of new ports; and when—most important of all—country roads carry traffic in such increasing quantities that seigneurs watch the traffic pass and wonder whether they might engineer their own Higham and their own Market Harborough.

The multiplication of new towns on roadside and riverside sites was the natural accompaniment of growing economic activity, and the choice of site for any particular seigneur was correspondingly limited. If an important artery of road or water touched only the edge of his estate, there was no choice at all but to lay out the town at the point of tangency. The magnetic attraction of a roadside site is clearly seen when it drew settlement to what had previously been open heathland or to the edge of an existing parish. If a road itself formed the parish boundary, many places show that a planted town would cheerfully straddle the old boundaries for its new purpose: Royston, Newmarket, Wokingham, Boscastle, Mitchell and Maidenhead all have this characteristic feature.

Where two major roads crossed (as at Dunstable and Baldock) the seigneur's choice was equally circumscribed. The town had to be on the arms of the cross-roads. When a road crossed the river, the optimal point for a town was at the crossing itself. If the seigneur had land at the crossing, the choice was made for him: if he did not have land at the crossing, the crop was not for his gathering.

When a king of France wanted to build a new port for embarkation of the Crusaders' fleet his choice was also circumscribed: it had to be on the Mediterranean and as far east as possible. In the early thirteenth century the Rhône estuary was the eastern frontier of France and the new port was placed on the western edge of the delta, even though this meant peopling the lonely marshes of the Camargue and the construction of a causeway to the town: thus Aigues Mortes was created. War between England and Scotland led Edward I to a desperate search for a site where a victualling port for his fleet could be built on the Solway Firth near the border. The search was truly desperate, for two successive sites were chosen: only to be abandoned when the seas overran them.

Occasionally the forces that suddenly advanced the commercial potential of a site were neither those of war nor developments within the European economy, but sudden freaks of nature. Thus the erosion of one Hastings directed its burgesses to another site two centuries before the waves began to evict the burgesses of Old Winchelsea. As if in compensation, the sea threw up an island off Spurn Head and suddenly made possible another Humber port with the ambition to behave, as its jealous rivals at Grimsby complained, "just as if it were a borough".

In less dramatic foundations than these we must look to developing traffic on road, river and sea as major stimuli to new ventures, and these three influences will now be considered in turn.

III

Wherever possible, water transport was preferred to road throughout the Middle Ages. There seems to have been no adequate technology of road-building and it was the strain imposed on the draught-animals and carts by stones and mud that raised land-transport costs and drove traffic to water even though a circuitous route had to be followed. The rivers of the English plains were linked together by the broader highway of coastal navigation, and most traffic to London from beyond the Chilterns and the North Downs first went down-river to the sea, then along the coast and finally up the Thames. West of London the Thames and its tributaries drew traffic down towards the metropolis, and in the west and north of England the Severn and the Humber estuaries were the gateways to and from productive hinterlands. In English Gascony at the great ports of Bordeaux and Bayonne the wine-fleets for north-western Europe awaited the concourse of barges coming down the great rivers from the wine-growing plains.

If the rivers were the arteries of medieval inland commerce, the roads were its veins, the necessary final stage in the journey to the many places that were not fortunate enough to lie on coast or navigable river. Generously as the English plains are supplied with rivers, not all of them were navigable in the Middle Ages, and the multiplication of market centres and inland boroughs—both organic and planted—could not have taken place without road transport to link them to waterways. In such an economy the junctions of roads and rivers, together with the coastal havens, would be obvious points for a seigneur to consider, but there are a small number of foundations where the dry road itself encouraged hopes, and it is significant that nearly all these were located on Roman roads, confirming the view that Roman roads were still in active use in the Middle Ages and not yet at their low point of disrepair. Bretford (Fig. 12) on the Foss Way, Royston and Baldock on the Icknield Way, and Dunstable on Watling Street were all placed on Roman roads and away from navigable rivers.

The new Stratfords, the places at the street-fords, bring us to the junction of road and water. Some of these junctions fostered river-ports, but there were Stratfords far above the head of navigation, where only swans sailed. Stony Stratford and Fenny Stratford were

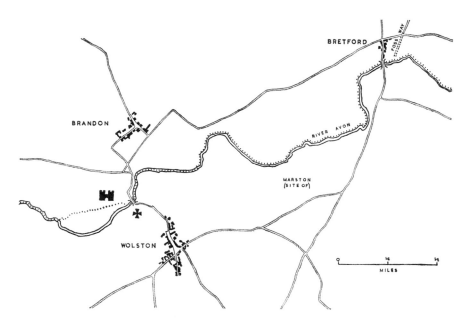

FIG. 12. BRETFORD, Warws. The small borough was placed where the Foss way crossed the Avon, but on the edge of Brandon parish, where the founder's castle lay near the village.

founded where the Watling Street was forced to wade: but in normal weather not to wade deeply. After storms traffic might have to wait at a ford; and it is never difficult to find ways of making money from waiting travellers.

The fords carrying Roman roads across rivers were not the only fords to engender towns. Newton Poppleford (Fig. 13) carried both its newness and its location in its name, and Colyford (Fig. 14) was planted on the same road only a few miles away. One of the abortive ventures outside Totnes was at the North Ford, and there was once a

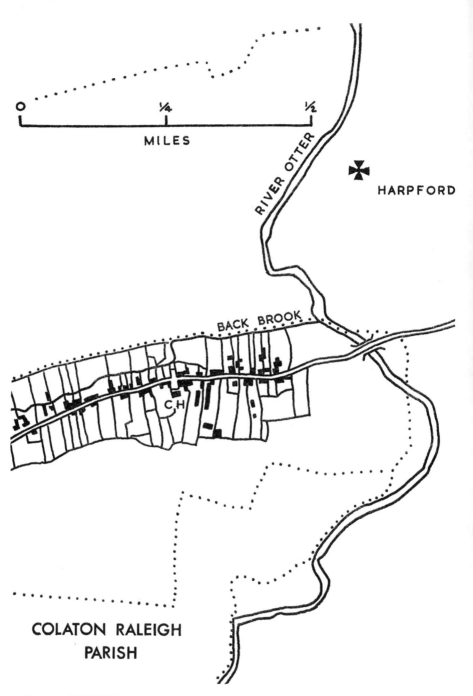

MILES

HARPFORD

RIVER OTTER

BACK BROOK

CH

COLATON RALEIGH
PARISH

FIG. 13. NEWTON POPPLEFORD, Devon. A borough set on a parish edge near the
Otter ford.

borough at Stoford. Not all fords were fatal to bastidors: a successful plantation was achieved at Camelford.

A ferry-crossing (such as that which linked the boroughs of Deganwy and Conway, that which crossed the Aire at Airmyn, or that which linked Devon and Cornwall at Saltash) was a classic site for commercial development that was founded on a delaying factor longer than a flooded ford: that is, the loading and unloading of small boats. If a bridge was built to replace a ferry, it might seem that traffic would then

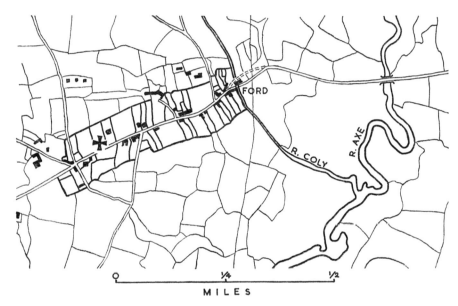

FIG. 14. COLYFORD, Devon.   A borough set on a main road adjoining a ford.

flow more smoothly, but bridges (like ferries) imposed tolls, and the collection of tolls imposed halts and delays.   At important bridges and ferries, where roads crossed frontiers or entered new lordships, the tolls and delays would be more serious.   Internal tolls were less important in England than in Wales, where lordships proliferated, and much less important than in Gascony.   It will be noticed from the distribution maps (Figs. 48–49) that a number of important plantations in England stand at county boundaries, but these were not frontier towns making up a host of petty Berwicks.   They were mostly at river-crossings, and their economic potential arose from the junction of roads with the river that happened to form a county boundary.

A bridge, ferry or ford was bound to act as focus for local routes on either bank of the river just as a coastal port draws inland roads to itself. Traffic wishing to cross a river had no option but to choose one of these limited number of crossing places, and at these major junctions of road and water there was much more economic opportunity than merely catering for benighted travellers: there was work for men to do

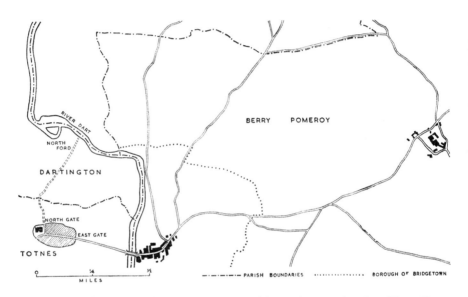

Fig. 15. BRIDGETOWN POMEROY, Devon. A borough set on the edge of Berry Pomeroy parish but at the Dart Bridge, facing the old borough of Totnes. There was also a small (perhaps abortive) borough at North Ford.

in transferring goods from horse and cart to the river-barges, and opportunities to put on sale what the laden barges had brought from up- or down-river. Thus the traffic on the Dart sustained not only the older town of Totnes but a plantation at Bridgetown Pomeroy on the opposite bank, as well as the unfulfilled hopes of two other boroughs on other demesnes only a quarter of a mile away (Fig. 15).

The importance of a river-crossing in engendering a town is shown clearly when the building of a new bridge caused the diversion of an old road to a new route, and the development of a new town at the new crossing-place. Thus, when the London to Colchester road was given a new bridge east of the old crossing at Writtle, the bishop of London (on whose demesnes the northern end of the bridge rested) created Chelmsford by leading the road straight into a great triangular market place which still gives form to the heart of the county town of Essex, now with a bishop of its own.

In Shropshire the crossing of the Severn near the *burh* of Quatford

FIG. 16. BOROUGHBRIDGE, Yorks., W.R. A borough set up by the new bridge over the Ure, but on the edge of Aldborough parish, the open fields of which are shown.

117

was replaced by a bridge a little further north and the *burh* was deserted for Bridgnorth. The Roman bridge that carried the Great North Road over the Ure near *Isurium* seems to have lasted until the twelfth century but when it finally collapsed a new site was utilised and the

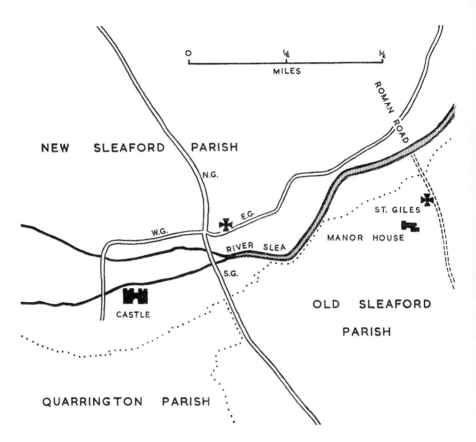

FIG. 17. NEW SLEAFORD, Lincs. Old Sleaford, abandoned for the new borough by the castle, lay near the church of St. Giles on the Roman road. *N.G.*, etc., mark the four main streets or *Gates* of the borough.

Great North Road had to be diverted. The Saxon borough near the old bridge declined to a village with the significant name Aldborough (*sc.* Old Borough), and the new town of Boroughbridge flourished by the new bridge (Fig. 16). A similar diversion seems to have produced

New Sleaford. The Roman road crossed the Slea river by a ford near the village of Old Sleaford until a bishop of Lincoln chose a site for his castle a little west of this crossing, built a bridge, diverted the road, created a borough at the crossing and left Old Sleaford to decline to a deserted village with only the site of its ruined church marked on the Ordnance Survey map. The *ford* element in the name New Sleaford is thus rather deceptive, as in some other ford plantations (Fig. 17). In the thirteenth century, Stratford on Avon and Stony Stratford were centred upon bridges, not fords.[7]

The names of several plantations emphasise the role of the bridge in their siting. Stockbridge was a borough that extended the full length of the long bridge, or bridged causeway, from which it was named. Uxbridge and Bridgetown Pomeroy are straightforward examples; and if Norman French were still spoken in England, no one would miss the significance of the borough of Grampound, *Grandpont* (Fig. 18). In Ireland two Norman burghal plantations, Rosspont (now New Ross) and Jeripont have the same syllable. The purest of all the bridge-boroughs is the Lincolnshire plantation on the east bank of the river Ancholme. Its older name of Glanfordbridge has given way to the single syllable of Brigg.

Some fortunate seigneurs were able to develop ports on the coast itself. The multiplication of sea ports in the twelfth and thirteenth centuries was stimulated not only by the export trade in corn, wool and minerals from the hinterlands of these ports but also by the use of the sea as a highway linking one place in England with another. The east and south coasts were particularly well placed: navigable rivers flowed down to them through fertile plains, and they faced the foreign countries that were then most important to English trade.

> The transport facilities of Medieval England enabled an east-coast port to extend its influence at times over a very considerable area, and the economic watershed of the country was thus thrust far to the west, so that cloth from Wales and wool from the Marches gravitated towards the North Sea as did lead from the Pennines.[8]

Table IV.2 analyses the character and location of the plantations that were ports, whether sea-, estuarine- or river-ports. Nearly half the

---

[7] An original ford is disclosed also by elements in the place-names Bridgeford and Wade-bridge (wade = *waeth*, ford).

[8] R. A. Pelham in H. C. Darby, ed., *An Historical Geography of England before 1800* (1936), p. 299.

English plantations fell into one of these categories, the greatest activity being on the south coast. One-third of the Welsh plantations were ports. In Gascony, where the undrained marshes of the Landes inhibited all coastal ports between the Gironde estuary and Bayonne, there was no opportunity to develop sea-ports, but the converging rivers

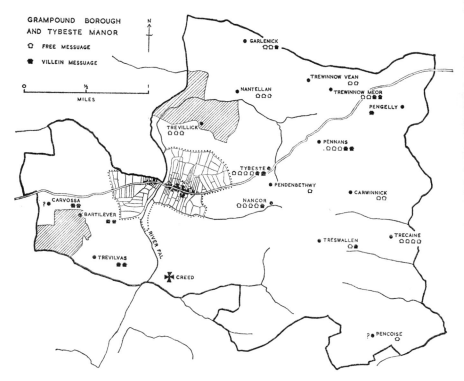

FIG. 18. GRAMPOUND, Cornwall. The borough was set at the bridge over the Fal, and was named after the *Grand Pont.* The scatter of farms in Creed parish (Tybeste manor), antecedent to the borough, is indicated by the free and villein messuages.

that flowed down through the vine-growing countryside to Bordeaux and Bayonne gave plenty of opportunity for the development of small river-ports to load the wine for its journey to Bordeaux and Bayonne. Of the two, Bordeaux was by far the most important, and twenty of the twenty-four river-ports in Table IV.2 were sited on rivers leading to the Gironde estuary. The bastide of Créon, south-east of Bordeaux, was sometimes known as *bastida inter dua maria*: the "two seas" were the

TABLE IV.2

PLANTED TOWNS: PORTS

	Sea ports	Estuarine ports	Inland river ports
England, north-western / west coast	1	2	1
south-western / east coast	5	13	7
north-eastern / south coast	19	15	5
south-eastern	13	7	4
Wales	0	1	8
Gascony		—	24
Total	38	38	49

Ports as proportion of all plantations

England: sea ports	15%	
estuarine ports	17	*England total:* 42%
inland river ports	10	
Wales: sea ports	15	
estuarine ports	8	*Wales total:* 32%
inland river ports	9	
Gascony: sea ports	0	
estuarine ports	—	*Gascony total:* 20%
inland river ports	20	

Garonne and the Dordogne, soon to meet in the inland sea of the Gironde estuary where the wine-fleet waited for the river barges.

In south Wales the mountains approach close to the indented coast-line, and the main coastal road crosses the rivers very near the head of the estuaries. It was at these crossings that the great chain of English castles was placed, and their accompanying towns could be victualled from the sea, like the later towns of Edward I in north Wales. In Cornwall and south Devon the coastline was also indented, and the coastal roads switchbacked between the valleys: it is not surprising, therefore, that Cornwall's plantations included so many river- and estuarine-ports through which the heavy mineral products of the moorland stannaries were exported.

On the long coastline of north-eastern England the distribution of ports at the time of the Norman Conquest left plenty of room for innovations.[9] A few acres from the commons of Lesbury were suffi-cient to house the burgesses of Alnmouth, a new port intended for the easier victualling of the castle and abbey of Alnwick (Fig. 19). The maritime origins of Alnmouth were remembered 300 years later when the earl of Northumberland's surveyor wrote:

> In auncyent tymes yt was taken forthe of this lordship of intente yt should be planted with suche persons as wold trafique by the sea.[10]

A little further south the same surveyor noted the origins of Wark-worth Newtown.

> At the first situation of the said borowghe, before the same was inhabited, yt was thought that in all the lordship there was not one so mete a place to be founde like the scyte of a borowghe as it is . . . and it was thought good for diverse causes that those persons which sholde trade ther traffique by sea (as maryners or fishermen) sholde inhabyte and dwell together, evene so was sett forthe one parcell of grounde for them to inhabit upon called the Newe-towne.[11]

The origins of the two Shields, facing each other across the Tyne, are also well documented, but the origins of Newcastle itself, their jealous rival, can only be deduced. On the Durham coast the bishop had estates at the mouth of every river, and by the end of the thirteenth

---

[9] Edward I's motives for acquiring a site to extend the town of Wyke on Hull, according to the chronicle of the dispossessed abbey, was directed at port development: *ut ibidem portum pro navibus et mercimoniis aptum stabiliret* (*Chronica Monasterii de Melsa*, ed. E. A. Bond (Rolls Series), ii (1867), p. 186.

[10] *N.C.H.*, ii (1895), p. 467.

[11] *Ibid.*, v (1899), p. 149.

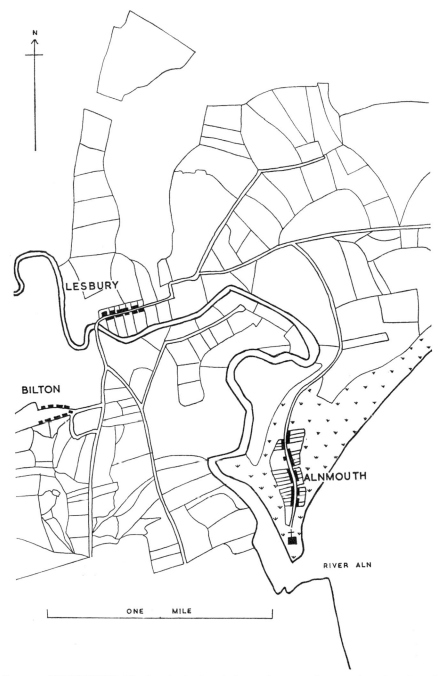

N

LESBURY

BILTON

ALNMOUTH

RIVER ALN

ONE   MILE

FIG. 19. ALNMOUTH, Northumberland.   A borough set on the strand at the edge of
Lesbury parish.

century had boroughs from Tyne to Tees. On the Yorkshire coast the cliffs were not hospitable until south of Bridlington where the earls of Aumale were able to create Skipsea Brough in north Holderness, and Hedon and Ravenserodd in southern Holderness; the Humber estuary fostered Wyke, Airmyn, Brough and Selby (see Fig. 48).

From the Humber to the Thames the east coast was already well provided with ports, but two newcomers on this coast, Boston and Lynn, were soon among the leading ports of the whole kingdom. Also looking to this coast, although considerably up-river, was the great fair-town of St. Ives, also a plantation. The coast between the Thames and the Solent was also well stocked with pre-Norman ports, and here the newcomers were mainly replacing eroded or inaccessible older ports (New Romney, New Hythe, New Hastings and New Winchelsea). Yet the Thames estuary sheltered the last of the medieval English plantations, an Aigues Mortes in miniature, Edward III's military port of Queenborough.

From Selsey Bill westwards the old-established ports had a less firm hold: a bishop of Chichester hoped (unsuccessfully) to engineer a town nearer the sea than Chichester itself; old Porchester was successfully challenged by new Portsmouth; the Isle of Wight acquired three port-boroughs, and the coast between Southampton Water and Portland Bill acquired five more (Fig. 49).

The English shores of the Bristol Channel were not hospitable to new ports, and the coast of north-west England also scored poorly. Here, it was not the competition of old-established ports that inhibited the proliferation of new coastal towns. The coast of Lancashire and Cumberland did not have the military importance that brought garrison towns to the neighbouring coastline of north Wales, and the hinterland, as the tax yields of the early fourteenth century show, was still poorly developed. Even the opportunities for traffic with Ireland did no more than create a modest rival to Chester in King John's new port of Liverpool, founded in 1207. Yet the language of Liverpool's charter made it quite clear that two types of English borough were accepted, a land-borough and "borough on the sea"; and Liverpool was not to be put off with any second-best.

> Know ye that all our lieges who have taken burgages at Liverpool shall have all the liberties and free customs which any free borough on the sea has in our kingdom.[12]

[12] *Ballard*, p. 33.

124

IV

The founders of towns were not always passive spectators of economic change, waiting for an opportunity to be presented to them as the result of political and economic action far outside their own control. The urban potential of a site was sometimes the result of a seigneur's own actions. It has been seen already that the construction of a new bridge and the diversion of roads could be turned to the seigneur's advantage. The intensive development of their rural estates could not help but improve the chances of any plantation whose modest aim was to be a local market centre for the products of the fields. The development of quarries and mines by a seigneur would also improve the fortunes of local markets and ports.

Besides the general encouragement of local economic development the seigneur might spend money on constructional work that had the indirect result of encouraging town development. It has already been seen that building of new bridges in Essex, Lincolnshire and Yorkshire encouraged the diversion of roads and the creation of Chelmsford, New Sleaford and Boroughbridge. There were other building ventures where the seigneur had no direct intention of fostering trade or towns, yet where the natural consequence of building was the enhancement of a site for a new town. The residence of a seigneur could not help being a place of public resort. A new residence for a great seigneur that was built away from an existing village promoted a concourse of social visitors, tenants, suitors at court, knights of the Honour and perhaps even the king himself; and with the visitors came servants, retinues and spectators. The suddenly inflated population had to be housed and fed, and if the seigneur was regularly in residence there were regular opportunities for traders and craftsmen established at his gate.

These magnetic forces were strong around the residences of bishops and abbots and even stronger around the residences of the king and the royal family, and they can be detected—though less strongly—around the manor houses of the smallest seigneur. The forces of attraction were strengthened if the seigneur's residence was fortified and could offer a place of refuge in time of war. In the earliest planted towns of Normandy and Norman England these focal residences of the seigneur were usually fortified. The Norman towns of New Windsor, Ludlow, Rhuddlan, Cardiff and Carmarthen (Fig. 20) stood like suppliants at

castle gates.   Feudal society was a military society and the great ones
of the land equipped their residences for warfare.   Yet their households were more than garrisons in comfortless castles, and the castle-
gate town was something more than a garrison town.   The royal
residence at New Windsor was a palace and a hunting-seat as well as a

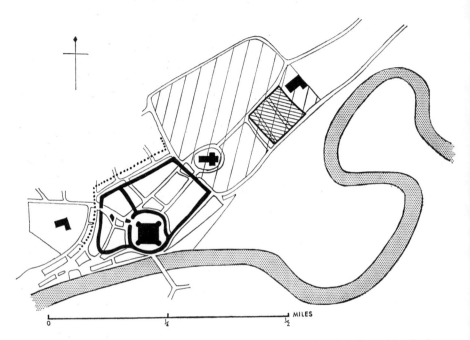

FIG. 20. OLD AND NEW CARMARTHEN.   New Carmarthen is indicated by the heavy
lines of the walled town and castle north of the bridge.   The dots show a watercourse
defence.   The lightly- and heavily-shaded rectangles mark two views of the extent of Roman
Carmarthen, fort or town.   Celtic Carmarthen, between the church at the west end of the
shaded area and the Priory at the east end, can also be seen to lie outside the area chosen for
the medieval borough.

fortress, and no king could afford a permanent garrison as numerous
as the burgage plots of walled Ludlow.   To people these, the town had
to attract and hold civilians.   The purely garrison town, all army and
camp followers, can be detected only in the little boroughs that crowded
themselves into the baileys of castles along the Welsh border where the
remote and elevated site of the town points to the victory of military
over commercial considerations.   Yet the grass that now covers sites

126

like Dynevor, Cefnllys (Fig. 21), Dolforwyn and Bere testifies to the fate of towns that fed only on war.

Other towns in the chain that stretched from Aberystwyth to Flint were planted by rivers and seas, and were ports and market towns as well as fortresses. They survive, for in the intervals between wars a

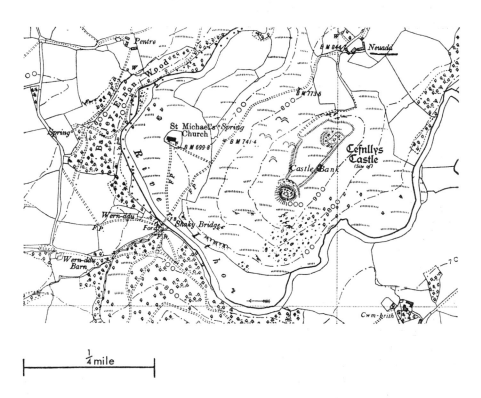

FIG. 21. CEFNLLYS, Radnorshire. The borough site has not been excavated, but it may have lain within the earthworks of the castle.

town could flourish only if there was a living to be made by its crafts-men and traders, and the domestic presence of a seigneur in a castle was a guarantee that there would be such a living to be made in peacetime.

The plainest statement that a castle and a new town were connected is seen in town names such as Newcastle on Tyne, Newcastle under

Lyme and Newcastle Emlyn. In Derbyshire the name of Castleton proclaims the same fact. In Warwickshire there is interesting documentary evidence that the Norman lords who built Kenilworth castle and endowed Kenilworth Priory were alive to the possibility of developing a borough at the castle gates. In the foundation charter of the priory (c. 1122) Geoffrey de Clinton stated that he had retained a little land in order to make a park to go with his new castle

excepta particula quam ego inde retinui ad castellum et ad parcum meum faciendum

but when Stephen confirmed this charter for Geoffrey's son (1135–54) the purpose was re-stated: the castle and park were now to be endowed with a fish-pond and a borough—

excepta terra in qua castellum eius situm erat et quam retinuit in suo dominio ad burgum suum faciendum et ad vivarium suum et ad parcum suum.[13]

The navel string that tied town to castle is also seen whenever a seigneur changed the site of his residence and a town followed him. New Windsor had not always been the favoured residence for kings of England: Edward the Confessor's palace was in the riverside meadows at Old Windsor, 2 or 3 miles from the Norman castle. The Conqueror placed his new castle on a cliff at the extreme north-west corner of Old Windsor parish where it abutted on Clewer, and part of the new borough at the castle-gate was taken in from Clewer parish. The abandonment of the Saxon *burh* at Burpham on the east bank of the Arun may have been caused by the creation of the Norman castle and town at Arundel on the west bank, just as (a little later) the construction of the bridge and castle at Bridgnorth caused the desertion of the Saxon *burh* at Quatford a mile or so down-river. New Buckenham was created outside a castle that had been moved from a site in Old Buckenham village, and when Edward I built a new castle at Rhuddlan he left the Norman motte and the Norman town outside the walls of his new town; no signs of the Norman road remain above ground and only the motte remains as a reminder of its site.

A castle was the accepted place of residence for a seigneur even in peacetime, and the duties and pleasures of peacetime continued to bring

---

[13] B.M. Harl. Ms. 3650, ff. 2, 3v. and 73; the recital in *The Stoneleigh Leger Book* (ed. R. H. Hilton (Dugdale Soc. Publns. xxiv (1960), pp. 114–116) has no mention of an intended borough.

a concourse to his gates. If he came for the sports of the chase or for tournaments he would still bring his household and guests. New Windsor was in Windsor Forest. The seigneur of Pleshey rode out to hunt in the Essex forest through the ring of defences that took in both his castle and his town. If the seigneur of Devizes looked westward from his ramparts he saw his palisaded deer-park, and if eastward, the burgage plots, market place and church of his castle-borough (Fig. 22).

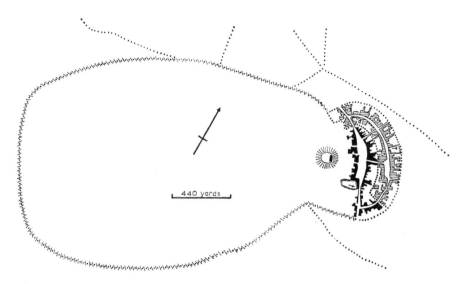

FIG. 22. DEVIZES, Wilts. A borough set at the dividing place, *de devisis*, of parishes (dotted lines) and outside the bishop's castle—with its great oval park-pale. The borough bounds also have semicircular features. There are two urban parishes, each with a market place; the houses in the inner parish are shaded black, those in the outer are cross-lined.

In the course of the enquiry that produced the Hundred Rolls of 1279 an Oxfordshire jury informed Edward I of the origins of New Woodstock:

> in the time of Henry II there was a certain empty plot beside the park of the manor of Woodstock, and since the king's men were lodged too far from the manor, the king gave divers parcels of land from the said empty plot to men who would come and build *hospicia*, giving them also a weekly market . . . and Henry III gave them a fair of three days' duration.[14]

14 *R.H.*, ii, p. 839.

The concourse for pleasure had produced a town. When Woodstock no longer sounded to the royal hunt there was little else to keep the town going, and a statute of 1576, seeking to remedy the decay of the little borough, recalled nostalgically that the town was

> formerly chiefly supported by access of the Queen's noble progenitors unto their manor of Woodstock.[15]

The monastery gate had the same power to draw traffic to it as the gate of a castle, palace or hunting lodge. Tenants, suitors and litigants had occasion to come to the courts of the abbot when abbots became great landowners; and the monastery had a further attraction for visitors if it became a place of pilgrimage, especially if its church became the centre of a popular cult. We have already seen that the bones of St. Edmund had the power to draw Edward I to Bury, and two centuries before Edward's pilgrimages Domesday Book described the enlargement of the Saxon town in order to play host to travellers. The English monasteries were normally sited in existing towns or on the edge of existing villages. (The particular case of the Cistercian houses is considered below.) The main contribution of monasteries to urbanisation, therefore, was to develop existing towns or to urbanise villages. This would seem to be the meaning of the statement in the Hundred Rolls that at Tavistock *abbas villam fecit levari*.[16] As Professor Finberg writes,

> the Domesday manor of Tavistock . . . came to an end at some date between 1105 and 1185 when one of the abbots, most probably abbot Walter, created a borough outside the monastery gates.

Rather earlier, an abbey founded in 1004 alongside the Trent at Burton (Staffs.) was able to turn the village into a borough and by the mid-thirteenth century to add several burghal suburbs to this nucleus. Yet there were exceptions: the abbey of Battle was set in open countryside, since a grateful king founded it on the site of his victory at Senlac Hill; William's descendants continued to favour the abbey and it was a popular place of pilgrimage. The monks saw their opportunity and laid out burgage plots for a lay settlement along the edges of a triangular market place north of their abbey gate. Royston stood at the intersection of two important Chiltern roads, but the town also prospered

---

[15] 18 Eliz. cap. 21.
[16] *R.H.*, i, p. 81.   H. P. R. Finberg, *Tavistock Abbey* (1951), pp. 17 and 197–198.

from the cult of St. Rohesia's shrine near the cross-roads, just as Dunstable's excellent roadside site was further improved by the important priory founded near the cross-roads.

The Cistercian foundations were also in isolated positions, but for reasons of policy. Solitude was chosen as an insurance against too much contact with the laity and with Mammon. The Order came to possess land within towns: Dr. R. A. Donkin has shown that Cistercian

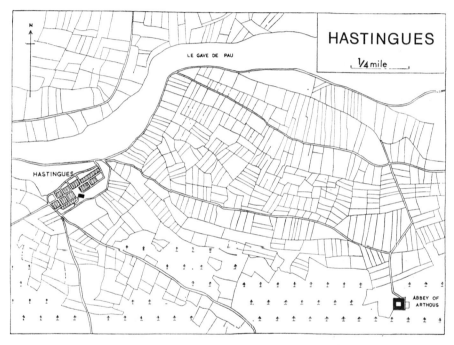

FIG. 23. HASTINGUES, Landes. A bastide set on the edge of the lands of Arthous abbey but convenient for a port on a river which flows west to Bayonne.

houses had property in forty English and Welsh towns, but the significant fact is that no abbeys were located in these towns. The statute of 1134 plainly banned such sites:

in civitatibus, castellis, villis, nulla nostra construenda sunt coenobia sed in locis a conversatione hominum remotis,

and if isolated sites were prescribed for the Cistercians it followed that the isolation could not be broken by founding towns at the monastery gate.[17]   Yet the Cistercians' business sense was too acute for them to remain aloof from such a profitable venture as town plantation, especially since their active work as colonists would make them well aware of the necessity for augmenting existing market facilities.   The Order was able to share in the urban movement by developing towns on its outlying properties, for the Cistercians had a highly organised system of isolated community houses (granges) as centres for agriculture, the labour force being composed of lay brothers.   Part of a grange territory could be given over for the site of a new town without much sacrifice of farming income and without the monastery itself infringing the statute of 1134.

In Gascony the Cistercian contribution to urbanisation was immense. Professor Higounet has identified forty-four French bastides in the Garonne valley that were founded by *paréages* between 1252 and 1325, usually on land belonging to a Cistercian abbey, and often at a grange. In English Gascony our Gazetteer shows twenty-four monastic bastides, nearly all of them Cistercian, and all except two founded by *paréages*. One of Edward I's *paréages* was with the abbot of Clairac for the foundation of a bastide to be named St. Damien but since the site lay near a grange, the name by which the town became to be known was simply Granges sur Lot.   Near another English bastide, Durance, the building of the grange can still be seen (though semi-ruined) in a woodland clearing half a mile from the little walled town that was built in 1325, after a *paréage* between Edward II and the abbot of St. Jean de la Castelle.   Hastingues (Fig. 23) also lay at a grange site.

In comparison with Gascony the English and Welsh Cistercian houses were very inactive.   The house at Meaux in Holderness founded the town of Wyke upon Hull by sacrificing part of the fields of their grange of Myton but their very success defeated them, for Edward I was attracted by the prospects of the town and forced the abbey to give up the site.   At Aberconway a Cistercian house also found itself providing the site for one of Edward's towns.   The site that Edward chose for his new castle and walled town of Conway was occupied by the monastery of Aberconway.   The king bought out the monks by giving them a new site further up the river in genuine soli-

[17] R. A. Donkin, "The Urban Properties of the Cistercians in Medieval England", *Analecta Sacri Ordinis Cisterciensis*, xv (1959), pp. 104–131; for monastic boroughs generally, see N. M. Trenholme, *The English Monastic Boroughs* (Univ. of Missouri Studies, vol. ii, no, 3, 1927).   See Skinburgh, Newton Arlosh and Beaulieu for new settlements connected with abbeys.

tude; he took the abbey church as the parish church of his new town and used the monastic buildings as offices and lodgings for himself and his household while the builders set to work on the castle and walls.

Only two other urban ventures are known to be connected with Cistercian houses: Kingsbridge, founded from Buckfast, and Wavermouth, founded from Holm Cultram. New Thame, the planted town that lay nearest to a Cistercian house, had no connection with the abbey of Thame, being a creation of the bishops of Lincoln; Neath, only a mile from Neath abbey, was founded not by the abbey but by an earl of Gloucester; and despite small urban holdings in Deganwy, Hedon, Boston, Newport, I.O.W., and Portsmouth, the Cistercians had no part in these foundations: their properties were donations or investments akin to their greater possessions in old-established towns like London, York and Chester.

The military order of the Knights Templar did not have great urban houses since the main business of its members was not residence in England but fighting in the Near East, but their benefactors presented them with estates, and these, if large, were worked from "commanderies" that were rather like Cistercian granges. The only urban venture of the Templars in England seems to be the successful Baldock, their New Baghdad in Hertfordshire, which was planted at a road junction on the northern edge of their manor of Weston. Their partnership in a Gascon bastide is commemorated by the names of La Bastide du Temple and by Le Temple de Breuil.

In French Gascony the buildings of a Templar commandery and the walled bastide that was built alongside it in 1158 can still be seen at Ste. Eulalie de Cernon (Aveyron), magnificently perched on a spur above a deep valley in the *causses*.

One or two other monastic foundations will be noted in the English and Welsh gazetteers, but no particular Order was outstanding. The most far-sighted of the monastic creations was that founded on his manor of Slepe by an abbot of Ramsey. Named St. Ives, it soon sheltered one of the four great fairs of medieval England.

V

The normal position for a village was fairly near the centre of its township, so that all the field-land could be reached with equal readiness: or, putting events in their historical order, the parish fields encircled the village that had created them. The planted borough, on the other hand, can now be seen as most typical when it lay on the edge of a rural parish.   It is as if a small piece, the borough bounds, has been bitten from the parish bounds at their edge; or as if the shadow of an eclipse has begun to overlie the full moon of the parish.   The act of sundering or separation of bounds may, indeed, be the origin of the name "Sunderland" at Bishop Wearmouth.

The intrusion of a town into a rural parish is strikingly preserved in the early nineteenth-century plans of the borough of Llanidloes (Mont.).   The town has a simple plan of gridded streets, all straight lines and right angles.   In marked contrast is the behaviour of the boundary of the rural parishes of Glynhafre Iscoed and Cilmachallt. It enters the town, wanders unconcernedly through it, utterly indifferent to the alinement of the streets and the position of the town church, and then out again on the other side.   It is quite clear that the rectilinear borough streets were laid out across the bounds of two parishes, and in a document of 1375 the borough of Llanidloes was described as "in Ughcoid (Iscoed)".

Towns planted on former Roman roads were particularly liable to find themselves straddling boundaries.   The Anglo-Saxon settlers rarely placed their villages on a Roman road, preferring a more private site a mile or so off the road.   Their fields extended up to the Roman road and it formed an easily defined boundary for parishes on either side of it.   A new town that had houses on both sides of such a road was bound to find itself in two parishes.   On the Watling Street this was the situation at Dunstable, Fenny Stratford and Stony Stratford.   Buntingford was divided between four parishes that met on the Ermine Street.

A testimony to the attraction of a parish-edge, roadside site is the conjunction of boroughs where the Exeter to Totnes road crossed a stream forming the boundary of the parishes of Woolborough and Teignwick.   The principal landowner in each parish projected a borough, one on each side of the stream, probably the nearest pair of plantations in Europe.   Each was called Newton (*Nova Villa*), one Newton Bushel and the other Newton Abbot.   The latter was sometimes called Shireborne Newton, and "Shireborne" emphasised the position of the town.   The stream that divided the boroughs, the Aller, formed the boundary of a lordship (*schire* = administrative district). Both boroughs prospered and they now coalesce in Newton Abbot; the Aller has been hidden away in a culvert beneath the market place.

A substantial number of planted towns lay on common land at the edge of parishes. There was more than one reason for this choice. Because the colonisation of a village fields had proceeded from the village outwards the land last to be cultivated was often situated on the perimeter of the parish. The land still awaiting cultivation was not idle, for it was available for commoning animals—pigs in the woodland, cattle and goats in the glades, sheep and horses on grass heathland— but it was easier for the founder of a town to forgo the produce or rent from land of this sort than to sacrifice the food-growing acres of the arable fields nearer the village. It was along the edge of parishes, as we have seen, that road and river traffic often passed, so that a site for a town on the commons brought the greatest hope of gain and the smallest sacrifice of demesne income.

Thus, when in 1218 the bishop of Winchester projected a town in north Hampshire to be set on the main road from Winchester to Oxford, he had a fairly wide choice of site. His two manors of Clere, High Clere and Burghclere, were extensive. The point on the road that he finally chose was not where the road came nearest to his villages, nor near his mansion-house, but where it came in from Berkshire over the Sandle ford and entered on common heathland. There he placed his *novus burgus de Sandelford*. When the earl of Aumale promoted a new Humber port his choice of site was limited. A convenient creek led from the Humber into the parish of Preston in Holderness, forming the southern boundary of that parish. A small part of Preston was cut out and assigned for the harbour, streets, market place, burgages and churches with which the earl's new town was furnished. The character of this part of Preston, the very edge of the parish, is indicated by the name of the new town, Hedon. (Hedon = *haeth-dun*, "the small hill overgrown with heather".) Another port that lies on the edge of an older parish is Harwich in Dovercourt, and the extensive green outside the walls suggests that Harwich, too, was planted on the heath of Dovercourt village. The little river port of Bawtry was almost certainly planted on the wastes of Austerfield (Fig. 24).

The exact site of the borough at the mouth of the Waren in Northumberland is unknown, but it was taken out of the grass commons of Bamburgh where they swept down to the sea. In 1274 a local jury testified:

Willelmus de Heron edificari fecit quamdam villam nomine Warmuwe in communi pastura villae de Bamburg tempore domini Henrici regis.[18]

[18] *N.C.H.*, i (1893), p. 194.

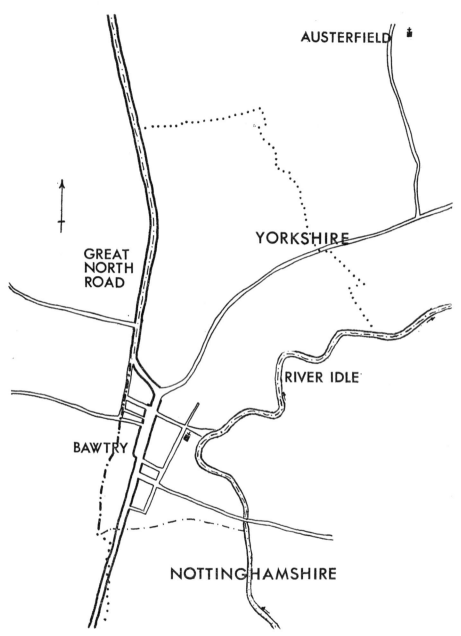

Fig. 24. BAWTRY, Yorks, W.R. A borough on the edge of two counties. It was a river-port, and the Great North Road has clearly been diverted from its original course into the market place; the parish and county boundary (— · —·) indicates the older route. The church of the mother-village is shown top-right. Scale: 4 ins. to the mile.

Near by, the more successful foundation of the port of Alnmouth occupied a similar site. The selions of the West Field of the village of Lesbury did not come right down to the sea edge: where the cliff sloped down to the estuary was a common grass pasture and there the burgages were laid out, the town being

> sett at an angle or a corner of the lordship of Lesburie, given forth by the lord of Alnewyk to one certain nombre of persons.[19]

Baldock on the northern edge of the parish of Weston (Herts.) was another town set at an angle or corner where the Great North Road crossed the Icknield Way, and the meeting of five parishes at Royston and four at Buntingford also suggest sites where the village ploughs had not yet reached.

Poole was set on Great Canford Heath, Liverpool on the common pasture of West Derby, and Petersfield on the common of Mapledurham manor. The parishes of Bigby, Broughton, Scrawby and Wrawby (Lincs.) met in the watery no-man's-land of the Ancholme marshes where the river was forded at the Glan Ford. The town of Brigg which came with the bridging of the river found itself lying in all four parishes.

The building of a bridge, as Section III has indicated, drew traffic and trade into a narrow funnel and much encouraged the provision of a town to cater for this traffic and trade. A new focus of this sort was very likely to be on the edge of a parish, for riverbanks were the commonest of all natural features to be taken for parish boundaries, and it was on the riverbank by the bridge that the town would most likely be placed.

This position for a town gave a particularly insular look to its bounds. On three sides it would be surrounded by the parish that it had invaded and on the fourth by the river from which it hoped to live. This was the situation at New Malton on the Yorkshire Derwent, and the insularity was accentuated by the wall that followed all the landward boundary of the town and by the steep cliff on the river side of the town. As soon as a burgess of New Malton stepped out of one of the three landward gates he found himself in the fields of Old Malton; the fourth gate led him to the Derwent bridge and over into the East Riding. Newport, I.O.W. (Fig. 25), and Henley, Warws. (Fig. 26), show the same features.

[19] *Ibid.*, ii (1895), p. 467.

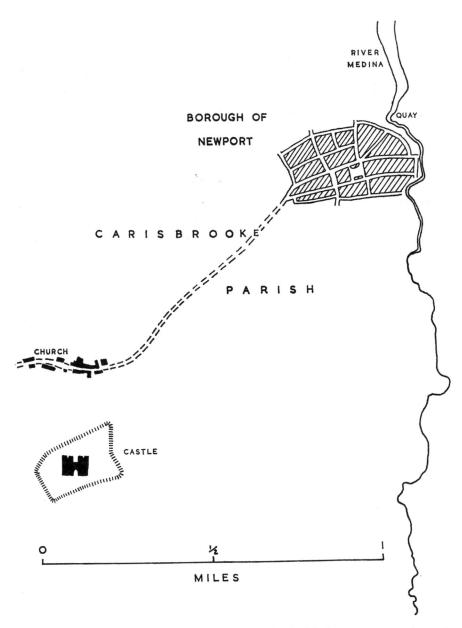

FIG. 25. NEWPORT, I.O.W.   A borough at the head of the Medina estuary, *novus burgus de Medina*, but on the edge of Carisbrooke parish.

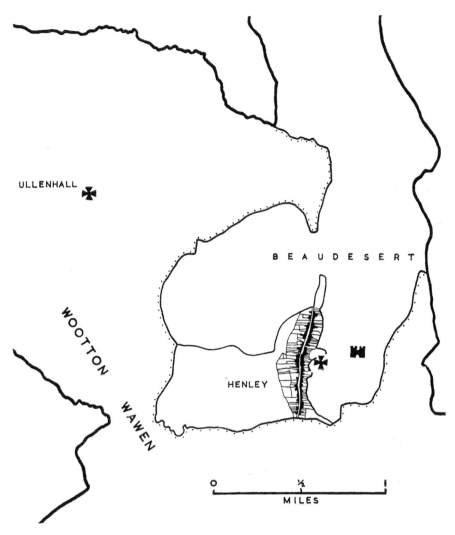

Fig. 26. HENLEY IN ARDEN, Warws. A borough on the main road, its territory cut from Beaudesert parish where the church and founder's castle stood. (Beaudesert itself may be an early castle-park cut from Wootton Wawen parish.)

One of the most famous English boroughs, Stratford on Avon, has bounds that are equally insular. On three sides are the fields of Old Stratford village, and on the fourth the Avon. The name "Old

Stratford" for the village reinforces the suspicion that the town might be a plantation; the pattern of streets points the same way; and the borough had no parish church of its own. If one asks, therefore, why one has to go outside Shakespeare's borough to see Shakespeare's tomb or why the civic procession has so long a walk from the Birthplace (in the borough) to the Birthday memorial service (in Old Stratford church), the answer is that an early thirteenth-century bishop of Worcester ordered it thus when he created his new borough of Stratford.

Winchelsea was placed at the very end of Iham parish because only there did a spur of land approach the sea, and New Winchelsea was designed to succeed Old Winchelsea as a port. New Romney also had a lonely position on the edge of the marshes, and Rye, probably a plantation, was completely isolated on its island. The Dutch plantations, the product of dams, were necessarily very insular.[20] On a modern large-scale plan of Holland their compact, densely-packed houses stand out in contrast to the light, scattered settlement of the polders around them.

For isolation, the unchallengeable town of medieval Europe was Aigues Mortes, placed where the kingdom of France reached furthest into the Mediterranean. The east bank of the Rhône was not then French. On the furthest edge of the Rhône delta and on the frontier with Provence Louis IX built Aigues Mortes, to be a place of assembly for the Crusading fleet and a victualling and supply port for the armies once they had reached their destination. In the marshy delta the edge of the sea was far away from any existing town or village, and the landward approach to Aigues Mortes was down the long causeway over the Camargue. No site in England, Wales or Gascony was as lonely as this.

Where there was no river to act as a frontier the planted borough was surrounded on all sides by rural parishes like besieging armies. An extreme case of isolation through late arrival is provided by Royston. The town was compactly gathered around the four arms of the cross-roads where the Ermine Street met the Icknield Way. It was a true no-man's-land situation. The Icknield Way formed the boundary between Hertfordshire and Cambridgeshire and the bounds of five parishes met at the place where the town was founded. It needed an act of Parliament in 1540 to free the town from this quintuple dependence:

[20] G. L. Burke, *The Making of Dutch Towns* (1956), pp. 53–63.

forasmuche as the Towne of Royston is a markett Towne situate and bilded to gither and extendeth itself into Fyve severall parrishes, wherof never a Parrisse Churche of them is within twoo myles of the said towne and somme of them be three myles.[21]

In the same way, and for the same reason, Sauveterre de Guyenne found itself at the junction of parishes.

Situations on the edge of counties, with some townsmen in one county and some in another, made for first-class wrangles. The collection of taxes and the administration of justice went according to county boundaries, so that a town straddling two counties easily provoked demarcation disputes. The appearance of a town in the tax assessments of two counties is not an infallible pointer to plantation (for an organic town might easily develop a transpontine suburb in another county), but where (as at Newmarket) divided tax assessments conjoin with the absence of early references to the place and a distinctive name, the origin of the town cannot be in doubt.

[21] 32 Henry VIII c. 44.

CHAPTER FIVE

Beau Regard: or, The Content of a
New Town

"For the most excellent proporcion therof being devyded in to
xxxix quarters the most part square, with streats very large and
broad, all strayght as the same wear layd with a line."
Report to the Privy Council on New
Winchelsea, 1570 (P.R.O. SP12/75, f. 70).

I

AFTER the site, what endowments remained for a founder to
provide for his town? The most important, its liberties and
privileges, form the subject of the next chapter where it will be
shown that there was considerable variety in provision, even though
groups of towns had similar endowments. Something of the same
mixture of variety and family-groups can be seen in the physical form of
the towns themselves, and to decide this form was an important responsibility of the founder. Once made, it was almost as irrevocable
as the choice of site.

The planted town was not the architectural prisoner of its past, for
it had no past. If the best was to be made out of the limited space
available it was natural to be orderly and to have a planned town.
The essence of Edward I's instructions to the town planners chosen for
the Bury St. Edmunds conference was that they should set out (*ordinare*)
a town in good order. When, as at Berwick, their new town was to
have its limits set by walls, there was an additional reason for eco-
nomical use of the available building space. In other towns (for
example Penryn (Fig. 27) and Kingsbridge (Fig. 45)) limits were set to
the burgage plots by sharp changes of slope and steep valley sides. It
was always awkward to build on a steeply sloping site, although (as
Conway[1] shows) needs must if the king drove hard.

[1] In this and subsequent chapters unsupported statements about particular plantations are
based on references given in the appropriate Gazetteer entries in Chapters 15–17.

142

The very choice of site helped to define the limits of the town if the site was at all restricted. Monségur, *mons securus*, was secure so long as the town streets were confined to the hill-top. Only a limited number of building plots could be accommodated, and any suburban extension of the town would have had to forfeit the protection of the hill-top and the steep cliffs. Since the hill-top was not exactly rectangular, the alinement of chequers could not be completely symmetrical (Fig. 28).

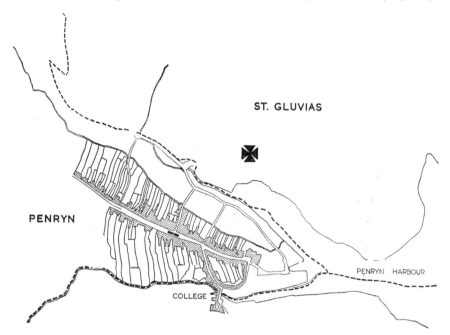

FIG. 27. PENRYN, Cornwall. The borough was set in St. Gluvias parish, and had no church of its own.

A site on the level plain could be more easily divided into regular chequers, the number limited only by the founder's assessment of demand. If the town was not walled, a suburban expansion could easily be accommodated by building over the fields and converting a few yards of field-road into a town street. Conversely, when towns shrank or failed to meet expectations, an area designed for building plots reverted to fields or vineyards (see Fig. 29).

Payments to officials to do the work of defining the line of streets and staking out the bounds of each building-plot occur from time to time

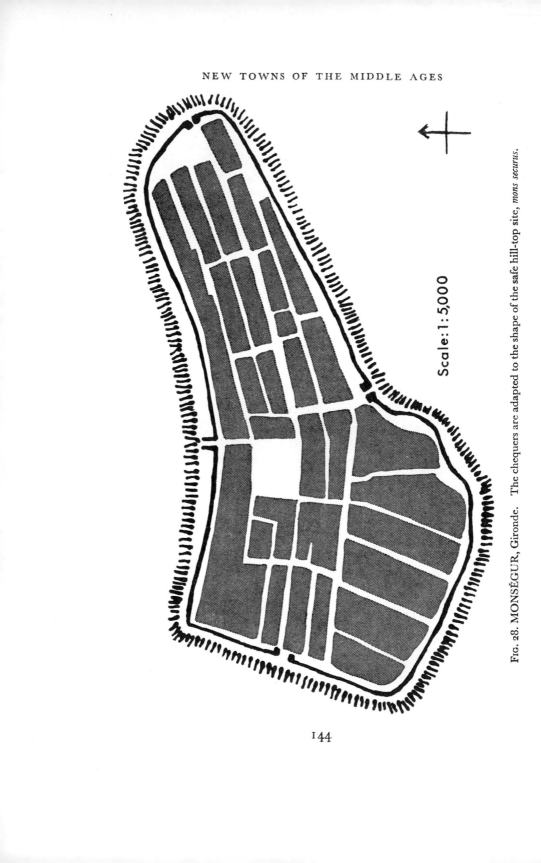

Scale: 1:5,000

Fig. 28. MONSÉGUR, Gironde. The chequers are adapted to the shape of the safe hill-top site, *mons securus.*

Plate 3. VILLENEUVE SUR LOT. Air photograph, showing the regular grid of chequers within the walls, and the modern suburbs. Across the bridges is Pujols.

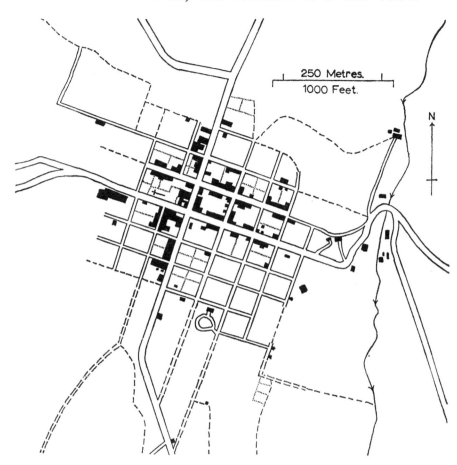

Fig. 29. ST. DENIS, Aude. A French bastide, much shrunken, but its chequers preserved as field bounds.

in the royal accounts, with the pence paid to the clerks who did the measuring, and the pence paid for the rope that measured out the building-plots. The very precise measurement of these *placeae* has already been illustrated from New Winchelsea, where the allotment of lands by these thirteenth-century clerks still determines the position of roads and the boundaries of plots and fields. No medieval plan of a new town has survived, and it is unlikely that the art of surveying had progressed far enough for anything elaborate to have been made, but the almost universal right-angles and the symmetry of the chequers would make a plan the less necessary.

Within the ordained limits of the town site the simplest way of setting out building plots and streets was in a rectilinear grid, which made no more demands on techniques of measurement than the ability to set out a straight line, to divide it into equal proportions, and to set another line at right angles to it. Documentary references to the actual operation of laying out and assigning the building plots of a new town

Scale:1:5,000

FIG. 30. STE. FOY LA GRANDE, Gironde. A riverside town on a level site, with uninterrupted chequers (*cp*. Fig. 28).

Plate 4. LA BASTIDE D'ARMAGNAC. The air photograph shows that only a few of the chequers in the right-hand side of the town are now built over. The market place is the white rectangle, centre.

are few, but in compensation there is the dumb witness of the sites in England, Wales and Gascony that have the simple rectilinear grid of streets (Plates 3 and 4; Fig. 30).

The rectilinear street-plan was a flexible one. It could be adapted to a square site as well as to a long, narrow site; rectangles of different size could be laid together to cover such hill sites as Monségur or Domme where the natural features did not leave a neatly rectangular level space.

If the roads of a new town were set out at right angles, then the internal divisions of the town were necessarily rectangular. The term commonly used for these empty blocks of land was Island (*insula*, *îlot*) although at New Salisbury the use of Chequer (Fig. 31, Plate 5) shows that the chess-board analogy had not escaped its planners. The term for the building plot within the Islands was usually *placea*, a word encountered in England, Wales and Gascony. The *placeae* within the Islands of New Winchelsea have already been illustrated in Fig. 1, p. 17. The commonest shape for the *placea* was also rectangular since it could most easily be marked out by lines drawn parallel to the sides of the Island. There was, however, no standard size of *placea*, and even in the most regular towns such as Monpazier there is more than one size apparent. In the crowded quarters of a town the house-frontages were short, but in the more open, residential areas the better-off might take a whole Island. One whole Island was commonly assigned for the church and another for the market place.

The prevalence of right-angled chequers and parallel streets does not mean that every planted town had exactly the same length and breadth, every street the same width, and every chequer the same proportions. Similarity of internal pattern is most marked in Gascony where Edward I and a small group of officials were actively concerned with a large number of plantations within a comparatively short span of years. The absence of modern industry has protected these small Gascon towns from drastic rebuilding and suburbanisation so that the original patterns of streets and chequers are much more easily appreciated than in England. In Wales, modern industrial development has distorted the medieval plan of towns in the south-east, such as Cardiff, but in the south-west, in mid-Wales and in the north, the walled towns are sufficiently well-preserved for their original plans to be quite plain. Histories of town planning have always leaned heavily on these rectilinear towns of Wales and Gascony for their illustrations, and it will not

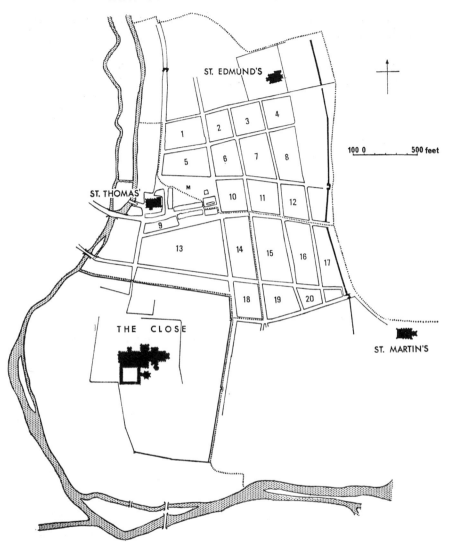

FIG. 31. NEW SALISBURY, Wilts. Cathedral, churches, market place and chequers are shown. For the parish bounds see Gazetteer, pp. 506–08. The names of the twenty chequers are those on Naish's plan of 1751 (see also plate 5):

1. Whitehorse 2. Gores 3. Parsons 4. Vanners 5. Blue Boar 6. Three Swans 7. Three Cups 8. Griffin 9. Mitre and Market Place (*M*) 10. Cross Keys 11. Black Horse 12. Swaynes 13. New Street 14. Antelope 15. Trinity 16. Rolfes 17. Barnards Cross 18. White Hart 19. Marsh 20. Pound

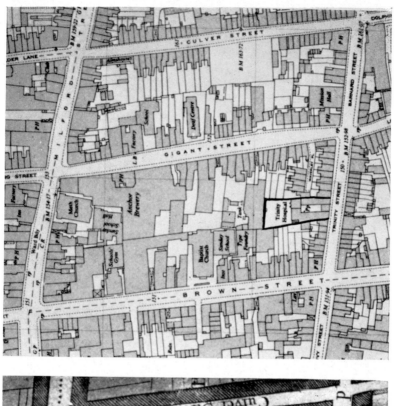

Plate 5. NEW SALISBURY. Two Chequers (nos. 15–16 of Fig. 31) and their subdivision into house-plots. Many of the divisions on Naish's plan of 1751 survive in the Ordnance Survey plan of 1954. The main north–south division of Trinity Chequer was by a rivulet which then ran down the middle of Milford Street, joining another in Brown Street.

be necessary to reproduce the whole range of plans here. More will be found in the books of F. R. Hiorns, Hughes and Lamborn, and Lavedan.[2]

All the entries in the Gazetteer chapters indicate the pattern [or absence of pattern] in each town plan. Classification of the varieties of bastide plan encountered in French and English Gascony was attempted by Lavedan, and his book has an extremely generous collection of town plans. Further analysis of form, and further plans, will be found in Professor R. E. Dickinson's *West European City* which (despite its title) is equally concerned with towns. A lavish collection of photographs and plans of Swiss plantations has recently appeared.[3]

Most of the Gascon towns were too small for the cartographers of the sixteenth and seventeenth centuries to think it worth while including a large-scale town-plan in their Atlases: there is, however, a plan of Cadillac in Braun and Hohenberg's *Civitates Orbis Terrarum*. It shows the original rectilinear bastide with chequers in the north-west corner obliterated by the new, Renaissance chateau, and streets ending abruptly at the chateau wall, rather as the streets of Berwick on Tweed were cut off abruptly by the mid-sixteenth century fortifications, almost contemporary with the works at Cadillac shown in this plan.

John Speed's *Theatre of the Empire of Great Britain* was published in 1611, and each county sheet had an enlarged plan of one or more towns in the county. Most English county towns were organic and not planted, so that it is in Wales that Speed's plans are most valuable in presenting the appearance of plantations just after the end of the Middle Ages. That of Flint is particularly useful (Fig. 6), since modern Flint is cut into by a railway and a main road, and the ramparts have been levelled. Speed's plan of New Radnor is also valuable since it shows the town less decayed than today, and the full grid-plan within the walls is clearly visible.[4]

The rigorously rectangular plans of the Gascon bastides and the rectangular chequers of the principal Edwardian towns in north Wales are so spectacular that histories of town planning sometimes give the

[2] F. R. Hiorns, *Town Building In History* (1956); P. Lavedan, *L'histoire de l'Urbanisme* (Paris, 1926, 2 vols.); E. A. G. Hughes and T. H. Lamborn, *Towns and Town Planning* (1923).

[3] Hans Boesch and Paul Hofer, *Flugbild der Schweizer Stadt* (Bern, 1963), esp, pp. 92–103.

[4] The following plantations are mapped in Speed's volume: Newport (I.O.W.), Launceston, New Salisbury, Richmond (Yorks.), Hull, Durham, Newcastle on Tyne (all 1611); Pembroke, Carmarthen, Cardiff, Monmouth, Brecon, New Radnor, Cardigan, New Montgomery, Harlech, Denbigh, Flint, Carnarvon and Beaumaris (all 1610). Other towns discussed in the head-notes to the Gazetteer are also mapped: Southampton, Peterborough and Berwick on Tweed (all 1611). *Tout*, Fig. 4, has the plan of Cadillac.

impression that every founder chose this type of lay-out for his town. Even in Gascony, where the type is most prevalent, it is not universal; in north Wales it predominates, but again it is not universal. Table V.1 shows that forty-six Gascon towns have clear grid plans, and these comprise only 37% of bastides. It is possible that a number of abortive and decayed towns in the light soil of the Landes, which now seem amorphous, were originally rectilinear, but the proportion could hardly rise above 50%. In England the proportion falls to one in seven. Historians of urbanism have always drawn heavily on a narrow selection of the towns named in Table V.1 without, perhaps, noticing how untypical of English plantations their plans are. For every New Sarum, New Buckenham and New Malton there were six plantations whose plans had no affinity with the chess-board.

The greater enthusiasm for a thorough-going grid plan in Gascony may be attributed in part to the narrow range of years within which they were founded. The work was being done in a hurry, and by a quite small group of people; 71% of Gascon bastides were founded by the king of England, alone or in *paréage*, and 15% more by the counts of Toulouse, alone or in *paréage*. Between smaller town-builders there was a good deal of competition, so that it is not surprising that a form of town that had gained royal approval was taken up by others. A good deal of rivalry took the form of imitation, and the form of a town was one of the features easiest to imitate when one was starting with a blank sheet.

About one-third of Welsh plantations have a clear grid-pattern, and it will be noted that the most striking examples of Welsh towns with rectilinear grids date from the late thirteenth century—also the years of the Gascon bastides—and were built by the same king. In England, the proportion of royal towns among the plantations is only 12%, compared with 35% in Wales and 71% in Gascony, and the spread of years is wider. In these circumstances, a variety of plans in England is not surprising. England has only one truly Edwardian grid—New Winchelsea—for Kingston on Hull and Berwick on Tweed cannot really be ascribed to the king. Edward's new town in Dorset may have been intended to have a gridded plan, but nothing has survived.

Table V.1 also shows that the grid plan was in use in England and Wales long before the first bastide was planted in Gascony at Marmande in 1182. There is nothing in the argument that the grid is a Mediterranean tradition which percolated slowly to England. Wallingford,

TABLE V.1

TOWNS WITH CLEAR GRID PATTERNS SURVIVING

ENGLAND		DATE OF FOUNDATION
Berkshire:	Wokingham	by 1146
Cornwall:	Lostwithiel	by 1190
Devon:	Plympton Erle	1194
Dorset:	Melcombe Regis	by 1268
Hampshire:	New Lymington	1184–1216
	Newport, I.O.W.	1177–1184
	†Newtown, I.O.W.	1255–56
	Overton	1217–18
	Portsmouth	1194
	Yarmouth, I.O.W.	c. 1170
Kent:	New Romney	by 960
Lancashire:	Liverpool	1207
Norfolk:	New Buckenham	1146–56
	King's Lynn	1086–95
Shropshire:	Bishop's Castle	1127
	Ludlow	1086–94
Sussex:	Rye	by 1086
	New Shoreham	1096–1103
	†New Winchelsea	1288
Warwickshire:	Stratford upon Avon	1196
Westmorland:	Church Brough	c. 1092–1100
Wiltshire:	New Salisbury	1219
Yorkshire:	†Hedon, E.R.	1138–48
	Wyke-on-Hull E.R.	1160–93
	New Malton, N.R.	1154–73
	Bawtry, W.R.	1199–1213

WALES		
Anglesey:	Beaumaris	1295
	Newborough	1303
Cardiganshire:	Aberystwyth	1277
Carmarthenshire:	Carmarthen	1109
Carnarvonshire	Carnarvon	1283
	Conway	1283
Denbighshire:	Holt	1282–1311
Flintshire:	Caerwys	1290
	Flint	1277
	Overton	1292
	Rhuddlan III	1278
Glamorganshire:	Cardiff	1081–93
	Cowbridge	after 1090
Monmouthshire:	Chepstow	1072–75
	Monmouth	1070–72
	Newport	by 1191
	Usk	by 1131

151

Montgomeryshire:	Caersws	?
	Llanidloes	1280–93
	New Montgomery	1223
	Newtown	1280–1321
	Welshpool	1247–52
Pembrokeshire:	Newport	c. 1197
	Tenby	early 12th century
Radnorshire:	New Radnor	?1257
	Rhyader	?1304–60

ENGLISH GASCONY

Dordogne:	Beaumont du Périgord	1272
	†Beauregard	1286
	Domme	1281
	Lalinde	1267
	Molières	1278–84
	Monpazier	1285
	Villefranche du Périgord	1261
Gers:	Fleurance	1274
	Montréal du Gers	1255
	St. Clar	1289
Gironde:	Cadillac	1280
	Créon	1315
	Libourne	1270
	Monségur	1263
	Pellegrue	1272
	Sauveterre de Guyenne	1281
	Ste. Foy la Grande	1255
Landes:	Geaune en Tursan	1318
	Hastingues	1289–c. 1303
	La Bastide d'Armagnac	c. 1283–91
	Ste. Quitterie	1289
	†Sarron	by 1318
Lot:	La Bastide Murat	1290–1304
	Montfaucon du Lot	1292–93
Lot et Garonne:	Aiguillon	1296
	Castillonès	1259
	Damazan	1250–69
	Durance	1320
	Granges sur Lot	1291
	†La Montjoie St. Louis	1299
	La Parade	1267
	Libos	c. 1320
	Marmande	1182
	Miramont	1278–86
	Monclar d'Agenais	1256
	Monflanquin	1256
	Puymirol	1246
	Vianne	1284
	Villefranche de Queyran	by 1281
	Villeneuve sur Lot	1264
	Villeréal	1265

Tarn et Garonne:	Castelsagrat		1255–62
	Dunes		1263–66
	†Montjoi		1255
	Valence d'Agen		1279

Note: † indicates good quality earthworks of decayed grid.

The following towns have streets based on a circular or semi-circular grid:

ENGLAND:	Wiltshire:	Devizes	1135–39
	Yorkshire N.R.:	Richmond	1109–14
GASCONY	Gers	Fourcès	1270–79

Wareham and Oxford were almost certainly Anglo-Saxon urban plantations with right angles and parallel streets that would do credit to any Gascon bastide founded three and four centuries later, and there are good examples of Norman grid-plans in England.

The paucity of full-blooded grid-plans in England becomes rather less extraordinary when comparison is made, not with the thirteenth-century towns of Gascony and north Wales, but with the twelfth- and thirteenth-century plantations of western and central Europe, from Normandy to the Elbe. In Alsace, in Switzerland, in south Germany, in Bavaria and in Austria there is a second form of town plan that is very prevalent, and which can also be recognised in England.

We shall call this type of plan "market-based", for whatever the shape of the market place, the burgage plots were concentrated around it. There were no other streets to divide the plots, and consequently no chequers. At the most a back-lane ran behind the burgages. The full grid-plan of the bastides was of course also focused on the market place: in a bastide of nine chequers, laid out in three rows of three, the centre chequer of the centre row was usually left unbuilt upon to form the market place where the booths and stalls could be set out on the day of the week prescribed in the foundation charter, and where the extended activities of the annual fairs could have elbow-room (Fig. 32). In pastoral areas in particular, a good deal of room was needed for tethering and penning animals that were brought in for sale.

The essential difference, therefore, between the grid-plan and the market-based plan more common to England is the fact that the grid-plan contains other streets and building-plots that move further and further from the market place until the town limits are reached. It is this succession of rectangular chequers that gives the envelope of the gridded town its rectangularity.

153

The grid-plan, therefore, assumed from the very beginning of a town that there would be enough development to occupy all this area.   In New Winchelsea and New Salisbury this principle must have operated. for the main peopling of these particular English plantations was by transfer from an older site and Old Winchelsea and Old Salisbury had too many burgesses to fit into the perimeter of one market place. Study of the Winchelsea rental (pp. 21–25) has shown that the more remote the plot from the market place, the lower the rent.   Although the gridded towns of Gascony were not peopled by migration from towns

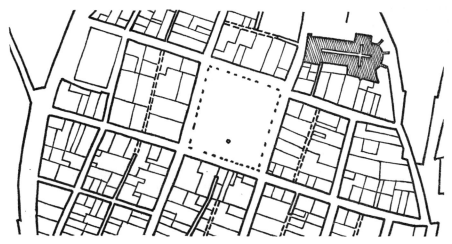

FIG. 32. MONFLANQUIN, Lot et Garonne.   Plan after G. Heritage, showing market place, *cornières*, subdivision of chequers (*ilôts*) into building plots, and the church.

that were being washed away by the sea, their founders clearly expected to find some recruits who would accept building-plots that did not adjoin the market place, and in most cases their expectations were justified and the chequers were filled with houses.   The same hopes are expressed in the multi-chequered Edwardian foundations in north Wales, and in the event most of these hopes were also justified.

The non-gridded English towns, on the other hand, display a much lower level of ambition.   When the plots alongside the market place were taken up, their founders' plan was completed and, if the town was walled, any further expansion was virtually ruled out.   In the small walled towns of southern Germany, Bavaria and Switzerland this modest ambition and modest achievement are widely encountered. A very common type of town is this: a long, broad, central market place, narrowing a little at the terminal gates; a town hall and church in the middle of the market place; a row of burgage plots on both sides of the market place; and four walls built at the far end of the plots, so that they, too, converge at the gates and give the whole town the shape of a cigar.

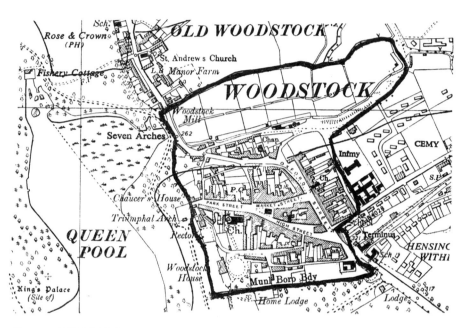

Fig. 33. NEW WOODSTOCK, Oxon. A triangular market place, at the gate of the former royal park, forms the basis of the borough. Old Woodstock is to the north.

The overall shapes of the non-gridded English towns are very varied, for they depend on the shape of the market place. If the market place was laid out as a triangle, with a castle or a monastery at the base of the triangle, the two remaining sides of the triangle had to accommodate all the burgage plots, as they did at Battle and New Woodstock (Fig. 33). On the rare occasions where the market place had a semi-circular shape, as at Devizes and Richmond, Yorks., the burgage plots abutted on to the semicircle like a fully opened fan. (In the circular bastide of Fourcès (Gers) the burgage plots made a complete ring.)

Where the market place was a rectangle much wider than a road, the arena of commerce approached the proportions of a football pitch.

The importance of having an ample and uninterrupted open space is clearly shown in those plantations where an existing road—sometimes of considerable importance—was turned aside from its course in order to bring it to the level ground chosen for the market place. A level space for a market-square was essential if carts and stalls were not to slide downhill. On the Great North Road, Baldock, Bawtry (Fig. 24) and Boroughbridge (Fig. 16) demonstrate this preference, for at the points of diversion the roads have sharp turns for traffic, even today. Chipping Sodbury (Plate 6) and Appleby have market places set well off the original main road in the same distinctive manner.

In many towns the site and shape of the market place were not dictated by the position of a castle or a monastery gate. The seigneur could plant his town along an existing road and use the road itself as the town's market place, setting the burgage plots to face each other across the road (Figs. 34–6). This allocation was simple if the road was already wide and straight, and simplest of all on a Roman road, as at Dunstable, Stoney Stratford, Wulvesford (Fig. 36) and Fenny Stratford. If the road was twisting it could be widened for a length corresponding to the need for building plots.

The full area and the original shape of a market place cannot always be appreciated by studying the present market area. The more spacious market places were always liable to encroachment as temporary stall-holders sought to build permanent shops. If a high rent was offered to the seigneur as lord of the soil of the market place, he would find it difficult to resist. The Norman market place laid out at Bury St. Edmund's was several times the area of the surviving open space (Fig. 34) and the plan of New Salisbury (Fig. 31) has clear evidence of encroachment upon a market place so important in the original concept that the boundary of the town's two parishes was set out to bisect it. At New Thame it was reported in 1279 that

> the bishop of Lincoln has raised a hundred feet of houses in the middle of the market place so that his rents might increase.[5]

Those who sought to set their shops in the middle of a market place were displaying the same anxiety to be at the centre of affairs that had

---

[5] *R.H.*, ii, p. 30. A petition from the bastide of Castelsarrasin in 1270 asked for the market to be kept open, and butchers forbidden to build permanent stalls (*A.P.E.A.*, p. 343).

Plate 6. CHIPPING SODBURY, Glos. The market borough (*chipping* = market) involved the diversion of the main road, and the setting out of burgage plots on both sides of a long, wide market place. At the top of the plate the road swings through a right angle to join its former course.

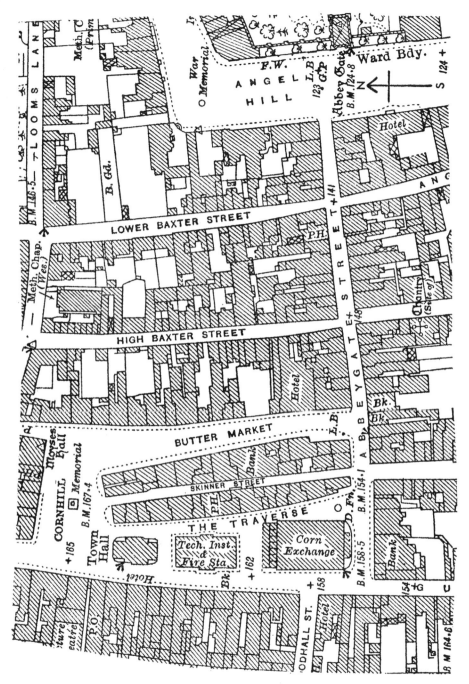

Fig. 34. BURY ST. EDMUNDS, Suffolk.   The chequers west of the Abbey gate, probably laid out in 1066–86.   Note the buildings that have encroached on the Market Place, probably following the line of booths and stalls.   Scale: 25 ins. to the mile.

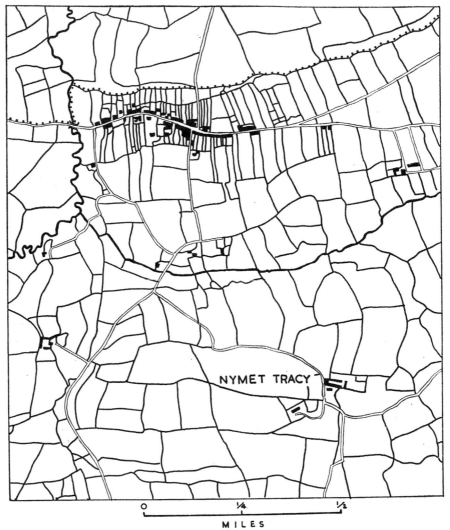

MILES

FIG. 35. BOW, Devon. A borough set on the edge of the mother-parish of Nymet Tracey.

concentrated older burgages around the edges of the market place in the non-gridded English plantations. Whatever the occupation of a townsman, he would want to be as near as possible to the centre of the arena. The full-time merchant would want his warehouse to be

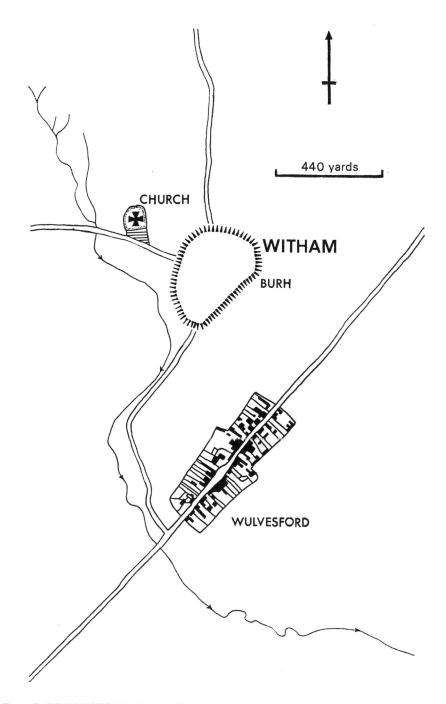

440 yards

CHURCH

WITHAM

BURH

WULVESFORD

FIG. 36. WULVESFORD, Essex. The borough is laid out on the Roman road. The Anglo-Saxon *burh* of Witham had been built further north, and the limits of its earthwork are shown. West of the *burh*, Witham church sheltered a small market place. The roadside borough site clearly rejected both the older centres.

accessible; the townsmen who were both artisan and trader—that is, the majority—needed a workplace, a house and a shop under one roof, and the shop to be in the fullest light of day to catch the eyes of passing customers; the retailer wanted to participate in the open-air display of a market-day by throwing open his windows and hanging out boards for counters to compete with the stalls and booths.[6]

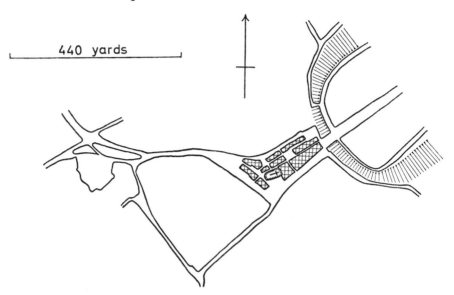

440 yards

Fɪɢ. 37. PONTEFRACT, Yorks., W.R. The first suburban lanes burst from the constriction of the walled borough, top right. A market place outside the west gate developed permanent lines of buildings (cp. Fig. 34), and acquired a church. In 1255–58 this area became the borough of West Cheap.

The triangular and rectangular market places, even when partially overbuilt in modern times, present few difficulties in recognition. The market place set in the ordinary course of a street is not usually difficult to identify, even when the market name has gone from the street and commerce has quite evaporated. If the placing of stalls was so important there was good reason to choose as level a piece of ground as possible. In many small plantations that are today no more than roadside villages a level stretch of road is often discernible within the old borough area, the natural slope of the main road being resumed outside the town limits. This temporary, and perhaps artificial, break

6 For higher rents in favoured precincts of New Winchelsea, see p. 25 above.

of slope is particularly marked where the main road is in the course of climbing the side of a valley after crossing a ford: see Colyford and Newton Poppleford (Devon) in the Gazetteer.

Another physical sign of town limits can sometimes be discerned on entering these ribbon-plantations: the points where the former country lane was converted into a town street may still be marked by a slight widening of the street when the borough limit is reached: the house-frontages step back to make room, just as the townsmen themselves stepped back on a busy market-day as the loaded carts swung into the town. If the town had gates, then they would be set at this limit, and their bulk would give a greater chance of influencing modern topography.

The former limits of a town can also be detected at the points where the road system was freed from the constriction of the walled town: where a fan of minor roads and footpaths suddenly breaks out (Fig. 38) we can be certain that we have passed through the town gate and are outside the walls.[7]

When walls survive, there is no problem of recognising old limits. When walls have disappeared or ditches have been filled in, there may still be significant indications of their former line. Sometimes there is a tell-tale change in the level of the ground: the town ditch of Flint on the west and south sides is quite unmistakable through a sudden dip in the lawns and flower beds of semi-detached houses. During its lifetime the wall or boundary ditch was an effective barrier to development across it, and all property boundaries would have to stop at the barrier. When the wall was pulled down, a narrow belt of ground became available for building upon, but the properties would be ill-aligned to the older building-plots within the walls, so the line of the old town-bounds leaves a shadow, as it were, on the modern map. When there has been extensive modern suburbanisation there is usually a contrast between the orderly alinement of building plots within the envelope of the older limits and the irregular shape of the piecemeal extensions beyond the wall.

Regular dimensions for building plots were not confined to plantations where the plots were gathered into chequers. The founders of market-based and ribbon-towns were just as assiduous in laying out

[7] In prosperous towns the concourse for fairs might be so great (as at St. Ives) that the fair-ground was extra-mural: but the charter of Saltash (*Ballard and Tait*, p. 250 (1246)) envisaged that the fair would be *in media villa*.

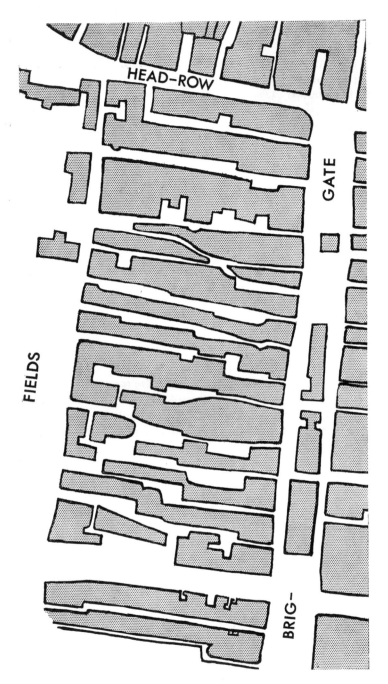

Fig. 38. LEEDS, Yorks., W.R.   Burgage plots of the borough of 1207 as shown on a plan of 1725, with the market street of Briggate encroached upon.   Scale: 48 ins. to the mile.

plots that (in a given town) tended to standard lengths and breadths. Simplicity of this sort facilitated the act of staking out the plots, and it accorded with the normal practice of a standard annual rent (usually a shilling a year) for the plots. If larger holdings were needed, they were obtained by amalgamating unit plots. It is this regularity of plot-length within a town that further emphasises the position of town bounds, for if a row of adjoining plots had the same length, the ends of the plots furthest from the street will join to make a smooth line.

Some charters specified the length and breadth of these plots, and where houses have not been disturbed by modern development the dimensions can usually be measured from a large-scale plan. A remarkable survival of these long, narrow plots is in the properties that line both sides of the market place that Maurice Paynel laid out in Leeds in 1207. They are shown diagramatically on John Cossins's plan of 1725, and in detail on the large-scale Ordnance Survey plan [5 feet = 1 mile] made in 1847. Many of the burgage houses became inns, and the inn-yards stretched the full length of the narrow plots, as they still do; a few have footpath rights-of-way through them; and several were taken for the Victorian and Edwardian shopping arcades (Fig. 38).

II

At Rhuddlan in 1279 it was proclaimed:

> To all the king's faithful subjects and tenants of the town of Rhuddlan, greeting! Master William de Louth, the king's clerk, is coming to view the empty building plots and others in the town, to assess the rents of the burgages and to demise them.[8]

It will be noted that the plots were empty ones. It was not usually the founder's responsibility to provide buildings for the first inhabitants. The burgage rents were usually for the empty plot, and no extra charge was made if more buildings were afterwards erected down the whole length of the *placea*, where there had initially been a yard, a garden or an orchard. The burgess himself met the cost of building, and thus became something of a shareholder in the success of the town, bearing part of the risk of the venture. In compensation, the townsmen holding by burgage tenure (p. 206 below) would be able to profit by the

---

[8] *Calendar of Various Chancery Rolls, 1277–1326*, p. 178.

increased value of buildings in a prosperous town whenever he came to sell out to someone else; and if he did not sell, his heir would enjoy the increased value without having to pay any part of it to the lord.

On the rare occasions where accounts show the founder in the course of building a house in a new town it will be found to be either for his own use or for housing his officers. When the fuller of New Alresford paid the bishop 10s. a year for his house—ten times the rent of the adjacent burgages—it is plain that this was no ordinary house.[9] It was akin to the bishop's bakehouse in the same town or the moneyer's house that Edward I built in Kingston on Hull. The occupants' rents bought more than a roof over their heads: they gave the right to the profitable exercise of fulling, baking and minting. Similarly, the miller of Kingston paid £5 6s. 8d. for the farm of the mill in 1303, as much as if he had rented 107 one-shilling burgages. (The king's return on the investment can be determined, for between 1302 and 1303 he had spent £61 5s. 7d. on building this new water-mill on the stream of the Ald Hull.) One of Edward I's improvements to Wyke on Hull, when he transformed it to Kingston, was a house for his bailiff: this cost £50; another, for the moneyer, cost £23 16s. 0½d.[10]

The obligation of the townsmen and not the founder to build the ordinary houses is made plain by the clauses in many charters, prescribing penalties for those who did not build and build quickly. Thus newcomers to Créon in 1316 were given a year to build on their plots under a forfeit of £5, half to the king and half to the town coffers.

The furthest assistance that might be expected from a founder was a reduction or remission of rent during the expensive years of building. The accounts for *Nova Villa de Dinevor* in 1303–04 show that there was one year of the seven rent-free years still to run:

> burgenses villae tenent burgagia et terras sine redditu a prima fundatione villae per vii annos unde iste annus est sextus.

Newcastle Emlyn had the same allowance, while the first burgesses of Beaumaris, Carnarvon, Harlech and Criccieth were allowed ten years rent-free.[12]

A concession from the founder which cost him very little was the provision of building materials from the local woodlands or quarries.

[9] Hants. Record Office, Pipe Roll no. 159270B m. 11, (formerly PRO, Eccles. 2/159270B).
[10] SC11/743; E372/152B, mm. 1–34.
[11] SC6/1218/1.
[12] SC6/1218/2; SC6/1211/2.

When fifteenth-century burgesses of New Malton set out their customs they claimed the right to take building stone from local quarries for the repair of their houses, and alleged that this right was "of the first foundation of the town".[13]   It was certainly the right of the townsmen of Créon:

> petrae sive lapides vel lapidicina si inveniantur in districtu dictae bastidae possint capi sine porestagio.[14]

At Barnard Castle the burgesses could dig in the road in front of their houses to get clay for building, while at Carnarvon unused stone from the castle was sold off cheaply to the burgesses for building their houses.[15]

In an area of abundant woodland, from Wales to eastern Gascony, there are many examples of seigneurs making building timber available to the burgesses.   This right was given in the Okehampton charter (1194–1242) "for any new burgage" and fortunate towns might find themselves given other rights of exploiting the wastes.   Rhuddlan got important rights in the forest of Bach y Graig, and in 1284 the king informed the burgesses of new Flint

> that they may have all their necessaries both for founding lead ore and for other business, without cost, from the woods and underwoods of eight Welsh townships adjoining, as well as common pasture therein.[16]

At Villeneuve sur Lot it would seem that some burgesses came like snails with their old homes on their backs, for a petition of 1270 asked that

> men who have come from homes elsewhere to live in the said bastide shall be able to bring wood, stone and tile at their own expense but without interruption from the officials.[17]

When the king was not the founder of a town he could still show it favour by a gift in kind: in 1221 Henry III granted wood from Gillingham Park to build a hall for the bishop in New Salisbury, and three years later he made another gift of timber for the new cathedral.[18]

[13] *Y.A.J.*, xxvi (1922), p. 326.
[14] C61/30 m. 4.
[15] *Ballard* and *Tait*, p. 61; SC6/1211/4.
[16] *Cal. Pat. Rolls, 1284*, p. 133.
[17] *A.P.E.A.*, p. 312.
[18] *Rot. Lit. Claus.*, i (1883), pp. 456 and 587.

To his new borough in Needwood Forest the earl of Derby gave one buck a year and a pipe of wine: these were to enhance the annual fair.[19]

In England it is unfortunately true that the more successful the plantation, the fewer are the modern remains of the original houses. Medieval Liverpool and medieval Portsmouth could be found only by excavation in the literal sense, and in other plantations the surviving buildings or fragments of buildings are visible only to knowledgeable local experts. Those who know the towns in our English Gazetteer intimately may be able to point to a few score of surviving medieval houses in the whole country, although there may be further timber houses concealed behind post-medieval façades.

It is significant that when the Historical Monuments Commission came to Carnarvon and Conway they found not a single medieval house surviving, despite the preservation of the castle and walls. The earliest surviving houses reported date from the sixteenth century: there are six survivors of this date in Conway and possibly one in Carnarvon. Neither town has been overrun by industrialisation, so that it is not surprising that even fewer medieval houses survive in more industrialised parts of the country.[20]

With so few surviving houses from the period of town plantation, very little can be said about the character of the private houses within the chequers. We cannot say whether the uniformity imposed on plot-size and street-width extended to house-design. There is nothing in England to match the group of thirteenth-century houses around the market place at Monflanquin (Fig. 32) although the reports of cellars under the turf in the abandoned chequers of New Winchelsea give hope that the house-plans of Edward's town might be retrieved by excavation.

When asked to describe the characteristic appearance of a Gascon bastide, an English visitor will certainly settle on two features: the rectilinear form of so many street-plans; and the prevalence of the *cornières*. *Cornière* is the Gascon word for the arcaded passages that line each side of a market-place. The roof of the arcade is formed by the overhanging first floor of the houses, and a series of arches give access from the shops to the open market place (Plates 2 and 7). The arcades are alined with the streets that enter the four corners of the market place, so that traffic reaches the market place only by first entering an

[19] *Ballard and Tait*, p. 129.
[20] *R.C.H.M.W. Caernarvonshire*, i (1956), pp. 58–69; ii (1960), pp. 156–158.

Plate 7. MONPAZIER.   *Cornières* and the market place.

arcade; but the impatience of modern traffic is forcing a breach at many corners.

Where there are no abrupt changes of slope it is possible to stand outside a town gate and see the entrance to an arcade at the far end of the street; and then to see, beyond the arches of the arcade, the continuation of the street from the market place as far as the opposing gate of the town.

The modern practice is to allow a shopkeeper the use of the arcade, on ordinary days of the week, rather like a pavement extension of a café, but on market days to allow new stalls to be placed under the arches as an extension of the floor of the market place. This is only possible when wheeled traffic has an alternative route into the *Place* through one of the corner-breaches already described.

Since some market places no longer have any medieval buildings alongside them, it would be rash to say that every bastide was given *cornières*, but it would be a fair assumption from the prevalence of survivors. Fifty years ago, before the motor car gave an incentive to widen streets and push back frontages, the historian Domengie noted that only two of the French and English bastides in the Agenais lacked *cornières*. The *cornière* feature has not been noted further north than the department of Dordogne: except, curiously enough, in the old quarter of La Rochelle. This town was an early Angevin plantation, but the age of the buildings in this particular street at La Rochelle is not apparent, for they have an impersonal and timeless stucco.[21]

Further shelter for commerce than the *cornières* could afford was given when a market hall [*halle*] was built in the *Place* of a bastide. In Gascony these are of open construction, being essentially a roof supported by columns. Most *halles* are of post-Revolution reconstruction, and one bastide has a *halle* that proclaims its origin in Marshall Aid, but a small number are genuine survivors from the thirteenth century. The fine wooden *halle* at Beaumont de Lomagne, for example, is a classified *Monument Historique*, and the most magnificent of all is at La Côte St. André (Isère), a bastide which was not, however, English.[22]

But neither *halles* nor *cornières* were confined to bastides. They were buildings that neighbouring organic towns possessed, and they rein-

21 G. Tholin, *Congrès Archéologique de France*, xli (1875), *sub loco*. Similar constructions on the eastern frontier of European colonisation are illustrated at Schweibus and Züllichau, near Berlin, in E. J. Siedler, *Märkischer Städtebau im Mittelalter* (Berlin, 1914), plate 121.
22 V. Chomel, "Le Marché et Les Halles de La Côte St. André", in J. Saunier and V. Chomel, *Notes d'Histoire Locale* (Crémieu, 1962–63), pp. 8–19, with plan.

HONITON

ST. MICHAEL'S ✠

O   ¼   ½

M I L E

Fɪɢ. 39. HONITON Devon.   The borough and the church of St. Michael, remote from it.

force the suspicion that there was no house-type peculiar to planted towns, and the same can be said of the churches. The surviving churches in such towns as Beaumont du Périgord and Villeréal are magnificent but not unique. The individuality of a plantation church was more pronounced in respect of its status and its relations with the nearest village church (Fig. 39). Indeed, the characteristic of a plantation was often that the town had no church at all.

III

The foundation of a new town created difficulties if the townsmen wanted an independent church, since the site was bound to lie in some existing parish whose rights would be infringed. For this reason, founding kings petitioned popes for support, and other founders came into conflict with abbots, bishops and archbishops.

It was not simply an English (or even an Anglo-Gascon) trait of obtuseness and quarrelsomeness. When the count of Savoy wanted to endow his new town of Monthoux with a new church that was independent of the rural parish church of Vetraz, he had to obtain papal bulls in 1245 and 1247. A third bull of 1249, two years after the foundation of the town, shows that the curé of Vetraz, backed by the bishop of Geneva, was still demanding the demolition of the town church.[23] A petition of 1270 from the townsmen of Villeneuve sur Lot complained that the abbot of Eysses had agreed in the original *paréage* that a chequer should be allocated for a church and cemetery, but that after the church was built the abbot began to refuse burial rights.[24]

All these resentments are well demonstrated by the disputes between the East Riding church of Hessle and the burgesses of a town on the eastern edge of Hessle parish near the Cistercian grange of Wyke. It was the new town of Wyke on Hull. Hessle church was 4½ miles to the west of Wyke, which probably came into existence between 1160 and 1180. By 1200 the townsmen had obtained permission to build the

[23] L. Blondel, "Les Fondations de Villesneuves ou Bourgs-Neufs aux environs de Genève", *Bull. de la Soc. d'Hist. et d'Arch. de Genève*, ix (1951), pp. 3–17. New castles sometimes intruded into parochial jurisdictions if their garrisons had their own church, and precedents for the small, "island" parishes of planted towns may have arisen in this way. At Durtal in Anjou, in the eleventh century, it was decided that the church of a castle could rightly claim authority and tithes from the area embraced by the wall, ditch or other surrounding works (F. M. Powicke, *The Loss of Normandy*, (1961), p. 191 fn.).
[24] *A.P.E.A.*, p. 312.

chapel of Holy Trinity in Market Gate. This town chapel had no rights of burial, for these were retained by the mother church. Before 1182 the church of Hessle was given to Guisbrough Priory, but the new owners were no less adamant, even after Wyke had been acquired by Edward I and enlarged into the chartered borough of Kingston upon Hull in 1299.

Fortunately for the burgesses, the archbishop of York visited the town in March 1301 and was surprised to encounter a funeral procession precariously carrying a coffin along the Humber shore with a high tide and a strong gale blowing. The archbishop notified the prior of Guisbrough that he intended to consecrate a churchyard in the town and prevailed on the king to grant land for a burial place. The king himself visited Hull in June 1301 and a year later he granted to God and the church of Kingston upon Hull a vacant *placea* on the west of the church. Holy Trinity still remained dependant on All Saints, Hessle, and it was only by an act of Parliament of 1661 that the town's church gained full parochial status.

The burgesses of Newport (I.O.W.) were in a similar position. Theirs was the *novus burgus de Medina*: it had been founded on the banks of the Medina near the edge of Carisbrooke parish. There was no town cemetery during the Middle Ages: it needed a plague in the reign of Elizabeth I before the funerals ceased to journey to Carisbrooke (Fig. 25).

Similar dependence can be seen in some Gascon bastides. The church in Castelsagrat was a chapelry of the village church of St. Michel d'Ursaud, a mile to the south east; Montjoi had no church, since the church of St. Martin de Posicastels was already in existence 50 yards below the walls; Villefranche du Périgord was situated in the parishes of Ste. Marie de Viel Siorac and Loubejac.

It needed the intervention of a bishop to elevate a town chapel to a parish church and to redraw parish boundaries, and when the bishop of Saintes resisted the elevation of the chapel at La Rochelle the king of England had to intervene on the town's behalf with the Pope. At Battle, where the town was founded by the Norman king's favourite monastery, the bishop of Chichester took a conservative stand when the monks wanted the chapel that they had built for the burgesses to become a proper parish church. In the time of abbot Ralph (1107–25) the matter was aired before the chapter of Chichester and the independence of the town church was granted.

When bishops were asked to elevate town chapels to the rank of full parishes they did not always act quickly. Their interests pulled in two directions. As lords of towns they could appreciate the ambition of a townsman to have his own church but they also had to safeguard traditional rights, and if the new town threatened to compete with one of their own towns the argument for change might fall on deaf ears. On the occasion when the intervention of the Pope was necessary, the opposition of the bishop arose from his concern that the upstart town of La Rochelle might trouble the future of his own city of Saintes, despite its solid Roman foundations.[25]

When an archbishop of York in 1315 forbade burials at the town chapel of Bawtry (Yorks.) in favour of the mother church of Blyth (Notts.) it was not because he had interests in the market tolls at Blyth. The reasons were nakedly economic, as he stated them, but what he feared was a diminution in the income of the clergy at Blyth (Fig. 24).

> *Inhibicio ne fiat sepultura in capellis de Bautre Austerfeld aut aliis dependentibus ab ecclesia de Blida seu eorundem cimiteriis . . . ex quo iidem religiosi debitis oblacionibus et aliis juribus defraudantur.*[26]

Yet it was a bishop, as an eighteenth-century incumbent of Bladon (Oxon.) recalled, who had built a rectory house in New Woodstock

> in charity to the Borough of Woodstock; to draw the Rector of Blayden (*sic*) to reside at Woodstock, and induce him by such residence to perform full service in their chapel; to which he is not otherwise obliged. The parish of Blayden (where the Mother Church is) contains in it . . . the Borough of New Woodstock.[27]

The cautious intervention of bishops in favour of the church of a new town can be illustrated from three Cornish boroughs. Grampound was founded within the parish of Creed. There may have been a town chapel before 1370 but that is the first occasion when a licence to have services in the town is recorded. The bishop gave a licence for ten months only. A year's renewal was granted in 1371, and again in 1372, 1373, and 1374. In 1375 it was renewed only for Sundays and

[25] P. Marchegay, "Chartes de Fontrevaud", *Bibl. de l'École des Chartes*, 4th ser. iv (1858), pp. 132–170 and 321–27: the contemporary chronicler, Richard of Poitou, wrote of La Rochelle as *vicum mirabilem de novo constructo*. When Pope Eugenius over-ruled the bishop in 1153 he gave as his reason the large population living in La Rochelle: *hominum multitudinum quae inibi ad habitandum noviter venit* (R. Dion, *Histoire de la Vigne* (Paris, 1959), pp. 338–341).
[26] *Register of Archbishop Greenfield*, ed. W. Brown and A. Hamilton Thompson (Surtees Soc. clii (1938), pp. 180–181.
[27] *Oxon. Record Soc.* xxxviii (1957), p. 18.

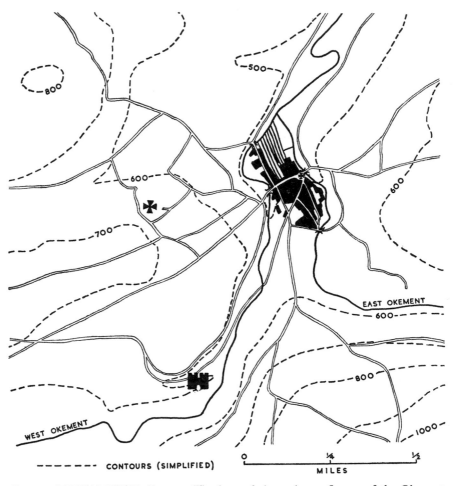

Fig. 40. OKEHAMPTON, Devon. The borough is at the confluence of the Okement rivers, with the parish church a half-mile away, above the town.

festivals. In 1745 the rector of Creed reported to his bishop that his only chance of a congregation for Wednesday and Friday prayers in Lent was to say them at Grampound, no one being willing to come across the fields to Creed. Yet the village church was the eventual victor, for the town chapel fell into disuse in the early nineteenth century (Fig. 18).

The situation at another small Cornish borough, Mitchell, was similar. In 1398 the inhabitants successfully petitioned the bishop for a renewal of a licence for their town chapel of St. Francis. Mitchell, they said, was partly in St. Enoder parish and partly in Newlyn, and at a great distance from the church of either. The main road through the town was much frequented by travellers who had nowhere else to worship. After annual renewals the chapel's licence was made perpetual in 1414, but (as at Grampound) the decay of the borough brought with it the decay of the town chapel and today the rights of St. Enoder and Newlyn over the few houses of Mitchell go unchallenged.

The townsmen of Penryn also strove for their own church: and with some hopes, for the founder of their town (1236) was a bishop of Exeter. Its site lay within the episcopal manor of Trelivel near the bishop's palace where he frequently came to stay. Town and palace were both in Budock parish. The bishop allowed the townsmen to build a chantry chapel of St. Mary in the middle of their High Street and in 1318 bishop William Briwere cut from Budock parish the new parish of Gluvias, made up of 2,000 rural acres and the borough. The church of this new parish was the old chapel of St. Gluvias which stood outside the town and across the river. The town continued to have its chantry chapel but in 1322 relations between the vicar of Gluvias and the burgesses had become so bad that the bishop had to refer the dispute to an arbitrator (Fig. 27).

The issue was an economic one. The town claimed that their chaplain was entitled to the offerings made in their chapel and that its fabric should be allowed to benefit from any legacies. The vicar of Gluvias found this too like a declaration of independence but the arbitrators gave the chaplain some (but not all) of the year's offerings and the burgesses were to administer some (but not all) of the legacies; as a token of dependence the burgesses were to pay the vicar one shilling a year from the chapel fund, and this offering was to be made publicly on St. Gluvias's day, at the high altar of the church.[28]

The foundation of New Montgomery within Chirbury parish in 1227 gave rise to a written agreement between the parson of the town and those interested in the advowson of Chirbury:

> touching the chantry of the newly built church at New Montgomery and the burial of the dead there, that is to say that the church shall

[28] The Cornish evidence is taken from Charles Henderson, "The 109 Ancient Parishes of the Four Western Hundreds of Cornwall", *J.R.I.C.*, n.s. ii (1956), pp. 121–127, 150–151 and 175–179.

13

always have its own parson whom the king shall present, and that it shall have the right of the font and of burial with the full rights of a mother church, but that every year the parson shall pay 30s. to the church at Chirbury . . . as compensation for what the church used to receive from the parishioners of (Old) Montgomery, with a penalty of half a mark for each half year that these payments come in default;[29]

we have already seen that the vicar of Icklesham was allowed £10 a year in consideration of tithes lost when the lands of Iham in Icklesham parish were taken for the site of New Winchelsea.

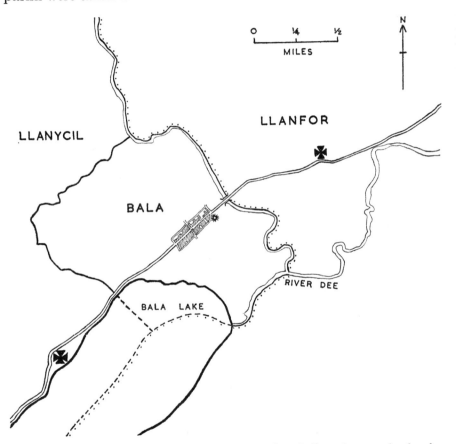

Fig. 41. BALA, Merionethshire. A church-less borough set half-way between the churches of Llanycil and Llanfor, its territory being cut out of the former parish. At the north-east edge of the borough is a motte.

29 *Cal. Chart. Rolls*, i, p. 101.

The resistance of the rural churches, their clergy, their bishops and their patrons was thus strong enough to deny churches to many planted towns, and to force others to accept chapels with dependent status. On rare occasions the new town found itself with a ready-made church, probably one that had been standing in an isolated position in an area of scattered settlement. This relation is sometimes indicated by the church chequer displaying distinct nonconformity to the general plan. At Vianne the church thrusts itself inconveniently across the main street near the gate. Part of New Salisbury lay within the parish of the older church of St. Martin, and although the bishop provided a new church in the market place, Fig. 31 shows that several chequers remained to be served by St. Martin. Edward I was able to take over the church of the Cistercian house of Aberconway, and to build Conway around it, having moved the monks to Maenan. The bishop of Salisbury was able to build his new cathedral in New Salisbury and to abandon the old, but Edward I's attempt to raise the church of the borough of Rhuddlan to the dignity of a cathedral was frustrated by the opposition of the bishop of St. Asaph.[30] It will be noticed also that the bishops of Winchester did not provide all their six new towns with independent parish churches.

The density of population in the great organic towns, together with civic and gild pride, led to an increase in the number of town parishes with a separate church. The planted towns sometimes show this pressure of population on church-room. In 1270 New Salisbury was given a third parish church; Hull had a second church, as we have seen, for the town that lay within the Aton fee; Winchelsea had two intra-mural churches, and a third just beyond the walls; Richmond (Yorks.) had a second church in the centre of the market place, since the original church was on the edge of the borough; Hedon had three churches; each half of New Malton had a church; Devizes had one for the castle garrison, and one for the townspeople (Fig. 22); when Lynn was extended northwards, the town acquired a second market place and a second church.

IV

The seigneur might feel that he ought to improve the access roads to his new town, especially if the novelty of the foundation meant that it was not well provided with established roads. This seems to have been

[30] J. G. Edwards, *Calendar of Ancient Correspondence concerning Wales* (1935), p. 264.

the case at Wyke on Hull where the town site, admirably placed for water-traffic at the junction of the Hull and Humber rivers, lay at a dead-end as far as land routes were concerned, being placed in the fields of a Cistercian grange on the marshy edge of Hessle parish, far from any village. After Edward I had acquired Wyke for development into the royal borough of Kingston, he used his authority to re-cast the local road system:

> no roads have yet been made to our new town by which merchants may bring their goods and merchandise or the men of the town lead away their goods; which is well known to turn to our loss and to the hurt of the town and to men dwelling there and to merchants wishing to come there.[31]

From the complaint of a local landowner it also appears that the landing-place of the Hull river-ferry was also changed in order to bring it more conveniently for the town.

The charter of Newborough (Staffs.) in 1263 described four new approach roads through Needwood Forest as *profitabiles ad burgum*, but no English plantation needed an approach road as long as that made through the marshes of the Rhône delta to Aigues Mortes. A short causeway had to be built on the landward side of Libourne after the foundation of the new town on the Dordogne bank, and one English plantation, Stockbridge, lay entirely on an artificial causeway, for the main street and the burgage houses are raised above the shallow streams into which the river Test is here divided. Each thread of the stream forms the boundary of a burgage plot, and each thread runs under the main street and market place. Emerging on the other side they perform a similar office for another row of burgage plots before being united again in the main flow of the river.

The diversion of roads to bring all passing traffic near to the siren song of the town's tradesmen has already been noted. These diversions sometimes necessitated the construction of a bridge: Bridgnorth would have been nothing without the bridge that brought traffic over the Severn on to the narrow ridge where the borough was built; Appleby would have been nothing without a bridge to bring traffic from the east bank of the river over to the market place that had been laid out under the shadow of the castle; at St. Ives (Hunts.) the old crossing of the river by a ford at Slepe was replaced by a new bridge bringing the London–Ramsey road straight into the town market place.

[31] *Y.I.*, iv, pp. 47–48.

If deflection of roads was important, how much more the improvement of river navigation and the construction of river-ports. Rhuddlan was given an artificial canal to connect it with the sea, and the very origin of Alresford Forum, as we have seen, followed closely on the canalisation of the river Itchen at the beginning of the thirteenth century and the construction of a great dam to regulate the flow of water. Below the dam the market place of the new town was laid out adjoining the canal wharves, and across the dam went the road from the village of Old Alresford to New Alresford (Fig. 11). In 1289 Edward I ordered his seneschal to accede to the petition from the bastide of Monségur, to build a port on the banks of the Dropt beneath the town cliffs and to clear away obstructions in the river. This was not altruism but an investment:

> *cum ipsi habeant multa bona venalia que vendere possent si portum haberent in flumine Droti, quod esset utilitas toti patrie et nobis.*[32]

The wharves on the Rother below the north cliff of New Winchelsea occupied a very similar position to the port of Monségur, and when Edward I enlarged the quay at Kingston on Hull he thought it no sacrifice to diminish some burgages and lose their rent in order to gain space for the extensions.

A very generous founder might provide a market hall, although in the more prosperous towns there were market-halls that also served as meeting places for the gild-merchant and were probably built at the gild's expense. As the recipient of the profits of justice, the seigneur had an interest in a building where courts could be held, and after Hedon became Edward I's, the accounts show him re-roofing the Hall of Pleas.[33] Prisons, toll-houses, bake-houses, and a public weighing-beam were other contributions that, like the heavy expenditure on town mills, show seigneurs looking (in the long run) to the revenues that would accrue from activity within such buildings. After the foundation of Lalinde Edward I permitted his seneschal to spend money on building mills and a fish-weir in the Dordogne, and subsequently a bridge. A bridge was provided for Ste. Foy la Grande and Villeneuve sur Lot on their foundation. Of minor public works we happen to have details of the expenditure on the town-well during the foundation of Hindon. Fourteen fathoms of digging cost 1s. 6d. a fathom; the

---

[32] *R.G.*, ii, 1618.
[33] SC11/743; E372/152B.

rope and iron-bound bucket cost 1s.[34]   The well at Baa has also left its
mark in the accounts; the king's clerk paid two men to seek springs,
to dig out a well, and then to carve a motif upon them.[35]

   To build a water-mill was another seigneurial investment, since the
lord had the same monopoly of milling within the town as on his rural
territory, unless the town charter specifically freed the burgesses, as
did that of Newborough (Staffs.) in 1263. Other charters (e.g.
Denbigh and Morpeth) prescribed the fraction of milled corn that the
townsmen should pay in multure; and while the charter of Barnard
Castle released the burgesses from the use of the lord's oven (another
monopoly of seigneurs), it insisted that they still ground their corn at his
mill: here there was a limit to the freedom of town air.

[34] Hants. Record Office, Pipe Roll no. 159277 m. xi.
[35] J.-P. Trabut-Cussac, "Date, Fondation et Identification de la Bastide de Baa", *Rev.
Hist. de Bordeaux*, pp. 142–143, citing E36/201, ff. 19 and 34.

CHAPTER SIX

Bonne Garde: or, The Security of a New Town

"Not Authority alone: for if the place, whereunto men are drawn through the Authority of any, afford them no commodityes, they will not abyde nor tarry there."

G. Botero, *Of the Greatness of Cities*
(trans. R. Peterson (1606), p. 11).

I

THE defensive works of a medieval town—walls, ditches and gates—fostered the pacific activities that formed the centre of town life. Townsmen placed a high value on good order, quite apart from their own personal safety. Without it, foreigners were discouraged from coming to trade; without it, debts remained uncollected and fraud remained unpunished; without it, craftsmen stood to lose their tools and their goods by theft. The same need for physical protection drew administration into the twelfth-century towns. Just as the moneyers had struck their coins in the shelter of the eleventh-century *burhs*,[1] so the judges came to the shire towns to hold the assizes. Few of the plantations in England could have hoped to reach the dignity of shire-towns but the same arguments were valid. The founder of a town had every incentive to make it a place of order and safety, a *sauveterre*.

English medieval town plantation begins and ends with defended towns: it begins with the *burhs* of the Anglo-Saxon kings and it ends with Edward III's Queenborough, a strongpoint and naval base for

[1] A gazetteer of mint-towns is given in J. J. North, *English Hammered Coinage*, i (1963), pp. 105–109, 136–139, 149–153 and 172–185, with maps. It will be noted that the coin of Aethelred II which would remove Bridgnorth from the list of planted towns if it were correctly placed, is possibly from Bristol (p. 173); coins from Cardiff, Devizes, Durham, Hedon, Lynn, Newcastle on Tyne, Pembroke, Rhuddlan, New Romney and Rye have dates which do not conflict with the foundation-dates suggested in our own Gazetteer. The coins from Launceston are, of course, from the pre-Norman settlement which was moved after the Conquest. (I am indebted to Mr. Michael Dolley for advice.)

the middle Thames estuary during the hostilities against the French. The physical endowments of the Saxon *burhs* have yet to be revealed by scientific excavation but the character of the new Norman towns is a little clearer. Eighteen of the first twenty-five plantations were located alongside a castle, and one of them took its name from the new castle on the Tyne.

At Launceston the power of the Norman landowner and the magnetic force of the castle were shown when an older market was moved more than half a mile to the new site. At Windsor the new castle-town spurned the meadowside site of Saxon Old Windsor, more than a mile away. At Trematon (and probably also at Skipsea, Richard's Castle, Belvoir and Oswestry) the small borough sheltered within the actual castle bailey: while at Pontefract, Richmond, Rye, Bridgnorth and Ludlow the civil area was more extended, needing its own circuit of defences to link it with the castle.

> What in 1068 was essentially a device of war, came to be a prominent feature of the new feudal administrative order which the Norman here established. Indeed, before the end of the eleventh century there had been erected in England at least 84 castles.[2]

At this stage, therefore, the function of a new castle-town was not different from that of an older town and its appearance resembled towns such as York and Northampton, that the Normans had strengthened by clearing away houses to make way for a castle in the new fashion. It was to such protective shelter in Lincoln, Norwich and Salisbury that William the Conqueror transferred the seats of bishops, and it was natural that county administration should become centred upon towns that could offer some guarantee of personal safety in a troubled world.

Yet the early twelfth century also shows some successful urban development without the shelter and encouragement of a castle and without a system of town defences. New Romney and Battle had shown the way, and now Boston, New Shoreham, St. Ives, St. Neots, Dunstable, Watford, Boroughbridge and New Thirsk followed.

Castle towns and defended towns did not cease to be founded in

---

[2] D. C. Douglas, *William the Conqueror* (1964), p. 217. The association of towns and castles had already begun in Normandy itself soon after 1025 (M. De Bouard, "Le Duché de Normandie", in F. Lot and R. Fawtier, eds., *Histoire des Institutions Françaises au Moyen Age*, i (Paris, 1957), p. 12; in Anjou there was a similar movement (F. M. Powicke, *The Loss of Normandy* (1961), p. 27).

England in the twelfth and thirteenth centuries, for there were still troubled frontiers on the north and west where the English were not strongly enough established to do without intimidating works. It was for the frontier town of Berwick, after all, that Edward I summoned his town-planning colloquium, and after the loss of Normandy the greater ports along the Channel coast were liable to become involved in hostilities: we have already seen that New Winchelsea, defended from the waves by migration to Edward's new site, wished also for walls to defend itself from the French. Its shattered parish church still bears witness to the violence of cross-channel raiders in the late fourteenth century. If the borders and the Marches needed fortified towns, then in Wales itself the English had always to look to their moats and walls. Almost every plantation in Wales, whether royal or seigneurial, lay in the shadow of a castle, and by integrating town- and castle-defences in his towns of north Wales Edward I was simply following and elaborating what the English had been doing ever since the first Norman penetration.

The evidence of walls and defences in the plantations of the borders and Wales is misread if these plantations are seen as no more than extended fortresses. No fortified town of any size could survive in peacetime without a flourishing local economy that went further than relations with the castle garrison. The charters of the Edwardian towns did not envisage them being peopled by soldiers, camp-followers and retired army contractors. Even during their construction Edward I took steps to encourage foreign and native merchants to risk coming beyond Chester, promising to refund any losses they incurred. Like the older castle-towns of south Wales, the Edwardian towns had market places at their centre, and were designed as part of a strategy that would woo the native Welsh by offering them a place for the sale of their surplus produce (see p. 82); and was not the walled frontier town of Berwick to be set out for the benefit of merchants?

One must avoid gaining the impression that walls could always guarantee safety. Berwick, where Edward I wheeled his token barrow of earth for the new defences of 1296, was given walls and a castle. Yet it was captured by Robert Bruce in 1318. The Scots had no difficulty in passing over the walls. The castle fell in five days, and it was fifteen years before the English re-occupied the town. Eleven years after its first works began, Carnarvon was captured by the Welsh. The capture of Bere stifled the development of the borough for ever.

In general, however, the walls and defences of planted towns are evidence of commercial life which was thought worth protecting, and which gained protection: the towns were not simply enlarged fortresses planted as part of some military design.

The cost of protection was always considerable. Professor J. G. Edwards and Mr. A. J. Taylor have translated the massive town defences of north Wales into the currency of man-hours, weight of stone, lengths of timber and pounds of lead: and it makes a very impressive total. Even with powers of conscription and commandeering, the Edwardian exchequer was strained nearly to breaking point. The seigneur who wished to put defences around his new town faced greater obstacles, economic and political, than did a king.

As military engineering, defensive and offensive, grew in complexity the cost of defence works rose. A simple earth castle was succeeded by a stone castle, and the stone castles then became elaborated. Earthen ramparts and wooden palisades were succeeded by town walls of stone, and plain walls of stone were then elaborated with corner towers and interval towers. Plain gates and posterns became elaborate gates and barbicans. The king, who had the greatest potential resources, was becoming committed to other expenditures, and found himself progressively dependent on Parliament for emergency revenues. Kings could not always live up to their promises made at the foundation of towns. M. Trabut-Cussac has collected many examples of Gascon bastides petitioning Edward II and Edward III to redeem the promises of the first Edward.[3] New Winchelsea obtained a grant of murage in 1296—seven years after the first plots had been taken up—and another was necessary in 1328. When the French raided the town in the late fourteenth century they found no stone wall to oppose them on the north side of the town, only an earth rampart on the cliff-top, and a crenellated wooden stockade.[4]

The seigneur who founded a town had less chance than the king of raising revenue from his feudal dependants, and less access to ready credit. Labour and materials had to be bought on the open market in competition with the king's powers to conscript and commandeer. It is not surprising that in England, where the risks of internal disorder were slighter than in Wales, the new towns founded after the end of the civil war in 1154 took on a more and more pacific air, and that the fully defended plantation lay only within the command and purse of kings.

[3] J.-P. Trabut-Cussac, "Bastides ou Forteresses?", *Le Moyen Age*, lx (1954), pp. 81–135.
[4] *Cal. Chart. Rolls*, iii, p. 147; *Cal. Close Rolls*, *1288–96*, p. 463; *Cal. Pat. Rolls*, *1413–6*, p. 368.

Plate 8. CARNARVON. The earth bank, wall, wall-walk and two towers at the south-east corner of the defences; built 1283–85 and rebuilt 1295. The stones are limestone, light brown sandstone and red sandstone blocks, perhaps from the Roman fort.

TABLE VI.I

PROPORTION OF ENGLISH NEW TOWNS WITH CASTLES, BY PERIODS

Date of foundation of town	Number of plantations	Plantations with castles	Proportion of castle towns
1000–1140	40	30	75%
1141–1200	40	13	33%
1201–1250	40	9	23%
1251–1368	52	2	4%
Total	172	54	31%

Since the same period saw a decrease in the proportion of towns founded by the king, the defended town played a smaller and smaller part in town plantation within England.   Table VI.1 shows the new towns divided into four chronological groups, three of nearly equal size. The earliest foundations appear closely tied to castles, three-quarters of the towns created before 1141 falling into this category.   The proportion then dropped, and by the end of the twelfth century the tie between castle and new town was much weakened, until after 1250 it hardly existed.   In Wales, on the other hand, the English continued to regard a castle and a town as natural associates, and four out of five towns in our Welsh Gazetteer had castles to defend them.   Even at the very end of the period the link was not broken (Plate 8).   In Gascony, it will be noted, only one town in ten was associated with a castle.

The typical defended town in Gascony, as Table VI.2 shows, was

TABLE VI.2

DEFENDED PLANTATIONS IN ENGLAND, WALES AND GASCONY

	Castle-towns			Without castle			
	with walls in stone or brick	other defences	castle only	walls in stone or brick	other defences	Total	As proportion of all plantations
ENGLAND	20	12	22	7	4	65	38%
WALES	25	6	40	1	0	72	86%
GASCONY	13	0	0	28	4	45	36%

protected by walls of stone or brick, but the final column indicates that the proportion of defended towns *in toto* was no greater in Gascony than in England. Wales is revealed as the member of the trio who is playing out of tune, and the Gascon individuality is expressed, not in its general belligerence, but in its indifference to castles and its greater trust in walls if a town did need defences. Table VI.2, it should be stressed, indicates the situation at the mid-fourteenth century, and M. Trabut-Cussac has shown that many bastides which were built without walls were becoming anxious for them in the early fourteenth century: the Table will therefore underestimate the pacific intentions of the original bastidors.

This view of Gascony, with two-thirds of its bastides never provided with defences, is bound to surprise many readers. Was not its political history full of frontier disputes and the revolts of turbulent landowners? and was not the war of St. Sardos an Anglo-French war that arose specifically out of a dispute over the foundation of a bastide? and are not the picturesque remains of the walled, hilltop towns the English visitor's characteristic impression of the modern Gascon landscape? Were not all the bastides designed as part of a plan of military strategy, their defences basic to their purpose, and an essential part of the endowments that the founder partners would have to provide? (Plate 9).

This argument is plausible enough to have persuaded a distinguished French historian and geographer that there was such a Grand Design,[5] and a distinguished archivist to liken them to the frontier works of France in the age of Vauban.[6] The reality—as Trabut-Cussac showed in a devastating critical article—was far different. Part of Trabut-Cussac's argument depends on his demonstration that the principal "fortress" foundations date from a period of accord in Anglo-French relations; and he sees nothing to support the statement that townsmen in most of the bastides were freed from military service so that they could guard the walls; and nothing to support the statement that the founders of the towns provided the townsmen with arms.[7]

His most important arguments, however, derive from the defences

---

[5] C. Higounet, "Bastides et Frontières", *Le Moyen Age*, liv (1948), pp. 113–121.

[6] O. de St. Blanquat, "Comment se sont créés les Bastides?", *Annales*, 1949, pp. 278–289.

[7] J.-P. Trabut-Cussac, *art. cit.* in fn. 3, above. It should be noted that Trabut-Cussac does not argue that *no* bastide was defended: he is challenging the assumption that all were designed as part of a scheme to set defended towns along a frontier. Higounet's article is, after all, titled *Bastides et Frontières*, not *Bastides et Forteresses*.

Plate 9. VILLENEUVE SUR LOT. The defences of the town as represented on a key-stone of St. Catherine's church.

themselves. He shows that many bastides were undefended until the wars of the fourteenth century forced Edward II and Edward III into reluctant expenditure on a provision that was no part of Edward I's thirteenth-century project. He shows that the earliest bastides, those of Alphonse de Poitiers, do not have ramparts mentioned in charters earlier than that of Monségur in 1265. Promises to provide a *prima clausura* are certainly found in charters, but these were for a gate or gates, and the date of building was left vague.

Gascony affords many instances of long delays before the king provided any defences.[8] Seventy years after its foundation Ste. Foy La Grande was petitioning the king for permission to erect town walls, its privileges lacking in this respect. The burgesses of Créon, founded in 1315, addressed a petition to Edward II:

> your said town, built by Amaury de Créon, is set between your enemies; and yet it is enclosed neither with walls nor ditches. It finds itself in great peril of being lost: may it please you to grant the tax on merchandise called *loude* so that the said town can be enclosed.[9]

Despite the *prima clausura* of its charter it was 40 years before anything was done for Monségur; despite its name, Bonnegarde was left exposed to attack and as late as 1340 was complaining to Edward III that even its castle lacked a complete circuit of walls. It was 53 years before Villeréal obtained its defences, 50 before Libourne, 40 before Castillonnès, 35 before Miramont and 25 before Villefranche de Queyran. Yet in these very years the kings of England showed no reluctance to spend money and to send constant orders from England concerning work on castles and other military sites in the duchy.[10]

Trabut-Cussac also demonstrates that when the inhabitants of bastides petitioned the king for defences, they were often seeking protection not against the king of France but against their immediate and unruly neighbours. Bonnegarde was burned in one of these local disputes; Vianne was attacked by men from its rival, Lavardac, an older town; Nicole was burned by the lord of Tonneins; Sauveterre was damaged by the lord of Benauges; Montréal du Gers was pillaged by the count of Armagnac.

[8] The cases cited below are from Trabut-Cussac, *art. cit.*
[9] SC8/263/13083.
[10] Table VI.2 has shown the proportion of English towns that were walled: much of the evidence for walling comes from murage grants later than the date of foundation. Edward I's Kingston on Hull, for example, had its first wall and ditch a quarter-century after the foundation, and it was another generation before the walls were completed. (*Cal. Pat. Rolls, 1321–4*, p. 7.)

This desire of the commercial and artisan classes for physical safety is clearly expressed in Gascon petitions and in the language of charters, and it also appears in one sense of the common town name, *sauveterre* or *salva terra*, that is, a safe place. (It was on just such grounds that the founder of New Eagle (Lincs.) hoped to justify the plantation of a town mid-way between Lincoln and Newark on the Foss Way: it would give travellers a place of refuge from robbers and felons who terrorised the main road.) At Pimbo in Gascony the abbot gave Edward I *carte blanche* to choose a site for a castle and then to lay out a bastide wherever he wished. The abbot explained that he was doing this to bring peace to a disordered district. In 1321 Edward II's seneschal was asked to search the archives at Bordeaux for a copy of the charter of Sarron since both town and charter had perished at the hand of the count of Armagnac.[11] A petition from Hastingues recalled the circumstances of its foundation: it was designed as a place where local commerce would be safe from bandits and from those who infiltrated from neighbouring, independent states to ravage the abbey's lands. In 1305 Arnaud Loup of Estibeaux petitioned Edward for a *paréage* to found Ozourt because the lord of Navailles was making so many outrages and terrorising the countryside.

The final argument against the bastides as part of a plan of frontier fortification is the evidence of their situation. Although the picturesque hill-top bastides of Gascony are much photographed, there are also bastides of the plain, the pure bastides of commerce. These were placed on river-banks, on level sites alongside main roads, and can occasionally be found in the most indefensible of sites, overshadowed by an adjacent hill. One such site is Villefranche de Rouergue where a hill just outside the walls affords a position from which to rain arrows into the market place: and the site of Villefranche, it will be noted, was most deliberately chosen, for the earlier settlement was on the opposite bank of the river.

Since it was the essence of a planted town that its site was deliberately chosen, an undefended and indefensible site implies that the founder was seeking something other than physical security. Rapid commercial development was most likely in towns that were easy of access, and the price paid for an accessible site might well be a poor defensive position. There were founders and townsmen willing to pay this price, as the low proportion of walled towns has already suggested. Half

11 C61/35, m. 13d.

these walled towns, in any event, lay in the Agenais. It has already been noticed in Table VI.2 that few Gascon towns had castles or were sited alongside castles. The exceptions may be briefly noticed: Domme is one such, almost a second Conway in the contortion that the rib of the hill imposed on the alinement of the chequers. Molières also had a castle, perhaps older than the town. Castelsagrat admits its castle in its name, as does Castelréal: the relation to the town at the latter site is

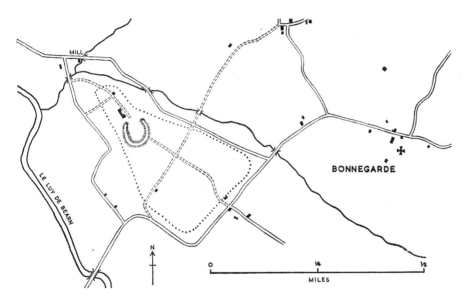

FIG. 42. BONNEGARDE, Landes. A deserted hill-top bastide of Edward I. Some earthworks of the castle remain on the kidney-shaped hill-top. Half a mile away a small village in the plain bears the same name. Crop-marks in air photographs show the pattern of roads meeting in the bastide, as indicated.

difficult to determine since the hill-top site has been totally abandoned. Bonnegarde is another fortified but deserted site, boasting of its defences in its name. The castle and town were laid out as one, and here Edward I spent the Christmas of 1288, but the empty hill-top indicates that the best defensive site could be inappropriate to the day-by-day livelihood of townsmen (Fig. 42).

The most successful of Edward I's towns in north Wales were those that did not sacrifice peacetime accessibility: Rhuddlan even sought it by an artificial canal. Diminished Harlech and the deserted hill-top at Denbigh demonstrate the same truth. Dolforwyn, high on the cliff above the Severn, might have seemed a perfect site to prince Llewelyn when fortifying his frontier, but it could not have competed with the riverside sites of Welshpool and Newtown, even if the English had not destroyed it (Plate 10).

Caus, one of those small border boroughs crowded into a bailey, is like a prehistoric monster crushed beneath the weight of its own armour. The ruins of the castle and outer fortifications have to be disentangled from the undergrowth and the roots of great oaks, and nothing is left at all of the burgages that once contributed their shilling a year to the lord of Caus. The craggy and deserted *bourgs* of Savoy and Switzerland point the same moral. The contrasting fates of two of Richard I's plantations in France indicate the same conclusion. Petit Andelys was founded, not on the hill alongside Château Gaillard, but in the meadows of the Seine below the castle. The town survives. St. Rémy was founded high on a river cliff alongside a castle: and it is deserted.

When commercial forces pulled the other way, an old defended site could be spurned by the founder of a new town.[12] Thus, Toulouzette was founded on the river bank, even though Nerbis stood on a nearby hill-top; Aire sur l'Adour replaced St. Quitterie. The migration from Old Sarum to New Salisbury is the most remarkable English example of the rejection of a defensive site. The traditional view, derived from writers sympathetic to the bishop, was that the proximity of castle and town at Old Salisbury had tested neighbourliness beyond endurance, but the disadvantage of a hill-top site in an age when river transport was dominant must also have weighed against the older site.

A contemporary poet, Henry d'Avranches, recited the troubles that the bishop's town had suffered up at Old Sarum by keeping company with the royal castle. It was, he says, like having the Ark of the Covenant in the Temple of Baal. This part of his complaint may be no more than a prejudice against the domination of the church by Caesar, but it was not all: the poem continues with a recital of the geographical and economic poverty of the hill-top site, *mons maledictus*. It was sodden with rain and dew; nothing would grow but wormwood; there was chalk in abundance but it dazzled the eyes and provoked thirst

---

[12] The villagers from the fortified site of Gardenat, or Gardemont, came down to the valley to occupy the bastide of Réalmont by agreement with the king of France in 1310–11 (*Lavedan*, p. 341).

Plate 10. DOLFORWYN.   The site of the abortive castle and town.

that the town wells could not satisfy; the hill was too steep for access. The accessible riverside site of New Sarum, on the other hand, was praised as most suited for a city: *mons maledictus* had become a garden of Eden.[13]

The new Salisbury defended itself by an outer ditch and bank on the east side, as any great town would feel necessary in the early thirteenth century, but the long perimeter and the absence of a great castle were in contrast to the compact site that the townsmen and bishop had abandoned at Old Sarum.

Two final examples may be given of planted boroughs that had the chance of a site beneath a castle but rejected it for an undefended site on a main road on the opposite side of the river from the castle. At New Thirsk the parish church and the Norman castle are on the west bank: the market borough is set on the high road that keeps to the east bank. At Downton the castle and residence of the bishops of Winchester lay on the east bank of the Avon, on the edge of the village. The borough of Downton was created on the west bank. In so far as these new sites lay in ambush for anyone, it was for traders, not soldiers.

II

Even in the older organic towns of England the lengths of medieval town wall surviving today are not numerous, and the losses in the planted towns have been no less. The walls of Kingston on Hull were removed between 1767 and 1784 to make way for a new dock; the walls of New Malton and a broken corner-tower have to be sought in the tangled thickets of a disused graveyard; one of the town gates of New Winchelsea has growing barley brushing its feet; and the walls of New Radnor were tumbling and grassgrown even when John Speed drew them in 1611.

Of course, town walls were always subject to refurbishment during the centuries when they had a defensive and not a decorative purpose, and it is singularly difficult to point with confidence to any plantation in England where the town defences are substantially as they were first designed. (Walls, it must be remembered, were often preceded by defences in earth and timber.) There has been neglect of some town walls

---

[13] The text of the poem with a translation will be found in W. J. Torrence, "A Contemporary Poem on the Removal of Salisbury Cathedral". *Wilts. Arch. Mag.* lvii (1959), pp. 242–246.

by their modern owners, but local pride has its own dangers. Over-enthusiastic restoration can easily confuse fact and fiction.

For substantial survivals one must therefore go out of England. Conway and Carnarvon are the pearls, and those who cannot visit them may now proceed by proxy through the lavishly illustrated reports of the Royal Commission. Yet there is no substitute for the walk along the ramparts of Conway and along the quayside at Carnarvon between the walls and the sea.

In Gascony, as one might expect, the Middle Ages linger longer, although some Gascon walls were tumbled into their moats by order of the restored Bourbons. Those who know Monpazier only through the plan, so often reproduced, will be surprised if they visit the town: its outer ring of houses stands naked to the wind, and the filled-in moats are transformed into an outer boulevard. Yet there are enough small, hill-top bastides where the gates and walls survive. A visit to Puymirol, Domme or Beaumont du Périgord can be confidently recommended. One can stand below the walls, sometimes of local stone, sometimes of red Toulousian brick, and, looking upward, feel the emotions that they were originally intended to provoke: pride from those within, and awe from those without. It is to other aspects of the contrast between Insiders and Outsiders that we must now turn.

CHAPTER SEVEN

Ville Franche: or, The Liberties of a New Town

"What is it that makes a borough to be a borough? it is a legal problem."

> F. W. Maitland, *Domesday Book and Beyond* (1897), p. 173.

"He who seeks to define a borough enters Ariadne's web."

> James Tait, *The Medieval English Borough* (1936).

I

A SITE, we have shown, was a founder's inescapable contribution to the endowments of a new town: public buildings, road- and river-improvements and town-defences were more optional provisions. These endowments facilitated forms of economic life that a village was not likely to engender. Yet the distinction between old villages and new towns, the superiority of the town for particular economic pursuits, went further than a difference in siting and a difference in physical assets. The attraction of a town as a home for craftsmen and traders rested on another difference between village and town, a distinction summed up in the well-known medieval saying that "town air makes free". The degree of freedom permitted in new towns was as varied as their physical endowments, but the basic minimum was the establishment of tenures that were attractive to an immigrant by being distinct from those of a manor.

To modern eyes the manor was an oppressive institution lacking many personal freedoms that are accepted as normal today, and it is true that medieval towns had an attraction for fugitive villeins. Where the convention was accepted that unchallenged residence for a year and a day conferred freedom on a town-dweller, the town's role as a place of refuge from oppression would not be forgotten. But the founders of towns were themselves lords of manors, not notorious for liberal

191

sympathies, and they would not have conceded liberties unless there were solid advantages for themselves. The financial gains to seigneurs from towns have already been discussed (pp. 55–97), but these gains arose only because traders and craftsmen had been attracted to the new towns, and from their prosperity the lords had prospered.

Useful as refugee villeins might be in providing an unskilled labour-force in a new town, its success depended essentially on a very different sort of immigrant: the man already possessing some knowledge of a craft or trade. If the project was to succeed, the number of such immigrants would have to be substantial and their recruitment rapid. A numerous influx in the first months was not only a good advertisement to induce waverers, it provided the essentials of urbanism: sufficient specialists to be able to meet each other's needs; sufficient numbers to engender purchasing power that would attract sellers to their markets; and sufficient products to turn aside buyers from their accustomed routes to venture in new market places. Hence the insistence of many towns that burgage plots must be taken up within stated periods or else fall forfeit.

To recruit new townsmen with experience of crafts and trades it was necessary to draw on existing skills, and to lure men from other places where they were already practising them. Who could such men be? where were they to be found? and what liberties, privileges and franchises did the founders of new towns offer them?

It is easier to answer the third of these questions than the other two. As later sections of this chapter will show, there is a body of evidence preserved in charters extended by founders to new towns. Yet these charters did not name the burgesses; for at the time of their issue it was uncertain who would come and build in the new town; or, indeed, whether anyone would come. A borough charter like that of Higham Ferrers, giving the names of the first burgesses, is quite exceptional, and it was possible at Higham Ferrers simply because its lord was not creating a new community but enfranchising an existing village, a classic case of an organic town.[1]

There was no legal reason why the names, occupations and birth-places of individual townsmen had to be recorded. Charters refer simply to "the burgesses" and to "those who shall come and take up burgages", and personal information available about recruits is scanty. Occasionally, as at New Lymington and New Winchelsea,

[1] *Cal. Chart. Rolls*, i, pp. 372–373.

there are lists of names in surviving rentals and surveys from the early years of the new town. Wealthier townsmen's names and occupations may appear in tax-assessments or in the records of litigation, but these are infrequent before the mid-thirteenth century. The element of chance in the recording of such information is illustrated by the thirteenth-century account-rolls from the estates of the bishops of Winchester. The *incrementa* of new burgage rents and market tolls were duly noted for six of the manors in Hampshire and Wiltshire when towns were planted: but in only two cases, Newtown, I.O.W., and Newtown in Burghclere, does the record name the first burgage-holders. For Newtown, I.O.W., 57 names were recorded (holding 73 plots) and for the other Newtown a bold heading *NOVUS BURGUS* in the manuscript is followed by the names of 52 holders of the 67 *placeae*. Yet for the other four plantations the record gives simply the number of burgages arrented or the number of shillings making up the borough rents.[2]

Although place-names occur as surnames in these rentals, an analysis of such names is not particularly useful except as illustrating the obvious fact that recruits came from near and far. Any significant statement about the proportions coming from different distances would need to rest on a much greater sample of evidence and upon certainty of the meaning to put on a place-name in a surname. One can be sure, for example, that "Eugenia and Richard de Stretley" who took up burgages in Newtown, I.O.W. had been living at Stretley in Calbourne, and that Stretley was near the town site, since the reeve was exonerated in the manorial accounts of the foundation year from the rents due from lands in Stretley, *tractae in burgum*. One can be sure that the "parson of Calbourne" was the parson of the parish in which the town had been planted, for there is no other place of that name in England: but what are we to say of "Andrew of the Monastery", and "Alexander of Weston" in the first rental of New Winchelsea. Nor can one be certain that a well-known place-name as a surname implies that the man had just migrated to the new town; it may refer to his birthplace, or it may even have been an inherited surname.

The case of William de Rowley, a burgess of Kingston on Hull, is a warning of possible misinterpretation of surname evidence. His

---

[2] Newtown, I.O.W.: Hants. Rec. Office, Pipe Roll 159292 m. 9; Newtown, Burghclere: 159275 m. 5d; Hindon: 159277 m. 11; New Alresford: 159270B m. 11; Downton: 159272 m. 7; Overton: 159275 m. 3d.

name suggests that he had migrated from an East Riding village a dozen miles away, but when he died without an heir the jury found that he came from Harwich "near London by ten leagues".[3]

The following place-names occur among the surnames of the first rental of New Winchelsea,[4] but since many inhabitants had come up from Old Winchelsea we cannot tell when these men (or their ancestors) left the place that formed part of their name.

Within 10 miles	*11–20 miles*	*21–50 miles*	*Over 50 miles*
Hastings (2)	Pevensey (3)	Canterbury (4)	Colchester
Brede	Folkestone (2)	Scotney (2)	Dartmouth
Broomhill	Biddenden	Dover	Harwich
Iham	Romney	Ewhurst	Lewknor
Rye		Gillingham	Lydham
		Mayfield	Portsmouth
		Sandhurst (Kent)	Rackley (Som.)
		Sandwich	Winchester

Doubtful

Weston
Pulham
Farleigh

The New Winchelsea rental also contains a few indications of occupations. Nicholas Pistor, *forester*, is an entry that suggests that occupational surnames had become hereditary, so that other surnames such as Cissor and Faber cannot necessarily be taken as giving the occupations. The occupations given are:

forester	carpenter
clerk	parson
fisherman	shoemaker (2)
butcher (3)	baker (5)
tanner (3, all in one Chequer)	shipwright

but there can be no statistical significance in this small sample.

A more complete occupational list exists for early settlers in Battle:[5] but the information is given for only 28 out of 115 tenants.

---

[3] *Y.I.*, iii, p. 3, but see the distribution of Stratford upon Avon surnames set out by Prof. Carus-Wilson (*Econ. Hist. Rev.*, 2nd. ser. xviii, (1965) p. 53.
[4] SC11/660.
[5] M. A. Lower, *The Chronicle of Battel Abbey* (1851), pp. 15–20; It has been observed (J. Tait, *The Medieval English Borough* (1936), p. 105) that three-quarters of these names were English. See also H. W. C. Davis, "The Chronicle of Battle Abbey", *E.H.R.* xxix (1914), pp. 426–434; J. S. Brewer, ed., *Chronicon Monasterii de Bello* (Anglia Christiana Soc., 1846), pp. 12–17.

Plate 11. FRANCHEVILLE (Newtown) ISLE OF WIGHT. "The seal of the community of Francheville of the Isle of Wight", a leopard on a ship, as it appears on one of the few buildings in the present village (see also Fig. 53).

smith (2)	shoemaker (3)
weaver	cook (3)
scourer	miller
herdsman	goldsmith
swineherd (2)	cowherd
steward	bellmaker
carpenter (2)	baker (3)
clerk	priest
secretary (2)	gardener

These lists, therefore, do no more than indicate a minimal range of skills. They can be usefully compared with the occupations of those who had come to live in the new houses of Bury St. Edmunds between 1065 and 1086:

seventy-five bakers, alebrewers, tailors, washerwomen, shoemakers, robemakers, cooks, porters and stewards,[6]

and with the crafts represented at Baldock in 1185:[7]

blacksmith, ironmonger, tailor, shoemaker, tanner, mason, cook, carpenter, mercer, weaver, saddler, goldsmith, merchant, and vintner.

Could these trades have been followed by immigrants from villages? or do they suggest that the skilled occupations of new towns had to rely on immigration from existing towns? The range indicated in this limited sample suggests that both sources could have been drawn upon. The arts of the bell-maker, the goldsmith, and the secretary were not to be learned and profitably practised in the ordinary village nor easily acquired as a part-time skill by an intelligent and observant villein. Some new towns were intended to be more specialised: the tradition at Alnmouth was that it had been

taken forth of the demesnes of Lesbury for such as would traffique by the sea,[8]

and the foundation of Bere Alston was to exploit the local veins of silver.[9]

In coastal villages the art of the fisherman and the shipwright would not be uncommon, but without knowing the size of the ships and the

[6] H. C. Darby, *The Domesday Geography of Eastern England* (1952), p. 198, trans. from the Little Domesday, fo. 372.
[7] B. A. Lees, ed., *Records of the Templars . . . in England* (1935), p. 66.
[8] *N.C.H.*, ii, p. 476.
[9] W. G. Hoskins, *Devon* (1954), p. 332.

size of the catch at New Winchelsea it is impossible to say whether fishermen and shipwrights from coastal villages could have made a living in New Winchelsea. The forester of New Winchelsea and the herdsmen of Battle—at the other extreme—could easily have been migrants from the villages of the Weald and the Downs. A middle range of occupations—shoemaker, baker, miller, weaver, carpenter, gardener, butcher, alebrewer, cook, tailor, and smith—could all have been followed in a village, as full-time or part-time specialists within the manorial system, just as the skills of porter and washerwoman in Norman Bury St. Edmunds would have been within the capacity of many migrants from East Anglian villages.

Since so few had access to education, one must suppose that there was much frustrated talent in the villages, and that occupations where acumen, rather than experience, counted could be successfully taken up by immigrants from the villages. An intermediate class, such as village bakers, carpenters and shoemakers, would possess the basic skills, and then be able to augment them rapidly to meet the needs of town customers. It must be remembered that many of the new towns were not large and would not aim at the sophisticated markets.

Other occupations, among them the more sophisticated, could be carried on only by men with skill and experience that derived from previous training, and the most likely place to acquire this training was in an older town. An eye-witness of the foundation of St. Rémy by Richard I recalled many years later how "many rich burgesses came to dwell in the new town".[10] If the recruits were already rich, then they were certainly not fugitive villeins and refugees from over the border. Something of organised recruiting is hinted in the account of the foundation of Battle in the abbey chronicle:

> a goodly number of men were brought thither out of neighbouring counties, and some even from foreign countries.[11]

One-quarter of the names in the first rental of the town are not English. Since there were Norman immigrants in old-established English towns after the Conquest, it would not be surprising to find them also in the plantations, especially those endowed with the privileges of Norman Breteuil. It is possible that Boston was first settled by Bretons.

Long-distance migration certainly occurred: a few English settlers are

[10] *Archives Historiques de Poitou*, viii (1879), p. 44.
[11] M. A. Lower, *op. cit.* in fn. 5 above, p. 15.

recorded in Gascon bastides; and rather more Gascons in Welsh towns. Naturally, a good number of immigrants to the new Welsh towns were from England, although south Wales had Flemish immigrants both in town and countryside. The larger and more commercial plantations, such as Lynn and Boston, were able to attract Jewish settlers, and the charter clauses that banned Jews from entry to towns in north Wales and Gascony are found only on the eve of the change in royal policy that brought about their expulsion from England in 1290.[12]

A tax list of 1292 shows at least nineteen taxpayers in Overton borough who had Welsh patronymics. Rhuddlan, on the other hand, had only one, Flint five, and New Mostyn none. Welshmen living in the displaced Rhuddlan may all have been removed, as the Welsh of Llanvaes were moved to Newborough to make way for Beaumaris. But apartheid was not universal in Edwardian north Wales: there were thirty-nine taxpayers in Caerwys borough who had Welsh patronymics.[13]

A likely source of recruits to new towns—although there is no direct evidence—would be from among the younger sons of burgesses in the older towns. From at least the mid-twelfth century, and possibly earlier, general demographic conditions were favourable to migration from older centres, and it was possible for new towns to develop without destroying older towns by the loss of skilled and semi-skilled townsmen. A period of population expansion was necessarily a period of migration for the many younger sons for whom there was insufficient employment or insufficient prospects near home. Migration from old towns to new was analogous to the contemporary migration of younger sons from the crowded villages of the English plains to reclaim the fens, settle the marginal lands and make the final attack on the remaining forests.

The town atmosphere in which such men had passed their boyhood and youth was itself an education in the basic skills that would earn a

---

[12] Nine borough charters in North Wales in 1284 excluded all Jewish settlers from the new towns, but those for Melcombe Regis (1280) and Newton, Dorset (1286) were more discretionary. A number of charters, such as that for Bridgetown Pomeroy in 1268, forbade burgesses to alienate their burgages to Jews, but there was no racial or religious discrimination intended, for alienation to monasteries was also forbidden (*Ballard and Tait*, pp. 49, 142 and 302). The expulsion of the Jews from England in 1290 was anticipated by the expulsion from Gascony in 1289 (*R.G.* ii, 1473).

[13] I draw upon an unpublished analysis of the tax-roll, E179/242/52, by Mr. G. R. J. Jones. There are details of settlers in the new towns of North Wales in A. Jones, *Flintshire Minsters' Accounts, 1301–28*, (Publns. Flints. Hist. Soc. iii (1913), pp. xxvi–xl. D. L. Evans (*Flintshire Hist. Soc. Record Series*, ii, (1929), p. xliv) says of the Hope charter of 1351: "this is the first borough charter in North Wales which specifically excludes Welshmen".

living in a new town. They had assisted in the workshop and at the counter, fetched and carried loads from the wharves and market place and thereby learned to recognise a good bargain and develop useful personal contacts. To attract useful men of this sort from older towns, bringing their skills with them, the founder of a new town would need to make bids higher than those sufficient for fugitive villeins and unskilled labourers: a legal status would be required that was at least as privileged as in the town that the recruits were leaving. It is to these endowments that we now turn.

II

The clauses from charters to be cited in the following pages will illustrate the connection between the needs of immigrants and the privileges granted by founders of new towns. It is important to realise that there were no privileges uniquely characteristic of plantations. Every privilege found in the charter of a plantation can be found in the charter of some other town that was not planted. This fact emphasises the similar economic base on which both organic and planted towns rested, and the importance of imitation when the founder of a new town was considering the endowments he would bestow. Many founders, of course, were already lords of well-established towns, and were well aware of the minimal endowments to ensure a prosperous town-life. Since others were simultaneously attempting to found towns, planted or organic, this would-be founder could not afford to be too mean in his endowments or his skilled townsmen might melt away. This threat was used to the king himself by the men of Hedon, which had come into Edward I's hands by 1280:

> they say on oath that they are straitened and impoverished . . . and if the king does not grant the privilege asked (that the town be demised to them in fee-farm) it may in a short while deteriorate in value: because many would wish to move away, and there are two good towns, Ravenserod and Hull, with good harbours, that are nearby and growing from day to day where they could go and dwell without being subject to such high taxes.[14]

Just as in their ambition some towns took on the names of existing towns—Baghdad, Cologne, Florence and Pavia—so also did flattery and ambition combine to take over the liberties of some successful

14 *Y.I.*, i, p. 216.

existing town for a model. The charter of John, bishop of Norwich, given to Lynn in 1204, reveals that the king himself had permitted the town to choose its own model:

> the lord king granted that we should choose a borough in England, whichever we willed; and then that our town of Lynn should have the same liberties as that town has: and we have chosen Oxford.[15]

Oxford and Winchester had been jointly taken as the models for the liberties of Portsmouth[16] when Richard I founded it in 1194, and at the foundation of Liverpool in 1207 his brother gave the new port the widest endowment that any newly christened town could desire:

> those who take burgages at Liverpool shall have all the liberties which any maritime borough in all our land has.[17]

The oldest and most famous of the chain of imitative endowments is that which began with the privileges of the Norman town of Breteuil[18] (itself in all probability a plantation).[19] These privileges of Breteuil are found in many organic towns of England after the Norman Conquest but they were also given to planted boroughs, particularly in south Wales and along the border. The intermediary was the city of Hereford to which William fitz Osbern first brought the liberties of Breteuil: Hereford's customs were then taken as the model for Cardiff, New Carmarthen, Haverford West, New Montgomery, Brecon, Denbigh, Rhuddlan, Llanfyllin, Welshpool and Dryslwyn. Cardiff in turn begat the privileges of Kenfig, Aberavon, Llantrissant and Neath; Carmarthen begat those of Laugharne and Cardigan; Montgomery begat Deganwy and Aberystwyth; Denbigh begat Ruthin; and Rhuddlan begat Flint, Overton, Hope and Caerwys. At their foundation, Carnarvon, Conway, Criccieth, Bere, Harlech and Beaumaris were privileged with direct reference to the liberties of Hereford, while Bala, Newborough, Nevin and Pwllheli enjoyed them indirectly.[20]

[15] *Ballard*, p. 32.
[16] *Ibid.*, p. 29.
[17] *Ibid.*, p. 33.
[18] M. Bateson, *E.H.R.*, xv (1900), pp. 73–78, 302–318, 496–523, 754–757; xvi (1901), pp. 92–110, 332–345.
[19] William, Duke of Normandy, built Breteuil castle c. 1060 and placed it in the hands of his seneschal and cousin, William fitz Osbern, who was later to become Earl of Hereford. Fitz Osbern was lord of Cormeilles, an urban plantation of the early eleventh century, and he now had the idea of creating a privileged town at the foot of the castle of Breteuil (R. Génestal, *La Tenure en Bourgage* (Paris, 1900), pp. 234–235 and 237).
[20] E. A. Lewis, *The Medieval Boroughs of Snowdonia* (1912), pp. 17 and 40.

A smaller chain is that in northern England connecting Leeds, Pontefract and Grimsby.[21] Leeds in 1207 obtained the liberties of Pontefract, and in 1194 these had been modelled on those of the organic borough of Grimsby. There are other small chains of affiliations: Wearmouth obtained the liberties of Newcastle on Tyne, as did Hartlepool; Winchester, which we have already seen as Richard I's model for the foundation of Portsmouth, was also the model for Petersfield, as York was for Appleby, Richmond for Barnard Castle, and Shrewsbury for Oswestry. Even when the liberties of an existing town were not taken over wholesale for a new town, there could be a partial imitation: the charter of Hedon, for example, prescribed that its burgage tenure should be akin to that of the king's burgesses in York and Lincoln.[22]

Imitative charters and parallel clauses could be expected when different towns had the same founder: thus, Edward I's charters to Flint, Conway, Carnarvon, Bere and Harlech have only small verbal differences, and four of these were issued on the same date.

The Gascon plantations show the same feature: the charter founding the bastide of Hastingues was granted when the king was at Bonnegarde (itself a bastide) and Hastingues obtained the privileges of Bonnegarde. The bastides of the Agenais were closely linked; the Alphonsian privileges of Montclar and Montflanquin can be seen in those of Valence d'Agen, Villeréal, Lalinde, Molières and Monpazier.

The three entries on the Gascon Rolls following the long recital of the thirty-two clauses of the liberties of St. Osbert in 1276 are very short: but they show the first links in a chain actually being welded:[23]

> the burgesses of the bastides of Castelnau in the diocese of Bazas have similar letters.
> The burgesses of the fortified place called Miramont in the diocese of Aire have similar letters.
> The burgesses of the bastide of Castetcrabe in Marsan on the Ladou river in the diocese of Aire have similar letters.

The same liberties were later taken for the bastide of Arthus.

Where a charter endowed one town with the liberties of another, it could afford to be very curt in its remaining clauses, since reference

[21] J. Le Patourel, *The Manor and Borough of Leeds, 1066–1400* (Thoresby Soc. Publns. xlv (1957)), pp. xxvii–xxviii.
[22] *Ballard*, pp. 23–34.
[23] *R.G.*, ii, 55–58: the text occupies 2½ membranes of the original roll; the editor wrongly allocated no. 58 to La Bastide d'Armagnac.

could always be made to the model charter, and in cases of disputed interpretation an appeal could be made to the authorities in the model town. The earliest surviving charter of a plantation, that of Dunstable, has only three basic clauses, the first being the most important:

> the men of Dunstable and their heirs shall have the liberties and quittances throughout his whole kingdom that the city of London or any borough of England has had from of old.[24]

The disappearance of documents makes it impossible to proceed to a complete analysis of the charters of plantations: Table VII.1 shows that more than half the planted towns in England have no surviving

TABLE VII.1

PLANTED TOWNS WITH EXTANT CHARTERS:
ENGLAND AND WALES

	1042–1215	*1216–1307*	*After 1307*	*Total*	*As % of all known plantations*
ENGLAND	34	34	3	71	41
WALES	7	20	17	44	52
Total	41	54	20	115	

charter and that Wales is scarcely more fortunate. The earlier the foundation, the greater chance of loss. Only at the very end of the twelfth century did the English Chancery begin to enrol charters, and thereafter a seigneur who issued a borough charter found it increasingly convenient to have it confirmed by the king and enrolled at the Chancery; some additional charters are known from the Patent Roll. Only in Gascony did the plantations come late enough for their charter to have a good chance of survival.

The early date of many English and Welsh foundations further circumscribes the evidence for urban privileges, in that many towns with surviving charters do not have charters from the actual period of plantation. Dunstable, with a charter issued c. 1119, seems to be the earliest plantation where the surviving charter is contemporary with the establishment of the town, although if the first charter of Newcastle on Tyne could be more closely dated than 1100–39 it might supplant Dunstable's. By 1119 there were at least thirty-nine plantations in

[24] *Ballard*, p. 23.

England, and eighteen of these have surviving charters, but always with a gap between the dates of foundation and the charter. Thus New Romney (founded before 960) has no charter earlier than 1154–89; Durham (founded 995–1006) none earlier than 1153–81; Hastings (founded c. 1069), none earlier than 1154–58. Five other boroughs that were founded by 1086 have charters as follows:

Hythe	1156
Pontefract	1194
Rye	1140–89
Launceston	1225–56
Okehampton	1194–1242

New Windsor, founded by William I, has no charter surviving earlier than the reign of Edward I. Gaps of two centuries are exceptional, but the five Domesday boroughs mentioned above have gaps ranging from at least 60 years to 170 years.

In Wales the position is worse, for Table VII.2 shows that New Montgomery, founded in 1223, is the earliest of the plantations to have an original surviving charter. Only Gascony has a large crop of charters contemporary with years when the bastides were planted. Even after the loss of Gascony, the English Chancery preserved the rolls on which the administrative orders from the king-duke were entered. Ironically, therefore, the municipal privileges of a lost territory are better documented than those of the United Kingdom.

Sufficient borough charters have survived, however, to make it clear that the range of liberties with which a borough might be endowed was wide, and a particular foundation often received only a few within the range. The classification used by Ballard, Tait and Weinbaum runs to 176 sub-divisions within thirteen main subject-sections.[25] The planted towns of England and Wales, as Table VII.3 shows, had endowments drawn from 116 of these sub-divisions, but only 24 of these endowments occur in more than 10% of the 115 boroughs whose charters are analysed, and 65 of the endowments are not found in more than three boroughs among the 115. It is not unreasonable, therefore, to concentrate attention on the endowments which were widely represented among the charters of plantations: even so, the great variety of form that the endowments take will be seen from the fact that no single privilege occurs in more than 45 (39%) of the boroughs.

[25] The subject-matter of the code used by *Ballard* is there set out on pp. vii–xi. In *Ballard and Tait* it occupies pp. ix–xiv.

TABLE VII.2

ENGLISH AND WELSH PLANTATIONS: CHARTERS
CONTEMPORARY WITH FOUNDATION

(a) Analysed in *Ballard*

Devizes	1135–39
Dunstable	c. 1119
Morpeth	1119–1239
Newport, I.O.W.	1177–84
Petersfield	1182–83
Portsmouth	1194
Radclive	1179–89
Yarmouth, I.O.W.	c. 1170

(b) Analysed in *Ballard and Tait*

† Aberystwyth	1277
† Beaumaris	1295
† Bere	1284
† Caerwys	1290
Camelford	by 1260
† Carnarvon	1283
† Conway	1283
† Criccieth	1284
† Deganwy	1248
† Flint	1277
Francheville	1255–56
† Harlech	1283
Newton Arlosh	1305
Knutsford, Nether	c. 1292
† Llanfyllin	?1293
† Montgomery, New	1223
† Newborough, Anglesey	1303
Newton, Dorset	1286
† Overton, Flints.	1292
Penryn	1236
† Rhuddlan III	1278
New Salisbury	1219
Sherborne Newland	1227–28
Skinburgh	1301
Warenmouth	1247
Wavermouth	1300
† Welshpool	1247–52
Weymouth	1244
Winchelsea, New	1288

(c) Analysed in *Weinbaum*

Queenborough	1368

† Welsh

The twenty-four most frequent endowments are treated in the next section of this chapter. A mere list could not explain how these endowments fitted the needs and ambitions of the first immigrants, so that both a statement of liberties and an explanation of their significance are necessary. The logical order for this purpose is not the same as that of Ballard's schedule but cross-references to it are given in brackets: a synoptic view of the Ballard schedule is given in Table VII.3. The italicised endowments are those most frequently found.

The liberties of the Gascon bastides are stated on the Gascon Rolls sometimes more fully and sometimes more curtly than in the normal English borough charter. Some entries record only that the king-duke has authorised his officers to inquire whether a bastide would be profitable, and if so, to create one. Thus Edward I's order from Westminster in June 1281 was sent to two officials who were to go personally to Lados and to set out a bastide there, if they could find a suitable place either on the king-duke's land or on land held from him; they were to proclaim the foundation and to concede to its first inhabitants whatever liberties and customs seemed fit and to make whatever regulations seemed fit to be made.[26]

The liberties granted by the king-duke in person, by his seneschals or by special officials are sometimes set out specifically in the Rolls: sometimes, as with the case of Nicole (June 1291), the town was simply given

> the liberties and free customs which we have given to the inhabitants of our other bastides in the Agenais [27]

in the same way that affiliation to named models is found in charters of English and Welsh plantations.

The Gascon charters of liberties have been better catalogued than those of England and Wales,[28] but there has been no analysis of their contents similar to that in the work of Ballard, Tait and Weinbaum. There is a brief discussion of the subject-matter of Gascon charters later in this chapter (p. 219) but, in general, they are very reminiscent of the liberties encountered in the pages of Ballard and Tait. It is only occasional references to vineyards, to the measures of Bordeaux

---

[26] *R.G.*, ii, 472.   [27] *R.G.*, iii, 1935 and 2087.
[28] *Gouron* is a catalogue compiled in 1935 for an area which excludes Périgord and Quercy; references are given to the volumes of *R.G.* that were then published, where the full texts of a number of charters appear; a fourth volume of *R.G.* was published in 1962. Other charters have been printed in local Historical Society publications. See also fn. 44, p. 219 below.

TABLE VII.3

ANALYSIS OF CONTENTS OF 115 CHARTERS OF PLANTATIONS

Number of charters containing each type of clause

Number of Subdivision in Ballard Schedule	1	2	3	4	5	6	7	8	9	10	11	12	13	14	15	16	17	18	19	20	21
SECTION I	—	1	*30*	5	—	3	8	*45*	1	—	—	—	—	—	—	—	—	—	—	—	—
SECTION IIA	*16*	*14*	2	3	2	8	*12*	2	*12*	1	—	1	1	5	*11*	4	*17*	1	1	—	—
SECTION IIB	1	2	3	2	9	3	2	2	5	1	6	—	—	3	3	2	6	1	1	1	1
SECTION III	*15*	2	4	*18*	—	2	—	1	—	—	8	—	—	—	—	—	—	—	—	—	—
SECTION IVA	1	1	*13*	*22*	*13*	—	—	—	—	—	—	—	—	—	—	—	—	—	—	—	—
SECTION IVB	1	*11*	4	9	*18*	8	—	2	—	—	—	—	—	—	—	—	—	—	—	—	—
SECTION IVC	5	5	3	4	1	1	1	—	1	—	2	—	2	—	—	—	—	—	—	—	—
SECTION IVD	3	1	*15*	3	1	1	1	1	—	—	—	—	—	—	—	—	—	—	—	—	—
SECTION IVE	10	9	—	2	1	5	*18*	*20*	1	—	—	—	—	—	—	—	—	—	—	—	—
SECTION VA	2	*15*	*17*	—	1	1	9	—	3	3	2	7	—	1	—	2	—	—	—	—	—
SECTION VB	*14*	—	7	5	10	2	—	—	—	3	—	—	—	—	—	—	—	—	—	—	—
SECTION VI	*14*	1	6	6	—	—	—	—	—	1	3	1	—	—	—	—	—	—	—	—	—
SECTION VII	—	5	—	1	—	—	—	—	—	—	—	—	—	—	—	—	—	—	—	—	—

Note: In the *Ballard* schedule the Sections comprise the following subject matter:: (I) Formation of Borough; (IIA) Burgage Tenure and Law of Real Property; (IIB) Tenurial Privileges; (III) Burgess Franchise and Residence; (IVA) Borough Courts; (IVB) Modes of Trial; (IVC) Procedure in Trials; (IVD) Punishments; (IVE) Distraints; (VA) Markets and Fairs; (VB) Guilds and Trading; (VI) Borough Finances; (VII) Borough Officers and Government. The same numeration was followed by Tait with the addition of some subdivisions to cover subjects arising for the first time after 1215; *Weinbaum* added two short sub-sections, (IVF) County Courts and Assizes; (IVG) Power to make Ordinances and Agreements.

and the customs of Issigeac, and the local place-names among the bounds of the towns' jurisdictions that bring the reader from an English atmosphere into that of south-western France.

III

Table VII.3 shows that the "affiliation" clause (*Ballard*: I, 8) is the one which occurs most frequently in the surviving charters. Almost as frequent are two categories that are related to each other, the grants of *liber burgus*, or free borough, status to a town (*Ballard*: I, 3). The key phrase is first encountered at Lynn in 1204:

> we have granted that the town of Lynn be a free borough (*liber burgus*) for ever;

and at the end of the century Edward I's charter to Kingston on Hull declared that

> for the betterment of our town of Kingston on Hull and for the use and convenience of our subjects there, we concede that it shall be a free borough.[29]

The meaning of these two words, which suddenly appeared in English borough charters at the very end of the twelfth century, was discussed at length by Tait. After reviewing the interpretations put upon them by Maitland, Ballard and Gross, he concluded that the words were designed to emphasise the contrast between the free town air and the unfreedom of the manor.[30] It was, therefore, more a declaratory banner than a statement of specific endowment, and it did not imply any standard array of franchises:

> the connotation of *free borough* varied from the privileges of London or Winchester to the mere burgage tenure of the humblest seignorial borough.

No similar declaratory phrase, at once self-congratulatory and self-advertising, runs through the Gascon charters. *Communitas* (commune), a word employed in such clauses as that giving the inhabitants

---

[29] Subsequent quotations from charters, if not given a foot-note reference, are from *Ballard*, *Ballard and Tait* or *Weinbaum*; the first of these volumes covers the period to 1216, the second ending in 1307. The passages quoted are in each case to be found in chronological order within the section and subsection of the editors' code, as repeated here (e.g. the passage from the charter of Lynn is at *Ballard*, p. 3, under the section-heading I, 3).

[30] J. Tait, *The Medieval English Borough* (1936), pp. 194–220.

of Créon a common seal, could be employed in other and non-urban contexts: *bastida* is thus left as the one word that came to sum up the distinctive status of urban communities of this novel sort. When the opponents of a new project wished to describe what they disliked, or when Edward wrote from Wales to his Gascon seneschal ordering him to explore the ground for a new town, the one word *bastida* was sufficient to indicate the full creation: site, endowments and liberties.

The full meaning of *liber burgus* and *bastida* can only be appreciated by studying the contrast between the free air of a town and the unfree air of a manor: it was this which made a new town a true *Villefranche*. The unfree air surrounded the town on all sides, and in this air some of the townsmen had been born and reared. There were some rural communities that had very light manorial burdens, particularly on late-colonised land and in the pastoral areas, but the generality of country dwellers had unfree tenures and bore services and payments of varying intensity. The self-interest of seigneurs, as we have seen (pp. 55–97), was well served by encouraging a limited number of free, urban centres to be established on their land, but their self-interest also demanded that the full burden of labour services should be asserted on their rural demesnes and that villein tenures be defended against erosion. This attitude, as Professor Postan has shown, was particularly marked in the thirteenth century, so that we have the paradox: the freedom of town air was being expanded in a limited number of centres just when the rural air was becoming increasingly sultry and oppressive.[31] The increase in population was at once furnishing the labour force for new developments in the economy and weakening the bargaining power of land-hungry tenants.

Later, with a contracted population and a large stock of towns achieved, the urban air was itself to take on an oppressive taint, and town institutions were often devoted to restriction, to hostility towards newcomers and to suspicion of innovation. Since the fall in population brought a great improvement in the bargaining power of rural labour and of rural tenants, the countryside itself was swept by a free air of its own, and the relative attraction of working and dwelling in towns was thereby diminished. Flight to freedom, on the lips of

---

[31] Professor Le Patourel has described a half-way house situation in Guernsey, between the freedom of burgage tenure and the villein; the inhabitants were sufficiently free to be able to indulge in commerce. In 1301 St. Peter Port, which had no municipal institutions, could therefore be described as *quasi burgus* (J. H. Le Patourel, "The Early History of St. Peter Port", *Trans. de la Soc. Guernesiaise*, 1934, p. 187).

urban textile workers, could now mean a flight from town to countryside, not from village to town. Yet this period when the direction of freedom changed, roughly the period after the Black Death, was also the period when new towns ceased to be founded. The context in which the privileges of new towns have to be studied remains, therefore, one where town air was designed to bring freedom to immigrants.

The welcome infection of personal freedom that could be picked up in town air is specifically mentioned in eighteen of the charters (*Ballard*: III 4). The charter of Haverford West put this most clearly and boldly:

> a man, whatever his status may be, who dwells there for a year and a day without being challenged shall be free.[32]

The challenge envisaged was from the villein's lord who might be reluctant to lose part of his demesne labour force, and many Gascon charters declared that no villein of the town's founders could qualify for freedom by undetected residence; the charter of Egremont likewise disqualified the king's villeins; and the villeins of the founding seigneurs were specifically disqualified at Plympton Erle and Bridgetown Pomeroy.[33] A surviving valuation of the Pomeroy estates in 1292 makes it possible to particularise the differences between the town air at Bridgetown Pomeroy and the unfree air at Berry Pomeroy, the manor from which the town had been cut.[34]

The superior position of the burgesses did not lie in any greater endowment of land: indeed, the fifty-eight villagers at Berry Pomeroy had an average of 30 acres of land each while a burgage tenement at Bridgetown occupied only a fraction of an acre. Nor was the link between urban tenement and agricultural land in itself distasteful. Specialists within village society, such as millers, and smiths, held field-land, and in many old-established towns the burgesses did not disdain land in the town fields and pasture rights on the town commons.

---

[32] *Ballard*, p. 104.

[33] *R.G.*, ii, 992; *Ballard and Tait*, pp. 141 and 143–144. The seigneur could profit from allowing some of his own villeins to people the new town: at Downton in 1210–11 a certain Odo paid 3s. "*ut possit remanere in foro*" and in 1211–12 another villein paid "*ut audeat remanere in foro*" (Hants. Rec. Office, Pipe Rolls 159270B m. 2d, and 159271 m. 5). For the villeins taking refuge in the new towns of seigneurs who were rivals of their own lord, see pp. 237 below.

[34] O. J. Reichel, "Berry Pomeroy", *Trans. Devon Assen.* xxviii (1896), pp. 367–368; see also C133/28/20 (1281) and C133/118/1 (1305).

What inhibited the efficient exercise of a craft and the pursuit of trade was not the possession of land but the obligations that went with a tenement if it was held by unfree tenure. Thus, at Berry Pomeroy there were thirty-eight villeins and twenty *operarii*. For the average villein's holding a rent of 10s. 9d. (or 4d. an acre) was paid. The holding of an *operarius* was similar in area, but he paid only a third of the villein rent since he owed considerable labour services, the *opus* of his name. The villeins, however, were not free of labour services: each ploughed the lord's demesne for three days a year, harrowed, hoed and carted for one day, and in autumn reaped for three days. The *operarius* owed these services and in addition had to plough, sow and harrow four acres of demesne, and then to work three days every week (except four) between Michaelmas and August.

The burgess at Bridgetown was quit of his obligation to the Pomeroys when he had paid his 1s. a year rent. The remainder of the lord's income from the borough (£7 2s. 11d. in all) was made up of tolls, market rents and the profits of the borough courts. The manor was still the more valuable of the two assets, being worth £26 10s. 6½d. a year.

The burden on the villager was clearly heavier than on the burgess even when the lord chose to allow labour services to be commuted for cash rents: the services of the *operarius* were valued at 8s. 8½d. a year, and those of the villein at 8½d.

The comparison, it should be noted, is not between a manor and the liberties of a great commercial borough. In 1292 there were only twenty-three burgesses in Bridgetown; it was never very large, and it always had to compete with the older town of Totnes on the opposite bank of the Dart. A second comparison between manorial obligations and burgess freedom can be made, for an even smaller and perhaps abortive project. About the same time that the Pomeroys were creating Bridgetown, Stephen de Bergstede, bishop of Chichester, was devising a new town at Wardour on the shore of what is now Pagham Harbour in Selsey. The burgage rent was to be 14d. a year and the townsmen were to be free to sell at all the bishop's markets and fairs without toll. Any villein of the bishop who was permitted to come and live in the town was given his freedom. From what was he free?

Within a decade of the foundation of Wardour a very full list of the customs of the bishop's manors was drawn up. Those for Sidlesham, from which the site for Wardour was taken, occupy fifty-two lines of print in the published translation. The custumal chose as its typical villein one Geoffrey de la Flete, and the duties which he owed were additional to a money payment of 4s. 4d. a year. The list of duties begins:[35]

> He shall work every day in the year when work may be done except Saturdays and holy days . . . in winter he shall plough and harrow 12 acres . . . in Lent he shall plough and harrow 12 acres. He shall go to the harvest work three times, each time with 4 men. He shall cart 2 loads of wood from Aldingbourne to Sidlesham. He and one other man shall mow as long as the bishop's meadow is being mown. He shall cart dung as long as is needed. In harvest he shall reap and bind half an acre. He shall hoe in summer till three in the afternoon. If he has to quarry marl he shall dig 8 feet long, 4 feet wide and 7 feet deep. He shall gather 50 trusses of straw and cart 100 trusses to Chichester fair. He shall fell one cartload of hedgewood and load it. If the bishop wishes to build at Sidlesham, Geoffrey shall cart the timber and the bishop provide two waggons. . . . [Many smaller duties follow.]

The real disability of village life for the exercise of crafts and trade is apparent. So long as labour services formed part of a tenant's obligations, then work on the lord's demesne took priority over work on the tenant's own land. That was irksome enough for a peasant, but for a would-be craftsman and trader it was crippling. The place where bargains and sales offered themselves was the market place and not the selions of the lord's demesnes. The time when strangers might pass by, or for the market-bell to ring, might be just when the lord's reeve was calling for work on the demesne. Ships made port, commercial news arrived, and hungry travellers drew near according to a timetable that took no account of whether villeins were free that day from the demesne works. A craft might demand continuous application to a task or a manufacture might need continuous supervision of a process: a demand for carting services and harvest work would then be a fatal interruption. Of these demands the generality of burgesses were free, and the ploughing and mowing services rendered at Egremont (*Ballard:* IIB, 16) are quite exceptional; light manorial services were also exacted at Saltash, Battle, Bretford and Morpeth.

The law took the view that villeins were chattels of their lord, and a lord had the right to dispose of his human chattels in the same way as any other chattels. The servitude was most noticeable in the restric-

[35] W. D. Peckham, ed., *Thirteen Custumals* (Sussex Rec. Soc. xxxi (1925)), pp. 22–32.

tions placed on the marriage of villein children, in the restrictions on place of residence, in the heriot (or death duty) and in the obligation to grind at the lord's mill and to bake at his oven, paying the appropriate tolls. Many borough charters gave freedom from the "suit of mill" and the "suit of oven" (*Ballard:* IIB, 17):

> every burgess can have his own oven and mill (Newcastle on Tyne)

> every burgess may bake and brew without licence and without toll and custom, and may build dove-houses, horse-mills and hand-mills; no burgess shall owe suit of mill, whether for fulling or dyeing clothes (Cardiff);

although some burgesses were less fortunate:

> they shall give multure at my mill, to wit, the thirteenth part of their own corn (Egremont);

> the burgesses ought by custom to bake in my oven (Leeds);

and the burgesses of Rye had to purchase from the abbot of Fécamp the right to brew ale in their own houses. The price was heavy: "six score marks of silver".

A villein had limited opportunities to amass personal property, but at his death his lord had a right to a heriot. A townsman who had been able to accumulate wealth, and who held much of it in the form of stocks of goods, household equipment and tools of the trade, would have been very vulnerable to such a death duty. Thus the liberties of a town frequently guaranteed that there would be no heriot or only a limited sum (*Ballard:* IIA, 17). At Lostwithiel

> his heir, by a relief of twelve pence only, shall hold his inheritance freely and in inheritance, and shall possess it in peace.

Since a burgess was not his lord's chattel he was also able to dispose of property without consulting the lord. This right appears in the clauses that gave freedom to make a will disposing of the burgage and other personal property (*Ballard:* IIA, 15). The burgage of the burgess who died intestate passed to his next of kin (*Ballard:* IIA, 16) without question:

> after his death his will shall have validity (Lostwithiel);

> if any burgess shall die, then his wife and heirs shall receive his tenements quietly (Okehampton).

Another valuable consequence of this free disposal of property was the ability to mortgage or to sell the burgage without the lord's permission and often without payment to him. This freedom would be particularly relevant in the case of increased capital values, for a burgess might wish to sell part of his burgage for a newcomer to build upon, while retaining his own house and shop; or he might want to raise credit by pledging his most valuable asset, the burgage (*Ballard*: IIA, 9).

> It shall be lawful for the burgesses to give, sell or mortgage their lands, houses and burgages, saving the right of the lord and except to religious houses (Haverfordwest).

> It shall be lawful for any burgess to sell his land and to go where he will (Wearmouth).

The villein was bound not only by the clock and the calendar but by the limits of the manor. Permission was necessary before leaving it, whether for a short journey or for residence, and permission involved payment. Personal mobility was essential in many of the urban occupations, especially that of trade, and the wealthier a town's merchants, the more likely that their business would call them to long journeys. The burgess was free to move at will, and the economic implications of the emancipation are set out in the charter of Bridgnorth (*Ballard*: VB, 5)

> they may come and go throughout all our land of England and may do all kinds of trading in buying and selling and bargaining, freely, quietly, well and honourably, in fairs and markets, in cities and boroughs and in all places.

The *liber burgus* thus emerges as a term of economic as well as constitutional significance.

IV

The superiority of burgage tenure over villein tenure went further than freedom from services that could hinder a commercial livelihood. It had elements of certainty which made it possible for the townsmen to plan ahead, to know the limit of his obligations to the lord of the soil, and to know that the lord could not vary those obligations in an arbitrary manner. The location and dimensions of the burgage plots were sometimes defined for greater certainty (*Ballard*: IIA, 1), but the most valuable certainty was the fixed rent payable for the plot, usually twelve pence a year (*Ballard*: IIA, 2). As we have seen, this payment was small compared with the rent of a villein holding, and it remained unvaried even when the demand for land increased and prices were rising.

The burgesses of Dunstable in the mid-thirteenth century, with population rising and land in heavy demand, were secure against revision of their rents, for the founding charter had declared a century and a half earlier that

all men going to live there shall give twelve pence a year for each acre.

More important, the capital value of a burgage could increase if a town prospered and more newcomers wished to take up residence.

It was certainly envisaged that a burgess might wish to make more intense use of his burgage. In the charter of 1155 to Scarborough a house placed gable-end to the street was to pay 4d. a year rent, but if the house was built with its longer side against the frontage it was to pay 6d. The foundation charter of Pontorson (Normandy), issued by Henry I, provided for the standard shilling-a-year rent for the plot, and then gave permission for more houses to be built on the *placea*:

faciat quisque pro placea sua vel domo per annum xij nummos . . . faciat in sua placea si libuerit plures domos.[36]

The Pontefract charter of 1194 envisaged a similar expansion of population and crowding of plots, and it may be noted that within a generation Pontefract acquired an extra-mural borough just outside the west gate (Fig. 37):

if anyone has more houses than one in his toft, and lets them to others they shall be free to buy and sell wares in the town but shall pay 4d a year to the reeve. He who dwells in the principal house shall be quit and free as if he were a burgess.[37]

Once the limits of the town were reached, newcomers could be accommodated by building over the rear part of plots if the first developers had simply built a house and shop on the street frontage of the long, narrow burgages; and thus the value of the plot rose. The most favoured positions—near the market place and on the roads leading to the market place—had always been limited, and the first grantees of these plots were exceptionally well placed for windfall gains

[36] E. J. Laurière, *Ordonnances des Rois de France* (1733), iv, p. 337 fn.
[37] *Ballard*, pp. 102–103.

in value. Of these increases in value the seigneur gained nothing unless he had retained some burgage plots in his own hand. Dr. Bilson's study of Kingston on Hull showed that holdings worth 43s. 4d. in 1294 were paying rents of only 29s. 4d. Another holding worth 30s. was paying 20s. In 1313 a holding was currently valued at twice its rent. In 1356 three messuages in *Hullstreet* were worth nine times their rent.[38]

The liberty next in order of frequency (*Ballard*: IVA 4) concerned the independence of the borough courts. In their charter of 1166 the burgesses of Truro were assured that

> they shall not plead in the Hundred courts nor in the shire court,

and at Cardiff (1147–83) the charter provided that

> the burgesses ought not to go to the court of the Hundred outside the borough for any sort of summons,

while the petty borough of Leeds received a more restricted independence in 1207:

> the said burgesses shall not go out of the borough for any action or for any suit, save only for the pleas of the Crown.

The borough court was more than a sign that the new community was separate from the manor, needing a different place and a different time for the meeting of its court. If the burgesses could not be called in question before other courts, then the privileges of the town—and the free status of the burgess—could not easily be called in question. It was not apprehension of some criminal accusation that made town craftsmen and traders so concerned about the character of their law-court, but their life was not likely to be free from civil litigation: disputed contracts, unpaid debts, irregular weights and measures, breaches of market regulations—all these might end in a court action, and townsmen would wish to be on equal fighting terms with their opponents or accusers; and particularly to be heard in a court where commercial matters were familiar, and where technical terms and the customs of the trade would be understood. If juries were involved, it was again better for townsmen to face a jury with more understanding of their problems than one composed of rural freeholders.

As important to the status of a burgess as his freedom from the

---

[38] J. Bilson, "Wyke upon Hull in 1293", *Trans. E.R. Ant. Soc.*, xxvi (1928), p. 97.

jurisdiction of the manor court was his independence of the financial and judicial institutions developed in the counties. Just as a summons before an outside court placed the burgess in hands that might be hostile or lack understanding, so the entry of the seigneur's financial officers gave an unwelcome opportunity to question the conduct of town affairs and to become familiar with the wealth of individuals in the community.

The sign of independence from officials was the *ne intromittat* clause (*Ballard*: IVA, 5)

> that in nothing shall they be answerable to the sheriff or constable concerning those matters which pertain to themselves (Newcastle on Tyne)

> They shall be quit of the shire and hundred courts, and of summonses and aids of sheriffs and serjeants and of all other secular exactions (Portsmouth).

Independence from the seigneur's financial officers was strengthened if the town community contracted to pay a fixed sum (the fee farm), taking upon itself the role of collector (*Ballard*: VI, 1). Provided this sum was paid annually, the king's sheriff or the lord's bailiff did not need to concern himself with collecting the individual items of revenue. Thus Richmond contracted to pay a fee farm of £29 in 1137–45, Appleby an unstated sum in 1200, while the fee farm for Newcastle on Tyne was progressively revised from £50 to £100 between 1201 and 1213.

Free courts and farmed revenues were not the same thing as self-government: but they went a long way towards it, and the course of negotiations, tax assessments and collection provided an educative exercise in how the few could speak for the many. The "legal title and the social force" that Unwin named as two of the three basic ingredients of a town were thus closely connected; in the exercise of lawful franchises the town soon could develop institutions and ambitions that were capable of assisting the town's further growth.

When mere villages were granted market charters it goes without saying that the founder of a new town would have to ensure this right as minimal; a town would also wish to have at least one fair a year, and the majority of urban grants were for both weekly market and yearly fair (*Ballard*: VA, 2 and 3). The most prosperous towns developed commercial activity that spread beyond the conventional few days at the patronal feast of a local church: Kingston on Hull's charter gave it thirty fair-days a year and the same number were enjoyed at its rival,

Ravenserodd: and the near-contemporary attempt to found a port on the Solway Firth began with a charter granting seventeen fair-days a year.

The importance of a market town's economy is brought out when the foundation of a town coincided with the deliberate removal of a market from another site. The charter of Launceston (1141–67) recalled

> the time when the count of Mortain removed the Sunday market from the town of St. Stephen to the new town of his castle of Dunheved and thus created the present Launceston at the castle gates.[39]

Domesday Book records that the same count of Mortain had removed the market of St. Germans to a nearby castle, that of Trematon:[40] and it is not surprising to find a new borough in the bailey. In 1278, after complaints that Welshpool market was damaging to the royal borough of New Montgomery, the markets and fair of Welshpool were removed to Trefnant, and in 1279 we hear of a grant of a burgage *in novo foro apud Treffnanz.*[41]

It was natural for a new town that was market-centred to be known simply as "The Market" or "New Market". New Alresford was first called simply "Alresford *Forum*", and Downton borough appears in the bishop of Winchester's account rolls as *Novum Forum* before it was *Novus Burgus.* The two Sodburys were differentiated as Old Sodbury and Chipping (i.e. Market) Sodbury. Since a market was such an essential part of a town's economy, the grant of a market charter is sometimes the only documentary evidence bearing on the date of a town's foundation if the borough charter itself is lost.

Among the earliest surviving English market charters are those for four plantations (Battle, 1106; Dunstable, 1131–33; King's Lynn, 1107–09; and St. Neots, 1100–35) and two of the earliest fair charters are for Norman plantations also (Belvoir, 1105; and St. Ives, 1110).[42]

Considering the importance of the markets and fairs it is surprising that so few charters of planted towns have a clause specifically mentioning them. There is a technical reason: markets and fairs could be granted in separate documents, and market grants to planted towns do appear on the Charter Rolls, the Patent Rolls, the Close Rolls and

[39] A. F. Robbins, *Launceston* (1888), p. 3.
[40] *V.C.H. Cornwall*, i, pp. 68b and 95a.
[41] *Cal. Welsh Rolls*, i, p. 179; *Cal. Chart. Rolls*, ii, pp. 211 and 263; J. C. Davies, *Mont. Coll.* xlix (1945), p. 133.
[42] These charters are printed in the two vols. of *Regesta Regum Anglo-Normannorum*; i (ed. H. W. C. Davis, 1913) and ii (ed. H. A. Cronne and C. Johnson, 1956).

the Fine Rolls. Even though a borough charter does not mention a market or fair, almost every clause presupposes that organised dealing was to be carried on within the new borough.

V

The two next most frequent clauses concerned another type of freedom, that from tolls (*Ballard*: VA, 7 and 8). Tolls and custom duties were lawfully exacted in most existing English towns and at rural markets and fairs: the revenues from these tolls were as much the incentive for the king and lords to allow these franchises as they were to be in the new towns. However, the burden of tolls was in practice much reduced by the king and seigneurs granting the equivalent of a passport for their townsmen to be free of tolls in towns, markets and fairs that lay on their estates. This practice, well-established in the older towns, was continued when new towns were founded. Thus the burgesses of Truro were freed from tolls at markets and fairs anywhere in Cornwall; those of Pembroke from tolls and customs paid at Bristol, Gloucester, Winchester and Rhuddlan, and from tolls on royal demesnes and in the counties of Devon and Cornwall; the men of Pontefract from tolls in the two lordships of Pontefract and Clitheroe. Wider freedom was given at Portsmouth when Richard I granted that the burgesses

> shall be quit and free of toll and pontage and stallage and tallage both by land and sea wherever they may come in all our land;

Devizes was freed from tolls and customs throughout the kingdom; and Hythe was also freed from tolls in Normandy.

As exemptions of this sort multiplied, the burdens of tolls fell more and more on other groups: on aliens; on traders from towns with narrow concessions or none at all; and on the great mass of countrymen who brought goods to town markets: and here again the villager encountered the superior position of the burgess. With the freedom to buy and sell within the town (*Ballard*: VB, 5) went the disability of those who were not free of the town:

> it is lawful for burgesses to buy whatever they wish within the borough and to sell without license of any person (Egremont)

no outsider shall keep a tavern in the town (Lostwithiel)

none but a burgess can buy cloth to dye or make or cut (Newcastle on Tyne)

no foreigner may cut up fish for sale (Newcastle on Tyne)

none, unless he be of the borough, shall buy green hide in the borough nor do any retail trade (Okehampton)

The distinction between the burgess and the non-burgess, between the insider and outsider, between borough and foreign, began as an essential defence, a guarantee of minimal rights for the exercise of town crafts and trade. By the late thirteenth century, when towns were still being founded, the self-consciousness of the burgesses was taking other directions.

In one direction lay self-government and elective assemblies. The new towns were not yet of that eminence, and many of the smaller plantations had only minimal independence. The range of freedom enjoyed when they came to choose the borough reeve is indicated by the following clauses (*Ballard*: VII, 1, 2 and 3):

if I wish to make a reeve, the burgesses shall elect him from those who dwell in the town (Lostwithiel)

the burgesses shall yearly of their own counsel elect and depose a reeve and a cryer (Okehampton)

the reeve of the town shall be chosen by the election of the burgesses (Egremont)

at Michaelmas the lord shall remove the reeve of the year and appoint another whomsoever he will, but the burgesses shall have preference if they are willing to give as much as the others (Pontefract and Leeds).

In another direction, towns were becoming increasingly restrictive in their outlook by the late thirteenth century, and it is reasonable to associate this attitude with greater competition. Towns multiplied, rural markets and fairs proliferated and, as increase in population and production began to level off, those who had power in a town were less willing to share it with newcomers. For self-protection the most powerful institution within a town was the gild merchant.

Free burgesses could properly band together for collective action, and the larger plantations followed the older towns in developing fraternities to speak for the town, to negotiate the fee farm, to bargain with other towns and foreigners, and to supervise the internal economy of the town.

At the time of their creation, the role of the gilds merchant was more supervisory than regulatory: the earliest reference to a gild merchant in the charter of a plantation is at Pembroke (t. Henry II), and this gild included merchants from other towns in the county; the next gild merchant to be chartered was at Lynn in 1204 but its membership was not defined; the gilds merchant of twelve other planted towns are mentioned in thirteenth-century charters (*Ballard*: VB, 1). Thus the charter of New Montgomery in 1226:

> the town shall be a free borough . . . and may have a merchant gild with a hanse and all customs pertaining to that gild, and none who are not of that gild shall practice the trade of merchant in the said borough except by consent of the burgesses.[43]

VI

The subject-matter of all the clauses that Table VII.3 showed occurring in more than ten charters has now been traversed, and a grant of burgage tenure can be seen to be more than a change in a man's legal status, and more than an increase in personal liberty and human dignity: it provided the minimum freedom to organise one's life as an urban specialist.

Most Gascon bastides, as Chapter 13 shows, were created as market centres for wine and other local agricultural produce; some were centres of administration. The Gascon countryside had tenures as servile as any in England, and the liberties necessary to maintain townsmen in the warmer Gascon air were not dissimilar from those encountered in England. Although Gouron provided a calendar of charters for the communes of Gascony he did not publish the text of any bastide charter. The printed Gascon Rolls, in Bémont's edition, supply many of these, and others have been printed in the journals of local learned societies; at least one appears in Rymer's *Foedera*; others are still in manuscript, their whereabouts being indicated by Gouron. The Gascon bastide charters have not been systematically tabulated by a French Ballard and Tait, but when Vigié printed the texts of three charters from Périgord he divided his commentary into eight sections, the headings of which are immediately recognisable to those who have studied English borough charters.[44]

1. Freedom from arbitrary feudal taxes and servile obligations.

---

[43] *Cal. Chart. Rolls*, i, p. 101.

[44] A. Vigié, *Les bastides du Périgord*, from *Mémoires Acad. des sc. et lettres de Montpellier*, 2nd ser. iii (1907), pp. 279–473; see also J.-P. Poussou, *Rev. de l'Agenais*, xc (1964), pp, 115–26 and 207–25.

2. Protection of the property of burgesses from seizure except by due course of law; freedom to deal; freedom to dispose of property.
3. Matters arising from the shared jurisdiction of the partners in the foundation (*paréage*).
4. Penalties for crimes, particularly against property.
5. Conduct of fairs and markets.
6. Mills and ovens.
7. Military service limited and defined.
8. Organisation of municipal government.

It is in this last group of clauses that the bastides diverge furthest from contemporary English and Welsh boroughs. Each bastide was to have a seal and to be regarded as a *communitas*; the royal bailiff and the elected jurats or consuls had their powers defined; and a ring of parishes in the surrounding countryside was usually placed under the jurisdiction of the bastide. These elements of representation and community organisation were not to be encountered in English and Welsh boroughs of comparable size, for it must be remembered that many of the Gascon bastides were no larger than a petty English borough. The king-duke's political motives in conceding liberties of this order are discussed elsewhere (pp. 235–36).

One small difference between Gascon and English charters should be noticed. If we take those for St. Osbert (1276), Beaumont du Périgord (1286), and Créon (1316) as typical of their respective generations and localities, we find that they have 32, 35 and 38 clauses respectively.[45] Ballard observed that the length of English borough charters was greatest in the petty boroughs, with Egremont, only a little raised above a village, having 29 clauses in its charter.[46] The three Gascon charters cited are lengthy because they descend to detail that in England would be thought more appropriate to by-laws: the width of streets; the scale of tolls; the scale of fines for thefts of different kinds; the punishments for adultery; the character of the houses facing the market place; and the king's rights to build a house in the market place for the vending of flesh and fish.

VII

A charter defined the liberties of the new town: in another sense they were also defined by its geographical limits. The founder of a town had good reasons, as we have seen, to ensure that boundaries were

---

[45] St. Osbert: *R.G.*, ii, 55; Beaumont: *Testut*, pp. 485–514; Créon: C61/30 m. 4.
[46] *Ballard*, p. xxii.

straitly drawn so that villeins should not trespass into freedom. The townsmen were equally anxious to confine their hard-won privileges. The townsmen of Newborough (Anglesey) thought it derogatory to their dignity to have Welsh bondmen living near their houses, and petitioned the king for their removal. In Cornwall, as Fig. 18 shows, the bondmen were tolerated a little nearer to the boroughs: but the burgages were none the less distinct in their compactness.[47] If the town acquired a jurisdiction separate from that of the surrounding county, there was an additional reason for defining the limits between borough and county, for the authority of a court to hear a particular case would depend on which side of the boundary a disputed bargain was struck or an indictable crime committed. The perimeter of the town was just as important when there were no physical defences: the maintenance of the boundary was a defence against the erosion of the town's liberties. If borough and county were separately represented in Parliament, the distinction was further emphasised; and if the town was reckoned a borough for taxation purposes, then property owners within its bounds were taxed at a higher rate than those in the county at large, and had good reason to know the bounds of liberty.

In 1590 one David Williams of Pwllheli, then aged sixty-eight, deposed that he had taken part in annual processions around the borough bounds about forty-eight times. As late as 1837 the Boundary Commissioners were told that the limits of Beaumaris and Conway were perambulated once every three years.[48] The importance of town boundaries had continued long after villeindom had passed away, and their definition had acquired renewed importance when corruption in municipal and parliamentary elections made it worthwhile to be a townsman with a vote. It is ironical that the only surviving evidence for the location of burgage plots at Old Sarum is a rough plan made when there was a dispute over the ownership of the empty plots that were returning their two members to the unreformed Parliament.[49] Similar eighteenth-century plans define burgages in Boroughbridge and Newtown, I.O.W., (Fig. 53)[50]

[47] M. W. Beresford, "Dispersed and Group settlement in Medieval Cornwall" *Ag. Hist. Rev.*, xii (1964), pp. 13–27.
[48] E178/3381, cited in E. A. Lewis, *The Medieval Boroughs of Snowdonia* (1912), p. 59. Perambulations still continue (*Daily Mail*, June 8, 1965, p. 3).
[49] *V.C.H. Wilts.*, vi, p. 66.
[50] B.M., Stowe Ms. 883; A. H. Estcourt, "The Ancient Borough of Newtown", *Proc. Hants. Field Club*, ii (1890–93), pp. 89–109, includes James Mallett's plan of 1768; see also PRO MR/489.

The limits of townships were also the limits of rating and relief under the old Poor Law and, as Rickman observed in his Preface to the first Census Reports, the administration of the Poor Law since 1597 had etched these bounds on popular memory as effectively as if large-scale plans had been drawn; and if a town's boundaries were also those of a parish, then they might also be important in determining whether or not a particular property paid tithes.

A curious effect of the bounds of a new town was seen in 1854 when the Hull and Withernsea railway came to Hedon. The station was built just within the borough bounds but the goods shed was placed a little further north, and outside the borough boundary. The reason? The charter of 1170 gave the right to take toll from "all goods unloaded within the borough", and although ships no longer came up the Hedon River and although the medieval Havens were silted and grass-grown, the borough lawyers claimed that merchandise from railway waggons would be liable for toll: rather than fight the claim, the railway company took evasive action.[51]

The bounds of Pwllheli and other boroughs of north Wales were cast wide: the perambulation of Beaumaris covered some 10 miles, and that of the Liberty of Conway some 18 miles. The Welsh boroughs, with jurisdictions covering large areas, have very few English equivalents, although frequent in Gascony where charters commonly name half a dozen parishes that were to come under the jurisdiction of a bastide. In Wales the largest areas occur where the lands of adjoining Welsh vills were appropriated to the boroughs. Carnarvon burgesses in 1305 owned 1,229¾ acres outside the walls and Beaumaris burgesses 1,486½ acres.

The largest territories attached to English plantations are found where there was abundant land locally, and no clash of interest between new town and older villages. The burgesses of Newborough (Staffs.) had pasture for their cattle in all Needwood Forest except in the enclosed hays, and those of Newport, I.O.W., had the use of the heaths of Parkhurst outside the wood itself. The burgesses of Pontefract were given 194½ acres in the town moor, and those of Maldon had rights in the marshes and pastures analogous to those enjoyed by the burgesses of Okehampton in the lord's wood, and the rights of the men of Swansea to set fish-traps on the sands. Pasture rights outside the town were also mentioned in the charter of Wearmouth.

51 M. W. Beresford, *History on the Ground*, (1957), pp. 140–141.

In England the perambulation of borough bounds was typically a matter of minutes rather than of hours. Some reasons for the compactness of the new towns have already been shown: no one wanted to be far from the market place, the centre of trade; the defended towns would wish as small a circuit as possible for manning. A lord who set his new town in the fields of a village could not deprive the villagers of too much land. After Newtown, I.O.W., had been cut from Calbourne the 132 villagers continued to farm the rest of the parish and to work on the lord's demesne of 288 acres of arable and 773 acres of pasture; the burgesses had only 26 acres of land beyond their burgages.[52] The earls of Aumale cut 321 acres out of the township of Preston in Holderness to make room for the borough and harbours of Hedon, but a survey of 1260 shows that the 5,820 acres of the fields of Preston had to support 77 villagers and over 3,000 sheep.[53] The same founders laid out the borough of Harewood alongside a village; the borough was confined to messuages along both sides of *Boroughgate*, and a few hundred yards to the north the street called *Bondgate* shows where the village remained undisturbed, the villagers cultivating 78 bond bovates in the fields. At Appleby the *Bondgate* is in a significant position near the mother-church, and on the Stainmore main road into Scotland: quite separate, and across the river, are the market place and the free burgages of the castle-town.

In the first Census tables of 1801 the small areas within planted towns contrast with the larger acreages both of rural townships and of organic towns (Table VII). Thus the united parishes of St. Leonard and St. Michael, New Malton, comprised 49 acres and all these acres were within the walls: in the surrounding parish of Old Malton there were 3,968 acres; the borough of Stratford on Avon comprised 109 acres but Old Stratford had 6,385 acres; Reigate borough was 65 acres in area but Reigate "Foreign" (*forinsecus*) was 5,941 acres; New Shoreham had 107 acres, Old Shoreham had 1,870 acres.

When in 1640 a petition was presented to give the town of Haslemere independent parochial status and separate it from the parish of Chiddingford in which it had been planted, Haslemere was described as

an auntient Burrough Towne having but a verie small quantitie of land thereunto belonging;[54]

[52] C145/62/1 (1303) and B.M. Add. Ms. 6166 f. 223 (1297–98).
[53] *Y.I.*, i, p. 79 (1260); *cp.* SC6/1078/8; SC11/730; E372/152B, m. 3.
[54] E. W. Swanton and P. Woods, *Bygone Haslemere* (1914), p. 368 from Loseley Ms. 757A.

TABLE VII.4

AREAS OF PLANTED TOWNS CONTRASTED WITH MOTHER
PARISHES, CENSUS OF 1801

	Acres	Area of mother parish
West Looe	4	2,661
East Looe	1	3,193
Okehampton	10	9,542
Bishop's Castle	11	5,638
Mitchell	15	7,022
North Shields	36	2,285
Newport, I.O.W.	59	9,579
Tregoney	69	2,300
Stony Stratford	70	4,240
Weymouth	77	1,702
Harwich	87	1,392
South Shields	90	4,225
Boroughbridge	95	2,241
Uxbridge	99	4,845
New Lymington	100	1,415
Lostwithiel	110	6,790
Hartlepool	137	2,465

and so small was the area assigned to the burgages of Market Harborough when they were cut from the fields of Great Bowden, that

the town having no fields has given occasion to some witty pleasantries among the vulgar, as, that "A goose could eat all the grass that grows in Harborough fields."[55]

The truly compact character of Harborough, never walled, and surrounded by fields, is shown by the terms used to describe the bailiff's holding in the town in a deed of 1365. His plot, the small croft with the tenement built on it,

stretches in length from the king's highway in the town as far as the edge of the field of Great Bowden.[56]

In England the jurisdiction of the borough was usually confined to these narrow areas, and the burgess was someone who held a burgage within the geographical limits of the town. Although the seigneur might receive revenues from both the old village and the new borough, the two were distinguished in the reeves' accounts as *burgus* and *man-*

[55] J. H. Hill, *The History of Market Harborough* (1875), p. 2.
[56] J. E. Stocks and W. B. Bragg, *Market Harborough Parish Records*, (1890), p. 47.

erium or as *intrinsecus* and *forinsecus*. In mid and south Wales, however, the distinction was a little blurred by a class of non-resident burgess described as *de vento* and sometimes *de vento et vico* (of the wind and street). These part-time townsmen fitted an economic environment where daily and weekly trading opportunities, such as feast days and fairs, made it profitable for "foreigners" to pay for the privileges of being considered burgesses. Many of the rentals, surveys and accounts of Welsh towns in the late thirteenth and early fourteenth century have such burgesses. At the new foundation of Newcastle Emlyn an account of 1303–04 described their status explicitly:

> from divers men called "burgesses of the wind" who hold neither burgages nor lands but pay 5s. 6d. in total so that they can enjoy the same liberty as a burgess.[57]

Another entry in the account shows that Newcastle Emlyn then had twenty-six full-time burgesses. Lists of burgesses of the wind survive for other boroughs of south Wales, and they were found in New Radnor,[58] and in Abergavenny:

> 40s. 9d. from the chensers of the borough so that they can buy and sell as if they were of the vill's liberties.[59]

The free air from the towns could sometimes be felt blowing up the valleys.

[57] SC6/1218/9 and 1219/4.
[58] SC6/1209/4.
[59] SC6/1094/11.

PART TWO

NEW TOWNS AND OLD

The planted towns had to compete with old-established towns and with villages that were being promoted to boroughs. The founders of the new towns were generally the lords of older towns, and the new towns were anxious to be as like their rivals as possible. This paradox of rivalry and imitation is examined in Chapter 8, and in Chapter 9 the achievements of the newcomers are measured in terms of their wealth and population in the early fourteenth century. Chapter 10 measures and attempts to explain the failures among the plantations.

CHAPTER EIGHT

Newcomers and Neighbours

"The men of this town, on account of the very great dignity of
the place, are called *Burgesses*."

Chronicle of Battel (Battle) *Abbey*,
(ed. M. A. Lower, 1851), p. 20.

CHAPTER 7 has shown that personal details concerning the
first inhabitants of the new towns are hard to come by. In the
mass, however, the immigrants have a discernible character,
and their migration is related to the economic environment of a general
rise in European population. This chapter considers the inhabitants
of the new towns in relation to their neighbours, the old-established
towns. We have already seen these older towns setting a pattern of
liberties for the newcomers, and providing them with some of their
recruits. We must now consider them as neighbours and rivals to the
new towns, before passing on to the rivalry that existed between the
newcomer of the day-before-yesterday and the newest newcomer.

I

A map showing the distribution of planted towns in a country (whether
England, Wales, Gascony, Holland, Bavaria or Eastern Germany) has
to be on a small scale, and, however small the dots are drawn, there is a
risk that the landscape will seem to consist of nothing but planted towns.
In Wales and Eastern Germany, where there were hardly any other
medieval towns except plantations, the small scale plans do not distort
the truth, but in England the planters of towns were certainly not
working on virgin soil. Their projects had to take into account the
existence of old-established towns and of villages that were concurrently
being elevated into boroughs. The inhabitants of the new towns had
to reckon with these rival towns in the same line of business as themselves. Newcomers had neighbours.

229

Even in Gascony, where the proportion of non-planted towns was higher than in England, the newcomers had their rivals to face in the same way. All the districts with bastides also had small towns and villages to which the king-dukes had given urban or quasi-urban charters of privilege. Marcel Gouron's catalogue of these Gascon charters of privilege gives details of 444 such places, and his catalogue excludes Périgord and Quercy completely. On this showing about one Gascon community in four was a bastide. The political and economic relationships were again those of neighbours and rivals.

In England the potential rivalry of the old-established and the newly-founded was of the same order. In 1086 Domesday Book named 111 places with some urban characteristics, and only two or three of these were newly planted since 1066. The stock of towns with Roman origins had been augmented by the Anglo-Saxon boroughs and by the county towns of the Danelaw. The Norman kings and their tenants in chief were quick to show willingness to develop markets and fairs in their villages and to confer borough status on any of their villages that had commercial prospects. There was no seigneur so dedicated to the cause of town plantation that he would deny urban development to promising villages elsewhere on his demesne. By 1350, when kings and seigneurs had developed about 170 planted towns in England, there were at least twice as many towns of organic growth, and Table III.2 has shown that great seigneurs, like the king himself, owned towns of both kinds.

We can now pass beyond the necessary distortion of small-scale distribution maps, where planted towns seem to dominate the landscape, and place the new towns of medieval England in their true economic context. They had not come to people an unurbanised desert, and in some cases the nearest neighbour to a planted town had been an urban centre for a very long time. Thus, Portsmouth was founded near Porchester, and Boroughbridge was a neighbour to Aldborough, the medieval borough alongside the *vetus burgus* that had been a Brigantine capital before the arrival of the Romans.

Fig. 43 shows the planted and organic towns that lay side by side in a busy area of southern England. In this area lay the old capital, Winchester, and by 1086 there were already boroughs at Christchurch and at Southampton, the principal port. By the end of the thirteenth century nine Hampshire villages had become boroughs by promotion, and ten other towns had been planted. An old-settled and long-

230

prosperous county now had twenty-two towns, eleven of them planta-tions.

With few exceptions, such as New Salisbury and Rhuddlan III, the new towns did not supplant the old towns: they supplemented them. They were planned additions to a stock of towns at a time when the economic situation gave opportunities both to new and to old. Just as agricultural expansion displayed itself through an increased

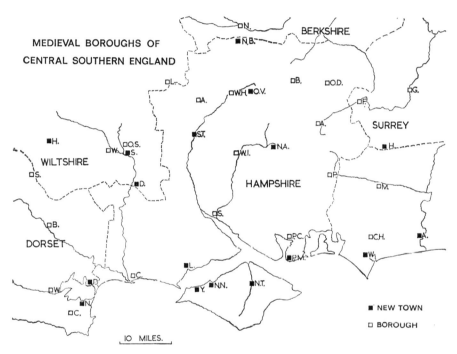

FIG. 43. THE MEDIEVAL BOROUGHS OF CENTRAL SOUTHERN ENGLAND.
Both planted and organic boroughs are shown.

number of plough-teams and farm animals, so urban expansion bore witness to great developments in the warehouse, in the workshop and on the wharves.

Yet there were two important, and related, differences between the character of new towns in the medieval period of expansion and that of the towns that developed during the Industrial Revolution. In the first place, the new medieval towns made conscious efforts to be as like

231

their older neighbours as possible, but the textile mill-towns and the towns of the Black Country had no reason to be traditionalist. In the second place, the medieval newcomers were practising the same arts, the same handicrafts and the same techniques of trade that were being practised in existing towns. The mill-towns were new and novel: the medieval plantations were only new.

By imitating their neighbour's franchises, the new communities showed that these liberties provided a practicable framework for living. The men of the new towns might have been refugees from the oppression of the manor, but they did not reject the conventions of contemporary towns. They did not reject the general tendency of older towns to confine the full benefits of citizenship to narrow groups, and they fashioned institutions that would lead to the same end. If there was an anti-urban sentiment, it was to be found not in the young towns but in the areas where rural industry was developing outside the jurisdiction of boroughs of any kind, old or new.

By imitating the crafts of their older neighbours, and by conducting much the same kind of trade, the newcomers showed that they were not driven into new centres in order to have freedom to practise a new technology or some unorthodoxy of commerce. The only industrial revolution that has been claimed for the Middle Ages in England[1] took place outside towns: important, but less revolutionary, changes took place in many technologies (such as building) but they were not the monopoly of any one type of town, and the architectural engineering of rural monasteries shows that building skills could be as highly developed in the countryside as in a town.

Compared with later periods of great technological advance and world exploration, the economic expansion of the Middle Ages in England consisted largely of doing traditional things in greater numbers. Yet expansion without a great deal of innovation is still expansion: colonisation is none the less progressive, even when the newly-won fields are growing the same crops as the older fields of a village. Newly-made ports, such as Liverpool and Portsmouth, did not have quays and physical equipment different from their neighbours, old-established Chester and Portsea, and there is no evidence that their warehouses and counting-houses housed any new expertise of trade. No one can doubt that the English economy was greatly assisted by the

[1] The "revolution" was the development of water-powered fulling mills on rural manors (E. M. Carus-Wilson, "An Industrial Revolution of the 13th Century", *Ec.H.R.*, xi (1941).

sheer increase in numbers of such ports; by the same light, the rural economies were aided by the sheer increase in the number of market places that came with the new towns.

II

We have seen that two counsellors whispered contrary advice into a seigneur's ear. One counselled the encouragement of towns and the bourgeois freedoms; the other counselled a firm hand on the unfree villagers and a strict discipline among the conscripted labour force of the demesne. This paradox was given logical consistency by Professor Postan's analysis of seigneurial reaction to rising prices and rising population in the period between the end of the civil war in 1154 and the late thirteenth century.[2] From the pressure of population on resources came rising prices for everything that came off the land, food and industrial raw materials alike. The high prices stimulated land-owners to use their demesnes to produce for the household, and to turn to the market as a place where surplus produce could be sold for useful cash. The scarcity of land enabled them to dictate hard terms to the peasants who occupied the non-demesne parts of the manor and who contributed their labour to the working of the demesne. The general bargaining power of peasant labour could not improve until the pressure of population eased; and that particular killing mercy was widely felt only with the Black Death.

Until then, the unfree peasantry could become townsmen only by flight or enfranchisement, and their best hope was in the town of another seigneur, since their own lord was often able to bar entry to his own villeins. If another seigneur was founding a town in rivalry to their own lord, they could go to this town and not find themselves on the list of proscribed immigrants, and thus in the multiplication of new towns and in the rivalry between competing founders there was some small hope that personal freedom might come to a few villeins even while the yoke was being more firmly fastened on the less fortunate. We have seen that *Francheville* (alias Newtown, I.O.W.) was no consolation to the villeins who continued to work on the bishop of Winchester's demesnes at Swainston manor.

The same ambivalent attitudes towards towns are visible among the

---

[2] M. M. Postan, "The Chronology of Labour Services" *Trans. Royal Hist. Soc.*, 4th ser. xx (1937), pp. 169–194.

landowners of Gascony. The contract for the foundation of Corneillas envisaged that there might be some risks in placing a new town so near to Valence d'Agen, that had only just been projected, and it called on Heaven to favour the recruiting campaign:

> *inhabitantes qui erunt inibi—Deo propitio—in posterum et ad bastidam predictam voluerint convenire.*[3]

In fact, the wrath of local seigneurs was capable of being as much an impediment as the wrath of God, and the anger of Gascon seigneurs was easily aroused when a recruiting agent for another seigneur's town seemed likely to seduce their own villeins. The lord of Madaillan near Villeneuve sur Lot declared that he had undertaken to found a new town at Cançon in 1255 simply because the bastides growing up around his seignory were threatening to rob him of manpower.[4] The map shows that six bastides were planted in that locality in addition to Villeneuve.

The first plantation of towns in the Agenais took place while that region was out of English hands, but on its resumption in 1279 Edward I inherited not only a stock of bastides created by the count of Toulouse but many unresolved complaints from landowners offended by the count's new towns. Complaints that had been investigated by the count's own officials in 1253 were headed *De Bastidis Novis*, and they form an anthology of anti-bastide feeling.[5] The barons and knights of the Agenais asked the count to ban his seneschal from beginning any more new towns on his own initiative, without the count's letters patent; the abbey of St. Maurin complained that its villeins were being received as townsmen into Puymirol;[6] a seigneur, Raymond Sextus of Lavaur, complained that the count had expressly promised not to receive his villeins into bastides, but the promise had been ignored in the Castres district;[7] the town of Montjoie, founded in 1255, complained that the arrival of the new town of Castelsagrat was bringing injury, but the count declared that he did not envisage any harm from the competition and would persist in his plan:

> *comes non intendit amovere bastidam.*[8]

[3] G. P. Cuttino, ed., *Le Livre d'Agenais* (Toulouse, 1956), p. 24.
[4] *Gouron*, 669; *Deffontaines*, pp. 147 and 153.
[5] *A.P.E.A.*, pp. 65–67.
[6] *Ibid.*, p. 67.
[7] *Ibid.*, p. 304.
[8] *Ibid.*, pp. 324–325.

In 1270 there were further complaints in the Agenais: the men of Azarco had been lured into the bastide of Montesquieu-Volvestre;[9] and in 1289 the foundation of Molières brought complaints to Edward I that the seigneur of Montclar's villeins were fleeing to the bastide and were being accepted there.[10] When the *paréage* for Marciac was drawn up in 1298 it was agreed not to receive any newcomers from four named villages—those of the seigneur concerned—in order not to depopulate his demesnes:

ut castra et villae non depopulentur prope bastidam.[11]

In 1278 Edward I ordered that no villeins of the Condomais should be received into the royal bastides, and in 1279 the villeins of the Viscount of Béarn were similarly barred;[12] in 1290 Bertrand de l'Isle's villeins were similarly barred from entry to the royal bastides of the Agenais;[13] in the previous year the king had appeased the complaints of the bishops, barons, knights and nobles of the Agenais by ordering his seneschal not to receive villeins in any royal bastide without their master's consent:

homines questales prelatorum, baronum, militum et nobilium contra eorum voluntatem, in bastidis nostris factis vel faciendis vel locis seu proprietatibus nostris non recipiatis.[14]

Gascon seigneurs were not irrevocably opposed to bastides. If the new towns could be tactfully sited, they were willing to enter into partnerships with the count and with the king-duke, the seigneur contributing the site and the other partner the legal authority. The private estates of Edward I as duke of Gascony were less extensive than those which he held in England as king, and even in the Agenais it was acknowledged that the barons and knights would have no cause for complaint if new towns were erected solely on the duke's demesnes there. The straitness of the demesnes, however, was always a powerful incentive to seek sites beyond them.

The declaration of intention and prohibition that Edward I made to his Gascon subjects must be seen in this political context. At the assembly of the estates of Guyenne, held at Bordeaux in 1278, the

---

[9] *Ibid.*, p. 341.
[10] *Ibid.*, p. 344.
[11] M. A. Curie-Seimbres, *Essai sur les Villes . . . sous le nom générique de bastide* (Toulouse, 1880), p. 275.
[12] *R.G.*, ii, 1652.
[13] *R.G.*, ii, 1777.
[14] *R.G.*, ii, 992.

nobles complained that the recent new towns of Henry III and his son had harmed their interest. In the same year the seigneurs with lands near St. Sever complained that royal officials were too zealous in seeking sites for bastides,[15] and the barons of the Bazadais were assured that no bastide would be built in their region without consent, although ten years later it was still necessary for them to ask for the attention of the royal officials to be drawn to this promise.[16] In 1279 a similar promise was given to Gaston, viscount of Béarn and Marsan, and it, too, had to be reiterated ten years later.[17] In 1282 Edward made an agreement with the abbot and town of Condom, promising not to found any new town in the region of Condomais unless they agreed.[18] Similar promises were made for Marsan in 1286, and a royal seneschal was ordered to cease the work that he had begun on a bastide within the barony of Gabardan.[19] On the other hand, the king-duke himself took action against seigneurs who had planted towns on their own land without consulting him, and thus the most enthusiastic of town planters is caught in opposition when his own rights were threatened.[20]

When territory passed temporarily out of the English king's control during war—as frequently happened on the Anglo-French border in Gascony—it was sometimes found, on recovery, that a local seigneur had founded a town either on his own initiative or by *paréage* with the king of France. For this reason Edward II ordered a retrospective enquiry into bastides built between 1294 and 1310; and in 1314 into those founded by the counts of Armagnac a generation earlier.[21] In 1310 the English complained not only that the king of France had seized the older bastide of Domme but also that in 1308 he had built Villefranche St. Louis (St. Louis en l'Isle).[22]

Opposition to particular projects of town plantation was not confined to English Gascony. Philip III of France quarrelled with his vassal, count Bernard of Astarac, over the foundation of Pavie in 1282,[23] and we have seen that Alphonse de Poitiers had to meet the grievances of the seigneurs of Agenais. Alphonse's plantations were not confined to

[15] E36/187 ff. 179–80.
[16] *R.G.*, ii, 57 and 61.
[17] *R.G.*, ii, 1652.
[18] *R.G.*, ii, 938.
[19] *R.G.*, ii, 881.
[20] *R.G.*, iii, 4874 and 4938.
[21] E36/187 f. 163; B.M. Cott. Ms. Julius E. 1, ff. 174–176
[22] *Albe*, pp. 402–403.
[23] C.-V. Langlois, *Le Règne de Philippe III* (Paris, 1887), p. 131.

this part of his lands: they extended into the territories that he held from the king of France. Indeed, it is sometimes said that Alphonse's policy of bastides was conceived as a move against his own sovereign in Paris, to counter a prohibition on fortified towns forced on him after the Albigensian wars. But Alphonse had opposition from other directions: in 1269 the count of Comminges was complaining of an Alphonsian project.[24] Alphonse appears himself in the role of an opponent of bastides: the abbot of Dalon, intending to found Tauriac in Quercy, found that Alphonse's enthusiasm for bastides did not extend to those which might threaten his own position.

Any local landowner who felt aggrieved by a local plantation could be expected to use what political influence he had to block the project. Bishops had additional weapons: in 1260 the bishop of Rodez excommunicated all the inhabitants of Alphonse's bastide of Villefranche de Rouergue in an effort to check its growth; the monastery of Montauriol petitioned Pope Eugenius III when they heard that Montauban was to be created; and Pope John XXII attacked Arthez (Tarn) as a danger to his castle of Lescure.

If a new project could not be blocked, there was another strategy available: it might be checked by a similar plantation on the territory of the aggrieved landowner. Three bastides of the counts of Comminges are said to have been checks to the king of France's towns (Mondilhan, 1264; Anan, 1270; Boulogne, 1283) and the count of Foix's foundation of Blajan in 1283 probably had a similar motive. Professor Higounet claims that after 1252 there was a deliberate counter-offensive of seigneurial bastides after a series of successful foundations where the king of France had contracted partnerships with the counts of Toulouse and certain Cistercian abbeys. Some difficulties arise in accepting this interpretation, however, when it is noted that the first three seigneurial bastides cited (Mazères, 1253; Labastide de Serou, 1253; Campagne sur Arize, 1255) are earlier than the first partnerships cited between the king, the counts of Toulouse and the abbots in 1256.

The widest repercussions of a conflict over the foundation of a bastide were those that followed the proclamation of St. Sardos in December 1322, since an Anglo-French war, lasting until 1325, arose on the issue.[25]

[24] C. Higounet, *Le Comté de Comminges* (Toulouse, 1949), i, p. 175.
[25] The following paragraphs are based on P. Chaplais, *The War of Saint-Sardos* (Camden Soc. 3rd. ser. lxxxvii (1954)).

The rights and wrongs of the issue were tangled. Before 1279, when the treaty of Amiens restored the Agenais to Edward I, the monastery of Sarlat had founded a priory at St. Sardos in the hills south of the river Lot. The king of France had earlier promised that the monastery and its lands would never be separated from the French Crown against its will, and it was now claimed that this right extended to the daughter-house of St. Sardos. In 1317 it became known that the priory was projecting a bastide outside the gate, and the seneschal of Saintonge reported to Edward II that such a town would be a French enclave in the midst of the Agenais, *eu milleu de tout Agenays*. The French moves, he counselled, were a threat to English security, *mout peril-losee a nostre sire le Roy*. The dispute was taken to the Parlement of Paris, which in 1322 ruled that the French king had every right to make a *paréage* with the prior despite the known opposition of the local seigneur, Raymond Bernard of Montpezat.

> *Abbas et gentes Sancti Sacerdotis dixerunt regi Francie quod ibi poterat fieri populacio seu bastida, et quod si regi Francie placeret facere ibidem villam, ipsi de dicto loco facerent pariagium cum dicto rege Francie.*

This declaration was reported to Edward II who was already in a difficult diplomatic situation, since the accession of a new French king in 1322 had revived the question of performing homage for the Gascon lands. There were already bastides near to St. Sardos: Granges sur Lot and Le Temple were each no more than 5 miles away. Indeed, they and La Parade can be seen from the gate of St. Sardos as one looks north across the Lot Valley. These and other towns of the Agenais, bastides and non-bastides, joined the lord of Montpezat in protest. Their main argument—that men would leave them for the dazzling attractions of life in the new French bastide—was not very flattering to themselves or to the lord of Montpezat.

> *Si hec pupulacio (sic) fieri paciatur in loco predicto, terra Agennesii amittitur, quia omnes aut quasi ipsius terre ad ipsum locum confluent propter privilegia que habitantibus per dominum regem Francie in ipso loco concedentur.*

The privileges of those who came to dwell in St. Sardos were pro-claimed in advance by the French seneschal, and he named October 16, 1323 as the day when the *executor* would perform the formal ceremony of raising the stake at St. Sardos. On this stake were to be the arms of France, and thenceforward all newcomers could take up their building plots. The stake (*palum*) was erected in readiness the previous evening but in the morning instead of the French flag (*penuncellum*) the French king's officer was found hanging from it, and the priory buildings were burned and looted. As it was reported to Edward:

> *Aucuns de voz officials de vostre duchee vindrent en la bastide de Seint Sacerdos et cele ardirent et destruyrent. Et son procurour qi illoeqes estoit prindrent et hastivement pendirent.*

There was no doubt that the seigneur of Montpezat was to blame for the foray, and the English seneschal was suspected of collusion since he had been in the company of Raymond Bernard in Agen three days earlier. He added to these suspicions by taking no action against the marauders and continuing his tour of the district as if nothing had happened. There was anger in Sarlat and in Paris. A judicial process against the seneschal began in the French courts but he refused to appear, as did Raymond Bernard. In February 1324 Raymond Bernard was condemned and the castle ordered to be seized. It was garrisoned by English troops by this time, and after some hesitation Edward ordered them not to give up the castle and he further delayed his appearance to do homage. The French king moved to confiscate his disobedient vassal's fiefs and war began.

The threat of a bastide in Gascony thus produced a two years' war between England and France. The threat of a new town at Dolforwyn in Montgomeryshire went almost that far in poisoning good relations between Edward I and prince Llewelyn in 1273. In the spring of that year, while Edward I was in Gascony, prince Llewelyn began work on a castle in Bettws Cedewain parish on the summit of a steep but flat-topped hill overlooking the Severn. The hill-top was large enough to fit a small borough within the castle-bailey, and this was Llewelyn's intention. The news of the project alarmed the English regents, who wrote to the prince forbidding him "to erect *de novo* a borough or a town or a market." Llewelyn sent a hurt reply: he was sure that if Edward himself had been in England he would have shown more understanding of the situation and sent no such harsh letter from his Chancery. The regents' reply was to besiege the castle and take it.[26]

Like St. Sardos, Dolforwyn had near to it other market towns that felt themselves threatened by the foundation project. As in the valley

[26] J. G. Edwards, ed., *Littere Wallie* (1940), pp. 23–24; id., *Cal. of Ancient Correspondence concerning Wales* (1935), p. 86.

of the Lot, so by the Severn these protestors included towns that had once themselves been new plantations, like New Montgomery, 6 miles to the east of Dolforwyn. The idea of a town in this locality must have lingered in English minds after the suppression of Dolforwyn. In 1280 a fair and market were established in the parish of Llanfair Cedewain, and the borough of Newtown was well established there by 1321.

It is not rare to find towns forgetting that they had once been new themselves, and seeking to block new projects. Hedon had been planted in the Humber estuary in the early twelfth century, but this did not prevent the burgesses joining with Scarborough and Grimsby in 1279 to oppose an even newer arrival, Ravenserodd.

> The men of Odd hold pleas and distrain for debts as if they were a borough[27]

ran the complaint, and the "as if" marks the indignant gulf between the Haves and the Have-nots.

It is not surprising that after the foundation of New Salisbury the remaining burgesses of Old Sarum complained that New Sarum was taking away their market, since it had already taken their cathedral; but Wilton also regarded itself as slighted by Salisbury.[28] In 1279, the same year that the complaints of Wilton, Grimsby and Hedon were heard, the men of Houghton Regis (Beds.) voiced their resentment against the town of Dunstable, even though that town had been planted some 160 years before.[29] Fears of this sort must lie behind the promise that Henry III made to Scarborough in 1256 that no new port or quay should ever be made between Scarborough and Spurn Point.[30] In the mid-thirteenth century, when new ports were still being planted on the English and Welsh coasts, a promise of this sort had some meaning: but in 1355, when the planting of towns had come virtually to an end, it is curious to see Edward, the Black Prince, appeasing the men of Bourg sur Gironde by promising that he would never create a bastide in their neighbourhood.[31]

The records of the royal courts in the thirteenth century contain hundreds of analogous disputes between rival market communities, with one place claiming that a neighbour's new market charter

[27] *R.H.*, i, p. 107.
[28] *R.H.*, ii, pp. 268 and 280.
[29] *R.H.*, i, p. 8.
[30] *Ballard and Tait*, p. 302.
[31] *Gouron*, 616.

infringed its own earlier charter. Only a few of these disputes concerned new markets that had come with new towns, for there were many villages that had grants of market charters, but occasionally the opposition to a new market is related to a new town or to a project for one. The grant of a market and fair to Trefnant (Montgomeryshire) in 1279 was deliberately intended to impede and perhaps supplant the market and fair of La Pole (Welshpool),[32] and if we enquire why Welshpool should be singled out for attack we find that it was because Welshpool was newly created and considered harmful to the town, markets and fairs of Montgomery. (If we pursue History further and enquire why Montgomery itself was called New Montgomery we shall find that its own origins gave it very little cause for moral indignation: it had been created by Henry III in 1223.)

Geoffrey Front-de-Boeuf was mayor of Bayonne and seneschal of the Landes for Edward II. In 1315 he founded a bastide that took his own name, Rondeboeuf (Landes). There were immediate complaints from two other bastides near by, St. Gein (1284) and Lias (1313), since their pasture rights in the forest were threatened by the new community. The local rivalry did not end here, for on the other side of the sometimes disputed frontier of Armagnac four more bastides were erected between 1313 and 1322 (Cazères, Arthez d'Armagnac, Barcellonne and Grenade). In a petition to Edward II (c. 1320) Rondeboeuf joined with its once-hostile neighbours, St. Gein and Lias, to complain of the threats from the counts of Armagnac:

les dites bastides marchent a les terres de le gentz del visconte de marssan dune part et a la terre del counte de Armanhack dirtre part.[33]

In this crowded frontier area, where so many towns turned out to be bastides, it is not surprising to find Edward II also enquiring into the circumstances in which two other towns, Marguestau and Monclar, had been founded by the count of Armagnac, allegedly without royal permission.

Newcastle on Tyne, despite the patent evidence of its newness in its name, was a fierce opponent of all rival ports of the Tyne. Thus, the new ports of North Shields and South Shields were both the subject of active litigation and frequent complaint to the king. In 1290 the petition and counter-petition were heard in full Parliament, and the pleadings occupy six columns of the printed *Rolls of Parliament*. In an earlier

---

[32] *Cal. Chart. Rolls*, ii, pp. 211 and 263.
[33] C61/30 m. 20; SC8/8/8767; *Gouron*, 1276 and 1399.

dispute recorded in 1275 a local jury had reported that the Priory of Tynemouth had created North Shields as a sea-port, probably about 1225:

> *Prior edificari fecit super unam partem rypae de Tyne quandam villam quae vocatur Northscheles . . . in qua villa plures mercandisas excercentur.*[34]

In the Parliamentary hearing the phrases clearly indicate plantation, adding bakers, fishers and brewers to those who practised trade in the new town. The Priory rent-roll, it claimed, had been augmented by thirty six marks a year and upward.

> *Predictus Prior levavit novam villam apud Sheles inter Mare predictum et Novam Castrum et habet ibidem piscatores, pistores et braciatores suos residentes de quibus Prior percipit per annum xxxvi marcas et amplius.*

On the south bank of the river, almost opposite North Shields, the prior of Durham had also appreciated the opportunity for augmenting the rent-roll of a rural manor by planting a town. In 1254 there was litigation before the judges of Assize between Newcastle and the Prior. The jury found that *quandam magnam villam* had indeed been founded here to the damage of Newcastle.[35] South Shields was in existence by 1235 and may therefore have been contemporary with its namesake across the estuary.

The passage of time brought even more curious ironies for the Cornish borough of Penryn on the Fal. Penryn had been founded about 1236 by the bishop of Exeter with the object of creating a town that would capture the trade of Truro, a little further upstream. In this context no one should be surprised to learn that Truro itself has many of the characteristic signs of an earlier plantation nor to find Penryn itself complaining of being strangled in its turn by a project further downstream.

The project is an interesting one, being one of the few in England in the 300 years following the Black Death. It produced Falmouth (originally Pennycomequick or Smitheck) and the projector was Sir Peter Killigrew. He procured the removal of the market from Penryn and the transfer of the customs house followed.[36] The petition against the town sent to Charles II in 1660 (the source of our

---

[34] *Rot. Parl.*, i, p. 26; *N.C.H.*, viii, pp. 284–315.
[35] *Feodarium prioratus Dunelmensis*, ed. W. Greenwall (Surtees Soc., lviii (1872)), p. 119 fn., *Three early Assize Rolls for Northumberland*, ed. W. Page (Surtees Soc., lxxxviii (1891)), p. 81.
[36] *Cal. State Papers Domestic, 1660–1*, p. 387.

information about the origins of Falmouth) attempted to discredit the project by associating it with Oliver Cromwell: but Falmouth stands.

A new plantation might be blocked, cursed, excommunicated, sued, besieged or fought with that potent weapon, imitation. It could also be harmed by the simple use of delaying tactics. The delays which local jealousies could cause are well illustrated by the foundation of Sauveterre de Guyenne (Gironde). M. Trabut-Cussac's researches[37] have shown that the ground chosen for the town and the surrounding gardens was in the hands of three separate owners, Jordan de Puch, the widow of the lord of Bergerac, and the abbot of Blasimont. The first two had already quarrelled, and de Puch probably hoped to get the king on his side by offering the site to Edward's agent, the abbot of St. Ferme. In 1281 the abbot of Blasimont joined in a *paréage*, which was to be void if the bastide was not built by November and endowed with all the franchises of Monségur. Petitions against the town began to flow to London, and in November Edward ordered a halt to construction until he had time to hear the complaints in detail. At the end of the month two envoys were sent to Gascony to make enquiries, and in February and March 1282 they took evidence at Bordeaux. It occupies fifteen feet of a parchment roll.

In July the king ordered the work to proceed, and in 1283 (two years later than the original intention) the town charter was sealed. Yet all was not calm; the charter gave six fairs a year, but this was unwelcome news to local towns and when, in 1284, the sergeants of Sauveterre and their heralds went to publicise these fairs at Sallebruneau fair, the heralds were attacked, their trumpets broken and the three sergeants wounded.

In the course of the evidence offered at Bordeaux in 1282 the local hopes for the town found succinct expression. The townsmen who had already begun to settle there said:

> The site of your bastide is good and convenient . . . and with time it will abound in land, meadows and vines; it will produce almost every commodity.

The abbot of Blasimont said:

> We firmly hope that the place will be populous and fertile, and at least that it will not be stifled by its neighbours who are your subjects.

[37] J.-P. Trabut-Cussac, "La Fondation de Sauveterre-de-Guyenne", *Rev. Hist. de Bordeaux*, ii (1953), pp. 181–217.

Sauveterre was not stifled, as its weekly market still testifies, but it had been delayed and harrassed by local feuds.

III

Rivalry between seigneurs has been shown as one of the motives that gave added force to town plantation. The rivalry sometimes went further than a general wish to plant towns in the economic catchment area of existing towns, and rivals may sometimes be found so close that the symbols on any small-scale distribution map jostle each other like stalls in a crowded market place. From the ramparts of La Parade, founded in 1267, one can see the church of Granges sur Lot down by the riverside. These economic rivals had the same royal founder, and from Granges it is no great step to Edward II's bastide of Felton (or Le Temple de Breuil). The same air photograph that shows the chequers of Castelsagrat, founded 1255–62, peeps also into the streets of Montjoi, founded in 1255. Baa (1287) and Camparian, founded in the same year, were placed so near each other in the forest of Bordeaux that in some documents it is difficult to discern whether they were the same place.

Outside the walls of the old walled town of Totnes two suburban rivals were projected, one across the bridge on the Pomeroy estates at Bridgetown Pomeroy and one across the ford on the Exeter road at North Ford. The parish of St. Stephen's, the first Cornish parish across the Tamar from Devonport, contains two planted towns, Saltash (c. 1200) and New Trematon (1066–86). East and West Looe were boroughs in different parishes and engineered by different lords, yet separated only by waters of the harbour and river that gave life (by 1201) to both projects. Kingsbridge (Devon) is very near Dodbrook (as Fig. 45 shows). The Yorkshire shore of the Humber estuary supported three plantations, at Ravenserodd, Hedon and Wyke; and the waters of the Solent nourished Newport, Newtown, Yarmouth, Portsmouth and New Lymington, and if this catchment area were extended a little as far as Selsey Bill and Poole Harbour, it would bring in three more plantations (Fig. 43).

The most striking confrontation of two rival plantations is to be found in Devon, in the two boroughs that now coalesce in Newton Abbot. The little river Lemon that once separated them is now hidden in a culvert, and on market-days the crowds pass indifferently from the soil of one borough to the other. But it was not always so. At the end of the twelfth century Torre Abbey received the manor of Wolborough from its founder and benefactor, William Brewer. To the north-east of Wolborough village and at the foot of the hill was the point where the Exeter–Totnes road crossed the Lemon. The river was here the boundary of manor and parish, and the town that Torre Abbey planted

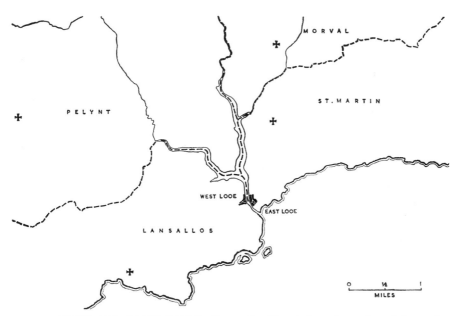

FIG. 44. EAST AND WEST LOOE, Cornwall. Two independent planted boroughs faced each other across the estuary. The parish churches of the older settlements are shown.

was sometimes called Schireborne Newton (scire = boundary; borne = stream). It first appears as *Nova Villa*, in a document of c. 1200, and was later called Newton Abbot after its founder.

On the other side of the stream, facing *Nova Villa*, was the manor of Highweek or Teignwick. In 1246 the lord of the manor obtained a grant of a market and another grant authorising him to create burgages and let them to anyone he pleased. This was *la Novelevile in parte pertinente ad manerium de Teyngewyk*. It did not acquire the name of its founder, a Theobald de Englechevill, but that of a later seigneur.

245

It was known as Newton Bushel before the borough and name were both absorbed into the neighbouring Newton Abbot.[38]

In Gascony, near the junction of the Lot and the Garonne, is the

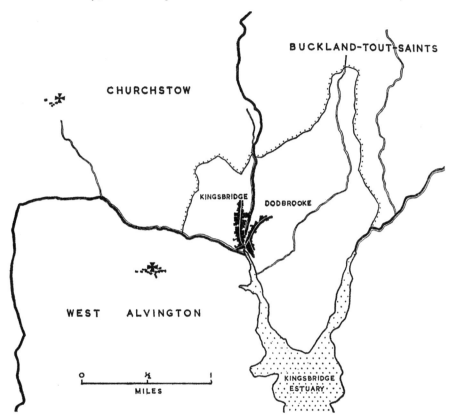

FIG. 45. DODBROOKE AND KINGSBRIDGE, Devon. Two adjoining and independent plantations. The parishes are indicated from which the boroughs' territory was taken.

little town of Aiguillon. Arthur Young was here in the year before the French Revolution:

> I viewed the chateau of the Duc which being in the town is badly situated according to rural ideas, but a town is ever an accompaniment of a chateau in France.[39]

[38] References to the sources for the Newtons are given in the Gazetteer.
[39] Arthur Young, *Travels in France*, ed. M. Betham-Edwards (1889), p. 65.

246

Although Arthur Young correctly deduced that the lord of Lunac had planted a town alongside the chateau, he did not know that a partner in the adventure was Edward I of England and that the bastide (founded in 1296) was sometimes called St. Edward as a compliment to its royal progenitor; nor did he know that the little town was a coalescence of two towns, like Newton Abbot, the second (or lower) town being a creation of a rival lord, the seigneur of Fossat.

In south Wales, the two foundations of Newcastle Emlyn and Adpar were almost as closely set, although the river that divided them is now the county boundary of Carmarthen and Cardiganshire. Newcastle was a royal foundation (1303) but Adpar a borough of the bishops of St. David's. Two boroughs also faced each other across the river at Kidwelly.

So long as the founder of a new town had no personal interest in some other town nearby he would be indifferent to any protests that the old-established towns made about "threats to our livelihood". Indeed the threat would not have been unwelcome if there was rivalry already between local seigneurs or between king and seigneur. The greatest number of towns in England belonging to a single lord were those of the Crown on royal demesnes and they were well scattered over the country-side. Here, if anywhere, the threat of the New to the Old would have been greatest, but the Crown does not seem to have been much deterred by any consideration for its own older towns. Exactly the same absence of scruple when tempted by new income from a new enfranchisement is seen in the readiness of English kings, especially in the thirteenth century, to grant markets and fairs to villages without any real guarantee that the trade of existing markets and fairs would not be encroached upon.

IV

Although events proved that in general there was room for both new and old, there were a few places that were suffocated by the proximity of neighbours, and their fate no doubt lent apprehension to other towns when projects for new plantations were disclosed. After all, New Salisbury had left Old Sarum high and dry; the new bridge and the new borough of Boroughbridge had taken the main road to Scotland away from the gates of Aldborough, and the traffic from its market place; Writtle had suffered from the new bridge and new town at Chelmsford; Porchester was never the same after Portsmouth had been founded; and the belief that a cunningly placed new foundation could bring an old city to its knees is nicely illustrated by an episode in the Albigensian wars as set out in one of the *Chansons*.[40]

In 1217 the city of Toulouse was being unsuccessfully besieged, and the captains of the encircling force were called together for a conference. Various strategies were suggested for the capture of this Troy, all but one of them military. One proposal, however, was more in the tradition of the cunning of Ulysses and the wooden horse. It was suggested that a much less expensive way of destroying Toulouse would be to found a new city a few miles further down the Garonne, leaving the merchants of Old Toulouse without trade and its craftsmen idle and starving. The plan was not put into effect, but nearby at Carcassonne the new town founded in 1247 on the plain below the old *bourg* did succeed in drawing from the hill-top all trade except that of tourism. As a guide book confesses,

> nowadays the living part is the lower town that is broadly spread out in its alluvial plain. Today the higher town is no more than a museum; the crowds of visitors give it momentarily a fleeting animation, but the life of older times has withdrawn from it for ever.[41]

The abandoned site of an older settlement near a new town cannot always, however, be taken as evidence that a war of attrition has taken place between rivals and neighbours. An old-established settlement, shrunken to a village in the shadow of its newer neighbour, does not always indicate an economic battlefield strewn with its dead, for there are a few cases where a new town was deliberately placed in a position more accessible for commerce, cheerfully abandoning the protective walls of some older, hill-top site. Réalmont, founded in 1311, replaced the fortified village of Gardenat (Gardemont or Almont) 3 kilometres to the north-west. The railway and the N.20 have also chosen the lower course by the river. Commerce has not made of Réalmont a flourishing City of the Plain, but from its quiet market place it is possible to see in the distance on a hill-top the two farms that remain as the sole occupants of the Gallo-Roman and early medieval sites.

The flight from Old Sarum to New Salisbury displays a similar wish to abandon an upland site for a lowland, and a similar attraction to a riverside site is seen at Okehampton where the Norman borough is

---

[40] *La Chanson de la Croisade Albigoise*, ed. E. Martin-Chabot (Paris, 1961), iii, p. 33.
[41] P. Morel, *The Sights of Carcassonne* (Paris, 1951), p. 8; see also J. Poux, *La Cité de Carcassonne* (Toulouse, 1931), ii, pt. 1, p. 127.

squeezed between the branches of the East and West Okement rivers, leaving the church of the Anglo-Saxon village isolated in the fields on the hillside above. In general, sites of this kind represent a re-assessment of the ideal situation for a town. The dead or dying town is here not an unsuccessful rival nor a neighbour, but an earlier version of the present town, sited to meet circumstances that did not continue to suit it. The misfortunes of these displaced or supplanted towns are considered more fully in Chapter 10.

There was a worse fate for a town than to have angry and powerful neighbours and rivals, dangerous as these could be. A plantation might fail to encourage economic development of the surrounding area and have no neighbours at all. As economic units, towns depended on social and economic intercourse with other settlements, even other towns. The small market town needed to have flourishing agricultural villages to bring their goods to its market but it also needed larger towns where in turn it could buy the specialities that it was too small to shelter. More: its economic life hinged on the existence of other towns that were ports, and even if rivals groaned when a new port was founded, the inland towns had every reason to rejoice. From the river- and sea-ports went the goods of the inland towns; through these ports came the greater merchants of the cities to do business with the lesser traders of the provincial towns.

In another situation towns could find their trade increased by a new foundation that was successful, for successful towns created or diverted inland trade-routes, unintentionally bringing travellers and traders past unfamiliar gates. Downton (Wilts.), on the west bank of the Avon, profited from the traffic that was diverted when the new bridges were built into New Sarum. Both Alcester and Stratford on Avon have good claims to be regarded as planted towns. The roads to them from the north came past the castle of Beaudesert, and the lord of Beaudesert successfully planted Henley in Arden at his castle gate. Who can say that without Stratford and Alcester there would have been much activity at Henley?

It was natural that there was resentment, violence, litigation and the language of warfare in the rivalries of old towns and new, neighbour and neighbour. Not only in medieval, but in later centuries also, trade was widely envisaged as being limited in amount, and simply shared out among combatants: if one town had more people in its market place, then someone else must be having fewer. Even the clearest natural advantage—in this view—would not survive long unless it was backed up by privilege, by some grant that gave a monopoly or a quasi-monopoly locally: just as in conventional warfare a town with a good site for natural defence would need to augment Nature with walls, gates and the accoutrements of a fortified town. In commerce a town needed market- and fair-charters and might hope also for the crowning defence afforded by a borough charter that included the maximum number of privileges and exemptions.

In this combative view neighbours were always rivals, whatever the true economic situation. Neighbours were seen as competitive even when they were in fact complementary. Resentment and complaint were the natural reaction to any novelty: and yet despite hostility the newcomers came. The hard truth was that the old towns could not hope for redress so long as Authority was prepared to welcome the newcomers. Among territorial lords, from kings downward, there was no one whose loyalty to old-established towns on the demesne was so strong that he set his face against planting newcomers to be neighbours and rivals.

This chapter has been concerned with the reaction of existing towns (some old and some quite new) to the arrival of further newcomers as their neighbours. The evidence has been drawn largely from the years when the new ventures were being promoted. What of the final array of towns? What peaks of success had been achieved by the newcomers? Where did newcomers actually succeed in winning a place for themselves alongside their neighbours? These questions are the subject of the next chapter.

CHAPTER NINE

The Ladder of Success

"Mere numbers are important. I am persuaded that we hurry the history both of our villages and of our towns because we fill them too full."

F. W. Maitland, *Township and Borough* (1891) p. 24.

"The greatness of a Citty is sayd to be not the largeness of the scite or the circuit of the walles; but the multitude and number of the inhabitants and their power."

G. Botero, *Of the Greatness of Cities,* trans. R. Peterson, (1606) p. 1.

I

FOR a planted town its survival was a test of its ability to succeed. In competition with old-established neighbours there were some projects that failed, and their misfortunes form the subject of the next chapter. In this chapter the surviving towns are examined more closely in order to see whether there is any measure of individual success. Data concerning the wealth and population of the planted towns are considered in relation to both kinds of competitor that the new towns had to face: their old-established neighbours and the other newcomers.

In our own day the towns that were first planted in the Middle Ages have developed a wide range of size and prosperity. Of England's 53 county boroughs, 9 appear in our Gazetteer; of England's 285 non-county boroughs, 30 appear. Of the 32 boroughs of modern Wales, 26 were planted in the Middle Ages. At the one extreme are prosperous towns like Liverpool, Portsmouth, Cardiff, Libourne and Villeneuve sur Lot: at the other are Bishop's Castle (with the smallest population of any English borough in the Census of 1961), Newtown, I.O.W., and Roquepine (shrunk to a few houses), Bere and Warenmouth (where nothing remains at all), and Ravenserodd long since drowned in the Humber.

But nearly five centuries have passed since the end of the Middle Ages, and one would expect some ebbs and flows of local fortunes during five centuries of economic change. Present fortunes need not reflect medieval fortunes, and present prosperity may owe nothing to medieval conditions. Is there any way by which the standing of these planted towns in the medieval economy can be assessed? An ideal vantage point would be somewhere near the beginning of the fourteenth century. We need to go back beyond the industrial revolution; and back beyond the great plagues of the mid-fourteenth century, and the general contraction in population that brought an end to the business of medieval town plantation.

Three planted towns, it will be remembered, were considered important enough to appear on the Hereford world map of c. 1290 when they were less than a generation old, and nine others were marked on Matthew Paris' map of Great Britain drawn half a century earlier.[1] These were personal assessments; are there other assessments of a new town's importance?

A town's own inhabitants assessed its stature in different words, depending on the occasion. If a privilege was being sought, the language would glow with praise and self-congratulation in the hope that nothing would succeed like loyalty, success and the clink of gold. If some exemption from taxation was in question, the language would be melancholy and nostalgic, sighing for the good old days when a town could afford a loyal tribute. Neither language proves very helpful in assessing the real progress of a town.

If quantitative measures are required, the limit is set by the availability of documents. The following pages attempt to use documentary information to assess the relative standing of the planted towns, and a number of sources will be discussed that offer different opportunities of making an assessment.

There were occasions when the royal administration had to make a selection of the most important towns of the kingdom. For example, on five occasions between 1317 and 1326 Edward II had cause to address important messages, orders and requests for aid to the magnates and towns of his Gascon dominion. The Gascon Rolls in the royal Chancery preserve a copy of the messages and a note of the persons and

---

[1] G. R. Crone, *Royal Geog. Soc. Reproductions of Early Maps* vii (1961), nos. 3 and 4. The nine were: Boroughbridge, Dunstable, Pontefract, Newcastle on Tyne, Orford, Carmarthen, Bridgnorth, New Windsor and New Salisbury.

places to whom they were to be sent. Table IX.1 shows that the bastides formed a high proportion of the towns that were considered worth addressing.

In England the writs summoning town representatives to a Parliament are another means of identifying the towns that were considered important enough to be consulted at that moment. In early Parliaments, when there were no traditions to draw upon, the choice is particularly significant. Of the towns that received writs of summons it is natural that the majority were old-established boroughs, county

TABLE IX.1

PROPORTION OF BASTIDES AMONG IMPORTANT
GASCON TOWNS, 1317–26

Year	Total number of Gascon towns addressed	Number of bastides addressed
1317	29	23 (79% of total)
1318	48	31 (75%)
1318	46	27 (59%)
1324	65	28 (43%)
1326	27	12 (44%)

Sources: 1317   C47/27/14
          1318   C61/32 m. 13
          1318   C61/32 m. 14
          1324   C61/35 m. 6
          1326   C61/38 m. 3d

towns and places with large merchant communities: but in addition to these, representatives of planted towns could have been observed in Parliament. King's Lynn was one of the twenty-seven towns represented in Henry III's Parliament of 1268. It is true that Lynn was then nearly two hundred years old, its one-time newness probably quite forgotten. Yet the Parliament of 1275 had members for Uxbridge and Stratford upon Avon, which were much newer, and among the 114 towns with members in the Parliament of 1285 were Devizes, Downton, Hedon, New Malton, Pontefract, New Alresford, Overton (Hants.), Portsmouth, Newport, I.O.W., and Yarmouth, I.O.W. Liverpool, Tregoney and New Salisbury were represented at all seven of Edward I's Parliaments, and Launceston probably had the same distinction.

Newcastle on Tyne, Appleby, King's Lynn and Portsmouth were absentees once or twice only.[2]

Some of the greatest planted towns in England and Wales were ports. One indication of their importance is that five of them were chosen as head ports for the Customs collections. These head ports were responsible for overlooking a stretch of coast on either side of them, England and Wales being completely covered by about twenty-three head ports. Six planted towns appear regularly in the records as head ports between 1275 and 1400: Boston, Hull, Lynn, Melcombe Regis, Weymouth and Newcastle on Tyne. In the same period Liverpool, New Shoreham and Haverford West appear on occasions. For a brief decade of glory (1368–78) the newly planted Queenborough (Kent) reigned as a head port supplanting Sandwich.[3]

It would not be very useful, except as a measure of ambition, to compare the areas contained within the walls or bounds of different towns. Even towns with old roots such as London and Leicester had intramural precincts that were densely built upon, and other precincts that were largely orchards and gardens. In the closely packed streets of York near the market places there were densities of between 106 and 120 persons per acre in 1377 (and the plagues were then only just ended): but other parishes within the walls of York then had densities of only three persons per acre and the average for the whole city was six persons per acre.[4]

In the new towns there must have been equivalent differences of density, as the study of New Winchelsea (p. 25) has shown, and in the new towns there was a greater chance than in an old town that the ambit of the walls would be thrown too optimistically. In an old town the walls came when the town was well developed, and they were tailored to fit. In a new town the area assigned to the chequers was essentially speculative, and empty building-plots were not unknown. A better indication of the comparative size of new towns, therefore, is the number of burgages that paid rent at any particular period. These data have to be derived from scattered sources, for there was no occasion when all the boroughs in the kingdom had to make a statistical return of their burgages. For the royal boroughs there is a good

[2] M. McKisack, *The Parliamentary Representation of the English Boroughs during the Middle Ages* (1932), pp. 1–23.
[3] E. M. Carus-Wilson and O. Coleman, *England's Export Trade, 1275–1547* (1963), pp. 175–193.
[4] Densities calculated from E179/217/13.

chance that the number of burgages will be stated in some rental of the town preserved among the Exchequer records; for the towns on the territories of bishops the burgages may sometimes be stated in the rentals compiled by Exchequer officials when the see was vacant and the temporalities of the see in the king's hands; for the boroughs on the territories of lay seigneurs the most frequent source of information occurs in the inquisitions *post mortem*. Extents or surveys of the possessions of deceased tenants-in-chief survive from the reign of Henry III onwards. A borough could be a valuable part of an estate, so that its income was stated alongside that of the rural manors. The exact number of occupied and empty burgages was often stated. Table IX.2

TABLE IX.2

NUMBER OF BURGAGES IN SOME WELSH BOROUGHS

	Number of burgage plots	*Year*
Abergavenny	239	1255
Abergwili	25	1326
Aberystwyth	157	1308
Adpar	96	1326
Bala	53	1311
Beaumaris	154$\frac{1}{4}$	1317
Caerphilly	116	1381
Cardiff	421	1296
Cardigan	172	1308
Carmarthen	281	1300
Carnarvon	63	1309
Cefnllys	20	1332
Chepstow	308	1306
Conway	124	1312
Cowbridge	276$\frac{3}{4}$	1306
Criccieth	25$\frac{5}{6}$	1351
Denbigh	120	1311
Dryslwyn	48	1360
Dynevor, Old	11	1301
Harlech	29$\frac{1}{4}$	1312
Haverford West	360	1324
Hay	183$\frac{3}{4}$	1298
Holt	204$\frac{1}{2}$	1315

TABLE IX.2.—(contd.)

	Number of burgage plots	Year
Kenfig	142	1281
Knighton	162⅓	1304
Lampeter	26	1317
Llandilo	41	1326
Llandovery	81	1317
Llanfyllin	30	1309
Llanidloes	66	1309
Llantrissant	198	1316
Llawhaden	174½	1326
Neath	128	1306
Nevin	c. 50	t.Ed.I.
Newcastle Emlyn	62	1316
New Moat	89	1326
Newport (Mon.)	256	1296
Newport (Pem.)	?46	1324
Newtown (Dynevor)	44	1308
Painscastle	50	1309
Pembroke	227½	c. 1300
Pwllheli	20	t.Ed.I.
Radnor, New	262½	1304
Talgarth	73	1309
Tenby	247	1307
Trellech	271	1306
	(?378)	(1298)
Usk	300	1306
Welshpool	225	1322

Note: Burgesses *de vento* are excluded: Carmarthen had 87, Cardigan 53 and Tenby 20 in the extents cited.

brings together the information for the Welsh boroughs, and it will be seen that the towns ranged in size from Cardiff's 421 burgages (in 1296) to the twenty in Cefnllys in 1332 and the eleven in Dynevor in 1301. Where it is known, the number of burgages in each English plantation is given in the county Gazetteers of Chapters 15–16.

It would be useful to know the number of burgages in each English borough, planted and organic, but no one has yet essayed the task of reading all the extents. The printed Calendars of Inquisitions Post Mortem do not always give this figure. One can, however, compare the 176 burgages in the new town of Chipping Sodbury in 1307 with other boroughs of the same lord in that year:[5] the organic borough of Fairford had 68 burgages, Thornbury had 100 and Tewkesbury had 145⅚ burgages. In 1304 the planted New Radnor had 262½ burgages when Cleobury Mortimer had 102¾ and Wigmore 140¼.

Another occasion when towns and boroughs were singled out from among the vills was the visit of the itinerant justices. On the Assize Rolls the boroughs often have separate entries with a distinct *burgus* rubric. Towns were represented by separate juries and the list of jurors in an Assize Roll is sometimes the earliest authentic record of a town's existence.

Penryn, Camelford and Mitchell appear in the Cornish Assize Roll of 1284 though not in that of 1201; but in 1201 Lostwithiel, Saltash, East and West Looe and Tregoney can be seen as already founded. Many small Devon boroughs first appear in the Assize Roll of 1238, and Durham boroughs in 1242–43. Stockbridge and New Alresford (Hants.) appear in the roll of 1236, not long after their foundation. New Thame (Oxon.) is not mentioned in the Roll of 1241 but appears in that of 1247. In Somerset the Roll of 1235 identifies the mysterious and short-lived borough *Caput Montis* (or *Chef del Mont*). These towns had made their mark and were already being treated differently from the mere vills and hundreds of the countryside.[6] Occasionally, even though a new town had not yet gained a separate jury, its existence may be testified by a case reported in the main body of the roll and involving some market offence. Thus an entry in the Devon Assize Roll for 1244 links two planted towns. A prosecution of offenders for illegal sale of cloth and wine in the borough of Plympton Erle reveals that the seller came from the Cornish borough of Tregoney.[7]

II

Another method, perhaps the most satisfactory, of judging the relative prosperity of a medieval town is to study its assessments for tax

---

[5] C133/28. For other towns see Tables III.1 and 2, above.
[6] J.I. 1/1171 and 1/113; 1/174; 1/775; 1/695 and 700; *Somersetshire Pleas*, ed. C. E. H. Chadwyck-Healey (Som. Rec. Soc. xi, 1897), pp. 28 and 52. Mr. C. A. F. Meekings of the P.R.O. kindly placed at my disposal his manuscript key to the contents of the medieval Assize Rolls, Class J.I. 1.
[7] J.I. 1/175 m. 41d.

purposes. The basis of assessment before 1334 frequently changed with each collection, and the absolute sums are not important except for comparison with rural manors. Within any single collection, a comparison of sums paid by different towns does say something significant about the towns as they appeared to their contemporaries, especially when the taxes were assessed by taxors or jurors and not arbitrarily imposed by the Exchequer.

In the twelfth century there is scattered information about the aids paid by boroughs to Henry I and II.[8] Between 1128 and 1186 there were four planted towns among the aid-giving boroughs: Bridgnorth, Newcastle on Tyne, Old Salisbury and Newport (Salop.). The first three of these towns date from the early years of the Norman Conquest and were thus about fifty years old when the record shows them paying aids, but Newport could have been only about a generation old when it appeared among the aids in the Pipe Roll of 1159.

The intensive taxation of the laity through an assessment of their personal wealth began in the late thirteenth century, and from this period the records of collection begin to survive more thoroughly. The assessments attempted to cover all the laity who possessed substantial personal possessions other than land, and the wealth of townsmen fell into this category. These assessments provide information about the taxable wealth of the laity in a very large number of towns, far exceeding the number of towns whose tallage or aid was recorded on the Pipe Rolls.

According to Willard there were 219 separate towns that were treated as boroughs for taxation purposes at one time or another between 1294 and 1336; in fact he counted Saltash and Ash as separate places, when they were one, and he omitted eight places that were ranked as boroughs in 1316. A total of 226 may therefore be accepted as the sum of all the most important English towns except in Cheshire and County Durham, where no tax was assessed, and the Cinque Ports that were also exempt. These exempt areas cannot have contained more than a dozen towns, making an approximate total of 240 towns for the kingdom.[9]

Forty-six of these towns appear as plantations in the Gazetteer of Chapter 15, being about one-fifth of the total of taxed boroughs. This

[8] F. W. Maitland, *Domesday Book and Beyond* (1897), p. 175.
[9] J. F. Willard, "Taxation Boroughs and Parliamentary Boroughs, 1294–1336", in J. G. Edwards, ed., *Historical Essays in Honour of James Tait* (1933), pp. 417–435.

is an impressive contribution to the total stock of important towns but it was not the end of the achievement. The decision to call a place a "borough" for taxation purposes (involving a higher rate of tax than for a non-borough) always had an arbitrary element, as Willard showed, and there were towns which were not taxed as boroughs. In 1334 sixty-six planted towns were not treated by the collectors as "taxation boroughs" but taxed as ordinary vills.

The assessments of 1334 are important because in that year the Exchequer made a deliberate effort to fix a quota for each village and town in the kingdom that would fairly reflect the wealth of the laity in each place.[10] The extreme northern counties were omitted through border troubles, but within a decade their communities had been assessed on the same basis; only the Palatines of Chester and Durham remain, in company with the barons of the Cinque Ports, outside this great record of local assessments; Cumberland was also re-assessed more than once but on the same basis as the other counties in 1334.[11]

These assessments enable most of the rungs in the ladder of success to be identified. The reason why we cannot identify every rung (apart from the exempt jurisdictions) is that places lying near each other or forming part of one manor could occasionally be assessed to one total sum. Thus part of the planted town of Stony Stratford was assessed with the village of Calverton at £5 and part with Wolverton at £6, with no means of knowing what fraction of this £11 came from the mother villages and what from their daughter town.[12] Newton Abbot was reckoned for tax purposes with Wolborough, the parish in which it had been planted, but there are no means of knowing how much of the 15s. was paid by the burgesses of Newton and how much by the villagers of Wolborough.[13] Of the 172 plantations in England, assessments survive for 91 places separately and for 21 places joined to others. Of all plantations in the Gazetteer, 65% are thus covered; among the remaining 35% are 13 towns in the exempt jurisdictions (8%), 23 very small towns in Cornwall, Devon and Northumberland (14%), and the abortive plantations (Table IX.3).

The ladder of success for 1334 is set out in Table IX.4. For comparison the assessments of organic towns of comparable size appear in

[10] J. F. Willard, *Parliamentary Taxes on Personal Property, 1290–1334* (1934).
[11] E179/90/4 (1336); E179/90/5 (1337–38); E179/90/7 (1338–39) all show diminishing sums, and by 1352 (E179/90/16) Cumberland was paying only half of the sums of 1336: ex. inf. Dr. R. E. Glasscock.
[12] E179/77/4. [13] E179/95/10.

TABLE IX.3

NEW TOWNS WITH SURVIVING TAX ASSESSMENTS, 1334

County	Number of new towns	No. of new towns with no tax assessments known	No. with separate tax assessments	With tax assessments but not separately
BEDS.	1	—	1	—
BERKS.	4	1	3	—
BUCKS.	2	1	—	1
CHES.	1	1	—	—
CORNWALL	19	8	11	—
CUMBERLAND	4	3	1	—
DERBY	1	—	1	—
DEVON	17	9	6	2
DORSET	6	1	5	—
DURHAM	4	4	—	—
ESSEX	4	1	3	—
GLOS.	3	1	1	1
HANTS.	11	1	9	1
HEREF.	3	1	—	2
HERTS.	6	2	4	—
HUNTS.	3	1	1	1
KENT	3	3	—	—
LANCS.	3	1	2	—
LEICS.	3	—	2	1
LINCS.	4	1	2	1
MIDDX.	1	—	—	1
NORFOLK	3	—	3	—
NORTHANTS.	1	—	—	1
NORTHUMB.	10	6	4	—
OXON.	5	—	4	1
SALOP.	8	3	1	4
SOM.	4	2	2	—
STAFFS.	2	—	2	—
SUFFOLK	1	—	—	1
SURREY	2	1	1	—
SUSSEX	9	5	4	—
WARW.	3	—	3	—
WESTM.	3	—	1	2
WILTS.	3	—	3	—
YORKS.	15	3	11	1
Total	*172*	*60*	*91*	*21*

TABLE IX.4

TAXATION ASSESSMENTS OF TOWNS, 1334

Planted towns	Shillings	Some non-planted towns for comparison	Shillings
Newcastle on Tyne*	1780		
Boston	1467	Lincoln*	1333
New Salisbury*	1000	Shrewsbury*	1067
King's Lynn*	666	Southampton*	673
Kingston upon Hull*	443	Derby*	400
Pontefract	360		
St. Albans	354		
New Sleaford	321		
Ludlow	320		
Dunstable	282	Bodmin*	266
Tickhill	250		
New Brackley	220		
Hungerford	201		
Ravenserodd*	200		
New Thame	183	Carlisle*	180
Baldock	177		
Stratford on Avon*	175		
Portsmouth*	168		
Truro*	161		
New Shoreham*	160	Huntingdon	160
New Windsor*	153		

Planted towns	Shillings	Planted towns	Shillings
Egremont	150	Sherborne Newland	90
Newport (I.O.W.)	145	Weymouth*	87
Newcastle under Lyme*	144	Market Harborough*	85
St. Ives (Hunts.)	142	Arundel*	85
Hedon*	139	Henley on Thames*	80
Watford	135		
Melcombe Regis*	127		
Battle	126	Devizes*	80
New Lymington	123	Overton (Hants.)	73
New Buckenham	123	Midhurst*	73
		Downton*	73
Lostwithiel*	116	Leeds (Yorks)	73
Richmond (Yorks.)	100	Royston	70
Harwich	97	New Malton	67
Chelmsford	92	New Alresford*	66
Wokingham	90	Northleach	59

TABLE IX.4—(contd.)

Planted towns	Shillings	Planted towns	Shillings
Plympton Erle*	58	Saltash*	27
Henley in Arden*	55	Colyford	25
Poole	54	Penryn*	27
Reigate*	54	Mitford	24
New Woodstock*	51	Newborough (Staffs.)	23
Stockbridge	50	Tregoney*	23
Kingsbridge	47	Okehampton*	22
Clitheroe	47	Felton	20
Buntingford	44	East Looe*	20
Bretford	41		
Liverpool	40		
Mountsorrel*	40	Yarmouth (I.O.W.)	19
Appleby*	40	Nether Weare*	19
Skipsea	40	Pleshey	18
Boroughbridge*	40	Newtown (Burghclere)	17
Honiton*	38	Old Sarum*	17
Launceston*	38	Newport (Devon)	13
Petersfield	34	Stoford*	11
Airmyn	33	Grampound*	10
Corfe*	29	Boscastle*	8
		Camelford*	6
Hindon	29	Mitchell*	5

Note: The asterisks indicate the towns that were assessed at the rate of one-tenth; in this Table their quotas have been adjusted proportionately to aline with those assessed at one-fifteenth of their wealth. Sums are to the nearest shilling.

italics on the right.[14] Lincoln and Shrewsbury's assessments were about the same size as the plantations of Boston and New Salisbury; while Derby's was near that of Hull. Larger than Newcastle's—the wealthiest of the plantations—were the assessments of York (2,160s.), Bristol (1,933s.) and London (14,667s.). These high rungs of the national ladder are out of sight in the Table.

If all towns in the kingdom are considered together, Newcastle ranked fourth, Boston eleventh, Lynn twelfth, Hull twenty-fifth and Pontefract thirty-fifth. Of the forty-two places in the kingdom that paid over £20 tax, five were plantations.

[14] The sums for Midland and south-eastern counties are taken from the tables in the Appendix (Vol. 2) of R. E. Glasscock, *The Distribution of Lay Wealth in S.E. England in the Early Fourteenth Century* (London Ph.D. thesis, 1963); the sums from other counties are taken from the county rolls in E. 179. The sums for the largest towns in 1334 are conveniently set out in W. G. Hoskins, *Local History in England* (1959), p. 176, but with the places paying at one-tenth not differentiated as in Table IX.4 here.

When this achievement of the planted towns has been acknowledged it still remains true that the majority of them achieved much meaner status. If the four great towns paying more than £25 are excluded, the average assessment of the plantations was 59s. and this was no more than the assessment of an average village of Wiltshire and Gloucestershire in the same year. Table IX.5 shows that one-third of the planted towns in Table IX.4 paid less than 40s. and 14% paid less than 20s. Evidently Newcastle, Boston, Salisbury and Lynn had a large number of poor relations, and it must be remembered that the eighty-one plantations for which there are no separate tax assessments are likely to have been petty boroughs on the lower rungs of the ladder.

TABLE IX.5

ASSESSMENTS OF NINETY-ONE PLANTATIONS WITH
SURVIVING TAX DATA FROM 1334

Size of Tax assessment s.	Proportion of towns %	Size of Tax assessment s.	Proportion of towns %
1– 20	14	121–140	7
21– 40	20	141–160	7
41– 60	12	161–180	3
61– 80	11	181–200	2
81–100	9	over 200	14
101–120	1		

Can any recipe for success be detected in Table IX.4? With Newcastle, Boston, Lynn and Hull at the head of the list, it might seem at first glance that ports were at an advantage, but the first ten include Salisbury, Pontefract, St. Albans, New Sleaford, Ludlow and Dunstable, plantations whose fortunes were certainly not based on their harbours; four of the six towns named would hardly ever have seen as much as a river barge.

Nor was any particular locality favoured. No county has two towns in the first ten (taking Yorks. E.R. and W.R. as separate counties). Nor was royal favour essential for the greatest success. Only one of the first ten towns was a royal foundation: despite its name, King's Lynn was a bishop's plantation. The most significant contribution to success seems to have been an early arrival.

Table IX.6 displays the foundation dates of the towns in the previous

TABLE IX.6

FOUNDATION DATES OF NINETY ENGLISH PLANTATIONS, ARRANGED
BY SIZE OF THEIR ASSESSMENT IN 1334. (TABLE IX.4)

	Before 1066	*1066–1154*	*1155–1200*	*1201–1300*	*After 1300*
First ten by size	1	7	0	2	0
Second ten by size	0	5	4	1	0
Third ten by size	0	6	3	1	0
Fourth ten by size	0	3	3	4	0
Fifth ten by size	0	1	4	5	0
Sixth ten by size	0	1	5	4	0
Seventh ten by size	0	3	2	5	0
Eighth ten by size	0	3	2	5	0
Ninth ten by size	0	1	2	7	0
Total	1 (1%)	30 (33%)	25 (28%)	34 (38%)	0

Tables. The ten towns at the head of the ladder show the importance of an early start most strikingly, and the bias towards a foundation earlier than 1154 persists in the next two divisions. Conversely, the smaller foundations are shown to be drawn largely from the period after 1154, indeed after 1200.

There are no similar figures for Wales in 1334, but if the number of burgages set out in Table IX.2 is accepted as an indication of prosperity, it is plain that the earliest were the most prosperous and the latest the least prosperous. Eight of the ten largest towns were planted before 1165; the dates of the other two are uncertain and may fall within the same period. On the other hand, none of the ten smallest towns was founded until after 1240.

The rewards of being early-established are also demonstrated by Table IX.7, an analysis of those Gascon towns whose order of wealthiness is established in Table IX.9. Nine of the ten wealthiest bastides were those in the Agenais, founded by the French count of Toulouse before the district became English; nine of the ten least wealthy were founded after 1270. When neighbouring towns continued to be planted in each successive decade, the importance of establishing one's position at an early date needs no underlining.

If the advantages of being first in the field were enjoyed by the earliest plantations, it is not surprising that the general performance of the organic towns was better than that of the plantations, for were not

TABLE IX.7

FOUNDATION DATES OF THIRTY GASCON BASTIDES ARRANGED BY
SIZE OF THEIR TAX ASSESSMENTS IN 1315–16.   (TABLE IX.9)

	Before 1240	1240–1249	1250–1259	1260–1269	1270–1279	1280–1289	1290–1299	After 1300
First ten by size	1	1	5	2	1	0	0	0
Second ten by size	0	0	1	4	3	2	0	0
Third ten by size	0	0	1	0	2	2	1	4
Total	1	1	7	6	6	4	1	4

the organic towns happily sited (in their former village form) earlier
than any plantation?   Being first in the field, of course, was not an
absolute guarantee of success, let alone pre-eminence.   An early
arrival could not erect insurmountable bars against a newcomer, as
Chapter 8 has shown, but the difficulties of the newcomers are well
shown by a study of a single English county, Hampshire, where the
total number of towns, new and old, is known.

In 1334 there were twenty-two towns in Hampshire that were liable
to tax, eleven of them plantations with foundation dates between 1150
to 1255.   None of these towns was so small as the petty boroughs of the
south-west, yet the disparity in wealth between the planted and the
old-established towns is generally evident.   Nine of the plantations
have surviving tax assessments, and the average sum paid was 83s.
The old-established "organic" towns averaged 219s.   The wealthiest
plantation, Portsmouth, paid 252s. but four of the organic towns paid
more than this, and Winchester paid four times as much.[15]

A study of the extreme failures and the abortive plantations is post-
poned to Chapter 10, but in fact few such towns would have tax assessments in 1334.   The towns at the foot of the ladder in Table IX.4
were not failures, but their achievement was very modest.   Is there
anything that they had in common?

It is plain that the lower rungs are dominated by the towns of the
south-west.   Eleven of the twenty-one lowest positions are occupied by

[15] E179/173/21 (incomplete) and E179/173/22. Omitted from the calculations are the
possible boroughs of Brading (V.C.H., v, p. 158); Romsey (J.I. 1/775); Botley (Commons
Journal, i, p. 252: 1603).

Devon or Cornish towns, and the seventeen plantations in these counties with no separate tax assessment are not likely to have been any bigger. Yet this smallness was not confined to the planted boroughs in the south-west. Their organic neighbours stood on no higher rungs of the national ladder. There is a good case for saying that the poor performance of these towns came not through being planted, but through being planted in Devon and Cornwall in a soil where the organic towns were also both small and numerous. It is shown in Table IX.16 that a county with numerous organic towns could still attract plantations. Yet to proliferate was not necessarily to prosper: one might envisage a Malthusian situation with hosts of small towns struggling to survive.

From this viewpoint the smallness of the south-western towns was the price paid for the ambition of the seigneurs who promoted too many villages and created too many towns. Another possible explanation (hinging on late colonisation and local markets protected by poor inland transport) has been put forward in Chapter 4.

Surviving records of tax assessment afford a second opportunity of comparing English towns. In 1377 Edward III levied a tax of fourpence per head on all over fourteen, the first of the three poll taxes. For the larger boroughs the records are almost complete, and in some counties they survive for almost every village and town.[16] It will be noted that the poll-tax population must have been smaller than that in 1334, since the Black Death and the pandemic had swept over Europe. The point at issue here, however, is not the absolute size of the planted towns in 1377 but their own ranking order and their position relative to organic towns (Table IX.8).

At the head of the ladder (where the 1377 records are most complete) there is little difference from the ladder of 1334. Newcastle, Boston, Salisbury and Lynn have shuffled places and Salisbury has come to the top, but none of the seven planted towns with more than 1,000 taxpayers in 1377 had ranked lower than ninth in 1334. Their peers among the organic towns are again indicated in italics on the right of Table IX.8.

[16] M. W. Beresford, *Lay Subsidies and Poll Taxes* (1963), pp. 19–29; the numbers of taxpayers are taken from the county files, E179, and from the enrolled returns for the cities and larger boroughs in E359/8B. Numbers for the largest towns are conveniently printed in W. G. Hoskins, *Local History in England*, (1959), p. 176. The sums and identifications of places in J. C. Russell, *British Medieval Population*, (Albuquerque, 1948) are unreliable. Miss L. M. Midgley is in course of transcribing numbers for the whole country.

TABLE IX.8

NUMBER OF TAXPAYERS IN 1377: PLANTED AND OTHER TOWNS

Planted towns		Other towns for comparison	
New Salisbury	3,226	Lincoln	3,569
King's Lynn	3,217		
Boston	2,871	Colchester	2,955
Newcastle upon Tyne	2,647	Canterbury	2,574
Kingston upon Hull	1,557	Southampton	1,152
Ludlow	1,172		
Pontefract	1,085	Lichfield	1,024
Tickhill	680	Carlisle	678
Newcastle under Lyme	550	Taunton	539
Hedon	482	Wakefield	482
Henley on Thames	377		
Richmond (Yorks.)	369	Loughborough	360
New Thame	325	Northallerton	312
Launceston	302	Horncastle	302
Devizes	302		
Uxbridge	262	Westminster	280
Market Harborough	258		
Plympton Erle	240		
Saltash	200	Modbury	210
East Looe	138		
Colyford	133		
West Looe	131	Ludgershall	117
Boscastle	101		

The proportion of planted towns at the top of the national ladder in 1377 is identical with that in 1334, seven out of forty-two. Unfortunately many poll-tax documents from smaller towns have perished, and Table IX.8 can show the taxpayers in only twenty-three plantations, but there is every reason to think that places paying only a few shillings tax in 1334 would have had only small populations in 1377: that is certainly the uniform pattern of village assessments in those counties where large numbers of poll tax documents survive. Villages with assessments below 30s. in 1334 (the level of the lowest twenty-two places in Table IX.4) rarely mustered more than fifty taxpayers in 1377.

A direct comparison between the wealth of the English plantations and those in Gascony and Wales is prevented by the fact that the taxes of 1334 and 1377 extended neither to Wales nor Gascony.[17] For

[17] The counting of hearths for tax purposes in 1328 was limited to the then frontiers of the French kingdom (F. Lot, "L'État des paroisses et des feux de 1328", *Bibl. de l'École des*

Wales, as Table IX.2 shows, the *extents* of inquisitions post mortem provide considerable but not complete evidence of the number of burgages in Welsh boroughs. No similar documents survive for Gascony.

In Wales, as Chapter 12 shows, there would indeed be no point in assessing the comparative standing of the planted towns and their organic neighbours. Almost every town in medieval Wales was planted. There were virtually no old-established rivals to occupy higher rungs on the ladder. Of the few towns that might claim to be organic or pre-Norman, none could muster burgages so numerous as the great castle-towns of Table IX.2.

In Gascony the relative standing of the plantations was higher than in England but not so high as in Wales. Gascony already had a number of old-established towns when the great development of bastides began after 1250. Some of these were Roman towns that had survived the early medieval period. Such towns appear at the head of the ladder in Table IX.9, but they were few, and the rest of the ladder (both higher and lower rungs) is crowded wth bastides. The construction of this ladder is made possible by the survival of an assessment[18] of the taxable capacity of the Gascon towns contained in a diplomatic dispatch sent to Edward II at the end of 1315 when aid was being sought for the expenses of the war with Scotland, the same need that in England produced the first attempt at a fiscal gazetteer, the *Nomina Villarum* of 1316.

The three columns of Table IX.9 are the divisions of the original assessment, the three areas of Gascony that centred on Bazas, Agen and Dax. The latter area, the Landes, was still thinly colonised and had few towns worth taxing; its second largest town was considered no more wealthy than the middle range of bastides in the Agenais.

Bordeaux and St. Macaire do not appear in the list, since their provision took the form not of cash but wine; Bayonne provided ships. At the head of each column, not unnaturally, are five old-established towns (La Réole, Bazas, Agen, Condom, and Dax), but thereafter the bastides (italicised in the Table) can be seen to predominate. Thirty-

Chartes, xc (1929), pp. 51–107 and 256–315). A few assessments for Périgord in 1365 are available: Beaumont had 230 hearths, Villefranche du Périgord had 190, Molières, 129, and Fonroque 41½ (*Testut*, pp. 33–56).

   [18] *R.G.*, iv, pp. 568–374 from C46/26/10; in the Landes there is an assessment for Marencin (£87) and for hearths in three areas of *terra regis* near Bayonne: the editor does not ascribe these payments to particular towns.

TABLE IX.9

ASSESSED TAXABLE WEALTH OF ORGANIC AND
PLANTED GASCON TOWNS, 1315–16

Bazadais	£	Agenais	£	Landes	£
		Agen	500	Bayonne	500 (or 4 ships)
La Réole	400	Condom	300		
St. Emilion	200	Marmande	225		
Bazas	200	Porte Ste. Marie	200		
Libourne	200	Monflanquin	188		
		Ste. Foy	175		
		Mézin	175		
		Fleurance	125		
		Puymirol	125		
		Le Mas	125		
		Villeneuve sur Lot	100		
		Villeréal	100		
		Turnon	100		
		Francescas	100		
		Gontaud	75		
		Montréal du Gers	75		
		Clairac	75		
		Castillonnès	75	Dax	75
		Monclar	75		
		Castelsagrat	75		
		Damazan	75		
		Villefranche de Queyran	50		
		Larroumeieu	50		
Sauveterre de Guyenne	40	Miramont	50		
		Vianne	38		
		Pouy Petit	38		
Langon	30	La Sauvetat (Gers)	25		
		La Bastide Castelamouroux			
Pellegrue	25	Valence d'Agen	25		
		Lamontjoie St. Louis	25		
		La Parade	25		
Castelnau sur Gupie	24				
Bouglon	20			Labouheyre	20
		Hautes Vignes	18		
		St. Julian de Colorbisse	18		
		St. Pastour	15	Mimizan	15
		St. Puy (Gers)	13		
		Aiguillon	13		
		Castelnaud	13		
		Sauveterre de Soverans	13		

TABLE IX.9—*(contd.)*.

Bazadais	£	Agenais	£	Landes	£
Castets Endort	12				
		Lagruère	10		
Caudrot	10	Peyrusse	10	*Sorde L'Abb-*	10
		Sauveterre (L.et.G.)	10	*aye*	
Pondaurat	8			*Hastingues*	8
Duire	6	*Nicole*	6		
Cocumont	5	*Larroque-Fourcès*	5		
		Réalmont (Montréal)	3		

three bastides appear, compared with 30 other towns, and the bastides are not concentrated in any one part of this Gascon ladder: on this score, the Gascon bastides look more successful than their English counterparts, but direct comparisons are not possible.

III

We have now identified the most successful plantations and placed the less successful on their appropriate rungs of the ladder. The greatest success, it is now plain, was reserved for a plantation that was founded early. The wealthiest towns represented in Edward I's Parliaments dated not from the great thirteenth-century expansion but from the earlier expansion in the two generations following the Norman Conquest. Similarly, the wealthiest bastides of Edward II's Gascony were not those of his father's foundation but those that Edward I had inherited from Alphonse de Poitiers.

If the greatest success came to planted towns that were first in the field, it does not follow that being first in the field was sufficient to ensure success. Otherwise organic towns would have swept the board, for they were promoted villages, and most villages were established long before the first urban plantations. The organic towns were never in so strong a competitive position as this. There were only four counties in England and Wales where organic towns had no planted neighbours, and one of these was tiny Rutland, amply equipped with the old borough of Oakham.

The characteristic smallness of planted (and other) boroughs encountered above in Devon and Cornwall suggests that the county might be a convenient unit for studying another aspect of success and failure in England. The units in the previous Table have been individual towns. Can anything be learned about the collective experience of a region by examining the array of towns within each county? In the next group of tables it is not the size of the towns but the number in each county that is the significant measure. When Maitland wrote "mere numbers are important" he had in mind the same subject as the earlier part of this chapter, the number of townsmen in a town, but mere numbers are important in another way, the different number of towns in each county.

Three measures of local merit in town plantation will be considered successively in order to identify the conditions where plantations flourished best. In the first of these ladders of success the highest places are given to counties with the highest ratio of planted to other towns. Table IX.10 assembles the county statistics, but it is first necessary to explain how English towns have been counted. (Readers not interested in this problem may pass on to page 274 where the commentary on Table IX.10 begins.)

TABLE IX.10

RATIO OF PLANTED TO ORGANIC TOWNS:
ENGLAND AND WALES

	All towns	Planted towns	Organic towns	Ratio
BEDS.	5	I	4	0·25
BERKS.	15	4	11	0·36
BUCKS.	11	2	9	0·22
CAMBS.	3	0	3	—
CHESHIRE	8	1	7	0·14
CORNWALL	38	19	19	1·0
CUMB.	8	4	4	1·0
DERBY	5	1	4	0·25
DEVON	69	17	52	0·33
DORSET	15	6	9	0·67
DURHAM	11	4	7	0·57
ESSEX	9	4	5	0·8
GLOS.	21	3	18	0·17
HANTS.	22	11	11	1·0
HEREF.	11	3	8	0·38
HERTS.	9	6	3	2·0
HUNTS.	4	3	1	3·0
KENT	17	3	14	0·21

271

TABLE IX. 10.—(*contd.*)

	All towns	Planted towns	Organic towns	Ratio
LANCS.	17	3	14	0·21
LEICS.	5	3	2	1·5
LINCS.	15	4	11	0·36
MIDDX.	3	1	2	0·5
NORFOLK	7	3	4	0·75
NORTHANTS.	8	1	7	0·14
NORTHUM.	20	10	10	1·0
NOTTS.	3	0	3	—
OXON.	9	5	4	1·25
RUTLAND	1	0	1	—
SALOP.	17	8	9	0·89
SOMERSET	25	4	21	0·2
STAFFS.	13	2	11	0·18
SUFFOLK	12	1	11	0·09
SURREY	7	2	5	0·4
SUSSEX	18	9	9	1·0
WARW.	7	3	4	0·75
WESTM.	4	3	1	3·0
WILTS.	15	3	12	0·25
WORCS.	8	0	8	—
YORKS. E.R.	9	6	3	2·0
YORKS. N.R.	11	3	8	0·37
YORKS. W.R.	16	6	10	0·6
Total	531	172	359	0·48

Wales				
ANGLESEY	2	2	0	
BRECKNOCK	4	4	0	
CARDIGAN	4	4	0	
CARMARTHEN	12	12	0	
CARNARVON	7	6	1	
DENBIGH	3	3	0	
FLINT	8	8	0	
GLAMORGAN	10	10	0	
MERIONETH	3	3	0	
MONMOUTH	11	9	2	
MONTGOMERY	8	8	0	
PEMBROKE	9	9	0	
RADNOR	6	6	0	
Total	87	84	3	

In order to calculate a ratio of planted towns there are two obstacles to face. Firstly, what is a medieval "town"? Tables IX.10–IX.18 include any place that passes *one* of the following tests: had it a borough charter? did it have burgages? was it called *burgus* in the Assize Rolls, or was it separately represented by a jury before the judge of assize? was it taxed as a borough? did it send members to any medieval Parliament? The tests are lawyers' tests rather than economists', but the selection is dictated by the nature of surviving documents that are more explicit about legal status than about economic structure. It would be difficult to think of any important town in medieval England, however, that would pass none of the prescribed tests.

The second difficulty is not in defining the test conditions but in applying them. No scholar has yet made an attempt to identify all English boroughs, even with tests as broad as these. The taxation boroughs and the Parliamentary boroughs can easily be identified, since tax assessments and writs of summons have survived in some quantity; the boroughs of the Assize Rolls have been identified in an unpublished study by Mr. Meekings; the charters copied by the Chancery clerks into their records have been calendared, and after 1200 only a few rolls are wanting; in addition, charters in private and local hands were sought out and calendared by Ballard, Tait and Weinbaum.

These documentary sources cannot fail to yield the names of all the major medieval boroughs. Yet, in making comparison with planted boroughs, some of which were very small, it is necessary to count the minor boroughs as well as the major. These minor boroughs were often given their charter by their lord without any reference to the Crown and with no enrolment of the charter on the Charter Rolls; they were too small to be taxed at the higher rate of a tenth, so that no trace of their burgality appears on the Subsidy Rolls; they were too petty to be summoned to Parliament or to meet the judges of assize. The main chance of identification that remains is the chance reference to *burgus* or *burgagium* in manorial accounts, rentals, deeds, lawsuits and extents. These records are not so well calendared as the great rolls of Chancery and Exchequer, and although they have yielded quite a number of boroughs not known to Ballard and Tait, there must still be others awaiting discovery. It may be no accident that the counties with the largest number of proved petty boroughs are those where local historians have been active: Professor Finberg in Devon and Gloucestershire,

Charles Henderson in Cornwall and the authors of the *Northumberland County History* at the other end of the kingdom.   If Hoskins and Finberg would produce Studies for Norfolk, Cambridgeshire, and Nottingham-shire to accompany their *Devonshire Studies* they might be able to make two boroughs grow where only one has grown before: except perhaps Rutland, where even these doctors may not be able to work a cure. The first column of Table IX.10 shows the number of places in each county identified as "towns", and the second column gives the number of planted towns among these.   The third column is obtained by sub-traction, and the fourth column shows the ratio of planted to organic towns in each county.   The average for England was 0·48.

If we now seek the thirteen English counties that show merit by having a high ratio of planted towns to organic towns we find them in the order of Table IX.11.

TABLE IX.11

COUNTIES WITH THE HIGHEST RATIO OF PLANTED
TO ORGANIC TOWNS

	Planted	Organic	Ratio
Carnarvon	6	1	6·0
Monmouth	9	2	4·5
Huntingdon	3	1	3·0
Westmorland	3	1	3·0
Hertfordshire	6	3	2·0
Yorkshire E.R.	6	3	2·0
Leicestershire	3	2	1·5
Oxfordshire	5	4	1·25
Cornwall	19	19	1·0
Cumberland	4	4	1·0
Hampshire	11	11	1·0
Northumberland	10	10	1·0
Sussex	9	9	1·0

Note: Eleven other Welsh counties had *all* their towns planted.

The best performances in England were surpassed in the eleven Welsh counties where every medieval town was a plantation.

Our first measure of merit may properly be criticised for ignoring the actual number of plantations in each county: the badge of merit might be granted to Huntingdonshire reluctantly when it is seen to have only three planted towns.   At the other extreme, what badge of merit

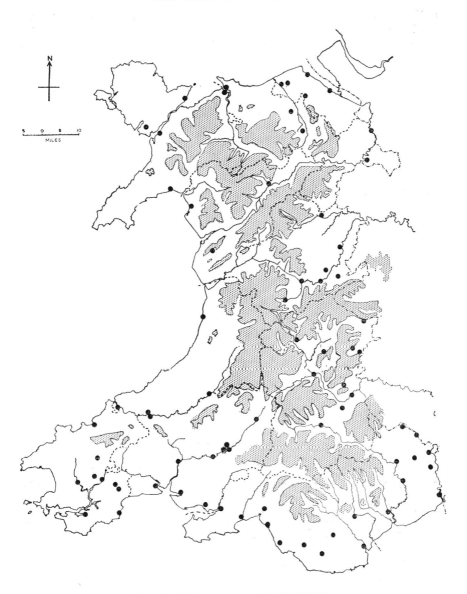

FIG. 46. WALES: PLANTED TOWNS.

is good enough for Wales with its eighty-four medieval plantations, distributed in every county? A second test of merit is more exacting. Table IX.12 selects counties with high ratios in Table IX.10 that also mustered eight or more plantations each. The sun now shines brightest on Cornwall and Hampshire, and upon Carmarthenshire and Glamorganshire. It will be noted that we have not entirely left the counties of mountain and moorland, and Northumberland runs third in England. Even if the Welsh intensity is attributed to political and military forces, it is not possible to explain Hampshire and Cornwall in this way.[19] The character of a local English economy that could support so many towns in high and waste places is discussed later (p. 347 and in the Gazetteer).

TABLE IX.12

COUNTIES WITH EIGHT OR MORE PLANTED TOWNS,
AND A HIGH RATIO OF PLANTED TO ORGANIC TOWNS

County	Number	Ratio
CORNWALL	19	1·0
CARMARTHENSHIRE	12	all
HAMPSHIRE	11	1·0
NORTHUMBERLAND	10	1·0
GLAMORGANSHIRE	10	all
MONMOUTHSHIRE	9	4·5
SUSSEX	9	1·0
PEMBROKESHIRE	9	all
SHROPSHIRE	8	0·89
MONTGOMERYSHIRE	8	all
FLINTSHIRE	8	all

The counties that do well by either of the two tests so far proposed, appearing in both Table IX.11 and IX.12, are: Cornwall, Hampshire, Northumberland, and Sussex together with Monmouthshire and five Welsh counties. Another criticism can now be voiced, and a third measure of merit devised to meet it. This criticism arises from the great difference in size between English counties, and the new measure of merit would not be awarded to a large county such as Yorkshire unless the number of its towns bore some proportion to its acres.

To obtain a measure which can be called "urban intensity", we can

[19] Nor were the Cornish plantations all pigmies: in 1300 there were 305 burgages in Lostwithiel, 118 in Saltash and 62 in Camelford: E158/8 and C133/95.

TABLE IX.13

MEDIEVAL URBAN DATA FOR ENGLAND AND WALES

County	Area in 1,000 acres (rounded)	Total number of towns	Number of planted towns	Number of organic towns
England				
BEDS.	300	5	1	4
BERKS.	450	15	4	11
BUCKS	480	11	2	9
CAMBS	560	3	0	3
CHES.	620	8	1	7
CORNWALL	870	38	19	19
CUMB.	970	8	4	4
DERBY	640	5	1	4
DEVON	1,650	69	17	52
DORSET	620	15	6	9
DURHAM	620	11	4	7
ESSEX	960	9	4	5
GLOS.	770	21	3	18
HANTS.	1,020	22	11	11
HEREF.	540	11	3	8
HERTS.	400	9	6	3
HUNTS.	230	4	3	1
KENT	970	17	3	14
LANCS.	1,030	17	3	14
LEICS.	520	5	3	2
LINCS.	1,690	15	4	11
MIDDX.	220	3	1	2
NORFOLK	1,300	7	3	4
NORTHANTS.	630	8	1	7
NORTHUM.	1,280	20	10	10
NOTTS.	520	3	0	3
OXON.	470	9	5	4
RUTLAND	97	1	0	1
SALOP.	860	17	8	9
SOM.	1,030	25	4	21
STAFFS.	690	13	2	11
SUFFOLK	940	12	1	11
SURREY	450	7	2	5
SUSSEX	900	18	9	9
WARW.	560	7	3	4
WESTM.	500	4	3	1
WILTS.	860	15	3	12
WORCS.	440	8	0	8
YORKS. E.R.	740	9	6	3
YORKS. N.R.	1,350	11	3	8
YORKS. W.R.	1,610	16	6	10

TABLE IX.13.—(*contd.*)

County	Area in 1,000 acres (rounded)	Total number of towns	Number of planted towns	Number of organic towns
Wales				
ANGLESEY	180	2	2	0
BRECKNOCK	470	4	4	0
CARDIGAN	440	4	4	0
CARMARTHEN	590	12	12	0
CARNARVON	360	7	6	1
DENBIGH	430	3	3	0
FLINT	160	8	8	0
GLAMORGAN	470	10	10	0
MERIONETH	420	3	3	0
MONMOUTH	340	11	9	2
MONTGOMERY	510	8	8	0
PEMBROKE	390	9	9	0
RADNOR	300	6	6	0

divide the area of each county by the number of its towns as they stood in the mid-fourteenth century. In this calculation notice must be taken of both planted and organic towns. For example, in Somerset (with 1,030,000 acres) there were four planted towns, a ratio of one planted town per 257,500 acres. There were also twenty-one organic towns in Somerset: the real achievement in Somerset was that the new towns were fitted into a county that would already have had one organic town for every 49,000 acres.

Table IX.13 gives the basic data for each county, and Table IX.14 calculates the intensity of the non-planted towns in each English county. The variation between counties is interesting. In Table IX.15, which sets out the extremes of experience, there are some strange neighbours.

To meet the objection that this crude counting of towns and acres fails to allow for the size of towns, some extra weighting can be given the great towns of 1334 and 1377. Yet, because the thirty-two greatest towns in England were spread among nineteen different counties, there are not many adjustments in ranking to be made. Following a system of weights described in the note to IX.15, it would be necessary to remove Norfolk, Leicestershire and Yorkshire E.R. from the very bottom of the ladder: but the group of counties with the

TABLE IX.14

DENSITY OF ORGANIC TOWNS ALONE: ENGLAND
'000 *acres per town*

BEDS.	75	MIDDX.	110
BERKS.	41	NORFOLK	325
BUCKS.	53	NORTHANTS.	90
CAMBS.	187	NORTHUM.	128
CHESHIRE	89	NOTTS.	173
CORNWALL	46	OXON.	118
CUMB.	243	RUTLAND	97
DERBY	160	SALOP.	96
DEVON	32	SOMERSET	49
DORSET	69	STAFFS.	63
DURHAM	89	SUFFOLK	85
ESSEX	192	SURREY	90
GLOS.	43	SUSSEX	100
HANTS	93	WARW.	140
HEREF.	68	WESTM.	500
HERTS.	133	WILTS.	72
HUNTS.	230	WORCS.	55
KENT	69	YORKS. E.R.	247
LANCS.	74	YORKS. N.R.	169
LEICS.	260	YORKS. W.R.	161
LINCS.	154		

greatest intensity of towns would still be the same after the adjustments, as the right hand column in Table IX.15 shows.

It could also be objected that the chosen measure fails to allow for the variation between acres, but it is difficult to see how these could be weighted when we know so little about the local fertility of soils in the Middle Ages; the most that can be done is to identify the counties that had notoriously poor agricultural land, low tax assessments in 1334, and small populations in 1377, and then see whether equal weighting of acres has kept them from the head of the ladder. A little more sympathy would have to be extended to Westmorland, Cumberland and Huntingdonshire; but at the head of the ladder it proves unnecessary to make any adjustment: there are no contenders near enough to be affected. Among the five counties at the head of Table IX.15, the achievement of the organic towns in Devon and Cornwall appears even more meritorious when the quality of their agricultural hinterland is taken into account. Clearly, something other than fertility of local soil sustained these towns.

TABLE IX.15

COUNTIES WITH EXTREMES OF URBAN INTENSITY IN TABLE IX.14

	'000 acres per organic town	'000 acres per organic town, weighted for great towns
DEVON	32	*32*
BERKSHIRE	41	*41*
GLOUCESTERSHIRE	43	*33*
CORNWALL	46	*46*
SOMERSET	49	*45*
HUNTINGDONSHIRE	230	*230*
CUMBERLAND	243	*243*
YORKSHIRE E.R.	247	*123*
LEICESTERSHIRE	260	*104*
NORFOLK	325	*163*
WESTMORLAND	500	*500*

Note: Forty-four towns are ranked as "large" according to data from 1334 and 1377 by the following criteria: having more than 1,000 poll-taxpayers in 1377 or an assessment of over 500s. in 1334. Two towns not taxed on these occasions, Chester and Durham, are also included. Bristol has been divided equally between Gloucester and Somerset, York between the three Ridings. A double weight is given to towns between 1,000 and 1,999 taxpayers in 1377; a triple weighting to those having between 2,000 and 3,999; a quadruple weighting between 4,000 and 7,900. If London were included, its weight would be sextuple, and should be perhaps divided equally between Middlesex, Essex, Kent and Surrey: it had 23,314 taxpayers.

How well did the planted towns fare in the five counties that have now emerged as most crowded with organic towns? Table IX.16

TABLE IX.16

PLANTATIONS IN THE COUNTIES MOST DENSELY
PROVIDED WITH ORGANIC TOWNS

	Density of organic towns ('000 acres per town)	Number of plantations	Ratio of number of planted to organic
DEVON	32	17	0·33
BERKSHIRE	41	4	0·36
GLOUCS.	43 (33)	3	0·17
CORNWALL	46	19	1·0
SOMERSET	49 (45)	4	0·2

Note: Brackets enclose weighted figures from Table IX.15.

280

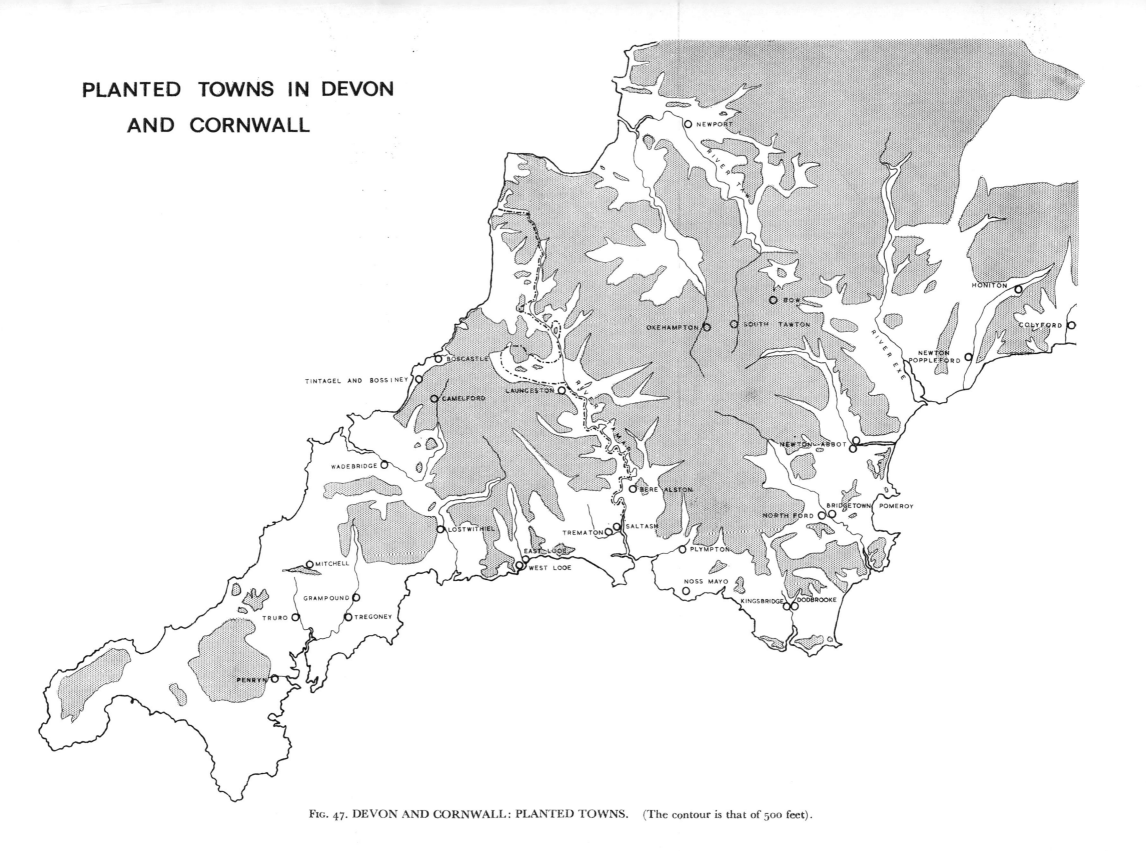

PLANTED TOWNS IN DEVON
AND CORNWALL

NEWPORT

RIVER TAW

HONITON

BOW

OKEHAMPTON   SOUTH TAWTON   COLYFORD

BOSCASTLE   RIVER EXE   NEWTON POPPLEFORD

TINTAGEL AND BOSSINEY

CAMELFORD   LAUNCESTON   RIVER

NEWTON ABBOT

WADEBRIDGE

BERE ALSTON

BRIDGETOWN POMEROY

NORTH FORD

LOSTWITHIEL   TREMATON   SALTASH

EAST LOOE

MITCHELL   PLYMPTON

WEST LOOE

NOSS MAYO

GRAMPOUND   KINGSBRIDGE   DODBROOKE

TRURO   TREGONEY

PENRYN

FIG. 47. DEVON AND CORNWALL: PLANTED TOWNS.   (The contour is that of 500 feet).

recapitulates the relevant parts of Tables IX.10 and IX.15. It shows that Berkshire, Gloucestershire and Somerset were counties where the organic towns did well, but the planted towns less well. On the other hand, Devon and Cornwall were able to maintain a large number of plantations. Cornwall wins honours by appearing in all lists of merit (see Fig. 47).

IV

These figures reinforce the argument at the end of the previous chapter. Districts with old-established or organic towns were not barred to the would-be planters of towns. Neighbours could not freeze out new-comers, whatever the language, the poses and the manœuvres of inter-urban rivalry. Cornwall, the county with the greatest number of plantations, had by 1334 the most intensive crop of towns in the whole country. The founders of new towns had chosen localities near those where other types of town were proving their worth. The same local economic conditions that encouraged lords to plant towns were encouraging the promotion of villages to boroughs, and the new towns supplemented the old.

Conversely, it will be noticed that counties without planted towns were often counties with few towns of any kind. Nottinghamshire, Rutland and Cambridgeshire had no plantations, and only seven other towns between them. The only counties where the planted town seems to have done poorly, even though other towns flourished, were Cheshire, Gloucestershire, Northamptonshire and Suffolk. In these four counties there were forty-nine towns by 1334: but only six of these were planted. Here alone might the gladiatorial language of inter-urban rivalry make sense. Elsewhere imitation and innovation were the sincerest forms of flattery by which the new acknowledged the existence of the old.

Yet to proliferate towns was not necessarily to ensure them a high rank of prosperity: the tax assessments of towns in Devon and Cornwall in 1334 show a modest egalitarianism in the jostling boroughs. No Cornish town, whether planted or organic, figured among the thirty wealthiest towns in those assessments. Devon was represented twice: by its county town, Exeter, a town as old-established as anywhere in the west; and by Plymouth, a town of rapid growth though apparently based upon two pre-existing villages.

A striking feature of the geographical distribution of these thirty

281

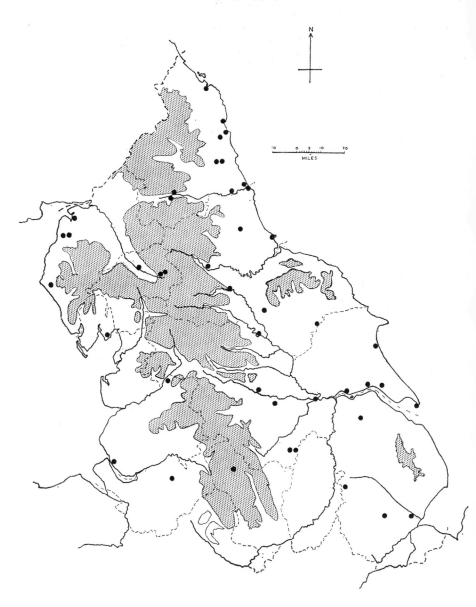

FIG. 48. NORTHERN ENGLAND: PLANTED TOWNS. Except along the coast, the
density is lighter than in southern England (Fig. 49).

FIG. 49. SOUTHERN ENGLAND: PLANTED TOWNS

highest-ranking English towns of 1334 is, indeed, their wide geographical dispersion. Only two counties, Lincolnshire and Yorkshire, appear as many as four times in the list; Norfolk has three representatives: all these, it will be noticed, are very large counties. Cambridgeshire, Gloucestershire and Hampshire (like Devon) appear twice, but eleven other counties have only one town in the list, usually the county town. Of the counties with most large towns, Table IX.13 has shown that Yorkshire was capable of supporting fifteen plantations, Devon seventeen and Hampshire eleven. Only Cambridgeshire seems to have possessed the secret of managing without plantations, but something of the secret must have had currency in Lincolnshire, Norfolk and Gloucestershire, none of which supported more than four new towns.

Finally, Table IX.17 attempts to bring the planted and organic towns of England and Wales into a single view by assessing the average catchment area enjoyed by the towns of each county. The method is similar to that employed in earlier Tables, the division of the total area of a county by the number of towns (of all kinds) that lay within it on the eve of the Black Death. Table IX.18 extracts from Table IX.17 the eleven counties with the densest distribution of towns, that is, with the smallest catchment areas. On this test, which is a very rough one, Devon and Cornwall are the plain victors, closely followed by Flintshire. It will be observed from Table IX.17 that seven of the counties of England manage a score no better than the four counties of Wales that were least hospitable to towns (Denbigh, Merioneth, Carnarvon and Brecon), and that two of these seven are counties which on other tests would have appeared among the most wealthy in England: Norfolk and Cambridgeshire!

Another way of presenting the material of Tables IX.17 and 18 would be to imagine each town at the centre of a circle that formed its catchment area, and that each town was so placed that the circles overlapped as little as possible. (The unrealism of this simplification is exposed in Fig. 50, below.) Then the 23,000 acres or 36 square miles of the average catchment area of a Cornish town could be contained within a circle of 3·4 miles radius; those of Hampshire within a circle of radius 4·8 miles, and the least-urbanised counties of Norfolk and Cambridge would need circles of 9·6 miles radius.

Calculations for Gascony cannot be carried out in similar detail, for the number of organic towns can be determined only approximately, and the areas of each Department are much larger than the ordinary

283

TABLE IX.17

AVERAGE CATCHMENT AREA OF THE TOWNS
IN EACH COUNTY OF ENGLAND AND WALES

In '000 acres

BEDS.	60	RUTLAND	97
BERKS.	30	SALOP.	51
BUCKS.	44	SOMERSET	41
CAMBS.	187	STAFFS.	53
CHESHIRE	77	SUFFOLK	78
CORNWALL	23	SURREY	64
CUMB.	121	SUSSEX	50
DERBY	128	WARW.	80
DEVON	24	WESTM.	125
DORSET	41	WILTS.	57
DURHAM	56	WORCS.	55
ESSEX	107	YORKS. E.R.	82
GLOS.	37	YORKS. N.R.	123
HANTS.	46	YORKS. W.R.	101
HEREF.	49	ANGLESEY	90
HERTS.	44	BRECKNOCK	118
HUNTS.	57	CARDIGAN	110
KENT	57	CARMARTHEN	45
LANCS.	61	CARNARVON	120
LEICS.	104	DENBIGH	143
LINCS.	113	FLINT	27
MIDDX.	73	GLAMORGAN	47
NORFOLK	186	MERIONETH	140
NORTHANTS	79	MONMOUTH	34
NORTHUM.	64	MONTGOMERY	64
NOTTS.	173	PEMBROKE	49
OXON.	52	RADNOR	50

run of English counties. The smallest, Lot et Garonne, is the size of Norfolk, and the Gironde is twice as large. In two Departments, the bastides lie on the very edge of the area, so that any calculation of an average catchment area is more than usually unrealistic. Table IX.19 shows the exceptional density of the bastides in the Agenais (Lot et Garonne), the product of effort by the seneschals of Alphonse de Poitiers and then of Edward I (Fig. 60 and Table XIII.2). The Gironde, dominated by Bordeaux, scores poorly, and the Landes scores well despite the extensive infertile areas that virtually inhibited colonisation (Fig. 62). If an index of general urban intensity on the lines of Table IX.17 is required for Gascony, it can only be provided for the

TABLE IX.18

MOST INTENSELY URBANISED COUNTIES,
TOWNS OF ALL KINDS

	'000 *acres per town, weighted**
CORNWALL	23
DEVON	24
FLINTSHIRE	27
BERKSHIRE	30
MONMOUTHSHIRE	34
GLOUCESTERSHIRE	37
DORSET	41
BUCKINGHAMSHIRE	44
HERTFORDSHIRE	44
CARMARTHENSHIRE	45
HAMPSHIRE	46

Note: *The weighting for great towns is given in footnote to Table IX.15

TABLE IX.19

DENSITY OF ENGLISH AND ANGLO-FRENCH BASTIDES BY DEPARTMENTS

	Area		*Number of bastides*	Density	
	sq. km.	'*000 acres*		*sq. km. per bastide*	'*000 acres per bastide*
LOT ET GARONNE	5,385	1,330	40	135	33
LANDES	9,364	2,313	30	312	77
DORDOGNE	9,224	2,278	18	512	127
GERS	6,291	1,554	11	572	141
GIRONDE	10,726	2,649	16	670	166
			115		

Note: In addition, the Department of Lot has two English bastides and one Anglo-French; Tarn et Garonne has two English and four Anglo-French, but all nine lie on the fringe of the Departments. Most of the bastides in these two Departments were French foundations.

areas as a whole. The five Departments of Table IX.19 have a total area of just over 10,000,000 acres, and if we take all the places with franchises calendared by Gouron as having some "urban" element within them, the average catchment area is about 23,000 acres, a figure very near that for Cornwall.

V

Finally, we turn from these averages and their generality to the realities of a small area where it is possible to locate all the planted towns, the organic towns, and the rural market-centres. Thus, the full array of competitors that faced a late thirteenth-century plantation can be set out and appreciated. Such a late-comer had to find not only physical room for itself, but—more important—an economic catchment area in its hinterland, along the coast and up the rivers. Figs. 50–52 examine the East Riding of Yorkshire, and the adjacent boroughs and market-villages of north Lincolnshire, the West Riding and the North Riding.

The first step was to draw circles of 5 miles radius centred on the towns, whether organic or planted. The countryman whose village lay within one of these circles had a journey of less than 5 miles if he wished to reach the market place of one of these towns; if two or more circles intersect, the villager had a choice of market places within a 5 mile journey. These areas of intersection are shaded in Fig. 50: B indicates an organic borough, and P a planted town. On this showing, there was a genuine rivalry between Beverley, Hull and Hedon, and some competition between Drax and Airmyn. The two latter places, however, were not important centres. Skipsea, New Malton and Ravenserodd, on the other hand, had no serious rival very near.

Fig. 50 deals only with competition from other towns. What of competition from villages that had market charters, very often accompanied by fairs? The crowded character of internal trade is indicated in Fig. 51 where circles, again of 5 miles radius, have been drawn around all such market centres, the towns being distinguished by firm lines. Clearly, the villager had very little choice in the north-west part of the Riding, but in a broad line running south-westwards from Bridlington there was much competition. The situation is summed up in Fig. 52 where areas that had a choice of six or more markets are shaded black. The white areas are those with no market lying nearer

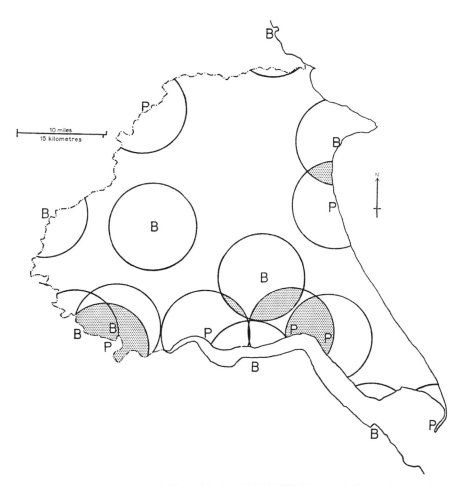

FIG. 50. TOWNS OF THE EAST RIDING OF YORKSHIRE. Circles are drawn with a 5 mile radius, centred on towns in the Riding or nearby. *B* indicates an organic borough, *P* a planted town. On this reckoning, only Pocklington of the organic boroughs had an unchallenged hinterland. See also Fig. 51.

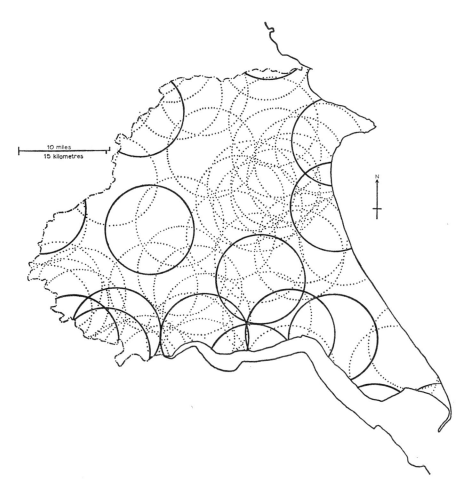

FIG. 51. RURAL AND BOROUGH MARKETS IN THE EAST RIDING c. 1350. Firm circles are drawn as in Fig. 50; dotted circles centre on other places with market charters. See also Fig. 52.

than 5 miles, and the grey areas indicate intermediate ranges of choice. The seven planted towns that were essayed in this crowded area are indicated by the letters A (Airmyn), B (Brough), H (Hedon), K (Kingston on Hull), M (New Malton), R (Ravenserodd) and S (Skipsea). Ravenserodd has sunk beneath the waves, and Hedon's municipal splendours rest in history rather than in surviving commercial life.

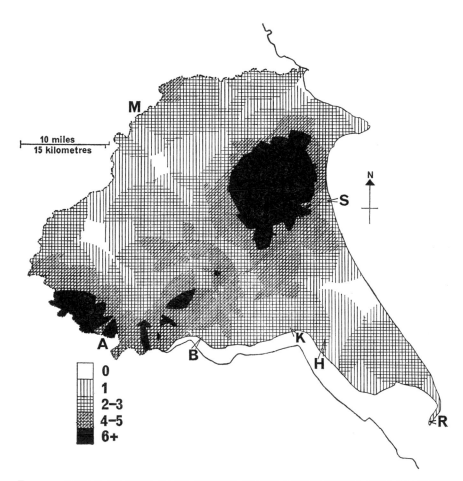

FIG. 52. AREAS IN THE EAST RIDING WITH MORE THAN ONE MARKET CENTRE AVAILABLE. The key indicates the intensity of rival markets. Letters indicate planted towns: A, Airmyn; B, Brough; H, Hedon; K, Kingston on Hull; M, New Malton; R, Ravenserodd; S, Skipsea, Wyke is not shown separately from Kingston.

One must be careful what one writes about Hedon, for one of my fellow historians was publicly—and justly—rebuked by its Mayor for describing it as a deserted village. There will be no disagreement, however, about the fate of the burgages in Airmyn, Brough and Skipsea. The next chapter considers the factors that put such new towns at the very bottom of the ladder of success.

CHAPTER TEN

The Procession of Failures

Glendower: I can call spirits from the vasty deep.
Hotspur: Why, so can I, or so can any man;
But will they come, when you do call for them?

Henry IV Part One,
Act III scene 1.

I

EVERY founder of a town had to be a prophet, hoping to discern existing and future opportunities of success: yet prophecies could fail, boroughs become rotten boroughs and the very names of towns pass into oblivion. The Chancery clerks of Elizabeth I who came upon Henry III's charter to Warenmouth assigned it to Sunderland (Bishop Wearmouth), for Warenmouth meant nothing to them.[1] John Norden, describing the Cornish borough of Boscastle to Elizabeth I, wrote:

> it is the meanest and poorest that can bear the name of town, for it consisteth of two or three houses. It hath been of more importance as appeareth by the ruins.[2]

Another Elizabethan surveyor had found Newtown, I.O.W., in 1559 to have "streats bothe of artificers and others cleyn dekeyed"[3], and in 1835 the Royal Commission on Municipal Corporations described Newtown again.

> The houses are merely cottages, of which there are about fourteen. The town has at some time been considerable as the names of the streets, the sites of which are still known, show.[4]

An eighteenth-century plan of Newtown (Fig. 53) shows the deserted

[1] J. Tait, *The Medieval English Borough* (1936), p. 350.
[2] J. Norden, *Topog. and Hist. Description of Cornwall*, ed. C. Bateman (1728), p. 78.
[3] SP12/7/58–9.
[4] *Appendix, Part II to the 1st Rep. on Municipal Corporations*, (Parl. Papers, 1835, vol. xxiv), p. 795.

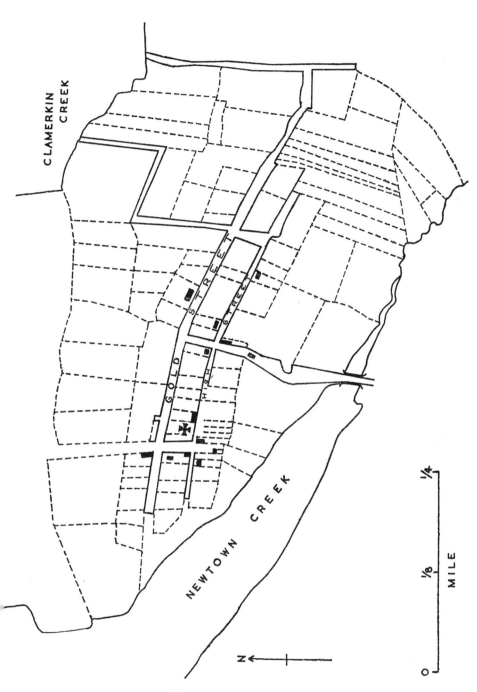

CLAMERKIN CREEK

NEWTOWN CREEK

GOLD STREET

HIGH STREET

SILVER STREET

N

MILE

0   ⅛   ¼

Fig. 53. NEWTOWN, I.O.W.   The decayed borough, from a plan of 1768.   Field divisions indicate burgage plots as laid out in 1256–57.

streets and the fields that retained the shape of the abandoned burgage plots, much as they do today.

A second plantation of the bishops of Winchester, Newtown in Burghclere, is even more thoroughly decayed. The church stands alone in a grass field just beyond the edge of the heath, and there is nothing on the ground that would indicate former burgage plots. The fortunate survival of an estate plan in the bursary of an Oxford college enables the site of the borough to be located, for in 1606, when the plan was drawn, the main road still passed through the old market place,[5] and the Tithe Award of 1839 has significant field names. All has now been absorbed into the parkland of Newtown House. A sudden turn in the line of the old Winchester to Oxford Road near the southern end of the park indicates where it was diverted from its course at the making of the park.

Another fallen borough that once straddled an important road is Bretford (Warws.), planted where the Foss Way forded the Avon. Another early seventeenth-century plan shows the remnants of the town, a handful of cottages.[6] Now, only the parish boundary indicates the line of the Foss Way through the borough, since the modern road has been diverted to the west, probably at the making of the bridge (Fig. 12).

The Gascon countryside has not been prosperous in the last century and its villages have seen a great exodus; most villages have decaying farmsteads and there are abandoned vine-terraces all over the barren, hilly country in the east. With the villages, the small market towns have decayed as the railway and the motor car have removed the invisible tariff that protected them from the competition of the large towns. Among these small market towns are many that were bastides, so that the fabled grass can actually be seen growing in market places that were hopefully laid out by the officials of Henry III and Edward I. *Cornières* have become shelters for farm-carts and Citroëns. Fig. 54 shows the emptiness of Beauregard (Dordogne), founded in 1286; empty chequers have become fields. The bastide of Roquepine (Dordogne), founded in 1283, was polygonal in shape but the outline is visible only in crop-marks on an air photograph (Fig. 55). Bonnegarde en Chalosse (Landes) was founded in the same year as Roquepine, occupying a flat hill-top overlooking the river Luy de

---

[5] Corpus Christi College, maps and plans; reproduced by O.S. in their series of cadastral maps, no. 331B, a copy of which is B.M. Map 188.e.2.
[6] B.M. Add. Ms. 48181, from Yelverton Mss.

Béarn and in the shelter of Edward I's castle. The hill-top is now completely deserted and the gnarled roots of huge old oaks clasp, and for a time preserve, short lengths of walling from the town gate (Fig. 42).

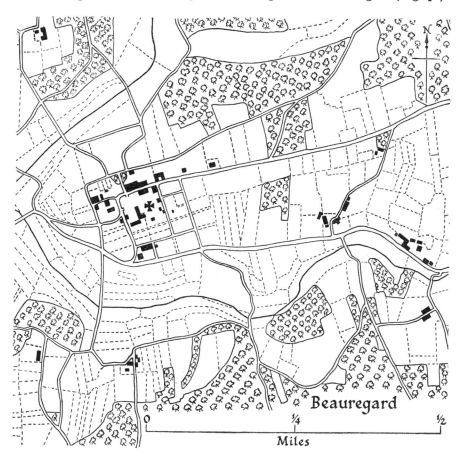

FIG. 54. BEAUREGARD, Dordogne. A decayed bastide, surrounded by clearings from the woods of Périgord. Former streets south of the church survive as deeply-cut hollow-ways among fields and vineyards of the present day.

Another castle of Edward I, Bere (Merioneth), has fallen into ruins that are being excavated for preservation by the Ancient Monuments Inspectorate of the Ministry of Public Buildings and Works: somewhere yet undiscovered, the slopes of the hill conceal the borough. Prince Llewellyn's market borough of Dolforwyn is all grass-grown (Plate 10).

Baa (Gironde), named in honour of Edward I's chancellor and visited by Edward himself while in course of construction, is now lost in the pinewoods south of Bordeaux; its neighbour Camparian has given its name to a farm, but all that remains of the town are a few earthworks in

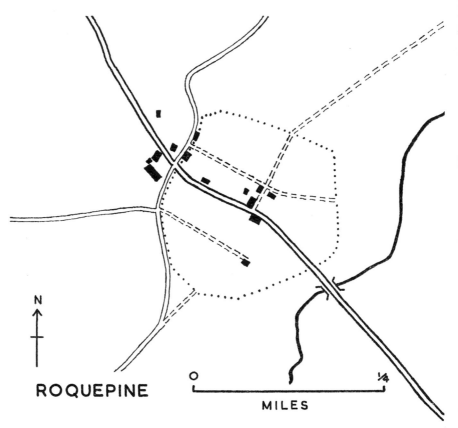

N
↑

ROQUEPINE

0   ¼
MILES

FIG. 55. ROQUEPINE, Lot et Garonne. A bastide reduced to two farms. The bounds can be recognised in air photographs as crop marks.

a meadow and the ruins of a church overgrown with trees and brambles (Fig. 56). The church of La Bastide Castelamouroux, also in ruins, is a bizarre companion of a hill-top farm. The trees in the churchyard have grown so tall and the undergrowth so thick that the church is invisible from a distance.

Exploration of hill-top thickets has produced a possible site for

Pugpito: long lost, since French historians do not seem to take easily to exploring thickets; ignorance of Sarron and Arouille is less excusable since the earthworks of their streets remain in grass fields alongside public roads. Several Gascon bastides remain unlocated, so abortive were they, or so thorough their decay: the Queenborough of the Gironde, Henry III's *Burgus Reginae*, is one of these; Cussac another.

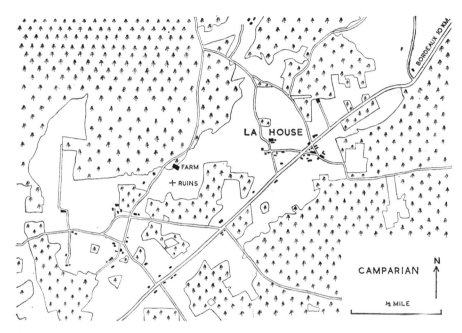

FIG. 56. CAMPARIAN, Gironde. The ruins of the church mark the site of medieval Camparian, which may have been a bastide (see Gazetteer). The bastide of Baa, with which it was certainly associated, lay to the north but no physical remains have yet been found.

England also has a small number of concealed sites. Nothing can be seen near the traditional site of Warenmouth (Northumberland). Edward I's Newton (Gotowre super Mare) is concealed somewhere in the Purbeck heaths. Ravenserodd has long gone under the waves, and on the Solway coast Skinburgh and Wavermouth were washed away within a few years of their foundation. Harlech, New Winchelsea and New Romney have also been destroyed as ports by the movement of the water: in these cases by its retreat.

The main vulnerability of riverside towns was to the silting up of estuaries. Hedon fell this way. St. Maurice, a bastide on the river Adour, suffered from the fickleness of the waters in a different fashion. Like its neighbour, Toulouzette, it lay at the head of a large meander. The river has now changed its course and St. Maurice is as high and dry as New Winchelsea. The catalogue of misfortunes could be continued. The Gazetteer chapters describe 23 English towns, 18 Welsh towns and 44 Gascon towns that have disappeared or dwindled to a handful of cottages. The Welsh plantations, it will be seen in Table X.1, had a failure rate of 21% (18 towns out of 84). The Gascon rate was higher still: 44 out of 125 (35%). The English rate was 13%: 23 out of 172.

It is important when judging the achievement of medieval town plantation not to be diverted by picturesque ruins of towns whose ports were choked in post-medieval centuries or by towns that perished in the French wars of religion. These late-deserted sites are of great archaeological significance, for they can be more easily explored for material remains than the valuable and crowded building land of a living town, but their failure is irrelevant to their founders' foresight. The important failures were the towns that were still-born and the towns that had only a few decades of life. Such failures do criticise the founders' foresight: they show what limits contemporary conditions set to the growth of towns in particular districts: and they show limits that the state of the economy set to urban growth in the mid-fourteenth century, the period when the very idea of town plantation wilted and faded away.

One sign that general, as well as particular, causes operated to produce unsuccessful plantations is the clear evidence of enfeeblement among some organic towns. It was of organic, and not of planted, towns that Ballard and Tait wrote:

> the creation of minor boroughs on so extensive a scale as characterised it in England had inevitably a strong element of experiment. The local lord was by no means a good judge of potentiality. His attempt to develop rural into urban communities was often futile, or at least premature.[7]

If Welsh plantations were burned in warfare, so were organic towns in Shropshire and Herefordshire. When the French burned New Winchelsea they also descended on older coastal ports. If the sea washed away new Ravenserodd, it also eroded the much older town of

[7] *Ballard and Tait*, p. lxxxviii.

Dunwich, perhaps the only place in England where sea-washed bones and skulls from a town cemetery can be picked up on the beach.[8] It was at Bridgwater, and not at some unsuccessful Somerset plantation, that in 1273 sixty burgage plots (12% of the total) were recorded as having reverted to farm land:

reducuntur in terram arabilem ad opus dominorum.

In Lancashire only four towns retained effective borough status at the end of the Middle Ages, whereas there had once been at least four times as many, perhaps six times as many.[10]

II

Two categories of failure among the plantations are particularly important. The first one will be called "abortive". Here, the promoter made the usual preparations, issued charters, granted liberties, proclaimed the empty plots and then found himself with no burgesses. The typical documentary reflection of such a situation is a charter of liberties but no subsequent mention of a town in the records of the church, the county, the Exchequer or the Chancery. Edward I's charter to Newton in Purbeck is the sole record of the town until its name recurs as the name of a single house and a belt of woodland in the late sixteenth century. Another plantation with a charter of liberties but no subsequent history is St. Osbert (Gironde). From London in June 1276 Edward I issued a long foundation charter that occupies six closely-set columns in the printed edition of the Gascon Rolls. There are thirty-two separate clauses defining the status and privileges of those who came to take up the building plots. Two other bastides (Castelnau sur Gupie and Castetcrabe) then had the liberties of St. Osbert conferred on them. This affiliation meant that the community of Castelnau had to test its liberties by reference to the charter of a non-existent place; Castetcrabe had less difficulty, for there is no record of that community after 1285, and it, too, may have been abortive.[11]

The second category of failure will be called "decayed". It will be reserved for those towns where the evidence of surviving documents,

---

[8] Lothingland is another eroded settlement, which may have been a town. It lay near Lowestoft (Suffolk) and may have been its predecessor (*Curia Regis Rolls*, xiii, p. 108).
[9] C133/2/7.
[10] Tait, *op. cit.*, in fn. 1, p. 352.
[11] *R.G.*, ii, 55–58.

buildings or earthworks show that the ground did become inhabited: to be "decayed", a place that was once a bastide or borough must now be reduced to a hamlet or less. The scatter of houses at Newtown, I.O.W., neatly fits this definition; the pattern of lanes and field boundaries sketch out the shadowy equivalent of a town plan; there is the additional documentary evidence of the early rent-rolls of the town to demonstrate that the ground was really occupied; the other decayed plantation of the bishops of Winchester, Newtown in Burghclere, also has lists of early burgesses to demonstrate that the project was not abortive.

There are some sites which so far it has proved impossible to distinguish between "abortive" and "decayed"; sometimes their terrain is a light soil with woodland for timber buildings, and the archaeological remains above ground are extremely difficult to detect. Several of the bastides of the Landes are in this ambiguous position, and it is in the nature of failed urban communities to be defective in record sources that would supplement the visual evidences.

There is another shadowy meeting place of categories when the very small foundations are considered. The ladder of success in the previous chapter has shown the lower rungs crowded. There had been large prizes for the few and consolation prizes of a sort for the remainder. Small towns, very small by modern standards, could survive behind the shelter of a monopoly or a seigneur's favours, but these would not last for ever.

Failure in such an environment, so favourable to the survival of small towns, is particularly significant. In the medieval environment the survival of the fittest was far from being the rule, and there were many shelters and crutches for the less athletic communities. Whether abortive or decayed, failures below the level of these protected and surviving small communities must point to some local disadvantage from which no parchment privileges could shelter the project. As the fate of Newton in Purbeck shows, even the favour of the most successful of all royal bastidors could not stave off mortality.

There are indications that the founders of towns themselves, particularly in the second half of the thirteenth century, had apprehensions. Some lack of confidence is shown in the *paréage* for the bastide of St. Justin. The abbey of Gimont offered the site but only on condition that the site was returned to the abbey if it failed to be peopled.[12]

[12] *Gouron*, 1778.

At Réjaumont the grant of land was to be void unless at least twenty houses were built,[13] and at Pugpito the contract was to be void unless twenty houses were built. The *paréage* for Sauveterre de Guyenne in April 1281 was to be void if the town was not commenced in November 1281.

To commence was not to complete: it was in fact November 1283 before the charter was sealed, and at once the town became involved in protracted litigation over rival jurisdictions.[14] Litigation could descend from the skies, as it did also at Lacenne and Hastingues,[15] and there was no insurance that a founder could take out against that hazard. What he could do was to use every goad to hasten the burgesses to fulfill their part of the contract and build upon their *placeae*. In 1289, four years after its foundation, Edward I was threatening defaulters at Monpazier with a £10 penalty, the proceeds to go towards the cost of the walls or the church;[16] latecomers at Domme were being fined in 1308, twenty-seven years after its foundation; in Fleurance, begun in 1274, the king found in 1287 that only 1,155 of the 2,000 building plots had been taken up.

It was apprehensions of this sort that brought penalty clauses and fixed time-limits into the *paréages*. Castelnau sur Gupie, as we have seen, obtained its charter in June 1276. The bastide was set in the parish of Artus, but in May 1289 the villagers were warned that if they wanted to take up residence in the bastide and claim its privileges they must do so within two years.[17] In August 1222 the same sort of pressure was being applied in England: the chapter of the new Cathedral of New Salisbury gave burgesses until Whitsun 1223 to build on their plots, on penalty of forfeiting the burgages.[18]

The delays, like the failures, were not always the fault of reluctant burgesses. The effective jealousy of a rival town or the anger of the king at a town erected without his consent could produce the same result. If petitions to the crown, litigation over title, or plain violence delayed a foundation for too long, some projector seized the opportunity to people another site nearby. If being early in the queue

---

[13] *R.G.*, iii, 2111.
[14] *Gouron*, 1918–22 and see p. 243 above.
[15] *Gouron*, 1103.
[16] *R.G.*, ii, 1403.
[17] *R.G.*, ii, 1097; references to the other instances cited here will be found in the Gazetteer entry.
[18] *Vetus Registrum Sarisberiense*, ed. W. H. Rich Jones (Rolls Series, lxxviii), ii (1884), pp. 10 and 21.

was so advantageous as the Tables in Chapter 9 suggest, delay could have fatal consequences.

In 1275 Edward I's seneschal of Gascony, Luke de Thenney, gave a foundation charter to the bastide of Castetcrabe. The liberties were generous, being basically those of Ste. Foy la Grande (1255) and the same as those given to Castelnau sur Gupie in 1276. But there was strong local opposition. Eight years later, from his new town at Rhuddlan, Edward I sent letters appointing three commissioners to recommence the work on the bastide, but two years later complaints of injury were being received from Constance de Béarn.[19] Today only a farm and mill in the commune of Bougue (Landes) bear the name of Castetcrabe. There is no local tradition of a site and no sign of any remains above ground, and it seems likely that the bastide was abortive.

Chapter 8 has shown how the jealousy of neighbours might arise, and in the case of the unhappy project of St. Sardos the jealousy produced a war between England and France. Prince Llewelyn was threatened with war by Edward I's councillors when they learned that he was beginning to build a market town alongside Dolforwyn castle. The abortiveness of this project is not a reflection upon the Welsh prince's judgement: indeed the reverse, for the nearby town of Montgomery thought well enough of the chances of Dolforwyn to want to kill it stone dead.

Towns could be planted very near to each other, even, as Chapter 8 has shown, an arrow's flight apart. The two towns that now make up Newton Abbot; the two Looes, and the twin boroughs of Kingsbridge and Dodbrooke show that such a position was not necessarily fatal. Yet there were situations where adjacent towns did not survive, although why one of the two succumbed is not always clear. Adpar faced Newcastle Emlyn: each had a castle of sorts, but the greater castle was the new castle and it is Adpar that is now a forgotten borough. Of the plantations that ringed Totnes, two have disappeared and Bridgetown Pomeroy has no independent urban life. The two adjacent bastides of Aiguillon have successfully coalesced, like Newton Abbot, but only one of the two Kidwellys has any life left in it. Villeréal killed the French foundation of Réalville, and in his old age one of the assassins petitioned Edward II for a pension as a reward for the murder.[20]

[19] *R.G.*, ii, 58, 643 and 864.
[20] SC8/114/5695.

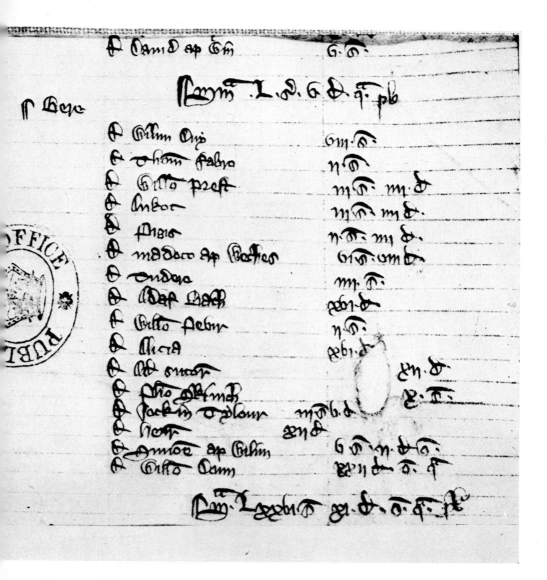

Plate 12. BERE. A planted town's tax assessment: sixteen of the wealthier burgesses with an assessment of each for tax in 1292, 76s. $11\frac{3}{4}d$. in all. This is one of the few evidences for the now deserted borough.

Since a town economy consisted partly of townsmen taking in each other's washing (in the best sense), the failure to recruit population early and quickly would have a damaging effect not only on the lord's revenue but upon the livelihood and morale of the burgesses. It was the poverty of Deganwy that made its townsmen reluctant to stay, and which forced the Exchequer to abate the tallage:

> villa de Gannoc nova est plantacio et quidem habitantes in eadem villa propter ipsius paupertatem recesserunt . . . Rex perdonavit tallagium.[21]

When Ravenserodd petitioned for a reduction of its annual payments to the Crown it claimed that the burgesses were fleeing not only the waves but idleness and lack of trade.[22] Pondering on the mixture of decay and prosperity in the cities of the Renaissance, Botero recognised that the strong will and the goodwill of the Princes had proved insufficient:

> for if the place, whereto men are drawn through the Authority of any, afford them no commodityes they will not abyde nor tarry there.[23]

The most powerful Authority and the most powerful bastidor could meet with failure. Edward I's failures are instructive in the context of his general success. The Welsh borough of Bere was chartered in 1284 on the same day as Harlech. Like most of the other Edwardian boroughs in north Wales it was the partner to a castle, in this case set on the spine of a hill that was even narrower and rockier than the site of Conway. Something of the strength of *Castell y Bere* is now beginning to emerge from excavations and restorative work.

It used to be thought that the civil settlement of Bere was completely abortive, and this view was supported not only by the absence of town walls but by the very small area of ground near the castle that was level enough to bear a town. The existence of a small borough is now attested by a list of taxpayers to the subsidy of 1292 where eighteen names appear.[24] This is a small number compared with a large walled borough such as Flint but it is a reasonable number if one compares Caerwys. The borough probably perished with the capture of the castle by the Welsh but other boroughs suffered in this way and were resurrected. The failure of Bere was probably due to its site, so unpromising for anything but warfare. It was far from the sea; it was

---

[21] *Cal. Close Rolls, 1251–1253*, p. 365.
[22] SC6/6/284; 68/3380; 87/4306; and 156/7763.
[23] G. Botero, *Of the Greatness of Cities*, trans. R. Peterson (1606), p. 11.
[24] E179/242/53.

served by no river; and it lay in a valley that came to a dead end in the screes of Cader Idris while less than 2 miles further south a parallel valley afforded easy access from the sea to Tal-y-Llyn lake and the lower passes: that way, if any, was the way of commerce.

Warenmouth, near Bamburgh castle, is another borough with an uncertain site. If (as seems possible) the town was intended to lie high up on the cliffs above the river, it had poor commercial interest while being too far from the castle to gain from military protection.

Edward I's intentions for his new town in the Isle of Purbeck were also good and his provision for the town was generous. It obtained a good borough charter with very full liberties for the new inhabitants and it was Edward's intention that the town should have its own church. Yet here again an examination of the heathy site alongside Poole Harbour has failed to yield unambiguous evidence for the exact location of the borough. There is no documentary evidence to confute the assumption that the town was still-born, but the final proof would be the discovery of abandoned earthworks and half-finished houses. This project had no military purpose and its commercial assumptions were not unrealistic: immediately inland were the busy quarries of Purbeck stone needing a quay from which to be shipped. Gotowre super Mare (as some of the early documents called the projected town) was much nearer to the quarries than Poole (an older plantation), but Poole flourished and Edward's town failed.

The distribution of failures in England, Wales and Gascony is a very scattered one. There is no great local concentration that would help to identify some great operating cause. We are left with individual explanations or with explanations that are more like conjectures. We can say that Poole succeeded while Newton was failing or that Newbury (Berks.) succeeded while the nearby Newtown (Hants.) was failing, but in most cases the documents are not illuminating.

III

What of the distribution of failures over time? Table IX.6 has suggested that success came more readily to those towns which were founded in the earlier decades. Table X.1 analyses the failures, using decade periods where possible. The total percentage of failures in England is small, and there is very little significance in their timing. Two of the three periods with four or more failures (1060–1100 and

1201–30) are long, and the failures are equivalent only to one each decade. The decade 1241–50, which lost half its eight plantations, was the most unfortunate.

The percentage of Welsh failures is little higher than in England, and they are very dispersed over the decades. The four decades that had total failures cannot be taken very seriously, as one plantation was attempted in each of them. If there was an unfortunate decade, it was again 1241–50.

In Gascony the death rate exceeded one bastide in three, and in two decades, 1271–90, the failures were both numerous and a high proportion of those attempted. The decades of Alphonse de Poitiers' foundations (1246–60) were the only ones to register no failures. The price paid for a vigorous pursuit of bastides by Edward I and his officers after 1271 was a good deal of miss in a mixture of hit and miss.

Yet there was one situation even worse than to have failed in establishing a bastide. It is revealed in Table X.1 and will be more fully analysed in the next chapters: there were decades, such as 1271–80 in

TABLE X.1

FAILURE OF ENGLISH PLANTATIONS BY BROAD PERIODS

Date of Foundation	Total plantations	Abortive	Decayed	Replaced	Total failures Number	Percentage
1060–1100	21	0	5	1	4	20
1101–1160	32	1	1	0	2	6
1161–1200	35	1	1	0	2	6
1201–1230	36	3	3	0	6	16
1231–1240	4	1	0	0	1	25
1241–1250	8	3	1	0	4	50
1251–1260	3	0	0	0	0	0
1261–1270	5	1	0	0	1	20
1271–1280	0	0	0	0	0	0
1281–1290	4	1	0	0	1	25
1291–1330	12	0	3	2	1	8
1331–1340	0	0	0	0	0	0
1341–1350	1	1	0	0	1	100
1351–1360	0	0	0	0	0	0
1361–1370	1	0	0	0	0	0
After 1370	1	0	0	0	0	0
Before 1066	3	0	0	0	0	0
Not dated	6	0	0	0	0	0
Totals	172	12	14	3	23	13

TABLE X.2

FAILURE OF WELSH PLANTATIONS, BY DECADES

	Total	Abortive	Decayed	Replaced	Total failures	
					Number	Percentage
before 1066	1	0	0	1	0	
1066–70	0	0	0	0	0	
1071–80	3	0	0	1	0	
1081–90	1	0	0	0	0	
1091–1100	4	0	0	1	0	
1101–10	3	0	0	1	0	
1111–20	3	0	0	0	0	
1121–30	2	0	0	0	0	
1131–40	2	0	1	0	1	50
1141–50	4	0	1	0	1	25
1151–60	1	0	1	0	1	100
1161–70	2	0	0	0	0	
1171–80	1	0	0	0	0	
1181–90	1	0	1	0	1	100
1191–1200	1	0	1	0	1	100
1201–10	1	0	0	0	0	
1211–20	2	0	0	0	0	
1221–30	2	0	0	0	0	
1231–40	3	0	1	0	1	33
1241–50	6	0	3	0	3	50
1251–60	2	0	0	0	0	
1261–70	1	0	0	0	0	
1271–80	10	1	3	0	0	40
1281–90	10	0	1	0	1	10
1291–1300	9	0	3	0	3	30
1301–10	3	0	0	0	0	
1311–20	1	0	0	0	0	
1321–30	1	0	1	0	1	100
1331–40	1	0	0	0	0	0
1341–50	1	0	0	0	0	
After 1350	0	0	0	0	0	
Not dated	2	0	0	0	0	
Totals	84	17	17	4	18	21

TABLE X.3

FAILURE OF GASCON BASTIDES, BY DECADES

	Total plantations	Abortive	Decayed	Not identifiable	Total failures Number	percentage
before 1246	1	0	0	0	0	0
1246–60	10	0	0	0	0	0
1261–70	17	1	2	0	3	18
1271–80	18	3	3	2	8	44
1281–90	31	3	12	2	17	55
1291–1300	11	0	3	0	3	27
1301–10	9	3	1	1	5	56
1311–20	18	1	3	2	6	33
1321–30	7	0	1	0	1	14
After 1330	3	0	0	1	1	33
Totals	125	11	25	8	44	35

England, when no attempts were made to found a single town, and others in which only one attempt was made in the whole decade (*e.g.* 1171–1210 in Wales). The period after 1330 was most significant of all: it was no longer a question of poor decades among a succession of good decades. Town plantation was ceasing. A black death was settling on English towns two decades before the Black Death itself. These changes were not local: Table XIII.8 shows that France outside Gascony was as much affected as Gascony, and studies in the Low Countries, Bavaria and Switzerland show the same trend in other parts of Europe.

Logically, one possibility would be that there was a revulsion against towns all over the Continent, so that economic life continued to expand, but in country industries. The development of the English cloth industry outside the towns was a feature of this period, and it is difficult to say how much this development compensated for the discouraging, chill wind that blew in towns. However, even the new cloth-working districts produced no one after 1330 who thought that it was worth trying to promote a brand-new town as a marketing centre.[25] In previous decades some very petty boroughs had been the summit of ambition; now, not even petty boroughs seemed worth planting.

[25] For developments in the cloth industry that produced settlement but not towns, see E. M. Carus-Wilson, "Evidences of Industrial Growth on some 15th Century Manors", *Ec.H.R.*, 2nd ser. xii (1959), pp. 190–205.

It seems more likely, viewing the contraction in town plantation in Europe as a whole, that opportunity had fled when the rate of increase of population and the colonisation of new land both began to slow down. There is some evidence for more than a slowing down: a retreat. The long-sustained increase in population and the clearance of additional farm-land had aided the multiplication of towns: now, without this support, the economy had enough urban centres to satisfy its needs: and there is some evidence that Europe was now over-stocked.

IV

England and Gascony each happen to have an abortive plantation of particular significance, not for its geographical situation but for the timing. The geographical situations were most promising.

The 16 miles of the Foss Way between Lincoln and Newark had no provision for travellers. The road passed through no village and (like many Roman roads) formed the boundary of parishes for almost all its length. The Knights Hospitallers were lords of the manor of Eagle, and a tongue of this manor's territory came down to the Foss Way near the present Half-way House Inn. Roadside sites between great towns on major highways had provided fertile soil for plantations elsewhere in England, and in 1345 the Hospitallers obtained a charter for the foundation of their new borough.

If the site was propitious the time was not. Within four years of the charter the first plague-infected rats were coming ashore at English ports. All over Europe the same disease was reducing the population. In a short space of time a quarter of the population of England was dead; the plague returned again and again; and by the 1370's the population may have been reduced by as much as one-third. Stagnation had been succeeded by a catastrophic contraction.

The Black Death and the subsequent plagues made the second half of the fourteenth century even more sterile for new towns than the first half. None of the basic encouragements for town plantation remained. In the countryside, fields were being abandoned and marginal villages were being deserted; the market towns were emptier and the market stalls were fewer; the seaports suffered from the reduced population and incomes of their European customers; and with the reduced population in England there was a general shortage of rural labour, at once taking

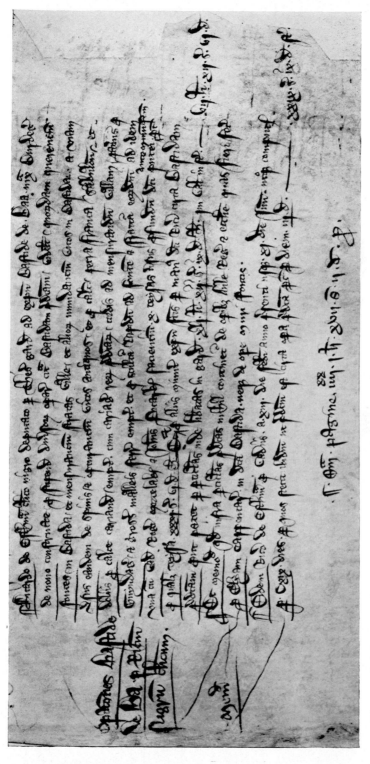

Plate 13. BAA. The foundation of a bastide: evidence from accounts for the wages of workmen at Baa, June 1287: including "measuring the streets" (line 3), "rope for measuring out the town" (line 5) and making a well (line 7). A note in lines 10–11 mentions other work on the King's Hall and the church of the bastide done by Elyas the carpenter. The main account covers the period from February 13 to June 11.

away some of those who might in earlier generations have wished to migrate to towns, and—more important—greatly diminishing the bargaining power of lords of manors. Demesne services lightened and then vanished, and when the village was less oppressive the towns lost some of their attraction as a place of refuge.

In this situation there was little incentive for lords to create boroughs by promoting villages, and very few successful organic towns date from the century following the Black Death. Roby (in Huyton, Lancs.) was a village whose lord's decision to foster a borough came too late. In 1304 it received a market charter and in 1372 a borough charter, but

> these attempts to improve the position of Roby appear to have met with no success, and there does not seem to be any further allusion to the borough or fair.[26]

With the fortunes of existing towns brought low, and the prospects of organic town creation so poor it is not surprising that the creation of new towns came to a virtual halt.

V

The sterile period was prolonged. After Queenborough in 1368 there is no certain evidence for a new town until the creation of Falmouth in 1613, although there was an abortive scheme in the reign of Elizabeth I for a new port at Dover. Two hundred and fifty years without new towns is in strong contrast to the 250 years before 1368, and even Falmouth was not the beginning of a revival.

For some time after 1349 this sterility was the undoubted product of economic contraction but historians are not agreed on the duration of the contraction. There are no useful figures for total population in the fifteenth century and the histories of particular towns and regions are varied enough to give ammunition both to the pessimistic and the optimistic school. The optimist in this context is one who believes that there was general urban stagnation for only a short time after the end of the plagues. The optimists have found a champion in Dr. Bridbury, whose book is boldly titled *Economic Growth*. He cites the statistics of dwindling town plantation in the late thirteenth century and the total cessation after 1370 but continues:

> it would be wrong to read too much into this decline . . . and total cessation of new foundations set upon land which had previously been agricultural.[27]

[26] *V.C.H. Lancs.*, iii, p. 175.
[27] A. R. Bridbury, *Economic Growth: England in the Later Middle Ages*, (1962), p. 70.

Myself a pessimist, I cannot help reading the evidence before and after the Black Death as a continuity. The common factor is the lack of enthusiasm for the positive act of wanting to create a town on the old medieval pattern.

Optimists and pessimists among historians would agree that by 1500 population was again on the increase and that there were a number of important growing points in the economy. Yet outside London, few of these were urban. The disenchantment with towns was as thorough as it could be. It is doubtful if there was ever a period in English history, except this one, when commercial and industrial innovation was so aloof from urbanism. From 1320 there were four centuries that could almost be christened the un-urban centuries.

The most rapidly expanding industry in the period after the Black Death was cloth, and it is well known that the cloth industry was taking to the countryside and becoming cottage-based: the wife of Bath was succeeded by the wives and husbands of Castle Combe. Industries such as coal, iron, copper, tin, alum and salt were tied to the location of their raw materials and to wood-fuel; and they did not produce new industrial towns. Industries such as brewing, brick-making and dyeing were tied to customers living in towns already established, and where town populations grew fastest (especially in London) these ancillary industries were attracted. The list of England's forty-two wealthiest towns in 1662 is very similar to that in 1523–27 and that in 1334. There were only eight changes in the ranking order between 1334 and 1662. Six of the newcomers to the list were old-established ports,[28] ship-building towns or dockyard towns: Deptford, East Greenwich, Portsmouth, Dover, Sandwich and Chatham.[29] Only Leeds and Gateshead had no smell of salt. The harbingers of the eighteenth-century factory-town, in respect of large numbers working in one work-place and under one direction, were the shipyards and dockyards of the Thames and Medway. None of these were new towns, but a near approach to a new town was Devonport near Plymouth, and its original name (by 1696) was significantly *Dock*.[30] Whitehaven was created soon after 1660, New Deal[31] between 1650 and 1670. This slow pro-

[28] A proposed new town at Dover (temp. Eliz. I) appears in a plan from the Hatfield House Mss. (I, no. 59), reproduced by A. H. W. Robinson, *Marine Cartography in Britain* (1962), p. 152.
[29] The data for 1334, 1377, 1524 and 1662 are set out in W. G. Hoskins, *Local History in England*, (1959), pp. 176–177.
[30] Id., *Devon* (1954), p. 456.
[31] Upper Deal has the Norman Church; E. Hasted, *Kent*, iv, p. 163, wrote of "a new town

gress from Falmouth in 1613 is feeble compared with some medieval decades, and not until Milford Haven in 1798 is there a new seaport that can be called the child of the Industrial Revolution.[32]

New boroughs were established in this period, but all were simply existing villages that had prospered and thought it worth while to obtain incorporation. In general, as Professor Carus-Wilson has put it, "the advantages of making and dealing within town walls were no longer what they had been". There was no strong technological reason why new industries should reside in new towns. Unlike their continental counterparts, English merchants and craftsmen no longer had to take the passage of hostile armies into account when planning where to establish themselves. With the decay of villeinage the country air became as free as the town air, and in many cases it was considerably freer. Where old-established towns were defending themselves against country competitors, the municipal privileges had atrophied into restriction. There were Tudor and Stuart industrialists who thanked God that they were not burgesses in a corporate town. Incorporation had come to spell oligarchy, conservatism and restriction of innovation. Walls had ceased to be a protection and were beginning to look like a prison.

One other direction of innovation must finally be mentioned. In the spa-towns, conditions favoured new residential building and indeed speculation and promotion. The clientèle of the spas when they came to take the waters wanted a standard of accommodation that was set by Bath, Cheltenham and Brighton. Lodgings in a converted cottage were no substitute, even supposing there were cottages near the mineral springs. Tunbridge Wells (1630–70) was not at Tonbridge. Harrogate was on a moor. In 1656 Dugdale recorded that the inhabitants of the village of Leamington Priors made much use of a spring of salt water for seasoning their meat; when the same waters began to bathe the human frame, the streets of a new town of Leamington Spa were laid out beyond the village; they form a perfect grid pattern that would not have disgraced any of Edward I's town planners.[33]

along the shore, New, alias Lower Deal", and reproduced a plan showing a street grid. (I am indebted to Mr. A. J. Percival for this reference.)
[32] Sir F. Ross, *The Town of Milford* (1954), p. 168.
[33] *V.C.H. Warws.*, vi, p. 155.

VI

In the sixteenth and seventeenth centuries, when the planning of towns had passed out of fashion in England and Wales,[34] there were still continental foundations. Why this divergent experience? There is no need to assemble a list of these continental towns, for they have been described in many studies of urbanism.[35] The majority of them were founded for reasons that were not important in England. Outside the mining towns of southern Germany and Austria, very few were industrial.

Some, like New Hesdin (Pas de Calais), were to replace towns that had been destroyed in war. England suffered no invasion in this period and her civil war did not obliterate towns. Freudenstadt in the Black Forest was built in 1599 specially for refugees from the religious wars, but the refugees who came from the Netherlands to Elizabethan England were comfortably absorbed in the empty houses and decayed workshops of Norwich and other old textile towns. England has no town as unlucky as Mannheim: founded in 1606, destroyed in 1632, rebuilt in 1648, destroyed in 1689, rebuilt in 1720.[36] The wars of Louis XIII and XIV, and the need to defend extended frontiers, produced a large number of French towns that were newly placed in positions that best suited new military strategy, their walls planned in geometrical patterns for the deployment of cannon fire, their barrack blocks and barrack square laid out with the same passion for the straight line. The gate of Neuf Breisach (Rhin), a town as rectilinear as any bastide, bears a scroll with the date and purpose of the town.[37] Appropriately enough for a town that had the air of a reborn Roman *castrum*, the scroll is in Latin.

XVI · X · MDCXCIX
SECURITAS ALSATIAE NEOBRISACUM

On the south-west coast, where the English navies might be expected to appear, the kings of France also built towns for *securitas*. Brouage

[34] It is possible that Longtown (Cumb.) and Coleford (Glos.) were also developed as market-towns in the Stuart period.

[35] E.g. R. E. Dickinson, *The West European City* (1951), ch. 18; *Lavedan*, vol. ii; G. L. Burke, *The Making of Dutch Towns* (1956), ch. vii; F. R. Hiorns, *Town Building in History* (1956), pp. 187–316.

[36] The chequers of Mannheim, numbered alphabetically and numerically, are still employed instead of street-names.

[37] There is a recent brief study by C. Cooke, C. Hennessey and D. Wardlaw, "Neu-Breisach: a study in change", *Journ. Roy. Inst. Brit. Archit.*, lxxii (1965), pp. 75–82.

(Charente Maritime) is one of these. It now lies high and dry among the marshes.

Towns of the same sort were founded in the watery lowlands of Holland. The village of Willemstad was designed to serve the large polder of Ruigenhilsche that was reclaimed in 1562. In 1583 William the Silent transformed the village into a fortress town, star-shaped with seven bastions and a harbour. Ten miles to the east, Klundert was built at about the same time: it was a nine-pointed star. Between 1597 and 1601 Coeworden, that had been destroyed by the Spaniards in 1592, was rebuilt as a perfectly concentric town, a seven-pointed star.[38]

The English kings had no need to embellish their frontiers with such towns. After 1603 they had no land frontier to concern them. The Welsh border had given no serious trouble once a Welsh Tudor was on the English throne; Mary and Elizabeth I spent money on the re-planning of Edward I's Berwick on Tweed, but within a generation of their construction the accession of James I in 1603 made its great walls and cannon embrasures superfluous.

Another reason for the multiplication of new towns in Europe after 1648 was its political fragmentation. The host of petty princes needed to reassure themselves and their subjects. Versailles, the leader of fashion, indicated that a true prince must have a fitting place for his court and that to build in the grand manner was truly princely. In the Rhineland and southern Germany small provincial capitals were the order of the day. Some were refurbished medieval towns but Charleroi, Charleville, Philippeville, Marienbourg, Saarlouis and Karlsruhe were compounded from the names of the princes that begat them. Richelieu imitated his king and named his foundation after himself (Richelieu, Indre et Loire). In the New World there had to be new towns. Appropriately enough it was a native of Brouage who founded Quebec, and a native of Cadillac founded Detroit. The English, who stood aloof from the continental town fever, did have their Jameston and their Charleston in the New World: but the New World, with its warfare and its international rivalries, was more like the mainland of Europe than the uninvaded fields of Jacobean England.[39]

Nearer home, but neither on the European mainland nor in England, there was another burst of town plantation by the English. It was in

[38] G. L. Burke, *loc. cit.*
[39] For the division of American colonial towns into chequers see C. O. Paullin and J. K. Wright, *Atlas of the Historical Geography of the U.S.A.* (New York, 1936), plates 40, 44 and 48B.

the true bastide tradition.   The towns of James I's Ulster plantation were just the sort of town that Edward I had planted in North Wales.[40] They were garrison towns that assisted the English to hold down the hostile natives of conquered territory yet they were also centres of commerce.   Although the word was unknown to their founders, the Ulster towns had true *paréages*.   The partners were the king as sovereign and the investors who provided the money, who laid out the streets and squares as if the thirteenth century had suddenly come again, and who arranged the recruitment of the burgesses.   The investors were the city companies of London, and the nature of the partnership is compounded into the name Salterstown and the name Londonderry. As the tablet in the porch of Londonderry Cathedral proclaims:

> If stones could speak, then London's praise should sound
> Who built this Church and City from the ground, 1633.

In Gascony the magic of the name London failed to give life to the bastide of St. Etienne de Londres.   It was left to Ulster to invoke magic more successfully, and the history of the new towns of the English may properly be said to end in the Ulster plantations of James I.[41]

VII

ENVOI

The planted towns of the Middle Ages, with so few imitators in early-modern England, made a curious, short-lived but effective reappearance in English political history during the agitation for Parliamentary and municipal reform at the beginning of the nineteenth century.   It was the growth of population in new industrial towns, often unincorporated and unrepresented in Parliament, that drew attention to the incongruously small and decayed medieval boroughs that still boasted

[40] T. W. Moody, *The Londonderry Plantation* (1939); G. Camblin, *The Town in Ulster* (1951); D. A. Chart, ed., *Londonderry and the London Companies* (1928); R. Common, ed., *Northern Ireland from the Air* (n.d., 1965).

[41] Its resurrection in the town-planning movement of the nineteenth century is another story.   The beginnings are related in W. Ashworth, "British Industrial Villages in the Nineteenth Century", *Ec.H.R.*, 2nd ser. iii (1951), pp. 378–387; and *id.*, *The Genesis of Modern Town Planning* (1954).

The grid plan was adopted at Middlesbrough, Barrow in Furness and other nineteenth-century urban novelties, but a symbolic beginning might be discerned in the plan, put forward in 1842 by Captain Vetch, R.E., to add streets to the edge of Birmingham in order to convert it to a regular polygon: *Sanitary Condition of the Labouring Population.   Poor Law Commissioners* (Parl. Papers., House of Lords, xxvi (1842)), p. 385, with plan.

mayors and corporation and still voted for their borough Members. Not all rotten boroughs were plantations, but in previous centuries the Crown had favoured a Parliamentary franchise for towns on the royal demesne, and many royal towns, especially in the south-west, were plantations. In the eighteenth century the franchise continued but the fewer the members of the corporation, and the fewer the inhabited burgage plots, the easier it was for a borough-monger to purchase votes. Thus the names of towns in our Gazetteer appeared frequently in the Blue Books when Parliamentary Reform was at its height.[42]

An analysis of the *Returns Relating to Parliamentary Representation*[43] shows that in 1831 five of the fifty-six Parliamentary boroughs with the lowest populations in the Census were plantations: Old Sarum (12 inhabitants), Newtown, I.O.W., (68), Mitchell (97), New Radnor (378), West Looe (593) and Bere Alston (not separately tabulated in the Census). When houses were counted in the Parliamentary boroughs several plantations again returned very low scores: Old Sarum had not a single house: "no house now remaining or male inhabitant actually residing". Mitchell had only twenty-four houses; Bere Alston, Newtown, I.O.W., and Bossiney all appear in 1832 in *Returns Relative to the 120 Smallest Boroughs*.[44] When the Boundary Commissioners reported in 1832 they found twenty-two burgesses in Beaumaris exercising the Parliamentary franchise, sixteen in Cefnllys (living in three farms and one cottage) and none at all in Adpar.[45]

Among the boroughs that lost their members by the Reform Act of 1832 were Appleby, Bere Alston, Bishop's Castle, Boroughbridge, Bossiney, Brackley, Camelford, Corfe, Downton, East Looe, Grampound, Haslemere, Hedon, Hindon, Lostwithiel, New Romney, Newtown, I.O.W., Okehampton, Plympton, Queenborough, Saltash, Stockbridge, Tregoney, West Looe and Winchelsea. The second Reform Act of 1867 disenfranchised Arundel and Reigate. The third Reform Act of 1885 took separate representation from sixteen Welsh boroughs that appear in our Gazetteer as plantations. The seats vacated by the representatives of these medieval plantations were occupied by the members for the new towns of the Steam Age.

[42] It was the planted borough of Grampound that in 1821 lost its Members in order to provide representation of Leeds, which by that date bore an un-medieval look. Maurice Paynel's plantation of 1207 never had the Parliamentary franchise.
[43] *House of Commons Papers*. no. 105 of 1831 (Report from the Select Committee on the Petitions for Reform in Parliament).
[44] *House of Commons Papers*, no. 38 of 1832, with plans.
[45] *Parl. Papers, 1832*, vol. xi, pt. vii, pp. 1, 35 and 191.

Like the Parliamentary franchise, the municipal privileges given to a town were not easily revoked. Cancelled charters like that to New Eagle are few. Shrinking communities clung desperately to the shelter of their privileges. When trade and traffic had deserted a town there was still the chance that municipal endowments could provide a supplementary income for the members of the corporation, and when a burgess could market nothing else there was always his vote to sell.

The Report of the Royal Commission on Municipal Corporations[46] (1835) is an anthology of critical invective against the corruption to which these towns had sunk. The borough of Bossiney "had no useful purpose"; at Grampound the votes were worth £280 each; at Kenfig only fifty-one burgesses resided; at Llantrissant the burgesses were "dissolute and venal"; at Looe

> the corporation has merely been kept alive for election purposes.[47]

No burgesses resided within the borough of Newtown, I.O.W. One would not think today, seeing its handsome William-and-Mary Town Hall, that when it was built the town had only a handful of burgesses, nor that in 1835 the commissioners would report:

> there is not an inhabitant capable of exercising any municipal function; there are probably not sufficient inhabitants of intelligence to make a court-leet jury.[48]

These were the mortal remains of the bishop of Winchester's new borough of 1255–56. At a time when the villeins of the bishop's manor worked out their servitude in the surrounding fields the town's seal had been the proud statement of its franchise. It was *Francheville de L'Isle de Whyt* (Plate 11). The device on the thirteenth-century seal of the borough had a ship and leopard. In 1835 the ship had ceased to sail and the leopard no longer leaped.

The Act of 1835 disallowed the municipal corporations of twelve planted boroughs. It is symptomatic of the less radical character of the 1835 Act compared with the Parliamentary Reform Act of 1832, that Newtown I.O.W. remained a corporation until the Act of 1885 when thirty-five other planted boroughs lost their corporations.

In 1835 the Municipal Corporations Act performed some curious rites. The lawyers had gone to work and disinterred the charters of

[46] *Parl. Papers, 1835*, vols. xxiii–vi.
[47] *Ibid.*, xxiii, pp. 267, 311, 451, 507 and 531–537.
[48] *Ibid.*, xxiv, p. 795.

corporations so long dead as to be utterly beyond corruption. Bere was solemnly disenfranchised even though there had been no mayor for over 500 years. Warenmouth was disinterred for reburial even though its name and location were helplessly forgotten. Kenfig ceased to be a municipal corporation even though the sands had choked the parish church many generations before. The burgesses of Skinburgh were solemnly deprived of their corporate existence and municipal officers, but the Solway Firth had dissolved the corporation more effectively by 1305. Ravenserodd was ritually deprived of its municipal officers but, like the town, they had been drowned four and a half centuries earlier by the waters of the Humber. Some very strange spirits were being called from the vasty deep.

PART THREE

FROM BEGINNING TO END

The town plantations of England, Wales and Gascony are now treated separately, and in chronological order. All three areas show a marked slowing down in the early fourteenth century and a virtual end to new towns with the Black Death in 1349, but there are important differences between the three areas in the dates when the peak of activity was reached. These chronologies are related to major political and economic changes.

CHAPTER ELEVEN

The Chronology of Town Plantation in England

Here *Time* and *Place*, like friendley foes doe warre
Which should shew most desir'd *Particulars*
But *Place* gives place, sith *Time* is greater farre;
Yet *Place*, well rang'd, gets glory by these warres.

John Davies, Poem Prefatory to John Speed's
Theatre of the Empire of Great Britain (1611).

I

IN all the previous chapters chronology has been subordinate. In some, the new towns have been treated in a general way, drawing illustrations from more than one period and not in chronological order. In others, some matters have had chronological treatment but no chapter has been wholly devoted to the march of events, and the Introduction began very near the end of the story, with Edward I and his colloquium of town planners in 1297.

The next three chapters, which precede the Gazetteers, move in a more conventional way. The main characteristics of medieval town plantation have been set out, and from this relatively firm base it is possible to look back towards origins, dim as they are, and to inquire when the activity of deliberate town plantation can first be discerned in the three countries, England, Wales, and Gascony.

The task is simplest in Gascony, for all but two of the bastides were founded after 1250, a period when documentary evidence is fairly generously available, and Chapter 13 tries to give a brief narrative to set the bastides in the general political and economic development of the area. For a different reason, it is useful to treat Wales separately from England: there is no serious problem of origins in Wales to be discussed, for there was only one English plantation in Wales before the Norman Conquest, the period that is the true dark age of urban history in England. The chronology of English towns in Wales was closely connected with conquest, native resistance, and reconquest, several times repeated before Edward I's final victories.   These events affected the economic life of some English towns near the border but were not of major significance in determining the timing of town plantation in other English counties.   Wales is, accordingly, given treatment separately in Chapter 12.

II

In 1936 James Tait wrote:

> Of the growth of boroughs we know little until the eve of the Norman Conquest.[1]

Since 1936 there has been some progress, and the evidence from literary sources and material remains has been set out by Professor Stenton and more recently by Mr. H. R. Loyn.[2]   It is now quite impossible to view the Anglo-Saxon kingdoms as mere collections of villages and their economies as mere subsistence agriculture.   Yet the evidence of craftsmen, traders, mints, walls, gilds and ports is not of the kind or quality that makes it easy to distinguish between a town that was an enlarged village and a town that was designed.

The earlier one travels back in time, the greater the risk that evidence will be damaged, or destroyed; habits of government such as produce bulky annual files of documents were slow to develop, and even the first generations of Norman government saw only the beginning of those records of central government that from the mid-twelfth century begin to throw a meagre light on the increase in English towns.   Surviving records of private justice and estate administration are very slender before the thirteenth century, and the Anglo-Saxon centuries are not the sole victims: the blanket of the dark lifts only slowly.   Were it not for the happy survival of Domesday Book, we should be as ill-informed about the state of all Norman towns as we are about those that lie in the northern counties for which Domesday Book is silent.

The non-documentary evidence that suggests a planted town is discussed elsewhere (pp. 382–85).   One of these evidences is the encirclement of a town by a rural parish to which the townsmen were still obliged.   The first claimants to be plantations are the Anglo-Saxon *burhs* of the

---

[1] J. Tait, *The Medieval English Borough* (1936), p. 31.
[2] F. M. Stenton, *Anglo-Saxon England* (1943), pp. 518–536; H. R. Loyn, *Anglo-Saxon England and the Norman Conquest* (1962), pp. 98–145; see also D. M. Wilson, *The Anglo-Saxons* (1960), pp. 80–83; P. H. Blair, *An Introduction to Anglo-Saxon England* (1959), pp. 277–300.

ninth century, but at the time most parish bounds were still drawn widely and vaguely. Many villages did not yet possess a church, and a town could have its church without infringing the rights of an existing church: it was not forced, like the later burgesses of Stratford on Avon, Liverpool and Hull, to make terms with a distant parish church. Tait noticed this feature of *burhs*:

> there seems to be no instance in the south-west in which the principal church of a borough was only the chapel of a rural church, as was common enough in new boroughs founded after the Norman Conquest.[3]

Ballard, however, deduced that the siting of Axbridge *burh* within Cheddar manor and Langport *burh* within Somerton manor were indications that towns had been planted within the territories of older communities:

> hence, from the earliest times we have to account for boroughs which were artificially created, and were not village communities which had acquired a burghal status.[4]

This sentence clearly distinguishes the "planted" and the "organic". Another *burh*, Maldon, was accepted as a plantation by Tait because it was a town without fields, an enclave of 81 acres, 165 of its 180 burgesses in 1086 possessing nothing beyond their houses.[5]

When there is no direct documentation to date the foundation of a town in the twelfth and thirteenth centuries, the event may nevertheless be sometimes apparent by comparing documents from different years and noting that a town has arrived in the interval. By the thirteenth century one can hope that documents will afford several glimpses of *Before* and *After*, but Anglo-Saxon documentation is much less generous, and too often the situation *After* is seen through light mist, and that *Before* in heavy fog. The achievement of recent historians of Anglo-Saxon town-life is to have made patterns from fragments, but these fragments do not greatly assist in distinguishing between promoted village and planted town.

The silence of documents is the classic moment for archaeological intervention. All power to the spade and trowel: let armies of archaeologists invade these semi-deserted Anglo-Saxon towns (such as Lydford, Eashing, Halwell, *Scaeftesige* or Burpham) where trenching operations do not need the eviction of the modern native population. Yet to ask

[3] Tait, *op. cit.*, p. 56.   [4] *Ballard*, p. xci.
[5] Tait, *op. cit.*, pp. 49, 71, 77 and 96.

for proof, by purely archaeological means, that a particular Anglo-Saxon town had no village antecedents may be posing a question too precise for the means available. Archaeology by its nature, is better at providing positive evidence than establishing essentially negative propositions such as the absence of a village before the foundation of a town.

These limitations on evidence, historical and archaeological, help to explain why authorities seem to contradict each other. When the recognition of a town plantation depends on a balance of probabilities there is plenty of room for other considerations to enter. If a historian is generally predisposed towards the view that Romano-British and Anglo-Saxon settlements were continuously occupied, he will naturally stress those *burhs* (eight of twenty-eight in the *Burghal Hidage* (p. 325)) that were set at Roman sites. If he regards the Anglo-Saxons as "individualists" not "dwellers in towns" he will be more ready to accept the idea that *burhs* were new and not simply the fortification of existing villages.

Maitland assumed both possibilities:

> in the one case the institutions that are characteristic of *burh* and *port* may have been superimposed upon those of an ancient village which had common fields. In another, an almost uninhabited spot may have been chosen as the site for a stronghold.[6]

Tait would have placed most *burhs* in the first, "organic", class:

> the new *burhs* founded by Alfred and his family, when not mere forts, were normally existing settlements, now for the first time surrounded by a wall or stockaded rampart.[7]

Thus he stressed that the charter to Worcester (885–900), envisaging fortification, was not the first creation of lay settlement there. Oxford, he claimed, had already attracted population, but Oxford's great topographer, Dr. H. E. Salter, believed that the town had been laid out on the furlongs of open fields,[8] rather as Norman Bury St. Edmunds was to cover the old ploughlands.

Professor Stenton wrote of Oxford and Wallingford:

> they were each founded on a compact block of royal land regarded as equivalent to eight yardlands. On the foundation of such a borough it seems that the defensible area was divided into plots—represented by the

[6] F. W. Maitland, *Domesday Book and Beyond* (ed. E. Miller, 1960), p. 239.
[7] Tait, *op. cit.*, p. 3.
[8] H. E. Salter, *Saxon Oxford* (Oxford Hist. Soc., c (1936)), pp. 7–10.

hagae and *mansurae* of Domesday Book—which were taken from the king at money rent by persons wishing to engage in trade.[9]

This is the very language of later medieval town plantation. Only the name for the house-plots is different: for *hagae* read *placeae*, and the passage would serve for an account of the foundation of New Winchelsea.

In his study of Saxon Oxford, Professor Jope leans more towards organic development outside the gate of St. Frideswide's monastery, comparing it with the development of Abingdon and (Saxon) Bury St. Edmunds. He sees the urban plan as an extension or colonisation of the initial settlement:

> it is not unreasonable to suppose that round about A.D. 900 some royal stimulus might have been applied to encourage the growth of a strong centre here for trade and defence.[10]

A Saxon origin for Wallingford, Ipswich and *Hamwih* (Southampton) does not seem to have been yet challenged, but Wareham is in dispute. One author declares that there is nothing Roman about the rectilinear town, but a recent archaeological account of Anglo-Saxon society says:

> Wareham was a town of some importance, and early Celtic inscriptions and remains of Roman habitation would seem to indicate that it was already old in Alfred's day.[11]

Twineham (Christchurch) was declared by the Victoria County History to have been a "ham" or village before it was a *burh*,[12] but Ballard put it with Langport and Axbridge as an example of the artificial creation of a borough.

With professional historians confused, it is not surprising that local historians have hesitated to recognise their towns as plantations. They also had to contend with an innate local patriotism in which longevity was a virtue for towns as well as antiquarians. The older a town could be proved, the greater was the credit. If it proved impossible to make it Roman—although a single coin was often enough to stimulate patriotic imagination—then it had to be early Anglo-Saxon. For Ludlow, a clear plantation of the early Norman period, a local historian felt impelled to make greater claims (the italics are not in the original).

---

[9] F. M. Stenton, *Anglo-Saxon England* (1943), p. 522.
[10] E. M. Jope, "Saxon Oxford and its Origins", in D. B. Harden, ed., *Dark-Age Britain* (1956), pp. 235–236.
[11] D. M. Wilson, *The Anglo-Saxons* (1960), p. 82.
[12] *V.C.H. Hants.*, v, p. 85.

That it was a town of note in the time of the Britons is evident from the British name it bears—*though we have no particular record of the matter*.[13]

While historians are in that mood it is of little significance that the name Ludlow is not British; and the absence of record matters less. The following modern account of the origins of Warwick can be recognised for what it is, a conjecture followed by a confession.

> We must picture its origin as late as the sixth century in a little cluster of dwellings by the weir. The recorded history of Warwick only begins in 914 when, late in the autumn, Aethelflæd, the Lady of the Mercians, fortified the hill-site.[14]

The passion for antiquity at any price was criticised by a perceptive local historian writing 200 years ago in Wiltshire. Dr. Davis's *Origines* poked fun at previous writers who had made his native town Roman or even pre-Roman in origin. What the evidence really showed, he said, was a scene "as dark as Erebus or Night". The town? it was one where the documentary darkness before the early twelfth century was perfectly natural, for only then did a bishop of Salisbury create a town alongside his castle and park. It was the planted *burgus de devisis*, the borough of Devizes.[15]

> As to your town, no doubt it was ancient, but not quite so old as the Flood, Babel, Babylon or Rome. The inhabitants are not the worse for not having long pedigrees of Roman blood in their veins; they may be contented with a descent no earlier than the Normans.

III

Circumscribed as it is, what does the evidence suggest for the motives of town plantation in England before the Norman Conquest? (For the moment the evidence of parallel activity on the continent can be left aside.)

The Anglo-Saxon kingdoms had within them the inherited and decayed urban centres of their Roman predecessors. The Roman towns were sited for Roman convenience, and the fate of Silchester demonstrates that a Roman site could be irrelevant to Anglo-Saxon needs.

---

[13] R. H. Clive, *Documents connected with the History of Ludlow* (1841), p. 1.
[14] H. A. Cronne, *The Borough of Warwick in the Middle Ages* (Dugdale Soc. Occ. Papers x (1951)), pp. 8–9.
[15] Dr. Davis, *Origines Divisianae*, cited in J. Waylen, *Chronicle of the Devizes* (1839), p. 22.

Yet a sufficient number of sites became Anglo-Saxon towns for it to be clear that advantages of geographical position seized upon by the Romans were also relevant to some Anglo-Saxon needs. Former Roman sites had natural advantages for defence or trade; they offered a free quarry for building materials, and also ready-made (if dilapidated) defences. Set on sites different from these, any other Anglo-Saxon or Danish town declares additional or different needs.

Two generations ago it might have been necessary to categorise all Anglo-Saxon towns as either military or commercial: in the one case all defences like a dinosaur and in the other as easily overturned as a market-stall. The prime need was undoubtedly military and political, as the word used for these towns demonstrated: they were *burhs*; and the same word was used for other fortified dwelling places that stood singly, like moated manor houses in later centuries, with no pretensions to urbanism. There are hundreds of place-names ending in *-bury* that indicate no more than this; the *bury* is no borough.

Looking back we can see that only those *burhs* were to survive where the military and political base was buttressed by economic life. Some *burhs* had acquired markets, fairs, traders and a church by the time of Domesday Book, and others were already abandoned. The initial decision, however, was military and political:

> the *burhs* originated in a conscious planned policy carried out by Alfred, and fully implemented by his son Edward and his daughter Aethelflæd, the lady of the Mercians, and her husband, Ethelred.
> Every borough which had arisen in southern or western England since the beginning of the Danish wars was created by an act of state.[16]

In other areas of lowland England the Anglo-Saxon chronicle records the construction of *burhs*. Thus in 912:

> In the summer king Edward went with some of his forces into Essex to Maldon, and camped there while the *burh* was being made and constructed at Witham.[17]

In southern England the *burhs* are known from a list, the *Burghal Hidage*, drawn up between 911 and 919. Eight of the twenty-eight places there named were at or near Roman sites, and two have yet to be identified; others—like Witham—were set within Iron Age hill-forts,

[16] H. R. Loyn, *Anglo-Saxon England and the Norman Conquest* (1962), p. 133.
[17] *The Anglo-Saxon Chronicle*, ed. D. Whitelock (1962), p. 62.

but it would require excavation to determine the degree of continuity of settlement. If an Anglo-Saxon *burh* is on a level site with no traces of Roman settlement there is some presumption that it was newly designed.

A marked rectangularity in plan, once a Roman origin has been discounted, is a helpful support in a claim for deliberate plantation. Salter accepted the plantation of Oxford on these grounds, although Oxford is also known to have had no open fields of its own, eight virgates having been taken from Headington. Lydford and Cricklade are also markedly rectilinear.

IV

There are also a few towns that have symptoms of plantation before the Norman Conquest, but these were not *burhs*. St. Albans has a strong claim to be considered: its Roman predecessor is quite clearly separate on the other bank of the river, and the Chronicle of the abbey has preserved the tradition that abbot Wulsin VI (c. 950) created the town. The circumstances are convincing. The Benedictine monastery was on a sloping site east of the river and the Watling Street passed through the centre of the Roman town on the west bank. The abbot diverted the main road and led it across the river to the monastery gate and then back to its old course nearly a mile south of the diversion. At the point of departure he built St. Michael's church and at the point of return St. Stephen's. To the north-east of the monastery he laid out a triangular market place and at the far end of it he built a third church, St. Peter's. Free timber was made available to any who wished to come and build themselves houses in the new streets.[18]

Other pre-Norman abbeys had a town at their gate. The mention of an existing village or town in some foundation charters destroys any claim for plantation. The abbey at Burton on Trent (founded 1002–04) was given a village among its first endowments but Abingdon, Peterborough, Whitby (*Streonesheal*) and Hartlepool may have sponsored their towns. It is very difficult at this early period to distinguish between the natural attraction of commerce to the monastery gate and its deliberate stimulation, and the evidence may be considered rather less certain than that for *burhs*.

[18] R. E. Pahl, "The Five Sites of St. Albans", *Amateur Historian* (1961), pp. 22–33; *V.C.H. Herts.*, ii, pp. 470–472.

One pre-Norman religious community did certainly create a town at the church door. The site at Durham, on the rocky peninsula above the Wear, was described by Symeon of Durham as unfit for any agriculture when the body of St. Cuthbert was first brought there (1003–06). What few peasants there were locally were to be found at Elvet on the opposite bank of the Wear. The peninsula was cleared of trees for the shrine and church, and by the Norman Conquest there was a town to the north of the church. Like the shrine and the church, the town was St. Cuthbert's, and its bounds cut off 58 acres from neighbouring parishes.

The town of Durham, surrounding the triangular market place outside the monastery gate, bears a strong resemblance to another monastic town about whose planted origin there is no doubt whatsoever. No village stood on the site chosen for the abbey, and the name of the abbey—like that of the town—celebrated an event that marked the end of the Anglo-Saxon period. This was the Sussex abbey *De Bello*; the town was Battle; and the battle had brought the Normans to England: for abbey and town were built on the hill of Senlac, a few miles from Hastings.

V

After the Norman Conquest the plantations in England became more numerous. Uncertain as the precise year of some foundations has to remain, there is no doubt that twenty-one new towns were founded between 1066 and 1100, and a further nineteen by 1130. Eighteen new towns had been planted in Wales in these years by the same authorities: the king, his bishops, his abbots and his barons. The greater amount of information that is available about these Norman towns makes the Conquest an appropriate moment to begin counting plantations in order to examine the significance of their chronology more carefully. It has already been noticed, for example, that plantation came to an end in the mid-fourteenth century (pp. 306–7). Were there other periods when enthusiasm waxed and waned?

The first necessity is to re-arrange the towns of the Gazetteer in chronological order. This is done in Appendix I (England). Little would be gained by studying single years, for in even the most intense period (Gascony from 1281–1290) the average rate of foundation did not exceed three a year, and in England no decade had an average as high as two a year. The left-hand columns of Table XI.1 set out the number of plantations by decades, whenever a foundation can be dated that narrowly. The earlier a plantation, the more likely that its charter or other documentary evidence must be assigned within a

TABLE XI.1

ENGLAND: CHRONOLOGY OF PLANTED TOWNS

	Assignable to decades		Assignable only to broad periods		
	Number	*Percentage*		*Number*	*Percentage*
1066–70	1	–	Before 1066	3	2
1071–80	2	1	Before 1070	1	—
1081–90	0	0	1066–86	9	5
1091–1100	2	1	1066–1130	10	6
1101–10	1	–	1071–1215	2	1
1111–20	3	2	1101–40	6	3
1121–30	1	–	1101–89	12	7
1131–40	1	–			
1141–50	1	–			
1151–60	1	–	1154–89	9	5
1161–70	1	–	1154–1225	23	13
1171–80	2	1			
1181–1190	2	1			
1191–1200	8	5			
1201–10	6	3			
1211–20	9	5			
1221–30	10	6	1225–72	9	5
1231–40	2	1			
1241–50	6	3			
1251–60	1	–	1261–1326	3	2
1261–70	3	2			
1271–80	0	0			
1281–90	3	2			
1291–1300	5	3			
1301–10	3	2			
1311–20	1	–			
1321–30	1	–			
1331–40	0	0			
1341–50	1	–			
1351–60	0	0			
1361–70	1	–			
After 1370	1	–			
			Not dated	6	3
Total	79	47	Total	93	
			Total: 172		

range of dates rather than to a single year. The English foundations suffer most in this respect and the Gascon bastides least; only two bastides in the Gascon Gazetteer were founded before 1251, and by the mid-thirteenth century the documentation is usually capable of yielding a single date or a narrow range of dates. The right-hand columns of Table XI.1 show that just over half the plantations in England demand either a range of dates longer than a decade (e.g. 1101–40, when there were six plantations) or one that overlaps decades (e.g. 1066–86, when there were nine plantations); yet 76% of the Gascon dates and 60% of the Welsh dates can be placed neatly into decades.

In order to compare country with country it is useful to bring all the data into decade divisions, by assigning a fraction of a foundation to each of the decades that its date-range spans (e.g. the five Gascon bastides that cannot be dated more closely than 1271–90 have been counted as two and a half in each decade, and then added to the number firmly assigned to each decade in the left-hand column of Table XIII.4). It will be noticed that in England, the country where this operation has to be most frequently undertaken (Table XI.2), such a procedure does not alter the pre-eminence of the two decades 1211–30, nor the close rivalry of the decade 1191–1200; in Wales the intensity of effort in the three decades 1271–1300 emerges from both the crude and the adjusted figures; and in Gascony nothing can oust the decade 1281–90.

Fig. 57 expresses Table XI.2 diagrammatically, and it will be seen at once that—so far as England is concerned—the distribution of plantations over time is remarkably even. Almost every decade before 1190 had the same share of the total plantations: four per cent. After 1190 came three decades with 8, 7 and 9% of the total plantations; thereafter only one decade had more than 3% of the total, and in fact no decade after 1310 had more than one plantation in it. It is relevant to refer also to Table X.1, p. 303, which shows that in four decades after 1230—1231–40, 1241–50, 1281–90, and 1341–50—the failure rate among new plantations was 25% or above.

The task of a commentator on the English figures is consequently a simple one. He must explain the even rate of plantation for twelve decades after 1066, pausing only to explain why the decades 1131–50 failed to conform. The doubling of the rate between 1191 and 1230 then has to be explained; and finally the lowered rate of activity (some of it abortive), and the rapid falling away in the early fourteenth century.

329

TABLE XI.2

ENGLAND: CHRONOLOGY INCLUDING CONJECTURED DECADES

	Assignable to decades	Decade conjectured	Total number	Percentage
1066–70	1	5	6	3
1071–80	2	4	6	3
1081–90	0	5	5	3
1091–1100	2	2	4	2
1101–10	1	5	6	3
1111–20	3	4	7	4
1121–30	1	5	6	3
1131–40	1	3	4	2
1141–50	1	1	2	1
1151–60	1	6	7	4
1161–70	1	5	6	3
1171–80	2	6	8	5
1181–90	2	6	8	5
1191–1200	8	5	13	8
1201–10	6	3	9	5
1211–20	9	3	12	7
1221–30	10	5	15	9
1231–40	2	2	4	2
1241–50	6	2	8	5
1251–60	1	2	3	2
1261–70	3	2	5	3
1271–80	0	0	0	0
1281–90	3	1	4	2
1291–1300	5	0	5	3
1301–10	3	1	4	2
1311–20	1	0	1	–
1321–30	1	1	2	1
1331–40	0	0	0	0
1341–50	1	0	1	–
1351–60	0	0	0	0
1361–70	1	0	1	–
After 1370	1	0	1	–
Before 1066	0	3	3	2
Not dated	0	6	6	3
Total	79	93	172	

The initial and continuous impetus is obviously connected with the Norman Conquest, and it is to the conqueror and his companions at Hastings that we must now return.

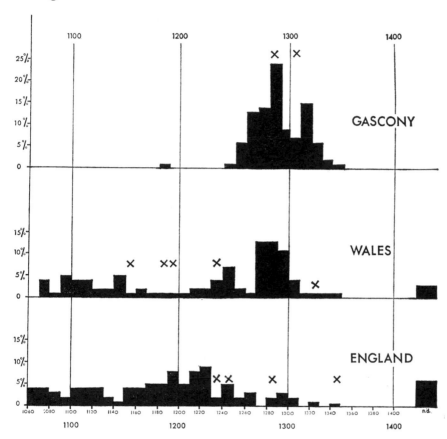

FIG. 57. CHRONOLOGY OF PLANTED TOWNS IN GASCONY, WALES AND ENGLAND. The diagram shows the proportion that can be assigned to each decade, 1060–1360; the cross symbols over certain decades indicate those with a high proportion of abortive and failed plantations.

VI

Duke William and his followers did not come to England innocent of the advantages of towns on their demesnes. For a century and a half before 1066 the Normans had been settled in northern France, where

331

old-established towns had roots as deep as (or deeper than) any Roman town in England.   There is also some evidence that the duke and his barons had learned to initiate new settlements in Normandy.   William himself had planted two *bourgs* at Caen alongside and beneath the old ducal *bourg*,[19] rather like the new borough of Mancroft that he was to add to Norwich, after negotiations very like those of a *paréage*.   The Norman town whose customs had most influence on the content of English charters was Breteuil sur Iton (Eure), and it is likely that this town was planted by William fitz Osbern about 1050.

He had the idea of creating a privileged town at the foot of his castle.[20]

Fitz Osbern was already lord of the *bourg* of Cormeilles (Eure).   It was the liberties of Cormeilles that Richard de Hugleville conferred on Auffay (Seine-Maritime) when it was founded in 1050.[21]

Historians of Normandy do not always make it clear whether a seigneur's *bourg* was a plantation.   Terms used in the record of a long dispute between Guy de Laval and the abbey of Marmoutier would suggest a plantation at Laval:

> Guy de Laval gave to the monks of Marmoutier certain land near his castle in order to make a bourg (*burgus*) of it.[22]

Ordericus Vitalis described Richard de Hugleville's foundation of Auffay (Seine-Maritime) in 1050 rather more ambiguously:

> He built a town at the place formerly called Isrelville on the river Sie and called it from the beech-clad hill above it, Auffay or *Alfagum*.   He introduced among his colonists the customs of Cormeilles.[23]

Auffay is laid out very regularly, with the church at the head of a long, broad market place, and the burgages on two facing sides: but what was "the place called Isrelville"?   The *bourg* of Dieppe, on the other hand, founded between 1067 and 1079, lay alongside a village of fishermen and salt-workers;[24] and there were fishermen by the bridge at Pont-audemer (Eure) at the beginning of the eleventh century, before the *bourg* was founded; the situation at another bridge-*bourg*, Ponts (Manche), is more obscure.[25]   There were at least twelve other *bourgs* founded in

[19] H. Legras, *Le Bourgage de Caen* (Paris, 1911), pp. 52–53.
[20] R. Génestal, *La Tenure en Bourgage* (Paris, 1900), p. 237.
[21] D. C. Douglas, *William the Conqueror* (1964), p. 65.
[22] M. Faroux, ed., *Recueil des Actes des Ducs de Normandie, 911–1066* (1961), pp. 344–348.
[23] Ordericus Vitalis, *Historia Ecclesiastica*, trans. T. Forester (1854), ii, p. 266.
[24] M. Faroux, *op. cit.*, p. 186; R. Génestal, *op. cit.*, p. 240.
[25] M. Faroux, *op. cit.*, p. 24.

Normandy before 1066, but no evidence has been encountered that would make the circumstances clear.[26]

For the Norman towns of England and Wales the surviving documentation, although not profuse, is more ample than for the Anglo-Saxon towns, and it reveals some unequivocal acts of urban plantation. Domesday Book records significant additions to the stock of towns, and the phrase *novus burgus* actually appears in its folios.[27] It also records the parallel expansion of urban populations by the development and extension of existing towns and villages: Northampton and Nottingham had new streets within a walled extension, oval in shape; Bury St. Edmunds, on a level site outside the monastery gate, was extended over the fields in a rectilinear grid plan worthy of any bastide. A famous passage in Domesday Book states that in 1086

> the town is now contained within a greater perimeter (*maiori ambitu*) including land which used (in 1065) to be ploughed and sown, whereon are now 30 priests, deacons and clerks together, and 28 nuns and poor people who daily pray for the king and for all Christian souls.[28]

In the twenty years between the Norman Conquest and the compilation of Domesday Book the town of Bury had doubled in value. The occupants of the new houses in the new streets were not exclusively clergy and nuns, for the account continues:

> there are 75 bakers, ale-brewers, tailors, washerwomen, shoemakers, robe-makers, cooks, porters, and agents (*dispensatores*). All these daily wait on the Saint, the abbot and the brethren. Besides whom are 13 reeves in charge of the abbey lands who have their houses in the same town, and under them five bordars. There are 34 knights, both English and French, and under them 22 bordars.

The town had begun to house the specialist trades most closely connected with the physical needs of the abbey; and the same trades catered for the pilgrims and tenants of the abbey estates when they came to Bury: they would be busiest on the days when the abbot held his courts, on the feast-days of the church and on the days of markets

---

[26] *Ibid.*, Index, under *bourg*; and see also S. Deck, "Formation des communes en Haute-Normandie et communes éphémères", *Annales de Normandie*, x (1960), pp. 207–228 and 317–329.

[27] Not exactly in the sense of a planted town: there were *novus domus et burgus* at Quatford (Salop.), the *burh* that was the predecessor of Bridgnorth; and *novus burgus* in Norwich, where earl Ralf's church was built: *D.B.*, i, f 252 and ii, f. 118.

[28] H. C. Darby, *The Domesday Geography of Eastern England* (1952), p. 198, prints the whole passage in translation. See Fig. 37, p. 164 above.

and fairs. The old Saxon town, according to Domesday book, had housed 310 persons, perhaps 310 households; the new development after the Conquest had more than doubled the population:

> Now altogether there are 342 houses on the demesne of the land of St. Edmund which was under the plough in the time of King Edward (the Confessor).

Lincoln had also been extended:

> outside the city are 36 houses and two churches which Colsuen built on the waste land that the king gave him and that was never before built upon.[29]

The new castles built by the Norman kings and their tenants were powerful stimulants to urban growth. Domesday Book records the new market that had developed outside the gate of the Suffolk castle of Eye, and at Tutbury, on the edge of the forest of Needwood,

> in the borough around the castle are 42 men making their living from their merchandise alone.[30]

In these cases, where the castle was built near a village, there was no need to engineer a plantation, but when a castle was built in open country, the town at its gates could claim no village ancestry. Thus J. H. Round described the site of Tickhill as

> a castle built on a site with no recognised name, being named from a manor a few miles away, and in later times it was often called "the castle of Blyth".[31]

The site of New Windsor was taken from Clewer parish, but from the very edge, so that there was never a possibility of Clewer village becoming the beneficiary of the presence of king, household and garrison in Windsor Castle.

The proportion of castle-towns in the early part of the chronological list of plantations (Appendix I) is high: 80% of the towns planted between 1066 and 1100 were alongside castles, and more than half of those between 1101 and 1135 were similarly situated. These groups

[29] C. W. Foster and T. Longley, eds., *The Lincolnshire Domesday* (Lincs. Record Soc. xix (1924)), pp. xxxiii and 6.
[30] *D.B.*, i, f. 248b.
[31] J. H. Round, "The Castles of the Conquest", *Archaeologia*, lviii (1902), p. 331. The Conquest brought two Norman names to towns in the area west of Shrewsbury: Old (and later, New) Montgomery; and Caus. The former was a place-name in Normandy (Dep. Calvados, cant. Livarot), and the latter a district-name (*cp.* Pays de Caux).

include important foundations at New Windsor, Old Salisbury, Bridgnorth, Arundel and Clitheroe as well as others that incorporated the "castle" in their name: Newcastle, Barnard Castle and Bishop's Castle; some of these towns lay within castle-baileys or were protected by earthworks continuous with the castle defences. These were the conquerors' decades, and it will also be noticed from Table XI.3 that the years 1066–1100 were those most dominated by royal ventures in town plantation. The royal proportion—one new town in three— was never again to be reached. The Table shows how the proportion

TABLE XI.3

STATUS OF FOUNDERS OF PLANTATIONS IN ENGLAND, BY PERIODS

	Kings	Bishops	Monasteries	Laymen
1086–1100	32%	4%	20%	40%
1101–88	19%	10%	11%	60%
1189–1215	6%	9%	18%	67%
1216–30	0%	30%	35%	35%
1231–1300	14%	14%	11%	61%
1301–50	9%	33%	33%	25%

Note: The periods of most active plantation are italicised.

of founders who were seigneurs, lay or clerical, rose after 1100. It is after 1100 rather than immediately after 1066 that Tait's comment has force:

> Not the least striking of the effects of the Norman Conquest in the field of municipal history was the wide extension of this class of dependent or seignorial boroughs. . . . The seignorial borough was, with rare exceptions, a post-Conquest creation.[32]

The chronological list shows another change after 1100, the increase in the number of new towns unsupported by any castle. These must have been influenced by the existence of local trade that might be profitably focused or by the belief that trade would come, given a focus. The town of Battle was the first of these commercial centres, but it might be regarded as untypical since there could be only one Senlac, and only one pilgrimage centre of this status. Boston, Lynn and Newborough (Staffs.) are more typical early commercial plantations.

[32] J. Tait, *The Medieval English Borough* (1936), pp. 342 and 350.

Boston and Lynn were estuarine ports set among marshland that was only just beginning to be reclaimed: Newborough, in the middle of Needwood Forest, was a child of agricultural colonisation on marginal land of another sort; St. Ives and St. Neots were commercial to their roots; and with Dunstable the long series of road-side plantation began.

Fig. 57 and Table XI.2 indicate that the two decades 1131–50 show a marked reduction in the annual rate of town plantation: for explanation it is not necessary to look any further than the civil war between Stephen and Matilda. If it was a time when "God and all his angels slept", further rises in population and the development of internal commerce could not be expected. During the period of medieval town plantation there was no other long civil war in England when war operated as a deterrent to growth, but this chronology of plantation in Wales and Gascony displays the relationship unambiguously.

The four decades after the end of the civil war in 1154 show a return to the old annual rate of plantation. Then came the three decades (1191–1200 and 1211–30) when the rate almost doubled, and the rate in the last of these decades was never to be equalled again.

There are no data to indicate annual changes in the growth of production or foreign trade during the twelfth and early thirteenth centuries. We can say only that Fig. 57 fits the hypothesis of a continued rise of population and production after the Norman Conquest, checked only by the civil war, and continuing into the thirteenth century.

It might be thought that the high rate of plantation in the reigns of Richard I and John was stimulated by the notorious financial difficulties of the two brothers. Yet it is difficult to put the charters to new towns in the same class as the enforced confirmation of charters to old-established towns for the sake of the revenue that came with re-issue. Richard I and John could not force a landowner to project a new town on his demesne. Their charters to new towns seem more akin to their grants that added to the number of places where markets and fairs could be held: the kings were willing enough to sell, but there were also eager buyers, and the kings' willingness shows them riding the wave, not creating it.

If the Crown's financial needs had been a chief cause of the uniquely high rate of town plantation it might also be expected that the royal demesnes would be exploited to the full by planting new towns. In fact, as Table XI.3 shows, the share of royal plantations fell steadily from 1086 to 1240. Richard I and John each founded only one town on their demesnes. These were Portsmouth and Liverpool, and military and naval considerations contributed to the foundation.

The great contributors to town plantation when it was at its most active were the landowners. Although the proportion of royal plantations in Table XI.3 increases again in the period after 1240, the figures are deceptive. There were actually six royal plantations: two of these, Warenmouth and Newton (Dorset), failed; New Winchelsea was a special case, being a replacement of an eroded port by a new town; Kingston on Hull was an annexe to the existing port of Wyke on Hull, and Melcombe Regis had rather the same relation to Weymouth, not 50 yards distant. Queenborough, the last of all the royal plantations, was a very special case, being part of a military strategy.

This unventuresome royal record in England is all the more significant if the Welsh and Gascon diagrams in Fig. 57 are examined, for the decade 1251–60 in Wales was surpassed only by the period of Edward I's great programme of castle-building in north Wales, and in Gascony the same decade was the first to see any substantial number of bastides on English soil. In both the Welsh and the Gascon plantations the Crown was a very active participant indeed.

One interpretation of Fig. 57 would be to make plantations in England diminish after 1240 because of a diversion of resources to Wales and Gascony. This argument would be plausible if there had been a fixed quantity of resources on which to draw. There is a sense in which the great Welsh defensive works of Henry III, and particularly of Edward I, drew on royal resources and made it less likely that money would be available for new royal towns in England. But the expensive defended towns of Wales were not typical of thirteenth century plantations in England, and the initial cost of a civil, commercial plantation was not great, as we have already seen (pp. 71–72). Nor was England starved of royal towns for the sake of Gascony: Gascony had its own financial resources on which the king-duke could draw without troubling the English taxpayer; and in Gascony the initial cost of a bastide was not great, and the device of *paréage* ensured that the king did not always have to provide even the site.

If we reject the hypothesis that royal plantations in England were starved for the sake of Wales and Gascony, we must conclude that Henry III and Edward I viewed the economic situation after the mid-thirteenth century in the same way as their subjects whose enthusiasm for town plantation also began to fade. If the demand for new towns

337

was an indicator of opportunity and optimism, then there seems no doubt that there was a distinct change at least as early as 1240. It may be no accident that four of the eight towns projected in England between 1241 and 1250 were failures, a rate not to be reached until the decade of the Black Death. These may not be the symptoms of an economy in decline, but they are remarkably like those of an economy saturated with towns. To go further and to say that the whole economy was therefore saturated is to enter on debatable ground.

One can envisage an economy where the optimum number of towns is reached before other productive forms have grown to their fullest extent. This would be most likely when a substantial sector of production and distribution does not need the services of towns. In the thirteenth century, raw wool was the principal export and probably the most valuable part of the agricultural surplus that came to market. The trade in wool was largely in the hands of visiting foreign dealers, and such a system of distribution did not need much from inland towns, although ports were vital for it. Raw wool exports, for which there are figures after 1279, did not reach their peak until 1305.

On the other hand, England may be seen as an economy where towns were so essential to growth that their greatest development cannot be far away in time from the greatest development of the whole economy, and any decline in the number of new plantations would indicate that the economy itself was less full of opportunities. If this is a true picture of England in the second half of the thirteenth century, then its saturation with towns does imply the onset of stagnation.

CHAPTER TWELVE

The Chronology of Town Plantation in Wales

"Concerninge the first buildinge of the castells and townes of this Countrie I had once determyned to have written thereof a parte by it self."

George Owen, *Description of Pembrokeshire* (1603), ed. H. Owen (1892), p. 84.

THE chronology of town plantation in Wales, summarised in Table XII.2 and Fig. 57, has some similarities with that observed in England. It began vigorously, and since there were virtually no old-established towns in Wales it was possible to maintain early rates of growth. There was also the same decline of plantation in the early fourteenth century, but in Wales more spectacularly, coming as it did soon after the three very active decades, 1271–1300. This activity at a time when plantation was quiescent in England is an obvious example of the powerful influence of political and military strategy not only on the siting but on the timing of Welsh plantation: the towns of these three decades were part of the final conquest of Wales by Edward I. These powerful influences are also apparent in the high proportion of Welsh plantations that were royal in decades when their counterparts in England were predominantly founded by the king's subjects.

The successful continuation of Welsh plantation into the second half of the thirteenth century may also be due to the different pace of rural colonisation in the two countries. Population density in Wales was far below that in England: warfare, climate, relief and poor soils had combined to hinder the colonisation of the interior of Wales, and adjectives like "saturated" which have been attached to the English economy of the later thirteenth century were inappropriate to north and mid-Wales; the coastal plains of the south were in this, as in so many respects, more like England.

339

I

The particular relation of plantations to political events[1] can be better shown if four periods are considered (see Appendix II, pp. 642–44). *Period I, from 921 to 1066*, gave the *burh* of Clwydmouth (Rhuddlan I) in 921. Nothing is known of its physical extent, since the Norman borough of 1073 replaced it, and the sites have not been excavated.[2] This early penetration of the coast of north Wales was the work of the earls of Mercia, but the English were then expelled by Griffith ap Llewelyn who was able to live in his palace at Rhuddlan and have his ships unmolested at the river-mouth, until in 1063 the English recaptured the town and began to invade Snowdonia. Harold was then called away to meet the Norman conquest of his own country.

Period II, from 1066 to 1135, was dominated by the rapid incursions of the Norman barons to whom William I had given the border counties. In piecemeal fashion the earls of Hereford, Shrewsbury and Chester moved west along the valleys, and by the death of William I in 1087 there were castles at Wigmore, Clifford, Ewias Harold, Chepstow, Old Montgomery, Bangor, Carnarvon and Aberlleiniog. In north Wales Robert of Rhuddlan was the chief agent of the earl of Chester in these conquests and at Rhuddlan he erected a motte and made a borough. A castle was built at Deganwy on the Conway but no town is recorded. In William II's reign (1087–1100) Bernard de Newmarch took Brecon and established a castle, priory, and town there while Philip de Braose obtained Radnor and set himself up in Builth. The lordships of Monmouth, Abergavenny and Ewyas Lacy also fell to three other Normans, and the earl of Shrewsbury moved up the Severn and through what is now Cardiganshire to establish the lordship of Pembroke. It will be seen from the Gazetteer that nearly all the castles so far mentioned were the sites for Norman boroughs.[3]

All except Rhuddlan were the property not of the king but of Marcher lords. William I went through south Wales to St. David's in 1081 but he established no royal castles or boroughs. William II was in Wales in 1096 and again in 1097 but neither expedition was

---

[1] The political narrative derives from J. E. Lloyd, *A History of Wales* (2 vols., 1911).

[2] See the Gazetteer, chapter 16, for references for towns mentioned here.

[3] Some confusion seems to lie behind the statement by Welsh geographers that the castle-town was brought by the Normans from "equivalent areas of conquest in southern France". (J. G. Thomas and H. Carter, "Settlement Patterns", in E. G. Bowen, ed., *Wales* (1957), p. 158.) The Normans had not conquered southern France, and there was no political link between English kings and southern French territories until 1154.

TABLE XII.1

WALES: CHRONOLOGY OF PLANTED TOWNS

	Assignable to decades			Assignable only to broad periods	
	Number	Percentage		Number	Percentage
1066–70	0	0	Before 1066	1	1
1071–80	3	4			
1081–90	1	1			
1091–1100	4	5			
1101–10	2	2			
1111–20	2	2			
1121–30	1	1	1100–30	4	5
1131–40	1	1			
1141–50	2	2	1147–54	1	1
1151–60	0	0	1147–89	4	5
1161–70	1	1			
1171–80	0	0			
1181–90	0	0			
1191–1200	0	0			
			Twelfth century	2	2
1201–10	0	0			
1211–20	0	0	1189–1215	3	4
1221–30	1	1			
1231–40	2	2			
1241–50	4	5			
1251–60	1	1			
1261–70	0	0	1215–72	3	4
1271–80	8	10			
1281–90	7	8			
1291–1300	7	8	Thirteenth century		6
1301–10	3	4	1272–1307	5	6
			1307–60	4	5
			Not dated	2	3
Total	50	58	Total	34	–
			Total: 84		

successful. The baronial conquests were not in defiance of the king's wishes, but he could not fail to see the threat of independent power. The second earl of Hereford revolted in 1075, and in 1102, soon after Henry I's accession, the earl of Shrewsbury and his brother Arnulf of Pembroke took part in a revolt. Their lands were confiscated and

341

TABLE XII.2

WALES: CHRONOLOGY INCLUDING CONJECTURED DECADES

	Assignable to decades	Decade conjectured	Total Number	Percentage
1071–80	3	0	3	4
1081–90	1	0	1	1
1091–1100	4	0	4	5
1101–10	2	1	3	4
1111–20	2	1	3	4
1121–30	1	1	2	2
1131–40	1	1	2	2
1141–50	2	2	4	5
1151–60	0	1	1	1
1161–70	1	1	2	2
1171–80	0	1	1	1
1181–90	0	1	1	1
1191–1200	0	1	1	1
1201–10	0	1	1	1
1211–20	0	2	2	2
1221–30	1	1	2	2
1231–40	2	1	3	4
1241–50	4	2	6	7
1251–60	1	1	2	2
1261–70	0	1	1	1
1271–80	8	2	10	12
1281–90	7	3	10	12
1291–1300	7	2	9	11
1301–10	3	0	3	4
1311–20	0	1	1	1
1321–30	0	1	1	1
1331–40	0	1	1	1
1341–50	0	1	1	1
After 1350	0	0	0	0
Before 1066	0	1	1	1
Not dated	0	2	2	2
Totals	50	34	84	

from this point the royal boroughs began.[4] The rural estates of Pembroke were developed for the crown in 1105–11 by the importation of Flemish immigrants, and by 1109 Henry had also acquired Carmarthen. There he built a new castle to the west of the Roman fort and created a new borough between the two. At his death in 1135 dependent English lords had been established in Kidwelly, Swansea, Llandovery, Nevern (near Newport, Pem.) and Llanbadarn. Boroughs were certainly to be found at the first two, and the others provided the base for later foundations.[5] At this stage, only fifty years after the conquest of England, the speed and degree of penetration by the Normans is striking, and the multiplication of towns no minor part of the achievement.[6]

Period III begins with the outbreak of civil war in England in 1135 and ends with Edward I's offensive against Llewelyn in 1274. The civil war in England gave an opportunity for the Welsh to re-establish themselves in west Wales. Henry II came to terms with Rhys ap Griffith (the Lord Rhys) who ruled from the Dovey to Haverford and Llanelly. It is not surprising that in this period of Welsh ascendancy the new towns came mainly in south-east Wales and Monmouthshire. Of the new western towns, the creation of Newport (Pem.) below the older castle at Nevern may date from after the death of the Lord Rhys in 1197. In 1212 King John intended a programme of Welsh castle building even larger than Edward I was to achieve; workmen were summoned, but the venture was cancelled.[7] Rhys's own family did not provide the leadership for a united Welsh opposition and the next successful defender of Wales was Llewelyn the Great (d. 1240). At the height of his power in 1234 he held all north Wales, most of mid-Wales, and territory in south-west Wales up to Cardigan and the gates of Carmarthen. Painscastle, Hay and (New) Montgomery, the plantations of 1223–37, are significantly all on the eastern frontier. Montgomery was created after Llewelyn had beseiged Builth in the autumn of 1223; Painscastle was built after the summer of 1231 when Llewelyn

[4] The economic interest of the English kings in the conquered territory is detailed in W. Rees, *South Wales and the March* (1924), p. 29.

[5] The Marcher lords had rights derived from conquest of lands that had never been within the allegiance of the English king: they thus had opportunities to institute fairs, markets and boroughs of their own volition (W. Rees, op. *cit.*, p. 43).

[6] "When the Norman is seen at the work of town-making, a new truth is added to Morgan's penetrating remark, 'the most thoroughly Normanised counties were those upon the Welsh border'." M. Bateson, "The Laws of Breteuil", *E.H.R.*, xv (1900), p. 74.

[7] *P.R.S.*, n.s. xxx (1955), pp. xv–vi.

took Radnor, Hay, Brecon, Caerleon, Neath and Kidwelly, and burned New Montgomery.

The treaty of Woodstock (1247) followed a series of successful campaigns by Henry III against Llewelyn's son, David, who died in 1246. In the campaign of 1241 the king regained the site of Deganwy, where David had razed the castle to the ground, and after the treaty of Woodstock a new castle and borough were built at Deganwy. A new castle was built at Dyserth after the same campaign, to replace the Norman castle at Rhuddlan, and in 1248 a borough was designed to accompany it. If New Radnor can be ascribed to the mid-century it may likewise have been a seal on reconquests. Cefnllys shows the Mortimers also strengthening their defences in the same decade, and Welshpool could only have been tolerated after Powys was under English influence.

The period for new works by the English was short. In 1255 Llewelyn ap Griffith became full ruler of Gwynedd (Snowdonia) and within two years he was able to command territories as extensive as those of Llewelyn the Great in 1234. In 1258 a council of Welsh rulers acclaimed him Prince of Wales, and in 1260–63 Llewelyn was able to harass the lordships of Builth, Brecon and Abergavenny. By the treaty of Montgomery in 1267 Henry III recognised Llewelyn's title as Prince of Wales. It was after this success that Llewelyn began to threaten northern Glamorgan; and the Clare castles at Caerphilly, the last of the pre-Edwardian towns, were a response to this threat. These years before Edward's return from the Crusade also saw Llewelyn himself essay the plantation of a borough at his new castle of Dolforwyn.[8]

Period IV opens in 1274 with Edward's return and the opening of his offensive against Llewelyn. The progress of his towns and castles from Flint to Aberystwyth has already been described in Chapter 2. The military and political context can be briefly restated. In 1276 Edward and the English armies moved up the Towy valley to Dynevor; in 1277 north Wales was crossed as far as Deganwy, and mid-Wales was penetrated by the Severn and Wye valleys as far as Builth, where a new castle (and perhaps a borough) appeared. In west Wales the army moved from Dynevor to Llandovery and over to Aberystwyth. A temporary peace was made at Aberconway in 1277, and its terms defined the boundary very much as in 1247, the previous high water mark of English power. Edward's first array of new castles and boroughs followed.

---

[8] He was forbidden to erect "castle, borough, town or market": *Cal. Close Rolls, 1272–4,* p. 51.

Llewelyn's brother, David, revolted in 1282, attacking some of the castles and towns that Edward had built since 1277. The English now

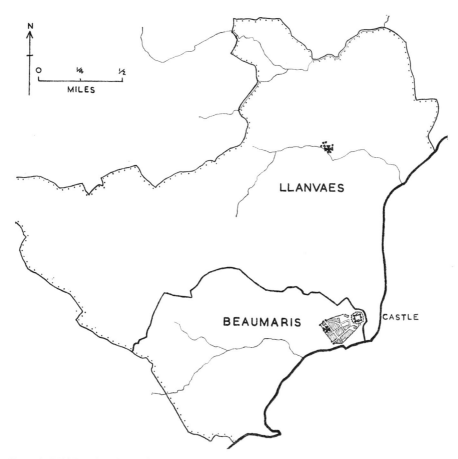

FIG. 58. BEAUMARIS, Anglesey. The last of the Edwardian plantations in north Wales. It supplanted the Welsh settlement of Llanvaes, a town whose population was moved to Newborough on the other side of the island.

overran the remaining Welsh territory. Llewelyn was killed in December 1282, David was captured in June 1283, and the second of Edward's array of castles and towns followed.

The Statute of Rhuddlan in March 1284 set out the form of government for that part of conquered Wales that Edward retained as royal demesne: the counties of Flint, Anglesey, Merioneth and Carnarvon were created, and the old counties of Carmarthen and Cardigan were enlarged to make new shires of the same name. The earl of Lincoln was granted the *cantrefs* of Rhos and Rhufoniog (the north of modern Denbighshire) and in imitation of the king the earl built a castle at Denbigh and matched it with a borough. At the same time Lord Grey was given the *cantref* of Dyffryn Clwyd in the upper Clwyd valley and this became the lordship of Ruthin where another borough was created.

It remains only to take note of the revolt of 1294–95 (after which Beaumaris was built to hold Anglesey), the last revolt on a national scale until 1400. In 1301 Edward of Carnarvon, then of age, was granted the entire lands of the Crown in Wales as well as the title of Prince of Wales, and thereafter the plantation of towns came to a halt until the Industrial Revolution.

II

The Tables in Chapter 9 have already revealed the remarkable intensity of urbanisation in medieval Wales. Many of its boroughs succeeded in attracting substantial numbers of burgesses to take up building plots, despite the risks to trade and the insecurity of personal possessions that the misfortunes of war so often brought. In England the two most intensely urbanised counties had one town for every 36 square miles; nine other English counties had urban catchment areas averaging less than 80 square miles. How did the Welsh counties measure against this scale?

Monmouthshire and seven Welsh counties had catchment areas within this limit. This was a very creditable achievement when it is remembered that the comparable English counties were in the lowlands, better equipped with soil, climate, inland waterways and coastal navigation, and nearer to the great centres of import and export.

The two English counties closest to Wales in their urban intensity were Devon and Cornwall, not counties of the plain but possessed of thousands of acres of moorland; their estuaries could be used for small ports, but their rivers were not great inland highways: is the conjunction accidental?

The highest density of towns did not go along with high densities of rural population. Devon and Cornwall, like Wales, were denied high densities of rural population by the limited amount of land suitable for arable cultivation. All other forms of exploitation of the land—from pastoralism to mining—produced sporadic clusters of population, but the minimum size of such clusters was generally smaller than for arable husbandry, and the wide open spaces between the clusters reduced the density of population. In Cornwall, especially, even arable cultivation was based more on small clusters of farmsteads than on villages, and the same pattern is recognisable in medieval Wales.

If the towns of Wales and south-west England were not supported and inspired by large populations of rural producers and consumers in their hinterland, why were they so numerous? In Wales, no doubt, some of the answer lies in the non-economic forces that created castles and castle-boroughs. Yet the similar densities in more peaceful Cornwall and Devon suggest that Welsh historians might test the evidence for another supposition which has been mentioned in the Cornish section of the Gazetteer.

Did the poor quality of inland transport slow down the movement of traffic? Did this in turn multiply the resting places that travelling merchants and traders needed? Did it also shorten the journey that countrymen were able to make to their weekly market? Did the carriage of ores, fleeces and hides present greater difficulties in this respect than the movement of grain in the lowlands? Was there any compensatory gain from the ease with which living animals, an important product of the pastoral economy, were moved by the drovers over tracks impassable to carts? Did the poor quality of local transport and the difficulties of navigation on the Atlantic coasts make it unlikely that any single port could engross the trade of a region? Did a host of small centres for export and import shelter behind an invisible tariff barrier of high transport costs? If there is anything in this line of argument, the proliferation of new small and medium-sized towns in Wales emerges as the natural companion of inefficient transport, and Cardiff could not aspire to be a London so long as the Taff was not the Thames.

CHAPTER THIRTEEN

The Chronology of Town Plantation in Gascony

Edwardus Dei gratia Rex Anglie,
dominus Hibernie et dux Aquitanie.
Royal style of Edward I.

I

IN previous chapters the Gascon bastides have mingled on terms of equality with the towns planted in England and Wales. There were enough similarities in motive and in form for this approach to be proper and instructive, but it is now time for a separate, if short, treatment of the political and economic influences upon town plantation that were local to south-western France.[1]

One term must first be defined. What was "Gascony" in the thirteenth century? How was Gascony related to the English king's title of duke of Aquitaine? The name Gascony derives from the Vascones who plundered and settled an area extending north from the Pyrenees almost to the Garonne. Its history in early medieval times is obscure. In the period after the break-up of the Carolingian empire it was ruled by an independent line of dukes who annexed the counties of Bordeaux, Agen and Bazas, though never very securely. This duchy of Gascony was united during the eleventh century to the duchy of Aquitaine which was centred upon Poitou, and these united duchies were inherited by Eleanor, the wife of Henry of Anjou. In 1154 Henry became king of England, and thereafter the kings of England ruled (in so far as they did "rule") the territory of Gascony as dukes of Aquitaine. For administrative purposes in the late twelfth and early thirteenth centuries their duchy was divided into Gascony in the south and

---

[1] A select bibliography of books and articles on town plantation and the Anglo-Gascon economy will be found in Appendix III, below.

[2] The political history and institutions of Aquitaine and Gascony are outlined in chapters ii, vii and viii of F. Lot and R. Fawtier, eds., *Histoire des Institutions Françaises au Moyen Age,* i (Paris, 1957); chapter iii deals with the county of Toulouse, part of which became involved with the English crown; see also J. Boussard, *Le Gouvernement d'Henri II* (Paris, 1956), chapter 4.

Poitou in the north, and when Poitou was lost to the French, only the southern territory (and not all of that) was left to Henry III as king-duke. The treaty of 1259, in which Henry accepted the loss of Poitou, acknowledged and gave currency to the name "duchy of Aquitaine" for those territories which still remained subject to him in the south: and in 1259 some other territories and jurisdictions were added to the fragment of his earlier duchy that Henry still held.[3] By the time of Henry III's death in 1272 some of these supplements were still not handed over, and it was only in 1280 that Edward I was able to appoint a single chief officer, his seneschal, for all these areas.[4]

This seneschal was sometimes called the seneschal "of Aquitaine", and the style of Edward as king-duke was always "duke of Aquitaine": yet despite this, contemporaries tended to use "Gascony" to describe all that he held in south-western France. Thus, the rolls in the English chancery that recorded the letters relating to southern France were called "Gascon Rolls", and the wine that came to England from Bordeaux and Bayonne was called Gascon also. This wider, general sense of "Gascon" is that employed in this book (Fig. 59).

From 1259 until the relationship was broken by war, the king of England as duke of Aquitaine owed homage and fealty to a superior, sovereign authority, the king of France. This relationship placed important restraints and qualifications upon the power of Henry, Edward I and Edward II in their duchy, making their position quite different from that which they enjoyed as kings of England. The use of the title king-duke will serve as a reminder of this difference. In the confusion of interlocking jurisdictions the Gascon seigneurs might at one time acknowledge the king-duke as their immediate feudal lord, and at another time the king of France, as they might be affected by war or diplomacy.

It is a paradox, to be discussed later in this chapter, that the most active period of town-building in the Gascon territories of the king-duke came at a time when the area of the duchy had seriously diminished,

---

[3] The history of Anglo-Gascon relations can be studied in E. Lodge, *Gascony under English Rule* (1926); F. M. Powicke, *King Henry III and the Lord Edward*, i (1947), pp. 156–258; id., *The Thirteenth Century* (1953), chapters 3 and 7. These works touch on economic relations, special aspects of which are treated by Boutruche, Carus-Wilson, Dion, James, Renouard, Sargeant and Trabut-Cussac in books and articles cited in Appendix II. One must also echo the regret expressed by Sir Maurice Powicke in 1953 (*The Thirteenth Century*, p. 274, fn.) that J.-P. Trabut-Cussac's thesis on Edward I in Gascony has not been published beyond a brief summary in École Nationale des Chartes, *Positions des Thèses* (Paris, 1949), pp. 151–158.

[4] J. Le Patourel, *E.H.R.*, lxxix (1964), pp. 789–792 and *History*, l (1965), pp. 289–308.

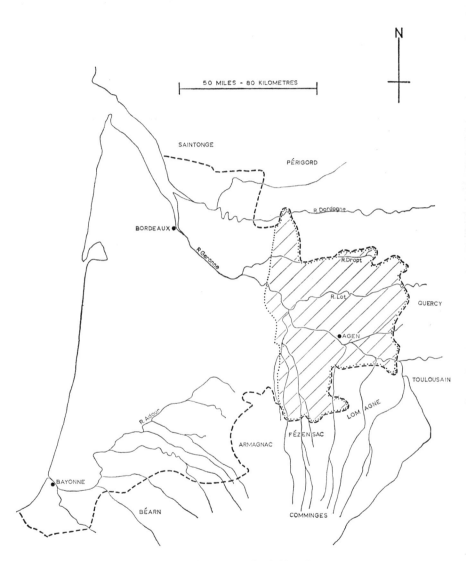

FIG. 59. ENGLISH GASCONY.   The names of neighbouring territories frequently mentioned in the text or Gazetteer are shown.   The shaded area is that of the Agenais (see Fig. 60).

and not during the period 1154–1202 when the duchy of Aquitaine was at its most extensive. The contraction began with the losses of 1202 and was accepted by Henry III in the treaty of 1259. Since virtually all the Gascon bastides have foundation dates after 1259, it is this reduced area with which our Gazetteer is mainly concerned. Yet this area was in its turn subject to fluctuation after 1259, for the treaty provided that certain territories and jurisdictions should eventually return to the king-duke. Some bastides had already been founded in these territories before they returned to Edward: we shall call these "Anglo-French" bastides, since their status was usually accepted by the king-duke, and their privileges confirmed or widened by him; restored to the duchy, these territories then shared in the general economic expansion, so that new, Edwardian (or "English") bastides were successfully founded within them.

The area under the jurisdiction of the king-duke was never again so large as it had been in 1202, but between 1279 and 1324 it included southern Saintonge; the Agenais; some territories and jurisdictions in the "Three Dioceses" of Limoges, Cahors and Périgueux; Bigorre (for a time); and a somewhat nominal suzerainty over Béarn and other great fiefs of the south-west.[5] After 1324, though with ebbs and flows, the tide flowed in favour of the kings of France, and by the end of the Hundred Years War the English were entirely expelled from south-western France.

II

The absence of English bastides in Gascony before the foundation of Marmande[6] in 1182 is not difficult to explain. Before 1154 there could have been no English bastides, for it was only in 1154 that the accession of Henry of Anjou to the English throne gave an English king any authority in territories so far south. If 28 years then elapsed before Henry's son, Richard, founded Marmande, a sufficient explanation can be found in the unsettled political conditions of the Angevin dominions. All three of Henry's sons rebelled against him at one time or another, and after being enthroned as duke of Aquitaine at Poitiers

[5] The complicated geography and diplomacy of these fringe areas is treated in *Albe*.
[6] P. Tamizey de Larroque, *Notice sur la ville de Marmande* (Villeneuve sur Lot, 1872), p. 4; *Gouron*, 1277 and 1279. It is possible that Richard also founded a settlement at the castle of Usa (Landes), where in 1249 it was claimed *rex Ricardus fecit Castrum Dusar in sua propria terra et populavit idem suis propriis hominibus, bonis moribus et consuetudinibus* (W. W. Shirley, ed., *Royal and Other Historical Letters* (Rolls Series, xxvii), ii (1868), p. 58).

in 1172 Richard had lived in Poitou with his mother who was increasingly estranged from the king. From his campaigns in the south of Aquitaine arose Marmande on the Garonne (1182).

Was Richard an innovator, bringing to Gascony an urban lesson learned further north? It would not seem so. Before the English connection began in 1154, Peter, viscount of Marsan, had joined the abbot of St. Sever in founding a *villa nova* at Mont de Marsan (1133),[7] and an earlier abbot of the same house had founded Mugron in 1074.[8] Some historians place the foundation of Nogaro as early as 1060,[9] and a *bourg neuf* had been added to Bayonne in 1120 after a *paréage* between a count and a bishop.[10]

These are single cases which can be paralleled in Normandy, Anjou, Maine and Poitou. Henry I planted at least two towns[11] in Normandy between 1100 and 1135; William, duke of Aquitaine, founded the port of La Rochelle between 1130 and 1150; Richard himself founded St. Rémy on the frontier of Maine in 1184, and two years before his death he founded Petit Andelys below his new Château Gaillard on the frontier of Normandy.[12]

These instances do not make a coherent movement of town plantation such as can be seen beginning just over the eastern frontier of Gascony between 1246 and 1255. The district known as the Agenais formed part of the dower given by Richard I to his sister, Joan, on her marriage in 1196, and by 1248 it was possessed by Alphonse de Poitiers as part of his extensive county of Toulouse. Seventeen bastides were planted in the Agenais between 1246 and 1271, besides many others elsewhere in the county.[13] There were no natural barriers between the Agenais and Gascony, and the economies of the two regions had a similar base.

---

[7] *Gouron*, 1443. C. Enlart, *Manuel d'Archéologie française*, ii (Paris, 1904), p. 242, dates the foundation to 1141.

[8] *Gouron*, 1493.

[9] *Gouron*, 1512, note; in no. 1443 Gouron dates this foundation to the early thirteenth century; Enlart, *loc. cit.*, says 1060.

[10] *Gouron*, 310; *Lavedan*, i, p. 300 considers Lavaur (Tarn) in 1098 the only large urban creation before Montauban (1141).

[11] Nonancourt (Eure) and Pont Orson (Manche).

[12] R. Crozet, *Villes d'entre Loire et Gironde*, (Paris, 1949), pp. 35–40 gives instances of four foundations, besides La Rochelle, in the period between 887 and 1152 and in territory between Normandy and Gascony which formed part of the Angevin Empire. The cumulative effect of the instances which have been brought together is to weaken any claim for the foundation of Aigues Mortes in 1241 as initiating town foundation in southern France.

[13] The "Alphonsian" bastides were not the result of personal effort by the count, for he was rarely in the south (*A.P.E.A.*, p. xlviii). Some of the responsibility of his seneschals for the bastides in the Agenais, Quercy and Toulousain is set out in *A.P.E.A.* pp. lxxiv–vi and lxxix. There is an interesting list of Alphonsian *paréages* in C47/29/1/10.

TABLE XIII.I

GASCONY: ENGLISH BASTIDES FOUNDED BEFORE EDWARD I'S VISIT OF 1273–74

	Date	Department
Marmande	1182	Lot et Garonne
Monségur	1263	Gironde
Montpouillan	1265	Lot et Garonne
Ste. Eulalie de Puyguilhem	1265	Dordogne
Castelréal	1267	Dordogne
Lalinde	1267	Dordogne
Pimbo	1268	Landes
Libourne	1270	Gironde
Beaumont du Périgord	1272	Dordogne
Pellegrue	1272	Gironde

TABLE XIII.2

BASTIDES ACQUIRED WITH THE AGENAIS IN 1279

Marmande	(founded 1182)
*Castillonnès	(founded 1259)
Damazan	(founded by 1269)
Donzac	(founded 1270)
Dunes	(founded by 1266)
Fleurance	(founded 1274)
La Bastide Castelamouroux	(founded c. 1269)
La Parade	(founded 1267)
Monclar d'Agenais	(founded 1256)
Monflanquin	(founded 1256)
Montréal du Gers	(founded 1255)
Puymirol	(founded 1246)
Ste. Foy la Grande	(founded 1255)
St. Pastour	(founded by 1259)
Villeneuve sur Lot	(founded 1264)
Villeréal	(founded 1267)

*Partitioned with the king of France until 1303.

The success of the Alphonsian bastides would be visible in English Gascony, but the absence of any imitation until 1263 is striking. Even then, the number of English plantations did not exceed those in the Agenais until 1276, and the Agenais was a very much smaller area than Gascony.

353

There is a strong presumption that the poor performance in English Gascony arose from the preoccupation of its ruler with domestic affairs in England and Wales. Henry III and Edward were not uninterested in Gascony: Henry III campaigned there and experimented disastrously by giving proconsular powers to Simon de Montfort; in 1254 Edward was given Aquitaine by his father on the occasion of the marriage to Eleanor of Castile, but he was not able to remain long in Gascony. The year of the charters to Monségur and Montpouillan (1265) was that of Simon de Montfort's Parliament and the battle of Evesham. Henry III's queen, who issued these charters in her son's name, was at that moment negotiating loans in Gascony to support the cause of her husband and son against the English barons.

After the defeat of Simon de Montfort, English domestic politics became less pressing but Edward's energies were then diverted towards the Holy Land. He left for the Crusade in 1270 and did not arrive in Gascony until the autumn of 1273. In his absence his seneschals had negotiated a small number of *paréages* in the duke's name but activity on an Alphonsian scale was yet to come. It did not depend on Edward's presence, for after an eight months' stay[14] he left Gascony in 1274 and did not return until 1286, but its timing suggests that it depended crucially upon the administrative reorganisation which Edward undertook during his brief stay in his Gascon inheritance and upon his appreciation of the political support that newly founded towns could give him against the notoriously fractious Gascon vassals.

The documentary evidence for Edward's close scrutiny of his assets is contained in part in a collection of records, printed by Bémont under the title *Recogniciones Feodorum*, that constitutes a survey of the rights and duties of his vassals taken at St. Sever, Lectoure, and Bordeaux between September 1273 and April 1274. These assets included eleven bastides already founded in the Bordelais and Périgord, and before the king left for England two more were projected in Périgord. It was from Northampton in November 1274 that Edward sent letters to his seneschals giving them general powers to acquire further sites for bastides and to endow them with liberties.[15]

Progress was not at first rapid, and the greatest gain between 1274 and 1280 lay in the acquisition of the Alphonsian bastides of the

---

[14] Some of his movements can be followed in H. Gough, *Itinerary of King Edward I*, i (1900), pp. 27–34; see also typescript *Itinerary* on shelves of P.R.O., 15/79D.
[15] *R.G.*, ii, 8.

Agenais.[16] This valuable increment came from a long-standing agreement with the king of France, made by Henry III in 1259, that the dowry given by Richard I to his sister in 1196 should return to the duchy of Aquitaine if the count of Toulouse and his wife died childless. The two died of plague within a day of each other in 1271, and eight years of negotiations and argument before the Parlement of Paris were to follow. The Agenais was solemnly transferred at a ceremony in Agen in 1279 (Fig. 60). Only Castillonnès was in doubt,[17] for the frontier ran through the town, but it was partitioned with the king of France, not becoming wholly English until 1303. The influence of political uncertainty upon the pace of town plantations is well illustrated by the progress of bastides within the Agenais between Alphonse's death and the restitution of 1279: there was one foundation (Fleurance) in the whole eight years.

A new project at Valence d'Agen was among the first fruits of the acquisition of the Agenais, being named after William de Valence, Edward's uncle and plenipotentiary at the business of the transfer. Back in London in November 1279, Edward sent his first seneschal of the Agenais, John de Grilly, a set of orders for bastide building very similar to those sent to the seneschal of Gascony in 1274 after the inquiry into fiefs.[18] (The lower Saintonge, between the Gironde and the Charente, also returned to Edward in 1279 but no bastides have been recognised within it. This nakedness can hardly be accidental, but no French historian seems to have commented upon it.)

The eight years of negotiations that ended in 1279 with the transfer of the Agenais did not resolve all the territorial matters on which the treaty of Paris had stated general principles. The translation of principles into action was delayed, not by ill-will between the kings of France and England, but by the vagueness of the rights which had passed with Joan's dowry in 1196. In 1259 it had been agreed that the lands of Alphonse in Quercy (or the diocese of Cahors) should pass to Edward if Alphonse died childless, but no transfer took place until after Edward's visit to Paris in 1286, on his way from England to Gascony. The king of France also agreed to surrender his own rights in the three dioceses of Cahors, Périgueux and Limoges, albeit with reservations. Some

[16] In 1271 the Alphonsian bastides as a whole were worth 3,810 £T., p.a. (*Histoire de Languedoc*, iii, p. 601).
[17] G. P. Cuttino, *Le Livre d'Agenais* (Toulouse, 1956), Introduction. Eymet was also retained by the king of France since it lay wholly in Périgord.
[18] *R.G.*, ii, 259.

FIG. 60. THE AGENAIS AND ITS BASTIDES ACQUIRED BY THE ENGLISH IN
AND AFTER 1279.
O: Bastides acquired at the reversion of the lands of Alphonse de Poitiers.
●: Other bastides acquired after 1279.
—·—· Limits of the *sénéchaussées* of the count of Toulouse in 1271 (after *Fournier and Guébin*; some
authorities do not include in the Agenais an area west of Donzac and Dunes, and south
of the Garonne, *i.e.* Brulhois and Condomois).

356

TABLE XIII.3

GASCONY: BASTIDES FOUNDED AFTER 1273-74

Montréal	c. 1272-94	Lot et Garonne
Pugpito	1274	Dordogne
Vacca Ferra	c. 1274-75	Dordogne
Castetcrabe	1276	Landes
Castelnau sur Gupie	1276	Lot et Garonne
St. Osbert	1276	Gironde
Near Mauvezin sur Gupie (or d'Agenais)	1278	Lot et Garonne
Molières	1278-84	Dordogne
Miramont	1278-86	Lot et Garonne
Valence d'Agen	1279	Tarn et Garonne
Fourcès	1279-86	Gers
Cadillac	1280	Gironde
Corneillas	1280	Tarn et Garonne
Villefranche de Queyran	by 1281	Lot et Garonne
Lados	1281	Gironde
Polinges	1281	Landes
Sauveterre de Guyenne	1281	Gironde
Bonnegarde en Chalosse	1283	Landes
Lacenne	1283	Lot et Garonne
Roquepine	1283	Dordogne
La Bastide d'Armagnac	c. 1283-91	Landes
Beaulieu (Pertus)	by 1284	Dordogne
Fonroque	by 1284	Dordogne
La Bastide Monestier (Villefranche)	by 1284	Dordogne
St. Gein en Marsan	1284	Landes
Vianne	1284	Lot et Garonne
Créon II	1285	Landes
Fourques	1285	Lot et Garonne
Monpazier	1285	Dordogne
Montbrun	1285	Gironde
Beauregard	1286	Dordogne
Baa	1287	Gironde
Camparian	1287	Gironde
Burgus Reginae	by 1288	Gironde
Artus	1288	Lot et Garonne
Lagruère	by 1289	Lot et Garonne
Arouille	1289	Landes
Boulogne (St. Pé-St. Simon)	1289	Lot et Garonne
Cussac	1289	Gironde
Larée	1289	Gers
Mauvezin d' Armagnac	1289	Landes
St. Clar	1289	Gers
Ste. Quitterie (Aire sur L'Adour)	1289	Landes
Souprosse	1289	Landes
Larroque	1289-93	Gers
Hastingues	1289-c. 1303	Landes

TABLE XIII.3—(*contd*).

La Bastide Murat	c. 1290–1304	Lot
Granges sur Lot	1291	Lot et Garonne
Nicole	1291	Lot et Garonne
Regalis Mons	1291	Lot et Garonne
Réjaumont	1292	Gers
Montfaucon du Lot	1292–93	Lot
Aiguillon	1296	Lot et Garonne
Levignac	1305	Lot et Garonne
Ste. Gemme	1305	Lot et Garonne
Ozourt	c. 1305	Landes
Salespisse	c. 1306–13	Landes
Labouheyre (near)	1307–18	Landes
Rovigna	c. 1307–27	Lot et Garonne
Betbezer	by 1308	Landes
Lias	1308	Gers
Nerbis	1314	Landes
Duire	by 1315	Gironde
Le Fleix	by 1315	Dordogne
Créon I	1315	Gironde
Rondeboeuf	1315	Landes
St. Barthélémy de Bellegarde	by 1316	Dordogne
St. Edouard (Baigts)	1316–17	Landes
Cazals	c. 1316–27	Lot
Sarron	by 1318	Landes
Geaune en Tursan	1318	Landes
St. Sauveur de Meilhan	1318–23	Lot et Garonne
Monguilhem	1319	Gers
La Bastide (Montpazier)	c. 1319	Landes
Villenave	c. 1319	Landes
Fonfrède	1320	Landes
Durance	1320	Lot et Garonne
Le Temple de Breuil (or Felton)	1320	Lot et Garonne
Montégut	1320	Landes
Libos	c. 1320	Lot et Garonne
Toulouzette	1321	Landes
St. Maure de Peyriac	c. 1324	Lot et Garonne
St. Maurice	c. 1326	Landes
La Bastide Chalosse	by 1327–29	Landes
Londres (St. Etienne)	after 1327	Lot et Garonne
Port de Lanne	1331	Landes
Pouriet (Arbanats)	1348	Gironde

transfer of rights took place at once, for it was holdings in the three dioceses that Eleanor had pawned in the crisis of 1265.

Edward himself visited Paris in 1286, on his way to Gascony, and his intervention produced a new settlement whereby lands to the value of £3,000 *tournois* should be assigned to Edward in respect of all the above claims. The first instalment of these was made up of two blocks of territory in Quercy: the bastides of Castelsagrat and Montjoi in the south-west, on the border with the Agenais; and a separate block of territory further north, beginning with the Alphonsian bastide of Villefranche du Périgord and continuing eastwards through the fortified towns of Cazals to the parishes depending on the *baillis* of Concorés and Vers. The two bastides on the Agenais border were then incorporated in the Agenais; Edward added another bastide to Quercy by purchasing land north of Vers in 1292 where Montfaucon was built in 1293; and between 1290 and 1304 La Bastide Murat was built nearby, possibly as a result of a *paréage* between the king-duke and the seigneur of Gourdon. These two were the easternmost of the English bastides.

Edward's visit to Gascony in 1286 was extended for three years,[19] during which thirteen more Gascon bastides were founded, making the 1280's the most active of any decade (Fig. 57). Edward visited many of the Alphonsian bastides that had been acquired since his last visit in 1273–74, as well as others further south (such as Bonnegarde) that had been planted by his seneschals in his absence. He also visited bastides in progress (such as Baa in March 1287).

III

Edward's keen interest in the Gascon bastides, which seems to have set off the foundation of bastides at a new pace, had a double origin. He was concerned to augment his revenues and he was concerned to increase his political power within the duchy. The bastides served both purposes.

It may be no more than a coincidence that the first two English bastides were chartered at a time when Henry III's queen was pawning Gascon lands, and only nine days before the battle of Evesham, but it is a useful symbol of the revenues expected from bastides that the earliest charters should be issued when the king and his sons were in such straits at home. Similarly, the customs revenues of Bordeaux were pawned in 1269 to help Edward go on Crusade, and the loan was prolonged to 1274 by falling back on the credit of merchants.[20]

[19] J.-P. Trabut-Cussac, "L'Itinéraire d'Edouard Ier en France, 1286–9", *B.I.H.R.* xxv (1952), pp. 160–203, shows Edward's movement during this period, correcting, supplementing and supplanting Gough's *Itinerary* for these years.
[20] F. M. Powicke, *Henry III and the Lord Edward*, ii (1947), p. 515; *id.*, *The Thirteenth Century* (1953) p. 281.

In Henry III's time Gascony was a drain on the English Exchequer, not a contributor. The position in Edward's reign is less certain but there is no doubt of his need to increase Gascon revenues and minimise losses. The Gascon bastides were to perform the same service that a plantation in England rendered its founder, the augmentation of his rent roll. The various ways in which towns contributed to seigneurial revenues have already been described in Chapter 3, and most forms of burghal revenues occur in the king-duke's Gascon accounts.

As a source of revenue the bastides were additionally welcome in that they called for virtually no expenditure by the duke, and, so far as founders were concerned, any future revenues came without effort on their part since initiative, effort and decisions lay with the townsmen. If the bastide proved abortive, the material losses to the king were small.

Edward also had a strong financial interest in the general development of commerce, particularly of exports, and anything that stimulated trade in the Garonne valley was good for Bordeaux and for its overlord. Accounts which survive from the year 1306–07, when the main complement of bastides had been achieved, show that the duchy revenues were then about £17,000 sterling. Almost half of this came from Bordeaux and the Bordelais, and nearly 30% from the Agenais. The Bordeaux contribution rested heavily on the prosperity of trade: three quarters of the £7,866 came from customs duties levied on goods that passed through or by the town quays. Between 1280 and 1300 the duties on wine at Bordeaux were from 6–10% of the value of the wine.[21]

The great feudal inquiry of 1273–74 was concerned not only with the payments and duties of Gascon vassals but also with their rights. The landowners of Gascony had a long tradition of independence, and political relations—if history was any guide—would not be easy for Edward. As duke of Gascony he had very few estates of his own, so that his economic and political strength lay in what he could do as feudal overlord. The relevance of the bastides in this situation was that they scattered the duchy with communities whose first loyalty was to Edward personally; communities made up of men with social origins and interests different from those of the Gascon seigneurs. In any

---

[21] J.-P. Trabut-Cussac, "Les Coutumes ou Droits de Douane perçus à Bordeaux", *Annales du Midi*, lxii (1950), pp. 135–150. The statement in M. McKisack, *The Fourteenth Century* (1959), p. 107, that in 1306–07 Gascony yielded a revenue greater than that of the English crown, rests on an assertion of Dr. Cuttino (*Speculum*, xxxi (1950), pp. 468–469): on inspection, the yardstick itself is defective, being the calculations of Sir James Ramsay.

conflict they might be expected to be on Edward's side, and a bastide's merchants and traders might also be useful if loans had to be sought.

IV

Some authors have attributed a prominent role to military strategy and dynastic rivalry in the development of bastides in English Gascony and the Agenais that bordered upon it.[22]   In this view a distribution map of the French and English bastides shows an advanced stage in a game of chess where neither Black nor White has lost any pieces.   This fortress view might have some validity where Black was England, and White was the Wales of prince Llewelyn, although even here there would need to be qualifications.   In Gascony M. Trabut-Cussac had no difficulty in showing that the geographical distribution of bastides is too general for them to mark out any political or strategic frontiers.[23] If any lines are to be discerned in Fig. 62, are they not the principal lines of inland commerce leading to Bordeaux and Bayonne?

M. Trabut-Cussac advanced other arguments based on the pacific tenor of foundation charters and on the absence of any serious defences at many bastides that were alleged to be on the frontier.   These arguments have already been considered (p. 184).   More relevant here is his demonstration that the timing of the bastides does not assist the fortress argument.

He examined the Alphonsian bastides of the Agenais, all but one of them founded after 1254 while Henry III and Louis IX were on good terms with each other.   In 1259 the treaty of Amiens assured the return of the Agenais to the English crown on the deaths of Alphonse and his wife, who was past child-bearing age.   If the Agenais was destined to be joined to English Gascony, what was the point of Alphonse designing towns to defend it against the English? or for the English arming themselves against the Agenais? and what in fact was the military state of these bastides when Edward I did receive them in 1279? most, says Trabut-Cussac, were undefended.   The defences, when and if they came, were asked for by the municipalities and not imposed by the

---

[22] C. Higounet, "Bastides et Frontières", *Le Moyen Age*, liv (1948), pp. 113–121; O. de St. Blanquat, "Comment se sont créés les Bastides?", *Annales*, iv (1949), pp. 278–289.
[23] J-P. Trabut-Cussac, "Bastides ou Forteresses?", *Le Moyen Age*, lx (1954), pp. 81–135. He did not deny that some bastides were fortified, only that they formed a Grand Design of frontier works directed against the count of Toulouse and the kings of France.

seigneur, and the fears of the municipalities were directed not across the frontier but at local seigneurs and local disorders.

Many of the royal bastides, it will be remembered, had been founded by *paréages*, partnerships with local landowners. The promotion of bastides therefore drew towards the king certain of his landowning vassals. *Paréages* with bishops and abbots—particularly of the Cistercian order—had been much used by Alphonse, and Edward continued this practice.[24] The partners, lay or clerical, shared the revenues of the town with the duke, and he was seen to have an accommodating spirit. Bastides did not appear as a naked weapon of aggression directed by an ambitious duke against all Gascon landowners.[25]

Edward's political needs also included centres for local administration within the duchy, and many of these units (*ballivia, bailliages*) had their headquarters in bastides. M. Trabut-Cussac has made a special study of the bastide of Créon and its administrative role.[26] In 1290 the king also decided that his recently acquired territory in Quercy lacked a centre for administration, and ordered a bastide to be founded for the purpose.[27] In the duchy accounts of 1306–07, to which reference has already been made, details are given of the farmed revenues of the *bailliages*. *Bailliages* centred upon bastides provided 70% of the total *bailliages* farms in the Agenais, and 50% in Périgord, Limousin and Quercy; while four bastides contributed one third of the total revenue of the Bazadais.[28]

We have noted the laggard progress of plantations in English Gascony compared with the earlier development in the Agenais, and in other parts of the county of Toulouse the most active period was twenty years ahead of English Gascony. Fig. 61 shows the distribution of bastides in other parts of the county of Toulouse and (in so far as evidence is available) for other parts of the kingdom of France.[29] It shows that the most active decade was the 1260's, whereas it was the

[24] C. Higounet, "Cisterciens et Bastides", *Le Moyen Age*, lvi (1950), pp. 69–84.
[25] This view can be seen in E. Lodge, *Gascony under English Rule*, deriving from F. B. Marsh *English Rule in Gascony, 1199–1259* (1912). Bémont's review of the latter in *Revue Historique*, cxiv (1913), pp. 382–383, exposed the weaknesses of the black-and-white view of kings and towns v. nobles.
[26] J-P. Trabut-Cussac, "Créon, Bastide Administrative", *Annales du Midi*, lxvi (1954), pp. 343–350.
[27] F. M. Powicke, *The Thirteenth Century* (1953), p. 309.
[28] See also E101/164/1, ff. 5–6.
[29] The dates are collected from many scattered printed sources; the articles by Professor Higounet cited in Appendix II have provided most of the dates for bastides in southern France outside Gascony.

1280's in English Gascony. The explanation that we have adduced for this late development is the preoccupation of the king-dukes with their English kingdom.

Another question is raised if Table XIII.6 and Figs. 57 and 61 are compared, for they show that even the activity in the county of Toulouse came very late in comparison with plantations in England itself. On the Toulousian side of the frontier there had been isolated plantations in the twelfth century (as at Lavour (1098), St. Nicholas de La Grave (1135), and Montauban (1144)) similar to those noticed in Aquitaine, Maine and Normandy. In the early thirteenth century the count of Toulouse had founded Verlhac, Cordes and Montech. One may regard the foundation of Puymirol in 1246 as the beginning of a concerted policy, or perhaps look for origins further east in the French king's own plantation of Aigues Mortes in 1241 to be a port of departure

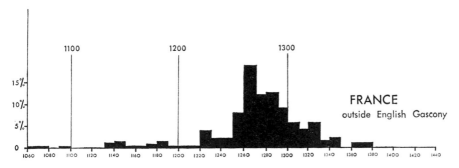

FIG. 61. CHRONOLOGY OF PLANTED TOWNS IN FRANCE, OUTSIDE GASCONY.

for the Crusading fleets. In any event, there was nothing continuous until Alphonse's officers began to negotiate their *paréages* in the 1250's, and this activity was beginning just when the peak had been passed in England itself.

We cannot blame the Welsh wars and the English barons for this particular delay, and the question arises: was there a general brake on development that affected all south-western France until the mid-thirteenth century? and was there some common economic basis for the rapid urban development that then took place on French and—albeit laggardly—on English territory, at a time when countries with more forward development were finding it hard to make room for additional towns? These questions can be answered by considering together two influences: the devastation within the most fertile parts of the south-west during the civil war of the Albigensian Crusade, between 1209 and 1244; and the increase in the area of vineyards in many parts of the Garonne basin after the English had lost Poitou. The evidence points to a retarded colonisation that took new vigour in the mid-thirteenth century. The economic life of the Garonne basin—including the tributary valleys of the Lot and Tarn—had always drawn strength from its

TABLE XIII.4

GASCONY: CHRONOLOGY OF PLANTED TOWNS

	Assignable to decades			Assignable only to broad periods	
	Number	Percentage		Number	Percentage
1181–90	1	1			
1191–1200	0	0			
1201–10	0	0			
1211–20	0	0			
1221–30	0	0			
1231–40	0	0			
1241–50	1	1			
1251–60	6	5	1251–70	3	2
1261–70	14	11	1251–80	1	1
1271–80	14	11	1251–90	5	4
1281–90	26	21	1271–90	5	4
			1281–1307	3	2
			1291–1307	1	1
1291–1300	9	7	1307–20	3	2
1301–10	4	3	1307–30	8	6
1311–20	13	11			
1321–30	4	3			
1331–40	1	1			
1341–50	1	1			
1351–60	0	0	1321–60	1	1
Totals	95	76		30	23
		Total 124			

Note: The decades 1241–70 include the Alphonsian bastides of the Agenais, acquired in 1279.

position in the corridor leading across southern France from Mediterranean to Atlantic. At the centre of this corridor was the old city of Toulouse, and at its western end, Bordeaux. The watershed lay east of Toulouse, so that the natural direction of river traffic was towards Bordeaux rather to the Mediterranean. Paradoxically, the bastides of the count of Toulouse were much assisted by developments taking place at the Bordeaux end of the corridor.

Until the 1230's, French wine for the English and northern European markets was grown in Poitou, the main centre being St. Jean d'Angély and the valley of the Charente. La Rochelle had been founded with this trade in mind, but with the separation of Poitou from the

TABLE XIII.5

GASCONY: CHRONOLOGY, INCLUDING CONJECTURED DECADES

	Assignable to decades	Decade conjectured	Total Number	Percentage
1181–90	1	0	1	1
1191–1200	0	0	0	0
1201–10	0	0	0	0
1211–20	0	0	0	0
1221–30	0	0	0	0
1231–40	0	0	0	0
1241–50	1	0	1	1
1251–60	6	3	9	7
1261–70	14	3	17	14
1271–80	14	4	18	14
1281–90	26	5	31	25
1291–1300	9	2	11	9
1301–10	4	5	9	7
1311–20	13	4	17	14
1321–30	4	3	7	6
1331–40	1	1	2	2
1341–50	1	0	1	1
1351–60	0	0	0	0
Totals	95	30	124	

English crown the wine merchants had to prospect other areas and other ports.[30]

Although French control in Poitou was by no means secure, this great province should henceforth be regarded as part of the domain of the French king. Hence Gascony became the centre from which Henry III and his successors maintained their fluctuating relations with those persons and communities of Poitou, the Limousin, Périgord and the lands to the south, who were induced from time to time to recognise their lordship.

[30] Y. Renouard, "Le Grand Commerce des Vins de Gascogne au Moyen Age", *Rev. Hist.*, ccxxi (1959), pp. 261–304 and "Vignobles, Vignes et Vins de France au Moyen Age", *Le Moyen Age*, lxvi (1960), pp. 337–351; R. Dion, *L'Histoire de la Vigne et du Vin en France* (Paris, 1959).

TABLE XIII.6

CHRONOLOGY OF TOWN PLANTATION, ENGLAND, WALES AND GASCONY
INCLUDING CONJECTURED DATES

	England	Wales	Gascony	Total number	Percentage
before 1066	3	1	0	4	1
	6	0	0	6	2
1071–80	6	3	0	9	2
1081–90	5	1	0	6	2
1091–1100	4	4	0	8	2
1101–10	6	3	0	9	2
1111–20	7	3	0	10	3
1121–30	6	2	0	8	2
1131–40	4	2	0	6	2
1141–50	2	4	0	6	2
1151–60	7	1	0	8	2
1161–70	6	2	0	8	2
1171–80	8	1	0	9	2
1181–90	8	1	1	10	3
1191–1200	13	1	0	14	3
1201–10	9	1	0	10	3
1211–20	12	2	0	14	3
1221–30	15	2	0	17	4
1231–40	4	3	0	7	2
1241–50	8	6	1	15	4
1251–60	3	2	9	14	3
1261–70	5	1	17	23	6
1271–80	0	10	18	28	7
1281–90	4	10	31	45	12
1291–1300	5	9	11	25	7
1301–10	4	3	9	16	4
1311–20	1	1	17	19	5
1321–30	2	1	7	10	3
1331–40	0	1	2	3	1
1341–50	1	1	1	3	1
After 1350	2	0	0	2	1
Not dated	6	2	0	8	2
Total	172	84	124	380	

It is not possible to say when the merchants gave up hope of the recovery of Poitou, but Henry himself clearly retained hopes when he campaigned in Poitou and Gascony in 1230, in 1242–43 and in 1253–54. In 1254 he gave Aquitaine to the rule of his son, the lord Edward, and

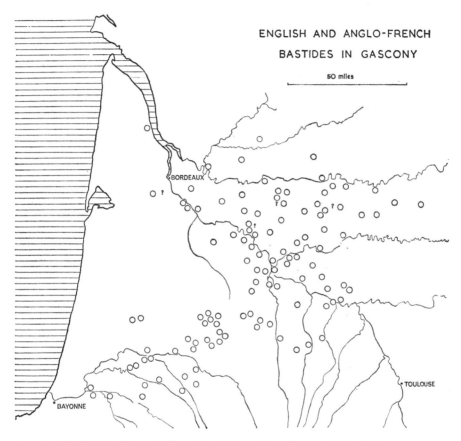

FIG. 62. ENGLISH AND ANGLO-FRENCH BASTIDES IN GASCONY. The map includes those acquired from the French (see Fig. 60) in and after 1279.

three years later there appeared the first signs that he might reconcile himself to the permanent loss of Normandy, Maine and Anjou as part of a general settlement with Louis IX. It was therefore only after the treaty of 1259 that the English wine trade could be said to be committed irrevocably to Gascony. The centre of the duchy of Aquitaine was now truly Bordeaux, and the unifying economic force was that of trade along the rivers that converged upon that city, and upon the smaller port of Bayonne at the south-western corner of the duchy.[31]

Wine was a commodity that depended on sea- and river-transport for efficient movement. The jolting of road transport was not good for the quality of the wine, and it greatly increased the losses from the bursting of wooden casks. Even on the sea-voyage to England the losses from burst casks ran as high as 5%, and the convoys carried carpenters to perform running repairs. The concern of Edward I and his son for river improvements on the Lot and the Tarn arose from their appreciation that the areas where wine could be grown for export were largely determined by the quality of river transport. In the early fourteenth century wine was coming to Bordeaux from as far up river as Montréjau on the Garonne, Pamiers on the Ariège, Albi on the Tarn, Salvagnac on the Lot and Souillac on the Dordogne. These places, it will be noted, lay beyond the frontier of English Gascony, extending into the counties of Toulouse and Comminges.

The traditional river-ports were quite inadequate for the volume of traffic that followed the increased cultivation of the vine for the Bordeaux trade. There was room for ports in the gaps between them on the smaller tributaries. Bastides planted away from older village centres were empowered to clear woodland, and themselves grow wine.[32] This ready market for wine brought a very high degree of specialisation to the agriculture of the south-west.[33] More and more resources were devoted to wine, relying on other countries—particularly England—for supplies of fish, hides, wool, cloth, and even corn. With this degree of specialisation and with poor land transport, the multiplication of small market centres was crucial for the local economies.[34]

[31] E. M. Carus-Wilson, "The Effects of the Acquisition and of the Loss of Gascony on the English Wine-trade", *B.I.H.R.*, xxi (1948), pp. 145–154. There was no great movement of colonisation of towns by Englishmen similar to that in the new towns of Norman or Edwardian Wales, or in Ireland. In peacetime the English administrators, soldiers and merchants living in Gascony did not number many hundred (R. Boutruche, *La Crise d'une Société* (Paris, 1947), pp. 134–135).
[32] There was a time-lag between the clearing of land, the planting of the vine and full production from the plant, which was usually six years (Boutruche, *op. cit.*, p. 32).
[33] It should also be noted that wine-growing imposed a discipline and a time-table that did not fit into the standard pattern of demesne works and communal husbandry (Boutruche, *op. cit.*, pp. 21–24). Thus, viticulture matched the freedom of town air.
[34] After becoming English in 1288, the men of the bastide of Castelsagrat wrote to Edward I asking whether they could now join the towns which sent wine down to Bordeaux; they had recently planted vines, even within the walled area. (SC2/119/38, cited in Dion, *op. cit.*, p. 383.)

The development of Gascon bastides was therefore a special case of a relation between town and country which has already been encountered in England and Wales: towns developed most rapidly and most closely together in areas where rural colonisation was delayed, and land transport was poor. Nor is the close crowding of the bastides any surprise when there was so much local jostling and rivalry for markets, and when the poor quality of land transport lengthened the time taken for journeys, making it possible for stopping-centres and collecting-centres to flourish at less than 10 mile intervals. If like begets like, the movements that occurred in the English lowlands in the twelfth century did not reach Devon and Cornwall until the early thirteenth century and north Wales until the late thirteenth century; cognate movements in Scotland and Ireland can also be inferred. Two other parallels, contemporary and better-known, are the new towns that accompanied the reclamation of the Low Countries, and the new towns that accompanied the great Germanic colonisation east of the Elbe.

In this view, the Gascon bastides of Alphonse and Edward prospered by the conjunction of two circumstances: the sudden demand of the English for wine after the loss of vineyards further north in 1224; and a generous supply of land in Gascony that could be put to this use.[35] But how was it that land on this scale was still available in the mid-thirteenth century, with the population of Europe (we are told) pressing everywhere towards the marginal lands? was it obtained by a massive change in land-use, such as that which gave England sufficient wool for its cloth industry? or was the vine planted in land that had never been cultivated?

Villages with conventional agriculture were well spread over the region, and there was doubtless some conversion of agriculture to viticulture when the advantages of specialisation were discerned and supplies of imported food became easily available in the markets. Gascony also had a good deal of land that was not suited to conventional food production, as the large areas still under woodland and scrub today will testify. It is one of the beauties of the vine that its roots welcome soils that other food-plants reject, and in this sense there was real colonisation.

[35] The protected market of England was not the only customer: Flanders, the Low Countries, Germany and Scandinavia were also supplied. The customs payments of 1308–09 from Bordeaux represent an export of over 100,000 tons; those of 1900 were about seven-eighths of this, and those of 1956 about half.

It also seems possible that the Garonne basis was laggard in conventional colonisation. Marc Bloch suggested that the easier opportunities in the great empty spaces of the Iberian peninsula had drawn away colonists in the twelfth and early thirteenth centuries,[36] and Professor

TABLE XIII.7

BASTIDES ACQUIRED FROM FRENCH KINGS OR SEIGNEURS AFTER 1279

Date of acquisition		*Year of foundation*	*Founders*
1286–87	Castelsagrat	by 1262	Alphonse de Poitiers
1310	Domme	1281	King of France
After 1279	Eymet	c. 1270	Alphonse de Poitiers
By 1298	La Bastide d'Armagnac	c. 1291	Count of Armagnac
By 1308	La Montjoie St. Louis	1299	King of France
1303–05	Regalis Mons (Rives)	1291	King of France
By 1314	Monclar	c. 1304	Count of Armagnac by *paréage*
1286–87	Montjoi	1255	Alphonse de Poitiers
By 1313	St. Jean de Cariet	by 1282	Count of Périgord by *paréage*
1303–05	St. Julien de Colorbisse	1300	King of France by *paréage*
By 1314	St. Justin	1280	Countess of Béarn by *paréage*
By 1329	St. Sardos	1323	Abbot by *paréage*
?1303	Sorde l'Abbaye	1290	Abbot by *paréage*
By 1293	Valence sur Baïse	1274	Count of Armagnac by *paréage*
By 1318	Villefranche de Longchat	by 1287	Prior by *paréage*
1287	Villefranche du Périgord	1261	Alphonse de Poitiers

For Castillonnès, finally acquired in 1303, see Table XIII.3

Higounet pointed out that the presence of so many Cistercian houses indicates plenty of land left for colonisation.[37]

There was one further circumstance that may explain how the south-west could turn itself so thoroughly to wine-growing at that particular time. Just when the English were being expelled from the Angevin

[36] Marc Bloch, *Les Caractères Originaux de l'Histoire Rurale Française*, (Paris, 1955), p. 14.
[37] Dr. Chaplais has drawn attention to the parallel between the English king's grants to encourage bastides and those to encourage individual settlers of *possessiones steriles vel quasi steriles* (P. Chaplais, "The Chancery of Guyenne", in J. C. Davies, ed., *Studies presented to Sir Hilary Jenkinson* (1957), pp. 72–73. The parallel between bastides and earlier *sauvetés* colonies has been discussed above, p. 186, and by C. Higounet in "Les Sauvetés de Moissac", *Annales du Midi*, lxxv (1964), pp. 505–512. B. Lyon, "Medieval Real Estate Development and Freedom", *Amer. Hist. Rev.*, lxiii (1957–58), pp. 47–61 discusses parallels with the *bourgs* and *hospites* of Maine, drawing on R. Latouche, "Un aspect de la vie rurale: l'établissement des Bourgs", *Le Moyen Age*, xlvii (1937), pp. 44–64.

lands of northern France, a long and bloody civil war was coming to an end in the south. The fierceness of the war arose from dynastic ambition and religious enthusiasm. In the so-called Albigensian Crusade the Pope and the king of France were in alliance to destroy the heretics and the count of Toulouse who supported them. The theatre of battle stretched from the Mediterranean into the Agenais, and approached near to Bordeaux. Vengeance, pillage and the extirpation of

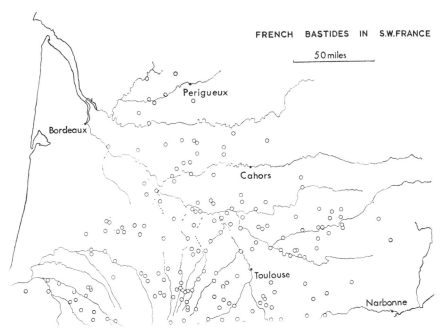

FIG. 63. FRENCH BASTIDES IN SOUTH-WESTERN FRANCE. This map should be taken with Fig. 62 in order to assess the full intensity of plantation in this area, largely after 1240.

heretics had profound effects on the rural population. Puymirol, the first of the count's bastides in the Agenais, was in the centre of a devastated area, and among those received into the new town were the monks of St. Maurin whose abbey had been destroyed in the war.[38] Villeneuve sur Lot, another early foundation, was sometimes known as *La Bastide de Pujols*, and the local tradition is that Pujols, on the opposite

[38] Y. Domengie, "Les bastides en Agenais", *Rev. de l'Agenais*, xlvii (1920), p. 260.

bank, had been destroyed in the Albigensian war. When the consuls of the town petitioned for a new bridge in 1270 they told Alphonse that they proposed to use the stone from the ruins of Pujols castle which, they said, was uninhabited "since the heresies".[39]

After they had made an abject peace with the king of France there was every reason for the counts of Toulouse to wish to repair their fortunes by the recolonisation of their county (which at that time included the Agenais), and although the treaty of 1229 forbade the building of walled towns it said nothing about *villes neuves*.[40] In this context the vine and the bastide of commerce were not incongruous allies, but after the king's brother had become count of Toulouse in 1248 it was less likely that walled bastides would be opposed in Paris.

V

From 1250 onwards, first in the county of Toulouse and then in the whole south-west, the development of bastides was rapid (Table XIII.8). The most active period in France generally seems to have been the 1260's, and in English Gascony the 1280's. Fig. 57 shows that the first check to the flow of English bastides came in the 1290's when the rate was less than a third of that in the 1280's. This check came from the outbreak of war between England and France in 1294, and disruption continued until 1297. Professor Carus-Wilson has shown how the fortunes of Gascon commerce rose and fell with the alternations of peace and fighting during the Hundred Years War, and the same effect can be seen in the numbers of towns planted during 1294–97 and after 1323 (Table XIII.5).

When war broke out in 1294 the matter at issue was not Gascon territory, but fighting spread to Gascony in 1295 and 1296. A truce was made in the autumn of 1297, and under its terms the greater part of Gascony, including the Agenais, remained subject to the French king. Edward's authority was limited to smaller areas centred on Blaye, Bourg and Bayonne in the west. No English bastide of any consequence was founded until after the conclusion of full peace in 1303 when the defeat lately suffered by the French king at the hands of the Flemings strengthened Edward's bargaining position. The Peace of

[39] *A.P.E.A.*, p. 312.
[40] Domengie, *loc. cit.*
[41] E. M. Carus-Wilson, *art. cit.* in fn. 31.

TABLE XIII.8

DATES OF 226 PLANTATIONS IN FRANCE EXCLUDING
ENGLISH GASCONY, 1041–1400, by DECADES

[see also Fig. 61 p. 363]

Decade	Number	Per cent
1041–50	5	2·2
1051–60	1	0·4
1061–70	1	0·4
1071–80	0	0
1081–90	0	0
1091–1100	1	0·04
	8	3·4

Decade	Number	Per cent
1101–10	0	0
1111–20	0	0
1121–30	0	0
1131–40	3	1·3
1141–50	4	1·8
1151–60	1	0·4
1161–70	1	0·4
1171–80	2	0·9
1181–90	4	1·8
1191–1200	1	0·4
	16	7

Decade	Number	Per cent
1201–10	1	0·4
1211–20	1	0·4
1221–30	9	4·0
1231–40	5	2·2
1241–50	5	2·2
1251–60	18	8·0
1261–70	43	19·0
1271–80	27	11·9
1281–90	28	12·4
1291–1300	20	8·8
	157	69·3

Decade	Number	Per cent
1301–10	13	5·8
1311–20	10	4·4
1321–30	13	5·8
1331–40	3	1·3
1341–50	4	1·8
1351–60	0	0
1361–70	1	0·4
1371–80	0	0
1381–90	0	0
1391–1400	1	0·4
	45	19·9

Paris restored his Gascon lands, bringing a small windfall of bastides (Table XIII.7) that had been built on them since 1294.

Edward himself did not return to Gascony after 1289, and in 1306 he handed over the duchy of Gascony to his son. The second decade of the fourteenth century witnessed unusual activity in the foundation of Gascon bastides particularly in the Landes, the south-western part of the duchy. The Gascon Rolls of this decade show correspondence passing between London and Gascony about the foundation of bastides that is reminiscent of the 1280's.

In a report made by the seneschal of the Saintonge in April 1317 two ominous statements appeared: the French were planning to set a bastide at St. Sardos *en milleu de tout Agenays*; and their proctors were agitating in the Parlement of Paris to re-open the question of ownership of the bastides of the Agenais,

> *la quele chose est mout perillosse a nostre sire le Roy.*

The foundation of St. Sardos was to lead to open warfare in 1323–25, and to a drastic reduction of English authority in Gascony. The questioning of the English title to the Agenais showed that the peace of 1303 had not finally settled the disposition of the territories left behind by Alphonse de Poitiers in 1271.

The War of St. Sardos went badly for the English. They were pushed back to a strip of coastal territory running from Saintonge to Bayonne, and the settlement of 1317 still left the French in possession of the Agenais and the Bazadais. Further negotiations over the fate of the Agenais were in progress when the Hundred Years War broke out in 1337. Thus, conditions were not encouraging for new English bastides after 1323: three were founded in the Landes between 1326 and 1331, but in an area least affected by the war. Several older bastides in the Bazadais and Agenais figure in a list of damaged towns that was prepared for the use of English diplomats in the peace negotiations of 1327.

The failure of new projects after 1330 arose from more than destruction by war and the uncertainties of intervening peace. The economic base that lay in the Bordeaux–English trade was being eroded by war, and, even before the reduction of population which began with the Black Death, Figs. 57 and 61 bear witness that plantation was wilting.

---

[42] *R.G.*, iv, pp. 578–579.

England, Wales, France and Gascony were at last in accord. A hard frost had settled on them all.

The single Gascon project of the 1340's, Pouriet (Arbanats), could hardly have been worse timed: Edward III's grant to Elias de Pomiers and his wife was made less than a year before the arrival of the Black Death in Europe. As a founder of towns Edward III had no success. His bastide of Londres proved abortive, and the gain of Calais in the north in 1347 was quite untypical of English fortunes at the end of the Hundred Years War. By 1453 all the bastides in our Gazetteer had been lost to England for ever.

PART FOUR

EVIDENCES

*Three detailed gazetteers set out the evidence for 172
English towns, 84 Welsh towns and 125 Gascon bastides.
In addition, some towns of doubtful origin are discussed, and
a preliminary chapter surveys the evidence on which assert-
ions of a planted origin for towns can be made. Documentary and topographical materials are given equal
stress.*

*Two Appendices set out the English and Welsh planta-
tions in chronological order, the data for Gascony having
already appeared in Chapter 13. Appendix III offers
a select bibliography of books and articles on town plantation in medieval Gascony, and Appendix IV is a very
brief account of town plantation in other European
countries in the medieval period.*

CHAPTER FOURTEEN

Symptoms, Doubts and Evidences

'History has still all the excitement of an unfinished excavation.'
Marc Bloch, *Feudal Society*, (Fr. L. A.
Manyon (1965)), p. 52.

I

UNTIL the *Nomina Villarum* of 1316 no English government attempted a gazetteer of vills and boroughs, and there was no *Nomina Villarum* for Wales and Gascony. The identification of a town as a plantation must therefore rely on documents that were drawn up for purposes other than the record of the presence or absence of a town. The later the plantation, the less the uncertainty, for the passage of time increased the number of occasions when something would happen in a town that caused its name to be written on parchment; and the later the document, the better the chance of its survival. In the eleventh and twelfth centuries the documents for the history of towns of all kinds, organic or planted, are few, and the identification of early plantations must rely on a conjunction of symptoms rather than on explicit evidence of a town being founded in a particular year. It must investigate all cases when the name of a town is missing from Domesday Book, even though the silence of Domesday Book is not conclusive proof that a town did not exist in 1086. It must watch the county volumes of the English Place-Name Society to see when their editors have been unable to find a documentary reference to a town before the twelfth or thirteenth centuries,[1] although there are occasional flaws in these volumes (see Wulvesford, Essex, in the Gazetteer). It must be on guard for the first appearance of a borough in the Exchequer

---

[1] It must be noted that when a planted town took its name from a river or estuary, there will be recorded instances of the place-name from a date earlier than the plantation. Yet there is no need to doubt that Richard I founded Portsmouth, and his brother, Liverpool, despite the earlier occurrence of the names of these natural features. Similarly there was a White Haven before the Lowther town of Whitehaven in 1693, and a Milford Haven before the town of Milford Haven. (C. and W. Hutchinson, *History of Cumberland and Westmorland*, ii (1794), p. 41, with plan; Sir F. Ross, *The Town of Milford* (1954), p. 168.)

tax assessments (Plate 12), in the Pipe Rolls, and in the Assize Rolls. It must observe the extents in the Inquisitions Post Mortem to see when a *novus burgus* appears on the demesne of a tenant in chief, and it must pay equal attention to the accounts of the manorial officers that form the great class of Ministers' Accounts at the Public Record Office. A single symptom is no more than ground for suspicion. It is by conjunction of symptoms that we move towards evidence.

When symptoms, rather than evidences, are in question there is room for disagreement between historians of towns, and it cannot be expected that all towns in the Gazetteers will be accepted as plantations by all critical readers. For this reason the documentary references have been given at some length, and the author has not concealed his own doubts on occasions. In counties where there are particular problems of evidence, such as Durham, with no coverage in Domesday Book, there is a longer discussion in the head-notes to the county.

II

Eye-witness accounts of town plantations are rare (Plate 13). In 1212 some jurors at Portsmouth recalled how Richard I had himself handed over the building plots to several inhabitants of the new town, and the sight of Richard at work about another new town was remembered fifty-five years after the event by two witnesses who had been present at the foundation of St. Rémy de la Haye. By chance, there is a record of witnesses recalling the first foundation of Ravenserodd on the Humber sandbanks, and others who remembered Colyford borough being laid out on the demesnes of Colyton.[2]

The borough charter, the document most closely connected with the foundation of a town, cannot always be relied upon to survive. It has been shown that only seventy-one places out of 172 in the English section of our Gazetteer have borough charters surviving, and that many of these are considerably later than the date of foundation of the towns. Of the 101 places without surviving charters, there are seventy-seven where there is explicit documentary reference to a *burgus*, *burgagium* or *burgenses*; or to the place being taxed as a borough; or to the representation of the place by members in a medieval Parliament; or to the place being acknowledged as a borough in the records of the itinerant judges

[2] The references for this and other particular statements about towns will be found *sub loco* in the appropriate Gazetteer, below.

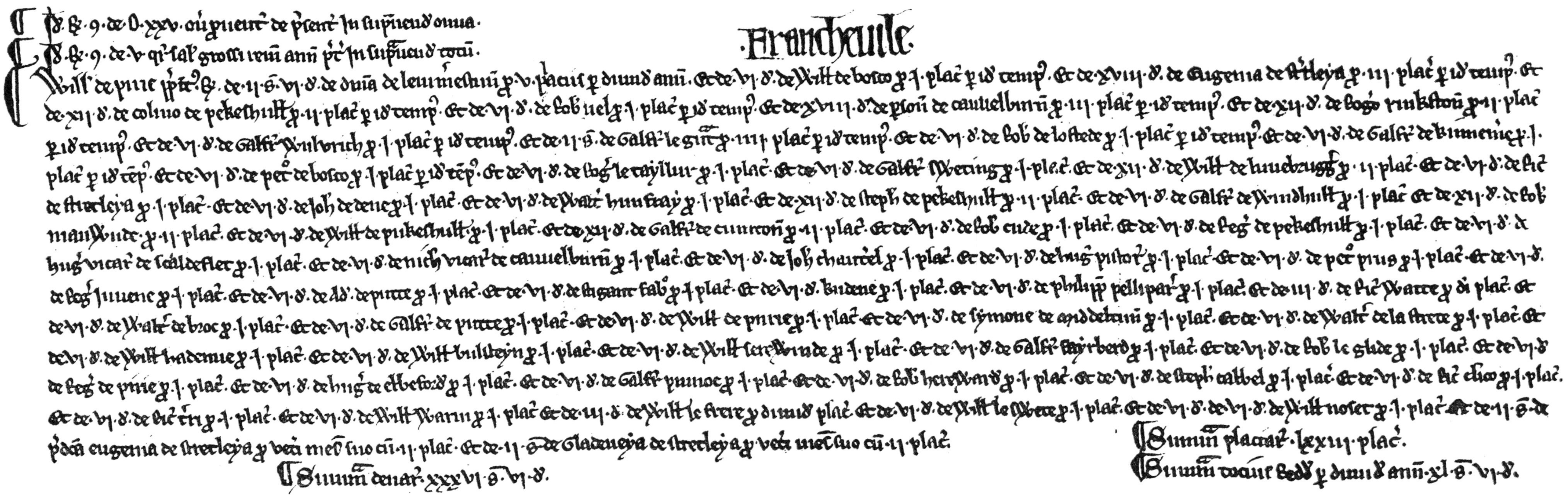

Francheuille

FIG. 64. FRANCHEVILLE (NEWTOWN) I.O.W.   Seventy-three building plots (*placeae*) are listed, each paying 6d. rent for the town's first half-year at Michaelmas 1257.

of assize. Thus, twenty-four remain unsupported, as places that were towns but not boroughs.[3] The twenty-four include St. Albans, Boston, St. Ives, Uxbridge, Wokingham, Brigg, Royston, Chelmsford, Stony Stratford, Newmarket, Wadebridge and Buntingford: about which the evidence cited in the Gazetteer seems conclusive; the twelve towns that a more scrupulous author might have transferred to the *Problems* head-notes are: Belvoir, Church Brough, Wymondham, St. Neots, Barnet, Beaulieu, Cogges Newland, South Shields, Airmyn, Kington (Heref.), and Maidenhead; Falmouth is included as a *jeu d'esprit*, an undoubted plantation, but hardly medieval, yet the first of a new series of English plantations so far removed in time from Queenborough (1368) that the gap needs to be marked by naming its limits.

The absence of a charter is not important when one of the other types of *burgus* reference is available. Of the six towns founded by bishops of Winchester between 1200 and 1256, only one (Newtown, *Francheville*, I.O.W.), has a surviving charter. The account-roll of the bishop's manor of Swainston for 1256–57 confirms that the town had indeed arrived: seventy-three burgages paid their first half-year's rent that Michaelmas (Fig. 64). The arrival of a borough may sometimes be reflected in the grant of a market-charter even when no borough charter was granted or has survived. Thus at Overton (Hants.) there was a market charter granted in 1218, and in the bishop's account roll of 1217–18 a *Burgus* rubric appears on the same membrane as the *manerium*. In the roll for 1218–19 a *Novus Burgus* heading appears for the first time among the entries for another Hampshire manor, that of Clere, and in 1220–21 a *Burgus* rubric under the manor of Knoyle where Hindon had been founded. Similarly, the foundation of New Alresford a decade earlier had caused the clerk to make a separate entry for Alresford *Forum* and then to have second thoughts, to cross out the entry under *Forum*, and to stitch two small membranes to the account roll and head them *De Burgo*.

Had not the bishop's account roll survived, these five plantations could only have been inferred, either from the names, from the absence of earlier documentary references or—most important—from their topography. Earlier chapters have shown that there were characteristic forms which the interior plans of planted towns reveal, especially the

---

[3] Of the Welsh plantations, forty-four have surviving charters. Of the forty places without charters, only three would fail to pass the test of burgality proposed above: New Mostyn, Bridgend and Loughor.

chequers and the grid-forms of streets. There were also characteristic positions for new towns to take up, in relation to older settlements. It has been shown that a planted town was likely to have a small area without field-land (although there are exceptions); it was likely to lie near the edge of an existing parish (although, again, there are exceptions); and it was likely to be surrounded by the territory of the rural village from which its site had been taken. It was also unlikely, in the first instance, to have a town church with full independence: the typical situation is dependence, as a chapelry, on the parish church of the village within whose limits the new town had beeen set. Documentarily, this situation of dependence affords a good chance that some record of dispute between village and town will have survived.

When there are no documents, the form, size and position of a town may be all that the argument can rest upon, unless and until the volume of medieval documents flowing into county and borough Record Offices from private estate archives brings, as it surely must, a few more references to the petty boroughs of the provinces.

III

The name of a town can also be symptomatic of its origins. Devizes, *burgus de divisis*,[4] emphasised in its name that parish-edge situation which has already been suggested as a characteristic of the late-arriving town, and the Newboroughs,[5] Newcastles, Newtowns and *Villesneuves* abound in the Gazetteer.[6] The discovery of a pair of names in the same locality, one Old and one New, is also calculated to arouse suspicions of plantation. Even if there were no Winchester pipe-rolls, the pairing of Old Alresford and New Alresford borough would call for some further enquiries. The existence of New Buckenham so near to Old Buckenham should also stir curiosity, even before the singular rectilinearity of New Buckenham, its situation on the edge of the common, and its absence of field-land are seen to point in the same

---

[4] Pipewell Abbey, Northants. was originally St. Mary *de Devisis* because it lay on both sides of a brook which divided Rothwell from Corby Hundred (*V.C.H. Northants.*, ii, p. 116).

[5] One *Novus Burgus* remains so far unidentified: in 1200 a charter was granted to the Templars to have a market in this place, but no Templar property with such a name has been traced (C53/12 m. 2).

[6] Just as the English *Newton* was given as a name to many townships in the Anglo-Saxon period that had no element of urbanism in their life, so *Villeneuve* is a frequent name for a village created in the course of medieval colonisation. The name itself, unsupported by documentary and/or topographical evidence, does not prove a New Town.

direction. When the Saxon town of *Burgh* suddenly became known as Aldborough it is prudent to look for a new borough, and to find it on the edge of the fields of *Burgh* at Boroughbridge. When Edward the Confessor's Windsor is neighboured by a New Windsor, and the village becomes known as Old Windsor, it is surely time to look more closely at the origins of the borough? and New Radnor, New Shoreham, New Romney and New Lymington are in the same category.

In a further group of town-names the urge to be distinctive and to advertise the virtues of the new town can easily be discerned in the choice of name for the christening. The choice of a name was no problem for the organic town, for it simply continued to use the name of the village. The planted town might, it is true, accept the role of yet another Newtown, Newcastle or Newborough, but there was considerable risk of confusion when (for example) Hampshire had at least three places calling themselves *Novus Burgus*. It was possible to define the town further—as Newport (I.O.W) became *Novus Burgus de Medina*—but there was another possibility, the full exploitation of which is best observed in Gascony.

Gascony had its plain Bastide names;[7] it also had its Villesneuves and its Villesfranches. *Burgus Reginae* was no more imaginative than Queenborough, Kent, but other Gascon names were as assertive as the trumpets of the heralds that proclaimed them. Libourne commemorated Sir Roger de Leybourne, a Kentish nobleman and old companion of Henry III and Edward I. St. Edouard invoked the name of a saint as well as the name of the reigning king-duke. Baa (although not very euphonious), carried the Latin name of the see of Bath, occupied by Robert Burnell, Edward I's trusted minister, co-regent and chancellor.

There was a certain panache in the invented names of towns that boasted of their excellent site. *Grande Castrum* is no more immodest, perhaps, than the Grosmont of Monmouthshire but *Mons Securus* (Monségur) showed great confidence, as did Bonnegarde and *Podium Mirabile* (Puymirol). Miramont, Beaumont and the Cornish Grampound (*Grand Pont*)[8] did not lack confidence in their site, but before the

---

[7] The name *Bastide* is found as the name of fifty French communes in eleven Departments, most of them in the south (*Dict. National des Communes de France* (Paris, 1959). It is also frequent as a hamlet name. The word bastide has a general sense in Languedoc of "a construction". In Provence it has the special sense of a (new) building high in the Alpine pastures.

[8] *cp.* Grandpont, the name of the causeway between Folly Bridge and Hinksey Hill, Oxford.

self-advertising name is dismissed as a gasconade it is necessary to see the English displaying immodesty in the Home Counties. At first sight there is nothing exotic about the name Baldock, even in the earliest spellings that we have (Baldoce, Baldac; 1135–68). It was a Templar foundation at the crossing of the Great North Road and the Icknield Way, an apt site for commerce. The Templars' hopes for their borough's prosperity emerge fully only when the meaning of Baldac is examined more closely.

> *Baldac* is the Old French form for Baghdad (Italian, Baldacco), and Skeat rightly suggested that the place was named by the Templars after the Arabian city.[9]

When William of Toulouse founded Toulouzette, he went to the other extreme and chose a diminutive of great Toulouse. Edward II's seneschal, Antonio de Passagno, was not so modest when he founded Geaune en Tursan in 1318. The seneschal came from Genoa, and the foundation charter commanded,

> *Janua perpetuo ab omnibus appellaretur.*[10]

The command is not strictly obeyed today in its Latinity, but the peasants who bring their baskets to market still enter the bastide past the road-sign that reads *Geaune*.

Similarly, Boulogne was intended to invoke something of the fame of Italian Bologna, Fleurance that of Florence, and Valence sur Baïse that of Spanish Valencia, and the invocation of commercial cities can also be observed in the names of bastides outside the limits of English Gascony. Without going far from Toulouse it is still possible to visit a Cordova at Cordes, a Pampelune at Pampelonne, a Cologne at Cologne, a Barcelona at Barcelonne, and a Pavia at Pavie.

The names of bastides, as Libourne has already shown, may carry within them the names of Edward I's friends, counsellors and officials. Lalinde was named after Jean de la Linde, seneschal for Henry III, and a bastide near Cazals, founded by William of Toulouse, was sometimes known as *Mons Tolasanus*. The seneschal, William de Montague, (Montaigu) gave his name to two bastides, one named from his Christian name (Monguilhem), and the other (Montégut) from his

---

[9] *P.N. Herts.*, p. 120. A lord of Puisaye, between Yonne and Loire, was in the same spirit in naming his colonists' villages, Jerusalem, Jericho, Nazareth and Bethphage (M. Bloch, *Les Caractères Originaux de l'Histoire Rurale Française* (1955), p. 11).

[10] C61/33, m. 4: not 34 as in *Gouron*, 995.

surname. Another seneschal, Jean de Grilly, named a bastide that he founded on his own demesne after his own name-saint: La Bastide de St. Jean. The name was soon supplanted by that of Cadillac (sc. head of an eagle, perhaps from the arms of the town), but subsequent events have brought world-wide fame to the name of Cadillac through the accident that the town of Detroit was founded by a native of Cadillac in the seventeenth century: and, so long as twentieth-century oil sheiks can afford Detroit limousines, Jean de Grilly's town will always be on men's lips.

Hastingues (Landes) commemorates English Hastings indirectly, for it was named, not after Hastings (Sussex) but after the family name of the lords of Abergavenny, one of whom joined with the abbey of Artous to found *Haurihastinggs*. Leybourne (Kent) is certainly aware of the connection between it and Libourne (Gironde), for its church has a stained-glass window presented by the people of Libourne, but it may be doubted whether Hastings is aware of Hastingues. Although the Gascon town has surviving walls and gates that Hastings could envy, there is now only one shop—and that not in the market place. The arcaded *cornières* that once sheltered the market-stalls are now so superflous that one serves as a place for hanging out washing, and another has been bricked up and taken in as an extra room for a house.

Gascony also had its new London, although there is even less likelihood that the Corporation of London will think of a civic exchange in the interests of tourism and Anglo-French accord. Their principal difficulty would be to locate their twin-town. The place is so decayed that it does not appear in the *Dictionnaire Topographique des Communes de France*. Three scattered farm-houses stand on a hill-top just off the N. 133, seven miles south-west of Miramont (Lot et Garonne). There are some faint earthworks in the orchards near these farms that the eye of faith might accept as remains of streets, and the church of St. Etienne acknowledges the full name of the commune and parish of St. Etienne de Londres on its war-memorial. The signwriters of the *Ponts et Chaussées* are not so anxious to acknowledge Anglo-Saxon influence, for all that the traveller on the *Route Nationale 133* is told by the road-sign at the cross-roads is that the lane that will lead him to "St. Etienne de L". The symptoms of a bastide could scarcely be more thoroughly concealed from a seeker for evidences.

CHAPTER FIFTEEN

Gazetteer: England

'Devizes we cannot find.'

F. W. Maitland, *Domesday Book and Beyond* (ed. of 1960), p. 259

INTRODUCTION

AS explained in the opening paragraphs of Chapter 3, there were contemporary urban developments which led to results that are not always easy to distinguish from a *de novo* plantation. The *Problems* sections in the county head-notes discuss some of the more difficult cases, and these are indexed below (pp. 392–93). Critical doubt is sometimes expressed in a Gazetteer entry itself.

It should be noted that a documentary reference to *Novus Burgus* is not in itself a proof of plantation. The words could be employed quite properly for a recent, "organic", promotion of an existing village to burghal rank; they have been taken to indicate a plantation only when there is topographical and other evidence (see Chapter 14) that seemed to rule out an antecedent settlement. *Novus Burgus* could also be applied to an extension of an existing borough—as in the *Novus Burgus* at Northampton mentioned in Domesday Book, and shown by Alderman Lee to be the Normans' addition to the pre-Conquest town (Frank Lee, "A New Theory of the Origins and Early Growth of Northampton", *Arch. Journ.* cx (1954), pp. 164–174). Extensions of this type have not been treated in the Gazetteers unless they were extensions to towns that were themselves plantations (see Durham, Lostwithiel, Lynn, Morpeth, Pontefract, Scarborough; and in the Welsh Gazetteer, Cardiff). Pandon near Newcastle on Tyne (*Ballard and Tait*, pp. 41–42) might also be mentioned as a suburban extension.

The arrangement of entries is alphabetical within counties. An alphabetical key giving the county of each place will be found below. Doubtful cases are discussed in the head-note to each county. Each entry gives the sheet number of the one-inch O.S. map (New Popular Edition) on which the town appears, together with a six-figure National Grid reference. The date on the left-hand side is that suggested for the plantation. References to works frequently cited follow standard abbreviations, for which see pp. xvii to xx. Sites in Monmouthshire will be found in the next chapter.

Alphabetical Index to Gazetteer

Name of Place	*County*
AGARDSLEY	Staffs.
AIRMYN ON HUMBER	Yorks. W.R.
ALNMOUTH	Northumberland
ALRESFORD, NEW	Hants.
APPLEBY	Westmorland
ARUNDEL	Sussex
BALDOCK	Herts.
BARNARD CASTLE	Co. Durham
BARNET, CHIPPING	Herts.
BASCHURCH NEWTOWN	Shropshire
BATTLE	Sussex
BAWTRY	Yorks. W.R.
BEAULIEU	Hants.
BELVOIR	Leics.
BERE ALSTON	Devon
BISHOP'S CASTLE	Shropshire
BOROUGHBRIDGE	Yorks. W.R.
BOSCASTLE	Cornwall
BOSTON	Lincs.
BOW	Devon
BRACKLEY, NEW	Northants.
BRETFORD	Warws.
BRIDGETOWN POMEROY	Devon
BRIDGNORTH	Shropshire
BRIGG (GLANFORD BRIGG)	Lincs.

Name of Place	*County*
BROUGH ON HUMBER	Yorks. E.R.
BROUGH, CHURCH	Westmorland
BROUGH, MARKET	Westmorland
BUCKENHAM, NEW	Norfolk
BUNTINGFORD	Herts.
CAMELFORD	Cornwall
CAPUT MONTIS (Downend)	Somerset
CASTLETON	Derbyshire
CAUS	Shropshire
CHELMSFORD	Essex
CLITHEROE	Lancs.
COGGES (Newland)	Oxfordshire
COLYFORD	Devon
CORFE	Dorset
DEVIZES	Wilts.
DOWNEND	Somerset
DOWNTON	Wilts.
DUNHEVED	Cornwall
DUNSTABLE	Beds.
DURHAM	Co. Durham
EAGLE, NEW	Lincs.
EGREMONT	Cumberland
EWIAS LACY	Herefordshire
EYNSHAM (Newland)	Oxfordshire
FALMOUTH	Cornwall
FELTON	Northumberland
FLOOKBURGH	Lancs.
FORD, NORTH	Devon
GLANFORD BRIGG	Lincs.
GRAMPOUND	Cornwall
HARBOROUGH, MARKET	Leics.
HARTLEPOOL	Co. Durham
HARWICH	Essex
HASLEMERE	Surrey
HASTINGS	Sussex
HAY	(see Welsh list, Brecknockshire)
HAYDON BRIDGE	Northumberland

Name of Place	*County*
HEDON	Yorks. E.R.
HENLEY IN ARDEN	Warws.
HENLEY ON THAMES	Oxfordshire
HINDON	Wilts.
HOLME	Hunts.
HONITON	Devon
HUNGERFORD	Berks.
HYTHE	Kent
KENNFORD	Devon
KINGSBRIDGE	Devon
KINGSTON UPON HULL	Yorks. E.R.
KINGTON	Herefordshire
KNUTSFORD, NETHER	Cheshire
LAUNCESTON (Dunheved)	Cornwall
LEEDS	Yorks. W.R.
LIVERPOOL	Lancs.
LONGTOWN (or Ewias Lacy)	Herefordshire
LOOE, EAST	Cornwall
LOOE, WEST	Cornwall
LOSTWITHIEL	Cornwall
LUDLOW	Shropshire
LYMINGTON, NEW	Hants.
LYNN, KING'S	Norfolk
MAIDENHEAD	Berks.
MALTON, NEW	Yorks. N.R.
MARAZION	Cornwall
MELCOMBE REGIS	Dorset
MIDHURST	Sussex
MITCHELL	Cornwall
MITFORD	Northumberland
MORETON IN MARSH	Gloucs.
MORPETH	Northumberland
MOUNTSORREL	Leics.
MOUSEHOLE	Cornwall
NEWBOROUGH	Staffs.
NEWBROUGH	Northumberland
NEWCASTLE UNDER LYME	Staffs.
NEWCASTLE UPON TYNE	Northumberland

Name of Place	*County*
NEWMARKET	Suffolk
NEWPORT	Devon
NEWPORT	Hants. (I.O.W.)
NEWPORT	Shropshire
NEWTON	Dorset
NEWTON (Warkworth)	Northumberland
NEWTON ABBOT	Devon
NEWTON ARLOSH	Cumberland
NEWTON BUSHEL	Devon
NEWTON POPPLEFORD	Devon
NEWTOWN (Burghclere)	Hants.
NEWTOWN (Francheville)	Hants. (I.O.W.)
NORTHLEACH	Gloucs.
NOSS MAYO	Devon
OKEHAMPTON	Devon
OSWESTRY	Shropshire
OVERTON	Hants.
PENRYN	Cornwall
PENZANCE	Cornwall
PETERSFIELD	Hants.
PEVENSEY (near)	Sussex
PLESHEY	Essex
PLYMPTON ERLE	Devon
POLRUAN	Cornwall
PONTEFRACT	Yorks. W.R.
POOLE	Dorset
PORTSMOUTH	Hants.
QUEENBOROUGH	Kent
RACKLEY	Somerset
RADECLIVE	Somerset
RAVENSERODD	Yorks. E.R.
REIGATE	Surrey
RICHARD'S CASTLE	Herefordshire
RICHMOND	Yorks. N.R.
ROMNEY, NEW	Kent
ROYSTON	Herts.
RUYTON, NEW	Shropshire
RYE	Sussex

Name of Place	*County*
ST. ALBANS	Herts.
ST. IVES	Hunts.
ST. NEOTS	Hunts.
SALISBURY	Wilts.
SALISBURY, NEW	Wilts.
SALTASH	Cornwall
SARUM, OLD	Wilts.
SHERBORNE NEWLAND	Dorset
SHIELDS, NORTH	Northumberland
SHIELDS, SOUTH	Co. Durham
SHOREHAM, NEW	Sussex
SKINBURGH	Cumberland
SKIPSEA	Yorks. E.R.
SLEAFORD, NEW	Lincs.
SODBURY, CHIPPING	Gloucs.
STOCKBRIDGE	Hants.
STOFORD	Somerset
STRATFORD, FENNY	Bucks.
STRATFORD, STONY	Bucks.
STRATFORD UPON AVON	Warws.
SWINDERBY	Lincs.
THAME, NEW	Oxfordshire
THIRSK, NEW	Yorks. N.R.
TICKHILL	Yorks. W.R.
TOTNES, LITTLE	Devon
TREGONEY	Cornwall
TREMATON	Cornwall
TRURO	Cornwall
UXBRIDGE	Middlesex
WADEBRIDGE	Cornwall
WARDOUR	Sussex
WARENMOUTH	Northumberland
WATFORD	Herts.
WAVERMOUTH	Cumberland
WEARE, NETHER	Somerset
WESTHAM	Sussex
WEYMOUTH	Dorset
WINCHELSEA, NEW	Sussex

Name of Place	*County*
WINDSOR, NEW	Berks.
WOKINGHAM	Berks.
WOODSTOCK, NEW	Oxfordshire
WULVESFORD (in Witham)	Essex
WYKE UPON HULL	Yorks. E.R.
WYMONDHAM	Norfolk
YARMOUTH	Hants. (I.O.W.)
ZEAL	Devon

Index to Places considered in County Headnotes and 'Problems'

Name of Place	*County*
ABINGDON	Berks.
ALCESTER	Warws.
ALNWICK	Northumberland
ALTRINCHAM	Cheshire
BERKELEY	Gloucs.
BERWICK ON TWEED	Northumberland
BIRCHINGTON	Kent
BOLTON	Lancs.
BOSSINEY	Cornwall
BRENTFORD	Essex
BRINKLOW	Warwicks.
BURFORD	Shropshire
CHIPPING	Herts.
CHIPPING CAMPDEN	Gloucs.
CHORLEY	Lancs.
CHUDLEIGH	Devon
CLIFFORD	Herefordshire
COCKERMOUTH	Cumberland
DARLINGTON	Durham
EWIAS HAROLD	Herefordshire

Name of Place	*County*
HUNTINGTON	Herefordshire
KENILWORTH	Warws.
LEEK	Staffs.
LONGTOWN	Cumberland
LOWESTOFT AND LOTHINGLAND	Suffolk
LYDHAM	Shropshire
MERRYFIELD	Somerset
NEWARK	Notts.
NEWBIGGIN ON SEA	Northumberland
NEWBRIDGE	Sussex
NEWBURY	Berks.
NEWPORT (North Curry)	Somerset
PATELEY BRIDGE	Yorks. W.R.
PAULL FLEET	Yorks. E.R.
PETERBOROUGH	Northants.
SALTFLEET	Lincs.
SCARBOROUGH	Yorks. N.R.
SELBY	Yorks. W.R.
SITTINGBOURNE	Kent
SOLIHULL	Warws.
SOUTHAMPTON	Hants.
STAPLETON	Herefordshire
STEVENAGE	Herts.
STOCKTON ON TEES	Durham
STOW ON THE WOLD	Gloucs.
STROUD	Gloucs.
SUNDERLAND	Durham
TEIGNMOUTH	Devon
TINTAGEL	Cornwall
TONBRIDGE	Kent
TUTBURY	Staffs.
WALSALL	Staffs.
WEOBLEY	Herefordshire
WHITSTABLE	Kent
WIGAN	Lancs.
WIGMORE	Herefordshire
WIGTOWN	Cumberland
WOTTON UNDER EDGE	Gloucs.

BEDFORDSHIRE

This county, small in area and far from the sea, has an old-established county town but otherwise no more than normal urbanisation. By the early fourteenth century Bedford was surpassed in wealth by Dunstable which can be regarded as one of the ring of new towns in the hills north and south of the London basin where the radial roads from the capital passed through gaps in the chalk. The Watling Street had followed the Dunstable gap, and near its crossing with the Icknield Street, the centre of Matthew Paris' schematic map of England, a new town was a profitable promotion.

DUNSTABLE   Bedfordshire   sheet 147   52/019219
c. 1119

In Camden's words, Dunstable had four streets pointing to the four corners of the heavens. North Street and South Street were simply the Watling Street north and south of the crossing, and East Street and West Street were Icknield Street. The borough and parish area is only 453 acres, being circumscribed by the rural parishes of Houghton Regis on the north and Kensworth and Totternhoe on the south.

These were royal manors, and c. 1119 Henry I created the borough of Dunstable from their fields. The nucleus seems to have been a royal lodge called Kingsbury. The Dunstable priory chronicle describes the King's motives: *volens praeterea constituere ibi villam, per omnes regni sui partes fecit proclamari ut omnes ibi accedentes ad morandum pro singulis acris darent duodecim denarios annuatim*; the new burgesses were to have the liberties and privileges of the city of London. "The length and breadth of the said streets was thus built upon by these people", concludes the chronicler. The foundation of the town was followed twelve years later by the foundation of the priory of St. Peter, and in the endowment charter (*Regesta*, ii, no. 1827) the canons were given the borough with four fields lying round the vill, the market and schools of the vill, and common pasture in four surrounding parishes; the king retained only his house and garden (9 acres in all). The priory and its precinct occupied virtually all the quadrant between East Street and South Street. There were to be fairs at St. Peter's tide and a weekly market. The north aisle of the priory church was given over to the use of the townspeople. The equipment of the town was complete.

In a monastic borough the relations between the townsmen and priory were often troubled (*Beds. Hist. Rec. Soc.*, iii (1916), pp. 121 sqq; and vi (1919), p. 86; H. R. Luard, ed., *Annales Monastici* (1865), iii, *passim*; see also *V.C.H. Beds.*, iii, pp. 349–350; *Dunstable Cartulary*, ed. G. H. Fowler, *Beds. Hist. Rec. Soc.*, x (1926)).

The development of the town until very recent times has hardly progressed beyond the original four streets and there is still very little behind the burgage plots on the east of Watling Street.

BERKSHIRE

To the four towns described below it is possible that Abingdon and Newbury should be added, although there is no certainty. In addition to the planted towns there were thirteen organic towns. Bearing in mind the area covered by forest and heath, the county was very well provided with towns and smaller market centres.

HUNGERFORD Berkshire sheet 158 41/337686
by 1131

There is no mention of Hungerford in Domesday Book. "The town grew up subsequent to Domesday Book" (*V.C.H., Berks.*, i, p. 301). But its growth was quick. A document of 1131 ("Cartulary of St. Frideswide", *Oxf. Hist. Soc.*, xxxi (1891) p. 330) concerns the burgesses of Hungerford, and another document of that period (*ibid.*, p. 324) speaks of "the church of Hungerford in which parish Eddington lies" (see also *Doc. France*, i, p. 124). *Eddevetone* was a Domesday vill. Eddington lies on the north bank of the Kennet, and the Oxford to Salisbury road (now the A.338) crosses the Kennet before entering the long, broad High Street of Hungerford. The church is a quarter of a mile to the west of the town.

There is nothing burghal in a survey of 1386 (E142/77 m. 10) but in another of 1590 (DL42/117 f. 31) Hungerford is called "mannor and burrough".

MAIDENHEAD Berkshire sheet 159 41/890812
by c. 1270

It is difficult to be certain whether the Domesday *Elington* or *Aylington* (*V.C.H., Berks.*, ii, p. 31) was on the site of the *Maidenhythe* which begins to be mentioned in the later thirteenth century. A bridge seems to have been built about that time, diverting the east–west road system from the previous crossing place at Babham End. The economic centre was thus moved south from the old market centres of Cookham and Burnham. (There was a William of Maidenhead in 1240–41: C. D. Ross, ed., *Cartulary of Cirencester Abbey*, ii (1964), p. 487.)

Two pieces of evidence support the possibility of a town plantation: the town lay in two parishes, for the north side of the road was in Cookham parish and the south in Bray; and there was no separate parish of Maidenhead until 1867 although there was a chapel, c. 1270, over which there was a lively dispute. The vicars of Cookham and Bray could not agree who was to serve it and the bishop refused a licence; in 1293, however, the inhabitants went ahead with building a house for a chaplain and were given six oaks by the king for it, but there is no evidence that a chaplain was appointed. In 1324 it was agreed that the chapel should be reckoned as part of Cookham and after the incorporation of the town in 1582 the advowson passed to the corporation (*V.C.H., Berks.*, ii, pp. 97–99; J. W. Walker, *A History of Maidenhead* (1909)).

WINDSOR, NEW Berkshire sheet 170 41/970768
1107–31

"It seems extremely probable that the tradition of royal residence at Old Windsor, which becomes explicit in the reigns of the Confessor and his Norman successors, had begun by the ninth century" (B. Hope-Taylor, *Medieval Archaeology*, ii (1958), p. 185).

This vill at Old Windsor was described in Domesday Book. Edward the Confessor had endowed Westminster Abbey with Windsor and 20 hides of land on the eve of the Conquest, and in 1067 William the Conqueror recovered the territory from the Abbey by exchanging it for lands in Battersea, but it was on the cliff overlooking the Thames in Clewer parish that he began to construct his motte and bailey castle. "The castle of Windsor", says Domesday Book, "is on the half hide of land taken out of Clewer's five." The peaceful meander and meadows by Old Windsor palace were unsuited for military defences. The attraction for a royal residence was the hunting in the adjacent forest and heaths. The deeds of exchange with Westminster Abbey in 1067 called the site *utilis et commodus propter contiguam aquam et silvam venatibus aptam* (B.M. Harl. Ms. 3749 f. 3).

The castle formed the focus for the town of New Windsor. The parish bounds show that it was cut out from Clewer, probably the half hide which Domesday Book (*V.C.H., Berks.*, i, p. 362) describes as appropriated from Clewer for the castle. The Easter Court of 1107 was the last to be held at Old Windsor: after that the new castle was fit for a royal residence. The first explicit reference to the new borough is in the Pipe Roll of 1130–31 (ed. Hunter, p. 126) when a virgate that had been exchanged was described as *capta ad burgum*.

The town prospered from royal residence and the consequent traffic up and down and across the river, although it frequently suffered disturbance from expansions of the castle and extensions to the parks: (*Cal. Lib. Rolls*, ii (1930), p. 122 (1242): iii, p. 328 (1251)). When Edward IV enclosed 200 acres for the park in 1467 (*Cal. Pat. Rolls, Edward IV*, i, p. 551) the townspeople were compensated with a fair and incorporation although their first borough charter dated from 1277 (R. R. Tighe and J. E. Davis, *Annals of Windsor* (1858), i, p. 104; see also *V.C.H., Berks.*, iii, pp. 1–70).

The earliest large-scale plan of the town, that by John Norden made in 1607, shows the main gate of the castle facing the two converging streets (now St. Alban's Street and High Street) which made up the core of the borough. The church stands squarely in the triangle made by these two streets, an area wide enough to take the market; indeed, the narrow streets north of the church, between the church and Castle Hill, are probably late-medieval encroachments on an original market place from church to castle gate. This area is level and sheltered by the castle. The suburban development down High Street and Thames Street to the bridge, and along Peascod Street towards Clewer, is attested by mid-thirteenth century documents, although in the plan of 1607 field land began at the end of the burgage plots on the west of High Street (BM. Harl. Ms. 3749, partly reproduced by Tighe and Davis, *op. cit.*). The advice of Mrs. S. Bond is acknowledged.

WOKINGHAM   Berkshire   sheet 169   41/815687
by 1146

This market town on the northern edge of the Berkshire heaths was formerly situated in two counties; part of the town was in Berkshire and part formed a detached part of Wiltshire. This unusual complexity, like the similar status of Newmarket, probably derives from the late foundation of the market and town. The bishops of Salisbury had a palace and park at their Berkshire manor of Sonning but the grant of a market by bishop Richard, the founder of New Salisbury, in 1219 (*Rot. Lit. Claus.*, i, p. 385) was at "Wokingham"; and the confirmatory charter of 1583 (*V.C.H., Berks.*, iii, p. 227) calls Wokingham "parcel of the manor of Sonning".

There is no reference to Wokingham in Domesday Book: the first reference so far noted is to a chapel of Sonning in 1146. The principal subsequent documentary references are set out in *Wilts. Arch. Mag.*, xi (1869), pp. 50–82.

There is a distinct grid of streets, with houses and gardens having the appearance of burgage plots, in the area west of the church. The Jacobean Town Hall, replaced by a New Hall in 1860, seems to have been at the junction of roads just outside the west end of the old town.

PROBLEMS

Of *Abingdon*, where a charter of Edward the Confessor mentions a borough (*V.C.H., Berks.*, iv, p. 437), Domesday Book says nothing except that there were ten traders dwelling in front of the church. The manorial centre was not Abingdon but Barton, and it is possible to see the development here as a miniature St. Albans: but the abbey Chronicle says that before the abbey was refounded (c. 950) there was the town of Sevekesham here (*V.C.H.*, iv, p. 430).

Newbury's name would seem to make it a prime candidate for inclusion alongside the Newboroughs and Newbroughs. Domesday Book assigns 51 *hagae* to the vill of "Ulvritone" where there were also twelve ploughs and a recorded population of twenty-two households. Ulvritone seems to have been south of the river, for it was from Ulvritone that Sandelford (on the southern boundary of the county) was cut (1194–1205, *V.C.H.*, i, p. 363). The first explicit reference to a borough is as late as 1189, but Newbury appears as a name in 1079–80 when part of Speen parish was called *Neoburia* (*ibid.*, iv, p. 134) by the lord of Ulvritone. The balance of evidence is for a change of name from Ulvritone to Newbury, but it is significant that the settlement was on land cut from two ancient parishes (Thatcham and Speen: *ibid.*, iv, p. 135) and a century after Domesday Book Reading Abbey sought to claim the town church for itself on the ground that it lay in Thatcham parish (*ibid.*, iv, p. 150).

BUCKINGHAMSHIRE

In addition to its two small plantations the county had nine towns; the two plantations were additions prompted by the same traffic on the Watling Street that encouraged Dunstable a little further south.

STRATFORD, FENNY   Buckinghamshire   sheet 146   42/883341
1202–4

Having descended from Dunstable and the Chilterns and crossed the sands of Woburn the Watling Street crosses two rivers within ten miles of each other, the Ouze and the Ouse. At each of these crossings a roadside town developed consisting (like so many towns at river crossings) simply of the houses on either side of the road. The first of these towns from the London side was Fenny Stratford, and Stony Stratford the other (*q.v.*).

The late arrival of Fenny Stratford is indicated by its division between the two parishes of Bletchley on the south and Simpson on the north, for the Watling Street (like other Roman roads) had for long been taken as the natural frontier, the no-man's land between the two villages' fields. A Monday market was granted to Roger de Caux in 1204, two years after the first reference to Stony Stratford, and a fair in 1253; the chapel of St. Margaret was not fully parochial (*V.H.C., Bucks.*, iv, pp. 274–283). Burgesses of a moiety of the town are mentioned in a survey of 1370 (C135/216/11), and the division into halves probably results from the frontier position of the town.

STRATFORD, STONY   Buckinghamshire   sheet 146   42/786405
by 1202

This account should be read in conjunction with that of the neighbouring Fenny Stratford, *supra*.

On the Northamptonshire side of the Ouse is the village of Old Stratford, and on the Buckinghamshire side is the town of Stony Stratford which lay at the frontier of two parishes, Wolverton and Calverton, straddling the Watling Street. In 1334 some taxpayers of the town were reckoned with those of Wolverton and some with Calverton. When an eighteenth-century Private Act set up the chapels of Stony Stratford as independent parishes they comprised 84 acres on the Calverton side and 69 on the Wolverton side, two tiny islands in the parishes where the townsmen had settled. On the Calverton side the church of St. Giles formed the focus for the July fair, and St. Mary Magdalen on the Wolverton side for the September fair. An earlier market, the date of which is unknown, was held on the Calverton side, and three transfers of land in 1202 and 1203 (*Bucks. Feet of Fines*, pp. 9, 25, and 27) speak already of messuages in Stratford and of "three acres on which Richard built his houses in Stratford": the plots had come from John of Calverton; (see also F. E. Hyde and S. F. Markham, *A History of Stony Stratford* (1948), with plan, p. 68).

CAMBRIDGESHIRE

So far, no plantations have been recognised in this county unless it be granted a share in Newmarket which lay on the heath at the Suffolk border, one side of the town street being in each county. This absence of plantations is difficult to explain when similar terrains in Hertfordshire and Essex supported new towns. Linton (not a plantation) was a type of small borough common in neighbouring counties; otherwise the county had only Ely and Cambridge as urbanised centres.

CHESHIRE

The single plantation in this county matches ill with the intensity of promotion of villages that gave seven organic urban centres. It is possible that *Altrincham*, with its charter of c. 1290 (Ormerod, *Cheshire*, i, p. 536) and a market of 1290, could have been a plantation in Dunham Massey manor. Until 1799 its church was a mere chapel of ease, but the prevalence in Cheshire of large parishes gave dependent chapels to the majority of villages, and makes this fact of less significance than in other centres.

KNUTSFORD, NETHER   Cheshire   sheet 101   33/750790
1292

By his charter of c. 1292 William de Tabley set up burgesses in Knutsford, each burgage plot consisting of 2½ selions of land; market and fair charters were also obtained from the king (Ormerod, *Cheshire*, i, p. 488).

It is difficult to be certain whether there was any existing village of Nether Knutsford to be enfranchised in this way. Ormerod considered that the Domesday entry referred to Over Knutsford, a mile to the south east; and two other documents rather in the form of *paréages*, cited by Ormerod (*ibid.*, pp. 489–490), suggest that William de Tabley engineered the market, fair, and burgages in one operation. Nineteen burgage holders are mentioned by name. There was no parish church here until one was created by an Act of 1741 (*ibid.*, p. 493).

The borough was situated on the southern edge of Tatton Park, the seat of the Masseys, and on the eastern edge of Tabley. It was the lords of the manors of Tatton and Tabley who were concerned in the agreement to share the profits of the new market in 1292.

A plan of the town will be found in D. Sylvester and G. Nulty, eds., *The Historical Atlas of Cheshire* (Chester, 1958), p. 35; the crofts shown may be vestigial burgage plots.

CORNWALL

The elevated rank of Cornwall whenever medieval boroughs are counted has been a feature that has often struck historians. In 1901 Miss Bateson wrote—not very tactfully (*E.H.R.* xvi, p. 335]—

> these private boroughs created by seignorial charter are commonest in the less civilised portions of England.

One sees what she meant. The same reluctance to equate Cornwall with the rest of England can be seen as far back as 1295 when a summons to send borough representatives to a Parliament was countered by the following modest self-abasement, no doubt brought on by the knowledge that taxation boroughs paid taxes at a higher rate than ordinary vills:

> nec sunt plures villae mercatoriae in comitatu Cornubiae nec ulla civitas est.

The remarkable intensity of small urban centres has already been signalled by the thirty-eight boroughs (Table ix.10), and some explanation must now be attempted. It has already been suggested that poor inland transport may have drawn market centres closer to each other than in the counties of the English lowlands; and the absence of old-established cities must also have been important (p. 346). Cornwall was not alone: Devon, its neighbour, was equally densely urbanised and had an even greater total of boroughs, and it is natural to look first at some common factor in their geographical position. Any explanation must also take into account the smallness of many of these south-western boroughs. As Prof. Finberg has written: "the petty boroughs of Devon and Cornwall exhibit a strong family likeness, and together constitute a local phenomenon which appears to have no parallel in other parts of England" (H. P. R. Finberg, "The Boroughs of Devon", *Dev. and Cornw. Notes and Queries*, xxiv (1951–52), pp. 203–209, and xxvii (1956), pp. 54–55).

In Cornwall the proportion of these petty boroughs that were planted is very high, for there were nineteen planted towns and nineteen organic towns. The Cornish plantations have another distinctive feature: they were often the only nucleated settlement centre in their area. In Devon the countryside was already settled with nucleated villages and scattered hamlets, and the planted towns had to fit into the interstices of these. In Cornwall the pattern of rural settlement was extremely scattered with no particular concentration either near the parish church or the principal manor house.

In Creed parish, for example, the church stood alone, and there was only a tiny group of houses at Tybeste, the manorial centre. When Grampound was planted on the edge of the commons it brought a nucleated settlement into the parish for the first time. In St. Stephen's parish (where two boroughs, Saltash and Trematon, were planted) there were fifty-eight houses in 1331 in fourteen different clusters: yet none of these clusters was chosen for town sites.

Thus the church as the centre of the parish, the manor house as the centre of the demesne, and the later planted town as the centre of commerce all occupied different sites and had different names:

Parish	Manor	Planted town
Lanteglos	Helstone in Trigg	Camelford
St. Creed	Tybeste	Grampound
St. Stephen	Trematon	Saltash New Trematon
St. Enoder	Degembris	Mitchell
Lanlivery	Restormel	Lostwithiel I
Lanlivery	Penknight	Lostwithiel II
Budock	Trelivel	Penryn
St. Breock	Pawton	Wadebridge
Minster	Talcarne	Boscastle
St. Martin	Pendrym	East Looe
Talland	Porbuan	West Looe

The contrast between the organic and the planted town can be seen in Helston and Helstone. Domesday Book shows the royal vill of Helston in Wendron parish already having a body of organised brewers, and the vill was certainly elevated to a borough by 1181 and perhaps by 1177 (C. Henderson, *J.R.I.C.*, ii, n.s. (1956), p. 205, and H. S. Toy, *The History of Helston* (1936), pp. 146 and 332). Helstone in Lanteglos parish, on the other hand, remained a small cluster of houses at the manor gate, and when a town was planted within the manor by the earl of Cornwall (c. 1260) it was placed at the ford over the river Camel, leaving Helstone and Lanteglos church equally isolated. The more normal, "English", burghal pattern where the castle, church, and village-turned-borough adjoin can be seen at Week St. Mary in the north-east of the county. The irregular shape of this borough strongly suggests a promoted village in the same category as Fowey where villeins were transformed into burgesses c. 1250.

Since most lay settlement was sited away from the parish churches it is not possible in Cornwall to use the church-less town as a definite symptom of plantation as it is elsewhere in England (including Devon). Even "organic" Helston was 2½ miles from its church at Wendron and had no parish church of its own until 1845. But Cornwall did have plantations with very small, field-less burghal areas—a test of late arrival elsewhere in England—and it did have towns whose bounds show that they were cut out from pre-existing parishes (Grampound from Creed, Saltash from St. Stephen's, Camelford from Lanteglos, Penryn from Gluvias, Bossiney from Tintagel, West Looe from Talland). There were also towns like Mitchell that were planted in no-man's-land on the edge of parishes: one side of the town street was in Enoder and one in Newlyn.

The two main incentives to occupy such a no-man's-land position seem in Cornwall to have been the attraction of road traffic and the widening opportunities for ports in the many small estuaries. The planted towns are strung out along the two roads that run east–west through the county, one near the north and one near the south coast. The southern line continues acrosss Devon from the Tamar crossing through Plympton to Colyton and Newton Poppleford on the Dorset border. The remaining plantations are ports, with a tendency to make new ports nearer and nearer the sea in order to use larger ships.

As Charles Henderson observed in his pioneer study of Cornish boroughs "(in Cornwall) towns were essentially plants of exotic growth, fostered and cherished by great landholders as profitable sources of revenue" (C. Henderson, *Essays in Cornish History* (1935), p. 19). The smaller landlords were not in fact slow to learn the same lesson, and the bishop of Exeter created a borough on his estate at Penryn. But the greatest landlord in the county was the earl (later the duke and eventually the Crown) and the spread of his estates gave ample opportunity for plantation at different profitable positions. By 1300 he had ten Cornish boroughs, seven of them plantations. Even in 1086 Domesday Book shows Robert of Mortain as an urban strategist: he had moved the market from outside the priory of St. Stephen's at Launceston to his new town, and again at St. German's he moved the market over to his castle-borough of Trematon. Lostwithiel, which became the duchy administrative centre, had been founded by the Cardinans, the second largest landowners in 1086, and the earl of Cornwall added a second borough alongside it.

Lostwithiel was far from a petty burghal plantation: there were 387 burgages in 1337. Launceston was also substantial: even after the Black Death it still had 302 taxpayers for the poll tax of 1377, indicating about 700 souls before the plagues. Saltash had 118 burgages in 1300 when Camelford had 62; the two adjoining boroughs of Looe (judging from the poll tax figure of 270) must have had about 600 inhabitants in the earlier fourteenth century; there were 60 burgages in East Looe alone in 1331. The ill-fame of some of the smaller Cornish towns in later centuries when they had become pocket boroughs has rather clouded their origin. Like every county, Cornwall had its petty boroughs (Mitchell, Mousehole and Penzance) but they were not all pygmies. Even Grampound, a name so often on the tongue of later Parliamentary reformers, had its 30 burgages in 1300, and Boscastle must have had at least 200 inhabitants at that time.

Initially, the plantation projects in Cornwall must have seemed extraordinarily successful. Neither medieval agriculture nor industry in Cornwall has yet been adequately investigated, and the economic basis of these projects can only be conjectured. It looks as if there was a happy conjunction: an area that had not been very densely settled for agriculture in Anglo-Saxon times, with much semi-marginal land that was capable of intenser exploitation when population pressure increased; and with more fields came more market opportunities, and with more markets came more towns. The true extent of this marginal occupation is only just beginning to emerge as medieval fields are recognised on the moors and the deserted medieval farm-groups disentangled from the prehistoric. But the lord who wanted to develop a borough on his estate would not have easily found a nucleated settlement where the characteristically concentrated activity of townsmen could be developed under the name and privileges of a borough. In no other English county was the creation of a new centre so natural a solution.

Towns could also feed on growing opportunities outside agriculture. The mining of tin was not urban, but mining was followed by marketing, and marketing by export: marketing and exporting were characteristically urban activities, and, with the poor state of land transport, the river- and estuary-ports were particularly important.

BOSCASTLE   Cornwall   sheet 174   20/098908
?1204

The topography and nomenclature are complicated. The borough of Boscastle took its name from the castle at the north-east end of the borough, but the town lay in two parishes, Forrabury and Minster. Neither of these had churches bearing these names, for Forrabury church lies on a hill about 200 yards west of Boscastle and was dedicated to St. Symphorian; Minster church was St. Merthian's (101905) a quarter mile east of the town. (Forrabury = fore-bury or *faubourg*.)

A charter was granted in 1204 to William de Botterell (*Lysons*, iii, p. 237) to have a Wednesday market at Talcarne (the manor in Minster parish) and when it was renewed and implemented with a fair in 1312 these were to be held at Castle-Botterell (or Boscastle) at St. James-tide. There was a chapel of ease in the town, which in 1306 was separately taxed as a borough although no charter has appeared. Norden's survey of Cornwall (BM. Harl. 6252) writes of "Forrabury" (i.e. Boscastle) as "the meanest and poorest that can bear the name of town, for it consisteth of two or three houses. It hath been of more importance as appeareth by the ruins" (*Lysons*, iii, p. 107).

The town lies on the side of a steep hill dominated by the castle site. There seems to be a crude grid, but formality is made difficult by the steep slopes and converging combes. There is more recent, but also decayed, settlement by the picturesque harbour north of the town.

CAMELFORD   Cornwall   sheet 186 20/105837
by 1260

Camelford stands where the old (low) main road from Launceston to the north coast and Bodmin crosses the Camel. The place-name is said first to occur in 1205 (*Layamon's Brit*, ed. F. Madden (1847), lines 28534–6) but with a *-ford* town-name it would be possible for the topographical feature to be on men's lips long before a town was planted.

In 1260 a royal charter (*Ballard and Tait*, p. 4) refers to the earl of Cornwall's recent grant of a market and fair and the creation of a borough here. The borough lay within the parish of Lanteglos, of which the isolated church is at 088824, 2 miles from the borough. Henderson (East Cornwall Ms. notes, R.I.C., p. 268) says that a church was built by the burgesses in 1312. This was probably the chapel of St. Thomas which used to stand on a site opposite the Bell Inn. Only recently has Camelford again had a church of its own. The original rural settlement was at Helstone (in Trigg) at 089814, and in the earl's accounts the *burgus* was usually entered next to the *manerium* of Helstone. At the Assize of 1283–84 the town was reckoned a *burgus* (JI/1/111 m. 42); similarly in 1279–80 (E142/7), in 1300 (E152/8)—when there were sixty-two burgesses—and in 1337 (E120/1). In 1306 it was taxed as a borough. Some villeins attached to Camelford were at Penmayn. W. G. V. Balchin, *Cornwall* (1954), p. 86, has an air photograph showing the long and narrow fields on both sides of the town. Despite his description of them as "former open fields" it is likely that they are fossilised burgage plots similar to those in Devon towns and to those shown by Balchin at Mitchell (*op. cit.*, p. 79) as "burgage plots", although truly fossilised open-field strips can be detected in the north-west of the borough (104840). See also M. W. Beresford in *Ag. Hist Rev.* xii (1964), pp. 13–27, and fig. I.

FALMOUTH   Cornwall   sheet 190 10/810325
1613

This seaport town is first cousin on the one hand to the Elizabethan ports which developed out of fishing hamlets on the Cornish coast, and on the other to such Stuart plantations as Londonderry in Ireland and the colonial ventures. Falmouth, like Portsmouth and Liverpool, was a haven name long before the town was founded. There is good witness to the previous non-existence of Falmouth in a plan of 1597 drawn by Baptista Boazio which survives in a copy dated 1801 (MPH 370). It is "the true description of ye Great Baie of Falmouth with the Headlands, Pointes, Rivers, Creekes, Baies as well of Sand as otherwise, Coves, Showles both of sand as otherwise". When the cartographer came to list "the Principal Townes next adjoininge" they were only three: "Trewro, Tregni, and Penrin". As a rival to these three, all further inland, Sir John Killigrew founded a town near the cottage known as Smithike or Penny-come-quick, a house indicated but not named on the 1597 plan.

There were petitions against the foundation made to the Privy Council on behalf of Penryn, Helston, and Truro. The town lay in Budock parish (plan in S. Lewis, *Topographical Dictionary*, v (1838), fig. xiv).

GRAMPOUND   Cornwall   sheet 190   10/934484
by 1296

Within the parish of Creed (church at 934472) the principal manorial centre was at Tybeste wherein Domesday Book recorded thirty plough teams and a population of sixty-one (*V.C.H.*, i, p. 89). The manor house was at 948486, as a plan of 1846 indicates (Cornwall Record Office, Truro: PDD 31), and the lands extended on both sides of the Fal, as the modern parish bounds continue to show. Through the parish ran the main road to Truro from east Cornwall, and the creation of the town probably followed the building of the bridge whose Latin name is preserved in the town name (*Grandis Pons*). Until Tregoney bridge was built in 1300 this was the lowest crossing of the river Fal by road (C. Henderson, *Essays in Cornish History* (1935), p. 20).

Grampound has no parish church, and the parish of St. Creed surrounds it: a chapel is mentioned in 1370, dedicated to St. Naunter. Although in use in 1812, by 1821 it was in ruins and pulled down. Only in 1869 was a chapel of ease built again. The fifteenth-century market cross stands still in the main street in front of the site of the medieval chapel (C. Henderson, *J.R.I.C.*, n.s. ii (1956), pp. 121–127). In form the town is simply the widened main street. The burgage plots are well preserved in the shape of the gardens of the houses on either side of the road. The present bridge is not the *grandis pons* but a replacement from the period of the turnpike. The main street swings out of its straight course north-westwards as it reaches the present bridge. The older direct course is marked by the wall of the school yard which has been built (since the plan of 1846) over the old road. On the far side of the river the old course leads straight to the disused road up a steep hill west of the town. As a grassy lane this disused track leads straight past Carvosse into the main road again near Probus, 2 miles west of Grampound. No traces of the piers of the bridge can now be discerned in the river bed. (See M. W. Beresford in *Ag. Hist. Rev.*, xii (1964), Fig. II, p. 22.)

The first charter dates from 1332, but the separation of borough and manor is plain in a survey of the earldom in 1299–1300 (E142/6 and 7), and in the accounts for 1296–97 (ed. Midgley, *Camden Soc.*, 3rd ser., lxviii (1945)) there were twenty-eight rent-paying burgesses. In 1300 (E152/8) there were thirty; and in 1337 (E120/1) the same number. The charter of 1332 gave (or perhaps confirmed) to the burgesses the manor mills, a gild merchant, two fairs and a weekly market. The Hundred Courts of Powder were moved into the town from Tybeste. Other evidence of a charter earlier than 1332 is the series of payments recorded in 1296–97 (Midgley, *op. cit.*, pp. 234–235) from eighteen persons *pro inquisitione habenda de statu suo pro carta domini Comitis de libertate habenda*. The sums were large: three payments of 40s., one of 33s. and three of 20s. The burgage rents were only a shilling a plot. There was a loss (*decasum*) of 6s. in the pasture *propter burgum*, and it was probably on the riverside pasture of Tybeste manor that the new town had been planted.

By 1306 the town was being separately taxed at a tenth of the value of the burgesses' moveable property while Tybeste continued to pay at the rate of one-fifteenth. The full survey of 1300 (E152/8 m. 2) shows Tybeste as a conventional rural manor with 22 free tenants, 28 customary tenants each holding 15 Cornish acres, and 21 villeins holding 6 acres and 1 ferling each. The manor had two water mills and a fulling mill, handed over to the burgesses in 1332 (Henderson, *loc. cit.*). There is still a water mill north of the town. The characteristic shape of fields west of the bridge on the abandoned main road suggests that the town extended equally on both sides of the bridge from which it was named, and this would give point to the enclave which the bounds of Grampound still show when they cross to the west bank of the Fal.

LAUNCESTON   Cornwall   sheet 186   20/332847
1066–86

Following the Norman Conquest, the earl of Mortain constructed a castle on the commanding hill-top of Dunheved, across the river Kensey from the Saxon town of Launceston St. Stephen. Domesday Book records that he moved the market from the old town to his new castle (*V.C.H.*, i, p. 72). In a later charter this transfer is recalled: "the earl transferred the Sunday market from the town of St. Stephen at Launceston to the new town (*novam villam*) of the castle of Dunhevet, the canons (of Launceston Priory) retaining for themselves and the burgesses of (Old) Launceston all the liberties of the borough except the market" (*Ballard & Tait* (1141–67), p. 379).

The old borough of St. Stephen is said to have decayed after the market was taken from it, yet it had 420 taxpayers in 1377 when Launceston had 302. A third borough subsequently developed on the north bank between the old and the new towns in the suburb of Newport. From 1529 this third borough, under the confusing name of "Launceston", duly returned two members to Parliament; the earl's castle-town had sent members since 1295.

The town was walled from the early thirteenth century and gated to form a common defence with the castle to which it formed an outer bailey and from which it takes its shape. The church of St. Mary in the town was made parochial in 1380. It was the new town which was represented at the Assize of 1201. In the fourteenth century the farm of the borough was 100s. (E152/8; E120/1). The increased importance of Launceston was probably followed by the building of Polson bridge, 2 miles to the east, which now carries the A.30. The precursor of the modern main road did not cross the moor but probably went on a lower route northwestwards via Camelford, Wadebridge and Mitchell (W. G. V. Balchin, *Cornwall* (1954), pp. 115–116; see also A. F. Robbins, *Launceston* (1888); air photograph in *Beresford and St. Joseph*, pp. 202–203).

LOOE, EAST   Cornwall   sheet 186   20/255533
by 1201

The borough formed a strip of 100 acres along the east shore of the estuary; its bounds show that it has been cut from St. Martin's parish. The church of St. Martin's lies 2 miles to the north-east and the manor was at Pendrym. East Looe had a chapel of

St. Keyne (or Kenna) at whose festival the borough fair was held. The borough is first recorded in 1201 (JI/1/1171). This fair was in existence in 1237 (BM. Harl. Ch. 58H47). In 1716 the bishop of Exeter gave lands in trust to endow the chapels in the Looe boroughs "so remote from their respective parish churches" (T. Bond, *Topography and Historical Sketches of the Boroughs of East and West Looe* (1823), p. 11). The rights of the mother church were still enforced when Bond was writing: "St. Martin's is the burial place for the town. Marriages are not solemnized in the chapel (of Looe). Children are frequently christened there, though sometimes objections have been made to this by the Rector of St. Martin's" (*ibid.*, p. 17).

The borough returned members of Parliament in 1340 and was incorporated in 1587. The founder of the town and its date are equally unknown. The market and fair claimed before the itinerant justices in 1283–4 (JI/1/111 m. 38) were in "Looe borough", and since another borough at West Looe occurs separately in the same document (as "Porbyham" and "Porbyghan": mm. 39 and 42) the first borough may be at East Looe. There were sixty burgesses in Otto de Bodrigan's borough here in 1331 (C135/29/3) and twenty-four taxpayers in 1327 (E179/87/37); in 1331 the borough was worth £6 a year to its lord who also held the advowson of St. Martin's church.

The town is made up of a single street along the shore, with narrow back lanes. The houses all stand on sand and shingle and are set deep down in it.

LOOE, WEST   Cornwall   sheet 186   20/253534
by 1201

This second borough was on the western shore of the estuary. Its mother church at Talland (228517) is even more remote from it than St. Martin's from East Looe. West Looe was often known as Porbuan (Portuan, Portbyhan, Porbyham, Porbyghan, etc.). The chapel of ease of St. Nicholas is now used as a church again after a period as a guildhall. The vill was represented by a jury at the Assize of 1201 (JI/1/1171). The Assize Roll of 1283–84 (JI/1/111 m. 39) records that Hugo de Trenryn claimed a free borough here, and a *burgus* is also recorded at m. 42 of the same roll. A charter of 1243 (*Ballard and Tait*, pp. 5, 137, and 249) issued by Richard, earl of Cornwall, confirmed the free borough granted to the town by Odo de Treverbyn, its lord. The town has a Michaelmas fair, and anyone residing unchallenged for a year and a day was to remain quit of all serfdom and servitude. The borough was formally incorporated in 1584 but the principal settlement was then, as now, on the east side of the estuary. In a survey of 1558 under West Looe (*Porpehan manerium cum burgo*) Humberston reported: "The verye towne of Loo is on the other side of the water or haven."

LOSTWITHIEL I and II   Cornwall   sheet 186   20/105598
I by 1190; II c. 1268

The modern town of Lostwithiel comprises two borough foundations welded into one by the earl of Cornwall's charter of 1268 (*Ballard and Tait*, p. 5) and now topographically indistinguishable within the grid of streets which make up the town. The survival of a plan of 1846 (Cornwall Record Office: PDD 11) makes it possible to match the charter evidence with that of the old boundaries.

On the south side of the town there is a stream which flows in a covered culvert down the north side of South street. This was the old boundary between rural Penknight (Penkneth) in Restormel manor and the borough of Lostwithiel. The borough existed in 1201 (JI/1/1171). The charter of 1190–1200 issued by Robert de Cardinan, lord of Restormel Castle (*Ballard*, p. 21), confirms the privileges given the burgesses by his ancestors on the day when they founded the town (*"die qua villam fundaverunt"*). Unfortunately this explicit account of a foundation does not say which ancestor (Hist. Mss. Comm., *Var. Coll.*, i (1901), pp. 327–328).

The burgesses of the new town paid 6d. a year rent; could freely inherit; could freely sell on payment of a 1s. fine; they had freedom from tolls; liberty of marriage for their children; and freedom to elect their reeve. They were also granted the monopoly of inns on dry land (*taberna extra navem*), a reminder of the fact that Lostwithiel was a port, near the highest point of the river Fowey reached by the tide and the lowest bridge across it. The town, with its church of St. Bartholomew founded by 1202 (*J.R.I.C.*, n.s. iii (1958), p. 307), was laid out in a grid of five streets to the west of the bridge with the quay on its eastern flank. It was unusual for a Cornish town to have its own church, although this church was not independent before the fifteenth century (C. Henderson, *Essays*, pp. 44–53). The town must have been closely packed: until 1878 a public path passed under the thirteenth-century west tower. The longest burgage plots are less than 30 yards long.

The mother church was at Lanlivery (080590), and on the west bank of the Fowey were two rural manors: the castle-manor of Bodardle with its centre halfway between the town and the castle; and the earl's manor of Penkneth with its Manor House half a mile to the south-west of the town. In 1268 the earl of Cornwall, who had just acquired from the de Cardinans Restormel castle and park together with Lostwithiel town and mills, issued a second charter by which that part of Penkneth which adjoined Lostwithiel was to be reckoned part of the new combined borough (E142/41; *Cal. Chart. Rolls*, iii, p. 479). The town's privileges were confirmed and enlarged including a Tuesday market. The two boroughs combined occupied only 100 acres, and Lanlivery parish surrounded them on all the landward sides. It would seem when the earl granted the second charter in 1268 that he either enlarged the physical area of the town by adding a street on the southern side (rather like Edward I's additions to the old town of Hull, *q.v.*) or he took the opportunity to legitimise a suburban cluster of his tenants who were parasitical on the Cardinan town.

The burgage rents, of 1296–97 totalled £8 2s. 7d., probably 325 sixpences (Midgley, *op. cit.*, pp. 241–242). The Bartholomewtide fairs brought 2s. 1d. in tolls that year. In 1300, 305 burgage plots were occupied (E152/8), and in a rental of 1337 no fewer than 387 were listed with rents totalling £9 13s. 5½d. (E130/1: a long list of names). Another list of 1331 (E142/41) discriminates between Lostwithiel with 7 messuages and 148 burgages and Penknight with its 212 burgages. The total of 360 accords with the other evidence, but it is surprising that Penknight should have more than Lostwithiel. From 1272–99 Edmund earl of Cornwall had his principal residence at Restormel, and Lostwithiel was virtually the Duchy capital. It is from this period that the church, the "Duchy Palace" and the "Shire Hall" date; also a lost charter of 1290 (E120/1).

The core of the town lies off the main road and is well preserved. The narrow lanes near the river and the Duchy prison are almost Gascon. The church occupies a complete chequer. Penknight is the farm, unnamed on the 1 inch O.S., at 102592. (*Cp.* Tybeste in Grampound.)

MARAZION   Cornwall   sheet 189   10/518306
1070–1215

The "mount of Cornwall", the island granted to Mont St. Michel in c. 1070, already had a Thursday market (P. L. Hull, ed., *The Cartulary of St. Michael's Mount* (Dev. and Cornw. Rec. Soc., n.s. v (1962)), p. xix). The next charter included two fairs at the Mount. In 1257–72 the earl of Cornwall's confirmation charter of three markets and fairs stated that these had been held at Marazion (Marghasbighan) but henceforward at Marchadyon (Market Jew). The former place was sometimes known as *petitmarche* or " *parvum mercatum* " (*ibid.*, p. 20) and in 1215 (*ibid.*, p. 46) a document refers to "burgesses of the vill of Marazion".

MITCHELL   Cornwall   sheet 190   10/860545
?1239

In 1239 a fair and market were granted by charter to the lord of Degembris, to be held at Meideshol. The farm of Degembris at 852568 marks the old manorial centre, two miles north of Mitchell and three west of St. Enoder church. The chapel of ease, in St. Enoder parish, probably dates from the same period. In 1283–84 the town was represented separately at the judicial eyre (JI/1/111 m. 42) and again in 1301 and 1305, when it was called *burgus*. In 1327 it was separately rated for the subsidy (C. Henderson, *Essays in Cornish History*, pp. 54–66). It may never have been very large, and Henderson thought that there were only eight burgesses. In the election of 1829, seven voters sent their M.P. to Parliament.

As the plan in W. G. V. Balchin, *Cornwall* (1954), p. 79, shows, the little town straddled the boundary of its two mother-parishes, rather like Royston and Devizes. It may have been planted on the common heath, a no-man's-land. Balchin suggests that the long fields in the eastern (St. Enoder) part of the town are burgage plots rather than the curved open-field strips which they first suggest to the eye. It will be noticed that they are S-shaped and not the reversed-S of the usual selion. (NB. The 1 inch map shows bounds altered since the large-scale O.S. plan reproduced in Balchin, fig. 11). The "town" is now simply a group of houses on both sides of the main road to Truro (A.30). The medieval topography of the borough is becoming obscured. The turnpike road leaves the medieval main road by the seventh milestone to Truro at the west end of the town, and the old road is now merely a grass track leading from the farmyard to the moor. The cross-roads which the old parish boundary follows, and which may once have marked the limit of the town, are also obscured, for the northern arm has been almost ploughed up and the southern arm is merely a farm road. A newer cross-roads at the east end of the town has replaced it. The chapel of ease dedicated to St. Francis in the main street has also gone (Henderson, *loc. cit.*, and *J.R.I.C.*, ii (n.s.) 1956, pp. 150–151).

MOUSEHOLE   Cornwall   sheet 189   10/470265
by 1267
See *Penzance*.

PENRYN   Cornwall   sheet 190   10/798342
1236
"Penryn was a speculation of the bishops of Exeter who built the town in their park, capturing the foreign trade of Truro. (C. Henderson, *Essays*, p. 22.)" It was cut out of Budock (later Gluvias) parish, the town being set between two streams on a narrow promontory at the landward end of the same estuary where Falmouth (*q.v.*) was later to be planted. The earliest charter is of bishop William Brewer in 1236 (*Ballard and Tait*, pp. 46, 55 and 95) and there is a second from bishop Walter Bronescombe in 1275 (*Register of Bishop Bronescombe*, pp. 220–221). The mansion house and demesnes of the bishop's manor lay on the south edge of the town near Glasney College, a college of thirteen canons founded by bishop Bronescombe in 1265. The bishops often resided here. A market and fair were chartered in 1259 (*Cal. Chart. Rolls*, ii, p. 16). In bishop Stapledon's register (i, 27) there is a rental of the *burgus*, which brought the bishop £7 13s. 2½d.; the market brought in more than three times that sum. The burgage rents were arrented at 1s. a year, making 153 burgesses in the year of Stapledon's rental. The bishop dispensed justice in the borough (JI/1/111 m. 38) but the profits of justice cannot be determined. The sums on the account roll of 1291 (SC6/1138/1) are worn away, and there are no details in the *sede vacante* accounts (E364/1 m. 3d (1222–23); E372/91 (1246–47)) other than the totals received from the vill and manor. In 1294 the borough was separately taxed. In 1372 (BM. Add Ms. 28859) Penryn borough was valued at £16 8s. 7¼d. when Penryn *forinsecus* was worth £76 9s. 6¼d., the same proportion of rural to urban values as in the bishop's towns of Ashburton and Chudleigh. The large rural manor of Penryn had developed from the Domesday manor of *Trelivel* (Treliver in 772353 in St. Gluvias parish). In Greenwood's plan of 1827 the market place was to the south-west of the Town Hall, standing in the middle of the single main street. The town is now by-passed on the north-east. From the by-pass the mother church of Gluvias can be seen on the hill across the river. A chapel of St. Mary in Penryn is mentioned in 1322 (*J.R.I.C.*, n.s. ii (1955), pp. 46–51 and 175–179).

PENZANCE   Cornwall   sheet 189   10/475305
by 1327
The only evidence for the inclusion of this borough and of Mousehole (470265), 3 miles south of it, is the situation of the borough within the old and large Domesday manor of Alwarton, but far from the manorial centre and also from the parish church at Madron, (453319). In 1327 (C135/3) an extent of Alwarton manor included 29 burgesses in Penzance and 40 in Mousehole. There were 13 boats at Penzance

rendering 1s. a boat or a quarter of fresh hake; Mousehole had 16 boats. There were 17 stalls of stranger fishermen in Mousehole who paid 6d. each. Marazion, 3 miles across the bay and opposite the pilgrim centre of St. Michael's Mount, was also a borough which may have arisen at the same period (*q.v.*). A market and fair at Portheness in 1267 (*Cal. Chart. Rolls*, ii, p. 75) may refer to Mousehole; a grant of 1300 (*ibid.*, p. 489) certainly does. See also *J. Brit. Arch. Ass.*, xxxviii (1882), pp. 354–370.

POLRUAN   Cornwall   sheet 186   20/125510

c. 1292

This little town lay in Lanteglos parish (Churchtown (145510) is the mother church). There was a fair here in 1292 (*Cal. Chart. Rolls*, ii, p. 422), and it was styled a borough (C. Henderson, *Essays*, p. 22). Henderson's East Cornwall parish notes (R.I.C. Mss., p. 265) cites a P.R.O. Charter of early thirteenth-century date with *totum burgum de Polruan*; the chapel of St. Saviour was founded by 1293. The place was not taxed as a borough nor represented at the Assize. It was not mentioned in Domesday Book. It faces Fowey, as the two Looes face each other.

SALTASH   Cornwall   sheet 187   20/432587

by 1201

The first known charter to this borough ("Ash") was issued by Reginald de Vautort II, who died in 1246, but the charter confirms to the burgesses the liberties and customs which they had "in the time of Reginald's ancestors"; unfortunately it does not specify which ancestors (*Ballard and Tait*, pp. xlvi and 16). However, Saltash was reckoned a borough in 1201 (JI/1/1171 m. 3d).

The site is one of the finest in the country, a long street on the hill above the Tamar, dropping sharply to the narrow foreshore at the ferry-point. It was this important crossing into Devon which focused routes here and gave the town its economic importance. In 1337 the annual value of the ferry, £10, was worth more than three times the burgess rents; the markets and fairs brought in £3 4s. 8d. (E120/1, m. 25d). The charter of 1246 fixed the burgage rent at 6d. a year (*Ballard and Tait*, p. 56). The fair was held *in media villa* (*ibid.*, p. 250).

The mother parish is St. Stephen's (416584), and a chapel for the townspeople was built overlooking the Tamar at the south-east end of the borough. Although the church was not independent until 1881, the architecture of its tower, the blocked south door and much of the chancel and nave are Norman, giving weight to the possibility that the market of 1086 (see *Trematon*) was placed here and that there was a twelfth-century town.

The main road traffic is now diverted to the north of the borough and it would be a bold car which would try to tackle the hill which took the medieval traffic. Although the building of the station and the Royal Albert Bridge have distorted the medieval street plan on the south of Fore Street, it is possible to see on the modern map a symmetrical line of burgage plots, each about 50 yards long and 10 yards wide, stretching for about 400 yards. There were 118 burgages in 1300 (E152/8).

The value of this borough to its lords is tabulated under *Trematon*. Agricultural land went with the burgage plots and common pasture was allowed after harvest in the lord's fields (*Ballard & Tait*, pp. 56 and 74).

TREGONEY   Cornwall   sheet 190   10/925450
by 1197

At first it would not seem that Tregoney would rank as a new town, for there is a manor of that name in Domesday Book. However, the small area of the parish of Tregoney St. James (69 acres) and the fact that it is surrounded on three sides by Cuby parish would suggest a late development. The name Tregoney, according to Henderson (*Essays*, pp. 21–22), means "the dwellings on the common by the river" but the only evidence of dwellings by the river is the ruined site of St. James's church near which, until 1278, was a small priory. There is a strong local tradition that the town was originally in the meadows and then moved to the east gate of the Pomeroys' castle. The castle has gone, but the broad street on the hill top is clearly a triangular street market-place with its apex at Cuby church, a few yards outside the borough boundary, and its base near the castle site. The borough had its chapel of ease (St. Anne's; also disappeared) but this was dependent on St. James in the meadows. From this, it would appear that a second settlement was planted on the hill-top to replace the Domesday village; if it coincided with the castle, then it was analogous to Launceston and Trematon. The castle is sometimes attributed to Richard I (*Lysons*, iii, p. 74). There were free and conventionary tenants in the rural manor. The date of the Pomeroys' castle is unknown, but by the Assize of 1201 (JI/1/1171) the town was reckoned a borough, and a borough fee farm of £3 14s. 2½d. was paid in 1304 (C133/118/1) and *placeae* were rented. In 1300 Tregoney bridge was built, supplanting Grampound as the point of lowest crossing of the Fal. The subsequent silting up of the Fal and the competition from Truro and Falmouth (after 1613) ended Tregoney's days as a river port. But the town still has character. The burgage plots stand out well as garden boundaries and there are good back lanes parallel to the market place behind the plots on the north-east and north-west sides.

A good church guide, *Tregony (sic.) and its Parish Church*, with a plan of the town by Charles Henderson, is available at St. Cuby's church. In his notes (*J.R.I.C.*, n.s., ii (1956), pp. 136–137) Henderson makes no mention of St. Anne's chapel. David Knowles, *Religious Houses of Medieval England*, (1940), p. 134, believes that there is no evidence of conventual life in the Tregoney priory.

TREMATON   Cornwall   sheet 187   20/410580
1066–86

Domesday Book (1086) records the transfer of a market from St. Germans to "a certain castle hard by" belonging to the count of Mortain. He had done the same thing at Launceston: removing a market from an exposed position outside a country church, on the land of the church, and setting it in the shadow and protection of the castle and on his own territory. At Launceston the count had also founded a town, but nothing is said of this at Trematon. In Domesday Book (*V.C.H. Cornwall*, i,

95a) the recorded population of 105 were linked to the twenty-four plough teams; only the market, worth 3s. a year, hints at anything non-agricultural.

Where was the market? was there ever a town of Trematon or was all the commercial life concentrated at Saltash (*q.v.*) where the Norman chapel suggests an early arrival of a populous community? The topographical evidence is slender. The hamlet of Trematon, a mile north-west of the castle, at 393597, was the old rural centre of the Domesday manor. It had no attractive commercial siting and was far from the protection of the castle. A better case can be made out for a small town of "Trematon" in the immediate vicinity of the castle, where the road from Saltash and St. Stephen's church to the castle crosses a narrow finger of the estuary. A few houses here are now called Forder. At neither site have earthworks of former houses and streets been observed.

It has been usual to consider that Trematon and Saltash (*Ash*) boroughs were the same place under two different names, the one the name of the original manor and the other the name of the new town. Some support is given to this view by such a document as E142/7 where (in 1279–80) the *vill* of Trematon was surveyed alongside the *borough* of Ash; or the fact that in 1283 it was the borough of Ash which was represented before the itinerant justices at the Assize (JI/1/111 m. 38): but in the earl's accounts of 1297–98 (Midgley, *op. cit.*, pp. 237–238) the boroughs of Ash and Trematon were separately valued; and again in the surveys of 1331 (E142/41) and 1337 (E120/1 m. 25d), the two *burgi* were separately assessed and a charter of March 1283 to Trematon *borough* was cited. Since Trematon "castle", "manor" and "park" were also surveyed in the same document, there is no possibility of confusion.

Although separately surveyed and accounted for, the Trematon borough could never have been very large. In comparison with Saltash it brought its lord very little income, and the figures would be compatible with a small borough within the bailey, on the Welsh pattern. In the extent of 1331 Trematon was described as "burgenses castri", paying 6s. 1d. rent.

The references to Ash and Trematon are:

1279–80	(E142/7)	"castle and vill of Trematon with the borough of Ash"
1296–97	(E119/1 m. 22d)	"borough of Trematon", "borough of Ash"
1300	(E152/8)	"borough of Ash", "borough of Trematon"
1300–01	(E372/146 m. 30)	"borough of Ash", "borough of Trematon"
1331	(E142/41)	"burgesses of the castle of Trematon"
1336–37	(E372/146 m. 30)	"Trematon borough", "Ash borough"
1337	(E120/1)	"boroughs of Ash and Trematon"
1369–70	(SC6/818/1)	"Trematon borough", "Ash borough"

Ash ferry was farmed for £10 in 1337 and a barge for the crossing was part of the manor stock (*instaurum*). There were the usual conventionary tenantry of the rural manor of Trematon, with rents about equal to those of the borough of Ash.

The gatehouse and shell-keep of the castle survive in the grounds of a private house, and from the motte there are fine views of the Tamar estuary, of St. Stephen's the mother church, of Saltash town and in the distance of the group of houses which make up Trematon village.

The survey of 1650 (E317 Cornwall/51, f.10) has "lands in ye Burroughe of ye Castle of Trematon" (5 entries); and lands in "Old Trematon" where there were thirty-eight conventionary tenants. "Ye whole manor is confused within ye parish of St. Stephens and is all inclosed in severall." See also M. W. Beresford, *Ag. Hist. Rev.*, xii (1964), Fig. III, p. 23.

Analogy, the last resort of the perplexed, is not helpful, for while Launceston town was planted immediately outside Launceston castle, the case of Restormel shows that a new town (Lostwithiel *q.v.*) could grow up some distance from the castle.

TRURO   Cornwall   sheet 190   10/825447

c. 1153

The earliest settlement here was at Newham in Kenwyn parish; Newham lies south of Truro town. The town of Truro, like Launceston, lay in the shadow of a castle, and like Penryn, on a tongue of land between two rivers. The castle, where the hill-top cattle market now stands, was probably raised by Richard de Lucy, lord of Kenwyn (Tregavran), chief justiciar in 1153, and may be one of the adulterine castles of the civil war period. In 1166 a charter from the earl of Cornwall confirmed a borough charter of de Lucy; both charters are now lost. Between 1174 and 1186 Henry II granted a charter and this, though also lost, is known from later recitals. It gave the burgesses freedom from tolls throughout Cornwall (1166 charter in *Cal. Chart. Rolls*, ii, p. 304; 1174–86, *ibid.*, p. 305; charter of 1285, *ibid.*, ii, p. 304). In 1201 the borough of Truro was separately represented at the Assize (Henderson, *Essays*, pp. 1–18). In 1259 the town's church of St. Mary was consecrated, its parish limits coinciding with the town. In 1262 Newham gave up its claims to have a meat- and cloth-market rivalling Truro, and in 1295 Truro was one of the five Cornish boroughs to have M.P.s: by 1311 Newham was reckoned a hamlet of Truro (C134/20/8).

The seigneurial character of the town survived. In 1307 the lord handed over half the profits of justice to the town but he kept the profits of the court baron and of the fair. The burgesses also had agricultural land like those of Helston, and were it not for the "enclave" parochial geography and the suppressed primacy of Newham, Truro would be assigned without hesitation to the ranks of the promoted village. Henderson veers to this view (*Essays*, p. 6) but Balchin (p. 83) to mine.

WADEBRIDGE   Cornwall   sheet 185   10/990725

1312

The town was known as *Wade* (*sc.* ford) before the bridge was built (c. 1470) and a weekly market and two fairs were granted to the bishop of Exeter at Wade in 1312 (*Cal. Chart. Rolls*, iii, p. 183). There was an episcopal manor and park here, centred on Pawton (960700), (*J.R.I.C.*, n.s., ii (1958), pp. 38–46). It had belonged to the western bishops since 835 and the bishops often stayed here on their Cornish itineraries. The river crossing carried the main Launceston–St. Columb–Truro road on which Mitchell and Camelford had also been planted. The site of the main town lay on the western edge of St. Breock parish but across the river there were some houses on the edge of Egloshayle parish. The two churches are each about a mile from Wadebridge. There is no record of the town being styled a borough in the medieval period.

PROBLEM

Tintagel and Bossiney were joined together and reckoned one borough (E143/7; E152/8; E120/1; but see SC6/818/1 for the borough of *Trenova*). The irregular sums paid in the rentals suggest that the 86 burgages of 1331 (E142/41) were agricultural holdings promoted; they seem to have been located indifferently in either of the twin places. On balance, I am disinclined to admit a plantation here.

CUMBERLAND

Half of Cumberland's medieval boroughs were planted, but we do not have a second Cornwall on our hands for the total was only eight. Cumberland did not carry a rural population of the density of Cornwall and its mineral resources were also less well developed. The sea gave Cornwall immediate access to the markets of London, southern England and western Europe, but Cumberland had a shorter length of coast, convenient enough for Ireland and Scotland but cut off from the populous and wealthier south by the long voyage round the Atlantic coastline of Wales. The proximity of Scotland was more a curse than a blessing since it involved Cumberland in border warfare. As the low tax paid per acre in 1334 shows, Cumberland and Westmorland rather than Cornwall were the truly marginal counties of England. It is perhaps significant that three of Cumberland's four planted towns were connected with warfare. Egremont was a Norman castle-borough while Skinburgh and Wavermouth were abortive attempts to provide Edward I with victualling ports for a naval offensive against Scotland. Newton Arlosh lay inland and was a civil settlement but hardly more than an attempt to save something from the wreck of Skinburgh and Wavermouth, and it never amounted to much.

PROBLEMS

Like other counties of the extreme north, Cumberland has a relative shortage of eleventh- and twelfth-century documentation, and the absence of a known reference to a town may not always prove that it had yet to be created. The name and early evidence for Egremont, however, is convincing but it may also be noted that the town of Cockermouth was ranked as a mere chapelry of Brigham (Hutchinson, *Cumberland and Westmorland*, i, p. 107) and that there is no reference to it before c. 1150 (*P.N. Cumb.* p. 362). It had 178 burgages in 1260 (SC11/730). Wigton, which was not mentioned before 1163 (*ibid.*, p. 166), may have had no church before the time of John (*Hutchinson*, p. 467). Longtown, in Arthuret parish, is also a possible plantation.

EGREMONT   Cumberland   sheet 82   35/010105
c. 1125

St. Bees priory was founded c. 1125 by William Meschin on a site near the sea and in the foundation charter he gave all the tithes "of my men who live in Egremont" (*E.Y.C.*, vii (1947), p. 29). The castle of Egremont had been built 3 miles further inland than the priory, at the western tip of the fells. Its name was probably taken from Aigremont in Normandy. Apart from the language of Meschin's grant it is uncertain when the civil settlement at the foot of the castle was founded. The town church was a chapelry of St. Bees. A borough charter was granted in 1202 by Richard de Lucy (*Ballard*, pp. 21 and 50) and its terms suggest that house-building was in progress. Those who failed to build within the year on the plots they had contracted to take were to be fined. In 1278 Egremont was separately represented before the assize judges (JI/1/131) but was called merely a *villata*. The town received a market and fair charter in 1267 (*Cal. Chart. Rolls*, ii, p. 75). The borough was semi-agricultural: in 1363 it was called a *villa mercatoria* but its ninety-nine burgesses then held their burgages by the service of reaping for one day in autumn, and those with ploughs had to plough for a day for their lord (C135/177/22; see also C135/119/12 (1350)). It must be confessed that these services suggest a promoted village more than an urban plantation.

The town is made up of very short burghal plots on either side of a wide market place street running north from the castle and church (Hutchinson, *Cumberland and Westmorland*, i, pp. 281–285).

NEWTON ARLOSH   Cumberland   sheet 75   35/198552
1305
This town was founded at "Arlosk", a grange of the Cistercian abbey of Holm Cultram. The abbey was an active coloniser of the forest, heath and marsh in the north-west corner of Cumberland but the depredations of the Scots had made it impossible for the monks to cultivate their lands effectively from the grange; the territory seems to have been cultivated by lay tenants and the abbey may have been glad to find a better use for the land (F. Granger and W. G. Collingwood, *The Register and Records of Holm Cultram* (1929); BM., Harl. Ms. 3891, ff. 10 and 21v; 3911 f. 19v). There had been two previous attempts at borough-making locally (see Wavermouth and Skinburgh). These had foundered on a poor choice of site, and in a petition to Parliament in 1305 the abbot stated that he had paid 100 marks to the king for a fair and market at Skinburgh but "the town together with the way leading to it is carried away by the sea" (*Rot. Parl.*, i, p. 161 b). The petition was granted, and fresh charters to Newton were issued (*Cal. Chart. Rolls*, iii, p. 55; *Ballard & Tait*, pp. xlvi–vii and 5–7). The bishop of Carlisle, who had granted a licence in 1301 for a parish church at Skinburgh, in turn cancelled his grant and in March 1305 substituted a licence for a chapel with parochial rights within the territory of Arlosh (W. N. Thompson, ed. *Register of John of Halton*, Canterbury and York Society, (1913), xii, p. 161). (The new borough was frequently called Kirkby Arlosh or Kirkby Johannis.) The burghal plots are still well-marked on the north side of the little village street. (Air Photograph in *Beresford & St. Joseph*, p. 214.)

SKINBURGH   Cumberland   sheet 75   35/c. 115560
1301
This borough at the grange of Skinburgh was the second of the three attempts by the abbey of Holm Cultram to plant on the Solway Firth a victualling port (E101/13/1

and E101/36 *passim*). Its charter was granted in 1301 after Wavermouth had proved abortive (*Cal. Chart. Rolls*, iii, p. 2) but by 1305 Skinburgh had been washed away and the approach road destroyed (*Rot. Parl.*, i, p. 161 b). Its privileges were transferred to Newton Arlosh, *q.v.* Skinburgh's charter had declared that merchants should have rights of access freely and that there should be a fair at the feast of St. John the Baptist. The church at Newton was also dedicated to St. John and the town was sometimes called Kirkby Johannis.

WAVERMOUTH   Cumberland   sheet 75   35/c. 140560
1300

The Scottish expeditions of Edward I caused the assembly of fleets in Solway Firth, and the estuary of the Waver was used as a port for victualling. The abbey of Holm Cultram had a grange at Skinburgh on the west side of the estuary and the conjunction of events may have encouraged the abbot to project a town similar to successful port foundations on the south coast. In March 1300 a borough charter was granted for *Wavremuth* (*Cal. Chart. Rolls*, ii, p. 488) but the site proved to be impracticable—probably through flooding—and in 1301 a fresh charter was issued for a borough at Skinburgh, *q.v.* The king himself had been at Holm Cultram for four weeks in the autumn of 1300.

DERBYSHIRE

This county, despite its more southern situation, was no more urbanised than Cumberland if towns are counted, and hardly more urbanised than Cumberland when towns and acres are counted together. It had the moorlands of the Peak but when population pressed, settlement was able to penetrate these as easily as the moors of Cornwall (see *Beresford & St. Joseph*, p. 95, for discussion of Chelmorton at the 1,100 foot contour). It also had lead-mining to correspond with Cornwall's tin but it had no coast-line and the Trent only skirted the county.

CASTLETON   Derbyshire   sheet 111   43/150830
1196

The castle of William Peverill in the Peak is mentioned in Domesday Book as the castle of *Pechefers* (=*Pechesers* (sc. Peak's arse: *P.N. Derbys.*, i, p. 56)). The stone castle which succeeded it is usually attributed to Henry II (1154–89). It stood within Bakewell Hundred but at the end of the twelfth century this district name changed to High Peak (*de Alto Pecco*). The first reference to a borough is in 1196 when the Pipe Roll records a payment of four marks "de cremento burgi de Alto Pech" for one whole year; there is no such payment in the previous year's account; thereafter the Pipe Roll has frequent references to the borough: *P.R.S.*, vii (n.s.) (1930), p. 273, to xxvi (n.s.) (1949) p. 127. In 1255 an extent of Castleton records 43⅝ burgages and 71 stall-holders in the borough: (SC6/1094/11).

We have, then, a borough taxed for the first time in 1196 and a contemporaneous change of the Hundred name; beyond that there is no evidence to suggest the exact date of the borough creation. No borough charter is noted in *Ballard* and *Ballard & Tait*.

There is a great market place (now partly encroached upon) below the hill on which the remains of Peveril Castle stand, and St. Edmund's church is at the north end of this square. On the east and south of the town there are the remains of the Town Ditch but on the west and north this function was performed by the Mill Race.

DEVON

The proliferation of medieval boroughs in this south-western county has already been indicated in the account of Cornwall above. Devon had the largest number of boroughs of any English county (69), and even after allowance has been made for the great area of the county it still emerges at the top of any national ladder with a borough every 23,000 acres, a density equal to that of Cornwall. Like Cornwall, Devon had a large area of infertile moorland, making these density figures even more remarkable.

In Devon the organic towns were three times as numerous as the planted towns, whereas in Cornwall the number was equal; the Devon plantations thus emerge as part of a general enthusiasm for boroughs among territorial landowners, particularly in the thirteenth century. It will be seen that only one of the seventeen plantations dates from before 1194 and the latest may have been founded in 1298 (and certainly no later than 1326).

In general, the Devon boroughs were small; one result of their smallness is the failure of their seigneurial charters to survive and a consequential imprecision in their dating. Smallness may also account for the frequency of boroughs with no separate tax assessments in 1334 by which their comparative wealth might be estimated. But the insignificance of their later municipal history and the small area embraced by the burgage plots support the occasional evidence of smallness that can be seen in the few surviving tax assessments or rentals: Newport with 13s. 5d. in 1334, Colyford with 25s., Newton Abbot with 15s. (including Wolborough village) and even Okehampton with only 22s. (adjusted rate).

None of these plantations seems to have been engineered by the Crown: one was founded by a life-tenant of the Crown and one on a piece of land granted to the founder by the king. Apart from one earl, a bishop, and two abbots, the other plantations appear on the land of lay seigneurs, many of them small landowners without estates in other counties. There was no one who contributed a cluster of boroughs like those of the earldom (duchy) of Cornwall.

What encouraged these landowners of the south-west to be so active in town plantation? The most likely explanation would seem to be a late but intense burst of economic development. Had the interior colonisation taken place as early as it did in the Midlands and south-east, Devon would have had more great towns to do the main work of marketing: but there were only four organic towns in 1100. The nature of this interior colonisation has already been described by W. G. Hoskins

(*Devon* (1954), pp. 58–59): "The twelfth and thirteenth centuries saw immense changes, comparable in magnitude and kind only with those of the nineteenth century. It was the great age of colonisation which took the form of the spread of settlement and of the cultivated area in the countryside and of the creation of new towns on a considerable scale." The development of industry was equally striking: "for a couple of generations Devon was the largest European source of tin: there was a veritable 'tin rush' on the Moor, and neighbouring landowners took advantage of it to create towns at strategic points." Tavistock and Ashburton, stannary towns for the weighing and stamping of tin, were elevated from villages to boroughs by their ecclesiastical lords, and a third stannary town, Plympton Erle, was created *de novo* by the earl of Devon. Like markets and fairs, the cloth industry—linked to the rural fulling mills—spread all over the countryside except the high Moor, and almost all the boroughs had small industries.

Devon had fewer coastal ports among its plantations than Cornwall, but the concentration of towns along the coastal road from the Tamar to the Dorset border is noticeable. Paradoxically, poor inland transport and the widespread high ground in the west and south-east of the county may have encouraged the multiplication of towns. If communications were slowed down by steep and rugged terrain, the number of nightly resting places on major routes was necessarily increased; nor could the large towns look to a hinterland all within a day's journey, and the role of the intermediate boroughs was thereby strengthened. The total of trade available to any one of them was sufficient to ensure survival, but insufficient to elevate any of them into great towns. Colyford in the late fourteenth century was the size of Looe or Boscastle.

PROBLEMS

Besides the new towns listed above it is possible that both Teignmouth and Chudleigh were medieval creations, although evidence of street-plans does not assist the argument. In 1308 Chudleigh was described as *novus burgus* in a rental (*Register of Stapledon*, i, p. 24) but it may be that a road-side settlement had been elevated by its episcopal owner. However, the first reference in *P.N. Devon* to the name is c. 1150. The bishops also owned West Teignmouth, where a borough was recorded in 1292 (*Register Bronescombe*, p. 473), and at East Teignmouth, adjoining, the Dean and Chapter of Exeter had a market and fair granted them in 1253. Neither place is recorded before 1148; but a charter shows a church at the river mouth in 1044 (Hoskins, *Devon*, p. 492). It has seemed best to accord these places organic growth, such as the bishops encouraged at Crediton before they finally gave the legal status of a borough to the mercantile core of their manor, leaving the rural part untouched. The parallel settlements, boroughs and manors, are well shown in the fourteenth century tax lists:

	1334 *Taxed wealth*	1377 *Poll tax payers*
Crediton borough:	81os.	185
manor:	42os.	83

Kingswear, although a small parish of 970 acres and clearly a late settlement in Brixham opposite Dartmouth, has also been excluded: it was never a borough; it was assessed at 26s. 8d. in 1334. Dartmouth itself was a late arrival as a town. The Clifton Dartmouth of the tax assessments was not there in Domesday Book. "There are clear indications that by 1200 or soon afterwards a borough had been formally created by the FitzStephens out of the casual assemblage of houses and shipyards . . . along both banks of the Mill Pool" (Hoskins, *op. cit.*, p. 383). This diagnosis indicates organic growth. At Tavistock the very language of town plantation is used in the Hundred Rolls (*R.H.*, i, p. 81): *quidem abbas villam fecit levari.* Prof. Finberg has shown, however, that the abbot simply tacked a new borough on to an old village (H. P. R. Finberg, *Tavistock Abbey* (1951), pp. 72–74 and 197–205).

BERE ALSTON   Devonshire   sheet 187   20/447667
1295–1305
The Domesday *Birlanda* lay in the triangle where Tavy meets Tamar. The older settlement within the present parish is at Bere Ferrers on the Tavy. Bere Alston is a hill-top town nearly 500 feet higher than Bere Ferrers. It originated as a mining settlement in the last quarter of the thirteenth century (W. G. Hoskins, *Devon* (1954), p. 332). In 1295 the lord of the manor, Reginald de Ferrers, obtained charters for market and fair and shortly afterwards set up a borough (H. P. R. Finberg, *Devon & Cornwall Notes & Queries*, xxiv (1951–52), p. 205). Each burgess paid 1s. a year. In all taxation records the two Beres were treated as one. There were twenty burgages in 1305 and the town returned members to Parliament from 1584 to 1832; the silver-lead mines continued to be worked until the late nineteenth century.

BOW   Devonshire   sheet 175   21/720018
1259–1326
In 1259 Henry de Tracey, lord of Nymet Tracey, obtained a grant of a weekly market and a three-day fair. Along the northern edge of Nymet Tracey parish passed the old (low) road from Exeter to Okehampton. This road provided a natural site for a commercial venue and a new settlement called Bow grew up there only 200 yards from the parish boundary of Nymet Tracey (W. G. Hoskins, *Devon* (1954), p. 341). Early in the fourteenth century Bow was called a borough (H. P. R. Finberg, *D.C.N.Q.*, xxiv (1951-2), p. 205); burgesses appear in a document of 1326 although as an urban venture Bow proved abortive; a fair, worth £3 in 1326, remained until about 1690. The village has a simple plan of pure ribbon development. It once had its chapel of St. Martin at whose feast-day the fair was held, but the villagers now worship at the mother church at Nymet Tracey. The pattern of burgages is well preserved in the garden plots; they are limited by the parish boundary to the north; the market may have been held at the cross roads where the street to the westward widens a little. The western edge of the town is delimited by the meadows of the Yeo which the main road crosses by Bow Bridge. The eastern limit was probably the road fork by the present chapel. The town was thus nearly half a mile long. The length of the burgage plots varied: in the north-west quarter of the town they

419

were cut to 22 yards by the slope of the ground: in the south-east they were nearly ten times as long. An inquisition of 1326 shows seven free and fifteen conventionary tenants in Nymet Tracey village which had 152 acres of demesne arable and 1,179 acres of grass. Bow then had thirty-four burgesses (C134/99).

BRIDGETOWN POMEROY   Devonshire   sheet 188   20/809604
c. 1250

Bridgetown was one of two boroughs which were engineered by territorial lords just outside the walls of the old town of Totnes, no doubt to profit from any overspill. Bridgetown was founded by the lord of Berry Pomeroy, a village a mile and a half to the east. He took a site along the main Exeter road at the east end of Totnes bridge. The foundation is attested by a charter of 1268 from the founder's son, Henry de la Pomeroy, which permitted an extension of his father's borough and defined the privileges of those who came to live in it. In 1267 the king had granted a fair to the town. The charter gives the new settlers the same rights as the burgesses in the core of the town, with liberty to buy and sell. Some of the settlers must have been men from Berry Pomeroy manor, for the charter stipulated that such men could be elected reeve only with the consent of their ex-lord. The Pomeroys were also the lords of Tregoney (*q.v.*).

The parish bounds show how Bridgetown was cut out of Berry Pomeroy, which surrounds it on three sides. The new borough and extension cannot now be distinguished but both were probably set along the main road. The small borough of North Ford (*q.v.*) was also an extra-mural appendage to Totnes.

In 1273 Totnes had 217 burgages (C133/2/7); in 1293 fifty-five tenants were named as burgesses of Bridgetown (*Book of Fees*, ii, p. 1308) but O. J. Reichel ("Berry Pomeroy", *Tr. Devon Ass.*, xxviii (1896)) has twenty-three burgesses in 1292. In 1305 the borough was worth £7 11s. 8½d. to its lord (C133/118/1; see also C135/238/9).

The Pomeroy charter is printed in *15th Report Hist. Mss. Comm.*, pt. vii, pp. 134–135.

COLYFORD   Devonshire   sheet 177   30/253927
1225–38

The main Exeter to Dorchester road crosses the Axe marshes and the river Coly in the south of Colyton parish. The ford on the Coly gave its name to the new town which was set up at the crossing. The lord of Colyton was Thomas Bassett, and in 1208 he obtained the grant of a fair. In the Hundred Rolls inquiry the town of Colyford was said to have been founded by Thomas Bassett on land given by the king (*R.H.*, i, p. 68), and in 1274 there were 112 burgages (C133/6/1) with a total rent of £4 15s. 7d. Twenty years earlier a bridge had been built to replace the ford. The town is mentioned in the Assize Rolls of 1238 and 1244, but there is no mention of it in the account roll for Colyton in 1224–25 (E364/1 mm. 1 and 3), so that the town may provisionally be assigned to this range of years, unless the fair of 1208 was connected with the new project.

The character of the town, which consists of two blocks of burgage plots on either side of the main road west of the bridge, has been fatally modernised but the burgage plots are still discernible in the broad gardens. The ford was at the highest point to which high tides flowed, and its site can still be seen, for the road to the present bridge splays away from the line of the main street, leaving a narrow lane a few yards long going straight on to the old crossing, where there are now steps. The burgage plots seem to have been just 16 perches long and the total length of the town was half a mile. The mother village of Colyton was quite large: 101 tenants alongside the 112 Colyford burgesses in 1274. The value of the two to their lord was about equal (C133/62/7).

FORD, NORTH   Devonshire   sheet 188   20/800610
? before 1250
In 1326 William Fitz Martin was receiving £11 17s. 2d. in rents from sixty-eight burgesses "at North Ford and elsewhere adjacent to the manor of Dartington" (Finberg, *art. cit.*, p. 206: C134/99). The manor of Dartington approaches the northern wall of the old borough of Totnes near the present railway station, as the parish bounds show, and the old ford was a few yards to the west of the railway bridge. The stream which divided Totnes from North Ford can still be seen at the foot of Castle Street, but no trace of North Ford borough has been discerned. The building of the station and sidings have probably destroyed any chance of archaeological discovery.

There are analogies with Bridgetown Pomeroy (*q.v.*) planted outside the east gate of Totnes. The ford is likely to be older than the bridge that gave rise to Bridgetown and it was to this crossing that the north gate of Totnes looked. The ford led straight across to the Exeter road, and it was quite a detour to go out of Totnes by the east gate and over the bridge. It may therefore be suggested that North Ford was an older extra-mural settlement than that at Bridgetown, east of the bridge (*q.v.*), and that its importance faded once the bridge-crossing was available.

In 1326 there were also fifty-eight tenants who were burgesses of Little Totnes, another extra-mural settlement in Dartington (C134/99). They paid £7 8s. 1d.

HONITON   Devonshire   sheet 176   31/163007
1194–1217
Between 1194 and 1217 the fifth earl of Devon founded a borough at Honiton (*R.H.*, i, p. 74, and *Testa de Nevill*, i, p. 263). The isolated position of St. Michael's church half a mile south of the town suggests that the burghal settlement was separate from rural Honiton which was a vill in 1066, and the complete alinement of the town along the London to Exeter main road makes it analogous to such bastides as Bow and Colyford.

In 1224 and 1225 there were burgage rentals: (E364/1 mm. 1 and 3) and in 1238 it was separately represented at the Assizes. In 1334 the borough was assessed for taxation at almost three times the value of the manor. In 1244 the borough was worth £5 15s. 4d. to its lord and the manor £19 8s. 5d. (C132/3/10; C132/14/13): in 1285–86 the values were £11 8s. 8d. and £7 14s. 5¾d. (SC6/827/39). Although the town has prospered in modern times it is still essentially a great street-town. King Street preserves one of the back lanes, parallel to the main road, which divided the burgages from the fields and gave access to the long, narrow building plots, the out-line of which can still be discerned in the garden boundaries. The western end of the town was probably set at the crossing of the little stream, the Gessage, which powered the town mill. The burgage plots on the north side were about 88 yards long and on the south side about 110 yards. No earthworks of houses or crofts could be discerned near the isolated church on the hill.

KENNFORD   Devonshire   sheet 176   20/920850
c. 1298

The name does not appear in Domesday Book, the first reference in *P.N. Devon* (p. 499) being 1298 when the place was mentioned in the Assize Roll. In an I.P.M. of 1274 for Kenn manor, however, two tenants had the surname Kenford. This document does not mention a borough (C133/6/1). In 1300 a market and fair charter was issued to Henry de Courtenay (*Cal. Chart. Rolls*, ii, p. 488), and by c. 1340 it was reckoned for some purposes to be a borough (Finberg, *art. cit.*, p. 206). In 1578 (SC12/6/61) there were only eight freeholders in the borough.

    The little town is one of those Devon plantations on a major road by a river crossing; the main road now by-passes it. The new settlement was in one corner of the parish of Kenn, the mother village. There is no sign of burgage plots.

KINGSBRIDGE   Devonshire   sheet 188   20/735443
c. 1219

The bridge here, linking the two royal manors of West Alvington and Chillington, is mentioned in 962 but the only settlement seems to have been at Dodbrooke until the abbot of Buckfast obtained a market charter for Kingsbridge in 1219. By 1328 Kingsbridge was reckoned a borough although never incorporated (W. G. Hoskins, *Devon* (1954), pp. 419–420; H. P. R. Finberg, "The Boroughs of Devon", *D.C.N.Q.*, xxiv (1951), pp. 205–206). The church of St. Edmund is mainly a thirteenth-century structure. The town had been founded on the eastern edge of Churchstow, a manor of Buckfast abbey. In the Hundred Rolls (*R.H.*, i, p. 79) Churchstow was recorded as having both a *novus burgus* rendering six marks and a Friday market. West Alvington also had burgages in 1304 (C133/114/4).

    The parish is significantly small: 150 acres gathered round the steep street climbing the hill from the head of the estuary. The line of burgage plots can still be discerned on the more level ground at the top of the hill, and a stream on the east marks the boundary with the older town of Dodbrooke. A charter of 962 mentioning Kingsbridge refers only to the bridge, which has now disappeared under a car-park although its approximate position can be deduced from the alinement of narrow approach lanes from the north-east and south-west. The 1334 assessment placed Kingsbridge at almost twice the wealth of Dodbrooke.

NEWPORT in Bishop's Tawton   Devonshire   sheet 163   21/565324
by 1291

One edge of the bishop of Exeter's manor of Tawton abutted upon Barnstaple, separated only by the tiny stream known now as Cooney Cut. Here, on the main road to Exeter, just outside the old borough of Barnstaple, the bishop planted his borough of Newport. A rental of 1291 (SC6/1138/1) includes a *firma burgi* for Tawton, and it is most likely that this sum was paid for the borough, of which this is the earliest record. Four years later a market charter was granted and a rental of 1307–08 (*Reg. Stapledon*, p. 23) includes a *burgus*, valued that year at £16 8s. 10d. In the subsidy roll of 1330 it was called *burgus* again (*P.N. Devon*, p. 27), and in 1334 was assessed at 13s. 4d. when Barnstaple paid £18 14s. 0d. In the rentals of episcopal manors in 1369–70 the place was still called a borough (SC6/1138/2).

To-day it is almost continuously welded to Barnstaple by buildings, although its separate character was still discernible in the plan made for the Boundary Commission in 1832. It was centred on the church, licenced in 1385, where the Exeter and South Molton roads join. The open space by the inn may be the vestige of the market place.

NEWTON ABBOT   Devonshire   sheet 188   20/858713
1196–1200

This town was planted shortly after Torre abbey received the manor of Wolborough from William Brewer (its founder) in 1196. To the north-east of Wolborough and at the foot of the hill was the point where the Exeter to Totnes Road crossed the little river Lemon. Here was the very edge of Wolborough parish where it marched with Highweek, and the town was sometimes called "Shireborne" Newton from the boundary stream which flowed along the north side of its market place. *Nova Villa* occurs in a deed of c. 1200 (E164/19 (Torre Cartulary), folios 13, 15, 16d). The market and fair charter dates from 1269 but in the Hundred Rolls (*R.H.*, i, p. 72) the jurors said that the *nova villa* had had a charter from King John as well.

The modern appearance of the town is described under Newton Bushel, *infra*. It will be noted that there is no medieval church.

NEWTON BUSHEL   Devonshire   sheet 188   20/858713
1246

The relation of Newton Abbot to this second borough is almost unique. In few places in Europe can there be two planted towns, their market places once separated by a stream and now welded into one with the stream hidden away in a culvert. The foundation of Newton Abbot (alias Shireborne Newton) has been described above, and in the same Hundred Roll as the account of the abbey's Newton there occurs the jurors' statement (*R.H.*, i, pp. 82 and 91) that certain tenants *de la Novelevile* partly belonging to Highweek manor (here called "Teignwick") claimed to have a grant from Henry III making the town a borough with a market and the assizes of bread and ale. No borough charter survives, but in 1246 there was a royal grant of a market to the life-tenant of the Crown (*Cal. Chart. Rolls*, i, p. 311) and another (*Cal. Pat. Rolls, 1232–47*, p. 495) authorising him to create burgages and let them to anyone he pleased.

Newton Bushel was separated from Newton Abbot by the little river Lemon, and its situation at the edge of Highweek parish mirrors the relation of Newton Abbot to

Wolborough.   The Lemon survives as the parish boundary and its old function as an important boundary is preserved in the name of Sherborne (sc. Shireborne) Road given to the north side of Market Square.   The river is now hidden from view in a culvert and emerges on the west side of Highweek Street.   The main shopping centre and the open and covered markets are now on the south side of the river in Newton Abbot proper, but the site of Newton Bushel market place has now become a cattle-market, partly open and partly covered.   There are some old houses, probably with medieval cores, facing it in Highweek Street.   Taking the Exeter–Totnes road (A.381) as the main axis of the original Newton Abbot borough, it is possible that the whole of the area between Courtenay Street and the Market Hall was once an open market space, later encroached upon by the shops of Bearne's Lane.   The rural shell of Teignwick is surveyed in C135/80/19 (1346).

NEWTON POPPLEFORD   Devonshire   sheet 176   30/080890
1226

Newton Poppleford is 12 miles west of Colyford (q.v.) on the Exeter–Dorchester road and it occupies an analogous position: west of a river crossing, once a ford and now bridged.   Its mother parish was Aylesbeare, 4 miles to the north-west.   In 1331 a chantry in Newton was reckoned to depend on Aylesbeare (Reg. Grandisson, p. 619) and in 1284–86 there is a reference to "villam de Aylesbear cum Popelford" (F.A., i, p. 324).   The first record of the name Newton is in 1305 (P.N. Devon, p. 592), but in 1274 there was already a borough here (C133/6/1), with 55½ burgages rented at 1s. each.   The grant of a market to William Brewer, lord of the manor of Aylesbere, in 1226 may signify the beginning of organised commercial life here (Rot. Lit. Claus., ii (1844), p. 132).   In 1239 the lord of Aylesbeare obtained a charter for a fair (Finberg, art. cit., p. 206).   In 1292 Newton villata paid 56s. o½d. rents in Aylesbeare manor; there was a fair worth 2s.; Aylesbeare customary tenants paid £5 17s. 6d. (C133/62/7).   In 1377 Newton rents were 62s. (C135/260).

The burgage plots are well preserved in the shape of gardens, 44 yards long on the north where there is a steep slope, and longer to the south.   Near St. Luke's church there is a widening of the road which probably represents the market place.   The eastern limit of the town seems to be marked by the beginning of the slope down to the river Otter, where a bridge has long replaced the ford.   The parish boundary runs behind the burgage plots on the north, parallel to the main road; on the south it also hugs the town and shows clearly that the settlement has thrust into the narrow tongue of Aylesbeare parish that gave access to the Otter meadows; the neighbouring parishes of Venn Ottery, Harpford, and Colaton Raleigh have similar tongues.

NOSS MAYO   Devonshire   sheet 187   20/550478
1286

The first recorded reference to Noss is in 1286 when a market was granted (B.M. Harl. Charter 58, I, 38).   In 1309 it was called a borough (C134/16/9): "burgus qui vocatus la Nosse"; burgess rents were £4 16s. 2d.; Yealmpton was worth £55 4s. 6¼d. and had 102 tenants.   The separate representation of Yealmpton at the Assize of

1244 (JI/1/175) may be a recognition of quasi-burghality, perhaps at Noss? Noss was again called a borough in 1359. (Despite its name, Newton Ferrers on the opposite side of the estuary is an older settlement, recorded in 1086.) For taxation purposes Noss was part of Yealmpton. The joint tax-paying population of 1377 was 295 (E179/95/43 m. 12). This is large, and in 1334 Noss and Yealmpton together paid 104s., also a large sum. In 1811 there were 78 houses in Noss (Revelstoke) and 187 in Yealmpton. Noss is now a small village along the estuary.

OKEHAMPTON   Devonshire   sheet 175   20/587952
by 1086

"Okehampton town was founded by Baldwin de Brionne, the Norman sheriff of Devon, shortly before 1086, on a new wedge-like site between the East and West Okement rivers, and the Saxon site was gradually abandoned except for the church (All Saints) which now stands alone" (W. G. Hoskins, *Devon*, (1954), p. 447). By 1086 there was a market and four burgesses were mentioned. (It will be noticed that the castle is one mile to the south-west, remote from both church and borough.)

No earthworks of the deserted Saxon village have yet been traced in the fields near the church, which is still in use. A later church at the east end of the main street of the new borough began as a chantry chapel; it was erected in view of the distance from the borough to the old church on the hill over the river, and the market place may have been in the splay of the main street near it. Markets are now held in a side-street to the north of the town. The borough-parish is surrounded by the large out-parish of Okehampton Hamlets. In 1334 the assessed wealth of these two units was about the same. In 1274 there were 140 burgesses (C133/6/1) and the borough was worth £8. The manor then had 79 villeins. In 1292 (C133/62/7) the borough was worth £7 5s. 1d. in rents, 16s. in tolls and 14s. 10d. other income.

PLYMPTON ERLE (St. Maurice)   Devonshire   sheet 187   20/545557
1194

The small parish area (232 acres) has clearly been cut from the older settlement of Plympton St. Mary, where the population of forty-five mentioned in Domesday Book probably lived. The church of Plympton St. Mary is on the A.38 (at 537564) but since the improvements of the eighteenth century the main road has by-passed Plympton Erle. The town was named after the earls of Devon who were lords of the manor in the twelfth century. It was an earl of Devon who, in 1107, built the castle on the abrupt hill. In 1194 the fifth earl made a borough here and gave the town a market and fair. The church was probably also built by the earls. Its dedication was to St. Thomas of Canterbury, St. Maurice being a post-Reformation alteration.

The church is immediately to the east of the castle, and from the castle-keep one looks down on the churchyard and the main street (Fore Street as at Saltash) that follows the edge of the castle ditch to the south. The church and castleyard occupy the full east-west width of the town, 440 yards, but only about half the depth (north-south) which is 240 yards. A back-lane north of Fore Street marks the line of the castle ditch. To the south of Fore Street the burgages abut on Long Brook.

Two blocks of houses south-west of the church may represent an encroachment on a market place. The town is full of character, although none of the secular buildings are medieval. It is what one imagines a Gascon bastide would have looked like if Gascony had remained English until today. It sent members to Parliament from 1295 to 1832 and was prosperous in the seventeenth and eighteenth century, as its buildings show. (J. B. Rowe, *A History of Plympton Erle* (Exeter, 1906), with plan of 1793 at end; Hoskins, *Devon*, pp. 461–462; *Pipe Roll Soc.*, n.s., vi (1929), p. 80, refers to burgesses in 1195; Finberg, *art. cit.*, p. 204; K. Ugawa, "The Economic Development of Some Devon Manors", *Tr. Devon Ass.*, xciv (1962), pp. 660–661.)

The rents from vill and borough were about equal in 1285–86 (SC6/827/39); in 1245 (C132/3/10) the borough was farmed at £24 2s. 2d. and the manor at twice that sum.

TOTNES, Little   Devonshire
by 1326
See FORD, NORTH

ZEAL, SOUTH   Devonshire   sheet 175   20/650935
c. 1264

In 1299 a market and two fairs at Zele Tony were granted to the lord of South Tawton, Robert de Tony (*Cal. Chart. Rolls*, ii, p. 479). The latter village lies under the northern slopes of Dartmoor, and the Exeter to Okehampton (high) road crossed the parish half a mile south of the church leaving the common moorland of South Tawton on the south of the main road. It was on this road that South Zeal was created; by 1315 there were twenty burgesses, *apud la Sele in precincta dicti manerii*, paying 35s. 4d. rent in all (C134/50). The shape and size of the town were perfect for its purpose; the burgage plots begin at the foot of the hill down which the main road comes, and end as it begins to rise on the western side. The houses lie well back from the road and the little chapel is in the centre of what must have once been the market place. Commerce, however, has been virtually banished since the modern road has jibbed at the descent into the town and taken to hugging the contours to the south. The fossilisation of burgage plots is almost complete. Their creation may be caught in a survey of 1264 (C132/31) which shows the lord of Tawton profiting from some revenue from a court at *Sele villata* and from 31s. 2d. from forty-two named tenants there, each of whom held plots of land (either ½, 1, 1½, 2, 3, 4, or 5 acres) at a flat 6d. an acre. The connection of these pieces of land with settlement is suggested by the fact that the last two entries in the rental are *pro quadam placia terrae*.

DORSET

This, the next county eastwards from Devon, shows a quite different pattern of urbanisation. It had no more than nine organic towns and six plantations, and a closer examination of the six shows that only three (Poole, Weymouth and Melcombe

Regis) were of any significance: and two of these were within an arrow's flight of each other. All three, it will be noted, were ports; and the abortive Newton was also planned as a port that would specialise in the export of Purbeck stone. Inland, the highroads of Dorset had nothing like the string of petty borough plantations in Devon and Cornwall. As ports, and successful ports at that, Poole, Weymouth and Melcombe achieved a middling place on the ladder of taxable wealth in 1334.

CORFE   Dorset   sheet 179   30/960820
1080–1215

The inclusion of this site is speculative. There is no mention of Corfe specifically in Domesday Book. It was separately represented at the Assize of 1288 (JI/1/213). Chartered only in 1571, the place was nevertheless taxed as a borough from 1307–32; a market dates from 1215 and a fair from 1246. The borough has the simple plan of two streets converging at the foot of the castle where the church stands.

There is some uncertainty whether "the hide in Kingston on which a castle had been built" refers to Wareham or Corfe (*Hist. King's Works*, i (1963), p. 21; D. F. Renn, "The Keep of Wareham Castle", *Med. Archaeol.*, iv (1960), p. 56; see also *ibid.*, iii (1959), pp. 120, sqq. for excavations of Corfe castle and a plan dating earliest parts to c. 1080). There is also the problem of the death of Edward the Martyr in 978 "at the gap of Corfe" (D. Whitelock, ed., *The Anglo-Saxon Chronicle* (1961), p. 79), but this phrase need not imply any settlement other than a royal residence.

MELCOMBE REGIS   Dorset   sheet 178   30/680790
by 1268

This was a separate borough, but the narrative is contained within that for Weymouth (*q.v.*).

NEWTON   Dorset   sheet 179   30/c. 011853
1286

This abortive plantation on the shores of Poole harbour was probably designed as a port from which Purbeck marble, quarried a few miles inland, could be shipped. But despite the privileges offered by Edward I to new settlers it seems unlikely that the town ever got far under way. There were other failures among Edward's plantations (see Bere, Wales) but it cannot have been military insecurity which deterred potential burgesses from coming to Newton. In the end, the port of Poole over the estuary was left unchallenged. No church of Newton seems to have been consecrated and no borough of this name was represented at the Assize of 1288 (JI/1/213).

In January 1286 Edward I was at Exeter where he appointed two men, one of them a Gloucestershire cleric, to lay out the new town with a physical equipment appropriate for merchants, who were to be granted the same privileges as Henry III's charter had given to the city of London: streets; lanes; a market place; a church; building plots; and a harbour. A charter was promised. The land was partly the king's already, and the remaining territory was acquired by him from Robert de Muchegros. On May 10 the town was granted two weekly markets and a fair at St. Lawrencetide (*Cal. Pat. Rolls, 1281–92*, p. 217; *Cal. Chart. Rolls*, i, p. 337).

When the estates of Corfe were surveyed in 1558 the name Newton had survived only as the name of a single cottage east of Ower quay, probably the present Newton Cottage (J. Hutchins, *Dorset* (1861), i, pp. 462 and 652). No harbour is shown on the Tudor coastal plan of Dorset (B.M. Cott. Mss., Aug. I, i, f. 31–3).

The presumed site of the borough is shown on the air photograph in *Beresford and St. Joseph*, p. 224, and the Rev. H. B. Cowl indicated in 1952 the foundations of buildings at about G.R. 011853 which may have been medieval; but the position is complicated by subsequent disturbance of this area for a light railway, now disused, and for a quay east of Goathorn Plantation. The name of this wood and peninsula preserves the name *Gotowre super Mare* of the 1286 grant.

Recent inspection of the footings of these buildings by the Royal Commission on Historical Monuments, Dorset, indicates that they are unlikely to be medieval. In addition, the Tithe Map of Studland shows that the main part of Goathorn peninsula lay in Swanage and not in Studland parish. Since Newton Copse and Newton Cottage on the western edge of the peninsula do fall in Studland parish there is a strong case for placing the intended site of Edward I's borough at the southern end of Newton Bay. It may be significant that modern charts show the only navigable channels from South Deep running into Newton Bay, and none on the east side of the peninsula. Since the borough was intended as a port for shipping out Purbeck stone the depth of water would be an important factor in siting the new port. (I am indebted to Mr. H. C. Bowen for a sight of the draft of the Royal Commission's report on Newton (1962) now published in *Med. Archaeol.* viii (1964), pp. 223–26, with plan.)

POOLE   Dorset   sheet 179   40/008904
c. 1170–80

The older medieval settlements in this area were at Kinson and Canford, both of which lie on the Stour, north of Poole, and separated from what is now Poole Harbour by heathland. Poole was founded in Longfleet tithing in Canford Parish. The mother church was Canford and the first mention of the chapel of St. James in Poole occurs c. 1170–80. The borough charter was granted c. 1248 by William Longespee, grandson of the probable founder of Poole church, and a number of documents prior to 1248 attest the presence of traders and seamen at Poole: for example, a bailiff and *probi homines* in 1224 (*Cal. Pat. Rolls, 1216–25*, p. 484). It is probable that (as at Liverpool and Portsmouth) the name of an estuary became attached to the new settlement.

The town is on a narrow peninsula between Holes Bay and Parkstone Bay. The church stands near the landward tip, and before the reclamation of land for the quays it was even nearer to the waterfront. On its landward side the splayed division of Market Street suggests a triangular market place, now encroached upon, as the original form of the town. West Street and High Street form an envelope to this area and may be original back-lanes or the limits of the marshland. W. G. Hoskins (L. D. Stamp and W. G. Hoskins, *The Common Lands of England and Wales* (1963), p. 38) suggests that the town was planted on the sea-edge of Canford common.

The town's first charter *inter alia* absolved the burgesses from the necessity to journey to Canford for the manorial court leet, and the burgesses themselves were allowed to plead "the hindrance of the sea" if any of them happened to be at sea when they should have been at the borough court. The presence of "stranger merchants" is also alluded to in the charter. (H. P. Smith, *The History of the Borough and County of the Town of Poole*, i (Poole, 1948), pp. 109, 113, 123-4, and 143-50; charter reproduced as Fig. 74; there is a large plan of the town in J. Hutchins, *Dorset* (ed. 1861), i, p. 1.)

SHERBORNE NEWLAND   Dorset   sheet 178   31/640169
1227-8

This little borough was created in 1227-28 by the bishop of Salisbury, fresh from the creation of New Sarum. Its charter (*Cal. Pat. Rolls, 1381-5*, p. 54, and *Ballard and Tait*, pp. 45 and 54) classified the *nova burgagia* into three types: north of the road from the chapel of St. Thomas to the bishop's castle the burgage plots were to be 24 perches by four and be rented at 1s. 6d. a year; on the south of the same road they were to measure 20 perches by four and be rented at 1s.; from the chapel to the bishop's barn there were to be smaller plots at 8d.

The road from chapel to barn is the street known as Newland which runs from the Green at the north end of Cheap Street across to the castle gate; at the Green is the chapel. This burghal project of the bishop was supplementary to the old-established town of Sherborne which was owned by the Abbey and it lay outside the town (J. Hutchins, *Dorset*, iv, pp. 204-300, and plan by H. M. Colvin in A. L. Poole, ed., *Medieval England* (1958), i, p. 62). It is analogous to the external *novus burgus* of Eynsham (1215) also called Newland.

WEYMOUTH   Dorset   sheet 178   30/680790
by 1244

There were originally two boroughs facing each other across the narrow *Waimouthe*, an estuary so named in a charter of 933. It was only by an Act of 1571 that a long friction between the two was ended by amalgamation into one borough to be called "Weymouth". The borough on the north bank (in Radipole parish) had been previously called Melcombe Regis and that on the south bank (in Wyke Regis parish) was called Weymouth. The division is shown by the fact that the customs collectors (e.g. in 1303) of "Weymouth" were responsible for a stretch of coastline from Weymouth south and westwards to Plymouth, while customs collected on the other side of the estuary at Melcombe were the responsibility (that year) of the customs collector based on Chichester, far to the east. Melcombe became an independent centre for the collection of customs on wool in 1331 and on cloth in 1365, but the impoverishment of the town caused it to be displaced as a Head Port by Poole in 1433 (E. M. Carus-Wilson and O. Coleman, *England's Export Trade 1275-1547* (1963),

29

pp. 182 and 191). This confused nomenclature is not eased by the fact that the modern seaside town of Weymouth is based on the north bank borough.

Leland had noted the connection between the distant parish church of Radipole and the late foundation of the borough on the sea edge of the parish: "the paroche churche ys a mile of, a manifest token that (Melcombe) ys no very old town" (J. Hutchins, *Dorset*, ii (1863), p. 447): and Hutchins drew the same conclusion for Wyke (*ibid.*, ii, p. 418).

The parish church of Radipole is at 670813 near the marshes at the head of the estuary; a chapel of ease existed in the borough at Melcombe in 1297 (*ibid.*, ii, p. 457) but it had no burial rights until an Act of 1603 (1 Jas. I, c. 30) erected Melcombe church into a full parish church and reduced Radipole to the rank of chapelry, a remarkable act of matricide.

On the south side of the estuary the inhabitants of Weymouth town were also dependent on the village church of the parish in which this borough had been founded. It was only in 1851 that the obligation to bury at Wyke Regis was lifted, although the townsmen had long had a chapel of ease, St. Nicholas', standing south of the town at the head of seventy steps.

A charter of Henry I had granted the port to St. Swithun's, Winchester, and it was to St. Swithun's that a market was granted in 1248 to be held at Weymouth in the manor of Wyke Regis (*Cal. Chart. Rolls*, i, p. 331). By 1256 (Eccles. 2/159292) Wyke "with the town of Weymouth" was in the hands of the bishops of Winchester (see also *Cal. Chart. Rolls*, ii, p. 9). It was called a borough in 1285 (*ibid.*, ii, p. 288) and had been represented by a jury of burghal size at the Assize of 1244 (JI/1/201).

The borough of Melcombe on the north bank received its charter from the king in 1280 (*Cal. Chart. Rolls*, ii, p. 223) giving all the liberties of the city of London; the manor had been acquired from Cerne abbey which already claimed a Tuesday market and a fair there. In 1268 Melcombe appeared as a borough at the assize (JI/1/202 m. 24d). It was these privileges of Melcombe borough that Edward I took as a model for his *nova villa* in Purbeck in 1286 (*Cal. Chart. Rolls*, ii, p. 337).

The north borough (Melcombe) has a very clear grid of streets remaining immediately north of the bridge but ending where the modern town opens out into the Promenade. The original core of the southern borough is less marked, but any rectangularity would have been restricted by the steep cliff above the river; the northern borough was laid out on a flat spit of land. Documents suggest that the southern borough had about 260 burgages at the beginning of the fourteenth century (C133/76/3; C133/128; C134/43; C135/152/5). The reeve's accounts for the rural part of Wyke in 1279–80 have survived (SC6/834/22).

COUNTY DURHAM

A study of urban chronology is made difficult by the absence from Domesday Book of any account of the territories of the prince-bishop. Boldon Book (*Surtees Soc.*, xxv (1852), ed. W. Greenwell), something of a substitute, dates from 1183 but by that time many of the boroughs were undoubtedly established. The difficulty is to decide when they were founded, and whether there were antecedent villages. The independent jurisdiction of the palatinate excluded Durham from records of litigation and accounting at the courts of the central government, the indispensable evidence for the chronology of settlement in other English counties. The palatinate had its own records but the early years are not well represented in them. The towns in this *List* are submitted, therefore, with some apprehension.

In this county even topographical aids conspire to confuse. Durham has a large number of "green-villages" which never claimed a market, let alone a burghal project: yet their severe rectilinear forms and the dominant position of the market place within them are a combination that elsewhere in England might be invoked as prima facie evidence for plantation. How impressive and suggestive of plantation by the bishop, for example, is the broad and straight market place of Stockton on Tees, placed at the gate of the bishop's castle, and backed by the quays of the riverport! Yet how confusing when a neighbouring village, Norton, still preserves a regular central green but turns out to be a village to which a market charter was granted within a generation of the Norman Conquest (*Regesta Regum Anglo-Normannorum*, ed. H. A. Cronne & C. Johnson, ii (1956), no. 925). No plantation here. Stockton itself has another feature of a plantation, the absence of a parish church (until 1713), but here again the peculiar settlement topography of Durham intervenes to raise doubts. Large parishes with many dependent hamlets are a feature of the county, and Stockton was one such hamlet in Norton parish. In 1183 there is no mention of a borough at Stockton, but there was a borough in 1283, 1308 and 1316 (*Surtees Soc.*, xxv (1852), ed. W. Greenwell, p. 383) and bishop Hatfield's survey of c. 1380 describes thirty-nine burgages in the town (*Surtees Soc.*, xxxii (1856), pp. 164–170). The chapel founded in the town c. 1230 may be a clue to the date of the lost charter but already in 1184 the vill was tallaged for £7, almost as much as the borough of Darlington (£8). Stockton may stand, therefore, as an example of organic growth, the elevation of a hamlet which prospered from the presence of the bishop's hall, the ferry and the river staithes. Darlington, a pre-Conquest village, had both a bond vill and a borough by 1183. Bishop's Auckland, a hamlet in South Auckland parish, became a borough by promotion between 1183 and 1242–3, when it appeared at the Assize (JI/1/223 m. 5).

Three other boroughs seem to be suburban offshoots of other towns: Gateshead's charter of 1153–95 elevated a forest vill that stood at an important river crossing opposite Newcastle on Tyne; there were forty merchant houses in Elvet, an eastern suburb of Durham, at the time of the foundation of the cathedral priory (1080–95) and a borough charter was given by the prior (1189–95); St. Giles was another small suburban accretion to Durham that was elevated to a borough by Bishop Hugh (1153–95) for the benefit of Kepyer Hospital.

Sunderland remains to be considered. The old port of Wearmouth was on the south bank of the estuary but the famous monastery was on the north. In 930 St. Cuthbert was given the vill of South Wearmouth by King Athelstan but it was badly damaged (and perhaps destroyed) by Malcolm of Scotland in 1070. The present parish church of Bishop Wearmouth indicates the centre of this vill, but the borough of the same name lay further to the east adjoining the staithes of the port. This borough may have acquired its other name simply because territory was "sundered" from South Wearmouth vill. Between 1180 and 1183 it was given borough status by bishop Hugh together with the customs enjoyed by Newcastle on Tyne, and in Boldon Book it appeared as "the borough of Wearmouth" (*Surtees Soc.*, xxv (1852), pp. xli–ii and 46). In Hatfield's survey of c. 1380 it appeared under its modern name *burgus de Sunderland* and the holdings surveyed under "Wearmouth" were those of the rural vill (*Surtees Soc.*, xxxii (1856), p. 137). The pre-eminence of South Wearmouth vill is emphasised by the fact that Sunderland had no parish church until an Act of 1719, and while the circumstances resemble those of a planted borough the evidence remains ambiguous (G. Garbutt, *History of Sunderland* (1819), has a plan showing the relation of Sunderland to Bishop Wearmouth; see also *Arch. Ael.*, 2nd ser., xiii (1892), p. 283).

There remain four boroughs that can be called plantations with a little more confidence, although the evidences for the first and third have some of the deficiencies already noted as characteristic of the county's towns. There is a good account of the episcopal boroughs in M. Hope-Dodds, "The Bishops' Boroughs" *Arch. Ael.*, 3rd ser., xii (1913), pp. 80–185.

BARNARD CASTLE   County Durham   sheet 84   45/052163
c. 1112

The castle stands high above the Tees, and on the east of the castle a broad street runs down from the general level of the plateau to the river crossing. At the north end of the town the main road turns sharply north-east and takes up again the course of the Roman road from Bowes to Binchester which must have crossed the Tees near by. There is no documentary evidence of settlement before the Norman Conquest and no traces of early work in the church where considerable excavation took place when the floor was lowered in the course of Victorian reconstruction.

The church was founded as a chapel of ease to Gainford, the parish in which the castle was erected by Guy de Balliol. This western frontier of the county was given to the Balliols by William II and was independent of the bishop's jurisdiction. Frequent conflicts of jurisdiction resulted. The first extant charter of c. 1175 refers to the liberties that the grantor's father, Barnard Balliol, had given to his town (Surtees, *Durham*, iv, pp. 71–72). Additional privileges modelled on those of Richmond were given to the town in 1215–27.

DURHAM   County Durham   sheet 85   54/273421
995–1006

In 995, when the body of St. Cuthbert was brought for safety, there was a settlement at Elvet on the south-east bank of the river on the outside of the great loop in the river Wear that now embraces the city. The rock top within the loop had no agricultural value. A church was built for the saint's bones by 1003 and by 1006, when there was a siege, there is mention of ramparts. Symeon of Durham said that houses were built and distributed by lot ("*unicuique mansionibus sorte distributis*") among those who had come with the monks. The existence of a *Forum* in 1040 suggests commercial

432

life in the Saxon town before the arrival of the first Norman bishop (1072) with his castle, cathedral and mint. The 58 acres of the borough lay to the north of the castle on lower ground and it is to the market place that the roads from both bridges climb (Air photograph in *Beresford and St. Joseph*, p. 184).

The agnostic conclusion of the *V.C.H., Durham* (i, p. 9) is: "there is no evidence at all as to the pre-Conquest buildings and streets save as regards the church itself". On the other hand there were "men of Durham" to rise against earl Cumin in 1069, when there were also streets to run with blood.

A second, extra-mural, borough of Elvet is described in its charter (1188–1219) (*Ballard*, p. 91) as a *novus burgus* lying "in Elvetehalge, that is from the way which lies near the house of the abbot of Newminster on the northern side towards Scaltoc". At the Assize of 1242–43 there were juries for three separate boroughs (Durham, Elvet and Durham Old Borough: JI/1/223 mm. 5 and 5d) as well as one for the *vicus* of St. Giles. The *Vetus Burgus* was associated with the building of St. Margaret's by the Prior, which may have revived memories of an older settlement?

HARTLEPOOL   County Durham   sheet 85   45/529337
1162–83
The first recorded mention of the name Hartlepool is in a charter of 1162–85 when Robert de Brus gave the liberties of Newcastle (*Ballard*, pp. 251–252). The Wearmouth charter of 1180–83 mentions the men of Robert Brus at Hartlepool but nothing else is known of a town before bishop Hugh purchased the whole wapentake of Sadberge in 1189. The headland at the end of the isthmus had been the site of a monastery from c. 640 to its destruction in 865.

The lords of the town were the de Brus and it was they who added the walls. Being the only royal borough in the county there were many conflicts of jurisdiction between the de Brus and the bishops of Durham. The appearance of the town, one principal street, a back street and several cross streets, supports the conjecture of a plantation: but it can be no more than a conjecture. The town church (St. Hilda's) was dependent on the parish church of Hart. There is an Elizabethan plan of the town at Hatfield House (Manuscript plans, vol. i, no. 4) and a copy in the B.M. Map Room. (*Rot. Chart.*, p. 86; Surtees, *Durham*, iii, p. 99; *V.C.H., Durham*, iii, pp. 263 sqq.; F. F. Wilson, *The Story of Hartlepool*, 1951).

SHIELDS, SOUTH   County Durham   sheet 78   45/365683
by 1235
South Shields, at the mouth of the Tyne, was a manor of the priors of Durham. Near it the Northumbrian town of Caer Urfa had been destroyed in Danish raids of the ninth century (*Arch. Ael.*, 2nd ser., xix (1898), p. 47). At the Assize of 1254 (*Surtees Soc.*, lxxxviii (1890), p. 81) it was claimed that the men of the prior of Durham had founded *quandam magnam villam* within the bounds of the port of Tyne. The previous judicial eyre had condemned it as a breach of existing rights but there were still 27 houses, 2 ovens, 4 bakers and men who merchanted fish and other things. The borough of Newcastle claimed damages. The bishop claimed that the place where the town was founded lay outside the jurisdiction of Newcastle. The jurors

found that Newcastle had suffered damages but whether the king had also lost tolls by the existence of *Sutcheles* they did not know. A particular grievance seemed to be the sale of bread to passing ships. Similar difficulties were encountered by the town of the priors of Tynemouth (North Shields) on the opposite bank. A rental of twenty-four tenants in 1235 was cited in 1464 (*Surtees Soc.*, lviii, p. 119, fn.) and this was accompanied by a disclaimer to a sudden foundation: *non subito illo anno fuerint dicta tenementa ibidem erecta.* In 1279 a jury found that towns had been built on both banks to the harm of Newcastle. It will be noted that St. Hilda's church at South Shields was until 1854 a chapelry of Jarrow.

ESSEX

A striking feature of medieval Essex is the development of markets and market towns on the main roads that radiated eastwards from London. Although the principal roads were Roman in origin, the medieval settlements upon them seem to have been late: the frontiers between parishes had already been set and the towns found themselves with the rank of chapelries in the parish of some distant village church. Thus, Brentwood was a chapelry of South Weald, and Romford of Hornchurch; Manningtree was probably in Bradfield, and Billericay in Great Burghstead; Harwich was in Dovercourt. Romford, which was five miles from its burial ground at the mother church, obtained permission to have its own town cemetery only at the beginning of the fifteenth century; Braintree was made a distinct parish at the beginning of the thirteenth century (Morant, *Essex*, ii, pp. 394–396).

At Brentwood a document of 1234, authorising Thomas de Canvill to have habitations on his side of the *via regia* such as the abbot of St. Osyth's had on the other side, suggests that new settlement was in progress along the main road that formed the edge of Shenfield manor (J. H. Round, "The Making of Brentwood", *Tr. Essex Arch. Soc.*, n.s. xvii (1924), pp. 69–74). The High Street of Billericay likewise lay in two manors (G. Walker, *The History of a Little Town* (1947), pp. 25 and 43; see also *Essex Review*, iii (1894), p. 180).

The normal canons of parochial geography cannot be applied in mid-Essex where the manor house and settlements were very scattered, nucleated villages few, and churches often isolated from every building except the manor. Some churches reflect the ambitions and piety of the separate manorial lords in the thirteenth century rather than provision for village communities. It is odd that towns were not able to achieve an independent rank for their churches if parochial status was so freely given to manorial chapels. The early history of settlement in Essex cries out for local study, and histories of small towns may then come tumbling after. Until then, the categorisation of certain towns as "planted" is bound to be less than satisfactory and all the towns named above may one day need to be included in the gazetteer (see W. R. Powell, "The Making of Essex Parishes", *Essex Review*, Jan. 1953 pp. 6–17, for an essential list of chapels and churches existing before 1300).

Otherwise the contribution of Essex to town plantation is slender; two of the four towns became substantial and one of these is now the county town: but Pleshey and Wulvesford were petty affairs.

434

CHELMSFORD   Essex   sheet 161   52/710068
1199–1201

This late foundation has had remarkable success, now being the county town. In 1086 there was a hamlet of four households (not near the present town), greatly inferior to its neighbour, Writtle, a royal manor with 150 households and later to have a royal palace. Chelmsford owed its urbanisation not to the Crown but to the bishops of London. The territory alongside Ceolmaer's ford was acquired by St. Paul's between 998 and 1066; the crossing of the Chelmer and Can near their junction had been used by the Roman road from Colchester to London, but the early dominance of Writtle suggests that the first medieval bridge was further up river and that traffic had to go round two sides of a triangle.

Miss Hilda Grieve (on whose researches this note is largely based) has argued that the building of a bridge c. 1100 diverted trade to a more direct route and gave the opportunity for the bishop to lead traffic through the triangular market place which he made by widening the road north of the bridge. Within three years, 1199 to 1201, a market and fair and freedom of tenure were granted, and in 1202 the justices in eyre met at Chelmsford.

Camden ascribed the bridge to bishop Maurice (1086–1107). It is significant that the Manor House and manorial chapel of Chelmsford were quite away from the site of the bridge and town.

John Walker's large-scale plan of 1591, showing the development of town houses along the side of the market place and the encroachment upon it of public and private buildings, forms the coloured frontispiece to the Essex Record Office's *Art of the Map Maker in Essex*; a black and white version with further notes and a photograph of the town are in *Beresford and St. Joseph*, pp. 203–206.

HARWICH   Essex   sheet 150   62/261326
by 1229

This little walled borough was placed at the end of a promontory which half closes the estuaries of the Stour and Orwell rivers. It was within Dovercourt parish: Dovercourt, a Domesday vill, is a mile to the south. The church of St. Nicholas in Harwich was a chapel annexed to Dovercourt. The earliest reference to the name Harwich is in 1229 (*P.N. Essex*, p. 339) and there were payments to the subsidy of 1238. A market and fair were granted to the earls of Norfolk in 1253 (*Cal. Chart. Rolls*, ii, p. 433) and a borough charter in 1318 (*Cal. Pat. Rolls, 1317–21*, p. 380; and Silas Taylor, *The History and Antiquities of Harwich* (1732), with plan of town facing p. 1). There are five or six small parallel streets crowded into the narrow neck of land; the landward gate is shown in Taylor's plan.

PLESHEY   Essex   sheet 161   52/665145
c. 1180

The name Pleshey (*plessis, plessier, plessees*) derives from the Norman French word for an enclosure made up of living trees or bushes with their branches interlaced; the purpose could be for defence or for retaining animals within the forest pale. The name as applied to the Mandeville castle is first noted in the mid-twelfth century; Geoffrey de Mandeville was killed in 1144 and his younger son, William, obtained leave from Henry II to fortify his castle at Pleshey wherein, in 1180, he solemnized his marriage. Mr. Rahtz's excavations suggest that the present earthworks in their massive form date from this period; the parish church also came into existence at that period as a chapelry of High Easter, the bishop permitting the chapel since Easter was too far off (J. H. Round, *Family Origins* (1930), p. 267).

The chapel had to serve more than the castle garrison or the staff of a hunting lodge, for the great earthworks, cast in circular form, were designed to embrace castle, church and a town. The site of the original church, it must be explained, is now vacant: for in 1393 a collegiate church was founded by the duke of Gloucester just outside the walls of the town and this became the parish church (*Cal. Pat. Rolls, 1391–6*, pp. 363 and 367–368).

No borough charter is extant, but burgesses and stalls in the market place are mentioned in a document of 1336 (C135/48); the extra-mural church of 1393 suggests that the earthen ramparts had ceased to have defensive function for the town; and the series of fifteenth- and sixteenth-century surveys of the town show that markets and shops still flourished (E179/107/17; E179/107/49 m. 8; DL29/42/820; DL29/74/1480; DL43/3/18–19; DL44/1; SC11/197).

Air photographs and a plan of the town and castle are to be found in P. A. Rahtz, *Pleshey Castle: first interim report* (1960), figs. 2–3; plates 1–2.

The town wall and the site of the first church have not been excavated; this work should give more precision to the date when the town was founded, but provisionally it may be assigned to the erection of the second Mandeville castle (see also *R.C.H.M. Essex*, ii (1921), p. 200; Morant, *Essex* (1768), ii, p. 461).

WULVESFORD in Witham   Essex   sheet 162   52/822146
c. 1212

This plantation, of which the name seems to have eluded even the editor of *P.N. Essex*, can plausibly be identified with the main street of modern Witham, Newland Street. Shortly after crossing the river Brain the old main road from London to Colchester widens to form the usual triangle of an elongated market, and the blunt end of the triangle can still be detected near the junction with the Maldon and Braintree roads. The ends of the gardens on both sides of this main road form the characteristic envelope of burgage plots, perhaps extending a little north of the Maldon road junction. It is significant that neither the parish church nor the earthworks of the Anglo-Saxon *burh* of Witham are anywhere near this modern centre: the few remains of the *burh* are cut into by the railway station; and the parish church is further away still, at what is now known as Chipping Hill. Alongside it are streets and another market place (now deserted) which must belong to Anglo-Saxon and medieval Witham.

The additional and separate town on the main road is first mentioned in a charter of John in 1212 giving the Knights Templar a Thursday market and a yearly fair *apud novam villam suam de Wulvesford in parochia de Wiham* (*Rot. Chart.*, p. 188) and this was confirmed in 1227 by Henry III (*Cal. Chart. Rolls*, i, p. 5). It is this confirmation that is mentioned in a later charter of 1379 (*Cal. Chart. Rolls*, v, p. 258) concerning a market "at Neulond in the manor and precinct of Witham" (see also C143/395/6). In 1213 John had granted the Templars "*terram de Newland*" (B.M. Cott. Nero E. VI., ff. 290–290v.). In addition to this market at the Templars' new roadside town, the old market of Witham continued until 1379 and it must have been this market which gave the distinctive name *Chipping* to the old village of Witham, although it is to be noted that the earliest form noted in *P.N. Essex* is Elizabethan (*Rot. Chart.*, p. 3: grant of market in 1199 with reference to a market *temp.* Henry I; *Rot. Lit. Claus.*, p. 386: change of day, 1219). Newland Street and Chipping Hill fairs were abolished in 1891 (HO45/B10730). In the 1185 survey of the Templars' lands (ed. B. A. Lees, *Records of the Templars*, p. 1 sqq.) the Witham property of the order is described in detail but without any revelation of a town such as the Baldock entries in the same survey reveal; the only *Wulvesford* is a surname, but if the new town was named after a ford there would be nothing strange in an earlier personal name deriving from the same ford. It may therefore be conjectured that the new town had come into existence just before 1212. The earliest Newland reference in *P.N. Essex* (p. 302) is 1213.

The most impressive evidence, however, comes in a rental of Witham (undated but t. Henry III) which has the bold rubric *Novum Forum* followed by fifty-six names holding plots of which the unit size is a half-acre (1s. rent). The occupational names indicate crafts and trade, and the rental also has a rubric *Scoppae* under which seventeen shops are arrented (DL43/14/1). A deed of 1284 (*Essex Fines*, ii, p. 48) concerned a messuage and three roods in Witham held by John Page *de novo foro de Witham*. The *Novum Forum* links Wulvesford with New Alresford and other near-contemporary Newmarkets, while the roadside site distinct from an older settlement is very similar to Chelmsford, Boroughbridge and Grampound. (The Essex County Record Office has court rolls of the manors of Newland and Witham from 1280: D/DBw/M98. I express thanks to Mr. W. R. Powell for discussion of Wulvesford problems.)

GLOUCESTERSHIRE

The high score for boroughs in the two counties (Devon and Gloucestershire) that Prof. H. P. R. Finberg has investigated may arouse suspicions that high scores elsewhere only await his coming. His study of Gloucestershire has revealed extensive development of boroughs: though not as many as Devon, yet more than most English counties. Yet the proportion of unambiguous plantations in Gloucestershire is small.

The various origins of Gloucestershire towns are discussed in Prof. Finberg's essay (*Gloucestershire Studies* (1957), pp. 52–88). The county has refurbished Roman towns such as Gloucester and Cirencester; abbey-towns such as Winchcombe (where the abbey was founded in 798); and towns that were already in existence by Domesday Book, like Tewkesbury and Berkeley. In the following 150 years a number of villages were endowed with markets and fairs by their lords and many of these places began to be treated as boroughs for taxation purposes or to regard messuages as burgages, even where no formal charter survives. Newnham and Newent are in this category. It would be surprising if among all this borough-making there were not attempts to found towns *de novo*. The best attested are those of Chipping Sodbury and Moreton in Marsh, but some of the characteristic features of planted towns occur elsewhere and arouse suspicions. The earthwork within which Stow on the Wold is placed dates from the Iron Age; the Foss Way passes through the town; and the church of *Edwardstow* dates from the very early eleventh century. In 1107–08 Henry I made it a *port* and a weekly market centre, but the very small parish area (33 acres) suggests strongly that there had never been an area of field-land belonging to the community; that it was non-rural from its beginnings. The same situation, a tiny urban parish in open countryside, is encountered at Northleach where the church actually stands outside the town in the parish of Eastington. Northleach's 43 acres seem to be an undoubted town plantation (Finberg, *op. cit.*, p. 57). Even Berkeley, where Domesday Book locates *unum forum in quo manent xvii homines*, may have been a plantation; perhaps the rural settlement was at Hame and the market and the market-dwellers separately placed (John Smyth, *A Description of the Hundred of Berkeley* (ed. 1885), iii, p. 207; "In many old deeds it is called *nova villa*" (*ibid.*, p. 84)).

In two cases, Wotton under Edge and Chipping Campden, the boroughs that were added to older village settlements were physically as well as legally separate. This may explain the remoteness of Chipping Campden church from the High Street; it certainly explains the isolation of Wotton church and the contrast between the knot of narrow winding streets by the church and the broad parallel streets of the market town.

Without doubt there was a borough at Chipping Campden; in 1273 there were 75¾ burgages (Christopher Whitfield, *History of Chipping Campden* (1958), p. 29; P. C. Rushen, *History and Antiquities of Chipping Campden* (n.d. (1911)), pp. 5–8) and the burgages were in the High Street sector of the town. The manor house and most of the demesnes (and probably the church) stood in the tithing of Berrington (Rushen, *op. cit.*, plan, p. 104). A charter of 1180, confirmed in 1247 (Whitfield, *op. cit.*, p. 18), granted a fair to "the burgesses" but no borough charter survives (*Cal. Chart. Rolls*, i, p. 340). But Campden in 1086, even before it became entitled to be "Chipping", was the largest place in the north Cotswolds except Blockley (Whitfield, *op. cit.*, p. 15) and the sources are not available which would tell whether this population occupied what was to be later the borough or simply the precincts of the church and manor house.

The origins of the borough at Chipping Campden are conjectural but at Wotton there is a folk-memory which tells of the town being burned in the time of John and re-built on a different site in 1253. The actions of the benefactress, the widowed Lady Berkeley, in 1251 and 1252 are just those that accompanied the foundation of so many seigneurial boroughs. In 1251 she obtained licence for a market and fair, and in 1252 agreed that burgage plots should be laid out, each of one third of an acre, paying her a mere 1d. a year rent. Her son confirmed the grant in 1282: "and this", noted Smyth (*op. cit.*, i, p. 117) "was the time and this was the manner of the New Town's beginning and building where it now standeth, the backer part of which is still called the Old Town". The parish church, the manor house and the cottages near them were outside the bounds of the borough. The only difficulty in accepting this as the time and manner of the borough is a reference to half a burgage in a document which I. H. Jeayes (*Descriptive Catalogue of the Charters and Muniments . . . at Berkeley Castle* (1892), p. 44) ascribed to the reign of John (five of the six witnesses to this charter, however, recur as witnesses to an almost identical grant (p. 117) which Mr. Jeayes ascribes to the next reign). If this document is correctly dated, there was indeed a seigneurial borough before the market, fair and reconstruction of 1251–52, and a fire may have been the occasion of the revision. (I am indebted to Mr. E. S. Lindley's *Wotton Under Edge* (1962), and to Mr. Irvine Gray for local information.) There is a photocopy of a fine, large-scale plan of the borough in 1763 at the County Record Office, Gloucester. It shows the curving and irregular street above and behind the straight High Street . . . Smyth's "backer part". The market place is set off the High Street in the New Town.

Stroud was also a rapid late medieval development: the first mention of it is in 1221 (*La Strode*) and in 1304 it gained rights of baptism and virtual independence from the parish of Bisley in which it had been a chapelry. It was not taxed separately in 1334. But what seems to have been developing here was not a town but a straggle of industrial centres down the Stroudwater (E. M. Carus-Wilson, "Evidences of Industrial Growth on some Fifteenth Century Manors", *Ec. H.R.*, 2nd ser., xii (1959), pp. 190–205; Atkins, *Gloucestershire*, i, p. 714).

MORETON IN MARSH   Gloucestershire   sheet 144   42/205325
1228–46

The Foss Way on its way northward from Stow on the Wold drops down into the Evenlode valley, where it is crossed by the main road from Oxford to Worcester (now the A.44). Here on the Henmarsh, the heathy commons of the parish of Bourton on the Hill, the abbey of Westminster founded the town of Moreton. The documentary evidence is unusually explicit. In the "Westminster Domesday" is copied a quitclaim (f. 321d) from Sir Thomas Gulafre and his men of "Becchesore" (i.e. Batsford) giving up all their rights in the common of the "new vill of Moreton", for which the abbot gave them 4 acres of meadow at the edge of Batsford in Bourton Park and also two burgages in the new vill at 6d, a year rent. The original document also survives (Westminster Abbey Ms. no. 8192).

This surrender of common rights is undated, but there are two pieces of evidence which point to abbot Richard de Berkyng as the founder: at f. 376 of the Domesday is an assignment of rents from the new vill of Moreton "which was made in the abbot's lifetime", the money to be used to celebrate his anniversary by ringing of bells and chanting, with wine for the convent and bread for the poor. (On the previous folio is a similar assignment by abbot Richard for a smaller sum—therefore probably earlier than the above—also from "Moreton".) Despite a reference to Morton Folet (Worcs.) (= Castle Morton) it seems likely that the Moreton involved is Moreton Henmarsh, and the document states that the new town was made and erected by the abbot. A similar statement for Moreton (Glosc.) occurs in the cartulary (B.M., Cott. Claud. A VIII, f. 48): *edificavit villam novam Morton in Henmershe*

439

in comitatu Glouscestriae; and John Flete's *History of Westminster* (ed. J. A. Robinson (1909), p. 104) quite clearly separates the account of Morton Folet (lines 4–6) from that of Moreton Henmarsh (lines 29–33).

Now Richard was abbot from 1222–46, and the beginnings of the new borough can probably be linked with the charter of Henry III given in February 1228 for a Tuesday market at Moreton (W.A.Ms. no. 1541), although an earlier grant of 1226 appears on the Close Roll (*Rot. Lit. Claus.*, pp. 159 and 165). A fair at St. Matthewtide was granted in January 1253 (W.A.Ms., Domesday f. 323).

Unfortunately the manorial accounts for Bourton on the Hill which have survived (from 1273–74) do not include the new town rents; there was a sum from the courts, the view of frankpledge and the *portmote*, but the location is not specified and may well have been at Bourton itself. (An extent of t. Ed. III headed "Moreton" (W.A.Ms. no. 22211) is for Morton Folet not Moreton Henmarsh.)

The town consists of the houses (burgage plots) on either side of the Foss Way, here widened to make a long market place; the church lies distinctly away from this street to the south-east in what is locally known as Old Town (cp. Wotton under Edge) where the Domesday *Mortune* may have been. Until 1512 there were no burial rights in this chapelry. The Domesday Book entry is composite, and if equally divided would give 1¼ ploughteams at Moreton.

NORTHLEACH   Gloucestershire   sheet 144   42/113147
1227

The borough of Northleach is usually supposed to originate in a market and fair charter of 1227 granted (*Cal. Chart. Rolls*, i, p. 30) to the abbot of Gloucester; a borough was developed at the village of Lechlade about the same year (H. P. R. Finberg, *Gloucestershire Studies* (1957), p. 66), but other documents date the market to 1220 and 1222 (*Historia et Cartularium monasterii sancti Petri Gloucestriae*, ed. W. H. Hart (Roll Series, 1867), i, pp. 26 and 103). About 1235 Northleach and Lechlade paid 8s. and 4s. respectively in order that offences should be tried in borough courts in place of Hundred courts. In an extent of 1266–67 Northleach had about eighty burgages; there were also *placeae* and stalls (*ibid.*, iii, pp. 176 sqq.). The borough area, the *intrinsecus* of the tax-lists (e.g. 1327: E79/113/5 m. 6d), comprised only 43 acres. The foreign or *forinsecus* included Eastington (*Calendar of Charters, Rolls etc. of the Muniment Room at Sherborne House*, (1900), pp. 58–63 and 171–183). There is a grant of half a burgage in Northleach in 1398 among these deeds, now in the County Record Office (D678).

The borough area comprises two narrow belts of land on either side of the road that is now the A.40 (London–Gloucester) and clearly represents the outline of burgage plots. The triangular market place and the church lie on the south side of the road. Like Stow on the Wold, the settlement did not lie along the Foss Way but on the east-west road crossing it.

But the case of Northleach is not without its problems. If there was no settlement at Northleach before the market and borough, where was the church of Northleach of 1100? (*Hist. et Cart. Glouc.*, ii, p. 40) and where were the 38 *manentes in Northleach* in the grant to Gloucester abbey of Ethelmund *subregulus*, even earlier? (*ibid.*, i, p. 4). At Eastington?

SODBURY, CHIPPING   Gloucestershire   sheet 156   31/727823
1218

The borough consisted of 107 acres completely surrounded by the mother parish of Old Sodbury, the church of which stands 2 miles east of Chipping Sodbury hard under the Cotswold scarp. The main road from London and the east descends the scarp, and a double right-angled bend shows where it has been diverted into the market place of the new town, distinguished from the old settlement by being "Chipping" (cheap = market; *cp.* Chipping (Herts.)). The borough is simply a single street (Rouncival Street leading into High Street) with the river Frome marking the southern limit of the burgage plots. The old course of the road before the town was laid out may be indicated by Slough Lane and Hoe Lane (F. F. Fox, *The History of Chipping Sodbury* (1907, map insert). The market street is very wide and it narrows at the limits of the borough. The church was a chapel of ease to Old Sodbury (Rudder, *Gloucestershire*, p. 672). In 1779, when Rudder was writing, the market was decayed. It had been granted to William le Gras (Crassus) in 1218 (*Rot. Lit. Claus.*, i, p. 368) and was confirmed in 1227 (*Cal. Chart. Rolls*, i, p. 43) together with an annual fair of eight days' duration. This grant of 1218 may date the foundation of the town but the earliest specific reference to a borough at Sodbury is in 1232 when William le Gras gave a burgage to St. Wulstan's hospital, Worcester. (The charter of 1227 in *Ballard and Tait*, p. xxvii, is not a borough charter but a market charter.) In 1221, however, the town was separately represented at the Assize, and 1218 remains the most likely foundation date.

In 1306 there were 176 burgages and in 1363 about 190 (C133/129 and C135/177/12). The rents of 1295 (C133/77/3) were £9 11s. 7d. so that there may then have been nearly two hundred burgages.

HAMPSHIRE

Hampshire was an old-settled part of England with as many boroughs as Gloucestershire, and it contained Winchester, the capital of the Anglo-Saxon kingdom. Here, if anywhere, it might seem that there would be little room for plantations. Yet half the county's twenty-two medieval towns were planted; three in the Isle of Wight and eight on the mainland.

The old-established position of Winchester may be thought to explain its exceptionally high tax assessments: £51 10s. 4d. in 1334 when Portsmouth, the wealthiest of the plantations, paid only £12 12s. 2d. Southampton was assessed at a sum only a little less—£51 2s. 4d.—and the medieval town has some elements of plantation in it. There is a grid plan within the walls, and a clear separation from an earlier Saxon site, *Hamwih* (or *Hamwic*). The relation of the Norman town to the *burh* of Hamtun is still uncertain. Full reports of the archaeological explorations have not yet been published: (see J. B. Morgan and P. Peberdy, eds., *Collected Essays on Southampton*

(1958), pp. 1–23, and plan, endpaper; F. J. Monkhouse, ed., *A Survey of Southampton and its Region* (1964), pp. 205–207 (by L. A. Burgess); and L. A. Burgess, *The Origins of Southampton* (Univ. of Leics., Dept. of Eng. Local Hist. Occ. Papers XVI, 1964).

The plantations of the bishops of Winchester in this area have been considered comparatively in M. W. Beresford, "The Six New Towns of the Bishops of Winchester, 1200–55", *Med. Archaeol.*, iii (1959), pp. 187–215. Four of these episcopal plantations lay in Hampshire.

It will be noted that seven of the county's eleven plantations were sea- or river-ports. Portsmouth was intended to be a naval port as well as a rival to Southampton for Solent trade; by 1334, Lymington's tax assessment was half that of Portsmouth, and the size of New Alresford's assessment shows that the head of a river navigation was also a well-judged centre for commerce.

The range of years of plantation is remarkably narrow. There was no plantation before 1170 nor after 1256. Half of the plantations occurred in the first two decades of the thirteenth century.

ALRESFORD, NEW   Hampshire   sheet 168   41/588328
1200

Old Alresford is a large parish, long and narrow, now wholly on the north of the river Alre. New Alresford is a much smaller parish of 693 acres on the south bank of the river and has clearly been taken from the mother parish. Bishop Godfrey (1189–1204) is credited with the construction of a large artificial pond, which still remains, in order to improve the navigation of the upper Itchen and the Alre as far as Bishop's Sutton, 2 miles east of New Alresford, where there was an episcopal residence.

Linked with the improvement of the navigation was a scheme to create a market town on the south bank of the river. In 1200 a charter was granted for a Thursday market and in 1202 for a fair. A chronicle describes the creation of a market place with a market hall at one end and a communal oven at the other end, partnered by a house for sifting flour from bran, a boulting house. The name of this town according to the chronicler was *Novum Forum*, "new market".

It was this new market from which the first surviving episcopal account roll of 1208–9 shows £18 7s. 8d. worth of rents but the reeve still accounted for these as part of (Old) Alresford. In the next surviving roll, that of 1210–11 (Eccles. 2/159270B), the reeve is caught hesitating. On the eleventh membrane he entered *Forum de Alresford* with forty-five houses each paying 2s. rent and four more newly arrented. There were also 477 acres of agricultural land reckoned part of the town, paying £14 18s. 4d. in rent. But there were signs of the shift in emphasis, apart from the market: 56s. 8d. was spent on making a new fulling-mill pond, while an old mill was pulled down and its pond filled in. These entries made, they were then crossed out and a small piece of parchment stitched to membrane nine. On it the same details were copied in smaller writing but the heading was significantly different. It now read: *de Burgo*, and subsequent rolls preserved the dignity. In 1236 New Alresford was separately represented by a jury at the Assize (JI/1/775 m. 19): wine was being sold at unlawful rates and measures in the town.

442

Thirteen years later the town was still growing: the rents had increased from 90s. to 31 9s.; the fuller's house and the bishop's house were empty but one new plot was taken up; the market tolls were yielding 66s. 8d. (Eccles. 2/159278 m. 1).

The site of the new plantation was probably determined by the limit of navigation and the too remote position of Old Alresford, nearly half a mile from the water. In 1269 the bishops of Winchester and Exeter joined Henry III in providing land for the construction of a road eastwards from New Alresford to Alton (*Cal. Chart. Rolls*, ii, pp. 122–123). In the fourteenth century Alresford was one of the ten great wool markets of the kingdom, a collecting centre for the hill country north-east of Winchester and Southampton.

BEAULIEU   Hampshire   sheet 180   41/386022
1204–27

The Cistercian abbey was founded by King John in 1204 on the east bank of a shallow river, 4 miles from the sea and surrounded by the New Forest. The situation fitted the remoteness prescribed by the Cistercian rule, and the rapid development of a lay settlement over the river so near the abbey was unusual in England; in France, also, the *bastides* in which the Cistercians were partners were usually not set at the abbey gate. At Beaulieu the little town developed on the west bank of the river facing the abbey; the letter if not the spirit of the Rule was obeyed. The foundation of the parish church in Beaulieu in 1227 sets a limiting date to the settlement.

LYMINGTON, NEW   Hampshire   sheet 180   40/324955
1184–1216

The manor of Lymington in Boldre parish was granted by Henry I to Richard de Redvers; it lay on the west side of the narrow estuary of the Lymington river and was a small Solent port facing Yarmouth (I.O.W.), another Redvers borough, and set between Southampton and a third Redvers borough at Christchurch. The principal economic asset, however, was the salterns at the estuary mouth (SC6/984/3) and the idea of developing a borough on the manor seems to have been William de Redvers'. His charter (c. 1184–1216) is known only by the confirmation issued by Baldwin de Insula which may date from 1256. In 1257 Baldwin obtained a fair (*Cal. Chart. Rolls*, i, p. 470), and a charter of 1271 by Isabella de Fortibus speaks of her brother's extension of the borough (E142/85).

This charter speaks of rents arising both from the old borough and from the extension (*tam de veteri burgo predicto quam de incremento eiusdem burgi*). The *incrementum* of the borough, it is also stated, was made by Isabella's brother, Baldwin, *ex parte boreali ecclesie de Lemington*. This statement is difficult to interpret since all the settlement in Lymington is alined east and west along the road that passes the church: north of the church there was nothing, even in the first Ordnance plans. The town church was a mere chapelry of Boldre (Dugdale, *Monasticon*, vi, p. 304) and so remained until 1870. See also E. King, *Old Times Revisited* (1879), p. 4.

The topography of modern Lymington ought to show a medieval village and burghal additions; the original centre, one would expect, lay near the church; and the burghal areas would then be: (i) the broad High Street running down from the church to the river and flanked by a back lane on either side: this would seem to be the mid-thirteenth-century extension; (ii) the group of streets at right angles to the High Street that lie alongside the river edge: this would seem to be the first borough. Mr. A. T. Lloyd kindly tells me that on a map of c. 1840 the west end of the church is located in "Old Lymington".

An extent (C132/47/24, undated in *Cal. I.P.M.*, i, p. 312) is probably that missing from the file of Baldwin de Insula in 1263 (*ibid.*, p. 175: C132/47/29/2). It comprises a rental of Lymington *burgus* with eighty-eight *placeae* and another of *Vetus* Lymington with sixty-nine entries.

An extent of the borough of New Lymington in 1300 (E142/85/3) lists 61 burgages followed by 36½ "new burgages". (See also SC6/984/3–5.) An extent of Old Lymington in the same year shows that it was a settlement with granaries on the beach and many salt-works (SC12/14/56).

NEWPORT   Hampshire (I.O.W.)   sheet 180   40/500890
1177–84

Newport, now the capital of the Island, stands 4½ miles from the sea in the estuary of the Medina where the Downs begin to close in on the river. The first borough charter was granted by Richard de Redvers II between 1177 and 1184, and its founder named it simply *novus burgus meus de Medina* (*Ballard*, pp. 252–253). The burgages were rented at 1s. a plot per year. The town church which stands in the grid near the market place cannot be earlier than 1172 for it was dedicated to St. Thomas of Canterbury; the monks of Carisbrooke Priory contracted with William de Vernon (d. 1216) to serve this church but it was not a parish church independent of Carisbrooke until 1858. De Vernon's charter describes the church as being *in novo burgo* (BM. Eg. Ms. 3667 f. 17d); in 1235 at the Assize it was called *novus burgus de Insula* (JI/1/775 m. 23) and in an extent of 1263 (C132/29/2 m. 23) 175 tenements are listed. The rents paid between 1224 and 1306 show that the town was worth about £27 a year to its lord (E364/1 mm. 1, 2 and 3d; SC6/984/1; E372/147 mm. 40–42; SC6/985/4; E372/91). The very low taxpaying population of fifty-six in 1379 may be due to the raids of 1378 (*Cal. Inq. Misc. 1337–88*, pp. 128 and 206) as much as to the Black Death and tax evasion.

"The three principal streets extend from east to west and are crossed at right angles by three others", reported Sir Richard Worsley in his *History of the Isle of Wight* (1781, p. 154).

The plan of the town in 1611 which forms an inset to John Speed's map of the Island, shows five parallel streets running east to west and two from north to south. The grid is broken in the north-east corner by a broad street of market width which runs down to the quay which had to be placed at the north-east corner where the Medina touches the borough. There is an encroached-upon quarter for the church and market place; and the dependent status of the church is shown by the absence of a graveyard. The bounds of the town on the east are the narrow Medina and on the north a small tributary.

NEWTOWN (in Burghclere)   Hampshire   sheet 168   41/478636
1218

This borough on the heaths of north Hampshire has disappeared as thoroughly as if the seas had arisen to overwhelm it.   The precise site is revealed only by a map of 1606 showing "Newtowne Street", a broad market street running up from the river-crossing at Sandleford before opening into the Heath (original plan at Corpus Christi College, Oxford, reproduced by O.S. in their collection of cadastral maps: A.O. 331B).   Houses still existed in 1593 and 1614 (J. N. Dalton, *Manuscripts in St. George's Chapel, Windsor* (1957), p. 316).

The parish bounds show clearly that the new town was cut out of Burghclere and the site was on the very edge of the county where the main road from Winchester to Newbury crossed the Enborne at the old ford.   Sandleford Priory lay across the stream, and in some account rolls of the founding bishops the town was called *nova villa de Sandelford* (e.g. Eccles., 2/159457) and it was sometimes called *Novus burgus de Alta Clera* because the bishop's palace was in Highclere.   The two Cleres were originally one parish (*V.C.H.*, iv, p. 294, and Eccles., 2/159270A).

The foundation of the town can be precisely dated.   The account roll of 1217–18 had no reference to anything urban and the only Sandleford reference is to a mill (Eccles., 2/159274) but in the roll of 1218–19 (159275) there is a bold heading *Novus Burgus* and then the names of the fifty-two burgesses who took up the sixty-seven plots at 1s. a year rent.   One held five, two held three, seven held two, and forty-two held one plot each.   The prior of Sandleford had invested in three.   In 1219–20 two more newcomers appeared in the accounts and more in that for 1220–21 (159276–7).   In 1225–26 the bishop built himself a house in the town and provided a chapel (159278–9).   By 1257 (159292 m. 27d) the burgages approached 130 and in 1283–84 may have reached 140 (159309).

As at the bishop's other Newtown the foundation of the borough was buttressed by a market charter from the king (*Rot. Lit. Claus.*, i (1883), p. 363: May 1218).

NEWTOWN (Francheville)   Hampshire (I.O.W.)   sheet 180   40/422907
1255–56

A large estate of 30 hides in the Isle of Wight was given to the church at Winchester by Egbert, king of Wessex, in 826.   It was centred on Calbourne on the north slopes of the Downs, and Domesday Book shows this manor still owned by Winchester. The bishop built a hall at Swainston within this manor and in the account roll of 1253–54 Swainston appears as a normal rural manor with the main source of income for the bishop still agricultural produce and rents (Eccles. 2/159291B).   In the next year's roll there is a short account for work at a house "in the new borough of Francheville" and in the same account the reeve is allowed 20s. for the missing rent of *Stretleya*, land *tractata in burgo* (159296 m. 5d).   Two Stretley tenants continued to hold their old houses adjoining the Haven and the new town seems to have been planted around them (159292 m. 9d).   Not all the seventy-three plots in the new borough were retained by their first tenants: seven were vacant in 1282–83–84 (159305–9) but after Edward I's new charter of 1285 the number of occupied plots passed the seventy mark (E372/147 mm. 27 and 40; SC11/579; BM. Add. Ms. 6166; C145/62/1).

30   445

The bishop himself issued a charter to the town (as "the borough of Swainston") in 1256, and in that year the account roll has the bold rubric *Francheville* for the rents from the town; a market and fair were secured from the king. The fairs are held at the feast of St. Mary Magdalen, the patron saint of the church that was built in the town but dependent on the mother church of Calbourne.

The king's role in the foundation had been purely that of a benevolent onlooker but the success of the town drew Edward I's attention to it, and bishop John of Pontoise was forced to relinquish the valuable manor in 1284 and pay a fine to retain his other temporalities. The burghal rights were worth about £29 a year to their owner at this time and in 1334 Swainston was taxed to a sum almost that of Portsmouth: (Eccles. 2/159291A–B; E372/147 m. 40; SC6/985/4; BM. Harl. Roll CC/21; *Cal. Chart. Rolls*, i, p. 274). From October 27, 1285 Edward resided in the Hall at Swainston for ten days and on the last day of his stay confirmed the foundation charter of Newtown. By this the burgesses acquired the liberties of the bishop's boroughs of Taunton, Witney, Alresford and Farnham (*Cal. Chart. Rolls*, i, p. 324).

In his paper, "The Ancient Borough of Newtown" (*Proc. Hants. Field Club*, ii (1890–93), pp. 89–109), A. H. Estcourt reproduced a plan of the decaying borough made in 1768 by James Mallett. He also mentioned a second plan, of Swainston, made in 1636. Mallett's plan shows the borough plots along both sides of High Street and on the north side of Gold Street, which was the broader of the two. Broad Street began at the stone bridge over the creek and formed the stem of a T, the cross-piece being formed by the other two streets. In the middle of Broad Street stood the Town Hall. The ruins of St. Mary's chapel were also indicated, together with twelve buildings which may all have been houses. At least forty-two vacant plots were shown together with the vestiges of holdings in a common field. To the north of the town was a large marsh.

At the I.O.W. Record Office the Swainston estate documents include a rental of 1574 (SW 1877) with *placeae*; rentals of 1666, 1701 and 1763 (SW 1047) with the tenements always distinguished by the surnames of forty-nine past burgesses (e.g. Slatford, Bruers, Dores, Bides); and a plan of burgages and lands dated 1818 (SW 1032). It seems to be based on the plan of 1768. There is a plan of 1793 in MR/489.

O. G. S. Crawford took an air photograph of the decayed borough in 1924 (*Wessex from the Air* (1928), p. 27) and a more recent photograph by Dr. St. Joseph is in the Cambridge Air Photograph Collection, no. HL67.

OVERTON   Hampshire   sheet 168   41/526497
1217–18

St. Mary's church, the rectory, Court House and Court Farm all lie on the north bank of the river Test about one mile west of its source. On the south bank there is a rectangular grid of streets which make up modern Overton, and from the bishop's account roll it is clear that a borough was laid out here in the fields of a village which probably lay near the church on the north bank.

The roll for 1213–14 shows Overton bringing in the usual type of rural rent, a

446

gabulum assisum of £19 2s. (Eccles. 2/159272 m. 1). The next surviving roll (1215–16) is defective, but in the roll of 1217–18 Overton emerges as possessing a borough in addition to a village (Eccles. 2/159274 m. 10). In the same year a market charter was granted (*Rot. Lit. Claus.*, i (1833), p. 363; *V.C.H., Hants.*, iv, p. 210) and a fair by 1246 (*Cal. Chart. Rolls, 1226–57*, p. 312). The first roll with a completely legible entry for Overton is that of 1218–19 (Eccles. 2/159275 m. 3d) where twenty-two burgages are listed, each paying 2s. a year rent. The original twenty-two burgage plots were held by only fourteen individuals, for one held three plots, and five other people two each. For permission to have a burgage 6s. 8d. was paid by a villein. Four and a half more *placeae* were taken up the next year (Eccles. 2/159275 m. 7). By 1223–1224 there were at least forty plots occupied. Meanwhile the reeve of the manor proper was allowed his 11s. rebate for the missing rents from the lands taken into the borough (159278 m. 6). The cash revenue from the village in 1208–09 was £43; in 1232–33 and 1235–36 it had passed £100.

There is a remarkable plan of 1615 in BM. Maps 188e2(3) (from Langdon Plans, ii, 25 and 28, at Corpus Christi College, Oxford; A.O. negative 328). Burgage plots were each about 3 roods in area. The main centre was the *Streete* leading to Winchester that ran south from the present main road. No other road, even the main east–west road, had continuous built-up frontages. There is good open-field detail on the plan but there was already no village near the church.

PETERSFIELD   Hampshire   sheet 181   41/749233
1182–3

A charter was granted to this borough by the countess of Gloucester between 1183 and 1197 (*V.C.H.*, iii, p. 113) giving the liberties and customs of Winchester to "my burgesses of Petersfield who have built and remain there and to those who shall build". This is near the language of foundation plans and building plots. The town is named after its church, St. Peter's, and was not mentioned in Domesday Book. It lay in the Rother gap at the north end of the parish of Buriton and within Mapledurham manor, the centre of which was also in Buriton. The borough bounds form a small enclave in Buriton, and may have been cut from Buriton's common. Buriton village lies 3 miles south of Petersfield under the scarp of the downs. The church was built or enlarged in 1170–80; it stands on the south side of the market square. By what may be no more than a coincidence, the first recorded mention of Petersfield is in the Pipe Roll of 1182, as a *villata*: *P.R.S.*, xxxi, p. 144.

The sums paid in borough rents a century later suggest that there were from 120–140 burgages (C133/77/3; C133/129; C134/42; C135/81/15; C135/230). The borough centre lies just off the London to Portsmouth road. (Portsmouth, of course, is also a late twelfth-century foundation; and Haslemere on the same road has symptoms of late foundation.)

PORTSMOUTH   Hampshire   sheet 181   41/635995
1194

Like Weymouth, Liverpool, and other towns with names embodying the names of estuaries, there was a "Portsmouth" before there was a town. The original "Portsmouth" was simply the anchorage at the mouth of the estuary of the Wallington river, an estuary with the Roman and early medieval town of Portchester at its northern edge hard under the line of the downs. This estuary, now called Portsmouth Harbour, was used particularly for naval and military expeditions while Southampton remained the unrivalled commercial port of the Solent. Richard I, for example, the future founder of the new town, landed here when he arrived back in England in 1189 and the foundation charter of 1194 was granted during a week's stay at Portsmouth on the eve of what was to be his final departure from England. Richard I's project of 1194 was for a civil settlement although a dock was built for the royal galleys (*V.C.H.*, iii, p. 186). As at his French foundations of St. Rémy de la Haye and Petit Andelys there are later law-suits to reveal what happened: *quando placuit domino regi Ricardo edificare villam de Portesmue ipse commisit placeas eiusdem ville pluribus hominibus* (*Curia Regis Rolls*, vi, p. 305). The plot at issue in this lawsuit of 1212 had not been built upon by its first assignee; the sheriff begged it from the king as a gift, leaving it to a servant to develop while he went off to the wars in Poitou. The Pipe Roll shows that houses were built for the king's use, including a *curia* (*Pipe Roll Soc.*, n.s. v, pp. 6, 7, 10 and 176; vi, p. 36; vii, p. 198; viii, p. 24; ix, p. 24), and by 1230 work was in progress on a castle tower (iv, p. 200). A grant of land was also made for the chapel of St. Thomas à Becket (now the Cathedral) in the High Street. The mother parish seems to have been St. Mary's, Kingston, and Kingston was the manor in which the town was planted (*V.C.H.*, iii, pp. 172–202). A grant of land for the chapel as early as 1180 is mentioned (*ibid.*, p. 197) but with no reference to support the statement.

The site of the new town lay on the south-west corner of Portsea Island facing deep water and at the very entrance of the estuary, available for large ships that could not reach Portchester: in a sense, it presaged the replacement of Hedon by Kingston upon Hull. The parallel streets of the walled town are now rather submerged in the extra-mural development of modern Portsmouth, but its appearance is well caught in the Elizabethan plan (reproduced in *V.C.H.*, iii, p. 186) and survives in the first edition of the O.S. plans. The mother settlement of Kingston has been absorbed in the growth of the dockyard town of Portsea to the north, and of modern Portsmouth around the railway station to the north east.

Richard I's foundation charter (Rymer, *Foedera*, i, p. 63) included a market and fair. The burgesses were given the privileges of Winchester and Oxford, and the first payments from the burgesses appear on the Pipe Roll of Michaelmas 1194, five months after the charter (*P.R.S.*, n.s. v, p. 6); in 1195 there was a substantial sum for pontage and for rents of *placeae* let for building, *de gersumis placearum que liberate sunt ad edificandum* (*ibid.*, vi, p. 36). In 1197 a farmed rent began to be paid, but difficulties were arising with the old-established port of Southampton which saw its customs revenue threatened by traffic at the new port and town, and in 1199 John's charter to Southampton (*Cartae Antiquae* (P.R.S., n.s. xvii), p. 31) gave the men of Southampton the farm of their own vill "*cum portu de Portesmue*", and they paid the first farm of £200 in 1200 (*ibid.*, xii, p. 206). But Portsmouth succeeded in limiting this grant to the waters of the port or estuary and not to the customs paid within the new town. In 1201 the men of Portsmouth paid John ten marks for confirming their liberties as granted by his brother, and entries then begin on the Pipe Roll for the separate farm of Portsmouth (*ibid.*, xii, pp. 195 and 206; xiv, pp. 107 and 113; xv, pp. 72 and 76, etc.). In 1230 the farm was raised from £18 to £20 (*Cal. Chart. Rolls*, i, p. 106) and John's charter confirmed (*P.R.S.*, n.s. iv, p. 196). A final settlement of the dispute with Southampton was made in 1239 (*Ballard*, pp. lxxvii–viii) and Portsmouth remained a "member" of the port of Southampton until the eighteenth century; the greater customs were collected at Southampton leaving only pontage and the petty customs for Portsmouth.

STOCKBRIDGE   Hampshire   sheet 168   41/355351
c. 1200

This plantation, in the north west corner of King's Somborne parish, occupied a remarkable position. Its burgage plots lay on either side of the straight causeway-like section of the Winchester to Salisbury road (now the A.30) where it crossed the floor of the Test valley. The original name of the borough was simply the *Strete*, for there were no other limbs to this road. It might better have been called the *Bridges*, for the Test divides into seven shallow streams, each of which is crossed by its own bridge; the divided streams are utilised as the boundaries of many of the burgage plots and there is a Venetian air about the back gardens, as if a rise of a foot in the level of the river would drown the whole project.

The main road, broad enough to make a market place of itself, had sixty-four burgage plots by 1264 (C132/21/12 m. 11) and ninety-seven in 1283 (C133/35/4); there were about the same number in 1361 (C135/160/5; DL29/682/11037); a survey of 1552 counted sixty-three (DL42/108 f. 15) and later in the century the borough began to return members of Parliament, a right it lost at the Reform Act: in 1591 there were 74½ burgages (DL42/116). In the latter survey the place-name *Streete* survives; the borough appears under this name in the 1332 taxation (E179/242/15a) but as "Stockbridge *burgus*" in the Assize Roll of 1256 (JI/1/778 mm. 23 and 57) and as "Stockbridge" in a transfer of burgages in 1242 (CP25(1)203/7 no. 288). When did the borough originate? In 1152 a charter was granted from *Stokbrigge* ford (*Sarum Charters* (Rolls Series), p. 23), but this merely attests a ford name earlier than those in *Ekwall*, p. 444. Richard I made a grant of a market *apud le Strete* in King's Somborne which was confirmed in 1200 (C53/2 m. 21); Richard also granted the manor to William Briwere; in 1221 Briwere obtained a grant of a fair to be held at the feast of St. Peter, the patron saint of the chapelry of Somborne that was situated in the town (C54/24 m. 8). If the distinction is of significance, a transfer of house property in 1226 (CP25(1)203/5) refers to messuages and not burgages, but a deed of 1233–37 mentions burgages (L. C. Loyd and D. M. Stenton, eds., *Sir Christopher Hatton's Book of Seals*, (1950), p. 325).

YARMOUTH   Hampshire (I.O.W.)   sheet 180   40/354897
c. 1170

This is the westernmost of the Solent ports of the Island. The mudflats which surround it give it even today an isolated appearance, accentuated by its regular street plan and the line of its walls. It occupies only 58 acres with no field-land for the burgesses (cp. Hedon, New Malton). It was chartered as a borough (c. 1170) by the 3rd earl of Devon (*cp.* Newport, Lymington) and was confirmed by Edward III (*Ballard*, App. p. 254; Worsley, *History of I.O.W.* (1781), appendices 41 and 45), and it is probable that the town received its present rectilinear form then. (The castle dates from the invasion scare of 1543–47 and is now a hotel: *V.C.H.*, v, p. 286). It has four gates called The Quay, Inner Town, Outer Town and Hither. There was a Monday market and a fair at St. James-tide. The church was originally at the east end of the town but was burned by the French in the raids of 1378 and rebuilt on the present site; it was again in ruins in 1543 and there were many Elizabethan complaints of decay. In 1559 it was said that there were scarcely a dozen houses left inhabited (SP12/7/58–9): the scapegoat was the ingrossing of trade by the port of Southampton. The town may not have recovered much from the damage of 1378; in 1380 it was let off its taxes (*Cal. Inq. Misc.*, iii, pp. 128 and 206). Only thirty-five tax-payers were assessed to the poll tax of 1379, but even the 1334 quota (19s.) was small. Perhaps Edward I, who acquired the property together with Newport on Isabella de Fortibus' death, thought that yet another rival to his borough of Newtown did not need encouragement. In 1300 a very full extent of the town lists 181 burgage plots held by 141 separate proprietors at an average rent of 6d. a plot (average size about one-third acre) (SC11/579). (See also SC6/984/1, 3 and 10; 985/4; E372/147 m. 40; BM Add. Ms. 6166 f. 153). There is an air photograph of the town in *Beresford and St. Joseph*, p. 193.

HEREFORDSHIRE

This is a county where the evidence is neither explicit nor easy to elucidate. In Domesday Book, for example, Wigmore castle is reported as having been built on the waste of *Merestun*, and a borough had been created with perhaps 140 burgages: but a Saxon owner of *Wighemore* manor is named, and the borough may have been no more than the village transformed to meet the needs of the castle. Yet the village is nearly half a mile from the castle: was there an early borough in the castle-bailey, as at so many border castles?; what was the relation of this Domesday borough to a Saxon *burh* of *Wigingamere*?

Clifford had 16 burgesses in 1086 but twice as many agricultural tenants: there seems a question of a plantation here. Ewias Harold, later to be a borough, had two messuages *in castello* in 1086 and these may have been the beginnings of the borough, but here again the village and castle are 400 yards apart on opposite sides of the valley, and the borough of the thirteenth-century surveys (A. T. Bannister, *History of Ewias Harold* (1902), pp. 37 and 113–122) would seem to be the modern village. Huntington, another medieval borough, seems also to be a case of a border castle stimulating burghal development (C132/34/8). Other places, such as Stapleton, a very petty borough, also depended on a castle; and Stapleton does not appear as such in Domesday Book: but the name does not sound like that of a new settlement. Weobley has a distinct separation between the castle-gate settlement and the church, which may result from the De Lacies' elevation of the village to a borough c. 1140. Mr. F. Noble also suggests Dorstone (314417). (For Hay see Brecknockshire in the Welsh List below.)

KINGTON   Herefordshire   sheet 129   32/294567
by 1267

The compact town of Kington is centred on the T-junction of High Street, Bridge Street and Duke Street. A plan of the town will be found in *R.C.H.M. Herefords.*, iii, p. 92. The castle and parish church are quite separate from the town, and it is probable that twelfth- and thirteenth-century Kington is represented by these former features, and that the bridge-head settlement is the "New Kington", so called in a document of 1267 (C132/34/8) when it was distinct from Kington *burgus*: the latter may be represented by the area near the church and castle at old Kington. Mr. F. Noble suggests that the name "Kington in the Fields" for New Kington implies that the town was laid out over former open fields: note Furlong Lane on the west of the grid. The castle was in royal hands from 1172 to 1203.

LONGTOWN (or Ewias Lacy)   Herefordshire   sheet 142   23/322291
by 1234

The earthworks and the castle occupy a commanding position on the eastern slopes of the Black Mountains near the present border of Herefordshire and Monmouthshire. Like Ewias Harold a little further east, this was an early Norman border castle. Domesday Book accounts for a small population here (*V.C.H.*, i, pp. 328–329) but nothing "in the time of Edward the Confessor". The borough chapel depended on the older settlement of Clodock. This borough church and the old town street adjoining it lie just outside the earthworks of the castle defences. A burgage is mentioned c. 1234 (Duncumb, *Herefordshire*, ii, p. 282), tolls of the borough in 1271 (C132/39/20), and by 1310 (C134/14/19) there were reckoned to be 100 burgages here. The town seems in every sense to go with the castle, but its date is uncertain: perhaps it accompanied the "new castle" of the 1186 Pipe Roll. There is a manuscript plan of 1718 in B.M. Maps, 2820(3).

RICHARD'S CASTLE   Herefordshire   sheet 129   32/484703
1066–86

Fifty-one persons were recorded in 1086 as within the *castellaria* of Auretone Castle; another twenty-three were in the castle itself. The *castellaria* may have been the settlement now known as Richard's Castle. There were 103 burgages in Richard's Castle in 1304 (C133/113/2) but no charter has been traced (Eyton, *Shropshire*, v, p. 225). The parish church, with a Norman chancel and nave, adjoins the castle (*R.C.H.M., Herefords.*, iii, p. 170). East of the churchyard there is a village green which probably represents the former market place, and in a field east of this are the footings of a town wall with at least one semicircular tower clearly marked. The line of this wall joins the castle defences at the north corner of the churchyard. Its course on the south, where there is a stream in a deep valley, is clearly defined. (Mr. F. Noble has kindly visited the site for this report. In 1962–64 excavations by Dr. M. W. Thompson included an examination of part of the town wall.)

HERTFORDSHIRE

The site of one Hertfordshire plantation, Buntingford, was described in 1367 as being "where there is common passage of magnates and people of the realm from north to south" (*Cal. Chart. Rolls*, v, p. 209), and this inland county within a day's journey from London brings us again to a succession of plantations along important radial roads. On one of these, a little north of the site where Buntingford was later to be planted, there was an interesting development in 1252 at a place that was known in 1322 as *New Cheping* (SC6/1147/9 m. 7). It is not quite clear whether the market and fair obtained by Bertram de Crioll (*Cal. Chart. Rolls*, i, p. 404) were intended to serve a trading post in open country or whether a permanent settlement was intended. If any settlement did occur it was smothered in favour of the market at Buntingford in 1360 (*Cal. Chart. Rolls*, v, p. 166) and Chipping is now merely the name of a few cottages, of no particular antiquity, on the Ermine Street. There seems to have been active rivalry between local landowners, for, six years after the charter to Chipping, the village of Buckland (the mother parish) obtained a market charter: perhaps the stimulus was the successful development at Royston a few miles further north on the same road. Stevenage may also have moved its site, perhaps with the market and fair granted in 1281 (*V.C.H.*, iii, p. 140).

BALDOCK   Hertfordshire   sheet 147   52/245340
1148–85

The northern boundary of the Domesday vills of Weston and Clothall was formed by the Icknield Street which followed the foot of the Chiltern scarp. At the junction of the two parishes the Icknield Street was crossed by an important road, Roman in origin, from London to the north (now the A.1) and for a short distance this latter road formed the division between Weston and Clothall.

    In the decade before his death in 1148, Gilbert de Clare, first earl of Pembroke, gave ten librates of land in Weston to the order of the Knights Templar, and the survey of their possessions made in 1185 shows that a town had been founded on this land *construxerunt quendam burgum qui dicitur Baudoc*; *Baudoc* is a corruption of Baghdad. When a later earl of Pembroke confirmed his ancestor's grant (c. 1205–19) he called the town of Baldock a borough (Dugdale, *Monasticon* vi, p. 820). In 1189 Richard I granted it the confirmation of a market first given "in the time of Henry II" (i.e. before 1189).

    The Templars provided a church for the new town, Weston being nearly 4 miles away. The alinement of roads shows that the London road has been diverted from its original course to bring it into the market place and past the church. The Icknield Way may also have been diverted, for it also leads straight to the church. There was thus a broad market on both the east and south of the church which formed the focal point of the town's streets. In the survey of 1185 the Templars owned "one stall (*seudam*) in the Market Place", but tenants paid rent for six others. The same survey lists smithies, and among the Templars' tenants were a blacksmith who made an iron ox-yoke each year, an ironmonger, a tailor, a shoemaker, a tanner, a mason, a cook, a carter, a mercer, a weaver, a saddler, a goldsmith, a merchant and a vintner: 122 tenants were crowded on 150 acres.

The project, which in 1185 can hardly have been more than a generation old, had certainly proved successful; it has affinities with the foundation of Royston 10 miles further east on another crossing of the Icknield Street with a north–south main road. It is interesting to compare the situation at Baldock in 1185 with that at the old centre of population at Weston; Weston appears as an ordinary rural manor with the Templars owning two carucates of demesne and exacting labour services from the villagers who were their tenants on two other carucates.

After the suppression of the Templars the town passed to the Knights of St. John of Jerusalem (E358/18 m. 50; *1338 Malta Return*, ed. L. B. Larking and J. M. Kemble (Camden Society (1855)), p. 172).

BARNET, CHIPPING   Hertfordshire   sheet 160 51/245966
c. 1199

At the north end of the single street which made up the original Barnet the two main roads to the north (now the A.1 and the A.6) diverge. The district which became Chipping Barnet was simply forest (*V.C.H.*, ii, pp. 329–337) until on this important route through the Chilterns the abbot of St. Albans obtained a grant of a market in 1199 (*Rot. Chart.*, i, p. 11). The church in the market place was founded as a chapelry of East Barnet (2 miles to the east) where the main manorial centre was located. The chapelry was not allowed to become a full parish until 1452.

The main road from London seems to have been turned off its straight course near St. John's church in order to lead it into the market street; a widening of this street near the A.1 and A.6 fork is shown as the market place on the first edition of the O.S. 6 inch, sheet XLV N.E.

BUNTINGFORD   Hertfordshire   sheet 148 52/364293
c. 1288

The town is named after a ford where the Ermine Street crossed the river Rib half-way between Royston and Ware. Like Royston, the town's late arrival is attested by the division of the site of the town between four older parishes (Layston, Aspenden, Throcking and Wydiall). The abandoned church of Layston, a mile from the town at 369301, shows how the new commercial settlement on the main road has supplanted the rural centre of population. A chapel in Buntingford served the townspeople from at least 1292. The beginnings of commercial life on this part of the Ermine Street seem to have been at Chipping (*Cal. Chart. Rolls*, i, p. 404 and v, p. 166), 2 miles to the north of this ford, where a market began in 1252; but by 1288 there were houses at the ford, and a chapel of St. Peter is mentioned in 1292. By 1360 the lord of the manor received licence to move the market from what was said to be an empty building plot to the Buntingford site: to be held in the main road by the chapel and in the roads that crossed it from east to west; this is analogous to the Royston site. The first edition of the 6 inch O.S., sheet XLV N.W., shows a compact group of burgages on either side of the main road north of the ford: on the west they are bounded by a back lane and on the east by water. The main road has been widened to a long triangle between the junction with the two roads mentioned in the 1360 grant. There was rivalry with Standon, and for a while in 1367 it looked as if Buntingford would have its market suppressed, but the market and a fair were confirmed by Edward III (*V.C.H., Herts.*, iii, p. 78), and by Richard II in 1378.

ROYSTON   Hertfordshire   sheet 148   52/356407
c. 1189

The site is again at the intersection of the Icknield Way (which follows the foot of the Chiltern scarp) and a road radiating northwards from London (in this case the Ermine Street). The place now occupied by the town was a true no-man's-land, for the county boundary followed the Icknield Way, and part of the town was in Cambridgeshire until 1897. Its late arrival is signalled even more clearly by the fact that five parishes met at the cross roads, the villages of these parishes being up to 3 miles away. Having no church of their own, it was to these distant churches that the townsmen had to resort, a difficulty plainly set out in the preamble to the Act of 1540 (*Statutes of the Realm*, 32 Henry VIII, cap. 44; see above, p. 141) when the former monastic church was bought for their own use by the townspeople. It was this house of Austin Canons, founded at *Crux Roys* in the late twelfth century, that had created the town. The priory lay in the south-east quadrant of the road junction at which Rohesia's cross was located, and in Barkway parish (*P.N. Herts.*, pp. 161–162). In 1189 the Priory obtained the right to hold a market and a fair; a second fair was granted in 1213 and a third in 1243, although the town was never given the privileges of a borough (*V.C.H. Herts.*, iii, p. 253).

The parish church is made up of the chancel and choir of the Priory church; the original shape of the market place is also discernible despite considerable encroachment: it is a cigar-shaped widening of the Ermine Street on both sides of the crossroads; a newer market place between the church and the Ermine Street has also been encroached upon, but its wedge-shape is clearly visible. (Air photograph in *Beresford and St. Joseph*, p. 169.)

ST. ALBANS   Hertfordshire   sheet 160   52/147073
c. 950

For the work of abbot Wulsin c. 950 at this town see p. 326, above.

WATFORD   Hertfordshire   sheet 160   41/115950
1119–46

"The town of Watford . . . similarly springs into existence as a market-town in the reign of Henry II without any earlier reference" (W. G. Hoskins, *T.L.A.S.*, xxv

(1949), p. 59). The earlier references to the name in *P.N. Herts.*, p. 103, are to the actual river ford.

The site is analogous to Uxbridge (*q.v.*) where a radial road from London crosses the same river, before making for a gap in the Chilterns.

The modern development shrouds the older features, but the first edition of the 6 inch O.S. shows the church half a mile north of the bridge with the characteristic widening of the main road to form a market place; a distinct kink in the frontages suggests where the market place terminated.

In 1248 it was separately represented at the Assize, a privilege reserved for boroughs and commercial communities, and in 1290 was taxed as a borough (E179/120/2). The town was developed, like St. Albans and Chipping Barnet, by the lords of the manor, the abbots of St. Albans. In Domesday Book the settlement centre seems to have been at Cashio but in a document of 1119–46 there is mentioned a parish of Watford (*Gesta St. Albani*, Rolls Series (1897), i, p. 95) and there is said to have been a market granted by Henry I (*V.C.H.*, ii, pp. 446–469), putting the origins of the town further back than Prof. Hoskins' date.

HUNTINGDONSHIRE

If Hertfordshire is a county of roadside plantations Huntingdonshire is a county of riversides. All its four medieval boroughs were accessible to river traffic. St. Ives was a plantation with a fair known all over western Europe, and St. Neots was able to survive a few miles further upstream; neither of these plantations was far from the county town. Even the petty borough of Holme fell into this class. The drainage of the fens has robbed it of the external appearance of a river-port but in a lawsuit of 1314 it was stated that "merchants came up the river from King's Lynn and especially to the King's town of Holme, situated on the river, with its market and fair" (*Cal. Chart. Rolls, 1313–17*, pp. 241–242 and *Cal. Close Rolls, 1313–18*, p. 119). For a small county with a good deal of undrained fenland Huntingdonshire had a very creditable record of urbanisation.

HOLME   Huntingdonshire   sheet 134   52/190880
by 1167

This petty borough, with its name meaning simply "a small island", is made up of a single street which encircles the edge of a small island in the former fenland just east of the Ermine Street. It lay on the eastern edge of Glatton parish and the boundaries show clearly that Holme was cut from Glatton's fenland tongue. The first mention of Holme is in 1167 (*P.R.S.*, xii (1890), p. 101) and the church, a chapelry of Glatton, has work from the same period (*V.C.H.*, iii, pp. 184–8). In 1279 (*R.H.*, ii, p. 650) there were eight burgesses and forty-two cottars in the town as well as five free-holders. Sixteen burgages appear in a reeve's account of 1359 (SC6/876/16). Burgages were still remembered in 1579 (DL43/4/1).

ST. IVES   Huntingdonshire   sheet 134   52/314713
c. 1110

This town was the creation of the abbots of Ramsey, who acquired the riverside manor of Slepe late in the eleventh century.   The church of Slepe still stands among a cluster of houses just outside the west end of St. Ives.   Early in the eleventh century the bones of St. Ivo were brought here but the commercial life of the town (and perhaps the town itself) dates from 1110 when a fair was granted for Easter week on the open ground between the church of Slepe and the new bridge.   The bridge probably diverted traffic from the old ford at Slepe, and the new town consisted of a T-junction of roads, one from the bridge northwards and the other from Slepe to the shrine of St. Ivo.   As the plan of 1808 (reproduced in *Beresford and St. Joseph*, p. 163) shows, these two streets formed the market place, but at fair-time the commerce coming up the Ouse from all parts of England and western Europe spread out over the adjacent fields.   The distinction between Slepe and the new settlement, the *vicus* or *strata*, continued to appear in the rentals of Ramsey abbey and in the Exchequer tax assessments.

A fuller account of the evidence, with air photograph, appears in *Beresford and St. Joseph*, pp. 161–164; see also J. A. Raftis, "Rent and Capital at St. Ives", *Medieval Studies*, xx (1958), pp. 79–92.

ST. NEOTS   Huntingdonshire   sheet 134   52/183603
1113–22

St. Neots shares many of the features of St. Ives, although its position further up-river gave it less chance of being visited by larger boats.   A fair was granted here between 1107 and 1122 (*Regesta*, ii, no. 1966) and by 1137 there were three fairs a year.   The mother parish was Eynesbury which almost adjoins the present town.   The Priory, refounded at the shrine of St. Neot in 1078, did not possess the whole of the manor until 1113.   There seems little doubt that the priory fulfilled the same sponsoring role for the new commercial centre as Ramsey for St. Ives.   The church of St. Mary became a separate parish church from Eynesbury in 1214.   An account of the sources and an air photograph will be found in *Beresford and St. Joseph*, pp. 164–165.

KENT

In this county, so early settled and so susceptible to the commercial influences of London, the Channel and the Continent, it is not surprising that towns came into existence early, in most cases too early to leave any clear record.   The three plantations that can be identified were all ports: the Weald at the centre of the county discouraged agriculture, population and traffic but there was a long coastline, with the Thames estuary penetrating almost up to London.   On this coastline were the old-established Cinque Ports, and the principal stimulus to any new foundation seems to have been the increasing difficulties that ships experienced in reaching some older ports when rivers silted up or changed their course, or when sandbanks blocked approaches. Queenborough was an exceptional case in this respect, as in its date. It was the last of the medieval plantations in England.

There are a few cases where some evidence for a later commercial centre exists in a slender fashion: Sittingbourne, a roadside development, in Milton Regis (900638) (E. Hasted, *History of Kent* (1782), ii, p. 610) where the first recorded reference is dated 1200; Tonbridge (590467) where the town was simply part of the outer defences of the castle (Hasted, iv, p. 342); Birchington (303690) has a tradition of removal from an earlier site at Gore End (Hasted, iv. p. 338) which may be akin to the removal of Romney and Hythe to new sites; Whitstable grew up on waste ground at the meeting point of three manors (Gordon Ward, "The Origins of Whitstable", *Arch. Cant.*, lvii (1944), pp. 51–55); Deal is a post-medieval plantation.

The old use of "borough" in Kentish place-names in the sense only of "tithing" or "minor settlement" should be noted. There is no urban or commercial implication in the late appearance of names such as Southborough (580420) in 1270.

HYTHE   Kent   sheet 173   61/160346
by 1086

The case for this former coastal town (one of the Cinque Ports) as a secondary development depends on the view taken of West Hythe, now a small village with a ruined church 2 miles west of the modern town. It is possible that West Hythe was the first Saxon port, succeeding the Roman *Portus Lemanis*, a little further inland. This was Hasted's view: "West Hythe which indeed, before the harbour of it failed, was the ancient Cinque Port itself" (*History of Kent*, iii, p. 412). In that event, the present Hythe would be to West Hythe as New Romney is to Old, and for the same cause: the retreat of the coastline. Plans of Hythe in 1684 and 1885 are reproduced in G. M. Livett, "West Hythe Church", *Arch. Cant.*, xxx (1914), pp. 258–259, and another of 1790 by Hasted, *op. cit.*, iii, p. 291. They show a very simple plan, based on a long street parallel to the sea (whose course is marked by the modern Rampart Road) with burghal plots on either side of it but confined by the steep slope of the former cliff to the north. Bartholomew Street and Dental Street delimit these narrow plots. The church of St. Leonard is above the town on the slopes of the cliff. In Domesday Book the 231 burgesses of Hythe were "in Saltwood". There are the earthworks of a castle (161359) half a mile further inland at Saltwood.

QUEENBOROUGH   Kent   sheet 172   51/914721
1368

This is an unusually late foundation, the only example in England between the Black Death and the early seventeenth century; there is slight evidence that the abortive *Londres* in Gascony was also founded by Edward III, and in 1372 La Bastide d'Anjou (Aude) was founded on French soil: but these were not propitious times for either country. Queenborough, founded as a town to accompany the new castle on the western edge of the Isle of Sheppey, was named after Edward's queen, Philippa, in the last year of her life.

The castle remains only as a circular patch of open ground near the railway station. From it, along the north side of a creek of the Swale, the broad High Street runs almost in a straight line to the river bank where there is a small quay. The ground is low everywhere and on the south of the creek are the mud saltings. The town can never have been more than the burgage plots on either side of the High Street; they are about 55 yards long and the width of a house. The parish church stands near the Town Hall on the north side of this street; in 1607 there were disputes concerning the tithes which had to be paid to the mother church of Minster, despite the town's royal foundation (*Arch. Cant.*, xxii, p. 181).

The town's foundation charter (*Cal. Chart. Rolls*, v, pp. 221 and 243) set out the events and motives: the king out of care for his subjects and realm and their protection has lately founded and fortified in a suitable place in the island of Sheppey where there is a broad and deep arm of the sea convenient for ships to put in at, a town and castle which he has named the Queen's Borough. In order that men might more readily come and live there he granted borough status, two markets a week, two fairs a year, the right to elect a Mayor and two bailiffs, together with independence from the jurisdiction of the Cinque Ports. All this, defence and commerce together, is very reminiscent of Edward I's towns in North Wales.

Fortunately, many of the accounts for the expenditure on the castle have survived, and although the king did not contribute much to the civil settlement the documents throw some light on the beginnings of the town.

In the early documents the castle is called "the castle of Sheppey", and Edward was clearly attracted by the need to defend the channels around the Island as well as the Medway estuary. The first stage was the purchase of the manor of Rushendon in August 1361 from Sir Walter Manny. It was not very useful as an agricultural asset: it had about as much marsh as it had arable and pasture together, but it had a suitable site for a castle (SC12/9/52). The first account dates from November of the same year (E372/207 m. 44) and in the first eight months of building more than £1,500 was spent. In the account for 1365–67, the heading mentions only the castle but the item of expenditure "for building and roofing 11 houses" suggests that the civil town was already appearing alongside (E101/483/23 m. 7).

In the account for January–August 1368 more roofs were tiled and the first stipend was paid to the chaplain *in ecclesia villae de Quenesburgh* (E101/483/25 m. 2). Later accounts (E101/483/26) make it plain that there were two chapels, one for the castle and one for the town. The town's chapel was dependent on Minster, the large Island parish (E. Hasted, *History of Kent*, ii (1782), pp. 656–660). It was in May 1368 that the town received its charter, its markets, its fairs and its Mayor, and in the building accounts for 1369 (E101/544/40) the work was described as in *castrum et villam de Quenesburgh de novo constructum et edificatum*. The castle was not yet complete. In the accounts for 1370–71 the collectors of customs are mentioned, so that trading must have begun (E101/483/27), and in those for 1373–74 (E101/483/29) a "markethous" for wool exports is mentioned. In July 1368 Queenborough replaced Sandwich as the Staple Port along the coast of Kent and Sussex from Gravesend to Winchelsea (*Cal. Fine Rolls*, viii, p. 28) and the customs duty on cloth was also collected at Queenborough instead of Sandwich from the same date (E. M. Carus-Wilson and O. Coleman, *England's*

Export Trade, 1275–1547 (1963), p. 193). This privilege lapsed in January 1378 and Sandwich resumed its traditional role of Head Port for this coast. The quantities of wool exported through Queenborough in this period totalled 1,649 sacks; the cloth accounts are incomplete. The king was at Queenborough in November 1374 and he ordered stronger fastenings to the door of the house "where the wool of the staple of Kent lay". The king had also ordered two new houses to be provided for Simon Waryn and John Segar whose houses had been pulled down to make way for the castle.

Work on the castle continued until after the end of the century but no substantial expenditure on the town itself has been noted: the stipend of the priest continued to be a charge on the royal funds (E101/484/1). See also *Hist. King's Works*, ii, pp. 793–804.

ROMNEY, NEW   Kent   sheet 184   61/065248
before 960

The port of Old Romney was silted up even before the Norman Conquest. The river Rother which once ran past the wharves of New Romney has now deserted the second Romney. Level ground in the orchard by the church shows where the wharves once were, and the former water edge is still marked by a change in level of the ground. The great Norman church adjoins the wharves and a long, narrow grid of streets parallel to the old estuary line makes up the town; not all the medieval area is still built upon. In 1086 there were 156 burgesses.

A century before the battle of Hastings New Romney had its mint, and the record of one of its churches is sometimes said to go back to 740 (Gordon Ward, "The Saxon History of the Town and Port of Romney", *Arch. Cant.*, lxv (1952), p. 12). In fact, New Romney may claim to be one of the earliest if not the earliest of the new towns in England. See also W. A. S. Robertson, "Romney, Old and New", *Arch. Cant.*, xiii (1880), pp. 349–373; see also xvii (1884) pp. 12–33.

A plan of the town in 1614 is printed in Major Teichman-Derville, "The New Romney and Cinque Ports Records", *Arch. Cant.*, xlii (1930), pp. 3–36. The original of this plan is in the custody of the Town Clerk.

LANCASHIRE

Besides the fourteenth-century taxation-boroughs of Lancaster, Liverpool, Preston and Wigan there were also burgages at Hornby (C134/62/6), Clitheroe, Bolton and Chorley (SC6/1094/11) and (for a time) at Manchester. Low densities of population, as in Cornwall and Devon, seem to have fostered petty boroughs and market towns. The southern part of the county between Ribble and Mersey was included in the Domesday survey but not in detail. Elsewhere the certain sequence of early and late settlement is even more difficult to establish. The very large parishes of medieval Lancashire also make it difficult to attribute plantation to a borough that was a mere chapelry.

The earliest reference to the following market towns is given in brackets: Ashton under Lyne (c. 1160); Bolton (1185); Bury (1194); Colne (1124); Wigan (1199).

The account of Wigan in *V.C.H.*, iv, p. 70, has some suspicious elements, especially the isolation of the town from the remainder of the parish and Hundred; *ibid.*, p. 286, disposes of the notion that the Domesday Book church of Newton was located at Wigan. Chorley, a chapelry of Croston, is not recorded before 1246 (*Lanc. and Ches. Rec. Soc.*, xlvii, p. 13) and four years later it was acquired by William de Ferrers, earl of Derby, and by 1257 there were burgages; the same William had made a borough out of the village of Bolton in 1253 and similarly transformed Higham Ferrers (Northants.).

The replacement of Penwortham by Preston as the local commercial centre took place after 1086, when there were six burgages in Penwortham, but no new settlement was created since Preston already existed in 1086 and the parish was mentioned in a charter of 1094 (W. Farrer, *Early Lancashire Charters*, p. 289).

CLITHEROE   Lancashire   sheet 95   34/743417

1086–1102

"The castle of Roger of Poitou" in the Domesday Book account of Barnoldswick is usually taken to refer to the castle that later formed the head of the important honour of Clitheroe: T. D. Whitaker, *A History . . . of Whalley* (ed. 1872), i, p. 237. The first extant borough charter dates from 1272–91 (*Ballard and Tait*, p. xxvii) but there were sixty-six burgages in an I.P.M. of 1258 (C132/21/13).

The town consists of one long market street north-west of the castle. The dependence of the town church upon Whalley is not in itself a proof of plantation since large parishes with dependent chapels are very common in Lancashire, even for places known to have existed in 1066 or earlier. The castle guards the upper Ribble valley, facing westwards (*sic*) an enclave of Yorkshire that extends between Ribble and Hodder. (See *V.C.H. Lancs.*, vi, p. 360, where the borough is ascribed to Henry de Lacy (1146–77) but note the charter of 1102 (W. Farrer, *Lancs. Pipe Rolls*, pp. 385–388) which distinguishes lands and messuages inside and outside the bailey; there was a chapel by 1120).

FLOOKBURGH   Lancashire   sheet 89   34/366758

c. 1246

This small market town on the road around the foot of the peninsula was developed on land belonging to Cartmel Priory, 2 miles to the north-east. The market granted to Cartmel in 1292 (*V.C.H.*, viii, p. 257) may indeed have been at Flookburgh but the first record of the place is in 1246 (*Lancs. Assize Roll*, Lancs. & Ches. Rec. Soc., xlvii (1904), p. 11). The town had no parish church of its own. The first reference to burgages that has been traced, however, dates from 1508–09 (DL43/4/9) and in 1609–10 there were sixty-five burgages. The place therefore has some of the symptoms of plantation but without final certainty. The final element of the name may, of course, be genuinely *burgus*. The village has a small open market place and a market cross, but no grid plan.

LIVERPOOL   Lancashire   sheet 100   33/342903
1207

In August 1207 the charter of Liverpool was issued by King John from Winchester, one of the oldest towns in southern England, in order to create a new borough at a creek of the Mersey at the other end of his kingdom. It was addressed to those burgesses who had wanted burgage plots at the vill of Liverpool and it gave them as wide privileges "as any free borough on the sea coast of England then enjoyed" (*Ballard*, pp. 32–33).

The older centre of this area was at West Derby, a little inland, where there was a motte and bailey castle. In August 1207 John had only just acquired the site of Liverpool by exchange: it was a block of land alongside the tidal creek already known as *le pool* and it may have formed part of the commons of West Derby. Here a new castle and a chapel were built for the new townspeople. A small grid of streets, now rather obscured by the seaward extension of the town, was placed in the neck of land between the pool and the estuary. A statement in the Pipe Roll for 1208 (W. Farrar, *Lancashire Pipe Rolls* (1902), p. 220) allowing West Derby £8 relief from its dues suggests that the king engineered some movement of people and possessions from West Derby to Liverpool: *et in defalta de Westderebi que est remota usque ad Lieurpul per breve regis et per inquisitionem viiif hoc anno.* The same allowance was continued in the accounts of 1209 and 1210. By 1227 Liverpool was tallaged at 11 marks compared with Lancaster's 13, and the fee farm in the charter of 1229 was set at 200s. In an extent of 1346 the number of burgages had grown to 168 (George Chandler, *Liverpool* (1956), for details, references and facsimiles of documents). The vill was separately represented before the Assize justices of 1246 (JI/1/404).

The new town lay in the parish of Walton on the Hill, with the church 3 miles distant.

LEICESTERSHIRE

This county has a poor crop of plantations. The best documented and described (Market Harborough) cannot be dated precisely, Mountsorrel can only be given a terminal date, and Belvoir hovers on the edge of being a town. This poor showing— almost as bad as the zero score of neighbouring Rutland and Nottinghamshire— cannot be attributed to paucity of information. The county has had its devoted local historians in Burton, Nichols, and Hoskins whose recent account of Market Harborough is one of the few local studies of urban origins.

BELVOIR   Leicestershire   sheet 122   43/820340
1076–1100

The priory and conventual church of Belvoir was founded by Robert de Todeni c. 1076, possibly within one of the two manors of Woolsthorpe (Lincs.) recorded in Domesday Book. By 1105 a fair was being held by charter (C. Johnson and H. A. Cronne, *Regesta*, ii (1956), no. 684). The priory church acted as the parish church.

Belvoir is described sometimes as a town and sometimes as a village: there were thirty-seven tenants in 1300 (C133/100/2) but none of them burgesses. Whatever its size, the settlement was burned during the Civil War on Guy Fawkes Day 1644. Nichols wrote in 1795 (*Leics.*, ii, p. 23) "the tumults of the last century so effectually demolished the village as well as the Priory as to leave in it scarcely the remnant of a building". It was then uncertain whether the site was in Leicestershire or Lincolnshire. The whole is now obscured by the castle, gardens and park of the dukes of Rutland.

HARBOROUGH, MARKET   Leicestershire   sheet 133 42/733872
1167–77

This plantation is the subject of detailed study in W. G. Hoskins, "The Origin and Rise of Market Harborough", *T.L.A.S.*, xxv (1949), pp. 56–68. Briefly, the town was placed in the fields of Great Bowden, a village 1½ miles to the north-east. The former main road from Northampton to Leicester crossed the Welland at Little Bowden, half a mile east of the present town. A new crossing at the new town shortened the route and diverted traffic from both Bowdens (see the plan in Hoskins, *op. cit.*, p. 57). The new road formed the core of the town, and the market place was in this street just south of the present church. The late arrival of the town is indicated by the dominant position of Great Bowden church in the lives of the townspeople: there is no burial ground at Market Harborough church, and the town church although elaborately constructed remained in Nichols' day a mere chapelry. It is also possible that the ridge road (now the A.427) approaching from the east via Oundle and Rockingham once made straight for Great Bowden but was diverted at the founding of Harborough to enter the market place at right angles to the main road already described. It will be noticed that there is a double turn in the Northampton road, now the A.508, as it first joins the Oundle road and then turns north into the market place. A similar pair of turns is prominent at Baldock.

The first recorded mention of the town is in the Pipe Roll for 1177 when *Haverberga* paid an aid of 7 marks, additional to the 8½ marks from Great Bowden; a mill at Harborough is also mentioned. The creation of a town able to contribute this sum must therefore be assigned to the previous decade. No charter is known.

Bowden was a royal manor and the plantation may have been by arrangement between Henry II and his justiciar, Robert earl of Leicester; and the purpose a resting place half way between the two towns of Leicester and Northampton. A market charter was granted in 1203, and the chapel was built c. 1250.

It is significant that the town had no fields, these still being occupied by the villagers of Bowden. (See also J. H. Hill, *The History of Market Harborough* (1875), p. 2; and J. E. Stocks and W. E. Bragg, *Market Harborough Parish Records*, i (1890), pp. 1–3; W. G. Hoskins, *Provincial England* (1964), pp. 53–67.)

MOUNTSORREL   Leicestershire   sheet 121 43/581151
by 1148

Six miles north of Leicester the main road to Derby, following the west bank of the Soar, passes under the lee of the crag that marks the easternmost outlier of Charnwood

Forest. Here a castle was built in the reign of Stephen or earlier, and the adjoining borough seems to have been a child of the castle. A grant from Ranulf, earl of Chester, to the earl of Leicester (made about 1148) included "the town and castle", and a treaty between the two earls (made 1148–53) confirmed the earl of Leicester's tenure of Montsorrel with the proviso that he should receive the earl of Chester "in the borough and baileys": H. A. Cronne, "Ranulf de Gernons", *Trans. Roy. Hist. Soc.*, 4th ser., xx (1937), pp. 131–132; the documents are in F. M. Stenton, *The First Century of English Feudalism* (1932), pp. 248–255 and 285.

Significantly, the town lay at the junction of two parishes, Barrow and Rothley, and half the town was in each. This division produced two separate chapelries, St. John the Baptist in Rothley for Mountsorrel Inferior and St. Nicholas in Rothley for Mountsorrel Superior. The latter chapel had fallen into decay by 1622 (*Nichols*, iii, p. 85). There was a market in 1292 (*Cal. Chart. Rolls*, ii, p. 423) and probably earlier, since in 1255 (C132/17/9) both North and South Sides of Mountsorrel had burgage tenements. The value of the burgages in the earl of Winchester's fee *versus partem australem* was then 44s. 9¼d.; that of the earl of Chester's fee *ad partem borialem* was £8 5s. 3d. The town was taxed as a borough from 1315; (see also E152/160/1: 1372).

LINCOLNSHIRE

The four Lincolnshire plantations had very diverse fortunes. One was beaten only by Newcastle on Tyne, for Boston became the second wealthiest of the medieval plantations in England; New Sleaford is still a local market town; Brigg corn prices are still quoted nationally; but New Eagle was founded at a fatal moment and its houses were never built.

Although it was not a borough, the port of Saltfleet may be an additional creation of the second half of the thirteenth century. It was at the coastal end of Skidbroke parish (sheet 105, 53/938455) and on the north side of Saltfleet Haven. The Haven was in existence long before the settlement that took its name: "It is not until the latter part of the thirteenth century that we find the name extended from the haven itself to cover a community which has grown up beside it" (A. E. B. Owen, "The Early History of Saltfleet Haven", *Rep. and Papers Lincs. Arch. and Arch. Soc.*, v, pt. ii (1954), p. 5), but (*ibid.*, p. 6) there was a previous nucleus of settlement before the market charter of 1268 (*Cal. Chart. Rolls*, ii, p. 100).

BOSTON   Lincolnshire   sheet 114   53/326442
1086–1113

The origins of Boston are confused: in 1086 Domesday Book described four manors at the mouth of the Witham: Frampton, Wyberton, Fishtoft and Skirbeck. All four were purely rural. The bounds of medieval Boston suggest that it was taken out of the parish of Skirbeck; the Domesday population of Skirbeck was thirty-two families; the only element in the Skirbeck entries to suggest something unusual is the mention of two churches and two priests. The parish church of Skirbeck is St. Nicholas' and the second church of 1086 was probably the church of St. Botolph which formed the nucleus of the medieval town of Boston (Botolph's Town). In 1090 Alan, earl of Richmond, gave the rectory of St. Botolph in Skirbeck to support the abbey of St. Mary at York.

If there had been any urban settlement by 1086 it is difficult to see why it was omitted from the valuation of earl Alan's manors; the first specific mention of Boston dates from 1113 when the Croyland abbey chronicle records a gift to the abbey by "a brazier of St. Botolph's town".

The medieval town extended for half a mile down the curving east bank of the Witham, alongside the main waterway to Lincoln and mid-Lincolnshire. When the Foss Dyke was not obstructed there was also a through passage to the Trent at Torksey and so to the north Midlands. At Skirbeck, as the earthworks of the old "Sea Bank" show, this river widened into its estuary.

South of the church was the great triangular market place, now overbuilt in its north-west corner. The town walls, begun in 1285 on the line of an earlier moat, took in the church, the market place and the short, narrow, parallel lanes which ran east–west on the landward side of South Street. A town plan of 1741 by R. Hall shows the line of much of the medieval Bar Ditch (*Medieval Archaeology*, ii (1958), p. 200). At the south end of the town St. John's gate gave on to the fields of Skirbeck. To the north of St. Botolph's church, Wormgate (= Withamgate) led to the riverside fields outside the town, again in Skirbeck parish which embraced the town on all sides. The Town Bridge (first documented in 1305) brought land traffic from the villages of South Lincolnshire, from Spalding and from London. Suburban development along the High Street and West Street on the west bank outside the manor of Boston had already taken place by the early fourteenth century as landowners began to let building plots to out-merchants.

From the north-east corner of the Market Place, Strait Bargate led to the causeway road across the fens to the Wolds; the sudden change of width to Wide Bargate indicates where the medieval gate stood. Wide Bargate itself broadens into Bargate Green, and when Boston Fair was known all over medieval Europe this and much space in the fields besides would have been needed for the streets of booths and stalls. John granted a charter in 1205, but the unchartered town was already prosperous. In 1190, when the manor was temporarily in the king's hands, the manor was farmed at 76s. but the fairs were worth £50 7s. 7d. If the sums paid in 1206 truly represent the value of the trade passing through English ports, Boston was already second to London, and in 1218 the fair was extended to eight days. In 1546 when Henry VIII made a free borough of all the area of the old Richmond manor he added to it the property which nineteen dissolved religious houses had held in Boston together with the lands of three Friaries.

It was for commercial purposes that so many monasteries, among them the greatest in eastern and northern England, had acquired a house or houses in the town for themselves. Croyland got its bells here, Bridlington, Bolton and Furness their cloths and skins, and Bardney its wine; Henry III's butler bought wine here for the king and rented cellars to store it, and in 1369 the wool staple was moved here from Lincoln. In 1309 the Norman church was replaced by a much enlarged fabric. The great tower (Boston Stump) was begun in the 1420's.

The Tudor town was diminished from the medieval glory. Leland wrote: "the Staple and Stiliard houses yet there remayne, but the Stiliard is little or nothing occupied". The export of wool was no longer of importance, and the quantity of cloth coming out down the Witham failed to compensate for the loss. In 1607 the Corporation asked that Boston should be counted among the "decayed townes". There was a revival in the nineteenth century with the drainage of the surrounding fens, and the building of the dock and the railway.

(The above account is based on M. R. Lambert and R. Walter, *Boston, Tattershall and Croyland* (1930), and A. M. Cook, *Boston* (1948).)

BRIGG (GLANFORD BRIGG)   Lincolnshire   sheet 104   54/001073
by 1183

Brigg, the short form, is now in common use, supplanting the town's original name as the bridge had once supplanted the ford. The charter of 1235 (*Cal. Chart. Rolls*, i, p. 214) contains the first mention of the -Brigg element. This charter granted a market and fair, but at the very first appearance of the name *Glanford*, in the Pipe Roll of 1183 (*P.R.S.*, xxxii (1911), p. 69) marketing was already in progress: it was for selling wine contrary to the assize that a fine had been levied.

Glanford does not appear in Domesday Book. The town was reckoned to be part of Wrawby parish and had no parish church of its own, but it is very significant of the late arrival of the town that four parishes met at the town site: "the town standing in four parishes had no place of worship nearer than a mile and a half" (T. H. Allen, *History of the County of Lincoln* (1834), ii, p. 224). The four parishes would have been Wrawby, Bigby, Scawby and Broughton. The shape of the boundaries suggests that there was an island in the Ancholme marshes to give the firm basis for a bridge-crossing The shape of the town is a triangle of streets east of the bridge-head. (See also A. N. Claye, *Brigg Church and Town* (n.d., c. 1900).)

EAGLE, NEW   Lincolnshire   sheet 113   43/889629
1345

In the Dissolution surveys the Hospitallers' lands in Swinderby were said to include Old and New Eagle (SC6/Henry VIII/7274 m. 9). Old Eagle is the present village of Eagle, and New Eagle is the site of the abortive foundation of a town on the Fosse Way, half-way between Lincoln and Newark, adjoining the present Half Way House Inn. The foundation charter (*Cal. Chart. Rolls*, v, p. 40) is dated July 6, 1345. It recalls the robberies and felonies prevalent on the Fosse Way; to make the passage safer "the Prior has requested that he may build a town or hamlet and settle men there upon his own ground in a place called Swynderby More, hard by the said Fosse Way and in his manor of Eagle". The charter authorised the erection of a chapel and "a town with houses about it, with *placeae* enclosed there". These were to be demised by the Prior to any man willing to come and dwell there "for the entertainment of travellers on the road". A weekly market and two fairs a year were also granted: an indication that more than the occasional traveller was expected.

A century later the Hospitallers offered to return the charter for annulment if in

465

return a market and fair in Swinderby village itself could be granted: T. Hugo, *The History of Swinderby* (1876), p. 15. There is now an inn for the entertainment of travellers, but alongside it are empty fields. No trace of former buildings has yet been noted, and the Black Death coming four years after the charter may have ended the hopes of the project.

SLEAFORD, NEW   Lincolnshire   sheet 113   53/067459
1123–47

The original ford over the river Slea was at 076461 where the line of the Roman road is shown on the O.S. map. The village of Old Sleaford, now completely deserted, stood at this crossing. Domesday Book records a valuable manor belonging to the bishop of Lincoln with 46 tenants and no fewer than eight mills. A church is also recorded. This was the church of St. Giles whose former site is indicated on the 6 inch O.S. just west of the Roman Road. The move to New Sleaford was probably associated with the building of a castle by Alexander, bishop of Lincoln (1123–47). A century and a half later, when this fact was reported by a local jury, they added "the bishop now has there a market with bakers and brewers". The town was not taxed as a borough but it was separately represented before the judges of assize in 1281–82 (JI/1/497). It would be useful to know whether the Sleaford fined for false measures in 1189 (*P.R.S.*, xxviii (1925), p. 78) was the old or the new town, but the record is not explicit. A very full survey of 1258 (Queen's College, Oxford, Mss.) lists 116 burgesses holding 97 tofts, 1 small house and 3 booths within the borough; 65 of the tofts paid 12 pence a year rent but 2 paid less and 20 paid more. It was noted as late as 1627 that the burgages were devoid of land in the open fields, which were presumably those of Old Sleaford (*cp.* Old Malton), "althoughe there be manie houses held of you by that tenure yet there is none that have anie thing in the open feildes save Two" (ex. inf. W. H. Hosford).

The focus of the road system after the abandonment of the Roman crossing was the junction of North Gate, South Gate, East Gate and West Gate in the centre of New Sleaford. There is a clear pattern of a market place east of this junction adjoining the church of St. Denis. This church is dated from the twelfth century.

MIDDLESEX

UXBRIDGE   Middlesex   sheet 160   41/055841
by 1145

The bridge which gave its name to this town is that by which the London to Oxford road (now the A.40) crossed the river Colne and passed into Buckinghamshire. The crossing lay on the edge of the parish of Hillingdon, a village a mile to the east, and a chapelry of Uxbridge in this parish is first mentioned c. 1145 (B.M. Cott. Vesp. B XXIV ff. 49 and 51); it was not until 1842 that the Uxbridge church became fully parochial. Leland noted that the town was but one long street, and here markets and fairs have been held since at least 1170. The Market House stands in a triangle of open ground next to St. Margaret's church (see plan in M. Robbins, *Middlesex*, (1953), p. 354). There is no evidence of a medieval borough here.

NORFOLK

For a coastal and old-settled county with a high density of population in 1086, medieval Norfolk was very lightly urbanised. The plantations are correspondingly few.

BUCKENHAM, NEW   Norfolk   sheet 136   62/088905
1146–56
The original parish of Buckenham covered more than 5,000 acres, part of the boundary being marked by an earthwork *Bunn's Bank* of indeterminate age. The parish is still sparsely populated with a small area of fen on the west and an area of common heathland on the east.

The parish boundaries show clearly that the 360 acres of New Buckenham have been cut from Old Buckenham and also from Banham and Carleton, perhaps in an attempt to give it a little field-land.

The creation of the new town is documented. William de Albany, who died in 1156, acquired land from the bishop of Norwich in order to build a new castle on the eastern edge of Buckenham parish nearly 2 miles from his existing village and castle. The stone of the old castle was used to build Old Buckenham Priory, founded c. 1146. The new site lay alongside the old road from Thetford to Norwich and has obvious commercial possibilities not enjoyed by Old Buckenham. About 200 yards east of the castle its founder laid out his new borough. It is a 200 yard square with a full street grid. There is a market place at the east where the road leads out on to the common. At first the new town used a chapel alongside the castle but the church of St. Martin was founded by Sir Robert de Tateshale; its later arrival is indicated by its position, for it lies outside the grid to the north of the town. The fairs were held on the common to the east of the town where the total stint of eighty cattle may represent the original number of burgages. Although no borough charter survives, the town was reckoned a borough (E372/92 m. 15: 1247–48). In 1305 there were 173 tenants (C133/123 m. 7). See also Blomefield, *Norfolk* (1739), i, p. 268. An air photograph appears in *Beresford and St. Joseph*, p. 207.

LYNN, KING'S   Norfolk   sheet 124   53/617197
1086–95
The first charter of Lynn, granted by John, bishop of Norwich in 1204, (*Ballard*, p. 32) speaks of the vill of Lynn, as being "all the parish of St. Margaret". In Domesday Book the entries for Lynn must refer to West, North and South Lynn (C. Parkin, *A Topographical History of Freebridge Hundred* (1772), pp. 113–115). St. Margaret's church and priory were founded by Herbert, bishop of Norwich, c. 1095 "at the request of the men of the town of Lynn"; and the bishop endowed his foundation

with the Saturday market and fair (*ibid.*, p. 126); a grant of tolls was made in 1107–09 (*Ballard*, p. 255; *Regesta*, i, no. 911). The town must then have been newly founded in the manor of Gaywood but its growth was rapid, for (1146–74) an extension was laid out to the north endowed with a second market place and a second church, the chapel of St. Nicholas. This chapelry made strenuous efforts to gain independence of St. Margaret but it was still subordinate in 1835. The grid of streets that makes up these two town plantations appears in the plan in W. G. Hoskins, *Local History in England* (1959), p. 83, and their duality is preserved in the surviving Saturday and Tuesday markets, one outside each of the churches. There is a good plan of the town as frontispiece to Parkin, *op. cit.*

WYMONDHAM   Norfolk   sheet 136   63/109015
c. 1107

Dr. W. G. Hoskins gives this town as an example of one founded on a common heath but no references are cited (L. D. Stamp and W. G. Hoskins, *The Common Lands of England and Wales* (1963), p. 40). Bartholomew's *Gazetteer* states that the town owes its origin to the Priory, founded 1107, but the phrase does not necessarily mean plantation; it probably derives from a more vague statement in James Bell's *Gazetteer* (e.g. ed. of 1835, p. 422). There was a rural vill in 1086 but the market place, about half a mile from the original village, was placed where the Thetford to Norwich main road crossed the common, a situation similar to that of New Buckenham. A fair was granted to the Priory by Henry I between 1106 and 1135 (Dugdale, *Monasticon*, vii, pp. 331–332). Market Street, even in the Census of 1801, formed a distinct division of the parish.

NORTHAMPTONSHIRE

This is another of the almost bare Midland counties. There is evidence that the urban settlement at Peterborough once lay to the east, and not (as now) to the west of the monastic church. The authority is Hugo Candidus (*Historiae Coenobii Burgensis*, ed. J. Sparke (1727), pp. 65–67, 76 and 88). Between 1133 and 1155 he writes of an abbot, *forum mutavit* and *villam mutavit*. *V.C.H. Northants*, ii, p. 425, points out that the parish church was not in its present position until 1402.

BRACKLEY, NEW   Northamptonshire   sheet 145   42/585368
by 1173

Brackley appears in Domesday Book, but the isolated position of St. Peter's church and the few accompanying houses which bear the name of Old Town suggest that modern Brackley on the hill is a secondary settlement, probably deriving from the castle which stood at the south end of the town. In 1202 the town was separately represented at the Assizes (JI/1/613) but already in 1173 (*P.R.S.*, xix (1895), p. 37) the assised rent of Brackley was £66 18s. 4d., far too large to have been paid by a mere vill. Burgesses are mentioned in the mid-thirteenth century when the name *Old*

Town was already in use for the area around St. Peter's. A chapel of ease, now destroyed, was built for the townspeople near the castle.

In the fourteenth century Brackley was a staple town for wool, and there must have been much resort to the Castle and town when the tournament ground at Evenley (1 mile S.E.) was in use.

Leland, who saw the Tudor town in diminished prosperity, said that at its heyday Brackley had had a circuit of 2 miles. The broad High Street is straight for nearly more than half a mile, and the road on the west of the town, parallel to it, has the character of a Back Lane similar to that at such street-towns as St. Ives (Hunts.). (See Baker, *Northants.*, i, 560; *Beresford and St. Joseph*, p. 209; E. R. Forrester, *Magdalen College School* (1950), for two eighteenth-century plans; Mr. Forrester's help in answering queries is gratefully acknowledged.)

NORTHUMBERLAND

This county was not covered in Domesday Book and it lacks the equivalent of Bolden Book. The early history of its towns and boroughs would be even more confused than those of Durham were it not for Hodgson's *History of Northumberland* and the magnificent volumes of the *Northumberland County History* whose authors gathered documentary material most assiduously.

Northumberland is revealed as a little Devon in the degree and timing of its urbanisation. Bearing its moorland in mind, its medieval boroughs were densely placed and ten of these were plantations. In Newcastle on Tyne the county had the second most populous of all the plantations, judged by the poll tax of 1377. By another criterion, the tax of 1334, it was the wealthiest of all the English plantations. Of the thirteen Northumberland boroughs recognised at the Assize of 1256, seven appear in the *List* below.

If Berwick on Tweed is reckoned part of Northumberland, should it appear? After all, was it not the occasion of the town-planning colloquium with which Chapter I began? No modern study of Edwardian Berwick has been noticed but the work carried out by Edward I after 1296 seems to have been a rebuilding rather than a new creation. There was certainly a town before the siege, a burgh of David I of Scotland (1124–53) and probably earlier. The plan of Edward's walled town is now obscured by the railway station and curtailed by the shorter circuit of the Tudor walls; it can be recovered from Johnson's plan of c. 1575 (B.M. Cott., Aug. I, ii, no. 14) (see also MPF 137 (c. 1545)). Some of Edward I's walls and towers can be seen among the allotments and golf course outside modern Berwick and his castle has remnants in the railway sidings.

It is possible that Newbiggin on Sea, a name first recorded in 1242 (*Book of Fees*, no. 1120), was a plantation. A market and fair were granted by Henry III (1216–72) (Hodgson, *Northumberland*, pt. 2, vol. ii, p. 216) and it was a borough in 1372 (C135/231/3).

Alnwick also poses certain ambiguities. Without Domesday Book it is not possible to be certain that there was no settlement here before the de Vescy castle of 1096–

1135. The historian of the town and castle wrote: "Of its existence as a town before the Norman Conquest there is no documentary evidence." (G. Tate, *History of Alnwick* (1866), i, p. 4.) There is also the fact that, like Alnmouth, Alnwick was reckoned to be within Lesbury parish. It is therefore possible that Alnwick was a castle-gate town like Ludlow and New Windsor. The first burgess charter dates from 1157–85 (Tate, *op. cit.*, ii, appendix 2). The abbey, which is not inside the town, was founded in 1147. There was a licence to wall the town in 1433 but progress was slow and the work incomplete in 1473.

M. R. G. Conzen, who has studied the morphology of the town, writes (privately): "*as a town* Alnwick cannot antedate the castle . . . it is not a simple case of a *de novo* town. In Alnwick's present town plans I see certain archaic features which, I think, carry us back to and indeed beyond, its Anglian origin, the latter being fixed by the place-name in the late settlement phase of Anglian Northumbria. In other words, as a village Alnwick antedates its Norman castle, as a town it is later." There is certainly no marked grid-plan.

ALNWICK   Northumberland   sheet 71   46/247105
by 1147

When Alnwick abbey was founded in 1147 it was given (Tate, *History of Alnwick* (1866), i, p. 153) land in "the borough of St. Waleric", and an undated charter (before 1178) granted William de Vescy a market at St. Waleric "which is also called Neubiginge". (*Percy Chartulary*, Surtees Soc., cvii (1911), p. 349.) This charter was granted by William the Lion, of Scotland, and there is a local tradition that William was shipwrecked here when coming back from the Somme and gave the saint's name to the new town which he founded at the spot. This story can be put in the same category as that of the legendary spirit who instructed a bishop of Salisbury where to set New Sarum.

In 1207 the king granted a Wednesday market here to Eustace de Vescy; it was Eustace's son, William, who assented to an agreement in March 1250 between Alnwick abbey and "the borough of Alnmouth" to end disputes about tithes of fish landed at Alnmouth. The abbot undertook to restore any ship's gear which was lost at sea including nets and spring herrings, so long as the fishermen paid tithes on their fish, gross of expenses (including repayment of loans). The abbey at Alnwick and the inhabitants of Alnmouth shared the cost of maintaining the three priests in the chapel of St. Waleric. About the same time, the foundation charter of the Carmelite house of Hulne granted the brothers the right to buy a barrel of herrings in Alnmouth market each year as freely as any burgess, choosing the time for the purchase which suited them best; other fish, food and small goods could also be bought freely if they were required for the brothers' sustenance. In 1256 the "villata" was separately represented before the justices of Assize by its own jury of twelve, and the cases heard there reveal tanning, stone-exporting and wine-importing (*Assize Rolls of Northumberland*, Surtees Soc., lxxxviii (1890), p. 68).

The plantation of a town which these documents witness was still a lively tradition in 1567 when the earl of Northumberland's survey reported that: "In auncyent tymes yt was taken forthe of this lordship of intente yt should be planted with suche persons as wold trafique by the sea. . . .The scite of the said towne doth marvelousleye weyre with the violence of the wynde and sea wherby the haven ys much indammaged and ys not nowe so good as yn tyme past yt was." The plan accompanying the survey shows thirty-eight houses on one side of the street and thirty-three on the other, with no other frontages than this single street leading down to the water's edge.

The chapel of St. Waleric has now become detached from the town through a change in course of the river Aln in 1806. Its roof was de-leaded in 1662 and it was in ruins by 1771. In the plans of 1567 and 1624 the chapel is some distance removed from the end of the town, and it may well have been a strand chapel for mariners and river-boatmen.

The survey of 1567 uses the words "taken forthe of this lordship", and the bounds of Alnmouth show that it has been cut out of the rural parish of Lesbury "sett on an angle or corner of the Lordship of Lesburye, gyven forth by the lord of Alnewyk to one certaine nombre of persons". It stood, in fact, on Lesbury common. Consequently the burgesses of the new town had to look to the fields of Lesbury for their arable land "ridge by ridge throughout . . . the sayd feldes". The 296 acres of Alnmouth consisted only of the beach, the town and the cliff-top grassland. The grazing ground was not enclosed until 1688. (See the full account with plans in *N.C.H.* ii, pp. 413–482 and air photograph in *Beresford and St. Joseph*, p. 192.)

The growth of Alnwick, up river, especially after it became the principal seat of the Percies in the early fourteenth century, was the main cause of the growth of a sea-port at Alnmouth, whence the castle-town could be provisioned and the grain and wool of the district transferred to coastal ships. The "free port" was annexed to the borough of Alnwick in 1452 (*Tate*, i, p. 239).

The harbour had been refurbished in 1529, but the uncertain course of the river complained of in 1567 had taken away much of the traffic. In the survey only twenty of the sixty households were headed by fishermen, the others were bakers, brewers and retailers. A generation earlier only ten had not fished for a living. In 1594 the earl of Northumberland wrote that all the burgesses were non-resident; indeed the place was "dispeopled". In a survey of 1614 it was "in great ruine and decay", although seventy-four tenements were listed in the East and West Rows, the two streets of the town. It is now a quiet little place, a dormitory of Alnwick and a seaside resort in the summer. Even so, there has been very little building outside the two sides of the main street.

FELTON   Northumberland   sheet 71   46/185005

c. 1200

This little town stands where the Coquet is crossed by the Newcastle–Berwick road, in a position corresponding to Warkworth and Morpeth further south. Old Felton, now only a farm, is at 180024 and there is a tradition that King John destroyed this place in anger after the barons of Northumbria had done homage there to Alexander of Scotland.

The present appearance of Felton is a very compact roadside settlement with plots

471

of the burgage type alined along the main road. The town was one of the thirteen in the county separately represented before the assize judges of 1256 (JI/1/642). Its market and fair were granted in 1200 (*N.C.H.*, vii, p. 229) soon after William Bertram II of Mitford had granted the church to Brinkburn together with land in Old Felton (Over Felton) and common pasture in Feltonshire (*Surtees Soc.*, xc (1892), pp. 2–3). There are references to burgage tenants in 1323 "who paid in time of peace 46s. but now 8s." (C134/83/5), and again in 1373 and 1377 (*N.C.H.*, vii, pp. 240 and 242).

The proposition that the present Felton is a new Felton is half accepted by the author of the account in the *N.C.H.* (vii, p. 375), when he writes: "a church and vill had probably existed at Felton from soon after, if not before, the Norman Conquest; and it may be inferred that the vill lying over a mile to the north of the church town called . . . Old Felton, is of yet earlier origin". But the evidence for a burghal plantation, as opposed to a daughter village, is still slender.

HAYDON BRIDGE   Northumberland   sheet 77   53/843645
c. 1323

This petty borough at the bridge over the Tyne may derive from the market and fair granted in 1323 (Hodgson, *Northumberland*, pt. 2, vol. iii, p. 362). Haydon was a township in the large parish of Warden; its church (or chapelry) was at 843653 (near the present Haydon and Tofts farms) and a mile north of the bridge. On the south side of the bridge was another settlement in Langley township, with another chapel. The two have now coalesced but it is significant that in 1365 there were burgages in Haydon "on both sides of the water" (C135/201/5 and 210/12). There is nothing very burghal about the arrangement of houses now.

MITFORD   Northumberland   sheet 78   45/168856
1100–57

If Hodgson's suggestion is correct (*Northumberland*, pt. 2, ii, p. 421) and Mitford marked the first crossing of the Wansbeck by the main road from Newcastle to Scotland— before the bridge at Morpeth—the town here must be older than Morpeth, indeed perhaps as old as the castle which was built in 1100 (C. Hunter Blair, "The Early Castles of Northumberland", *Arch. Ael.*, 4th ser., xxii (1944), pp. 116–68). There was a market charter in 1157 and burgages are recorded in the early fourteenth century and in an undated charter (*Newminster Cartulary*, Surtees Soc., lxvi (1876), p. 29).

MORPETH   Northumberland   sheet 78   45/197859
1199–1239

This borough occupied a position similar to Warkworth: the main coastal road to Scotland crosses a river by a bridge which brings it into a flat piece of ground protected by the double bend of a river meander. But at Morpeth the castle (and parish church) are on the opposite bank to the town. If the castle was founded in 1090 (C. Hunter Blair, "The Early Castles of Northumberland", *Arch. Ael.*, 4th ser., xxii (1944), pp. 116–168) it is credible that the borough town on the other bank is a separate creation, probably from the time of the market charter in 1199 (Hodgson, *Northumberland*, pt. 2, ii, p. 421). There is a curious tradition at Bockenfield, 8 miles further north, that Morpeth market was first held at this (now deserted) village and then transferred (W. Whellan, *History, Topography and Directory of Northumberland* (1855), p. 613), but Hodgson thought that Morpeth had displaced the older castle-borough of Mitford at the place where, before the bridge, the road to Scotland had crossed the Wansbeck. The borough charters that have survived begin with one from Roger de Merlay II (1188–1239) in terms that suggest the town was already established (*Ballard*, p. 21); two others (Hodgson, *Northumberland*, pt. 2, ii, pp. 480–482) from the period 1239–66 (*Ballard and Tait*, p. 48) describe forty-three and forty-six borough tofts respectively, and in terms that suggest extension of the borough by encroachment upon former open-field land. Most convincing of all is a phrase in a charter of Roger de Merlay III to Newminster abbey (*Surtees Soc.*, lxvi, p. 6) giving a piece of land *ad capud novae villae de Morpath quam fundavi*. Newminster, founded in 1138, is only half a mile west of Morpeth, and in the short biography of Roger de Merlay II (*ibid.*, p. 271) the Cartulary notes *burgum de Morpath decoravit*.

NEWBROUGH   Northumberland   sheet 77   53/874677
1221

"Newbrough was, I think, founded and formed into a borough by the Cumin family about the beginning of the reign of Henry III when they obtained a charter for a market at Thornton which was the name of the estate upon which this new *burgh* was founded." (J. Hodgson, *History of Northumberland*, pt. 2, vol. iii, p. 391.) There were certainly still burgages there in 1369 (C135/207/12) but the present settlement, half a mile south of Thornton castle, is without any distinct character. A document of c. 1320 mentions a *novus burgus* here (*Hodgson*, iv, p. 383) and Edward I was here himself in the summer of 1306. "The novus burgus of Thornton in Tynedale (arose) from the grant of a market charter in 1221," A. H. Smith, *E.P.N.S.*, xxv (1956), p. 60. The market charter at Thornton to which Hodgson refers is that of 1221.

NEWCASTLE UPON TYNE   Northumberland   sheet 78   45/249640
1080–1130

"The origin of this ancient town is a subject entirely open to the conjectures of the inquisitive", wrote E. Mackenzie in his *Description and Historical Account of . . . Newcastle Upon Tyne* (1827), and few of the many subsequent accounts of the town have been as candid. Since 1827 no new evidence has been noted that would establish the connection between the pre-Norman settlement at "Monkchester" and the Norman town outside the gate of the new castle which followed the Conquest. The first record of the name (*Ekwall*, p. 339) is from 1130 but the castle was built in 1080 (C. Hunter Blair, "The Early Castles of Northumberland", *Arch. Ael.*, 4th ser., xxii (1944), pp. 116–168). A recent history, however, comes to the same negative conclusion: "so far as we know there was no Saxon village on or near the site of *Pons Aelius*. This silence of contemporary records is a little baffling." (S. Middlebrook, *Newcastle*

Upon Tyne (1950), p. 9.)   It is less baffling if one admits the possibility that the town was as new as the castle.

NEWTON in Warkworth   Northumberland   sheet 71   45/249065
by 1249

This seems to have been a small suburb of Warkworth planted on the north side of the bridge.   In 1249 (C132/9/1) there were certainly both the borough of Warkworth and a *nova villa*, and in 1293 a market and fair (*Surtees Soc.*, cxvii (1909), p. 311), while in 1310 (C134/17/6) there were tenements "*que vocantur villa Novi Burgi*". Nothing has been noted on the ground, and the site is now partly occupied by a cemetery.   But in Elizabethan times the tradition of the new town remained.   In the survey of 1567 (*N.C.H.*, v, p. 149) the town was accounted a fisherman's suburb: "it was thought good for diverse causes that those persons which sholde trade ther traffique by sea as maryners or fishermen (owners of shippes and merchaunts onely excepted) sholde inhabyte and dwell together.   Evene so was sett forthe one parcell of grounde for theme to inhabit upon, as this daye called the Newe-towne, and nowe, althoughe not inhabited, the grounde or rigge therof is nowe used and occupied by the burgesses of Warkeworth."   It was explained that the main part of the borough of Warkworth between bridge and castle, south of the river, was for merchants and handicraftsmen.   In another survey of 1570 (E164/37 f. 151), when the main borough consisted only of mean buildings inhabited by poor fishermen, the site of the suburban borough was described merely as a parcel of land called "Tenterhughe et Newtowne" with 119 selions of land in it (these are the *rigges* of the 1567 document), and this suggests that the new town had been projected on an open-field site, and that the land had returned to field use.   In a rental of 1498 (*N.C.H.*, v, p. 162) twenty tenants shared 139 selions in New-town.   The land known as New-town is a block of about 50 acres, clearly cut from Birling parish (*ibid.*, v, pp. 161).   In 1567 it was "lyinge amonge ye erable land of Birling".   It is shown on Robert Norton's plan (*ibid.*, p. 136).

SHIELDS, NORTH   Northumberland   sheet 78   54/355680
1225

The town and port of North Shields comprised 33 acres taken from the demesnes of the priory of Tynemouth, lying along the north bank of the Tyne estuary; and the development is paralleled at South Shields (county Durham) on the opposite bank. In both cases there were acute conflicts of interest and jurisdiction with the burgesses of Newcastle and most of the information about the origins of North Shields derives from complaints in 1275 (*R.H.*, ii, p. 18) and the Parliamentary proceedings of 1290 (*Rot. Parl.*, i, p. 26).   There is supporting evidence from the Tynemouth Cartulary in 1267 (f. 116b, cited in *N.C.H.*, viii, p. 286).   The physical appearance of the town, crowded on to the shore, is well set out in a survey of 1564–65 (*ibid.*, pp. 293–294): "litle howses builded under the watterbanke, and they have nether groundes belongynge unto them nor yet anye rowme on the backside to make onye gardines or orchardes but only howses for fishermen, and on the fore partes litle kyes and shores maid before everye howse for ther cobles and ther geare to ly at and to drye ther fishe and geare upon".

The prior began to build here in 1225. The fishermen who came to settle on the demesne provided the monks with fish in return for the privilege of having houses and their own boats. There seem to have been twenty-seven houses, a quay, mills, and a small port soon after 1225. Between 1267 and 1280 thirty-two more houses were built; and sixteen between 1280 and 1290; in 1292 there were said to be a hundred, and in 1296—after judgment had gone against the Prior—there were still thirteen wealthy enough to be assessed for the lay subsidy (E179/158/1; eight free tenants were assessed in 1294: E179/242/80). The adverse judgment of 1296 did not permanently cripple the town; but its sixteenth-century condition shows it no larger than it had been in the late thirteenth (*N.C.H.*, viii, pp. 284–315). The town had no other church than that of the mother parish until 1836 (*ibid.*, p. 360).

WARENMOUTH   Northumberland   sheet 71   46/ c.160357
1247

In April 1247 Henry III granted to the new borough of Warenmouth all the liberties that John's charter had granted to Newcastle upon Tyne (*Cal. Chart. Rolls.*, i, p. 320) including a gild merchant. The new town must have come into existence, for in 1257 the sheriff was able to render £5 as the fee farm and seven years' arrears also (*N.C.H.*, i, p. 194). In 1293 a jury stated that the town was built on the common pasture of Bamburgh, and it seems likely that the town was intended as a port of supply for Bamburgh (*Ballard and Tait*, pp. xlvii and lv). In 1256 the town was separately represented before the assize judges (JI/1/642). In 1296 there were three inhabitants in the *Nova Villa* of sufficient wealth to be assessed for taxation and there were burgages in 1330. The farm of the vill was still set at £5 in 1279 (*N.C.H.*, i, p. 119); in 1328 it was described as "burned completely" but worth 50s. (SC6/950/3); only 40s. 3½d. was being paid in 1331 (SC6/950/2). It is not known when the place decayed: it may have perished in the siege of Bamburgh in 1464, and in 1472 the crown granted a "tenement called *Newe Towne*" which may be the predecessor of the present farm at G.R. 162355. Newton Hill is the name given to the furzy pasture above the farm but it is unlikely that the town was on this hill, so inaccessible to the sea; a more likely site is the cove at Heather Cottages (1 inch O.S. map) just below the farm. In 1575 (E178/1729) an Exchequer commission was sent to view the "see towne" of Bamburgh, but all memory of the former new town had gone. One witness declared that "the place called the towne is not knowne unless it be the towne of Bamburgh"; and another: "There is at this day no place or towne of that name, the Cee Towne." In the course of a Commons debate in 1621, mention was made of "a desolate town called Newton in Northumberland", probably this borough, that was still assessed to pay an old fee farm of 50s. (W. Notestein, F. H. Relf and H. Simpson, *Commons Debates of 1621* (New Haven, 1935), ii, p. 191.)

NOTTINGHAMSHIRE

No plantations have yet been noticed in this county, although the topography of Nottingham itself affords clear evidence of a Norman extension to the Saxon borough.

Newark, whose name is suggestive, appears in Domesday Book, and *P.N. Notts.*, p. 199, asserts that the "new work" from which the town was named was a pre-Conquest fortification.

OXFORDSHIRE

COGGES   Oxfordshire   sheet 158   42/364098
1212–13

The old village of Cogges, now largely deserted, stood near the church, just across the Windrush from Witney. The formation of a new settlement on the Witney–Oxford road is indicated by a charter of 1212–13 (L. C. Loyd and D. M. Stenton, eds., *Sir Christopher Hatton's Book of Seals* (1950), pp. 76–78). It was only 5 miles from the Newland suburb planted at Eynsham (*q.v.*) in 1215. At Cogges twenty-three holdings of 2 acres each were cut from the demesne next to the main road (*via regalis*) and rented out at 1s. an acre with a provision for building upon them, thereby "setting out to create a village of some importance" (*ibid.*, p. 78). The houses on the main road north from the church are still known as Newland, and this venture by Robert Arsic was probably a suburban imitation or supplement to Witney, where the borough was itself very new at this time: it probably dates from 1208–09 (H. Hall, *The Pipe Roll of the Bishop of Winchester* (1903), p. 17). But the venture at Cogges failed, for nothing urban is suggested by the Cogges entries in the Hundred Rolls in 1279 (*R.H.*, ii, pp. 867–868).

EYNSHAM, (Newland)   Oxfordshire   sheet 158   42/434096
1215

The charter of 1215 (*Eynsham Cartulary*, ed. H. E. Salter (Oxford Hist. Soc., vols. xlix (1906) and li (1908)) i, pp. 60–61) assigned a block of demesne land outside the vill of Eynsham which was to be divided into acre plots, each plot paying 4s. per year. The purpose was *pro utilitate et promocione domus nostrae*. By 1366 there were thirty-one houses in the *novus burgus* (*ibid.*, ii, pp. 177 and 50–56); about the same time there were 300 houses or so in the old town (*ibid.*, i, p. xliv). This extension of the town is clearly visible in the map of 1782 printed by Sir Edmund Chambers, *Eynsham Under the Monks* (Oxfordshire Rec. Soc., xviii (1936)), where the topography of Newland is discussed (*ibid.*, pp. 84–88). A plan showing the relation of Newland to Eynsham is given by H. M. Colvin in A. L. Poole, ed., *Medieval England* (1958), i, p. 63, drawing attention to the analogy of Newland borough at Sherborne (*q.v.*). The allocation of demesne plots at Cogges (*q.v.*) two years earlier should also be noted.

HENLEY ON THAMES   Oxfordshire   sheet 159   41/763827
by 1179

"It is a singular circumstance", observed its historian, "that this place is not mentioned in Domesday Book." (J. S. Burn, *A History of Henley on Thames* (1861), p. 5.) J. G. Jenkins, the editor of the *Missenden Cartulary* (Bucks. Arch. Soc. Rec. Br. i (1938),

p. 16), says in connection with a charter of Stephen, supposed to have been issued at Henley on Thames (1136–45), "there is some doubt about the existence of Henley as early as this". The first certain reference to Henley occurs in the Pipe Roll of 1179 (not 1184 as *P.N. Oxon.*, p. 74): an interesting if ambiguous statement that the king bought the land of Henley "for making buildings": (*ad facienda edificia*: *P.R.S.*, xxviii (1907), p. 95).

In 1196 (*ibid.*, n.s. vii (1930), p. 75) Henley was tallaged with Benson, and in 1199 John granted away both Benson and "the town and manor of Henley" (Burn, *op. cit.*, p. 7). Six years later there was a pavage grant and there was certainly a bridge over the Thames by 1234. In 1279 (*R.H.*, ii, p. 751) Henley is described merely as a hamlet of Benson with a chapel, but in 1297 the earl of Cornwall's revenues from the town included the tolls of markets and a fair as well as payments by a guild of 46 merchants (L. M. Midgley, ed., *Ministers' Accounts of the Earldom of Cornwall* (Camden Soc., 3rd ser., lxvi (1942), p. 91). There is no mention of a borough in 1272 (C132/42/1) but in 1300 (C133/95) 13s. 2½d. rent was paid for burgages; "gildesilver" was also paid. No charter is known before that of 1568 (Burn, *op. cit.*, p. 11). The borough consisted of a street west of the bridge that broadened into a market place after intersecting a north–south road running parallel to the river bank. The church stands near the bridge.

THAME, NEW   Oxfordshire   sheet 159   42/706058

1219–21

Thame was a large manor in Domesday Book belonging to the bishop of Lincoln, and south of the village there was a large episcopal park. Bishop Alexander gave this park for the site of a Cistercian abbey in 1139–40 and in 1146 founded a prebendal household near the church at Thame itself. At that time Thame was a village just south of the bridge over the Thame, near the present parish church; the main road from Oxford to Aylesbury passed the church.

Just as Alexander's new castle at Sleaford gave rise to New Sleaford (*q.v.*) so these two developments at Thame may have given the first stimulus to urban development along the road (now the High Street) leading from the village to the abbey. At this period the bishops were developing their newly acquired village of Biggleswade (Beds.) into a borough (*V.C.H., Beds.*, ii, p. 212), but there is no further documentation at Thame until the market of 1183–86 (*V.C.H., Oxon.*, vii, p. 191) and a market charter of 1215 granted in recompense for damage done to the bishop's property during the Interdict. More significant is the licence of 1219 for the bishop to divert the Oxford–Aylesbury road, bringing it from Lashlake down into the centre of High Street and adding almost a mile to the journey (*Rot. Lit. Claus.*, i, p. 402). It was in 1221 that bishop Hugh "made on the king's highway in the *Forum* of Thame an encroachment where he raised houses to increase his rent, to the length of 100 feet in all" and in 1251 eighteen shops were erected in the roadway (*R.H.*, ii, pp. 31 and 280). A survey of 1230–34 records sixty-three burgages paying the shilling rent, and the markets and profits of the courts were then worth £17 4s. 1½d. Thame was separately represented at the Assize of 1241 and 1247 (JI/1/695 m. 24d and 700 m. 3):

32   477

wine and cloth were on sale here. A very detailed survey of 1258 (Queen's Coll. Oxford, Ms., 366 ff. 23d–25) lists seventy-six burgages.

It is significant that the area of New Thame is only 50 acres, having the appearance of being cut from the large rural manor. No separate church was necessary for the new town since it was contiguous with the older village. The broad market street is nearly half a mile long and the encroachments upon it are very spectacular. In all the extant tax assessments from 1306 to 1523 the value of New Thame exceeded Old: by 1662 Old Thame and Priestend had seven householders paying the Hearth Tax while New Thame had 149.

WOODSTOCK, NEW   Oxfordshire   sheet 145   42/445168
1154–74

The river Glyme, 6 miles north-west of Oxford, divided the parishes of Bladon and Wootton. Woodstock park, the wooded area between these two villages, was enclosed with a stone wall by Henry I. The chronicler Henry of Huntingdon ascribed the foundation of Old Woodstock to Henry II but there was a meeting of the Anglo-Saxon witan here c. 1000 (A. Ballard, *Chronicles of Woodstock* (1896)). Old Woodstock, which still exists, is on the north bank of the river. The borough of New Woodstock lies on the south bank, centred on a long triangular market place with its apex at the park gates. The origins of this town (*primo statuta fuit villata de Wodestock . . .*) were described in the Hundred Rolls of 1279: "King Henry II visited the manor house of Woodstock for love of a certain woman called Rosamund, and there was a waste place without the said park and manor, and because men lodged too far, the king gave places to divers men to build hostelries there for the use of the king's men" (*R.H.*, ii, p. 839). The land was acquired from the Templars (*Ballard*, p. xci, and *Plac. Abb.*, p. 24).

A Tuesday market was granted by Henry II and John gave a fair. If the date of Rosamund's death is 1176 (*D.N.B.*, xi, p. 75) and her liaison with the king began in 1174, then the foundation may lie between 1174 and 1176, but the king had frequented Woodstock earlier in his reign (*Hist. King's Works*, ii (1963), p. 1010, and plan p. 1011).

In 1279 there were 137 houses, and 108 householders' names are known. The church of St. Mary was founded as a chapelry of Bladon before the end of the thirteenth century, and the borough sent two Members to the Parliaments of 1302. There is no surviving charter of date earlier than 1453 but borough rents were paid in 1230 (*P.R.S.*, n.s., iv (1927) p. 258) and in 1296 Woodstock was one of the nine taxation boroughs in the county.

RUTLAND

No plantations have been noted in this county, England's smallest.

SHROPSHIRE

In this border county the most fruitful period of plantation seems to have been the early twelfth century; the later examples are both petty creations. Ludlow is an important creation, the earliest Norman town that was rectilinear in shape and divided by an interior grid. It remained prosperous in the fourteenth century and it should be remembered that this border county was significantly different from those of the northern hills. Its sheep pastures produced the best quality wool and there was every incentive to develop market centres since there was no great concentration of clothmaking inside the county. Petty boroughs such as Lydham and Burford (*Eyton*, iv, p. 318, and xi, p. 280) seem to be promoted villages. Clun may be a burghal addition, north of the river near the castle, to the Domesday village south of the river near the church. At the end of the thirteenth century there were only three taxation boroughs, two of them plantations and the third the county town.

BASCHURCH NEWTOWN   Shropshire   sheet 118   32/424221
by 1227

At Baschurch there are two distinct centres of settlement. Baschurch village is near the church (422218) but Newtown is 400 yards to the north-east near the cross roads. Could the charter of 1227 (*Dugdale*, iii, p. 522) giving the churches of Baschurch, Ness and *novus burgus* refer to this place? There were burgages in *Nova Villa de Baschurch* in 1339 (*Eyton*, x, p. 133).

BISHOP'S CASTLE   Shropshire   sheet 129   33/323890
1127

The castle on which this town depended was erected c. 1127 in the western part of the large, 18,000 acre manor of Lydbury North, now a village 3 miles south-east of Bishop's Castle (*Eyton*, xi, pp. 203–206). The church of the castle-town shows the usual dependence on the mother church of the older settlement. The town consists of a simple grid of streets on ground steeply falling from the castle; the church is half a mile from the castle at the lower end of the principal street, although the side- and cross-streets of the grid no longer come this far south. The town was not given borough status until 1573 though Lydham, a few miles to the north, became a borough in 1270 (*Cal. Chart. Rolls*, ii, p. 146). Burgages to the number of forty-six appear in an extent of Bishop's Castle made in 1285 (*Camden Miscellany, xv* (Camden 3rd ser. xli (1929)), pp. 29–30). In 1961 it had the smallest population of any English borough and its municipal status has now lapsed.

BRIDGNORTH   Shropshire   sheet 130   32/717927
1086–1101

The succession of settlement and river-crossings in this locality is very interesting. In 896 there was a bridge over the Severn (*Ekwall*, p. 377) at *Cwatbrycg* (Quatbridge), which would explain why an Anglo-Saxon *burh* was built on the east bank at this crossing in 912, a year before Tamworth and Stafford. In 1086 Domesday Book records the *burgus* of Quatford with a *novus domus* but worth nothing; the entry appears under Eardington, a village on the opposite bank, and the fact that Quatford also lay in Eardington parish (*Eyton*, i, p. 110) emphasises the planted character of this *burh*.

479

It is not known how long the bridge at Quatford continued, but the use of "Bridge-north" to describe a second town to the north further upstream suggests that it was not completely forgotten in the thirteenth century. This second town of "Brug" (Bridge) must have followed the transfer of the military centre from Quatford in 1101, when Ordericus Vitalis records that the rebel Earl Robert *oppidum Quatford trans-tulit*, but the foundation of a new collegiate church at Quatford by Robert's father in 1086 suggests no move was then intended. In 1102 the king besieged and defeated the rebel earl at Bridgnorth and the town passed to Henry I. Henry II's charter of 1157 (*Ballard*, p. 5) is a simple one, giving the burgesses all the liberties and customs that they had in the time of Henry I (1100–35): so that the new borough and the new bridge could have been very close in date (*cp.* the other borough of the bridge at Boroughbridge, Yorks., also with a shift from an Anglo-Saxon borough and a decayed bridge).

The town of Bridgnorth originally lay in Morville parish, repeating the pattern of Eardington and Quatford; and the late arrival is reflected in the dependent status of the town church at Bridgnorth.

Eyton was well aware of the significant topography of Bridgnorth: "Bridgnorth was in every respect a mere transfer of . . . Quatford. The Castle, the Borough, the Collegiate Church, even the Bridge followed one another from Quatford to the site selected by the ambitious and restless Norman (Robert de Belesme, earl of Shrews-bury)" (*Eyton*, i, p. 242). Eyton, however (i, p. 131), seems to place the *burh* at Panpudding Hill (715925) in Oldbury. Excavation seems to be the solution. The town, castle and church are crowded together on the west bank, occupying the river cliff west of the bridge. The castle earthworks can be seen at the top of the pro-montory, adjoining the castle church of St. Mary Magdalene; and the broad market street runs northwards and inland. The castle church became parochial by 1472. The town church of St. Leonard was founded soon after 1102. St. Mary's parish now includes the southern part of the town and a considerable area on the east bank; the church of St. Leonard, which stands within the line of the old walls (1st ed. 6 inch O.S.), also has a large extra-mural parish, on the west bank. It is significant also that the borough bounds (before 1832) took in the eastern bank of the Severn as far as and including Quatford. (S. Lewis, *A Topographical Dictionary of England*, v (1838), plate 78. See also J. F. A. Mason, *The Borough of Bridgnorth* (1957).

CAUS   Shropshire   sheet 118   33/338078
by 1200

This is a castle-borough analogous to such Marcher petty boroughs as Cefnlys and Dolforwyn. It is situated at the east end of the Long Mountain and commands the valley road from Shrewsbury to Montgomery. The ground falls steeply to a small valley on the north and the castle crowns the ridge. The castle comprised a huge motte with two deep ditches, and three courts related to the contours of the hill. Below the centre motte, with its rock-cut ditch, is an inner court with a well; remains of twin towers can be seen among the undergrowth and a bridge crossed a wide ditch into the middle ward; there is a western gateway at a lower level.

The town probably stood within the outer bailey but no certain remains can be seen (*cp.* Bere; Dolforwyn; Cefnllys in the Wales *Gazetteer* below).

In 1086 the district was comprised in the manor of Alretone, which Roger fitz Corbet held from earl Roger de Montgomery, and there was a castle here by 1140. A market charter was granted to Robert Corbet, lord of Caus, in 1200 and a fair in 1248. On Thomas Corbet's death in 1273 there were twenty-eight burgages in the borough (C133/7/8) and in the record of the taxation of 1292 (E179/242/48) there are the names of the chief taxors, the lord, his bailiff and the twelve jurors of "the town and castle of Caus". In 1300 there were thirty-four burgages *infra muros villae*, each paying 1s. 2d. (C133/94/6). A chapel in the castle was built between 1261 and 1272. This chapel is mentioned in 1372 (C135/230), as well as £4 13s. 5d. of rents from burgesses (see also C135/85/14 (1347)). A borough chapel of St. Margaret was founded in 1272 (*Reg. Swinfield*, Cant. and York Soc., vi (1909), pp. 162–164): ex. inf. Mr. J. B. Lawson. In a document of 1387 the town was already in decay (L. F. Chitty, *Arch. Camb.*, civ (1955), pp. 199–201). A survey and a rental of 1521–2 (E36/150 mm. 111 and 181) reported that "the castel ther standing veray goodly upon height is in grete ruyne and decay"; and the rents of the "burrogh of Caurs" were assessed at 39s. 3d, but 23s. 6d. could not be collected. A similar picture is given by an account of 1540–41 (Anon., "The Lordship of Cause", *Trans. Salop. Arch. Soc.*, liv (1953), pp. 332–350.) Nine burgages paid rent but twenty-four other burgages had been in total decay "for many years past". Miss Chitty considered that the Corbets named the place after the Pays de Caux in Normandy.

LUDLOW   Shropshire   sheet 129   23/512746
1086–94

This town has long been known as a classic example of Norman town plantation. Its plan and history were thoroughly described in W. H. St. John Hope, "The Ancient Topography of the Town of Ludlow", (*Archaeologia*, lxi (1909), pp. 387 sqq. with plans); the plan is conveniently redrawn in A. L. Poole, ed., *Medieval England* (1958), p. 58. *Eyton*, v, p. 233, assigns the castle to the years 1086–94 and the Lacys must have planted the town at its gate almost immediately. (Recent work by Mr. E. L. Morley would limit this first borough to Dinham, west of Mill Street.) There is a broad market place eastwards from the castle to the church, its former width now partially obscured by encroachments. The church was given a chequer to itself in the north-east corner of the town, which was almost a perfect rectangle, with five parallel streets at right angles to the market place: two of these streets are now obscured by subsequent extension of the castle and by reversion of the south-east corner of the town to gardens, but their course is clearly shown in the plan cited above. The castle and town are bound in one by an encircling wall and together occupy a bluff overlooking the Teme at its junction with the Corve.

A Ludlow Corporation rental dating from 1482 is useful for setting out the burgages in Streets and Rows (*rangia*) (Shropshire Record Office). Note: the D.B. "Lude" was not Ludlow (H. C. Darby and I. B. Terrett, *Domesday Geography of Midland*

England (1954), p. 118). The thirteenth-century town walls seem to have excluded part of the street grid on the south.

NEWPORT   Shropshire   sheet 119   33/743193
1129–35

Henry II's charter of 1163–66 to *Novus Burgus* (*Ballard*, p. 17) confirms the original grant "in the time of King Henry my grandfather" (i.e. 1100–35) and Henry I is said to have visited the town twice. There is no mention of the place in Domesday Book: it lies on the edge of the county within the manor of Edgmond and alongside one of the meres (now drained). In 1159 and 1173 *aids* from the borough are recorded on the Pipe Rolls (*Eyton*, ix, pp. 129 sqq.) and in 1203 (JI/1/732) the borough was one of those recognised at the Assize; cloth was then being sold there. Its contribution to the Exchequer was increased in 1228 (E373/72 m. 12), and in 1274 (C133/8/6) its rental was £5 18s. 6¼d. In 1279 its tallage was stated to be 26 marks (*R.H.*, ii, p. 65).

A church is mentioned here 1129–48 and a priest, stated to be *novi burgi*, witnessed the first charter. The town was elevated to full parish status in 1221. The economic origins of the town are suggested by its obligation to carry fish from the vivary to the royal household, and by the three fishes *naiant in pale* that make up the town's arms. The church is dedicated to St. Nicholas, patron saint of fishermen. It stands in the middle of the long, broad market place that comprises the borough.

OSWESTRY   Shropshire   sheet 118   33/290297
c. 1100

The existence of the Iron Age fort of "Old Oswestry", linked to the Dee by Wat's Dyke, emphasises the strategic importance of this site where the Shropshire plain meets the Welsh hills. The medieval town, walled in its day (*Cal. Pat. Rolls, 1247–58*, p. 609) lay just over a mile south of Old Oswestry, taking its name from St. Oswald's tree or cross. "My distinct impression", wrote Eyton, "is that Oswestry as a town owed a name indeed to the Saxon legend which had consecrated its site, but owed its foundation to the Normans . . . the vill and church being built upon that part of the old manor of Maisbury which had previously been known as Oswald's tree" (*Eyton*, x, p. 319). The town was also known from its church as Blancminster, and the first known charter (1190–1200: *Eyton*, x, p. 324; *Ballard*, p. 81) shows William fitz William fitz Alan defining his burgesses as those "who received messuages from my bailiff for the improvement of my market". The market was worth £20 a year by 1271 (C132/42/5; see also E142/87/2: 1302). For the shilling burgages surviving in 1393 see W. J. Slack, *The Lordship of Oswestry* (1951), pp. 142–152.

The manor of Maesbury, in which Oswestry stands, was waste in 1086 but there was a castle of *Luvre* (*sc. l'œuvre*, "work" as in New-wark, South-wark). A charter of earl Roger to the monks of Shrewsbury records that the first Norman sheriff had previously given them the church of St. Oswald and the tithes of that vill (*Eyton*, x, p. 319). Castle, church and vill must have been very close together in time. The town has no grid shape: there is one cluster of streets near the castle and another street, in which St. Oswald's church stands, lies rather detached to the south-west: the two may represent *Luvre* and *Oswald's tree*. (There is a plan of the town in W. Price, *The History of Oswestry* (1815), p. 83, which shows a line of walls that definitely excludes the church.)

RUYTON, NEW   Shropshire   sheet 118   33/394223
1304–10
The vill of Ruyton is recorded in Domesday Book; the creation of New Ruyton in the early fourteenth century must have been an addition to the village, of the Eynsham type. "Edmund, earl of Arundel, purchased and reconstructed the manor with the design of founding a borough" (*Eyton*, x, p. 111). The borough charter dates from 1308 and a document of 1304–10 concerns seven burgages in the *nova villa* of Ruyton on the fee of the canons of Haughmond. It may be significant that in 1311 a market and fair were granted (R. L. Kenyon, "The Borough of Ruyton", *Tr. Salop. Arch. and Nat. Hist. Soc.*, 2nd ser., iii (1891), pp. 237–252). A mile or two away the abbot of Shrewsbury was creating burgages in the *nova villa* of Baschurch (*Eyton*, x, p. 133). The distinction between New and Old Ruyton was known to Miss Bateson ("an ancient distinction almost lost sight of": *Eng. Hist. Rev.*, xx (1905), p. 340). New Ruyton may be the area to the north-west of the castle and church.

SOMERSET

Somerset was colonised by the Anglo-Saxons before Devon and Cornwall, and there is a distinct difference in the urban pattern. Somerset had a number of important Anglo-Saxon centres and the additional plantations listed below were insubstantial additions to this stock. Organic promotion also went on: Montacute was transformed from a village between the arrival of Robert, count of Mortain, and 1102. He built the castle on the steep Lutgaresby Hill and the village of Bishopton at the foot changed both its name and character. It took the castle-name *Montagud* (*de monte acuto*). Similar development may be detected at Nether Stowey, a borough before 1222. It is not certain whether the *borough* of Merryfield (340178) mentioned in an extent of East Coker in 1274 was an abortive borough in the urban sense. No borough appears in later extents of the manor (*Cal. I.P.M.*, ii, pp. 97 and 326). A brief survey of urbanisation in Somerset is provided by Sir William Savage, "Somerset Towns", *Proc. Som. Arch. and Nat. Hist. Soc.*, xcix–c (1954–55), pp. 49–74. This article suggests that there might be an abortive plantation at Newport in North Curry (sheet 177, 31/317236). Chard has some symptoms of a planted town, including a town church lying outside the original borough bounds (plan in *Report of Boundary Commission* (1837), unpaginated), but on balance it seems to be a case of an episcopal borough tacked on to a village in 1235: *Proc. Som. Arch. and N.H.S.*, xviii (1883), pp. 28–78.

CAPUT MONTIS (Downend)   Somerset   sheet 165   31/310414
by 1159
Among the boroughs of the Assize Roll of 1225 (*Som. Rec. Soc.*, xi (1897), pp. 28 and 52) appears *burgus de capite montis*. It would be natural to take this for Montacute,

did not Montacute appear distinctly elsewhere in the roll. The editorial identification is with "Chesdulmunt", (*ibid.*, p. 67) which is in turn equated with the Domesday "Doneham" and the little hamlet of Downend in Puriton. The connection is closer when (as Mr. I. P. Collis has pointed out to me) the tithing fined in 1225 for the flight of a murderer was *Dunevde*; (*ibid.*, p. 98) and this may be a misreading of *Dunende*.

The "borough" appears again under its Latin name in the Assize Roll of 1242–43 (*ibid.*, p. 292) but in the *Nomina Villarum* of 1316 (*Som. Rec. Soc.*, iii (1889)) there is no mention of this place in Puriton Hundred. There is a messuage mentioned c. 1216 in the vill *de capite montis* (*Som. Rec. Soc.*, xiv (1899), p. 163) and see *Som. Rec. Soc.*, xliv (1929), p. 254, for tenements in Downend (1280)).

The down does indeed end here. The site is at the extreme western end of the ridge of land which ends abruptly above the reclaimed marshland between Bridgwater and Burnham. There is an earthwork which looks like a small motte and bailey castle, and above it a small grid of lanes makes up the hamlet of Downend, although the southern slopes and hill top are destroyed by modern quarrying. The river Parrett would have flowed past the site, which would have been the best waterside landing in Puriton. A small excavation was carried out in 1908 (A.G. Chater and A. F. Major, "Excavations at Downend", *Proc. Som. Arch. and N.H.S.*, lv (1909), pp. 162–73). The lords of Puriton became the lords of Nether Stowey, another small Somerset borough with a rather longer life.

In a perceptive note written in 1907 (*Proc. Som. Arch. and N.H. Soc.*, liii, pp. 174–178), W. H. P. Grenfell drew attention to the payment of 10s. which appeared on the Pipe Roll of 1161 as due from Philip de Columbers for *burgriht*. Since the de Columbers had not yet developed their borough at Nether Stowey (Collinson, *Somerset*, ii, p. 396) this payment may refer to *burgus de capite montis*. The *burgriht* payment first appears in 1159, two years earlier than noticed by Grenfell: (*P.R.S.*, i (1884), p. 20).

RADECLIVE   Somerset   sheet 165   31/395548
1179–89

In 1189 Richard I granted a charter to Reginald, bishop of Bath "that he may make a borough on his own land of *Radeclive* . . . with a market and other free customs and liberties that any borough has that is on our land in England '. Nothing seems to have come of this liberality although Edward II confirmed the charter in 1324. In Speed's map of Somersetshire "Ratclyffe" is marked on the bank of the old course of the Axe in Compton Bishop parish, and the farm of Rackley may now indicate the site. The curving parish boundary shows where the river used to run, and it approached the steep slopes of Compton Hill just west of the modern farm; the hill may be the "clyffe" of the old name. The borough would have been a small riverside market on the edge of a manor which had the bishop for its lord. In 1179 the Pope had confirmed to the bishop *villam de Cumton* (i.e. Compton Bishop) *cum portu de Radeclive* (*Som. Rec. Soc.*, xxxix (1924), p. 159) so that this riverside port within Compton parish may have become the borough of 1189. The 1st ed. 6 inch O.S. (1888) marks a farm named "New Town" east of Rackley at G.R. 409550, sheet XVII SW.

The village of Compton Bishop is a mile to the north. Rackley is now on a farm track, for the road to Loxton has been diverted to higher ground. There are faint signs of earthworks in the orchard to the north-east of the farm but little room on the slope for more than a row of houses along each side of the road. (The little borough of Weare, *q.v.*, was founded soon after on the same river a mile upstream (*Ballard and Tait*, p. 380). It may be no more than a coincidence that a Walter of Rackley figures among the burgesses of New Winchelsea in its first rental of 1290 (SC 11/660): no other Rackley than this is mentioned in any modern English gazetteer.

STOFORD   Somerset   sheet 178   31/567135

by 1273

In an inquisition of 1273 (C133/2/7) there were seventy-four burgages in the borough of Stoford; in a number of other documents this Stoford is linked with the manor of Barwick, 2 miles south of Yeovil (e.g. C135/200), and in 1348 (C135/91) the lord of the manor drew 30s. from the tolls of St. Mary's fair here. There was still a "borough of Stoford" in the musters of 1569 (*Som. Rec. Soc.*, xx (1904), p. 107) with eleven names, compared with Barwick's nine, but the place is now no more than a roadside village.

The railway line cuts through the western end of the three parallel streets and rather obscures their unity, but the general pattern is that of the Gascon *bastide du commerce*, a simple grid along a road (Yeovil–Dorchester) opposite the ford in the river Yeo from which the borough was named. The borough is one of those that stand at the boundary of two counties, and the ford crossing into Dorset may have had more importance than the present lane would suggest. The north–south road through Stoford on the Somerset bank cannot have been of any significance when the Roman road from Yeovil southwards was in use, and the borough may therefore date from a diversion of the road. The present main road (a turnpike?) has reverted to the Roman course.

The date of foundation is unknown; the borough was not named in the Assize Rolls of 1225 and 1242 (*Som. Rec. Soc.*, xi). Apart from the document of 1273 cited above, it was taxed as a borough in 1327 (but not in 1306 and 1316: *Som. Rec. Soc.*, iii (1889)) although it appeared as a vill in 1316; (see also *Som. Rec. Soc.*, xli (1926), pp. 19 and 69). A document concerning bounds of a *Stoford* in 1231 (*Cal. Close Rolls, 1227–31*, p. 587) mentions *Thrippe* in association. No Thorpe appears on the map near Stoford, but there is no Stoford visible near *Thrupe* in Croscombe which has been suggested as an identification. The alleged grant of a market in 1227 (John Batten, *Hist. and Topog. Coll. relating to South Somerset* (1894), pp. 5–18) is an error for Shalford, Surrey, as *Cal. Cl. Rolls, 1227–31*, p. 92, demonstrates.

WEARE, NETHER   Somerset   sheet 165   31/406537

1195–1225

This borough is known from the confirmation of its charter in 1418 which cites a charter of Edward I of 1278–79. Weare was a "free borough" in 1279: *R.H.* ii, p. 138. It was given the privileges of the borough of Hereford as these had been set down in writing by the burgesses of that city. The instigator was a certain Anselm de Gournay, knight, then serving with Edward I in Scotland. The king freed the burgesses from customs on their merchandise and recorded that Sir Anselm and the burgesses possessed this right by grant of Henry I to Maurice de Gaunt whose sister was Anselm de Gournay's grandmother (Collinson, *Somerset*, i (1791), p. 184). It is unlikely that Henry I was the grantor since Maurice's father, Robert de Weare, did not die until 1195; Maurice died in 1230. It would seem that the borough must date from the beginning of the thirteenth century, nearly contemporary with the bishop of Bath's town of Radeclive a mile to the north-west (*q.v.*). In 1225 Weare was separately represented at the Assize. It was certainly a borough by 1264–5 (*Cal. Inq. Misc.*, i, p. 266). In 1316 Weare was reckoned a *burgus* in the Nomina Villarum, and in the Lay Subsidy of 1327 (E179/169 m. 5) it had ten tax-paying families and a total assessment of 9s. It sent members to the last three Parliaments of Edward I.

The mother village of Weare lies a mile to the south-east and formed a separate tax unit. In its old course, as the parish bounds still show, the river Axe came near to the Bristol to Taunton road before doubling back north to Axebridge. Nether Weare would thus have occupied a peninsula of land adjoining the old crossing of the river. It can never have been very large. The rectilinear burgage plots seem to be preserved in the shape of the gardens to the north of the road, as in the smaller bastides of Devon and Cornwall which lie on main roads.

The text of the charter is printed in *E.H.R.*, xv (1900), p. 308. Grants of burgages in the town, with some topographical detail, are printed in C. D. Ross, ed., *Cartulary of St. Mark's Hospital, Bristol* (Bristol Rec. Soc., xxi (1959), nos. 208–221; see also p. xxix). These date from 1316–29.

STAFFORDSHIRE

It was originally intended to include Tutbury in this list. The Domesday Book entry for Tutbury, as it stands, suggests a small castle borough without any agricultural settlement. In 1086 Henry de Ferrers, lord of Tutbury, had in his borough around the castle forty-two men making a living in his market (*in burgo circa castellum sunt xlii homines de mercato suo tantum viventes*). When he founded Tutbury Priory (1087–1100) he endowed it with the "parish of the castle" and the tithes of the tolls of the castle and his wines (A. Saltman, ed., *The Cartulary of Tutbury Priory*, Wm. Salt Arch. Soc. 4th ser., iv (1962), p. 63). The "parish of the castle" was probably the whole of the market town. A parish church forming part of the Priory endowment was built for the town near the castle (*ibid.*, p. 23). It was certainly a borough, for Robert de Ferrers II's charter to Newborough in 1141 refers to Tutbury simply as "the old borough" (*ibid.*, p. 75). In *V.C.H., Staffs.*, iv, p. 48, it is suggested that the entry for *Burtone* which follows that for Tutbury in Domesday Book is a scribal confusion for *in Burgo* and not an account of Burton on Trent (which was not a Ferrers manor). This *Burtone* had "half a hide in the castle" which again fits the Tutbury situation, but not that at Burton where no castle is known.

If this suggestion is accepted, then the case for Tutbury as purely burghal falls since there had been twelve ploughs at *Burtone* in 1065.

The case of Walsall may need further investigation; *Shaw*, ii, p. 70, calls the omission of Walsall from Domesday Book "singular" but there seems to have been a separate manor *t*. Henry II (?1159); the "men of Walsall" are mentioned in the Pipe Roll of 1179 but the first charter was not until c. 1198 (E. J. Homeshaw, *The Corporation of the Borough and Foreign of Walsall* (1960), pp. 8–13).

The terms of the grant to Leek in 1214 (*Wm. Salt Arch. Soc.*, ix, n.s. (1906), p. 310) are similar to those in new towns: timber was made available to newcomers and building plots were rent-free for an initial period (here three years): but the event was probably the burghal development at an existing settlement, and the stimulus the migration of the abbey of Dieulacres from Cheshire.

NEWBOROUGH   Staffordshire   sheet 120   43/135254

1100–39

Henry de Ferrers founded the borough of Tutbury before 1086, and between 1087 and 1100 he founded the priory of Tutbury (A. Saltman, ed., *The Cartulary of Tutbury Priory*, Wm. Salt Arch. Soc., 4th ser., iv (1962), p. 63). His grandson Robert, the 2nd earl of Derby, granted to the priory in 1141 the tithe of the rents paid for the burgages of the new borough which his father "had caused to grow" (*accrescere fecit*). His father had died in 1139. Robert now added all the tithes of the parish of Newborough to his grandfather's gift of the tithes of Tutbury (*adjeci omnem parochiam de Novo Burgo sicut de veteri*) making it plain that the town planted on the one virgate at Agardsley was New in relation to the (slightly) older borough at Tutbury (*ibid.*, p. 75). In a confirmation of the priory's foundation charter (1150–59) Robert stated that he too intended to make the new borough grow further and that the priory should share in his good fortune if the income from market tolls and the fair should increase (*ibid.*, p. 65).

The borough seems to have been part of a project for the extensive assarting of the Forest of Needwood that lay south of Tutbury between the rivers Dove and Trent.

The priory exchanged most of its land in Newborough with Robert de Ferrers III c. 1260 probably under threats, and this is the context of the charter of 1263, previously thought to be the first borough charter. In 1263 earl Robert allotted 2 acres of arable and 1 acre *in burgo* to all who wanted to take burgages in his free borough of "Agardsley", (*Cal. Pat. Rolls, 1374–77*, p. 460). This name recalls the one virgate at Agardsley in 1086 (*V.C.H., Staffs.*, iv, p. 48) which must have formed the territorial basis for the second Ferrers borough.

Fourteen burgesses were wealthy enough to be taxed for the subsidy of 1332, about two-thirds of the number and wealth assessed at Tutbury that year. But these tax payers were only a minority of the burgesses, for 101 burgages paid £7 11s. 6d. in 1313 (DL29/1/3 m. 5) and several other *placeae* were mentioned in the same account roll; the same number of burgages occur in 1370 (SC6/988/14) and 1415 (DL42/4 ff. 164–6d). The number became conventionalised, for a survey of 1609 (DL44/825) said: "there are within this manor fyve score and one burgages," but the rents were being collected only from twenty-five. In 1377 ninety-three poll-tax payers were recorded.

A survey of the Honour in 1559 (BM. Harl. Ms. 71, f. 8) also records 101 burgages in Newborough but a good deal of nostalgic speculation in the surveyor's introductory remarks on the district as a whole suggests grass-grown market places and some empty burgages. This survey is quoted extensively in Shaw, *Staffs.*, i, p. 44, and seems to come from a lost part of the other volumes of that year's survey that now form DL42/109, 110 and 111.

The village of Newborough straggles along a country road and has nothing burghal remaining in its appearance. The moated site north of the village at Newborough Hall may represent Agardsley manor house.

NEWCASTLE UNDER LYME Staffordshire sheet 110 33/846460
1154–62

The castle newly built below the "lyme" or elm woods in Trentham parish dates probably from 1149 (T. Pape, *Medieval Newcastle under Lyme* (1928), p. 2), and on the Pipe Roll for 1167 (*William Salt Arch. Soc.*, i (1880), p. 48) the *novum oppidum* indicates that a town had been created at the New Castle *sub Lima*; in 1169 the "men of New-castle" are mentioned; in 1171 the pool of the Novum Oppidum was strengthened; and in 1173 the *burgus* contributed to the tallage (*ibid.*, i, p. 69). The earl of Chester built the castle but it had reverted to Henry II in 1154 and the new borough was royal. It is almost certain that the "new market of Trentham" in 1172 (*Pape*, p. 34) was at Newcastle. There are two documents which show that the new town was located at Trentham parish: a papal confirmation of the endowments of Trentham priory in 1162 includes "a certain small township (*viculus*) of Newcastle which is of the territory of Trentham parish" (*Wm. Salt Arch. Soc.*, xi (1890)) pp. 303–304); another document, dating from 1175–82 (Pape, *op. cit.*, pp. 35 and 139) also assigns Newcastle chapel to Trentham; it was only later (c. 1215–32) that the chapel was made dependent on the parish church at Stoke.

There were probably 160 burgages in the new town: this was the number in 1212 (*Wm. Salt. Arch. Soc.*, 3rd ser., ii (1911), p. 386). In 1199 wine was being sold at unlawful prices in Newcastle and in 1203 cloth of substandard quality (JI/1/800 m. 6d and 799 m. 3). In 1187 the tallage paid here was the greatest in the county. In 1174 there was a payment to the king *pro novo foro* (*Wm. Salt. Arch. Soc.*, i (1880), p. 71). In 1235 a Gild Merchant was chartered (*Cal. Chart. Rolls*, i, p. 213).

Farrer (*Lancs. Pipe Rolls* (1902), pp. 414–415) assigned a borough charter to 1173 but *Ballard*, p. xxxvii, shows that this was the charter of 1235. The 1173 charter is known only from the borough charter of Preston (Lancs.) which was modelled upon it in 1179 (*Ballard*, p. 27).

Plans form the frontispieces to Pape, *op. cit.*, and T. Pape, *Newcastle under Lyme in Tudor and Early Stuart Times* (1938). Together they show that the castle was virtually surrounded by the pool made by damming the Lyme Brook and that the borough was on the hill, beginning at the Upper and Lower Green, perhaps within the bailey, and continuing past the church into High Street, Holborn and Nether Street. There is no marked grid. The borough comprised only 544 acres. Burgesses had arable land and commons within the borough and neighbouring parishes (J. G. Jenkins in *V.C.H.*, viii, p. 51).

SUFFOLK

Suffolk has only one definite plantation and that may be regarded as half Cambridge-shire's. The low urbanisation of the Norfolk countryside affords neighbourly confirmation. Two other places have curious features that may derive from plantation. The evidence is as follows:

ORFORD. The local historian who knew it best (V. B. Redstone, "Orford", *Proc. Suff. Inst. Arch.*, x (1900), pp. 82–96 and 205–229) recognised that the place was unmentioned in Domesday Book but that by 1102 Robert Malet, the Domesday lord of Sudbourne, had granted the market and tolls of Orford to the priory of Eye (Dug. *Monasticon*, iii, p. 401). "At first sight this formed a new settlement or town," wrote Redstone (p. 84), but continued: "I do not think this to have been the case." Writing in 1900 he would naturally assume that new towns were extraordinary and that very positive proof would be necessary before Orford could be admitted into that exceptional class. With so many authentic cases of Norman plantation, the prima facie evidence should at least be considered for Orford. The chapel in Orford town was not parochial but a chapel of ease to Sudbourne: "it appears strange," commented Redstone (p. 88) without perhaps realising how common these dependent urban churches were. A charter of the early twelfth century (BM., Stowe Charter no. 407) concerns a house built on Orford causeway, and with it the early documenta-tion of the site ends. In 1164 the town was farmed for £24, a considerable sum, and extensive work began on the castle in the next year. The place was certainly a borough later: (SC6/1003/3 (1306) and SC12/15/16 (1316)); in 1313 it was taxed as a borough. A plan of 1601 (BM. Maps 5210/3 sheet 28) shows the town on a large scale: it had a simple grid focused on the castle.

LOWESTOFT AND LOTHINGLAND. It would be natural to think of Lothingland simply as the name of the whole island or district west of what is now Lowestoft (as O. S. Anderson, *English Hundred Names*, i (1939), p. 84). The *homines de Lothingland* taxed to the aid of Henry II in 1168 and 1187 (*P.R.S.*, xii (1890), p. 33, and xxxvii (1915), p. 61) may suggest some more coherent and compact unit. (The *Burc* in Lothingland of the 1168 Pipe Roll is presumably the village of Castle Burgh near the site of the Roman station in the north-west of the island.) In 1203 there was a manor of Lothingland (*Curia Regis Rolls*, ii, p. 153) and in a law-suit of 1228 (*ibid.*, xiii, pp. 108–111) it was declared that the place where Lothingland market used to be held was now eroded by the sea and the earl of Salisbury had transferred it to another place. I am content to leave the site of Lothingland market at or near Gorleston, where the Hundred Rolls (*R.H.*, ii, p. 160) suggest that there was a market in the late thirteenth century: but there is still the problem of the isolated church at Lowestoft, "even in fine weather out of reach of a considerable part of the population" (Suckling, *Suffolk*, ii, p. 92). It is quite uncertain, however, when or whether there was a settle-ment by the old parish church. "A new town has sprung up on the beach," says

Suckling (*loc. cit.*), but specifies no dates. In 1570 the beach-side community must already have been substantial, for it petitioned the bishop for a chapel to be consecrated in the town (*ibid.*, p. 59). The town church is St. Peter's and the distant church St. Margaret's.

NEWMARKET   Suffolk   sheet 135   52/645635
1217–23

The traditional origin of Newmarket is a removal of the market from Exning, 3 miles to the north-west, on account of the plague, and the date usually given is 1223, when Richard de Argentein was granted a fair at his manor *de novo mercato* at the feast of St. Giles (C60/18 m. 3); this was confirmed in 1227 (C54/36 m. 17) when the sheriff of Suffolk was also ordered to come to the Argentein manor of Newmarket once a year to hold a view of frankpledge (*Cal. Chart. Rolls*, i, p. 11). This provision may have arisen from the border situation of the town, the north side of the street being in Suffolk and the south side in Cambridgeshire (cp. Devizes and Newton Abbot, *q.v.*). Another document dealing with the fair in 1227 (*Cal. Rot. Lit. Claus.*, ii, p. 106= C54/35 m. 20) confirmed a market here (*quam consuevit habere*). In the *Nomina Villarum* of 1316 (*F.A.*, i, p. 154) part of Newmarket was assigned to John de Argentein and part to the prior of Fordham; part lay in Ditton: these entries are in the Cambs. portion of the documents. In 1283 a chapel is mentioned as being "on the Suffolk side" of the town (C133/33/16); in that year the market was worth (with its courts) £5.

Ekwall, *Oxford Dict. Eng. P.N.* (1960), p. 340, has a reference to *novum mercatum* in 1200 (*Selden Soc.*, lxvii, p. 305 (1943)). As a personal name, references can be traced further back: one occurs in 1161 (*P.R.S.*, iv (1885), p. 37) but many of these New-market names are not localised in Suffolk or even in East Anglia; indeed, they are frequent in the south-west, where there is no town of Newmarket although many villages were then acquiring their new markets and those living in new market places could easily acquire that surname. The only positive evidence for an origin earlier than 1223 is a reference to Newmarket in 1217 (W. Rye, ed., *Cambs. Feet of Fines* (1891), no. 10).

There is no significant form in the alinement of houses in the present town nor in pre-Ordnance Survey plans (e.g. BM. Maps K.8/74 by I. Chapman).

SURREY

We seem to have another old-settled county with few opportunities for the medieval economy to support more towns.

HASLEMERE   Surrey   sheet 169   41/905329
1221

In 1640 when a petition was presented to separate the town from Chiddingfold parish, Haslemere was described as "a Market Town, an auntient Burrough Towne having but a verie small quantitie of land thereunto belonging" (E. W. Swanton and

P. Woods, *Bygone Haslemere* (London, 1914), p. 368, from Loseley Ms. 757a). These facts of parochial geography and the distance of Haslemere borough from the nearest chapel at Piperham together make a prima facie case for a plantation at the southern edge of the bishop of Salisbury's woodland manor of Godalming. The bishop acquired the manor just at the time when the Haslemere market was initiated: *Sarum Charters* (Rolls Series (1891)), p. 165. The market charter of 1221 to Haslemere is in fact eighty years earlier than that of Godalming. The plan of the borough (Swanton and Woods, *op. cit.*, p. 240, from plan of 1735) is extremely regular with the burgage plots distinguishable on either side of the High Street. One of these burgages was granted c. 1230 (*ibid.*, p. 49). The town is explicitly called *burgus* in 1377 (SC6/1010/7). See also *V.C.H., Surrey*, iii, pp. 45–49.

REIGATE   Surrey   sheet 170   51/254503
c. 1170

To begin with the circumstantial evidence: there was a tiny borough area of 65 acres in the shadow of the earls of Warenne's castle; the older centre of settlement probably lay near the church which is 600 yards east of the castle and outside the borough bounds.

The succession of events may be this: the substantial Domesday manor of *Cherchefelle* (or *Crichefeld*), the head of its Hundred, was near the parish church; the church, as the church of *Crechesfeld*, was given to the Priory of St. Mary Overy c. 1164–1202 (Dugdale, *Monasticon*, vi, p. 172) and the charter refers to a burgage. The earls of Surrey were given the manor c. 1088 and at an unknown date built a castle on a hill facing the church. The first known reference to Reigate is c. 1170 and the name Crichefeld passed out of use at the end of that century (*cp.* the change of name at Piperham to Haslemere *supra*). The parish church was substantially rebuilt c. 1180.

By 1240 Reigate Priory had been founded south of the town; by 1276 there was a market, and shortly afterwards the prescriptive right to a fair was acknowledged, suggesting that the commercial development of the town was some generations old by then. It was called a borough in 1291 and sent members to Parliament in 1295. It was mentioned in an Assize Roll of 1225 (JI/1/863 mm. 4, 4d and 6) and was separately represented at the Assize of 1235 (JI/1/864 mm. 15–15d). The triangle of streets at the junction of High Street and West Street indicate the Old Market, and the east-west alinement of the town suggests that the main local route which determined the site was a road under the scarp of the downs.

SUSSEX

The only problem in this county seems to be the origin of the borough of Newbridge, now only a farm in Pulborough (*P.N. Sussex*, pp. 48–49). In 1375 the fair was known as "the borough fair" (C135/249/2) and there may have been a chapel here (*S.A.C.*, xii, p. 185). There is no mention of burgages, however, in the fines printed in *Sussex Rec. Soc.*, ii (1903), pp. 65, 68 and 85; xxiii (1916), pp. 29, 36, 106, 154, 237 and 240.

All the plantations but one were coastal or estuarine and were much influenced by changes in the coastline and the course of rivers. There is a marked concentration of dates in the decades following the Norman Conquest.

ARUNDEL   Sussex   sheet 182   51/015070

c. 1071

In Domesday Book the name of the place is simply "the castle of Arundel", which is stated to have existed in the time of Edward the Confessor. £4 was then its annual value: but by 1086 the value had risen to £12 from the "borough, the river-port and the custom from ships". What is not clear is how the £4 arose: was there any civil settlement alongside the castle and mill? The town plan is of a close seigneurial pattern. There were castle and town churches. "In the reign of Edward the Confessor the whole property of the place seems to have comprised the castle and mill" (M. A. Tierney, *The History and Antiquities of Arundel* (1834) p. 690). The Norman town would seem to have lain on both sides of the High Street. This street runs down from the Town Gate of the castle to the river quay by the bridge. It splays out near the bridge into a triangle now encroached upon by building, but probably the site of the market. There is haphazard building along the quay with no through road. The two parallel streets which follow the contours, west of High Street, are Tarrant Street and Maltravers Street but they do not seem part of the original plan.

On the opposite bank of the river was the Saxon *burh* of Burpham, now merely a hill-top with defensive earthworks, and Arundel may be seen as a replacement for it.

BATTLE   Sussex   sheet 184   51/749158

1070–71

As a thank-offering for victory William the Conqueror founded the abbey of St. Martin to stand on the battlefield of Hastings, endowing it with all the land in a 3-mile circle, and with six manors and three churches. The Chronicle of the abbey recalled how "this noble-minded king, regardful of the interests of his Abbey, appointed a market for the town of Battle to be holden on the Lord's Day, to be quit for ever from all exaction and to be entirely under the management of the monastery...". Thus, by William's death in 1089 the abbey had begun to develop the commercial opportunities which lay outside its gate. A Sunday market was granted by William I in 1070–71 (H. W. C. Davis, *Regesta Regum Anglo-Normannorum*, i (1913), no. 61). Those who resided there were to be answerable only to the abbot and monks, and the abbot and monks only to God.

No doubt the flow of visitors to the abbey provided the biggest part of the townspeople's incomes, but the town also stood on a road leading across the Weald from the port of Hastings; this road was probably diverted round the abbey precinct. At the end of the Middle Ages Battle had two fairs a year and was beginning to be a market centre for the Wealden iron industry.

The Chronicle also describes how the town was first peopled: "a goodly number of men were brought hither out of the neighbouring counties, and some even from foreign countries. And to each of these, the brethren who managed the building allotted a dwelling place of certain dimensions around the circuit of the abbey; and these still remain as they were first apportioned, with their customary rent or service." The chronicler then details the 115 houses of his day (c. 1180): sixty-five on one side of the main street leading north from the abbey gates; twenty-one on the other side of the same street; five houses on the eastern side of St. Mary's church (which had been founded (1107-24) on the south-eastern edge of the town) with ten beyond it; and fourteen houses facing the church. Even today numbering is continuous from the abbey gate northwards up the west side of High Street and then back down the east. "On account of the very great dignity of the place," the Chronicle continued, "the men of this town are called burgesses." In the town were two guild halls, and a third out of the town for the use of the country folk (*rustici*). There is no evidence that the townspeople were ever burgesses in any legal sense: it was an abbey plantation, and there is no borough charter.

The town consists of one street widening into a triangular market place, overlooked by the great Gatehouse of the abbey. In the original rental a large proportion of the names of townsmen were English; their labour services were limited to a day's haymaking in the 30-acre meadow away at Bodiham, the repair of the mill and the provision of eight bushels of malt. The standard rent was 7d. for each house. The occupations named were: shoemaker, weaver, cook, scourer, miller, herdsman, goldsmith, shoemaker again, swineherd, cowherd, sewer, bell-caster, carpenter, shoemaker, cook, baker, smith, baker, clerk, baker, swineherd, cook, secretary, priest (on E. side of St. Mary's), gardener, secretary, shoemaker and carpenter. As the Chronicle (ed. *Lower*, p. 32) says: "these, who in other respects are free, have from that time been accustomed to pay the Abbey the fixed charge of the land, with certain customary services."

The king gave ships to fetch building stone from Caen. The monks did not think the site a very good one because it was high and waterless, but the king was angry and insisted on using the actual place of victory. There are hints in the Chronicle that things went slowly, that William lost interest "by reason of his being concerned with so many things of importance" and that the bishop of Chichester was hostile; the abbey was not consecrated until 1095.

Initially, the townspeople worshipped in the abbey church, and the parish church, which stands outside the town on the Hastings road, has the air of an after-thought.

A plan of 1724 (BM., Maps, 5405/30) shows plots east and south-east of the church where there are now no buildings; the survey of c. 1180 listed houses here. A very detailed rental of 1429 (E315/56 f. 9 sqq. and 57 ff. 1–14) gives much topographical information especially on the division of the burgages among the three "boroughs" of Montjoye, Middleburgh and Sandlake (*i.e.* Senlac), a division that also appears on the tax assessments of the early fourteenth century.

The principal source for the early history of Battle is the Chronicle. The Latin text of the crucial passage forms pp. 12–18 of J. S. Brewer, ed., *Chronicon Monasterii de Bello* (1846), and was translated by M. A. Lower in *The Chronicle of Battel Abbey* (1851); see also Eleanor Searle in *Ec. H.R.*, xvi, n.s. (1963), pp. 290–300.

HASTINGS   Sussex   sheet 184 51/824095
c. 1069

In 1182 and 1183 the castle of Hastings was described as that of "New Hastings" (*P.R.S.*, xxxi (1910), pp. 88 and 106; xxxii (1911), p. 138). It was so called because the Norman town had replaced an earlier port, which was being submerged by the sea at the time when the count of Eu was building his castle on the cliff. The new Norman town lay in the Bourne valley below this castle. Parallel and further west was the Priory valley, at the southern end of which may have been the Saxon town. Even the Bourne valley was not immune, for the first St. Clement's church was washed away just before 1286. The medieval town consisted of two parallel streets, High Street and All Saints Street, running north up the valley with St. Clement's church at the seaward end and All Saints in the market place at the northern end. This town was walled on the seaward side and had three gates (Plan of 1746 in *S.A.C.*, xii (1860), p. 196, and plan of 1824 in W. G. Moss, *History and Antiquities of Hastings* (1824)).

William the Conqueror's first act, on the eve of the battle of Hastings, was to protect himself on the seaward side by building a "castle" at the water edge. (The motte and bailey shown in the Bayeux tapestry is probably anachronistic, being the count of Eu's castle built c. 1069.) The Saxon town had been developed by the Norman abbey of Fécamp to whom Canute had given the town c. 1017 (*E.H.R.*, xxxiii (1918), pp. 342–4). It was mentioned in the laws of Athelstan (928) and in the Burghal Hidage. The Liberty of Hastings (which may be presumed to be the extensive Fécamp manor of *Rameslie*) had a curious shape. It extended westwards from Hastings in a narrow coastal strip and terminated eastwards at Iham where the land route to another Fécamp town, Rye (*q.v.*), crossed the Brede and the marshes. On the eve of the Conquest Edward the Confessor had taken Hastings itself from Fécamp in view of the strategic importance of the site; in 1085 William I compensated the abbey with a grant of a manor so valuable as to suggest that Saxon Hastings was an important place.

The western extension of Hastings territory suggests that Bulverhythe (*sc.* the harbour of the burgesses) was the first of the Saxon ports in this locality and that the Aspen estuary silted up and forced the town to move further east to the Priory valley. If this suggestion (L. F. Salzman, *Hastings* (1921), p. 6, and *V.C.H.*, ix, pp. 1–33) is correct, there have been three Hastings on this turbulent and fickle coastline, just as there were two Winchelseas, two Romneys and two Hythes.

MIDHURST   Sussex   sheet 181 51/885215
by 1184

Midhurst presents some difficulties and ambiguities. The earliest references occur in documents from the end of the reign of Henry II, and in them Midhurst is associated with Easebourne, the rural parish in which it lay (*P.R.S.*, xxxvii (1915), pp. 109 and 113; *Cal. Pat. Rolls, 1358–61*, pp. 534–535). It was tallaged in 1184, and in 1279 the local jurors said that it had been a borough from time immemorial (*Placita De Quo Warranto* (1818), p. 756). Its market charter was in fact granted in 1223 (*Curia*

Regis Rolls, xi, no. 891) but markets sometimes flourished before being regularised by charters. The town was treated as a borough for taxation purposes in the late thirteenth century, and at the Assize of 1248. No borough charter has been noted.

The opportunities at Midhurst for a commercial centre were derived from its site on the London–Chichester road at a crossing of the upper Rother in a narrow valley between the Weald and the South Downs. The streets to the west of the main road and castle form an indistinct grid.

PEVENSEY (near)   Sussex   sheet 183   51/640045
1207

In the Pipe Roll of Michaelmas 1207 (*P.R.S.*, n.s., xxii (1944), p. 41) the barons of the Cinque Ports were charged with a debt of 40 marks for a licence to make a town near Pevensey and to have a market each Sunday and a yearly fair. A year later this sum was unpaid (*ibid.*, xxiii (1945), p. 72) and no mention was made in later years' accounts. The charter of April 27, 1207, is known only from a copy made in 1313 (*Cal. Chart. Rolls*, iii. p. 220) since the charters of King John's eighth year are missing. In this charter the king permitted the "barons" of Pevensey to make a town on the beach between Pevensey and Langney (*"faciant unam uillam super galetum quod iacet inter portum de Pevenesei et Langeney"*) and to have a market and fair there. Langney lies south-west of Pevensey (632020). The port of Pevensey has been long silted up and the silting may have inhibited the new town. The village of Westham consists of a very straight street leading directly from the west gate of Pevensey castle and its church is only 200 yards from the parish boundary of Pevensey, but its architecture is earlier than 1207: the south wall and part of the transept are Norman. The site of the new town must therefore be regarded as undiscovered.

No later references have yet been found. The *banleuca* of Pevensey is often mentioned in fourteenth-century accounts but it has not been possible to determine whether this was a district or a suburb (SC11/663).

RYE   Sussex   sheet 184   51/921203
by 1086

From c. 1030 the manor of *Rameslie* belonged to Fécamp abbey (*E.H.R.*, xxxiii (1918), p. 344); the exact centre of the manor is not known but in 1086 the abbey had within it a *novus burgus* (now generally identified with Rye: *V.C.H., Sussex*, i, pp. 49 and 391), and early in the twelfth century the first mention of (Old) Winchelsea occurs: the dating of c. 960 from a coin (*Ekwall*, p. 522) is now impossible since the coin came from Winchcombe (*V.C.H.*, ix, p. 62). The estuary of the rivers Brede, Tillingham (and possibly Rother) formed a natural harbour, the *Camera* or Camber. (Old) Winchelsea was created at the coast, east of the present Rother estuary where the parish of St. Thomas the Apostle still preserves the name. (For the development of the second Winchelsea see below.) Rye was placed up-river at the first island to be encountered: similarly the second Winchelsea, after the experience of coastal erosion, was placed on its island hill at Iham. The two towns, with a single overlord, were

495

treated as one for many administrative and fiscal purposes and may have come into existence together.

The first record of the name Rye dates from 1130: it means "the island" (*Ekwall*, p. 398) and the town consists of a clear grid of streets within rectilinear walls, all placed on a small block of raised ground between the river Tillingham and the present course of the Rother. (There has been erosion in post-medieval times at the eastern side of the town.)

The early twelfth-century work in the chancel of the parish church would not be incongruous with a foundation between 1066 and 1086. The first charter (*Ballard*, p. xxxi) coincides with that of Winchelsea (1154–58: *V.C.H., Sussex*, ix, p. 34). There was a mint here in 1142. With its streets accommodating themselves to the slopes of the hill and to the edges of the cliff, the town is more like a hilltop in Gascony than the usual English port-town; it is a Ludlow already provided with its moats by Nature. Although the foundation was engineered by a Norman abbey there is no parallel along the Norman coast, unless one counts Mont St. Michel.

SHOREHAM, NEW   Sussex   sheet 182   51/216052
1096–1103

The church of Old Shoreham stands at 208060, one mile north-west of New Shoreham church: the borough of New Shoreham, only 170 acres in area, has obviously been carved out of the older parish (T. W. Horsfield, *Sussex* (1835), ii, pp. 208–214). The pre-Conquest church at Old Shoreham was part of the foundation endowment of Sele priory; when Philip de Braose confirmed this and other grants the endowment included St. Mary *de Portu* at New Shoreham: the town's foundation is thus limited to 1096–1103. (H. Cheal, *The Story of Shoreham* (1921), p. 12.) The obverse of the town seal has "Nova Shoreham Brewes" commemorating the founder, de Braose. Another seal (*S.A.C.*, x (1858), p. xliv) has a ship on its reverse and a motto giving the town the name of "Hulk's Mouth".

The movement of site was probably due to the progressive movement of the shingle across the mouth of the Adur. In the later Middle ages the continuation of the action of the sea moved the mouth of the river further east, past New Shoreham to Kingston, while the southern block of the borough grid was eroded by the action of the river. In Camden's time the "greater part" of the borough was drowned. Only the most northerly of the east-west streets of the grid remain (along the shore line) but the ends of the ten parallel north-south streets can still be seen; Cheal suggests (*op. cit.*, p. 23) that the town, like Bury, was laid out on a furlong of open fields (of Old Shoreham), being 220 yards square. This receives some support from the description of a Templars' holding in the town as "a selion of land on front of the House in Shoreham which extends nearly from the gate of that House to the sea". (B. A. Lees, ed. *Records of the Templars in the Twelfth Century* (1935), p. 240; (1184–85).) A conjectural plan appears as endpapers in Cheal, *op. cit.* Another plan is given in B. Green, "New Shoreham", *Sussex Arch. Coll.*, xxvii (1877), p. 98.

New Shoreham was taxed as a borough from 1295, but no charter survives. The place was already reckoned a borough in 1279 (*R.H.*, ii, p. 203) and probably in 1248 (JI/1/909a, m. 25).

WARDOUR   Sussex   sheet 181   c. 40/857964
1262-7

Between 1262-67 bishop Stephen of Chichester granted to all his tenants and the inhabitants of his new town of *Wardur* that they should hold their land freely at 14d. an acre a year with freedom to buy and sell, to come and go.   The villeins of the bishop who lived there were made free and allowed to sell at all markets and fairs belonging to the bishop without custom or toll (*Sussex Record Society*, xlvi (1942-43), p. 340). The document appears under the heading *Sidlesham* which was one of the episcopal manors in Selsey, between Chichester and the sea.   Chichester itself had no harbour and this foundation may have been an effort to establish a port on what is now Pagham Harbour, for the traditional site of Wardour is by the Ferry House half a mile south of Sidlesham.   The land here, by the causeway across the former channel which divided the isle of Selsey from Sidlesham, is too wet to have been the site; it could have been 400 yards north where the ground rises at the old coastline.

No surviving account roll from the bishop's manors is detailed enough to show any revenue from Wardour within Sidlesham and it is not possible to say how soon the town failed (E364/19 m. 2d; SC6/1131/11; E372/90 m. 9; E372/112 m. 1).   It is ominous that there is no reference to Wardour in the carting services of the Sidlesham and Selsey manors in 1276 (W. D. Peckham ed., *Thirteen Custumals* (Sussex Rec. Soc., xxxi) pp. 13-32) nor in the terriers of 1327-28 (*ibid.*, pp. 126-133).   I do not think Wardour could be equated with Chalder Farm (*Chaluare, Chalfore* in the custumals, pp. 23 and 127).

WESTHAM   Sussex
See Pevensey (near).

WINCHELSEA, NEW   Sussex   sheet 184   51/905175
1288

The history of the foundation of this town, the planned successor to the storm-beaten Old Winchelsea, has been many times related, principally in W. D. Cooper, *The History of Winchelsea* (London, 1850) and *V.C.H.*, ix, pp. 62-75.   Cooper's frontispiece is a plan of 1763 by Charles Stephens and recently a bold attempt to reconstruct the original alinement of each burgage plot has been made by Mr. W. McL. Homan (*Sussex Archaeological Collections*, lxxxviii (1949), pp. 22-41).   The basis of all work on the beginning of the town is the rent roll of the town drawn up in 1292 (SC11/673) and the records of the negotiations by which Edward I acquired the hill-top site (Cooper, *op. cit.*, pp. 29-35).   Possession of the burgage plots was formally given in July 1288, the king promising that for the first seven years the townsmen should live rent free.   A full year's rental was reckoned at £13 18s. 5½d. for the town and 13s. 0¼d. for the extra-mural properties on the north side of the hill.

The rental of 1292 has a full list of names and it cannot be maintained that the document is merely a prospectus. Those like G. E. Chambers (*Arch. Journ.*, xciv (1938), p. 177) who believe that the whole site could never have been built upon are those whose archaeological imagination jibs at the possibility of two thirds of a medieval town site being now under grass. The real shrinkage of population began only with the destruction done to the town by French raids (principally those of 1337, 1359–60 and 1380: Cooper, *op. cit.*, pp. 69–80 and 90–91). In these raids the church was partially destroyed, never to be rebuilt; many houses were destroyed and the town seems never to have fully recovered; the project of the walls was never completed, and in 1415 the king allowed a murage grant to fortify the town on a lesser perimeter, the site of the town being too large for "necessary habitation" (Cooper, *op. cit.*, p. 96). A contributory factor was the retreat of the sea and the silting of the estuary. This retreat of settlement can be documented: in 1342 a list of ninety-four vacant *placeae* was compiled (E101/530/3 and SC6/1032/6); another in 1364 (SC11/676) showed more than 130s. of "decayed rents"; and in 1367–68 (SC11/677) 436 tenements had their rent affected; a document of 1369 (E142/85/2) shows rent reductions of over £12 from 387 tenements. By 1575 there were not more than sixty inhabited houses (Cooper, *op. cit.*, p. 107).

A series of accounts upon the Pipe Roll demonstrate that the full total of the rental of 1292 (£14 11s. 5¾d.) was received at the Exchequer from January 1293 to October 1297, when the account ends (E372/150/m. 32d; the subsequent years' accounts (1298–1306) are in B.M. Add. Ch. 18963). In addition, the profits of justice in the town courts brought in from £2 to £4 a year; the tolls of the markets and fairs also from £2 to £4 a year; the ships' customs from £5 to £7. The only sign of emptiness is the statement that nothing could be raised from the sea tolls at Old Winchelsea. It is clear that Edward in fact did not fulfil the promise of seven rent-free years that the townspeople alleged.

(Air photograph and plan in *Beresford and St. Joseph*, pp. 221–225.)

WARWICKSHIRE

Like its Midland neighbours, Warwickshire had a small number of plantations. Four other claimants have been considered but rejected.

SOLIHULL does not appear in Domesday Book but it is difficult to determine whether the village existed under the name of Ulverley (where there were 8 hides) or whether there has been a transfer of settlement to the Warwick–Birmingham road (*V.C.H.*, iv, pp. 214–249). It is, however, a parish in its own right with no obvious signs of being cut from another. A map in R. Pemberton, *Solihull And Its Church* (1905), marks some of the houses near the triangular market place, "The Borough". A deed of 1381 (Warw. Cty. Record Office, CR84/23/30), which Mrs. Gooder has transcribed for me, conveys a messuage *infra burgum de Solihull* and places it *inter messuagium et vicum altum ville burgi.*

ALCESTER is also missing from Domesday Book but, like Solihull, it lacks other supporting features which might give it a claim for inclusion in the main list below. It was certainly a borough, well placed for commerce at the crossing of the Ryknield

Street and the Roman road which came in from Old Stratford and the Foss Way. The connection with Roman Alcester is unknown; there were legends of an early eighth-century town being destroyed for its wickedness: this may be a myth derived from remains of the Roman settlement. The parish church of Alcester was among the endowments¦ of Alcester abbey, founded in 1140 (Dugdale, *Monasticon*, iv, pp. 175–177) and since the church seems to have been an independent parish church (*V.C.H.*, iii, pp. 8–22) one must assume that it had a village.

BRINKLOW has more suspicious features. It was an important enough market centre to be considered a taxation borough in 1307. It does not appear in Domesday Book where the local centre of population seems to have been at Smite. The motte and bailey castle of Brinklow built alongside the Foss Way on the eastern edge of Smite parish was a natural attractive force for a new settlement, and by 1135 the parish church of Smite had a chapel at Brinklow. This was then given to Kenilworth Abbey (*Cal. Pat. Rolls, 1397*, p. 55) but c. 1150 all the land in the parish of Smite, except *Brinckelawe*, was given to the new Cistercian abbey of Combe which was built within the parish and which then depopulated the villages of Upper and Lower Smite (B.M. Cott. Vit. A. I, f. 40 and D. XVIII; *Cal. Chart. Rolls*, i, p. 352). When (by 1169) Knightlow Hundred was formed from three smaller Hundreds, Brinklow became the seat of the court of the sub-hundred or *leet* (*P.N. Warw.*, p. 95). It will be noticed that Bretford (*q.v.*) was founded only a short way down the Foss Way but at the more advantageous situation where land and water routes met.

KENILWORTH. It seems from the language of Henry I's confirmation of the foundation charter of Kenilworth Priory that Geoffrey de Clinton had retained some lands for himself, when endowing the Priory, with the purpose of building a castle, making a park, laying out fishponds and making a borough: *ad burgum suum faciendum*. This may be the Castle-town separated from the Priory by the Abbey Fields (*V.C.H.*, vi, p. 135). In 1086 Kenilworth had been a small three-virgate hamlet in Stoneleigh (*The Leger Book of Stoneleigh Abbey*, ed. R. H. Hilton (Dugdale Soc., xxiv (1960), p. 114)).

BRETFORD   Warwickshire   sheet 132   42/429771
by 1199

Bretford lies just within Brandon parish where the Foss Way crosses the Avon. The de Verdons were lords of Brandon castle, about 2 miles west of the bridge (*V.C.H.* vi, pp. 273–280) and the borough project seems to have been theirs. No borough charter is known, but a market was granted in 1227 (*Cal. Chart. Rolls*, i, p. 58); the first reference to the place-name so far noted is a foot of fine for a messuage in 1199 (*Dugdale Soc.*, xi (1932), pp. 157–158). A leper hospital may have been built here c. 1180; it later became an ordinary chapel (*V.C.H., loc. cit.*). An extent of 1274 (C133/7/1) has no mention of burgages, but in the Hundred Rolls of 1279 (E164/15 f. 11v) nineteen burgesses are stated to hold 31½ burgages: Theobald de Verdon was overlord of borough and market and had a fair. The existence of burgages is confirmed by a long rental (SC12/16/8) (1307–27) which lists 23 burgages, 21 cottages, 24 *placeae* and 21 curtilages, as well as 1 messuage. The standard burgage rent was then 6d.; a curtilage together with a *placea* was rented at 8d.   There were seventeen tenants wealthy enough to be taxed in 1332 (E179/92/5 m. 9), some of the names being the same as those in the rental.

It is not possible to say when the borough fell into decay since later extents (C133/56/1; C134/14/19; C135/45/21; C135/152/5) give no details of a borough.   The amount paid in 1332 (37s. 6d.) was not trivial, but the hamlet is now quite small and there are no substantial earthworks which would indicate the extent of the former burgages.   It can hardly be doubted that the burgages were ranged along the Foss Way, and, since the modern road is set off from the old course of the Roman road, excavation may one day elucidate this petty borough.   An old plan (? c. 1615) of the fields of this area forms B.M. Add. Ms. 48181 (from Yelverton Mss.).   The burgages had already disappeared.   (Acknowledgement is made to Prof. Hilton for the reference in the unpublished Hundred Rolls.)

HENLEY IN ARDEN   Warwickshire   sheet 131   42/152660
1185–1220

The borough of Henley consisted of the burgage plots on either side of the road (now the A.34) from Stratford on Avon to Birmingham where it passes under the shelter of Beaudesert castle.   The castle on the opposite bank of the river Alne was built by Thurstan de Montfort between 1135 and 1141.   In 1141 a grant of a Sunday market at Beaudesert was obtained from the Empress Matilda and this may have encouraged commercial settlement on the other side of the stream.   The first explicit mention of Henley is in a grant of the mill c. 1185 (B.M. Harl. Ms. 506 f. 122).   A fair was granted in 1220 and the jurors at the Assize of 1232 (JI/1/951a m. 1) reported as a novelty the collection of tolls at Henley market; cloth was being sold there that year (m. 1d).   In the tax assessments of 1332 Henley was rated at about half the population of Stratford on Avon.

The shape of the township bounds shows clearly that the borough was cut from Wootton Wawen parish, and there was no church at Henley until 1367 when the bishop of Worcester permitted a chapel of ease to be built at the townsmen's charge in view of the inconvenience in reaching Wootton Wawen in bad weather.

The borough was burned in 1265 (*Cal. Inq. Misc.*, i, p. 931) and when surveyed in 1296 (C133/76/4) had sixty-nine burgesses and two watermills.   Tolls brought in £4 in a year and the total value of the borough was £15 13s. 4d. compared with £6 2s. 1d. at Beaudesert where there were twenty-nine tenants.   The history of the town is given at length in William Cooper, *Henley in Arden* (Birmingham, 1946).

STRATFORD UPON AVON   Warwickshire   sheets 131 & 144   42/550202
1196

The *Street* which forded the Avon and gave its name to the Anglo-Saxon village was a Roman road branching from the Foss Way near Eatington and running north-westwards to Alcester and the Ryknield Street.   The village of Stratford was focused on the church, which still lies well outside the core of the town, and there was no town until in 1196 the bishop of Worcester granted burgages at a shilling a year rent to all who would come and occupy them, and also created a market (Dugdale, *Warws.*, p. 680).

"Three streets running parallel and three at right angles to the river seem to be an example on a small scale of medieval town planning, modified by modern encroachments" (*V.C.H.*, iii, p. 222). The important encroachment is the occupation of the triangular market place once formed by Henley Street, Mere Street and Wood Street, westwards from the site of the old market cross (where High Street meets Bridge Street). The street leading from the borough towards the church is appropriately called Old Town, for here was the old township. The fields of the township extended on three sides of the borough, and the river on the fourth.

The separate jurisdictions of rural parish and urban borough were a continuous source of friction. The draft charter of 1600, never achieved, sought to bring all the parish into the borough (*ibid.*, p. 221–222). The townspeople had to use the church at Old Stratford (*Dugdale*, ed. of 1730, p. 696) until a chapel of ease was built in the town: this was not until 1855.

An extent of the manor in 1182 (M. Hollings, ed., *The Red Book of Worcester* (Worcs. Hist. Soc., iii (1939), pp. 260–262) is cast in purely agricultural terms. But in 1251–2 (*ibid.*, iv (1950), pp. 471–497) a pair of extents shows the contrast between *Stratford Vetus* and *Stratford Burgus*. In the former the bishop's assets were made up of 220½ acres of demesne arable, 27 acres of meadow, 7 acres of pasture, three corn-mills and a fulling-mill. In Stratford borough, on the other hand, the bishop drew rents from nearly 250 burgages and from 54½ other building plots (*placeae*); rents were also paid by fourteen shop-holders, ten stall-holders, and by the tenants of two ovens and two dye-vats. The dimensions of the burgages were fixed by the foundation charter as 12 perches by 3½ perches (about ¼ acre), and the borough would therefore occupy some 70 acres. The bishop's income from these 70 acres of urban development was £16 0s. 6d. in 1251–52 while Old Stratford manor was worth £20 19s. 6d.

There was an already well-established town at Warwick only 8 miles away; but in the second half of the twelfth century Alcester and Henley in Arden came into existence as commercial centres in addition to Stratford, and again no more than 8 miles away. Alcester and Henley served the Forest of Arden that was being rapidly colonised in this period (J. B. Hartley, "Population Trends and Agricultural Developments from the Warws. Hundred Rolls of 1279", *Econ. Hist. Rev.*, 2nd ser., xi (1958), pp. 8–18; R. H. Hilton, *Social Structure of Rural Warws.* (Dugdale Soc. Occ. Papers, ix (1950)). Stratford—like Warwick—was placed to serve both Arden and the Felden, the open-field arable parishes to the south of the Avon, while down the *Street* merchants could reach the Cotswold pastures. Its prime advantage was its position at the junction of these roads with the navigable Avon, then a part of the great waterway system of the Severn valley, looking to Bristol and Gloucester.

Since this Gazetteer was compiled Professor Carus-Wilson has published a study of "The First Half-century of the Borough of Stratford-upon-Avon", *Econ. Hist. Rev.* 2nd ser., xviii (1965), pp. 46–63), with a plan of the town and a diagram showing the location of the place-surnames of the burgesses of 1251–52.

WESTMORLAND

APPLEBY   Westmorland   sheet 83   35/685202
c. 1110

The pattern of the streets is a simple grid lying between castle and church in the manner of Ludlow and New Windsor.   The market place is the broad main street. The town is surrounded on three sides by the river Eden.   The north end of the town is not much above river level, and a bridge at right angles to the main street brings in traffic from the east bank; this awkward turn derives from the alinement of the main street which in turn was determined by the narrowness of the river loop and the space between the castle gate and the church.   The castle is on a knoll 100 feet above the water, and the main ditch of the Norman earthworks is still 30 feet deep in places (W. D. Simpson, "The Town and Castle of Appleby", *Tr. Cumb. & Westm. Ant. & Arch. Soc.*, xlix, n.s. (1950), pp. 118 sqq.).

On the east bank of the river, where the busy main road to Stainmore from Carlisle passes, is the church of St. Michael which incorporates stone-work of c. 1000, and the small settlement around it was described in a law-suit of 1265 as "Old Appleby where the villeins dwell" (Nicholson & Burn, *History of Westmorland* (1777), i, p. 313). The new town on the west bank is dominated by the castle and must have come into being with it.   The new town was provided with its own church, St. Lawrence, which faces the castle along the length of Boroughgate.   The lower part of the tower is probably part of the original twelfth-century church; the two churches are mentioned in a grant of 1120 (M. W. Holdgate, *A History of Appleby* (1956), p. 17, with plan). From 1136–57 and from 1174–75 the town was in Scottish hands, and the church was rebuilt by Henry II's command in 1178 after the town returned to English possession.   The great keep of the castle was wholly or partially rebuilt at the same time (*R.C.H.M., Westmorland* (1946), pp. 4–14, with plans).   The first borough charter was granted c. 1179 by Henry II when Chief Justice Glanville was the territorial lord.   A second charter was given by John in 1199 and two members were returned to the Parliament of 1298.   The town was separately represented at the Assize of 1254 (JI/1/979 m. 13).   In 1276 the lord of Westmorland claimed that the town was included in a grant which John had made to his ancestors but a jury declared that the grant referred only to Old Appleby and not to the new borough (Nicholson & Burn, *loc. cit.*).

BROUGH, CHURCH   Westmorland   sheet 84   35/793138
c. 1092–1100

W. D. Simpson has written: "the plan of Church Brough shows an unmistakable if incomplete attempt to lay out a town, in dependence upon the castle, in the normal manner of a *ville neuve* with the central market place . . . streets entering at its four corners and a church placed apart at one side."   The church at Brough was in fact a chapelry of Kirkby Stephen, the old civil centre of the district, four miles to the south. The new town was placed on the eastern edge of the Roman fort of Verterae within whose banks William II's castle had been built as one of a line of defences along the

Stainmore road into Scotland after his acquisition of Westmorland and Cumberland in 1092.

The secondary development of Market Brough is discussed below. Church Brough has declined in importance and is now little more than a cluster of farms around the church and castle; the former market place is discernible in the plan (W. D. Simpson, "Brough under Stainmore" *Tr. Cumb. & Westm. Ant. & Arch. Soc.*, n.s., xlvi (1946), p. 230; Nicholson and Burn, *History of Westmorland* (1777), i, pp. 564–566; air photograph in *Beresford and St. Joseph*, p. 132).

BROUGH, MARKET   Westmorland   sheet 84   35/795147
by 1196

Church Brough depended on the Norman Castle and the Roman road which must have crossed the beck nearby. It would seem that in the late twelfth century the Stainmore road was passing about half a mile north of Church Brough, where the A.66 now runs, and that a commercial community was growing up or had been planted along it just to the west of the bridge. In 1196 the burgesses of Brough were tallaged at 18s. while the "villata" of Brough Superior paid 9s. In 1198 the two settlements again appear in the Pipe Roll and in 1200 Lower Brough paid 25 marks for a Sunday market and a two-day fair at the feast of St. John the Baptist; in 1202 the borough paid 40s. and the villata 20s. In 1203 the king granted away the castle to Robert de Vipont.

Market Brough is now the principal centre, and Dr. Simpson suggested that the crucial point was the destructive visits of the Scots in 1314 and 1319; a market charter of 1330 may represent the reconstruction of commercial life at the new site only, the older town at Church Brough falling into its present decay. Modern Market Brough is a small town, with a simple grid plan, and kept prosperous by the arterial road.

The documents do not always make it clear which Brough was which. An extent of 1314 (C134/39) distinguishes between Lower Brough with 24½ tofts and Brough under Stainmore with a castle, a fair, 20 customary tenants and 10 tofts. The reference to the castle would make Lower Brough the present Market Brough, and it was Lower or Lesser Brough that in 1198 and 1200 paid twice the tallage of Upper Brough; in 1196 Lower Brough had burgesses while Upper Brough was called simply *villata*. It is clear that by 1196 the roadside settlement had surpassed the older settlement by the church (W. D. Simpson, "Brough under Stainmore" (*Tr. Cumb. and Westm. Ant. & Arch. Soc.*, n.s., xlvi (1946), p. 230; *P.R.S.*, n.s., vii, p. 98; ix, p. 140; xii, p. 34; xiv, p. 257; xv, pp. 156–157).

WILTSHIRE

"When we get to Wiltshire we are in the classical land of small boroughs," wrote Maitland (*Domesday Book and Beyond* (1897), p. 175). Three of these small boroughs were plantations and New Salisbury is pre-eminent for the boldness of its foundation, though far from petty. There is reason to think that its predecessor, Old Sarum, had also come into the world by the same path. (I am obliged to Mr. R. B. Pugh for discussion of Wiltshire problems.)

DEVIZES   Wiltshire   sheet 167   41/005615
1135–39

"If the town must be linked with the castle, the former had better be fixed to the true date of the latter," observed a realistic mid-eighteenth-century historian of this town, noting also the absence of early documentation (Dr. Davis' *Origines* quoted in J. Waylen, *Chronicle of the Devizes* (1839), p. 21). The plural name of the town in Waylen's title emphasises the original meaning of Devizes, *burgus de devisis*, the borough at the dividing lines or boundary of two manors, Bishop's Cannings and Potterne.

Bishop Roger of Salisbury built a castle here c. 1120 to replace another mentioned as burned in 1113. Roger's castle was besieged by Stephen in 1139 and then held after the war by Matilda. The Empress was herself at Devizes castle in 1141 and 1142 and may have granted a borough charter then. In April 1149 she returned the manor of Cannings to the bishop but retained the castle borough and parks which lay within the manor (*Sarum Charters* (Rolls Series), p. 15) and her son, Henry, confirmed the grant except for the borough and parks which he retained. In 1152 (*ibid.*, p. 22) Henry agreed with the bishop that the castle should remain in the former's hands for three years or until judgement in the disputed ownership was given. In the meanwhile Henry was to pay the bishop the same sums as the borough had yielded to bishop Roger. This establishes firmly that there had been a borough here before Roger's death in 1139, and Matilda's charter (*Ballard*, p. xxiii) cannot have been earlier than 1135. In 1157 (*Sarum Charters*, p. 29) the king finally acquired Devizes by exchange: "the castle with two parks and the borough as the same are at present divided and enclosed by the dykes".

The oval circuit of the boundary ditch of the Old Park still survives for a circuit of some 3 miles, and the castle earthworks are integrated with it. On the opposite side of the castle is another regular curve, rather that of a half moon, made by one of the main streets of the town, New Park Street. As Waylen observed (*op. cit.*, p. 295) "the disposition of the streets is somewhat singular, and possibly exhibits traces of original design. Those which are curved may almost be said to be segments of circles described about a point on or near the keep of the castle." It is as if the outer limit of the streets was constrained to follow the pale of a small park, perhaps the second of the two twelfth-century parks; but the line of the outer ditch of the castle defences is an equally plausible explanation for the curve (see *Wilts. Arch. Mag.*, li (1945), pp. 39–40). At the south-east end of this curving outer street, New Park Street, was the first (Thursday) market place alongside St. Mary's; the latter was probably the townsmen's church. The present market place forms the chord of the arc, and at its southern end, under the shelter of the castle, is the church, which probably began as a garrison chapel. Near it the market place has been much encroached upon, but the original shape is plainly to be discerned (E. Dove's large-scale plan of 1759 is B.M. Maps K43/33).

DOWNTON   Wiltshire   sheet 167   41/175215
1208–09

In the bishop's account roll for 1208–09 nineteen rents were recorded for *placeae* in the New Market at Downton and it was noted that eleven other plots had been rented for the first time that year (ed. H. Hall, pp. 20–21).   In 1210–11 the next surviving roll has the rents of 39s. from thirty-nine *placeae* (Eccles. 2/159270B m. 2) "in burgum"; forty burgage plots were accounted for (Eccles. 2/159271 m. 5) in 1211–12, but seventy-two in 1213–14 when the manorial reeve was allowed 6s. off his account for three pieces of land which had been taken in from the fields to the new borough, *terrarum tractarum in novum burgum* (Eccles. 2/159272 m. 7).   In the account of 1215–16 the roll (Eccles. 2/159273 m. 4) has seventy-nine burgage plots and for the first time the separate heading "Borough of Downton", the previous years' entries being among the normal manor accounts.   In 1217–18 (Eccles. 2/159274 m. 1d) there were eighty-one burgages.   One of the newcomers was a weaver, and there was a fulling mill on the Avon.   In 1218–19 there were eighty-nine burgages and it was noted that fourteen others were pledged to begin their payments next year (Eccles. 2/159275 m. 7d).   Twelve of these did pay in 1219–20 when twelve more newcomers were also noted (Eccles. 2/159276 m. 8).   In 1232–33 the rents were £5 19s. 3d. and a second weaver was paying a pound of pepper a year for permission to stay in the borough (Eccles. 2/159283 m. 15 and 159284 m. 6), and by 1244–45 the bishop was receiving £19 6s. from the borough (Eccles. 2/159287 m. 2).   This sum was still small compared with the net profits of rural Downton.   In 1208–09 830 acres of the demesne had been sown with cereal crops and the bishop's sheep flock numbered 1,764 head (ed. Hall, pp. 20–21).   After the borough had been laid out alongside the river the agricultural output continued: the accounts for 1232–33 record 832 sown acres and over 2,000 sheep; 1,396 fleeces had gone to market.   The manor was still producing a net profit of over £150 (Eccles. 2/159283 m. 14).

The map still shows the clear distinction between the two Downtons.   On the east bank of the Avon are the parish church and the earthworks of the bishop's castle near which the Anglo-Saxon hundred moot had been held.   There was a substantial village here in 1086 with a recorded population of 131, and it was an old episcopal property.   The rents for its messuages and agricultural lands continued uninterrupted after 1210 except for the three plots mentioned above.

The straight broad street on the other side of the river would seem to represent the bishop's new borough, placed in the same relation to an older settlement as New Alresford, created a few years earlier.   The fourteenth-century tax lists account separately for borough and *forinsecus*.   Andrews' and Drury's county map of 1773 shows a lesser settlement called "Street" on the west of the river; and in 1576 the tax collectors ("Two Sixteenth Century Taxation Lists", ed. G. D. Ramsay, *W.A.S. Record Branch*, 1954, pp. 116–117) drew a distinction between "Downton Burgus" and the much larger units of "Est Ende" and "Church Tithinge".

HINDON   Wiltshire   sheet 167   31/910327
1219–20

In the bishop's account roll for 1218–19 (Eccles. 2/159275 m. 7d) the entries for the manor of Knoyle are of the usual agricultural type, but in 1219–20 the reeve claimed 6s. 11¾d. as *defectus* since the lands concerned had been taken "into burgage" (*in burgagium*). A croft and a virgate of Roger de Hinedon had been deleted from the rent roll as well as half a virgate belonging to Ada de Hinedon (159276 m. 8). In the account roll for 1220–21 (Eccles. 2/159277 m. 11) a new heading appears: *Burgus Hinedon*, bringing the bishop 49s. 8d. for the year. The only cost to the bishop, apart from the loss of Ada's and Roger's rent, was 21s. for making a well 14 fathoms (*teisae*) deep and 1s. for the rope and an iron-bound bucket. The roll for 1223–24 is badly torn. In 1224–25 (Eccles. 2/159279 m. 2d) the rents for Hindon borough had increased to £4 3s. and six newcomers were pledged to pay the sixpences for their plots (*placeae*) in the next financial year. In 1225–27 the accounts show the town solidly established with £4 10s. rents (159280 m. 4d and 159281 m. 1d). It must have continued to expand, for the rents of 1231–32 (159282 m. 6d) were £5 16s. 6d. In 1235–36 a roofed stall was being rented in the middle of the market place for 2d. (159284 m. 5) and by 1244–45 (159287 m. 20d) the total rents were £6 4s. 9d. The borough was not separately represented at the Assize of 1249 (JI/1/996) but on m. 27d there is a case from the "vill" of Hindon. The borough elected members of Parliament from 1378 to 1832 (M. G. Rathbone, ed., *List of Wilts. Borough Records* (1951), pp. x–xi).

The bishop owned a chain of manors in the south-west of the county from East Knoyle to Fonthill Bishop, and if the etymology suggested by *P. N. Wilts.* is correct, Hindon was merely a hill-name; the two messuages of Ada and Roger would have been on the ridge road from Salisbury to Knoyle and Mere, and the new town took its name from the hill.

The town was never very large. In 1334 it was taxed only at 28s. 9d., a quarter of the sum from the two Downtons, and in 1377 it mustered only seventy-seven poll-taxpayers. At the time of its disenfranchisement in 1832 there were just over 150 houses in the town. A few years earlier, Hoare (*Modern Wilts.*, i, p. 194) had noted "one long street lined on each side by numerous public houses"; "the Town does not comprehend above 200 acres of land"; "the town church is still parochially dependent on East Knoyle where most of the people of Hindon are married."

Knoyle itself continued to grow agricultural produce. In 1234–35 it gave the bishop a net revenue of over £100 with 557 acres of demesne sown with cereals, and 2,672 sheep. This was no abnormal year: in 1235–36 the net revenue, the head of sheep and the sown area were about the same. These sums are a considerable improvement on those of 1208–09 but whether as a result of the town plantation or not cannot be shown.

SALISBURY, NEW   Wiltshire   sheet 167   41/142295
1219

The transfer of the cathedral from its former hill-top site at Old Sarum to a new town in the meadows is perhaps the best-known example of town plantation in medieval England. Plans of the rectilinear new town have often been published (e.g. A. L. Poole, ed., *Medieval England*, i (1958), p. 60).

The most recent account of the town by Sir Francis Hill and others (*V.C.H.*, vi (1962)) throws a new light on the events of the foundation period. The settlement history of this area now appears to have four stages. First, an original urban centre, the capital of its shire, at Wilton which is 3 miles west of modern Salisbury. Secondly, the Anglo-Saxon town of *Searisbyrig*, not yet satisfactorily located but perhaps near the Roman road at Old Sarum (*q.v.*). Thirdly, the royal Norman borough located outside the Iron Age hill-fort with a new cathedral and a new castle inside these earthworks. Fourthly, the bishop's borough planted in the Avon meadows at the transfer of the cathedral to its present site in 1219.

Two other important revisions to the traditional account of New Salisbury must also be made. Firstly: the removal in 1219 was not a sudden act of pique or hostility but seems to have been envisaged for at least two decades. Secondly: the site which the bishop chose for New Salisbury was known as "Old" Salisbury before the transfer and some early manorial centre near St. Martin's church seems indicated; it would be the centre of the bishop's extensive manor inside which all three Salisburies had been created. This problem is discussed further under *Sarum, Old*.

Quarrels between the cathedral clergy and their castle neighbours were endemic in the proximity of the two communities at Old Sarum. A poem by a court poet of Henry III on the removal compared the uneasy situation to the Ark of the Covenant being set in the Temple of Baal (*Wilts. Arch. Mag.*, lvii (1959), pp. 242–246). The Osmund Register states that Richard I gave sanction for a removal of the cathedral to the new site and approved the allocation of new sites for the canons' houses. There would be nothing strange in a king who had planted Portsmouth and two towns in France approving of a new Salisbury. Nor was town plantation strange to bishops of Salisbury. Devizes and Sherborne Newland were their creation and by 1219 their neighbour, the bishop of Winchester, was actively planting towns in the area, two of them in Wiltshire. Political troubles and the king's absence overseas seem to have delayed the Salisbury project until the early years of Henry III's reign.

In 1217 the Pope received a petition from the dean and canons and issued an approving bull in March 1219. A churchyard at the intended site was at once consecrated and a wooden chapel erected while work on the stone cathedral was put in hand. The first stone was laid in 1220, three altars consecrated in 1225 and the old cathedral abandoned in 1227. The king granted a market charter in 1219 and a fair charter in 1221. The first charter to the new borough that adjoined the Close was granted by bishop Richard in 1225 and confirmed by the king in 1227. The Close, one-third of an acre, was nearly as large as the area allotted out for the city.

The city's new site occupied a small area in the south-west corner of the bishop's manor where the villeinage may have been living, near to Milford. The manor lands continued to surround the walls of the new town as the lands of Old Stratford surrounded New Stratford, another creation of a bishop, on the Warwickshire Avon. The church of St. Martin was outside the line chosen for the city defences and would appear to have served Milford before its transformation into a town church. The church of Stratford on Avon also lay outside the town.

A second church, St. Thomas's, was built to serve the central part of the new city and in 1269 a third, St. Edmund's, to serve a new parish formed in the north of the city as population grew. The original market place lay alongside St. Thomas's church but in 1269, when the new parish was created, the market place was carefully divided between the parishes of St. Edmund and St. Thomas.

The rectilinear division of the city into building blocks is still plainly discernible even though the market place has been partly encroached upon by streets that once must have been rows of stalls (Oatmeal Row, Ox Row, Fish Row). Naish's plan of 1716 (*V.C.H.*, vi, p. 114) and Lucas's plan of 1833 (BM. Maps 5730 (i) and (ii)) name these building blocks "Chequers" and reproduce their traditional names (e.g. Rolfe's Chequer, Trinity Chequer, Swayns Chequer, Cross Keys Chequer). Within the Chequers the average building plot was 7 perches by 3, and the rent of a plot was the standard shilling a year.

Speed's plan of 1611 shows in many of the streets the water courses described a little earlier by Leland as "little Streamlets and arms derived out of Avon". The city had the air of a shallow Venice, for the wheeled traffic kept to the beds of these streamlets while small bridges were provided for pedestrians. A similar diversion of shallow streams in a valley site was made between the burgage plots of Stockbridge (Hants.), *q.v.*

The 1227 charter envisaged that the city would be "enclosed with adequate ditches". No stone wall seems to have been built.

The success of New Salisbury quickly diminished the economic importance of the royal Norman borough on the hill. Although the king confirmed the liberties of his borough in 1229 and granted it a new fair in 1246, the tallage had to be reduced in 1246 and further in 1260. Wilton also suffered from competition from a second valley-bottom site. Its fee-farm was reduced in 1230 and its mint closed in 1250. Once, Wilton had three market days a week: New Salisbury's charter had been granted only one, but in 1240 Wilton was complaining that there were daily markets at its rival (*Plac. Abb.*, p. 112).

SARUM, OLD   Wiltshire   sheet 167 41/138327
1075

It has recently been suggested (*V.C.H.*, vi (1962) p. 51) that the now-deserted Norman borough on the hill was also a plantation. The cathedral was built here within the defences of the old Iron Age site by William I in 1075 when the bishopric was created from the united sees of Sherborne and Ramsbury. The payment of a "third penny" in 1086 suggests a borough but the first known charter dates from 1100–35 (*Ballard*, p. xxxi). The site of this borough has long remained uncertain and archaeologists had been puzzled at the absence of any remains of civil settlement alongside the cathedral. Plans (*V.C.H.*, vi, pl. 66) now place burgages outside the earthworks. This royal borough was not large: in the twelfth century its tax was less than that paid by Wilton.

Geographically, this borough lay within the extensive manor that kings of Wessex had given to the predecessors of the Norman bishops. The king's selions and the bishop's selions lay intermingled in the common fields of Stratford-sub-Castle and the mill was shared between king and bishop. The bishop's manor was a large triangle of territory between the Avon and the Bourne; it probably had a villein settlement near Milford and it was this settlement to which the otherwise puzzling references to *Old* Salisbury in 1185 and 1188 may be assigned (*P.R.S.*, xxxiv (1913), and xxxviii (1925)). Otherwise to speak of "Old" Salisbury thirty-four years before the creation of New Salisbury would be nonsense. Indeed, there are other references to this manor as "Old Salisburies" in the plural, perhaps from twin settlements at Milford and near what were later the town mills of New Salisbury.

The topography of the successive Salisburies has its mysteries even after Norman Salisbury has been located. The site of the Roman town eludes the spade and there is no satisfactory location for the Anglo-Saxon *Searisbyrig* (*Hist. King's Works*, ii (1963) p. 824). This town is no myth: Edgar's Witan met there in 960, Aethelred II had his mint there, the Danes raided the town in 1002, and early in the eleventh century the church of St. Ethelreda was founded in it. If it were proved to lie in the meadows, then the creation of 1219 would indeed have been a penitent's return to an Old Salisbury. (See also: J. Musty and P. A. Rahtz, "The Suburbs of Old Sarum", *Wilts. Arch. and Nat. Hist. Mag.*, lix (1964), pp. 130–154.)

WORCESTERSHIRE

No medieval plantations have been found in this county.

YORKSHIRE, EAST RIDING

Although the East Riding had its inland towns, these were organic promotions of villages. Its plantations, large and small, were all ports. (Even Skipsea, now inland, had its Hythe on the shore of the mere.) As Holderness was drained and cultivated, the coastal ports prospered and traffic down the river Hull was increased. The beneficiaries of the economic development of the catchment areas of Trent and Ouse were the Humber ports, from Airmyn to the remarkable venture at Ravenserodd off Spurn Point, a borough now covered by the waves.

Paull Fleet (54/166264) may claim to be added to the list of plantations although its urban status is in some doubt (see C132/24/6; E179/239/219 m. 1d; and J. R. Boyle, *Early History of Hedon* (1895), p. 845, and App. 1).

BROUGH ON HUMBER   Yorkshire, E.R.   sheet 98 /936267
by 1239

It is argued below that the *Brough* of the place-name Skipsea Brough indicates a true *burgus*, for there are documents to authenticate the presence of burgages at Skipsea. Mr. J. W. Cox has suggested to me that the same must be said of Brough in Elloughton. The strongest case for the presence of a manorial borough here, or an attempt to found one, rests on two documents of 1239. In the first (*Cal. Chart. Rolls*, i, p. 245) Walter Gray, archbishop of York, was granted a Thursday market and a fair at St. Matthewtide to be held *apud manerium suum de Burgo super Humbre*. I was inclined myself to treat this as a village, a place-name latinised from an Anglo-Saxon *burh*, "a defended place", the defences being the earthworks of the Roman town. But the second document in Gray's Register (*Surtees Soc.*, lvi (1870), p. 251) is absolutely the language of borough foundation: "we have given to our burgesses *in burgo super Humbre* the liberties of Beverley and burgage plots 21' by 28' at a yearly rent of 4d".

Brough has other suspicious features. It had no church of its own in the Middle Ages. It lies on the very edge of Elloughton and Brantingham townships, and the placing of the Roman town here indicates an effective ferry route from Lincolnshire even though the principal ferry before and after the Norman Conquest was at North Ferriby, three miles further east. Perhaps the archbishop was attempting in 1239 to engineer a return to the Roman route? The opportunity was given him by the possession of the manor of Elloughton that touched the Humber for a short distance here. The attempted borough does not seem to have had much life.

There are, however, obstacles to the acceptance of Brough as an innovation in 1239: a document of 1202 (*Surtees Soc.*, xciv (1897), p. 47) which conveys land in Brantingham, Ellerker and *in Burgo* supports the view that the *burgus* was simply the *burh* latinised; and in the Cartulary of Meaux (BM., Ms. Cott. Vit. C.VI.) there are references to Brough which are dated 1160–80. These mention houses and a street but have nothing burghal. But no earlier references appear. (Note the name *The Burrs* on 1st ed. O.S. 6 inch map, sheet 238a, in the fields N.E. of the station). The accounts of the archbishop's manors at the end of the thirteenth century have no suggestion of a borough (SC6/1144/1; E372/152B m. 17).

HEDON   Yorkshire, E.R.   sheet 99   54/190289
1138–48

The site for this town was taken by the earl of Aumâle from the heath on the edge of the South Field of the village of Preston in Holderness (*E.R.R.O* DDCC/141/68 f. 14; DDCC/285 f. 13). The focus was the creek, the little Hedon river, that led up from the Humber into Holderness, giving shelter from storms and pirates. In 1115 there was a tenant of the earl, "at the river of *Heldone* and the passage of the Humber" whose services were given by the earl to the monks of Beauvais (H. W. C. Davis, *Regesta Regum Anglo-Normannorum*, ii (1956), p. 123). At this time neither Hull nor Ravenserodd was in existence: Hedon was the first essay at a Yorkshire port in the estuary.

The town had the form of three parallel Havens constructed artificially, with two streets between, also running north-south, and at least three east-west cross-streets. There were three parish churches and two extra-mural hospitals. Plans of the town are given in J. R. Boyle, *Early History of Hedon* (1895), pp. 179 and 197.

The first charter known is that of 1167–70 (*E.Y.C.*, iii, p. 45) but fairs were in progress outside the town near Magdalen Hospital a decade earlier; there were chapels in 1160–62 (*ibid.*, iii, p. 35) and certainly a house in 1148 (*ibid.*, p. 150), and other grants (*ibid.*, iii, pp. 30, 41, 43, 45) suggest that the site was occupied soon after 1138.

The medieval remains of the town and its contraction in face of the competition of Ravenserodd and Hull are described in M. W. Beresford, *History on the Ground* (1957) pp. 125–150; an air photograph will be found in *Beresford and St. Joseph*, p. 201.

KINGSTON UPON HULL   Yorkshire, E.R.   sheet 99   45/100285

1293

This narrative continues that begun under Wyke (*below*), the port established by the Cistercian abbey of Meaux at the junction of the Hull and Humber rivers. This town was sometimes known as Wyke and sometimes as the Port of Hull or *Le Hul*, but after its acquisition by Edward I in 1293 it became known as Kingston upon Hull.

Between 1260 and 1293 the Crown acquired a two-thirds interest in the lordship of Holderness, including the towns of Hedon and Ravenserodd. In the spring and summer of 1292 Edward I was in the area on his way to and from Berwick, and in November 1292 he ordered a valuation of the vill of Wyke to be made (J. Bilson, "Wyke-upon-Hull in 1293", *Tr. E. R. Ant. Soc.*, xxvi (1928), pp. 52–53 from E36/274 f. 171). This was made in January 1293 (*ibid.*, pp. 53–54) and at the end of that month Meaux granted all its rights in Wyke to the king, together with permission to take land outside the town for the building of 40 foot wide approach roads, (*ibid.*, pp. 55–59). The king's purpose was "to increase the fitness of the port for ships and traffic" (*Chron. Melsa*, Rolls Ser. (1886)), ii, p. 186). In exchange the abbey acknowledged that it had been given "great profit" by the king but no details were specified. The abbey's "well content", there expressed, was not long lived. The *Chronicle* (*ibid.*, ii, pp. 183–187) develops two grievances of the monks. About 1286 abbot Roger had leased the vill of Wyke and the grange of Myton to William de Hameldon, dean of York, for twenty years. The abbot repented and sought to cancel the lease. After much negotiation and counter-offers William surrendered the property in 1291 but charged a high price including a grant of the grange of North Dalton for the remainder of his life. The monks reckoned that they had lost £1,000. This conflict may represent the two parties' knowledge that the king was anxious to acquire the site.

But the king's price for the site did not satisfy the monks either (E159/68 m. 9). The manor was valued at £24 8s. and the vill of Wyke at £78 14s. 8d., £103 2s. 8d. in all. When the monks came to receive their income from the exchanged lands in Pocklington, Weelsby (Lincs.) and Wawne they found that the royal valuations of £50, £30 and £5 respectively were too optimistic by £32 14s. 9d. a year. They also complained that they lost more than half a year's rent from Wyke in the year of the take-over, another £51 11s. 4d. It was eleven years before the king made his final offer: the church of Skipsea and £30 worth of licences in mortmain. The lands which Edward had given to Meaux, it will be noted, were not sacrifices from his ancient demesne but taken from the recently acquired Aumâle lands.

The first rental of the town of Wyke was drawn up in March 1293 (Bilson, *op. cit.*, pp. 61–65) showing 111 tenements. The king's scheme for improvements included new approach roads in three directions: towards Beverley (north), Hessle (west), and York (north-west), and this land was valued (*ibid.*, pp. 65–67). On 19 March the king formally took possession of the vill of Wyke and the remaining Meaux lands within Myton. In 1297 three tenements were taken into possessson at the east end of Kirk Lane for enlarging the King's Quay at a cost of £10 8s. 11d.; and a new residence for the royal bailiff was built at a cost of £50. In July 1293 two markets a week and a six-week fair were granted; and in 1300 houses were got ready for the establishment of a Mint and an Exchange (E372/152B, m. 1d). On April 1, 1299, the town was granted a borough charter (*Cal. Chart. Rolls*, ii, p. 475), the same day as its rival, Ravenserodd. Kingston was called *burgus*, however, in the bailiff's accounts for 1293 (E372/152B m. 34). A final piece of royal construction was the new water mill on the Ald Hull, built in 1302–03 at a cost of £61 5s. 7½d., but immediately rented at £5 6s. 8d. a year.

Although the town had the chapel of Holy Trinity, the rights of the mother church at Hessle were strictly claimed, and burials had to take place there. In 1301 the archbishop intervened and informed the patrons of the church that he was going to consecrate a churchyard alongside Holy Trinity (*Reg. Corbridge* (Surtees Soc., xxxviii (1925), pp. 161–162, 167 and 196)). The king granted a vacant plot for the enlargement of this churchyard in 1302 but the church was not fully parochial until 1661 (13 Chas. II, cap. 2).

The roads planned in 1293 were slow to be built, and fresh inquisitions as to ownership and value of land were taken in 1302 (*Y.I.*, iv, pp. 47–50), and building was in progress in 1305 (Bilson, *op. cit.*, p. 73).

The king's other improving project was the physical enlargement of the town. In the bailiff's account of 1296 (E372/152B) each of fifty plots is described as *nova placea extra villam* although comparison with the rentals of 1320 and 1347 (SC11/746; Bilson, *op. cit.*, pp. 75–101) shows that they were physically within the bounds of the town. It is clear that the western streets of Kingston upon Hull—roughly those west of Holy Trinity—were developed after the acquisition of Wyke in 1293 and "their rectangular lay-out may have been due to the vogue of this type of planning which is characteristic of Edward I's new towns" (*ibid.*, p. 82). Yet the rental of 1320 shows that only twenty-one plots in this western area had actually been occupied, and the expected rents had not been achieved even for these (*ibid.*, pp. 95–97; compare also SC11/773 (1305) for fallen rents of other plots). The average revenue from the town for the twelve years 1293–1305, clear of ordinary running expenses, was £113 12s. (E372/152B mm. 1 and 34). This was a little above its take-over valuation of £103 2s. 8d. The royal tile-yards produced 54,350 tiles in 1303–04 and 92,000 in 1304–05.

The rentals of 1302–06 (SC11/743-4) give the dimensions of plots, confirming the inequality in size and absence of rectangularity shown in the conjectural plan (Bilson, *op. cit.*, endpiece).

The old core of Wyke along the river Hull, and Edward I's additional streets both lie away from the modern shopping centre and railway station. The old town has lost its walls, their line being occupied by gardens and a dock. Within this line are the remains of the offices and warehouses of the port, its burgage plots fully built over before the bombs of World War II laid them open. The Humber shore and not the Hull now carries the main docks.

RAVENSERODD   Yorkshire, E.R.   sheet 105   45/ c.400100
1240–50

Set on a sandbank, *un sablon entre la mere et le Humbre* (SC8/68/3380), the borough of Ravenserodd probably stood somewhere to the west of Spurn Head. As the chronicle of Meaux Abbey said, "the town of Ravenserodd occupied a position in the utmost limits of Holderness between the sea and the Humber. It was distant from the mainland a mile or more. For access it had a sandy road no broader than an arrow's flight yet wonderfully maintained by the tides and the ebb and flow of the Humber." The origin of the town was stated by a jury of 1276 (*R.H.*, i, p. 107) to have been "forty years and more ago when the casting up of the sea caused stones and sand to accumulate, and on them the earl of Aumâle built a town". Between 1235 and 1249 Meaux Abbey had been given a plot of land in the new town in order to put up buildings suitable for a store of herrings and other fish (*Chron. Melsa* (Rolls Ser.) ii, pp. 29–30, and iii, pp. 121–122), and in 1251 (*Cal. Chart. Rolls*, i, p. 353) the earl obtained a charter for a market and fair. A farm of 52s. in 1260 and the increments in 1264 and 1265 (C132/24/6; SC6/1078/8) suggest from 100 to 120 burgages. Larger rents were paid a decade later (SC6/1078/16–7). An origin in the decade 1240–50 is also suggested by evidence given by a jury in 1290 when the king was hearing complaints from the royal borough of Grimsby about the town "*de novo constructo*" no more than 5 miles away as the crow flew (*Y.I.*, ii, pp. 112 115).

"In the reign of king Henry (1216–72) at first by the casting up of the sea a certain island was born which is called Ravenserodd. And afterwards fishermen came to dry their nets there and men began little by little to dwell and stay there, and afterwards ships laden with divers kinds of merchandise began to unload and sell at the town. And now, inasmuch as the island is nearer the sea than Grimsby and as ships can unload there more easily, nearly all ships do stay, unload and sell there. About thirty years ago (i.e. c. 1260) there were not more than four dwellings. The countess of Aumâle is lady of the island. The men of Ravenserodd take tolls as if the place were really a borough (*ad similitudinem burgi*)."

Among those who treated Ravenserodd as if it were a true borough were the royal tax collectors. The tax of 1297 from the burgesses of Ravenser amounted to £16 and from Ravenserodd another £5 13s. 7d. (E179/239/219 m. 1).

The Grimsby men lost their suit, but on the death of Isabella de Fortibus in 1293 the Aumâle estates passed to the king, and in 1299 on the same day as Kingston upon Hull's charter, Edward I granted Ravenserodd identical privileges (*Cal. Chart. Rolls*, ii, pp. 475–476). For the charters they paid £200 (N. Denholm-Young, *Y.A.J.*, xxxi (1934), pp. 403–405). In 1304 the borough was summoned to send its two representatives to Parliament.

The topography of Ravenser, Ravenserodd and Old Ravenser (three separate places in the taxation of 1297) is impossible to determine certainly, since all three have now been eroded. Old Ravenser lay on what was then the mainland (J. R. Boyle, *Lost Towns of the Humber*, (1889), p. 10). Odd (that is, "headland") was the original name of the new town, but it was frequently called Odd near Ravenser and then Ravenserodd and even Ravenser. It was reckoned to be in Easington parish; the town had no parish church of its own.

The sea which had thrown up the site began to claim it again. In 1346 two thirds of the town was said to be washed away. In 1347 200 houses were reported destroyed since 1334 and the borough's tax assessment was reduced from £15 to £5. Within twenty years there was no borough to tax at all. The Chronicle of Meaux said: "All men daily removing their possessions, the town was swiftly swallowed up and irreparably destroyed by the merciless floods and tempests. This was an exceedingly famous borough devoted to merchandise and very much occupied with fishing, having more ships and burgesses than any on this coast."

The stages of destruction can be followed in: SC8/6/284; 68/3380; 87/4306; 156/7763; *Rotulorum Originalium Abbrevatio*, ed. H. Playford, ii (1810) p. 188; C135/143/23; *Chron. Meaux* (Rolls Series) iii, pp. 247 and 283. A recent study of the erosion is G. de Boer, "Spurn Head", *Tr. Inst. Brit. Geog.* xxxiv (1964), pp. 71–90, esp. fig. 4.

SKIPSEA   Yorkshire, E.R.   sheet 99   54/165550
1066–1102

Before the drainage of the Hull marshes Holderness was virtually an island, for the upper waters of the river Hull penetrated almost to the sea near Lissett and Gransmoor. On this slightly higher ground at the north end of Holderness Harold had a large manor at Cleeton. In 1086 there were twenty-eight ploughs. After Harold's defeat William I gave the manor to Dru de la Beuvrière, and it was to Dru that the Chronicle of Meaux attributed the building of Skipsea castle (*Rolls Series* (1866), i, p. 89). The castle stood on the very western edge of Cleeton township only a few yards from the fields of its hamlet, Dringhoe. When the borough settlement of Skipsea Brough was created, its houses—of which a few survive—were over the Dringhoe boundary (O.S. 1st ed. 6 inch sheet 180). The village of Skipsea proper is quite separate, lying within what were Cleeton fields, and since Cleeton has been completely eroded the village may simply be Cleeton transplanted. A similar separation between a bond village and the seigneur's castle is seen at Burstwick where the lords of Skipsea transferred their seat in 1221 (*P.N.E.R.*, p. 33; N. Denholm-Young, "The Yorks. Estates of Isabella de Fortibus", *Y.A.J.*, xxxi (1934), p. 402).

The first reference to the castle is in 1098–1102 (*E.Y.C.*, iii, p. 27) when there was also a castle-church. Later in the twelfth century, when the earls of Aumâle were lords of Skipsea, there was certainly a castle-borough (*ibid.*, iii, p. 72 (1160–75)); land *in burgo* and a toft *in burgo* were given to the monks of Bridlington. The erosion of Cleeton (T. Sheppard, *Lost Towns of the Yorkshire Coast* (1912), ch. xxi) seems to have been complete by 1260 when forty bovate-holding bondsmen of Cleeton were "dwelling in Skipse" (*Y.I.*, i, p. 82) together with thirteen cottars. The same document clearly distinguishes three burgage-holders in Skipsea borough, and its New Hythe (*sc.* landing-place) was still worth 20s. a year even though the castle was razed in 1221 and the seigneurial household had left this part of Holderness. Ships could still sail the lake.

The final link between this landing-place on the lake, the borough at Skipsea, and the eroded village of Cleeton is given by the description of this hythe in the Pipe Roll of 1306–07: *novae hydae burgi de Cleton* (E372/152B mm. 3 and 6).

Skipsea Brough is now only a group of houses gathered at the south entrance to the castle earthworks (see plan in *Y.A.J.*, xxiv (1917), p. 359).

WYKE UPON HULL (later Kingston)   Yorkshire E.R.   sheet 99   45/100285
1160–93

Wyke upon Hull was the port which Edward I took over and enlarged in 1293 as his town of Kingston upon Hull (*q.v.*). But Wyke itself, at least a century older, was also a planted town, promoted by the Cistercian abbey of Meaux at the point where the river Hull entered the Humber. Down the Hull came the traffic from Holderness, the eastern Wolds and Beverley, the principal old-established town of the area. Meaux abbey, the active drainer and coloniser of the marshland, would particularly appreciate the seaward vent. The earlier foundation at Hedon by the lay seigneurs of Holderness was another expression of the same commercial potentialities but it foundered on the narrowness of the Hedon creek. The Hull at Wyke was a broader river, and its last few hundred yards were straightened to give a more direct access to the estuary.

The *Chronicle of Meaux*, written at the very end of the fourteenth century (Rolls Series (1866), i, p. 169) describes how this new course of the river Hull ran on the east of Wyke along what had previously been a mere creek, the *Sayercryk*. The old course was blocked up: *vix sewera valet nuncupari*, "making it hardly worth calling a drain".

The first interest of the abbey in the site came by a grant from Robert of Meaux (1160–82) of arable land, pasture, fishing rights, a saltern and a house within Myton. By 1210 the monks had acquired all the ten bovates of demesne. This land, some enclosed and some within the open fields, was farmed in the usual Cistercian fashion by lay brothers living in Myton Grange, probably the hall granted them by Robert of Meaux. The site of this grange was still visible in a meadow at the time when the Chronicle was being written and the name of the meadow was *Grangewyk*, "wyk" being simply the name for a creek.

In 1193 (*P.R.S.*, n.s., iii (1927), p. 69) the wool of Yorkshire monasteries contributed for the ransom of Richard I was gathered for export at a place called *portum de Hulmo*, the first mention of a place of that name; four years later large quantities of wool also left "Hull" (J. Bilson, "Wyke-upon-Hull in 1293" (*Tr. E.R. Ant. Soc.*, xxvi (1928), p. 40)), and in 1203–05 Wyke ranked as the sixth among the thirty-five seaports whose merchants were taxed by John. In the accounts of the New Custom levied from 1275–90 Hull usually ranked as third port of the kingdom, coming after Boston and London (*ibid.*, p. 45). It was the port through which archbishops of York obtained their wine, and when the king was at York his household was similarly provisioned.

Almost as soon as documentation begins, there was a dispute between the abbot of Meaux and the parson of Hessle which reveals that there was a chapel of the Holy Trinity in Wyke (alias the chapel of Myton) that lay within Hessle parish: "*Hesel in cuius parochia villa ipsa de Kyngeston pro parte dicitur esse sita*" (*Reg. Corbridge* (Surtees Soc., xxxviii (1925)), pp. 161–162). And when the abbot obtained a charter for a market and fair in 1279 at Wyke near Myton it is significant that the fair was to be held at the feast of Holy Trinity (*Cal. Chart. Rolls*, ii, p. 214). A space of 7¼ acres was reserved within the town for the fair ground (Bilson, *op. cit.*, p. 54, from E36/274 f. 171). On the eve of its acquisition by Edward I in 1293 Wyke had 109 messuages and *placeae*, all of them on land belonging to Meaux. In the north of the town there was a small enclave of land belonging to Sir William de Aton which had on it three messuages and three villein tofts: this island of unfreedom in the midst of burghality is explained below.

The tenements of the valuation of January 1293 were collated by Bilson and L. M. Stanewell with those of later rentals and inquisitions and placed on a conjectural plan (*ibid.*, end-paper). Bilson observed (*ibid.*, p. 81): "the lay-out of the town proves conclusively that it was not developed from an agricultural hamlet, but that it had its origin with the port." This plan shows the houses set along two main streets parallel not to the Humber but to the Hull; twenty-nine of the burgages backed on to the river and the only public access to the river bank was where the four short streets (east–west) parallel to the estuary ended at the river. Holy Trinity chapel marked the western limit of Wyke. The Aton enclave is shown in the north of the town; by 1327 it had its own church of St. Mary. In 1333 it was still reckoned to be in North Ferriby parish (*Y.A.J.*, xxiv (1917), p. 277), and was not separate in all respects until 1868.

A second valuation of March 1293 (Bilson, *op. cit.*, pp. 60–61, from E36/274, f. 172b) concerns Myton, the hamlet of Hessle within whose fields and marshes Wyke had been built. Myton was still an agricultural community. The two principal land-owners in it were the abbot of Meaux, who had ten bovates of land and two wind-mills, and Sir William de Aton who had seven bovates in the fields and six houses in Wyke town, one of which was rented to the archbishop. It would seem that the island made when the *Ald Hull* was shortened by the New Cut also contained some of the Aton acres in the fields of Myton, and these had to be accepted within the town.

The additions made to the town after its acquisition by Edward I in 1293 are described under Kingston upon Hull, *supra*.

Mr. J. W. Cox points out to me that a passage in the Hundred Rolls misplaced in the printed text (*R.H.*, i, p. 106) discloses an interest by archbishop Walter de Gray in the port of Hull, in the time of Henry III. References to *burgus de Humber* (cited above under *Brough*) may indicate a burghal community in or near Wyke. The main difficulty in this view is that there is no record of Edward I buying out an archiepiscopal interest in Wyke, and in the rentals the archbishop simply leased houses from others: but see C. Frost, *Notices relative to Hull* (1827), pp. 120–121.

YORKSHIRE, NORTH RIDING

To the inland towns, all still important, that were planted in this Riding it may be necessary to add Scarborough, its principal port, although the evidence is very ambiguous. In view of the importance of the town a brief discussion is appended.

Scarborough was probably founded in 966–67 (*P.N. Yorks. N.R.*, p. 106) as a

Danish stronghold but this settlement may have been extinguished in Harold Hardrada's attack of 1066 (A. Rowntree, *History of Scarborough* (1931), p. 52) and not restored before the building of the castle (1136). The place does not appear in Domesday Book when the centre of population still seems to have been at Falsgrave, to the south-west. A borough charter was granted in 1155 (*Cal. Chart. Rolls*, i, p. 417). In Henry III's charter of 1256 a distinction was made between an Old Borough and a New. Newborough Street preserves the name of this division but the walls marking the western limit of the Old Borough were taken down in 1817 (*V.C.H., Yorks. N.R.*, ii, p. 538).

MALTON, NEW   Yorkshire, N.R.   sheet 92   44/786716

1154–73

New Malton, a walled borough, was surrounded on three sides by the fields of Old Malton, a village which lies more than a mile to the north-east, and on the fourth by the river Derwent. The borough was created north of a bridge which linked the East and North Ridings. The bridge itself led to a narrow shelf of land under the river-cliff on the north bank where there was room for neither market place nor houses so that the town was built on more level ground a little west of the bridge and below the castle. There were two town churches: St. Leonard's on a slope at the castle end of the borough and St. Michael's on more level ground at the west of the central cross-roads where there was room for a large market place. The town walls formed a rough pentagon with the river along the south side. The short burgage plots on the north-west side of the Market Place are well preserved as inn-yards although the actual wall that limited them has disappeared. In the north-east part of the town the O.S. 6 inch plan shows the line of the wall but it is now marked only by a change in level of the ground. Nothing of the castle remains except a short length of wall overlooking the bridge, and a wall tower. The important road junction in the centre of the town produces Yorkshire's most notorious traffic bottleneck at summer week-ends.

The creation of Old Malton is best described by the fortunes of the castle. This was built early in the twelfth century by the de Vesci's, the first Norman lords of Old Malton, at or near the western end of a Roman fort which had guarded the same river crossing. In 1135 the archbishop of York, acting for Stephen, besieged and captured Matilda's garrison and destroyed the castle. Eustace fitzJohn, son-in-law of Ivo de Vesci, rebuilt the castle after the war and probably founded the borough; he also founded the Gilbertine Priory in Old Malton. The two town churches, which remained dependent on the mother church at Old Malton, have architectural features of the mid-twelfth century also.

The first documentation of the new town is in a grant to Old Malton priory (Dugdale, *Monasticon*, vi, p. 970, no. v; B.M. Ms. Cott. Claud. D. xi, ff. 45 and 47) which refers to "Old" Malton and to the chapels (i.e. in the town) belonging to the village church; a charter to the weavers of York (1154–73) reveals that the weavers of Malton were then making striped and dyed cloth and uses words that suggest that the borough was built on royal land (*Cal. Pat. Rolls, 1345–48*, p. 300). The town paid

517

tallage in 1184 when the Pipe Roll records both *homines de Veteri Mealton* and *burgenses de Mealton* (*P.R.S.*, xxxvii (1915), p. 91). At the Assizes of 1219 onwards (*Surtees Soc.* lvi (1937), p. 1047) the borough was separately represented by jurors.

A late fifteenth-century custumal of the borough (*Y.A.J.*, xxvi (1922) pp. 326–333) purports to date from "the fyrst ffundaycon". It assigns waste on either side of the town as a quarry for building the burgage houses, the walls and the four gates.

RICHMOND   Yorkshire, N.R.   sheet 91   45/172009
1109–14

The first specific reference to Richmond comes from the first decades of the twelfth century (charter of 1109–14: *E.Y.C.*, i, p. 25). The river cliff above the Swale was chosen for a castle which became the head of the extensive Honour of Richmond. Earl Eadwine, the last Saxon owner of these estates, had treated Catterick in the plain and Gilling on the edge of the moors as their natural centres, but these sites were rejected by the first Norman earl for a site that was probably still uninhabited in 1086, being within the fields of *Hasse* (Aske) and *Hindrelac*; the land of *Fontenais* was also in or near the site (*E.Y.C.*, iv, p. 22). The parish within which the site lay was probably Easby (*E.Y.C.*, v, p. 163). Compare earl Eadwine's seat at Ledstone (W.R.) abandoned for Pontefract by his Norman successor.

A fine drawing of the castle in a late fifteenth-century *feodary* (B.M. Ms. Cott. Faust. B vii, f. 85 v) shows the positions (*placeae*) to be taken up along the walls by the knights who held their lands in return for the duty of defence. The burgage *placeae* of the townsmen were placed more vulnerably outside the castle gate, on the perimeter of the semicircular market place, making one of the few semicircular boroughs in England. As Leland described it in the early sixteenth century: "The compass of the ruinous walls is not half a mile about, so that the town compasseth little but the Market Place, the houses about it and the gardens behind them."

Trinity church stands in the centre of the market place as the town church; the castle has its own chapel. Trinity church must have been erected by 1135–36 when it was given by earl Stephen to St. Mary's, York. This earl's gift was "the *churches* of Richmond", indicating that St. Mary's, the parish church that stands on the lower site by the river, was already in existence. Between 1136 and 1145 earl Alan III granted the burgesses of Richmond their fee farm at £29 (*Ballard*, p. 220). A second charter of the same period (*Ballard*, p. 16) ascribes the first liberties of the borough to the time of earl Alan's uncle (Alan) and father (Stephen), i.e. 1089–1136. There are valuations of the borough in 1282 and 1285 (*Y.I.*, i, p. 230, and ii, p. 38).

Richmond, Surrey, was not a Norman town. The name was given to the royal estate at Sheen by Henry VII in honour of his Yorkshire earldom, thus bringing two Richmonds into the field.

THIRSK, NEW   Yorkshire, N.R.   sheet 91   44/430824
1135–45

At Thirsk two important roads from south to north come within a few yards of meeting each other acrosss the Cod Beck. On the east bank is the York to Yarm road and on the west the road from Boroughbridge and Topcliffe to Northallerton and Darlington. The position of the church and Mowbray castle on the west bank makes it virtually certain that here was the original settlement, as described in Domesday Book. The other settlement, on the east bank, has several features that strongly suggest a second, burghal, plantation. "The fifty old burgage tenements which till 1832 gave their possessors the right of sending two members to Parliament were all in this part of Thirsk." (J. J. Sheahan, *History and Topography of the City of York and N. Riding*, ii (1857), p. 151). There are no records of any burgages in documents concerning the western site (*V.C.H., Yorks. N.R.*, ii, pp. 58–70). The eastern settlement had no parish church, merely the chapel of ease of St. James at the head of an enormous rectangular market place, now abandoned to commerce except as a night resting-place for long-distance lorries. This eastern borough was already in existence in 1145 when its chapel and the parish church of Thirsk were given by Roger de Mowbray at the foundation of Newburgh Priory in Coxwold. The charter mentions a Bar on the Kilvington road out of the borough, and this can only have been the eastern route (Dugdale, *Monasticon*, vi, p. 318). This foundation charter also distinguishes throughout between the "vill" of Thirsk and the "borough" of Thirsk.

No closer dating of the borough foundation is yet possible. (A phrase in a charter of Henry II to the York Weavers (*Cal. Pat. Rolls, 1345–8*, p. 200) may mean that Thirsk was a royal borough, that is, founded before the Mowbrays acquired the manor from Henry I.) The Mowbray castle was built before 1130, but the borough is not subcastellar. It was the older vill that lay under the castle; and the establishment of a borough on the other side of the river suggests that defence and commerce had different optimal sites. (The purpose of the moated site on the mill island, east of the river, is uncertain. It may have been a motte.) More precision might be possible if there was some significant development along the York–Yarm route in the early twelfth century which suddenly made it more attractive to traffic. It is, of course, possible that the Mowbrays built a bridge at Thirsk to link the two roads and projected a borough at the junction. They had other property at Kirkby, on the north bank of the Ure opposite Boroughbridge where a new bridge was creating a new borough. It will be noted that the east-bank main road at Thirsk is diverted in and out of the market place very much like that of Boroughbridge.

The greater use in post-medieval times of the western road has made the west-bank village into the present town; but not, as we have seen, a borough. It is on the west bank that markets are still held, and the shopping centre is also there. For this reason, the de-commercialised east bank settlement is now called Old Thirsk and the west bank, New Thirsk: but the original order of things can be in little doubt. (The close arrangement of houses around the market place of the west bank town is, however, disturbingly burghal in its appearance.)

YORKSHIRE, WEST RIDING

The same economic expansion that created the new boroughs of the Humber, Aire and Ouse was also encouraging smaller manorial boroughs inland at Ripon (SC6/1141/1), Otley (SC6/1141/1, 7 and 10), Bingley (E. E. Dodd, *Bingley* (1958), p. 20, and C133/2/7), Bradford (C134/22; SC6/1085/17; DL10/5; see H. I. Judson, *The Early History of Bradford* (London Univ. M. A. Thesis, 1933)), and Harewood (SC6/1077/26). These were organic developments of villages by promotion or by addition of a borough to a village nucleus.

PATELEY BRIDGE hovers on the border line of categories. The first mention of the bridge here is in 1320 (*Cal. Chart. Rolls*, iii, p. 422) but the "paths" of 1175 in the place-name (*Y.A.S.R.S.*, xxxix, p. 58, and *P.N. Yorks.*, *W.R.*, v, pp. 149–150) may have led to an earlier ford across the Nidd. The Nidderdale road intersects here the road across the moors from Ripon and Fountains to Craven. It was a natural market centre for locally-mined lead. The market village stands in the civil parish of Bewerley a township of the large parish of Ripon.

It was originally intended to include SELBY in the main list but further evidence has set it aside. In view of the importance of the town the discussion is appended. "It is quite impossible to believe that there was any settled monastery or town at Selby at any time in the year 1068," wrote E. A. Freeman (*The Norman Conquest*, iv (1876), p. 794). The legendary history printed as a Preface to *Y.A.S.R.S.*, x (1891), describes the sheriff sailing by on the Ouse, seeing Benedict's cell, and leaving the monk a tent to cover himself with before taking him to the king to obtain a grant of land. Nor does the foundation charter mention any vill of Selby: rather it seems to have been a field-name within the great and marshy parish of Snaith. William I gave the abbey simply *ipsam Selebiam, videlicet unam carucatam terrae de Snaith*, together with six bovates and half a carucate elsewhere; the archbishop of York had given Monk Fryston and *Salebia minor*, 7 carucates out of his great manor of Sherburn in Elmet. The main town was often called Over Selby in distinction to this Little Selby, but the names are now merged (*The Coucher Book of Selby* (*Y.A.S.R.S.*, x (1891), p. 11; *V.C.H., Yorks.*, ii, p. 210, fn.)).

The broad market place runs from the west gate of the abbey; Micklegate is another broad street north of the abbey church abutting on to the abbots' staith on the Ouse bank; the name Bondgate on the northern edge of the town probably indicates the homes of the agricultural population. The town was not reckoned a borough but it had a full commercial life as a river port. In the *Year Books of Richard II* (ed. T. F. T. Plucknett (1929), p. 81) it was noted: "the vill of Selby where he dwells is a merchant vill, wherein are divers wine taverns and a Street to the city of York and divers other vills of the said county."

The language of the foundation charter and the archbishop's gift poses no problems if we accept "Salebia" as a minor place-name given to riverside fields. But there is an earlier document which pushes the balance of conjecture the other way, suggesting a vill of Selby (or indeed two, since if Upper surely Lower also?). There is a survey of the archbishop's properties (c. 1030) which comprises *inter alia* "all upper Selby and two oxgangs in Flaxley, half Barlow, all Brayton except half a ploughland" (*E.H.R.*, xxvii (1912), p. 15). The grouping of the names makes it certain that this is the territory within Sherburn from which the archbishop's gift at the foundation of the abbey was made. The places where "all" was given are places that were villages in 1086, and it is difficult to resist the conclusion that (*pace* Freeman) there was a

Selby in or near which the abbey was built, unless, of course, the vill of 1030 had been wasted by 1069.

AIRMYN   Yorkshire, W.R.   sheet 98   44/725251
by 1253

The principal evidence for this foundation is an allegation in the course of an action against the abbot of St. Mary's, York, heard in the Curia Regis in Michaelmas term 1253 (KB26/151 m. 27v). The men of Airmyn (Ermine) claimed that the abbot was forcing them to perform customs and services other than those which had been performed when the manor was in the hands of the king. The days to which the men of Airmyn looked back must have been those of Henry I; the charter granting land between Ousefleet and Airmyn to the abbey survives (W. Farrer, ed., *Early Yorkshire Charters* (1914), pp. 270 and 361).

The old custom, claimed the men of Airmyn, was that they were quit of the payment of "pence", and that the yearly rent was only a penny. The abbot was now exacting hens, eggs and other services, and distraining for arrears. On the abbot's side it was claimed that at the time of Henry I's gift there was no town, and none until the abbot's predecessors founded a town and set villeins there; the townsmen had always been the abbey's villeins. The men of Airmyn said that there had always been a town on the royal manor.

It is likely that the abbot was correct. Airmyn lies on the edge of Snaith parish, a single line of houses spread out for half a mile along the east bank of the river Aire just before it joins the Ouse. The Airmyn entries in Domesday Book clearly refer to the modern Little Airmyn in Drax parish on the opposite side of the river (*V.C.H.*, ii, pp. 270 and 298) and the first charter granted land not *in* Airmyn but *between* Airmyn and Ousefleet. Another sign of late settlement at the present Airmyn is a complaint heard before the archbishop in 1311 (*Register Greenfield*, i, Surtees Soc., cxlv (1931), p. 135). The inhabitants and abbey tenants at Airmyn in Snaith parish were forbidden to proceed with their plan to build a chapel in the town, which would damage the rights of the mother church at Snaith.

The lowest bridging of the Ouse to-day is at Booth Ferry bridge near Airmyn, and the ferry must always have been important, taking traffic from the whole of the East Riding across to the narrow ridge of dry land by which travellers to Doncaster and the south avoided the marshes of Trent and Ancholme. There was a second ferry which crossed the Aire at Airmyn (C143/244/1), and in the poll tax of 1379 two of the fifteen villagers wealthy enough to be taxed were ferrymen. The widow of one of these was accused in 1394 of charging double rate for taking a man and a horse in her barge from Airmyn to Little Airmyn (*Selden Soc.*, xl (1923), p. 306).

Apart from distance (6 miles) the Airmyn people had other impediments to attendance at Snaith. The parish had a great deal of low-lying land in it, subject to winter and spring flooding. In 1362 it was stated that the only highway from Airmyn to Ousefleet was along the river-bank itself (*ibid.*, p. 292). In 1318 the archbishop relented from his decision of 1311: he wrote to the abbot of Selby (to whom Snaith church belonged) exhorting him to provide a chapel at Airmyn in view of the way in which townspeople were being deprived of the sacraments. A chapel dedicated to St. David was founded, and in 1363 the abbots of St. Mary's and Selby came to an agreement about the division of the tithes. Carlton and Rawcliffe, two other out-townships of Snaith, also obtained chapels in the fourteenth century, and in 1499 Airmyn was granted the right to bury at Hook, 3 miles away (G. Lawton, *Collectio Rerum Ecclesiasticarum* (1842), pp. 155–159).

Airmyn was a small port as well as a ferry-town. In 1317 it was named as one of eight places which supplied "merchants and sailors frequently going on the water of Ouse" (*Y.A.S.R.S.*, lxxxi (1932), pp. 41–42).

BAWTRY   Yorkshire, W.R.   sheet 103   43/652930
1199–1213

The first mention of Bawtry as a place-name is found in a charter to Roche abbey of 1199 (*Cal. Chart. Rolls*, i, p. 146). Like its neighbour, Tickhill (*q.v.*), Bawtry occupied a border situation between Yorkshire and Nottinghamshire; the lords of the territory were Yorkshiremen with their seat at Hexthorpe near Doncaster, but the chapel of Bawtry, given to the canons of Blyth by John de Busli (1199–1213), was always reckoned part of the Nottinghamshire parish of Blythe. In 1213 de Busli's son-in-law, Robert de Vipont I, obtained livery of this land and it was he who created the borough. His charter, granted 1223–38, is known only from a paraphrase in J. Hunter, *South Yorkshire* (1868), p. 70, and is not cited in *Ballard* or *Ballard and Tait*. Robert's widow, Idonea, confirmed to her free burgesses of Bawtry all the tofts of her husband's grant at 1d. a year rent; the burgesses were granted a meadow, a carr and estovers in the turf moors, and for the confirmation they paid Idonea 16 marks. She promised to maintain the burgesses "in the liberties granted by king John to her husband". The king certainly granted a market charter, known only from its confirmation in 1293 (*Cal. Chart. Rolls*, ii, p. 433); and a fair in 1213–14 (*Rot. Ob. Fin.*, p. 495). Its date must be 1213–15, and there may have been an accompanying borough charter? "Liberties" sounds a wide term for Idonea to use if only the market grant was meant. Idonea's great-granddaughter, wife of Roger de Leyburn, claimed a market and fair here in 1276 as well as the assize of bread and ale; she also confirmed the other Idonea's charter. In 1315 the townsmen were claiming burial rights at the chapel (*Register Greenfield*, (Surtees Soc. cliii (1937), pp. 180–181)).

Bawtry's position on the Great North Road made it the first place in Yorkshire after crossing the river Ryton, but the town was a mile north of the bridge. Its economic focus seems to have been not the Great North Road but the river Idle whose meanders come up to the eastern edge of the borough. The Idle was navigable upstream into Nottinghamshire and downstream to the Trent; a ferry over the Idle was one of the manorial perquisites. The boundary of Yorkshire drives a narrow wedge into Nottinghamshire here, but it is significant that it goes no further than the southern end of the town; it makes no attempt to follow the Great North Road down to the Ryton bridge. Bawtry seems, therefore, to have been founded as a river port.

The shape of the town is a perfect grid formed by High Street, Low Street and Wharfe Street with a wide market place in the line of the main road and the church on the eastern edge near the river quay. If the parish boundary marks the course of the Roman road, then there has clearly been a diversion at the north end of High Street to bring the North Road into the market place. The old route lay a little further west.

In 1247, after Idonea's death, the extent of her possessions described demesne and villein land in Austerfield but "in Bautre no demesne, but in rent of assize eight marks; also a mill, a market, and all manner of other variable profits which are worth yearly twelve marks" (*Y.I.*, i, p. 12). The town may have been planted, therefore, not on the demesne but on part of the waste of Austerfield. Austerfield was of some antiquity since a Synod was held here in 702 (*P.N. Yorks, W.R.*, i, p. 46), another fact that suggests a strong route focus in this area. The poll tax of 1379 shows that Bawtry developed into a flourishing little town of merchants and craftsmen.

BOROUGHBRIDGE   Yorkshire, W.R.   sheet 91   44/395665
c. 1145

The town resulted from the construction of the bridge over the Ure that is said by *P.N. Yorks. W.R.*, v, p. 82, to be first recorded in a charter of 1155 granting Fountains Abbey freedom from tolls (*E.Y.C.*, i, p. 72) but actually mentioned in 1145 in the foundation charter of Newburgh Priory (Dugdale, *Monasticon*, vi, p. 318). The name *Ald*borough in 1145 also suggests that a new borough had already been founded. An older crossing place a little to the south-east had been used in Roman times and was still in use until the early twelfth century. The main roads to Scotland from London and from York met at Roman Isurium and within its walls the Saxon town of Burgh sheltered. Until the new bridge at Boroughbridge (Pont de Burgh) was constructed the main road to Catterick and Newcastle left Burgh by the north gate.

The new bridge completely altered the economic centre of gravity: Burgh became Aldborough when a new borough was developed on a narrow piece of land, 95 acres in area, to the south of the bridge (Sir T. Lawson Tancred, *Records of a Yorkshire Manor* (1937), p. 138). As a survey of 1631 put it: "the borough lieth within the said Manor of Aldborough and is part thereof, being compassed about with the Demesnes and fields of Aldborough and having no demesne, fields or other lands" (*ibid.*, p. 151). The new town was provided with a chapel which was not long in surpassing the mother church in importance (R. Kettlewell, "Notes on a Tithe Map of Boroughbridge", *Y.A.J.*, xxxvii (1950), pp. 387–401).

The street plan suggests that there was a deliberate leading of the re-alined road-system into the new town's market place. The point chosen for the new bridge was a curious one and must have been dictated by some strength in the banks, for, after crossing the Ure, the road from Scotland has to cross a small tributary, the river Tutt. A site 200 yards further east would have avoided this double crossing. As it is, the road from the north crosses the bridge, turns sharply east to cross the Tutt and then turns again southwards to enter the market place of Boroughbridge. A tithe map of 1846 shows this market place and the now-destroyed chapel which stood near it (*ibid.*, plate facing p. 400). There is a plan of 1709 showing the pre-enclosure alinement of main- and field-roads (B.M. Stowe MS. 883). After its eighteenth-century turnpiking the Great North Road by-passed the market place on the west, but the grid of the little town can be plainly seen. In 1963 another by-pass took traffic still further away from the old market place.

Boroughbridge was the head of the Ouse navigation in the late twelfth and thirteenth centuries, and the river down to York was part of the property of the lords of Aldborough and Boroughbridge. "No ship can pass without payment" declared the jurors at the eyre of 1218–19 (*Roll of Justices in Eyre 1218–9*, ed. D. M. Stenton, (Selden Soc., lvi (1937), nos. 1076–77 and 1108)), and charters show that the lord of the manor had permitted the hospital of St. Leonard at York to have free passage for ships bringing its victuals down river from its estates in north Yorkshire (*Cal. Chart. Rolls*, ii, p. 443).

Alongside the bridge were the lord's three water mills, one of which may have been converted to fulling by 1211 (*Pipe Roll. Soc.*, n.s., xxviii (1953), p. 157). Of the lord's income from Boroughbridge in 1300 the mills contributed almost a third, and the tolls of market and river-freight almost another third: from the burgesses the lord claimed only suit of court (*Y.A.S.R.S.*, xxxi, pp. 128–129 (I.P.M. of earl of Cornwall)): "They render no rent." To the Parliament of 1300 they sent two members.

The earliest date for the bridge is given by the Newburgh charter of 1145; in 1165 the Pipe Roll records for the first time a payment of two marks (£1 6s. 8d.) *de ponte Burc* alongside the usual payment from Aldborough and Knaresborough (*P.R.S.*, viii (1887), p. 51). The same sum was paid in 1169 towards the aid for the marriage of Henry II's daughter, but on that occasion (*P.R.S.*, xiii (1890), p. 37) it was paid by "the burgesses of Ponteburc". One indication that Boroughbridge was only small in 1169 is the size of the payment in aid: it was no more than the rural village of Ouseburn. Pickering paid twenty-seven times as much and Scarborough sixty times as much. But in the thirteenth century it became the head of a deanery, and important meetings, such as that of the local clergy to discuss Pope Nicholas' taxation in August 1293, were held in the church at Boroughbridge and not in the mother church at Aldborough (*The Registers of John le Romeyn* (Surtees Soc., cxxviii (1917), p. 16)).

LEEDS   Yorkshire, W.R.   sheet 96   44/303334
1207

The borough created by Maurice de Gant (or Paynel) in November 1207 was physically separate from the old-established village of Leeds. This physical separation is still marked by the remoteness of the parish church from the main shopping centre in Briggate, the broad market-street running northwards from the bridge. The pre-burghal village was centred on Kirkgate, and the manor of Leeds Kirkgate was still "a severall and distincke Mannor from the Queenes Mannor of Leedes" in 1600 (E123/26 f. 7; E134, 41 Eliz. Hil. 5, Yorks.). The sixty burghal plots lay on both sides of Briggate and are well preserved in the long, narrow innyards and the Victorian arcades that have replaced some of them. The significance of the topography of Leeds was first demonstrated by G. Wooledge, "The Medieval Borough of Leeds", *Thoresby Soc.*, xxxvii (1945), pp. 288–309; the charter and other documents are printed in J. Le Patourel, *The Manor and Borough of Leeds, 1066–1400* (*ibid.*, xlv (1957)).

PONTEFRACT   Yorkshire, W.R.   sheet 97   44/462226
by 1086

The urban history of Pontefract is confused by a change of name (Tanshelf to Ponte-fract) and by the existence of two boroughs after 1255–58. The argument that follows begins with the topographical evidence and attempts to fit to it the docu-mentary evidence.

The appearance of modern Pontefract on a large-scale plan shows the clear pattern of a castle-town west of the Castle ruins. This town had Micklegate as its central street, wide enough for a market place. North Street and South Street were placed symmetrically, with a significant curve at their western end where they came to join Micklegate (as Finkle Street and Baxtergate) just inside the old west gate. The curving lines of two other streets, Back Northgate and Walkergate, made an enclosing envelope for the town, suggesting that they followed the inside of the defences.

It is remarkable that the original parish church of the town, All Saints, lies outside this envelope (and indeed probably outside any defences) on the north-eastern edge of the town. Since a church was mentioned in Domesday Book (at Tanshelf) and since it seems generally agreed that the name Pontefract has replaced Tanshelf, I conclude that this church marks the site of the pre-urban village. A marginal note to a manuscript by Simeon of Durham, writing c. 1137, equated *Taddenesclyf*, Ponte-fract and "Kirkby" (*Surtees Soc.*, li (1868), p. 77). Since the wapentake met at Osgot's Cross, next to the present St. Giles' church—also outside the town, but to the west of it—I suggest that Tanshelf-Kirkby stretched from All Saints up to near where St. Giles now is. I also suppose that it was at this *Asgautr's Cross* that King Edred met the archbishop and all the councillors of the Northumbrians in 947.

The fundamental importance of the town site derives from its defensive position near to the various places that the road from London to Scotland has chosen to cross the Aire (by ferry, ford and bridge). The replacement of the village of Tanshelf by a town so shaped that it must have been integral with the building of a castle is there-fore to be related to the coming of Ilbert de Lacy and the establishment of Norman Pontefract as the centre of his fee.

The third feature to be noticed is the extra-mural group of streets (Wool Market, Salter Row, Beast Fair, Shoe Market Street, Market Place, etc.) to the west of the place where Horse Fair narrows into Bridge Street, the west gate of the castle town. Apart from the names cited and the narrow "Middle Row", the appearance of these streets around St. Giles are as good an example as one could find anywhere in England of a former market place now encroached upon by streets. Indeed, this market stretches north-westwards out along an approach road as "Corn Market". I assume that these streets formed the second borough, that of West Cheap (*sc.* "the west market") chartered in 1255–58. St. Giles, which stands inside it, was once a dependent chapelry of All Saints; All Saints was damaged in the Civil War and its inconvenient position to the east of the town caused the Act of 1787 to elevate the chapel of St. Giles to be the parish church of Pontefract.

Apart from modern O.S. plans, the best idea of the original topography of the two boroughs can be gained from the eighteenth-century plans from the Harewood archives, made in the days when identification of a burgage tenement was crucial in electioneering at the proprietary borough (Leeds City Archives, Harewood Mss.).

For the purposes of classification I would therefore assign the first castle-borough to the type of Richmond (Yorks.), where a village is superseded by a town so thoroughly based on a new castle that nothing of the pattern of village streets remains: only the (virtually isolated) church. This was the borough which received the charter of 1194 (*Rep. Hist. Mss. Comm.*, viii (1881), p. 269) but *burgus* references occur earlier (e.g. *E.Y.C.*, iii, p. 191).

Pontefract also illustrates the shift of an administrative centre from a Saxon manor to a Norman castle-town. Earl Edwin, the last Saxon owner of these estates, had his seat at Ledstone. Similarly, Norman Richmond superseded Saxon Gilling and Catterick.

The second borough, West Cheap, is analogous to other burghal extensions beyond the limits of a successful borough—not incorporated within extended walls as at Norman Nottingham and Northampton, but left detached as at Sherborne Newland (Dorset) and Eynsham Newland (Oxon.). These were also thirteenth-century extensions.

TICKHILL   Yorkshire, W.R.   sheet 103   43/593930
by 1086

The Norman castle of Tickhill and the Honour of Blyth depending on it guarded the southern entrance to Yorkshire as that of Richmond in the north. Domesday Book has no mention of Tickhill but it seems likely that the thirty-one burgesses at *Dadsley* were centred on the castle. But the site of Dadsley village is generally placed near Dadsley Well Farm (589942). Eastfield (594942)—north of Tickhill but east of Dadsley—also suggests that the rural centre was not near the castle, even if the castle-borough of 1086 was still known by the name of the village. The agricultural tenants in Dadsley and its two members in 1086 (sixty-six in all, with twenty-four ploughs and three mills) make it certain that Dadsley was a substantial place. Its site is now quite deserted, though the traditional site of the church mentioned in Domesday Book is in Tickhill North Field (J. Raine, *The History of Blyth* (1860), p. 18; O.S. 1st ed. 6-inch map, sheet 291: "site of All Hallows church"). Raine perspicaciously compared Tickhill as a new castle-town with Barnard Castle and Castleton, *q.v.*

In a document of 1121–27 (*E.Y.C.*, iii, pp. 130 and 143) the church of the castle of Tickhill is mentioned. It will be noticed that by the time of an undated charter (before 1232) in *Cal. Chart. Rolls*, i, p. 170, Dadsley was the name not for a vill, but simply *terra*. Tickhill was consistently reckoned a borough (*e.g.* SC11/544 (1340)).

A web of roads leading in from the fields, the typical road-system of a village, can be discerned: with the coming of the castle the burghal streets of Northgate and Westgate cut across them.

CHAPTER SIXTEEN

Gazetteer: Wales

INTRODUCTION

ALMOST every Welsh borough appears in this section of the Gazetteer. There were 87 medieval boroughs in Wales and Monmouthshire: 84 appear in this Gazetteer. With such a long list it might seem that the last vestiges of caution have been thrown aside on crossing the border. Has the distinction between planned and organic (always difficult to draw) been abandoned? Paradoxically, a planted origin can be discussed with more certainty in the towns of Wales and Monmouth than in England, even though the documentation is scantier. Thus, E. A. Lewis' detailed study of the medieval boroughs of Snowdonia is prefaced by a survey of Welsh towns in general, concluding:

> The rule (is that) in our Welsh medieval boroughs the majority in the circumstances of their origin was purely artificial.

There is also a cleaner sheet to begin with: Welsh historians seem to be agreed that in the Anglo-Saxon period only one *burh*—Clwydmouth (Rhuddlan I)—had been created within Wales. Further, almost every borough in Wales was associated with a castle, and the date of castle-building was frequently recorded by contemporary annalists, whether Welsh or English. Even when the exact date of a castle is uncertain a minimal date can often be arrived at from some reference in the annals to its siege or its capture. In medieval Wales, warfare was a principal preoccupation of any annalist.

The classic statement of the tie between castle and town is that in George Owen's *Pembrokeshire*. Of the Norman lords in south Wales and the Marches he wrote:

> And the saied lordes, att their first coming to those lordships by conquest, espyenge out the fertile partes in ech countrye, builded their castles for themselves and townes for their owne soldiers and countryemen which

came with them to remayne neere about them as their guarde, and to be allwayes ready to keep under such of the countrye inhabitantes as wold offere to rebell . . . and by this means all the townes and castles in most part of Wales . . . were first built.

As we have already seen (p. 181) this barracks-view of the Welsh towns underestimates the role that the market places came to take in the castle-towns, but as a simple statement of origins it passes muster.

The castle and accompanying towns were created by the English kings, by their barons and by those native Welsh landowners who accepted English overlordship; and on occasions (as the Appendix to the Gazetteer shows) the Welsh princes in opposition to the English kings were not ashamed to imitate them by encouraging towns on their own demesnes.

Is it possible for there to be "organic" towns in Wales, as opposed to plantations? In the south, where English occupation was oldest and most continuous, villages did develop on the English pattern, especially in Pembrokeshire, and it would have been possible for one of these to be promoted to a borough. Wiston may be one such.

In native Welsh society any town-like elements in the economy were most likely to develop organically alongside the *maenor* residence of a prince or chief. Some of these *maenors* had their castles, and in the thirteenth century they sheltered boroughs even before being taken over by Edward I. This was the situation at Nevin and Pwllheli but not enough is known of the topography of these pre-Edwardian boroughs to reveal whether the arrangement of streets and burgages were those of a planned addition or an organic transformation of rural holdings. If the site of Llanvaes could ever be excavated it would afford useful evidence on this point. A cautious view on the admission of these native Welsh villages is taken in the Appendix to the Gazetteer.

As in England, the differing wealth and political position of the founders produced Welsh castles and towns of every size. The burgages, the distinctive features of town life, were found in petty boroughs like Cefnllys that did no more than fill a castle-bailey, as well as in the great planted towns of the Edwardian conquest that can be set without shame alongside the finest of the Gascon plantations and alongside Aigues Mortes itself. As Table IX, 2 has shown, Cardiff was the largest borough, with 421 burgages in 1296; Chepstow, Usk, Trellech and Haverford West had 300 or over; while in the 200–299 range came Abergavenny, Cowbridge, Holt, Newport (Mon.), Pembroke, New

Radnor, Tenby and Welshpool. It will be noticed that none of the Edwardian towns of north Wales for which information is available was as large as the towns mentioned, most of which were earlier in date; nor is there any reason to think that Caerwys and Flint were any larger than Conway and Beaumaris. There is no information for Rhuddlan, the oldest of the boroughs in north Wales. Its fee farm was large, but not all the sum is attributable to burgage rents: tolls and the profits of justice made up an unknown proportion of the £40.

At the other end of the scale came the petty boroughs of mid- and south Wales. The small episcopal boroughs of the south-west were clearly smaller than many English villages, and the boroughs that had been developed within the earthworks of a castle (Cefnllys and Old Dynevor) were pygmies. If we knew more of Bere, it would probably fall in the same class.

The uplands that made up most of medieval Wales were lightly populated. In consequence, a borough could have large out-districts for which it was the unchallenged commercial centre, whereas in England the hinterland of most towns was small, besides being peopled with non-burghal market villages and served by rural fairs. The Welsh boroughs were distinctive in housing a number of burgesses who were only occasionally resident: "burgesses of the wind" as the documents describe them, or *chensers*. These men either shared their time between different towns or resided normally in the up-country, coming into the borough at the buying and selling seasons.

It might be thought that the large number of burgages revealed in the boroughs of south and west Wales were swollen by the inclusion of these burgesses of the wind. But the surveys counted these men separately: there were 53 at Cardigan in 1308 as well as the 172 ordinary burgesses; at Carmarthen there were 87 of them alongside 184 ordinary burgesses; at Tenby, 20 alongside 247.

Chensers were not found in Edward I's plantations in north Wales (which chronologically come very near the end of borough-making in Wales) for these particular towns were designed to have all the trade of their districts centred on their market place and in the hands of their own burgesses. Thus the older rural market at Llanfor was forced into the new market place at Bala in 1310, and the general position is summed up in Edward I's order:

No markets, no fairs nor any other places of trade indeed, for the selling and buying of oxen, cows, horses, etc., excepting small articles of food shall be held elsewhere in north-west Wales than in the towns of Conway, Beaumaris, Newborough, Carnarvon, Criccieth, Harlech and Bere.

Only genuine travellers and those dwelling very remote from the market were permitted to buy and sell locally, and Beaumaris burgesses were much disturbed at the wide use made of this exception by the Welsh in the Anglesey country-side.

The Edwardian towns of north Wales came late enough in the thirteenth century for them to feel inadequately supplied with defensive institutions unless they had a gild merchant, a fellowship with a membership fee, able to offer its members a collective monopoly of trading rights within the town. The boroughs of the south and west, earlier in date, display a whole range of municipal liberties and privileges from the petty to the most elaborate. With founding lords of differing political power, with different potentialities in their hinterlands, with different dates for their foundation there was nothing approaching a standard bundle of rights that all inhabitants of new towns could expect; the nearest approach was in the affiliation of the Hereford (Breteuil) liberties.

The geographical distribution of Welsh boroughs is visible in Fig. 46 and in the county arrangements of the *List* below. As would be expected, the mountainous character of much of the country severely limited the places where towns could flourish. Lines of communication were canalised along the coastal fringes and in the half dozen river valleys that afforded inland communication. Strung along these valleys and on the narrow coastal plains were to be found the majority of boroughs, for the routes taken by travellers determined trade (one motive for town plantation), while the same narrow lines of communication were what the castles were erected to defend (and here we have the other main motive for Welsh towns).

With land communications so difficult it was natural for ports to be highly esteemed as sites for towns; and in Wales that they should need castles to defend them. The ports would deal with whatever imports and exports the local economy could support and through the port would come the victuals and military stores for the castle-dwellers. The Edwardian boroughs of north Wales were provisioned by sea, and Rhuddlan had an artificial canal to bring sea-borne traffic to it. Edward replaced an older castle at Llanbadarn by a new castle at Aberystwyth accessible to the sea.

Political considerations determined some sites. Towns that now lie on county boundaries were placed there when the same boundary was a national or local frontier. Adpar faces Newcastle Emlyn across the Cardigan-Carmarthenshire border and the bridge joining them now causes boundary disputes only between county highway authorities: but it was once the boundary of Ceredigion and the passage was more fiercely contested. Nowadays Old Radnor seems to be in the middle of nowhere, but it was a Norman border castle long before its valley-road successor, New Radnor. Offa's Dyke, visible from the ramparts of Old Radnor, emphasises an older frontier tradition. Deganwy was a borough where English soldiers and merchants looked across the Conway to an unconquered Wales: Matthew Paris wove into his chronicle a letter home from an officer of Henry III's garrison saying just this. Builth, Loughor and Hay are other boroughs that stand on county boundaries that were once the boundaries of lordships. Even in those parts of south Wales where rebellions against the English were fewer, there were still local landowners to quarrel with each other, and in their rivalry they valued castles and towns as much as Gascon nobles valued their bastides.

The pattern of native rural settlement was such that most rural communities did not have a parish church in their midst. The towns, on the other hand, so much influenced by the English experience of their founders, considered that a church for the burgesses was essential. It was a rare fortune (as at Conway) to find a ready-made church on the place where the town was to be laid out. The planted towns in England, as has been shown, often had to do without a church of their own or else accept a dependent chapelry status for their town church. These symptoms of late arrival are also visible in Wales. Bala had no parish church until 1811 although it was important enough to be an assize town: it had been planted on the edge of Llanycil parish. Caerphilly borough had no parish church: the chapel of St. Martin was in Eglwysilan parish. The first of the two plantations at Kidwelly had no parish church. At Montgomery there was an agreement of 1227, four years after the town's foundation, ending a dispute with Chirbury church. The church "newly built in Montgomery" was to have rights of burial and "the full rights of a mother church". Kenfig had to obtain the goodwill of Tewkesbury Abbey to get itself a town church.

The Welsh boroughs thus emerge in many respects as kin with the contemporary plantations of England and Gascony; the family resemblance is unmistakable, and if the medieval borough plantations in Ireland find their historian, another member will have a good hope of being reunited with the family.

Note

The entries follow the same form as in the previous chapters. The same standard abbreviations (see pp. xvii to xx) are used. Monmouthshire is included in this chapter. An alphabetical key follows. With the border so often disputed in medieval times, the full significance of a Welsh county gazetteer appears only when the *Lists* for the English counties of the Marches are also taken into account.

In all counties, William Rees, "A Bibliography of Published Works on the Municipal History of Wales and the Border" (*Bull. B.C.S.* ii (1925), pp. 321–382) is a useful reference list of work in print at that date. The same author's *Historical Atlas of Wales* (1959) is very useful for the limits of English power at different periods and for the boundaries of the Marcher baronies.

Wales—Alphabetical Index to Gazetteer

Name of Place	*County*
ABERAVON	Glamorgan
ABERGAVENNY	Monmouth
ABERGWILI	Carmarthen
ABERYSTWYTH	Cardigan
ADPAR	Cardigan
BALA	Merioneth
BEAUMARIS	Anglesey
BERE	Merioneth
BRECON	Brecknock
BRIDGEND	Glamorgan
BUILTH	Brecknock
CAERPHILLY	Glamorgan
CAERSWS	Montgomery
CAERWYS	Flint

Name of Place	*County*
CARDIFF	Glamorgan
CARDIGAN	Cardigan
CARMARTHEN	Carmarthen
CARNARVON	Carnarvon
CEFNLLYS	Radnor
CHEPSTOW	Monmouth
CONWAY	Carnarvon
COWBRIDGE	Glamorgan
CRICCIETH	Carnarvon
DEGANWY	Carnarvon
DENBIGH	Denbigh
DOLFORWYN	Montgomery
DRYSLWYN	Carmarthen
DYNEVOR, OLD	Carmarthen
DYSERTH	Flint
FLINT	Flint
GROSMONT	Monmouth
HARLECH	Merioneth
HAVERFORD WEST	Pembroke
HAY	Brecknock
HOLT	Denbigh
KENFIG	Glamorgan
KIDWELLY (Old Town)	Carmarthen
KIDWELLY (New Town)	Carmarthen
KNIGHTON	Radnor
LAMPETER	Cardigan
LAUGHARNE	Carmarthen
LLANDILO	Carmarthen
LLANDOVERY	Carmarthen
LLANELLY	Carmarthen
LLANFYLLIN	Montgomery
LLANIDLOES	Montgomery
LLANTRISSANT	Glamorgan
LLAWHADEN	Pembroke
LOUGHOR	Glamorgan
MONMOUTH	Monmouth
MONTGOMERY	Montgomery
MOSTYN	Flint

Name of Place	*County*
NARBERTH	Pembroke
NEATH	Glamorgan
NEVIN	Carnarvon
NEWBOROUGH	Anglesey
NEWCASTLE EMLYN	Carmarthen
NEW MOAT	Pembroke
NEWPORT	Monmouth
NEWPORT	Pembroke
NEWTOWN (Dynevor)	Carmarthen
NEWTOWN	Montgomery
OVERTON	Flint
PAINSCASTLE	Radnor
PEMBROKE	Pembroke
PWLLHELI	Carnarvon
RADNOR, NEW	Radnor
RADNOR, OLD	Radnor
RHAYADER	Radnor
RHUDDLAN I	Flint
RHUDDLAN II	Flint
RHUDDLAN III	Flint
RUTHIN	Denbigh
SKENFRITH	Monmouth
SWANSEA	Glamorgan
TALGARTH	Brecknock
TEMPLETON	Pembroke
TENBY	Pembroke
TREFNANT	Montgomery
TRELLECH	Monmouth
USK	Monmouth
WELSHPOOL	Montgomery
WHITECASTLE	Monmouth
WISTON	Pembroke

ANGLESEY

The two plantations in this county were closely connected, since Newborough would not have arisen had not Beaumaris ejected the Welsh from Llanvaes.

BEAUMARIS   Anglesey   . sheet 107   23/605761
1295

This castle-town replaced the Welsh town of Llanvaes that was moved from Rhosfair to form Newborough (*q.v.*). It is discussed above pp. 49–50. The charter of 1296 is printed in E. A. Lewis, *Medieval Boroughs of Snowdonia* (1912), pp. 279–82 (wrongly dated as 1295: see *Cal. Chart. Rolls*, ii, p. 465). The town and castle have been described in detail with photographs and plans in *R.C.H.M., Anglesey* (1937), and the early surveys of the town analysed in E. A. Lewis, *op. cit.*, pp. 49–51.

NEWBOROUGH   Anglesey   sheet 106   23/424656
1303
The foundation of Newborough in Rhosfair followed upon the removal of the Welsh town of Llanvaes to make room for the English borough of Beaumaris (*q.v.*). An extent of Rhosfair on the eve of the removal has survived (SC11/768–9), and on the Pipe Rolls of 1306–07 (E372/176) the inability to render the traditional payment is explained: "Just over 90 acres of demesne have been assigned to certain Welshmen in compensation for the burgages they used to hold in Llanvaes. The inhabitants of that town have been moved by the king to Newborough and their lands assigned to Beaumaris castle." H. R. Davies, *The Conway and Menai Ferries* (1942), pp. 24–26 cites the Pipe Roll of 1302–03 as the first to show these lessened rents of old Rhosfair, and that of 1303–04 as the first to show the burgage rents being paid. Their sum £8 8s. 5¾d., was exactly that of Llanvaes, no doubt a deliberate equivalence. Rhosfair itself was already a village with a market and fair (E352/94 m. 22d) but these ceased with the arrival of a new borough. Other details of the exchanges are given in *Record of Carnarvon*, pp. 74, 83–89, 177–181, 218 and 223–224. The interval between the foundation of Beaumaris in 1295 and the charter of Newborough in 1303 (E. A. Lewis, *Medieval Boroughs of Snowdonia* (1912), p. 283) may be due to the reluctance of the men of Llanvaes to move and the reluctance of Rhosfair to cease its independent trading.

BRECKNOCK (or BRECON) SHIRE

Brecon, Builth (and perhaps Hay) derived from the early thrust westwards of the Normans under Newmarch that by 1100 had annexed virtually all the modern county. In later centuries the area was held by the families of de Breos (of Builth) and de Bohun with periods of re-occupation by the Welsh princes.

There was a small borough at Crickhowell, of uncertain origin: *Cal. I.P.M.*, vii, p. 317.

BRECON   Brecknockshire   sheet 141   32/044287
1087–1100
Although only two corner-towers of the original ten survive, the oval outline of the walled borough of Brecon is clearly preserved in minor topographical features, particularly the change of level which marks the ditch on the southern, eastern and northern sides. On the east division is the stream called Honddu. The triangle of the once great market place, now encroached upon, contains St. Mary's church, and the burgage plots are well preserved in the narrow courtyards of the back streets.

The Norman castle was built c. 1092 on the west of the Honddu, and facing the

Usk crossing, probably by Bernard Newmarch who was also the benefactor of the monks of Battle Abbey to whom he gave lands in the town together with the church of St. John that adjoined but was outside the fortifications.   This later became a priory.

The question remains whether the walled town on the east bank was planted.   In his *Illustrated History of Brecknockshire*, (1886) pp. 9 and 25–27 E. Poole ascribed the town's foundation to Bernard Newmarch, and this seems to be supported by the account of the grant to Battle as it is set out in the Battle Chronicle (ed. M. A. Lower (1851), p. 38).   The grant is said to be a possession in *Vetus Villa*, and it is unequivocally made up of land between the castle and the priory church, i.e. wholly on the west bank.   Was the compact walled town on the east bank a *nova villa*?   The monk · to whom Bernard gave the land increased "the talent of the small possession given to him", and this must have been due to the concourse of people at the market town across the stream.   The tradition is that the Norman walls were built of stone from the Roman fort, Brecon Gaer, three miles west of Brecon.   In one of the grants to Battle Abbey it was correctly described as *vasta civitas*.   Bernard Newmarch came from a place in Normandy whose very name, Neufmarché, fits in well with ideas of new commercial centres, but nothing can be made of this coincidence.

The first recorded charter was in 1276 but burgesses were known in 1100 (William Rees, "The Charters of Brecon and Llandovery", *Bull. Board of Celtic Studies*, ii (1925), p. 244).   In 1336 it was described as a *villa mercatoria* (C135/48) held at farm for £60; the market tolls were worth £5 19s. 3d.   See also William Rees, "The Medieval Lordship of Brecon", *Trans Cymmrodorion Soc. 1915–16* (1917), pp. 212–216.

BUILTH   Brecknockshire   sheet 141   32/040510
1095–1102

The charter of 1278 (*Cal. Chart. Rolls*, ii, p. 209) granted a gild merchant and other privileges to a borough that already existed.   Its age is not known.   It cannot be earlier than 1095 when this territory became English, and the castle the headquarters of Philip de Breos, "lord of Builth" (*Lloyd*, ii, pp. 402–403 and 436).   After many vicissitudes it was rebuilt by Edward I, beginning in 1277, but the building accounts do not mention the making of a town.   On this very flimsy evidence the town may be considered Norman.

It lies below the castle on the north and west but has only a rough approximation to any regular plan.

HAY   Brecknockshire   sheet 141   32/230425
? 1237

This little borough has the characteristic remote church (at 226421).   This church of St. Mary "at the Hay" (*i.e.* forest clearing) was in existence at the beginning of the twelfth century, and the parish comprised the manor of Hay Anglicana which had been carved out of Llanigon parish, probably in 1130 (W. E. T. Morgan, *Hay and Neighbourhood* (n.d., c. 1933), pp. 13–14).   A town or vill of Hay does not appear in Domesday Book and the first urban reference is in a document of 1237 when a murage grant was made (*Cal. Pat. Rolls 1232–47*, i, p. 178). A castle was built c. 1100 and in 1234 a chapel of St. John was founded within the walls. Since there is a Norman motte near the isolated church of St. Mary (Morgan, *op. cit.*, p. 15) it is possible that there was no town of Hay before the walls of 1237, but Llewelyn is said to have burned the town of Hay in 1233 (*Lloyd*, ii, p. 674) and the murage grant may, therefore, simply be for rebuilding.

There is a "town" in an inquisition of 1265 (C132/34/8). In the tax collection of 1292 (E179/242/48) Hay was also reckoned a town and in 1298 (C133/92/7) there were 183¾ burgages in the town. By 1336 (C135/48) the assessed rent of the borough was £12 13s. 4d.

The town stands on the south bank of the Wye, and is tightly compacted within a triangle which marks the original walls; there are castle remains, and there were three gates.

TALGARTH	Brecknockshire		sheet 141	32/155337

by 1309

This is a doubtful case; there are three parallel streets to the west of the church which may represent a grid of a planted town. It was undoubtedly a borough, for in an inquisition of 1309 there were seventy-three burgage plots, sixty of which were inhabited and paying 1s. a year rent each. There were markets and fairs as well as an agricultural population of villeins, cottars and Welsh: C134/15/10. The difficulty is to know whether this was a Welsh or an English venture. The site, before the Norman conquest, was the chief royal residence of Brycheiniog.

CARDIGANSHIRE

Until Edward I's wars there were only two pockets of English territory in Ceredigion. One lay near Roger de Montgomery's castle at (Old) Cardigan at the southwestern tip of the county, although no town seems to have accompanied this castle. The second lay in the north around Gilbert de Clare's castle of Llanbadarn. Here again, no town accompanied the first castle. The ventures at Adpar and Lampeter seem to show a Welsh lord and the bishop of St. David's attempting small commercial boroughs.

ABERYSTWYTH	Cardiganshire		sheet 127	22/580815

1277

This borough, originally called Llanbadarn after the parish in which it was planted, is treated above, pp. 37–41. Work was begun in July 1277. The modern development of the town is studied by H. Carter in *Trans. and Papers of the Inst. of Brit. Geographers*, xxv (1958), pp. 239–253. The charter of December 1277 is summarised in *Cal. Chart. Rolls*, ii, p. 206; the rental of c. 1300–10 (SC12/17/72) is printed in *Bull. B.C.S.* xv (1954), pp. 282–293 by I. J. Sanders.

537

ADPAR   Cardiganshire   sheet 139   22/309409
by 1326

This riverside borough faces Newcastle Emlyn, over the river Teifi; there are now no remains of the borough, even as burgage plots, merely a small group of modern terrace houses and single shops. On the east of the bridge, the *tumulus* of the 6 inch O.S. plan is probably a motte of the bishops of St. David's whose borough this was (Black Book of St. David's, *Cym. Rec. Ser.*, no. 5 (1902)). But the only space for a borough of ninety-six burgages (as it was in 1326) would be the flat terrace to the west of the bridge. It is now completely characterless. The corporation of Adpar was dissolved for venality in 1741. (See also Newcastle Emlyn, *infra*; and D. C. King, "The Castles of Cardiganshire", *Ceredigion*, iii, pt. 1 (1956), p. 58.)

CARDIGAN   Cardiganshire   sheet 139   22/178460
c. 1165

The site of the first castle, built by earl Roger de Montgomery in 1093 at the mouth of the Teifi after the Norman invasion of south Wales, lies a mile west of Cardigan (164465 near Old Castle Farm). The date of transfer to the present site is uncertain, but may be under Gilbert de Clare, c. 1110–15 (D. J. C. King, "The Castles of Cardiganshire", *Ceredigion*, iii (1956), pp. 50–69). The borough beneath the walls of the larger, later castle may have been founded by Gilbert de Clare in 1165 (D. J. M. Peregrine, "Cardigan's Ancient Borough", *Ceredigion*, ii (1955), pp. 117–118). The charter of John in 1199, sometimes said to be a borough charter, was a release from toll, passage and custom duties for the burgesses for the next four years provided that they remained loyal to the king (*Ballard*, p. 193, from *Rot. Chart.*, p. 63). This was renewed in 1230 (*Cal. Chart Rolls*, i, p. 116). The first extant charter is that of Edward I in 1284 at the time of the charters to Criccieth, Harlech and Bere (*Cal. Chart Rolls*, ii, p. 280).

By this time the town was substantial: in 1274–75 it had had 128½ burgages (C145/33/31); in 1279–88, 130 (E142/51 and SC11/771). By 1308 it had grown to 172 burgages (SC6/1218/6); see also *Bull. B.C.S.* xv (1954), pp. 282–293.

In shape, the town consists of an elongated triangle of streets from the castle eastwards to the church. The castle overlooks the bridge. The town wall survives in portions, and is said to be based on Roman work, although there is no sound evidence. The historical topography of this county town still needs elucidation. There is a useful town plan, of French origin (? late seventeenth century) in B.M. which shows the town contained within the walls except for a suburban ribbon outside the north gate and more substantial development between the east gate and the present church ("Le Colege").

LAMPETER   Cardiganshire   sheet 140   22/578481
1271–7

This borough was established in the rural commote of Mabwynion and its position was probably associated with the castle (now in the grounds of St. David's College) and the bridge of Pont Stephen. The site was on the border of Ceredigion and

Ystrad Tywi where Cardigan and Carmarthenshire now meet. An account of the founding of the borough is contained in a survey of March 1317 (E142/87): *quidam Res ap Mereduth ante conquestum Walliae tenuit totum commotum de Mabwynon et infra certas metas in eodem commoto ordinavit quemdam Burgum apud Lampeder talpontstephan*. . . . Rhys succeeded his father in 1271 and made peace with Edward in 1277 (*Lloyd*, ii (1911), pp. 750 and 758). In the first extant rental (1301–02: SC6/1218/1) there were small markets and fairs and 19½ burgages; two years later there were 20 (SC6/1218/2) and by 1317 only 26; 11 customary tenants also then lived in the town, and there were Welsh tenants in Maenor Lampeder.

The High Street has clear remains of burgage plots on either side, with a characteristic back lane on the north (now Market Street). The church of St. Peter is a little removed from the town; what was believed to be an earlier motte and bailey castle, Castell Bugad, is now considered entirely natural.

CARMARTHENSHIRE

The hold of the English in this area was also limited. The most permanent hold was on the area surrounding New Carmarthen itself and the coastal plain defended by Kidwelly. The undisputed acquisition of the northern cantrefs and the foundation of English boroughs within them was deferred until the victories of Edward I.

ABERGWILI Carmarthenshire sheet 152 22/440230

by 1326

The editor of the *Black Book of St. David's* considers the small borough here to have been "planted". There were twenty-five burgesses in 1326. Bishop Beck founded the collegiate church here but there was no bishop's palace until the time of Bishop Barlow (1536–48). The village is now a single street on the main road eastwards from Carmarthen along the north side of the Vale of Towy, with the north-eastern end overlaid by the railway. Nothing can be seen to suggest that the area of settlement had ever been larger.

CARMARTHEN Carmarthenshire sheet 152 22/413200

1109

About 1109 Henry I acquired the strategic site of Carmarthen where the Roman roads of west Wales joined and where the lowest crossing of the Towy was made. In 1093 a castle had been built at Rhydygors, a ford one mile south of the Roman fort, but Henry rejected this site for a new castle on a cliff overlooking the present bridge. Around the castle he founded the walled borough that the charter of 1109 (*Ballard and Tait*, p. 66) distinguished from "Old Carmarthen", that is the *clas* of Celtic Carmarthen. There is no doubt that Celtic Carmarthen lay in the north-east of the walled town but there is some doubt whether it occupied all or part of the shell of Roman Carmarthen, Moridunum. (See *R.C.H.M.W. Carmarthen*, p. 248, and E. G.

Bowen, "The Lay-Out of Carmarthen Town", *Arch. Camb.*, c, (1948–49), pp. 118–122 with plan; another view in E. A. Lewis, *Tr. Hist. Soc. West Wales*, iii (1913).)

The interior plan of Henry I's town consisted of two parallel streets running from the castle to the gates nearest Old Carmarthen, and a market street north-westward from the castle-gate. The town had no church of its own. A Norman church (St. Peter's) seems to have been already built at the west end of Old Carmarthen, and it was not disturbed. It did not remain isolated, for in 1148 a new priory church of St. John was founded further to the east so that Old Carmarthen became part of a medieval suburb. In the tax list of 1292 (E179/242/48) the priory lands were entered as *de suburbis*. At that time there were between 155 and 184 burgages in Carmarthen (E142/51; C145/33/31).

DRYSLWYN   Carmarthenshire   sheet 140   22/554204
?1271–89

Virtually nothing remains of this borough which once comprised burgages within the castle defences as well as extra-mural burgages down in "Briggestrete" (SC6/1158/10 (1360)). In 1360 there were thirty-four of the former and fourteen of the latter. It is not certain when the town was founded, for in the first extant rentals and account (E372/146 (1298–1300); SC11/773 (1302–03)) there were already between 34 and 43½ burgages, and in the account for 1301–02 (SC6/1218/1) the burgesses were said to hold their lands *per cartam regis*. No charter is known, however, earlier than 1324 (*Cal. Chart. Rolls*, iii, p. 461) which was a grant of markets and fairs, declaring that the town was already held at fee farm. A break in political continuity which may have made an English foundation possible was the death of Meredith ap Rhys in 1271 (*Lloyd*, ii, p. 750). Again, the English captured the town from Meredith's rebellious son in 1287, and the constable's accounts for 1287–89 include expenditure on the ditch surrounding the castle and the town (E372/134, cited in *Hist. King's Works*, ii (1963), p. 641, fn. 6). The area within the formidable hillside earthworks must have been constricted.

DYNEVOR, OLD   Carmarthenshire   sheet 140   22/612217
1276–80

There was a small borough attached to the old Welsh castle. This borough "of the Upper Town" was chartered by Edward I, c. 1288, but there is evidence of a market and fair at least as early as 1280, very soon after the castle was surrendered to Edward in 1276, so that there may have been a mature borough in Meredith's day (*cp.* Lampeter). There is just sufficient level ground outside the castle to fit in burgages and a market place but they were probably within the defences as at Cefnllys and Dolforwyn. There were still eleven burgages in 1301–02, when the new Town on the lower site (*Newtown*, Carmarthenshire, *q.v.*) was four years old. The principal documents concerning the two boroughs are printed in translation by E. A. Lewis, "Dynevor", *Tr. Hist. Soc. West Wales*, i (1911), pp. 146–224, and ii (1912), pp. 105–133. See also *R.C.H.M.W.*, *Carmarthen*, pp. 107–111, and *Hist. King's Works*, ii (1963), pp. 643–644.

KIDWELLY (NEW TOWN)   Carmarthenshire   sheet 152 22/407067
c. 1130
see Kidwelly (Old Town) *infra*.

KIDWELLY (OLD TOWN)   Carmarthenshire   sheet 152 22/409070
1106-15
The castle of Kidwelly, on the north bank of the river, was begun by Roger, bishop of Salisbury, between 1106 and 1115 (*Lloyd*, ii, p. 430, fn.). The bishop was acting as the agent of Henry I. "There is no evidence of any occupation before the grant to Roger" (C. A. Ralegh Radford, *Kidwelly Castle* (1956), p. 8). An earthwork which formed the bounds of the old Norman town enclosed about eight acres; about 1280 the southern half, which may have been the only part with burgages built upon it, was walled, and in the following century the gate-house (which still spans the road) was built. The plan is a simple triangle of streets in front of the castle; the modern road by-passes the old town on the north-western side (see plan in Ralegh Radford, *op. cit.*, p. 10). There was no town church, and the borough was in St. Ishmael's parish, the church being 4 miles to the west (362084). When Leland visited the town in the early sixteenth century it was walled but desolate. What commercial life there was had migrated to the New Town south of the bridge.

The earliest known charter to Kidwelly is by Henry of Lancaster (before 1309) (*Weinbaum*, p. 141) but there were burgage rents in 1283 (C133/35/5) totalling £3 13s. 6d., and an undated charter printed in Clark, *Cartae*, i (1885), p. 161, concerns *unum burgagium* in the vill of Kidwelly; two weekly markets and a fair were granted in 1268 (*Cal. Chart. Rolls.*, ii, p. 113). Other later references to the burgages are C135/161 (1361) and DL29/573/9063 (1399). There is a detailed house-by-house survey of 1609 in DLMB 120, printed by W. Rees, *A Survey of the Duchy of Lancaster Lordships in Wales, 1609-13* (1953).

The *New Town* across the bridge centred on the Priory church of St. Mary founded about 1114 by the bishop of Salisbury, presumably to serve the town across the river. This part is now more prosperous than the castle-town, although nearly all the medieval houses in it have now been pulled down. In Leland's day the New Town, though decayed with the haven, was three times the size of the Old (*R.C.H.M.W.*, *Carmarthen.*, p. 54). The influence of the bishop seems to have made the church of the New Town fully parochial. Its streets are included in the survey of 1609, when about 164 burgages were occupied (Rees, *op. cit.*, p. xxvii). See also D. D. Jones, *History of Kidwelly* (1908).

LAUGHARNE   Carmarthenshire   sheet 152 22/301108
before 1278-82
The verdict of the Historical Monuments Commission is that the town arose in the early thirteenth century along with the rebuilding of the castle; and the church of St. Martin at the other end of the town is probably of the same period. The town received its first charter 1278-82 (*Ballard and Tait*, p. xxix) from Guy de Brionne, but there is no other useful evidence. The town consists of one principal street running

up the east side of the valley, with a further group of houses (possibly suburban) at the harbour.

LLANDILO   Carmarthenshire   sheet 140 22/629223
by 1326

There is only a very slight case for including this town here: it is involved in the complex topography and chronology of the neighbouring but abandoned borough of Newtown in Dynevor (*q.v.*). This part of the vale of Tywi has a number of castles and petty boroughs which have been ascribed to both English and Welsh founders. In the *Black Book of St. David's* forty-one burgesses were recorded in Llandilo in 1326 together with a market and fair (ed. J. W. Willis-Bund, *Cym. Rec. Ser.*, no. 5 (1902), p. 263).

Despite an irregular hillside site, the town is made up of two main streets intersecting at right angles, with the burgages embraced in an oval envelope, a smaller version of Brecon and Abergavenny. The church and churchyard occupy much of the south western quadrant and a market-green the north western. The development of the town in the thirteenth century seems to have been the work of the bishops of St. David's (*R.C.H.M.W., Carmarthen.*, pp. 107–111) but the church was important before the Norman Conquest.

LLANDOVERY   Carmarthenshire   sheet 140 22/767343
?1276–1316

In form this borough consists of a long triangular market place with burgage plots along the northern and eastern sides. On the north, Garden Street perfectly preserves the back lane of the plots, and the beginning of Queen Street, together with Victoria Street, do the same on the east and shortest side. There may have been burgages on the western end of the south side, but the eastern half of this part of the market place contains the outer bailey of the castle. There may once have been burgages along the whole length of the long south side, but the eastern half of this flank is now occupied by pens and folds of the cattle market. The original triangle has the usual type of encroaching buildings, and open-air trading has been moved to the new site. But it is appropriately enough still in the shadow of the castle, and on fine days the farmers' wives sit on the castle-mound drinking cups of tea, while the bargaining echoes in the sheds.

The date of the town's foundation is not known; the first recorded charter comes from the end of the fourteenth century, but the town could have followed the Norman castle whose periodic misfortunes in war are first recorded in 1113. About 1185 Rhys had *burgesses* attached to his castle (*Lloyd*, ii, p. 606, fn.). The castle finally became English in 1276 (*Lloyd*, ii, p. 758) giving another possible date for a burghal plantation. An inquisition of December 1316 reported seventy-eight burgages here at 1s. a year rental; the fairs were worth 53s. 4d. and the markets 40s. A reassessment was ordered the following month (C134/56/3 m. 9) when eighty-one burgages were returned, and the tolls increased to £7 6s. a year.

It will be noticed that the borough has no church: the parish of Llandingat surrounds it, and the church is at 746340; a second church at 770352 within the Roman fort, although in Llandingat parish is actually the parish church of Llanvair ar y Bryn, an area of scattered settlement in the valleys north and west of Llandovery.

LLANELLY   Carmarthenshire   sheet 153   22/505004

n.d

This little castle-borough (DL29/573/9063) of the lordship of Carnwallon stood on the boundary of Glamorgan and Carmarthen. It had markets and fairs but there is no record of a charter, and it was very small before the coming of heavy industry to the neighbourhood. It has now been overwhelmed, and the original medieval streets near the market place cannot be disentangled.

NEWCASTLE EMLYN   Carmarthenshire   sheet 139   22/311407

1303

This borough faces the episcopal borough of Adpar across the Teifi, the county boundary. The castle, after which it is named, occupies the whole of a narrow peninsula formed by a meander in the river, and the town follows the curve of the river cliff which it occupies; some of the burgage plots come down to the river edge with steep gardens. Holy Trinity church dates only from 1843, for the new town was planted in an already existing parish, Cenarth (270415).

The "New Castle" was built c. 1240 but for sixty years there was no urban settlement alongside it, only the houses of a Welsh *trev* which occupied the hillside before the castle site was chosen. In accounts for Michaelmas 1303 the king received no rent from the new borough since the plots were not yet arrented, but a year later there were twenty-six burgages paying their 1s. a year rent (SC6/1218/9), in 1305 there were fifty-four, and by 1316 (SC6/1219/6–7) there were sixty-two as well as twenty-four other tenants of lesser status. The first tolls from the fair are recorded in 1308 (SC6/1218/6). Confirmation that there was no borough here before 1303 is found in the tax roll of 1292 when the only taxpayers were those in the castle (E179/242/48). Accounts for 1298–1300 (E372/146) speak only of the *commote* of Emlyn. A rental of 1303 (SC11/773) is probably the list of the first burgesses: there were five burgesses who held two burgages each, and one who held five; the rest held one each. In the accounts of that year (SC6/1218/9) it was noted that as well as resident burgesses there were also burgesses "of the wind" who lived outside the town but who paid to share its privileges: *de diversis hominibus dictis burgensibus de vento qui burgagia nec terras tenent sed ut gaudere possint eadem libertate.*

(See Gruffyd Evans, "The story of Newcastle Emlyn", *Y Cymmrodor*, xxxii (1922), pp. 58–170.)

NEWTOWN (Dynevor)   Carmarthenshire   sheet 140   22/ c.615225

c. 1298

There was a small borough attached to the old Welsh castle, once the capital of south Wales, possibly within the defences as at Cefnllys and Dolforwyn. This borough "of the upper Town" was chartered by Edward I, c. 1288, but there was a market and fair at least eight years earlier. There is sufficient level ground outside the walls of the cliff-top castle to have burgages and a market place, but the site could not have been so accessible as the bishop of St. David's nearby borough at Llandilo; and easier accessibility as well as an anticipation of more pacific conditions may have encouraged the foundation of the second borough, *Nova Villa* or Newtown, in a lower position but within Llandyfeisant parish.

A very full rental of 1302–03 (SC11/773) sets out the thirty-two English burgesses, who held their thirty-five burgages *in villa inferiori quae vocatur Nova Villa*, together with twenty-five other tenants of the New Town. By 1308 there were forty-four burgages, and by 1363, when the town received its first formal charter (*Cal. Pat. Rolls, 1391–6*, p. 504), there were forty-six (SC6/1158/10 and 1165/5).

The old borough, at the time of the foundation of the new, was much smaller, and perhaps was always small. There were eleven burgages in 1301–02 (SC6/1218/1) when the New Town was four years old. It is possible to date the new foundation because in the account of Michaelmas, 1304, it was explicitly stated that no rent would be due from the newcomers for the first seven years and that the sixth had begun on November 2, 1303 (SC6/1218/2; *burgenses villae tenent burgagia et terras sine redditu a prima fundatione villae per vii annos unde iste annus est sextus.*

The town was founded within Llandyfeisant parish and within the rural area of Maenor Deilo on the north bank of the Tywi. The isolated church is at 622222, within the park of the modern mansion of Dynevor Castle, and the site of the New Town is generally thought to have been overwhelmed by the mansion and its gardens. Certainly nothing has been observed in the parkland to suggest a borough site elsewhere, and the traditional name for the mansion locally is Dre Newydd. In 1563 there were still reckoned to be 12¼ burgages (SC12/17/83), and in 1651 (E317, Carmarthens. Nos. 6 and 15) there were eleven houses in Newtown.

The principal documents concerning the borough are printed in translation by E. A. Lewis, "Dynevor", *Trans. Hist. Soc. West Wales*, i (1911), pp. 146–224, and ii (1912), pp. 105–133. See also *R.C.H.M.W., Carmarthen*, pp. 107–111.

CARNARVONSHIRE

The only territory where the English were able to plant a town before the Edwardian conquests was the fragment of the county east of Conway that comprised the Llandudno peninsula. Here on the east shore of the estuary, where the coastal road took to the ferry, was the western limit of Norman penetration in the late eleventh century and the disputed site of Gannoc in the thirteenth.

CARNARVON   Carnarvonshire   sheet 115   23/478628
1283

Work on the new castle and town defences began in June 1283. The king and queen arrived in July and came again the next April. The town wall was probably complete by the end of 1285, and the heaviest expenditure of men, materials and money was over by the autumn of 1288. The castle, still incomplete, was overrun in the Madoc revolt of 1294. After its recapture there were two seasons of energetic building, and in 1301–02 the main bridge into the town from the east was rebuilt and fortified in stone.

By 1330 the castle and town were very much as they appear in Boydell's engraving of 1750 (A. J. Taylor, *Caernarvon Castle and Town Walls* (Ministry of Works Official Guide-book, 1953, plate 2); *cp.* the air photograph in *Beresford and St. Joseph*, p. 218).

As at Conway and Beaumaris, the building of the town displaced an older community: there was already a Welsh castle and princely residence here. A survey of the old Welsh *maenor* (SC6/1171/7 m. 5) also shows that there was a Welsh commercial centre. There was a port and also a *curia burgi*. There were also extensive agricultural holdings in the surrounding fields within Llanbeblig parish, and after the foundation of the new town, when commercial life had been taken within the walls, over 1,300 acres of this field land was assigned to the burgesses.

Unlike the monks of Aberconway or the townspeople of Llanvaes the Welsh of Old Carnarvon were not assigned a new resting place in compensation. Speed's plan of 1610 clearly shows extra-mural streets which may be the successors of the Welsh *tref*. The original scatter of settlement before the Norman castle, and the house of the Welsh princes at the riverside, is suggested by the isolated position of the parish church of St. Peblig nearly a mile from the modern town on the Beddgelert road, a little south-east of the Roman fort of Segontium, the *gaer* from which the town of Carnarvon was named.

The castle and walls are described architecturally and historically with plans in A. J. Taylor, *op. cit.*, and *R.C.H.M.W., Caernarvonshire*, ii (1960), pp. 115–158, esp. figs. 98–99. The text of the charter (1284) is printed in E. A. Lewis, *Medieval Boroughs of Snowdonia* (1912), pp. 279–281, also pp. 46–48. See also K. Evans, "Y Porth Mawr", *Tr. Caern. Hist. Soc.*, iii (1941), pp. 33–43; G. P. Jones, "Trading in Medieval Caernarvon", *ibid.*, x (1949), pp. 3–11.

CONWAY   Carnarvonshire   sheet 107   23/782775

1283

The crossing of the Conway estuary was an important stage in the coastal route of north Wales, and, while the Conway was the frontier between the English and Welsh, the castle of Deganwy, on the east bank of the river, was important. Alongside that town a borough had been developed (*q.v.*). After the defeat of Llewelyn, Edward I planned a castle and town on the west bank and for that purpose acquired the site of the Cistercian abbey of Aberconway. (See pages 42–44, above). The abbey church was given to the burgesses for their church.

The town, houses, walls, castle and church are minutely described and illustrated in S. Toy "The Town and Castle of Conway", *Archaeologia*, lxxxvi (1936), pp. 163–193, and in *R.C.H.M.W., Caernarvonshire*, i (1956), pp. 38–74. The chronology of building is set out in J. G. Edwards, "Edward I's Castle Building in Wales", *Proc. Brit. Acad.*, xxxii (1944), pp. 15–81. The charter of 1284 is printed in E. A. Lewis, *The Medieval Boroughs of Snowdonia* (1912), pp. 279–281. See also J. Griffiths, "Documents relating to the Early History of Conway", *Tr. Caern. Hist. Soc.*, viii (1947), pp. 5–19; and R. W. Hays, *The History of the Abbey of Aberconway* (1963), pp. 61–77. An Elizabethan plan of the town is reproduced in *Arch. Camb.*, xcvi (1941), p. 164, from the Hatfield House manuscript plans, I, 62. There are similarities to Domme (Dordogne), built in 1281, where the castle and town have also to adapt themselves to a steep, narrow ridge of land overlooking a river. Despite its breach by the railway, the three modern bridges on the river side, and the perpetual stream of road traffic, the character of the walled town is still well preserved. The walls are complete although the ramparts are not all restored and the full circuit cannot be walked. The western corner of the town is 100 feet higher than the east wall, and the sloping ramparts are an unusual feature.

CRICCIETH   Carnarvonshire   sheet 115   23/499377
1284

The charter was granted on November 22, 1284 (*Cal. Chart. Rolls*, ii, p. 280). In 1308 there were twenty-three burgages here (SC6/1170/6); and only four more by the mid-century (SC6/1173/1). The origin and present character of this small borough are further discussed at p. 47 above. See also B. H. St. J. O'Neil, "Criccieth Castle", *Arch. Camb.*, xcviii (1944), pp. 1–51, and 258; and *R.C.H.M.W.*, *Caernarvonshire*, ii (1960), pp. 57–65.

DEGANWY   Carnarvonshire   sheet 107   23/782795
1248

There was certainly a town planted near the castle in the mid-thirteenth century but although the castle was destroyed by 1263 early rentals of Conway borough include *placeae* in Deganwy (SC6/1211/2: SC6/1170/4; SC12/17/87–8). The market tolls at Deganwy exceeded those of Conway and its fairs were worth about one-third of Conway's in tolls. Deganwy then had a Monday market and an October fair. The main Conway ferry was also at Deganwy. These evidences point to a surviving commercial life on the north bank of the estuary, perhaps at or near the ferry which had given rise to extra-mural building on the south bank also. The modern settlement of Deganwy which is on the estuary shore below the castle has no old buildings, no walls and no grid-plan; although it is suspiciously churchless, being a township in the ecclesiastical parish of Eglwys Rhos. A chapel in the town was part of Henry's plan (*Hist. King's Works*, ii (1963), p. 625).

Burgages were ordered to be assigned in 1248 and 1251 (*Cal. Close Rolls, 1247–51*, p. 55, and *Cal. Pat. Rolls, 1247–58*, p. 84) and markets and fairs granted in 1250 (*ibid*, pp. 314–315).

There was a borough charter in 1252 (*Cal. Chart. Rolls*, i, p. 378) dating from the period when Henry III was re-establishing the English position in Flintshire and Denbighshire after the treaty of Woodstock (1247) (see also *Dyserth, infra*). This charter has the language of a town foundation. "The burgesses are to have half an acre of land in the borough on which they are to build their house and make a curtilage; two acres of arable outside the town are also given them; they may enclose the town with a wall and ditch; the bondmen who come and settle are to be free after a year and a day's residence; the town is to have a gild merchant and all the liberties of New Montgomery." (In 1251 Deganwy had been promised the liberties of Chester: *Cal. Pat. Rolls, 1247–58*, p. 84). In 1252 the borough was assessed at 10s. for tollage but released through its poverty (*Cal. Close Rolls, 1251–53*, pp. 149 and 365; *Cal. Pat. Rolls 1247–8*, p. 125). The language in the royal letter is explicitly that of plantation: *villa de Gannoc novella est plantacio et quidam habitantes in eadem villa propter ipsius paupertatem recesserunt. . . .* In 1258 Henry retained the castle but in 1263 it fell to the Welsh and was confirmed to them by the Treaty of Montgomery in 1267. It became English again only in 1277 by the Treaty of Aberconway.

NEVIN   Carnarvonshire   sheet 115   23/308407
See *Appendix* at end of Gazetteer.

PWLLHELI   Carnarvonshire   sheet 115   23/374361
See *Appendix* at end of Gazetteer.

DENBIGHSHIRE

The three plantations in this county all followed the Edwardian conquests.

DENBIGH   Denbighshire   sheet 108   33/052658
1283–90
The residence of Dafydd ap Gruffydd probably occupied the summit of the hill where Denbigh castle now stands. The castle and medieval borough were planned as a unity, like Carnarvon, and the first stage, the protecting town walls, was probably incomplete when the Welsh recaptured Denbigh in 1294; on the suppression of the rising it became English again. A charter was granted between 1283 and 1290 by Henry de Lacy, earl of Lincoln, to whom Edward had granted in 1282 a large tract of neighbouring country. It lists the forty-seven burgages which are to be taken up by the first thirty-nine burgesses, some of whom were to have more than one unit; with each burgage went a curtilage and agricultural land in Lleweni. The hill-top was remote from the rural church of Llanfarchell and the town and garrison shared the chapel of St. Hilary on the green outside the castle gate; the tower of this church and a few cottages are the only buildings remaining within the town walls except for the unfinished Elizabethan church which the earl of Leicester commenced as part of a project to move the see of St. Asaph to Denbigh—as abortive a project as Edward's attempt to settle the see at Rhuddlan.

It is just possible for a motor car to make its way up the hill to the walled town, and its inaccessibility was an incentive for commercial traffic to find a less exhausting home. Even in 1334 the *Survey of Denbigh* (ed. P. Vinogradoff and F. Morgan (1914)) describes (p. 52) "a borough of Denbigh inside the walls as well as a merchants' town (*villa mercatoria*) outside the walls". The walled town then occupied

9½ acres and the extra-mural town 57 acres. A survey of 1530 shows that most of the town was by then in the suburbs, and Camden's description of the deserted upper town confirms this.

The survey of 1334 deals only cursorily with the borough, but in 1311 (C134/22) there were 120 burgesses each paying 4d. a year rent. It is very informative about the mixture of native Welsh settlement and English manors in the agricultural area around Denbigh. In the Hamlet of Neuburgh, part of Lleweni, there were twelve (or perhaps sixteen) *placeae* in addition to the ordinary peasant holdings. The name does not appear on the modern map, and it is not certain whether the survey has recorded an abortive attempt to lay out a small borough beyond the suburbs of Denbigh, or whether it is the remains of a Welsh commercial settlement, older than Denbigh, such as the twenty-one burgages and three placeae at Llanrwst indicate.

The town walls of Denbigh are preserved in their full circuit and are in the care of the Ministry of Works. Access to them is given by the custodian on request, and the walk along their circuit is most attractive. Over the great gate of the castle there is a large carved figure, much smoothed by the weather, which is said to be Edward I. He looks down on an empty town beyond which can be heard the hum of modern Denbigh.

There is an air photograph with commentary in *Beresford and St. Joseph*, pp. 219–221. See also John Williams, *Ancient and Modern Denbigh* (Denbigh, 1856), for the charters and surveys.

HOLT   Denbighshire   sheet 109   33/410540
1282–1311

This castle and town stand on the west bank of the Dee, facing Farndon in Cheshire. The old name of the town, *Castrum Leonis*, resembles such Gascon names as Castrum Comitale and La Bastide Castelamoroux. The historian of Holt accepts it as a planted town contemporaneous with the building of the castle by the earl of Surrey in the late thirteenth century. (A. N. Palmer, "The Town of Holt", *Arch. Camb.*, 6th ser., vi (1906), pp. 217–240 and vii (1907), pp. 1–34; 311–334 and 389–440). There was a borough charter in 1411 (text: *ibid*, pp. 26–31). The town was surveyed in 1315 when there were 204½ tenants paying a shilling an acre and 159 "burgesses" so that the charter of 1411 must be a formal confirmation of some older, lost grant.

The town has some of the street plan of a true *bastide*. The Dee bridge is at one end, the castle and market place at the other and the castle between the market and the river. The site is analogous to Overton (*q.v.*) and the borough seems to have been carved out of Hewlington manor. The thirteenth-century church of St. Chad is placed within the town grid.

RUTHIN   Denbighshire   sheet 108   33/125584
1282

The boundaries of the borough show that it has been cut out of the parish of Llan-rhudd-dyffryn-clwyd at the southern end of the Vale of Clwyd. In 1282 this lordship was granted by Edward I to Reginald de Grey who founded a new church in the town for the burgesses. Edward himself was here in August 1283. The church was rebuilt in 1310 as collegiate (*R.C.H.M.W., Denbigh*, p. 181). It stands at the north end of the long street which leads north from the castle gate; beyond it the ground falls steeply and the only level ground is taken by the High Street and market place; the width of the street which drops down to the bridge suggests that it, too, once contained the market. There is no charter extant before the late fourteenth century (*Weinbaum*, p. 146), and no other evidence for the plantation of the town has been encountered. A. J. Taylor (*Studies in Building History*, ed., E. M. Jope (1961), pp. 104–133) suggests that a new castle was built on or close to the "red fort", the native centre of the commote of Dyffryn Clwyd; see also *Hist. King's Works*, i (1963), pp. 327–329.

FLINTSHIRE

The first two Rhuddlans indicate the early but impermanent penetration of the English and Normans along the coast of north Wales. Dyserth is a product of the same mid-thirteenth-century movement westward that produced Deganwy, but the main burst of town plantation, including a third Rhuddlan, came with the Edwardian armies.

CAERWYS   Flintshire   sheet 108   33/128728
1290

The charter was granted in 1290 (*Cal. Chart. Rolls*, ii, p. 372) giving the town the privileges of the royal town of Conway and the seigneurial town of Ruthin. The town is not military in character, but it has a full rectilinear plan, with a small market place at the centre and the church taking up half the south-west quadrant. In 1292 there were forty-three taxpayers in the town and thirty-seven others in the out-township (*forinsecus*) (E179/242/52). The rents of the borough at the end of the first decade averaged £5 a year, the profits of justice less than 20s. and the tolls o markets and fairs ranged from 20s. to 40s. (SC6/777/1 and *Lancs. and Ches. Rec. Soc.*, xcii (1938), p. 198).

Mr. G. R. J. Jones suggests to me that the borough was planted in the territories of two places mentioned in Domesday Book among the berewicks of Rhuddlan: *Cairos* and *Coiwen*, which he places at 116746 and 123737 respectively. Excavations in progress in 1963 at Hen Caerwys (140741) suggest a medieval settlement of some sort there. (See also above, p. 48).

DYSERTH   Flintshire   sheet 108   33/060800
1248

A new castle *de Rupe* was built here near the coastal end of the Clywdian range after the campaign of 1241 to replace the Norman castle at Rhuddlan (*Cal. Lib. Rolls*, ii, p. 129; *Cal. Pat. Rolls*, i, p. 258). Seven years later, following the peace at Woodstock, Henry III ordered burgage plots to be allocated near the castle for anyone who would come and take them (*Cal. Close Rolls, 1247–51*, p. 55) and in 1251 the borough was given the liberties of Chester. This municipal activity is paralleled at Deganwy in the same period. Rents were received from Dyserth at this period (E352/43). There is no settlement at all near the castle now, but there is a village half a mile to the south-west. The castle was destroyed by Llewelyn in 1263, and if there was a borough separate from the modern village site it may have perished with the castle. The village has no very clear pattern of burgages. Dyserth does not appear at all in William Rees "Bibliography of Published Works on the Municipal History of Wales", *Bull. B.C.S.*, ii (1925), pp. 321–382. In the tallage of 1252 when Deganway *burgus* first appears, Dyserth had only "the forinsecus of the castle" which may well imply the modern village. The vill of Dyserth had twelve taxpayers in 1292 (E179/242/52).

FLINT   Flintshire   sheet 108   33/244730
1277

The building of Flint has been briefly treated above, pp. 37–40, and fully in J. G. Edwards, "The Building of Flint", *Flints. Hist. Soc. Pub.*, xii (1951), and "Edward I's Castle Building in Wales", *Proc. Brit. Acad.*, xxxii (1944), pp. 15–81. See also A. J. Taylor, "The Building of Flint: A Postscript", *Flints. Hist. Soc. Pub.*, xvii (1957), pp. 34–41, and Sir J. E. Lloyd, "Notes on Flint", *Arch. Camb.*, xcv (1940), pp. 57–59; the charter is printed in *Cal. Chart. Rolls*, ii, pp. 276–277.

The site lay in the territory of two vills, Redinton and Ondeston, and within Northop parish. It obtained its own church of St. Mary, the most popular dedication in the English towns of Wales. The castle, which was integrated with the town, is described in *Flint Castle* (Ministry of Works Guide, 1946). An air photograph appears in *Beresford and St. Joseph*, p. 216.

The royal revenues from the borough in the early fourteenth century, when the medieval population was probably at its peak, was about £36. (A. Jones, ed., "Flints. Ministers' Accounts", *Flints. Hist. Soc. Pub.*, iii (1912–13)). The number of burgages is not precisely known. In 1292 the town mustered seventy-six taxpayers wealthy enough to be assessed, with a total of £23 10s. 6½d., almost the same number and sum as Rhuddlan (E179/242/52). Northop paid £7 9s. 2¾d. and had thirty-six taxpayers in its vills.

MOSTYN, NEW   Flintshire   sheet 108   33/160804
by 1292

The only evidence is the double entry in the Lay Subsidy for 1292 (E179/242/52) of Mostyn Welshry (18 taxpayers, 71s. 3¼d.) and *Nova Villa de Moston* (20 taxpayers, 91s. 8d.). Similar pairing is to be found at Caerwys (*q.v.*). The taxpayers of New Mostyn may have included sixteen English tenants of 1308 who held 280 acres of land cut from the demesne (C143/74/22). The map shows no patterned settlement: Mostyn village extends along the north side of a small valley, running inland. Tremostyn is at the south-west corner of Mostyn park (140800). Mr. G. R. J. Jones tells me that no personal name in the New Mostyn subsidy of 1292 is obviously Welsh, whereas the "Welshry" has at least sixteen.

OVERTON   Flintshire   sheet 118   33/373418
1292

A castle at Overton in Maelor Saesneg existed soon after 1138 (*Lloyd*, ii, pp. 583–584, fn. 44), but it is not certain whether there was a village at Overton before the creation of the borough by Edward I's charter of 1292 (*Cal. Chart. Rolls*, ii, p. 414). Edward stayed at the castle in September 1283 and October 1284. In July 1279 (*Ibid.*, p. 213) a market had been granted to be held at Overton manor in Maelor Saesneg, and the tax roll of 1292 (E179/242/52) preserves the distinction between the borough with its fifty-six taxpayers and the *forinsecus* with twelve. The sum paid by the burgesses in that collection was about half that of Flint, and the numbers also suggest that they cannot have been very recent arrivals. On the other hand the document in *Cal. Close Rolls, 1293*, pp. 285–286, states that Reginald de Gray went to Overton to distribute burgages to those wanting to take them up. They were given timber from the royal forest for their new houses and land to assart and cultivate; for the first ten years of residence they were to be free of the fee farm payment to the Crown. This is the very language of town foundation. The language of another charter of 1282 (*Cal. Chart. Rolls*, ii, pp. 422–423) is also of vacant land and burgesses coming from outside to settle on it (see also G. J. Howson, *Overton in Days Gone By* (1883)). These two charters describe lands with Welsh names, or with former Welsh tenants, which were given as building plots in the lifetime of Queen Eleanor (d. 1290), lady of the town.

The main street ran from the castle to the bridge (*id.*) in 1292. The castle stood on a cliff edge which has been eroded by the Dee (*R.C.H.M.W., Flints.*, p. 111). The main road still runs through the town, and indeed, is forced to make a right-angled turn into the borough grid by the church, but the place has no urban character now.

RHUDDLAN I   Flintshire   sheet 108   33/c. 029776
921

It is very likely that the burh of Clwydmouth was located here. The site has not been excavated.

RHUDDLAN II   Flintshire   sheet 108   33/026776
1073

This was the *novus burgus* of Domesday Book created by the earl of Chester. The motte survives as Twthill and other features are discussed at p. 37 above.

RHUDDLAN III   Flintshire   sheet 108   33/024780
1278

"At Rhuddlan we have the remains of two castles and two defended towns" (A. J. Taylor, *Rhuddlan Castle*, (1957), p. 12). The relation of the two is discussed above

p. 40. The second (the third if the Saxon *burh* is included) was built alongside his new castle by Edward I after the surrender of Llewelyn in 1277. The charter (*Cal. Chart. Rolls*, ii, pp. 276–277) dates from September 1278 and was based on the liberties of Hereford. The riverside meadows were being enclosed and burgages laid out on the north side of the castle earlier that year (*Cal. Welsh Rolls*, p. 165; *Cal. Pat. Rolls, 1278–81*, p. 259) and were being built the next March (*Cal. Welsh Rolls*, p. 180). Edward's town, with its rectilinear street plan, also had an artificial canal which replaced the meanders of the river and enabled ships to come up with the tide: *magnum fossatum qui ducit a mare usque castrum* (A. J. Taylor in E. M. Jope, ed., *Studies in Building History* (1961), pp. 104–133). Edward also hoped—but in vain—that the town might have a cathedral: A. J. Taylor, "Rhuddlan Cathedral", *Flints. Hist. Soc. Publ.*, xv (1954–55), pp. 43–51.

GLAMORGANSHIRE

The conquest of this area by Robert fitz Hamon, later earl of Gloucester, was the first and most permanent of the Norman invasions of south Wales. Following it came a number of important town foundations including Cardiff, the headquarters of the Marcher lordship. Its lordship passed later into the Clare family; the late arrival of Caerphilly indicates that the northern part of the present county was disputed territory.

ABERAVON   Glamorganshire   sheet 153 21/765902
?1147–83

The town may be the *novam villam in Margam* of an undated charter (1147–83) (Clark, *Cartae*, i, p. 106). The foundation of castle and borough may be due to Caradog, lord of Rhwng Nedd ac Afan in the early twelfth century (*Lloyd*, ii, p. 440). The liberties of the near contemporary foundation of Kenfig were conferred on this town later by a charter from a local lord, Leysam ab Morgan (1288–1313) (*Ballard and Tait*, p. xxv) (Clark, *op. cit.*, iii, p. 922). The modern development of the site has been even more thoroughly destructive of topographical evidence than at Llanelly or Swansea. A hundred years ago this borough had degenerated into a dilapidated river port but it has since been transformed by the development of Port Talbot.

BRIDGEND   Glamorganshire   sheet 154 21/903799
by 1197

The town of Bridgend comprises two settlements, one on each bank of the Ogmore river, here crossed by the main road through south Wales. Each settlement depended on a castle. On the east bank was Nolton in the parish of Coity and the castle may have been built by the lords of Coity castle, the de Turbevilles. On the west bank was Newcastle of which the ruins remain on a cliff north of the bridge. Next to the castle is the church of St. Illtyd which is parochial. The town must have comprised the vicinity of the castle; in a charter of 1197 it was called *Nova Villa* (Clark, *Cartae*, ii, p. 231) and two years later another charter parallels this castle-town with *Vetus Villa* (for Nolton) (*id.*, p. 236). There is too much modern building to be able to discern anything from the topography. See H. J. Randall, *Newcastle, Bridgend* (M.O.W. guide). "Oldcastle" is a late and literary name for Nolton.

CAERPHILLY   Glamorganshire   sheet 154   31/157868
1271

The present castle, a magnificent ruin, was commenced by earl Gilbert de Clare in 1271; an unfinished building, begun in 1268, had been destroyed by the Welsh. The area had been much in Welsh hands after the Norman conquest of the Glamorgan plain and it is likely that the town began with the Clare castle. It is significant that there was no parish church in the town; a chapelry of St. Martin was in Eglwysilan parish. No borough charter is known, but there were 116 burgages in 1281 (Clark, *Cartae*, iii, p. 845) and 80 burned burgages in 1296 (C133/73/3), 44 burgages in 1306 (C133/120): 95 in 1314 (C134/43) and 98 in 1347 (C135/105). There were probably rather fewer in 1375 (C135/252 printed by W. Rees in *S. Wales and Mon. Rec. Soc. Pub.*, iv (1957), pp. 31–50).

From the first edition of the 6 inch O.S. plan it can be seen that the old part of the town consisted of the street at the east of the castle, in front of the gate, and the narrow triangle at the upper end (now cleared for a car park) must have been the market place.

CARDIFF   Glamorganshire   sheet 154   31/182763
1081–93

The problem here is whether Robert fitz Hamon's town, begun in 1081, had any relation or continuity with the Roman settlement or that of the native Welsh princes of Morganwg, the last of whom was dispossessed by Robert fitz Hamon. A charter of c. 1102 (Clark, *Cartae*, i, p. 37) describes a branch of the river Taff as running *iuxta burgum* and there was an addition to the borough, probably on the north-east which was described in a charter of 1147–48 (*ibid*, i, p. 104): *de novo burgo quod feci ubi gardinum meum extra villam de Kardif*. A tradition embodied in a monastic chronicle (*ibid*, iii, p. 858, from P.R.O. KRMB 1) was that in 1081 *edificata est Kerdiva sub rege Willelmo primo*, but it is not clear whether it was Cardiff town or castle that was built that year and *Lloyd* (ii, pp. 396 and 402), discounts the possibility of a successful settlement before 1087.

Cardiff was the largest of the medieval boroughs of Wales. In 1281 (Clark, *Cartae*, iii, p. 813) there were 380 burgages; in 1262 (*ibid*, ii, p. 657) there were 405 and in 1296 (C133/77/3) there were 421, and about the same number in 1306 (C133/130); in 1316 there were reckoned to be 380 (SC6/1202/9).

The bounds of the walled town are clearly visible both from the wall where it survives and from the line of streets near the Glamorganshire Canal (which follows the moat). The plan is that of a rectilinear grid at the south gate of the castle, with the market place in the central street and the church in the eastern street.   This church (St. John's) was originally the lesser of the two borough churches, a chapelry to the Benedictine priory of St. Mary which stood at the south-western end of the town on the banks of the Taff until it was swept away by a flood in 1607.   See also W. Rees, *Cardiff, a History of the City* (1962); and for a mid-seventeenth-century plan of the town, *Arch. Camb.* 6th ser., i (1901), pp. 318–319.

COWBRIDGE   Glamorganshire   sheet 154   21/994747
1090–1262

This small walled town of 33 acres has its medieval topography well preserved despite the growth of shops and coaching inns over the burgage plots along its single street, the main road from Cardiff into west Wales.   The borough boundary and the town wall follow the end of the two lines of burgage plots, and the whole is clearly cut out of the rural parish of Llanblethian whose church is at 985740, a mile to the south-west of Cowbridge.   The bridge in the borough name is that which marks the east end of the old borough, and beyond which a suburb, the East Village, has grown up along the main road.

The very substantial parish church was no more than a chapel of ease to the mother church of Llanblethian.

The south gate is the only one remaining of the three which Leland saw entire, but there are lengths of the wall to be seen along the perimeter of the borough.   The town has a poor military position and must have been purely a civil settlement devoted to roadside commerce, markets and fairs.   The military stronghold was at Llanblethian, a castle built by Sir Robert St. Quentin shortly after the Norman conquest and the local tradition is that he built the town.

Within this narrow limit of the walls there were $277\frac{3}{4}$ burgages in 1306 and 1314 (C133/130 and C134/43), and if the *redditus* of other documents was calculated on the same basis of a shilling per burgage, there were 58 burgages in 1262–63 (SC6/1202/1); 135 in 1281 (Clark, *Cartae*, iii, p. 828); 233 in 1296 (C133/77/3) and 151 in 1349 (C135/105).

With such good topographical evidence it is disappointing to note that no firm date can be advanced for the foundation of the town in the absence of a borough charter. (The charter of 1201 indexed at *Rot. Chart.*, p. 87, is for Corbridge.)

The right-angled corner of the town wall at the south-west end of the town, and the central position of Church Street leading in from the south gate, must indicate that the town originally comprised only the houses between the present Cattle Market and the bridge.   On this basis, both East and West Village, both of which are within the present borough, were suburban in the middle ages.   They comprise Eastgate Street and Westgate Street respectively.   It is remarkable in so busy a roadside town that there has been virtually no building outside this envelope.

The West Gate was removed in 1754 and the East Gate had gone by 1775; the north moat was filled in during 1853 (L. J. Hopkin-James, *Old Cowbridge* (1922), plan, p. xvi).

KENFIG   Glamorganshire   sheet 153   21/801826
1140–47

This is an extraordinary site: the castle ruins, churchyard and all the other remains of the borough are overwhelmed by the sands and overlooked by a marshalling yard and a steel works.   It is possible to discern what may have been streets and the boundaries of tenements in the sands, but the work of the wind and rain upon the sand dunes is able to construct almost any archaeological pattern at the wish of the imagination.   It is a great pity that this interesting site has not been thoroughly excavated.

The site of St. James' church and graveyard will be found on the 6 inch O.S. map, and from there it is possible to make one's way through the relics of wartime barbed wire to the edge of the railway sidings where the ruins of the castle are thigh-deep in sand.

Burgesses were recorded here in 1184–85 (Clark, *Cartae*, i, p. 172) when the place was subject to one of the frequent burnings inflicted upon it.   In 1281 (*ibid*, iii, p. 835) there were reckoned 142 burgages, and the same number in 1306 (C133/130), 1314 (C134/43), 1349 (C135/105) and 1359 (C135/45).   In 1316 forty-two burgages were said to be burned and empty, the same number as in 1281, so that the accounts and extents would seem to be satisfied with a conventional reckoning.

In the end, the sands were more virulent than the Welsh.   In the early fourteenth century other local villages began to complain that the sands were swallowing their lands, and in 1336 Margam abbey complained to the Pope of their loss of lands locally.   Leland found the town "almost choked and devoured with the sands that the Severn sea there casteth up" and in 1572 there were only three burgages remaining, the borough petitioning the Queen about the "overthrow, blowing and choking up of sand in drowning our Town and Church".

The first church was built for the town by earl William of Gloucester; an undated charter (1140–47) reveals burgages in Kenfig (Clark, *Cartae*, i, p. 103) and the permission which Tewkesbury Abbey gave by another undated charter (1147–54) confirms the date when the town came into existence: this second charter allowed the church of St. James to be set up (*erigere*) (B. M. Cott., Cleo. A. VII).   About 1250 a chapel of St. Mary Magdalen was founded at the south-east end of the town, and this has given its name to the settlement of Mawdlam, at the edge of the higher ground which still defies the sands.   (See T. Gray, *The Buried City of Kenfig* (1909); plan between pp. 58–59; and pp. 86–93; pp. 99–115.)

LLANTRISSANT   Glamorganshire   sheet 154   31/047834
by 1262

The date of the castle and the borough is unknown: it was already a borough in 1262 (Clark, *Cartae*, ii, 1, 659), and in 1306 (C133/130) there were 145 burgages as well as the sites of 5½ others.   In 1316 there were reckoned to be 198 burgages of which 47½ had been wasted in recent warfare; and in other accounts there were said to be 170 (SC6/1202/6, 7 and 9); the market was said to have been granted in 1313.

The town consists of a market street, with encroachments, on the north of the castle, and these together with the church and Guild Hall of 1773 occupy the hill-top; there is another street, called High Street, which winds down the hill-side. The castle site is now occupied by an ivy-grown tower, three allotment plots, beehives and gardeners' huts. The castle occupies a commanding site with excellent views to the plain and the Bristol Channel.

LOUGHOR   Glamorganshire   sheet 153   21/564979
after 1100

This small castle town was within the site of the Roman Leucarum; the first castle, on which the town depended, was built in the south-west corner of the fort shortly after 1100 by the earl of Warwick, but destroyed by the Welsh in 1150. The church of St. Michael was just west of the castle on the constricted ridge, and the borough occupied the remainder of the fort area, and also developed in ribbon fashion along the main road. There was a medieval ferry across the estuary here (DL29/573/9063) into Llanelly. The bridge was built with the turnpike road.

NEATH   Glamorganshire   sheet 153   21/752976
1100–30

The first charter which is known is that of the earl of Gloucester, (1147–73), but the castle (and perhaps the town) date from the earlier part of the century. It stands on the east bank of the river Neath facing Neath Abbey and the site of the Roman Nidum over the river. The abbey was founded by Richard de Granville in 1130 and among its endowments was the chapel of the castle, later the town church. The core of the town is the rectangular pattern of streets east of the bridge and between the main road and the parish church of St. Thomas.

In 1262 (Clark, *Cartae*, ii, p. 662) there were just over a hundred burgages; in 1281 (*ibid*, iii, p. 837) eighty had been burned in one of the frequent Welsh attacks on the town but seventy more seem to have been able to pay rent; in 1306 and 1314 (C133/120 and C134/43) there were reckoned to be 128 burgages in Neath, and in 1349 about 150 (C135/105).

SWANSEA   Glamorganshire   sheet 153   21/656929
1116

The castle here was built, like that of Llanelly, by the earl of Warwick in 1116 (*Lloyd*, ii, p. 430), and the tradition is that the earl also founded the town. The first known charter is by William, earl of Warwick (1153–84) (Clark, *Cartae*, i (1885), p. 136). The parish church of St. Mary near the site of the castle was rebuilt in 1739 and most of the centre of the town is equally transformed by more modern rebuilding.

There are plans of the medieval town and walls, together with notes on the excavation of the castle, in W. L. Morgan, *The Castle of Swansea* (1914), esp. pp. 2 and 36; see also W. L. Morgan, *An Antiquarian Survey of East Gower* (1899), p. 87. W. H. Jones, *History of Swansea* (1920), pp. 77–78 would seem to support the view that the town was a foundation *de novo*: "there was probably no permanent population at Swansea" when the Norman castle was first built; the name was in vogue for some land at the mouth of the river.

MERIONETHSHIRE

The English towns of this county all followed the subjection of the princedom of Gwynedd by Edward I.

BALA   Merionethshire   sheet 117   23/926360
c. 1310

Even without documents, the topography of Bala would strongly suggest a town plantation. The town consists of one absolutely straight main street with a back lane parallel to it on either side. The township area is small: apart from some marsh land it is less than a square mile, and it has clearly been cut out of the large parish of Llanycil (914349) which has 12,800 acres.

The borough charter of 1324 recites the circumstances of the foundation of the town (E. A. Lewis, *Medieval Boroughs of Snowdonia* (1912), pp. 283–287). Notorious groups of wrongdoers and thieves had beset travellers at "Penthlyn" and the king had ordered his justiciar to set out (*ordinare*) the town of Bala as a free borough to quieten the district. The borough was given a weekly market and two yearly fairs; the town could be surrounded with a ditch and a mortared wall. The burgesses could elect their own mayor from among themselves.

The justiciar concerned was Roger de Mortimer, and the year of foundation about 1310 (Lewis, *op. cit.*, p. 55, citing SC6/1231/5) when fifty-three burgages were measured out, thirty-four of them on the royal demesne of Penllyn and nineteen on freehold land. The markets and fairs held previously at Llanfor (938367) were moved to the new town (*cp.* Trematon and Launceston two centuries earlier).

The royal demesne here, before the foundation of the town, is mentioned in a sheriff's account of 1291–92 (SC6/1231/11), and Edward I was at Bala for most of June 1284. After the foundation of the town the burgesses paid a fee farm of £10 12s. a year (SC6/1203/1) and rented the remaining demesne lands of the Crown in Bala township for £3 0s. 10d.

The town straddles the main road from Dolgelly down the Dee valley, just north of the marshes where the river leaves Lake Bala to be joined by the Afon Tryweryn. A small motte, Tomen y Bala, suggests that this position had earlier been of some military interest but the flat site of the borough would have been easily over-run even if the wall had been built; there is a strong likelihood that it was never built.

BERE   Merionethshire   sheet 116   23/667085
1284

The charter of November 1284 (*Cal. Chart. Rolls*, ii, p. 280) places this borough in the same class as Conway and Carnarvon, but the scale of Edward's ambition must have been nearer that for Harlech, also chartered on the same day.

The historical evidence for the existence of a civil settlement until 1293 is discussed above pp. 47–48. (See also E. D. Evans, "Castell y Bere", *J. Merioneth. Hist. and Rec. Soc.*, iii (1957), pp. 31–44. I am indebted to Mr. Evans and to Mr. A. J. Taylor, Chief Inspector of Ancient Monuments, for discussion of this site.)

The borough may have been within the castle defences as at Cefnllys or Dynevor; another possible site is the western slope of the hill outside the castle gate where the ground is now rough and tree-covered.

HARLECH   Merionethshire   sheet 116   23/582311
1283

The castle building began in 1283, and the charter was issued in November 1284 on the same day as those of Bere and Criccieth (*Cal. Chart. Rolls*, ii, p. 280; the date in E. A. Lewis, *Medieval Boroughs of Snowdonia* (1912), p. 282 is erroneous).

This was a small borough (see pp. 46–47, above) and it may not have been walled. It had no church of its own, and is now an amorphous collection of houses at the castle-gate. No sign of a grid of streets could be detected in the surrounding fields, and the hill-side is too steep to be able to accommodate very many more houses.

MONMOUTHSHIRE

The early date of the plantations in this Border county attests the successful hold of the English. The present county was divided among several Marcher lords.

Note. Raglan, although not mentioned as a borough in William Rees' bibliography (*Bull. B.C.S.*, ii (1925), pp. 369–372), did have sixty-eight burgesses in 1354 (SC11/970); there is no evidence that it was planted.

ABERGAVENNY   Monmouthshire   sheet 142   32/300140
1087–1100

This walled town has the dimensions and some of the character of Brecon, of which it is a near-contemporary. Each has a Norman castle standing in an elevated position overlooking the Usk, and a compact town of oval shape delimited by walls and the changes of slope which show where walls and ditches have once been; each town also has an extra-mural priory of the same period (c. 1090). The founder of Abergavenny was Hamelin of Ballon (J. A. Bradney, *History of Monmouthshire* (1907–32), i, pp. 144 sqq.). North, South and East gates can be distinguished, and there were two principal parallel streets. The curving western end of the wall and burgage plot is still (1961) preserved in the waste ground between Baker Street and Nevill Street, but it is likely that new housing schemes will cover this feature; on the southern side the burgage plots end abruptly at the cliff-top and wall.

In 1255 (SC6/1094/11) there were 230 burgages and five *placeae* with the standard 1s. a year rent; the market brought in £10 11s. 6½d. and the fairs £4 6s. 10d.; four plots were empty. The great out-manor was worth £301 8s. 11¾d. that year. There is a long list of taxpayers in 1292 (E179/242/56), and in 1325 (C134/91) the rent roll was a little more than in 1255; by 1368 (C135/200) it had shrunk a little, and the markets and fairs were about a third of their former value.

CHEPSTOW   Monmouthshire   sheet 155   31/536940
1072-75

This port at the mouth of the Wye, where Offa's Dyke meets the Severn, has changed its name; until the early fourteenth century it bore the name of the Clare's castle outside which it was placed, Stroguil (Striguil). The change of name emphasises its commercial character: *ceapstow* = market place. Its name is thus akin to Chipping, Chipping Sodbury and the *Novum Forum* (New Alresford) and Newmarket.

The walled town, which included a church, comprised 113 acres, and there is the same problem as at Monmouth (*q.v.*) that is whether the situation described in 1086 in Domesday Book was wholly a consequence of the coming of the castle or whether there was an earlier village here? A bull of Pope Honorius cited by J. A. Bradney, *History of Monmouthshire*, iv, p. 22, speaks of the original church of Chepstow being at Llangynfarch. The present parish church of St. Mary at the lower end of the market place was originally the church of the Benedictine Priory, founded by 1077. In the early fourteenth century there were 308 burgages here (C133/127: 1306).

J. G. Wood's *The Lordship, Castle and Town of Chepstow* (Newport, 1910) supports the view that the town was a consequence of the Norman castle: another Ludlow, Windsor or Richmond. "It has been persistently asserted by writers, of more or less pretension, that there was a town in Welsh and Saxon times. I believe this to be entirely erroneous" (p. 7). "There is no mention before the Norman Conquest. It is mentioned in Domesday Book in such a way that leads me to infer that it had then recently arisen" (p. 6). The Domesday Book statement is that earl William made the castle and that in his time it returned 40s., and that from ships going up to the wood; but in the time of his son, earl Roger, the town returned £16. Since William left England at the end of 1070 and his son forfeited the town in 1075 the limit of dates is narrow.

GROSMONT   Monmouthshire   sheet 142   32/406243
1154-89

King Stephen acquired this manor and Llantilio (see *Whitecastle*), and building of castles began here, and at Whitecastle and Skenfrith, in the reign of Henry II. Of these three strong points in the Monmouthshire triangle only Grosmont shows surviving signs of a small urban and commercial life. There is still a moderate-sized village, and the church, part of which is disused, bears witness to something more important in its past. It was completed by Eleanor of Provence. There is a small market hall in a triangle of streets which looks like an encroached-upon market place, and to the east, behind the gardens, stands the castle overlooking the Monnow. There was a small medieval borough here (*Cal. Inq. Misc.*, i, p. 8 (1250); SC6/1094/11 (1257); C135/169/3 (1362); DL29/594/9506 (1370) and W. Rees, ed., *A Survey of the Duchy of Lancaster Lordships in Wales, 1609-13* (1953)).

MONMOUTH   Monmouthshire   sheet 142   32/508130
1070–72

"Under the shadow of the castle and at the point where the converging rivers, the Monnow and the Wye, offered a defensive site, a borough of considerable importance had grown up during the late eleventh and twelfth centuries, and by the early fourteenth century Monmouth had been converted into a walled town" (W. Rees, ed., *A Survey of the Duchy of Lancaster Lordships in Wales, 1609–13* (1953), p. xi). The castle was built in 1070 by the earl of Hereford, William Fitz Osbern, at the same time as Wigmore, Clifford, Ewias Harold and Chepstow. At Wigmore and Clifford the castles sheltered a chartered borough (*Lloyd*, ii, p. 375) so that it would not be impossible for the towns of Chepstow (*q.v.*) and Monmouth to date from the same period.

Domesday Book records the castle and church as well as plough teams, and the difficult question is whether there was any settlement here before the Norman Castle and its dependent town? The Roman *Blestium* may have been near the bridge in what is now the suburb of Over Monnow; this suburb beyond the Monnow Bridge, and enclosed by the Black Dyke, is a very peculiar appendage. J. A. Bradney, *Hist. of Monmouthshire*, i (1907), has an account of the town which would accord with a view that there was a Norman plantation. The foundation charter of Monmouth Priory, however (Dugdale, *Monasticon*, iv, p. 595), could be interpreted as indicating a church of St. Cadoc existing before the castle.

The accounts for the borough in 1256–57 (SC6/1094/11) are printed in A. J. Roderick and W. Rees, "The Lordships of Abergavenny (etc.)", *S. Wales and Mon. Rec. Soc. Pubs.*, iv (1957), pp. 6–9. A full survey of the burgages in 1610 (266 in all) is printed in W. Rees, *op. cit.*

The "mouth" of the Monnow in the place-name is its convergence with the Wye: and this name is recorded in an eleventh-century document (E. Ekwall, *English River Names* (1928)).

NEWPORT   Monmouthshire   sheet 155   31/311882
by 1188

The *novus burgus* recorded by Giraldus in 1188 accompanied the new castle that guarded the river crossing, an earlier Norman motte being near the original *maedref* or serf village at Gwynllwg (Stowe Hill). The borough was planted in St. Woolo's parish and had originally no parish of its own. The castle was there by 1185 (W. Rees, *The Charters of Newport, Mon.* (1951), p. xi) and an undated account from the late twelfth century mentions the tithes of *nova villa* and its mill (Paris, Bibliothèque Nationale, ms. Latin 4221 f. 170). The exact date of the borough (which was probably contemporary) is unknown; the first written charter is that of 1385 (J. H. Matthews, *Cardiff Records*, i (1898), 2) but a charter of 1324 mentions burgesses (*Cal. Chart. Rolls*, iii, p. 461). The name of the place (*novus burgus*) in 1188 is sufficient evidence that there was a twelfth-century borough. In 1263 there were 242 burgages (SC6/1202/1); in 1296 sixty-six out of 256 were wasted in war (C133/77/3); in 1306 there were 228 able to pay rent (C133/80); and in 1314 275 (C134/43).

The town was prosperous enough in the nineteenth century to have its medieval features overlaid, but there is a good grid of streets south and west of the bridge near the old castle site. See also C. J. O. Evans, *Monmouthshire, its History and Topography* (1953), p. 428, for an undocumented date of c. 1126 for the first mention of *novus burgus*.

SKENFRITH   Monmouthshire   sheet 142   32/455203

after 1190

This is a marginal case for inclusion, since the borough can never have been very large: indeed, the burghal element may simply have been a privileged tenure within the royal manor which depended on the castle. The castle is first mentioned in the Pipe Rolls for 1190 and the first record of the church is in 1207.

There is now only one house between the castle and church, alongside the Monnow. The position is a flat riverside one, and the focus of military interest must have been the bridge.

TRELLECH   Monmouthshire   sheet 155   32/500055

c. 1150

This village on the plateau between the Monnow and the Usk was once a substantial borough, with 271 burgages in 1306 (C133/130). It has a simple street plan with slight banks and ditches around the perimeter of the former burgage plots. The town was named from three standing stones, and the first appearance of the name noted by the *Oxford Dictionary of English Place-Names* is the mid-twelfth century.

There was certainly a borough in 1288 (SC6/1247/21) and the amount of the *redditus* even suggests that there were 378 burgages (and a new one let that year) (see also SC6/925/24 undated, of the same period). There were 102 destroyed by fire in 1296 (C133/77/3), but even so, the 271 burgages of 1306 and the 265 of 1314 (C134/43) make a very substantial number.

J. A. Bradney, *History of Monmouthshire* (1907-32), ii, pt. 2, pp. 129-130 describes a second street, now only earthworks, running north to south on the west of the motte of Tump Terrett, where foundations of houses could be also seen.

USK   Monmouthshire   sheet 155   32/376008

by 1131

This town, of which the first mention is in 1131, was named after the river on whose east bank it stands. The castle is at the north end of the town, and the south eastern quadrant was occupied by the Priory, of which the church remains as the parish church. A square between church and castle gate has the air of a market place, but New and Old Market Street, in the west and south of the town, suggest that the commercial centre at one stage was alongside the river (where remains of the Roman fort of Burrium have been discovered).

The town is quiet and spacious, but in medieval times it was large. In 1262-63 the borough rent was £7 1s. 6d. (SC6/1202/1) suggesting 141 burgages, and in 1306 there were 294 and six new burgages that year (C133/130); the destruction of 180 recorded in 1296 (C133/77/3) seems to have been only temporary. In 1314 there were 296 burgages rented (C134/43). This gave Usk three-quarters of the number of burgages in Cardiff at that time, and all Bridge Street, the Market Streets and Maryport Street would have been needed to fit in these building plots. There is a plan of the town in J. A. Bradney, *History of Monmouthshire*, iii, p. 33.

WHITECASTLE   Monmouthshire   sheet 142   32/380165
after 1185

This borough is akin to Skenfrith in its hardly-urban character; the castle was begun in 1184–85 (C. A. Ralegh Radford, *White Castle* (1946), p. 1) and medieval records show occasional mention of burgages among the tenantry in Llantilio Crossenny, a parish whose centre is 2 miles to the south-east of the castle. In the duchy of Lancaster surveys of 1609–13 (ed. William Rees (1953)) it was reported that "there is noe markett towne within the said mannor of White Castell" although there were still tenants holding in free burgage. A number of medieval documents which describe Grosmont (*q.v.*) as a borough fail to give Whitecastle burghal status (SC6/1094/11 (1256–57); C134/43 (1314); C135/105 (1349)). Whatever the original intention, it is uncertain whether there was ever a town at the castle gates; but in the adjoining fields is a complex of earthwork "baileys" that need investigation. "Further enclosures protected by much denuded earth banks and ditches lie east and west of the central area" (Ralegh Radford, *op. cit.*, p. 6).

MONTGOMERYSHIRE

When this county was created by Henry VIII it took its name from New Montgomery which, like its predecessor Old Montgomery, lies near the western edge of the county. Neither the Norman who founded Old Montgomery nor Henry III, who founded New Montgomery, was able to establish himself further westward, and the other planted towns of the upper Severn valley were the work of Welsh princes of Powys, some of whom accepted English sovereignty and others of whom were influenced by English example.

CAERSWS   Montgomeryshire   sheet 128   32/030920
n.d.

This small village, on the Severn half-way between Newtown and Llanidloes, has a very formal rectangularity in its street pattern. Leland reported that it had once been a borough (*Mont. Coll.*, ii (1869), p. 66). The town church is Victorian, and before its erection the town lay on the edge of Llanwnog parish. The Welsh *maenor* of Is Coed commote was in Caersws. B. H. St. J. O'Neil suggested that the street plans of Machynlleth, Llanidloes, Newtown and Caersws all show the lord of Powys imitating Henry III and Edward I in town plantation ("The Castle and Borough of

Llanidloes", *Mont. Coll.*, xliii (1933), p. 63). The grid pattern is continued into the surrounding fields and lanes.

DOLFORWYN   Montgomeryshire   sheet 128   32/153951
1273

Llewelyn attempted to found a market town *de novo* at his new castle of Dolforwyn in Bettws Cedewain parish in 1273. It was prevented by the English. (See p. 44 above for references.) The site has the same character as Cefnllys, a narrow hill-top across which ditches have been cut to make a first defence, with additional defences of stone in the inner bailey. The burgages could only have fitted themselves in at the western end of the hill where there are some signs of small rectangular buildings under the turf. No excavation has been reported and all trace of the town had certainly gone by 1330 (SC6/1206/2). The commercial hopes of Llewelyn must have rested on the Severn valley route at the foot of the castle hill and perhaps the existence of Strata Florida's grange at Abermule opposite.

LLANFYLLIN   Montgomeryshire   sheet 117   33/142195
?1293

This small market town was once an assize town. In 1309 and 1310 it had thirty burgages (C134/10/16 and 17/1). In 1293 a market and fair had been chartered (*Cal. Chart. Rolls*, ii, p. 433), and Robert Williams, "A History of Llanfyllin", *Mont. Coll.* iii (1870), p. 91, assigns the borough charter to the following years. R. Richards (*Mont. Coll.*, xlix (1946), p. 174) concurs, as do *Ballard and Tait*, p. xliii. There was a church here in 1291 so that the borough must have been added to a Welsh parish; there may or may not have been a settlement by the church. This is a marginal candidate for inclusion in the list. Its charter served as model for the Merioneth borough of Dinas Mawddwy (B. G. Charles, "Merioneth Records—I", *J. Merioneth Hist. and Rec. Soc.*, i (1949), pp. 44–68).

LLANIDLOES   Montgomeryshire   sheet 128   22/954846
1280–93

Llanidloes is the most westerly of the plantations of mid-Wales. To the west of Llanidloes the Severn cuts its way across the slopes of Plynlimmon, and over the watershed the rivers lead down to Aberystwyth and the coastal bastides.

  In his study of the town and castle (*Mont. Coll.*, xliii (1933), pp. 47–65, B. H. St. J. O'Neil wrote: "it is unlikely that a town of any size would grow in such a remote part of the Severn valley until the period of Edward I's deliberate policy of urbanisation". He ascribed the broad streets of Powys boroughs like Llanidloes to a deliberate imitation of Edward by his nobles.

  The late arrival of Llanidloes is attested not only by its deliberate grid of streets (there is a good plan in O'Neil *art. cit.*, p. 50). The mother church of Llandinam lies 6 miles distant. The borough took into its parish small portions of Glynhafren and Cilfachallt townships. Its four main streets meet at the Market Hall, and the town church occupies part of the north west quadrant. The western arm of the grid leads to the Severn bridge and there was a castle on the south side of the town overlooking the river. The beginnings of the town can be approximately determined. There was a charter granting a market and fair in 1280; in an inquisition of 1293 the place is called a town (C133/64/16: 59s. 2d. assessed rents; £6 fairs; £5 6s. markets; £1 6s. 8d. pleas of court); and in a second inquisition post mortem in 1309 there were sixty-six burgesses recorded, each paying a shilling a year rent; no borough charter is known before 1344 (*Mont. Coll.*, xlix (1945), p. 123); in 1375 two fairs and a market were held in the borough (C135/237/1).

The "Lanthelas" of SC6/1146/13 (1332) is this borough (identification by fairs of St. Luke and St. Thomas). There were then sixty-five burgages, each paying 1s. a year; fairs worth £4, profits of justice at £2 and market tolls at £3 6s. 8d.

MONTGOMERY, NEW   Montgomeryshire   sheet 128   33/223965
1223

In 1086 Domesday Book records that earl Roger de Montgomery had a castle (which he had built), three hides of demesne and £6 of Welsh rents. This motte was at *Hen Domen*, within 400 yards of the river Severn where it enters the Welsh mountains; and only a mile from where Offa's Dyke crossed the Severn. The castle became "Old" Montgomery in 1223 when Henry III began a new and more elaborate castle 1½ miles S.E. of the motte, 300 feet above the plain and in the shadow of the hill-fort of Ffriddfaldwyn (*Cal. Pat. Rolls, 1216–25*, p. 386). The king planned a town alongside the new castle, for in November 1223 he issued a safe conduct to all who would bring victuals for sale to the castle and promised to all who would stay and dwell there the liberties of the borough of Shrewsbury (*ibid*, p. 414). The king himself visited the town at this time, and it was surrounded with an earth and timber wall (A. J. Taylor, "Montgomery Town Wall", *Arch. Camb.*, xcix (1946–47), pp. 281–283, correcting B. H. St. J. O'Neil and A. H. Foster-Smith, *ibid.*, xc (1940), pp. 217–227). Within the walls there was as straight a grid of streets as the slope would allow; the market place (now Broad Street) was towards the southern end of the town and the church at the south-east corner. The site lay in Chirbury parish and there was a consequent dispute with that parish church. From the town graveyard it is only a short distance to the eastern side of the town ditch, and from it a watchman's view of the Long Mountain and the valleys leading towards England.

The borough charter dates from February 1227 (*Cal. Chart. Rolls*, i, p. 10) and was a royal grant based on the liberties of Hereford. Soon after, the borough must have been granted to Hubert de Burgh, earl of Kent, for it was his charter which was confirmed by the king in 1229 (*Cal. Chart. Rolls*, i, pp. 100–101). The burgesses took the town and its markets and fairs at farm for £40 a year; "all merchants shall come safely to the town with their merchandise"; "the constable of the castle shall purchase necessaries by the consent of the townsmen but shall in no way defer payment beyond twenty days".

For rivalry between New Montgomery and other towns in the Severn valley *see* Newtown; Dolforwyn; Welshpool *supra* and *infra*.

The castle was burned by the Welsh in 1231 but regained at the treaty of Woodstock in 1247. After the surrender of Dolforwyn in 1277 Edward I visited Montgomery and in 1279 the palisade which had stood round the town was removed to the castle bailey and a good wall made for the town (A. J. Taylor, *art. cit.*, and *Hist. King's Works*, ii (1963), pp. 739–742).

By 1364–65 the town rents had risen to £21 15s. 11d.; fairs brought in £1 4s. 0d., and the profits of justice £3 18s. 0d.: (SC6/1206/3).

NEWTOWN   Montgomeryshire   sheet 128   32/108918
1280–1321

The full appreciation of the origin of this town necessitates a short account of Dolforwyn, the bastide that Prince Llewelyn was prevented from completing by the English in 1273. Dolforwyn (see also p. 563 above) was planted in Bettws Cedewain parish (32/153951) on a hill overlooking the Severn opposite to a grange of Strata Florida abbey, Abermule (*Mont. Coll.*, xlix (1945), p. 110). At that time the argument was used that a second town in this part of the Severn valley was a threat to New Montgomery, but there must have been second thoughts since in 1280 Edward granted a charter for a market and fair at Llanfair Cedewain near the site of the future Newtown (*Mont. Coll.*, xxviii (1894), pp. 145–164). The chapel of Llanfair stood on the south bank of the Severn, the mother church of Llanllwchaiarn a mile to the east on the opposite bank. On the south bank were the glebe lands and also two mottes, *Gro Tump* opposite Llanllwchaiarn and a second to the west of Llanfair. The position of these older castles suggests that the crossing was of some significance. The new town was focused on the bridge at the north end of its principal street, Broad Street, and the town plan still shows the basic rectilinear grid. The church is now in ruins and has been replaced by a newer church (St. David's) on the south side of the town. The churchyard has the tomb of Robert Owen, who was born here in 1771. It is unlikely that the founder of New Lanark knew that he had been born, and was to die, in a planted town. The first mention of *Nova Villa* as such is said to be 1321 (R. Williams, "Dolforwyn and its Castle", *Arch. Camb.*, 6th ser., i (1901), p. 314). Certainly in 1331 (SC6/1206/2) there is a reference to *nova villa de Kedenwyng* (i.e. Cedewain); in 1364–65 (SC6/1206/3) the borough paid an assized rent of £6 8s. 8d. and the markets and fairs were farmed for £24 a year; the profits of justice in the borough court were £11 13s. 3d. (also C136/20) (1382) where the total value was also c. £41.) There are accounts of the later history of the town by R. Williams in *Mont. Coll.*, xii (1879), pp. 87–108, and xxxii (1902), pp. 175–202; for the street lay-out in 1798 see *ibid.*, lvii (1962), p. 144.

TREFNANT   Montgomeryshire   sheet 117 c. 33/185038
1278

This abortive borough was the intended beneficiary of the removal of the market and fair from Welshpool in 1278, after complaints that Welshpool was damaging the commercial prospects of Montgomery; there was a grant of a burgage in the "new market at Treffnanz" in November 1279 (*Cal. Welsh Rolls*, p. 179) but in 1282 the Trefnant market and fair were revoked by the king on the grounds that Montgomery's allegations had proved unfounded (*Cal. Chart. Rolls*, ii, pp. 211 and 263, and J. C. Davies, *The Welsh Assize Rolls, 1277–84*, (1940), pp. 148 and 235, citing JI/1/1147 and SC6/1152/2). The locale of the grant is disputed by local historians. According to J. C. Davies, *Mont. Coll.*, xlix (1945), p. 133, it was Trefnant in Castle Caereinon (i.e. c. 185038); T. S. Jones and R. Owen (*ibid.*, xxxi (1900), p. 142) placed it in the lower part of Llanerchydol (see also Davies, *op. cit.*, p. 153) near the western end of Welshpool (c. 215075) but this seems a very short distance for the proposed removal to be effective. There were still inhabitants in 1292 (E179/242/52) when eighteen taxpayers paid 37s. 1¼d. Rents of Trefnant "vill" (but only 5s. 6d.) appear in 1332 (SC6/1146/14) in the commote of South Llanerchydol.

WELSHPOOL Montgomeryshire sheet 117 33/224075
1247–52

In 1252 Griffith ap Gwenwynwyn was allowed to move his market at Pool from Fridays to Mondays: this is the first information about the town (*Cal. Close Rolls, 1251–3*, p. 142). In 1278 he was ordered to remove his market and fair from Pool to Trefnant (*q.v.*) and his market was said to be held by the charters of "preceding kings of England" (*Cal. Chart. Rolls*, ii, pp. 211 and 263). The earliest known charter was granted by Griffin (?1263–74) (M. C. Jones, "The Feudal Barons of Powys", *Mont. Coll.*, i (1868), pp. 303–312) and may be connected with a removal of the centre of affairs from the motte and bailey castle (230073) near the Severn, which was dismantled by Prince Llewelyn in 1233, to the present High Street on the edge of the park of Powys Castle. Powys Castle was probably begun c. 1273 (R.C. H.M.W, *Montgomery*, p. 182). If this conjecture is correct there is a parallel to the removal of Old to New Montgomery. The borough of Welshpool (or Middle Pool) is a narrow grid of streets on either side of the High Street. St. Mary's Church, also late thirteenth century, is off the north side of the main street.

At Griffith's death in 1293 Pool was called *villa mercatoria*; the borough rents totalled £12 15s. 7d. (C133/64/16); there were three fairs a year (the third had been added in 1282 (*Cal. Chart. Rolls*, ii, p. 263)) which brought in £6; the weekly markets were worth the same amount; and the brewers' tolls another £6. In 1309 (C134/10/16) there were 173 burgesses; in 1292 (E179/242/52) there were 106 taxpayers in the borough paying £20 15s. in all; in 1322 (SC6/1146/14) there were 225 burgages paying 1s. a year each; fairs were worth £10, markets £6. In 1353 (C135/124/9), 1360 (C135/151/16) and 1374 (C135/237/1) the borough was farmed for £10, the fairs for £10 and the market for £14; the town was revalued by the Exchequer since, by accident or design, the original return only accounted for two of the three fairs. See also M. C. Jones in *Mont. Coll.* vii, xii–xvi, xix, xxi, xxiv and xxix.

PEMBROKESHIRE

Although the most westerly of Welsh counties, Pembrokeshire was early subjected to the English and powerfully influenced by them in its settlement and cultural history. It was through the English king that refugees from Flanders were planted after 1106 but they seem to have been settled in the country villages rather than in towns. The towns are mainly early, although a thirteenth-century bishop of St. David's seems to have imitated his English peers; it was, after all, a bishop of Salisbury who had founded Kidwelly.

HAVERFORD WEST   Pembrokeshire   sheet 138 12/952157
1110–17

The first charter known is that of William Marshall (1189–1219) (*Ballard*, p. xxix), but the town may owe its origin to Gilbert de Clare (1110–17). The urban parish of St. Mary, the church in the middle of the triangular market place, comprises only 30 acres, and its bounds mark out significantly the envelope of burgage plots on either side of the High Street. The continuation of the High Street eastwards to the bridge is a nineteenth-century improvement: the original bridge over the Cleddau was to the north-east of the castle, and at the east end of the borough the main road turned north up Bridge Street to the old bridge. The second large church, St. Thomas, to the south of the borough, was an extra-mural Priory church founded by Robert fitz-Tancred.

There may have been as many as 360 burgages in 1324 (C134/83). By a charter of Edward IV the town was created a county of itself, and later the assizes and quarter sessions for Pembrokeshire were held there, and by the nineteenth century it was virtually the capital of the county.

LLAWHADEN   Pembrokeshire   sheet 138 22/071174
1290–92

The borough of Llawhaden was founded by Bishop Bek of St. David's (1280–93) who also transformed a simple ring motte castle into a great fortified mansion designed to be the bishop's principal country residence. (*Black Book of St. David's*, Cym. Rec. Ser. no. 5 (1902), p. xix). There were burgesses here in 1292 (E179/242/48), and 174½ burgages in 1326. There is no mention of the borough in an extensive charter dealing with the bishop's markets and fairs in 1290 (*Cal. Chart. Rolls*, ii, p. 343).

The original core of the episcopal estate was the church of St. Aeddon which stands away from the village down by the Cleddau (075175). The borough, now only a small village, was planted on the level ground above the river, running westwards from the castle gate; there is a decayed market square.

NARBERTH   Pembrokeshire   sheet 152 22/110145
c. 1150

The evidence for this foundation is slight, but in Samuel Lewis, *Topographical Dictionary of Wales* (1840), ii, *sub. loco.*, it is stated that in the time of William II this place was the head of the lordship of Arnulph de Montgomery and that his follower, Stephen Perrot, built himself a castle to the south of what is now Narberth. The grandson of this Stephen is said to have built the present Narberth Castle and "under the immediate protection of the castle . . . built habitations which formed the origin of the present town". The church is ascribed to the same period. A survey of the Mortimer manor of *Le Neuhous* in 1331 (E142/73) states that there were ten free tenants *ad modum burgenses* holding fourteen burgages and paying 14s. a year rent; the manor, about which nothing else appears, lay in the barony of Llawhaden and the borough may have been at Narberth (or perhaps Llawhaden).

The small town is simply a long broad street with a market place at the castle gate. There is no striking symmetry of plan. (See *Cym. Rec. Ser.*, vii, pt. 2 (1914), pp. 71–115.)

NEW MOAT Pembrokeshire sheet 138 22/064254
by 1219

There is now little to show that this small village was ever a borough. However, the ground between the village and the church has a number of earthworks: on the east of the road are the remains of the motte from which the place is named, a castle of the bishops of St. David's and on both sides of the road some banks and ditches some of which are the remains of a manor house and some (I think) those of burgage plots. There were eighty-nine burgages here in 1326 (*Black Book of St. David's*, Cym. Rec. Ser. v (1902)), and the perimeter bank, which has sometimes been thought Roman, is probably the outer limit of this considerable settlement. A charter of William Marshall, earl of Pembroke (d. 1219), speaks of a burgage here (*Cal. Chart. Rolls*, ii, p. 469). The southern limit of the borough seems to be marked by the church of St. Nicholas, some parts of which are early thirteenth century.

NEWPORT Pembrokeshire sheet 138 22/058390
c. 1197

Kemmes (Cemais) was a Marcher lordship in what is now north Pembrokeshire.

The first Norman lord of Kemmes was Martin (de Tours) and his castle stood just above the village of Nevern (082403). In 1190–95 Martin's son, Robert, built a castle 2 miles to the west, overlooking the estuary of the Nyfer (*Lloyd*, ii, p. 425) and the town was probably founded at the same time. A borough charter of William fitz Martin c. 1197 was confirmed by his son Nicholas c. 1241 (*Baronia de Kemeys* (Cambrian. Arch. Assn. (1862)), pp. 49–51; *Ballard and Tait*, p. xxxi). The church of St. Mary was a contemporary foundation.

The two parallel streets run north from the castle gate, although there are now no houses in the part nearest the sea; the western street seems to have been the market place. The pure rectangularity of the grid has been broken by the modern road from Cardigan to Fishguard which cuts these streets at an angle. Otherwise, the burgage plots are perfectly preserved in outline. It looks as if space was left for eighty. If the burgages were let at the usual shilling, there were forty-six occupied in 1324 (C134/88/18), but another extent shortly after (C134/99) suggests that the 1324 document was an undervaluation of the borough.

The town was taxed as a *burgus* in 1292 (E179/242/48). The author of the *Guide* to St. Mary's church was much puzzled that there were no references to the church before the early thirteenth century; in fact it is not surprising, since there was no town or church before that date.

The eclipse of Newport by Fishguard is said to date from a sixteenth-century pestilence but these myths are not very reliable.

PEMBROKE   Pembrokeshire   sheet 151   12/984014

1110

The confirmatory charter of Henry II (*Ballard*, p. 18) is of a grant made "to the burgesses of Pembroke" by Henry I. It was Henry I who made Gilbert de Clare the first earl of Pembroke in 1110. The earl rebuilt Arnulph de Montgomery's castle of 1093 beginning the great structure which still dominates the western end of the narrow peninsula on which the walled town stood. The town and the castle are a unity in the fashion of Ludlow and Richmond of which they are probably contemporary. The width of the peninsula afforded room only for one long, broad street and for the burgage plots sloping down to the water on either side. The envelope of walls embraced the whole. There were three gates, one at each end of the main street and one on the north leading to the Mill Bridge. The Norman church of St. Mary stands at the corner of Bridge Street. At its east end, the main street broadens and there is a strip of buildings encroaching.

In the early fourteenth century there were between 200 and 227½ burgages in the town (C134/4; C134/83; C135/91–2; SC6/1208/5 m. 12), and this number conforms approximately with the vestigial bounds of burgages visible on the 6 inch O.S. plan.

TEMPLETON   Pembrokeshire   sheet 152   22/113115

by 1283

This is a very regular street-village with long plots behind each house but it is not called a borough in W. Rees, "Bibliography . . ." (*Bull. B. C. S.*, ii (1925), pp. 321–382). Yet there were "burgesses of the wind" recorded here in 1283 (C133/32/7) and also in later accounts: "A Calendar of the Public Records relating to Pembrokeshire", *Cym. Rec. Ser.*, vii, pt. 2 (1914), p. 95. The village is in Narberth parish (*q.v.*) and from its name may have been a manor of the Knights Templar. No reference has been found to it in the Templars' Inquest nor in the great French cartulary of their possessions.

TENBY   Pembrokeshire   sheet 152   22/134004

early 12th century

This compact walled town with its castle on the headland still retains much of its original walls, with corner towers and a western gate; and within the walls the narrow streets have not been too transformed by the popularity of the town as a seaside resort. The town has several times been attacked and despoiled since its foundation and the walls have been more than once restored, and they probably antedate the first murage grant of 1328 (*Cal. Pat. Rolls, 1327–30*, p. 248). The number of burgages is recorded as 247 in 1307 (C134/4/1); 220 in 1324 (C134/3) and 252 in 1348 (C135/9/1). These burgages were packed tight along the narrow streets. The falling contours allow only Frog Street to run exactly parallel to the long side of the town wall; High Street forks at the Church and market place, with one street keeping high and the other dropping to the castle on the headland; and there is a third line of streets at the cliff edge which follows its curves.

There is no documentation of the origins of this town, but the Elizabethan antiquary, George Owen, preserved the plausible tradition that the town was contemporary with Haverford West and Pembroke, created by the Norman earls. There was a Welsh stronghold here before the Conquest and possibly a fishing village (*Lloyd*, ii, p. 265). "The street plan of the medieval town within the Town Wall suggests the typical plantation . . . but the beginnings of the town can be seen before . . . 1093." W. G. Thomas, "Tenby", *Arch. J.*, cxix (1962), pp. 316–318 and 324, with plan.)

WISTON   Pembrokeshire   sheet 138   22/021180
1135

This small group of farms was once a borough, although by prescription only, there being no charter. It was probably, therefore, a creation of the Norman or Flemish possessor who built the castle (before 1135). The church of St. Mary is of that period also.

RADNORSHIRE

Like Montgomeryshire this county was named by Henry VIII after a planted town of the thirteenth century that had a Norman predecessor. The plantations at Cefnllys and Painscastle date (like New Montgomery) from Henry III's Border warfare; the others seem belated and minor foundations of the late thirteenth century.

CEFNLLYS   Radnorshire   sheet 128   32/088613
1240–46

Two miles east of the modern town of Llandrindod Wells the river Ithon makes a great sweep around the 1,000 foot high hill on which the Mortimers' castle of Cefnllys was built between 1240 and 1246. The site is now remarkably isolated. The hilltop is covered with the massive earthworks of the castle of which no stonework remains above ground. One of the first documents to afford any detail is the survey of 1304 (C133/114/8 m. 14) when there was a watermill on the Ithon and twenty-five tenants in the vill of *Keventhlis*. These probably correspond to the twenty burgesses of 1332 (C135/29/5); the place was also called a borough in the survey of 1360 (C135/154). In 1383 ten decayed burgages are referred to as "Stakeburgeis" (SC6/1209/14) but 48s. 6d. was paid in rents of other property in Cefnllys.

Since one of the tolls of 1304 was called pontage, it is likely that there was a bridge across the Ithon here, probably at what the map now calls "Shaky Bridge". Tracks lead south and west from this point. An older crossing may have been at "Alpine Bridge" 2 miles further north, for a motte, the predecessor of the Mortimer castle, guards this point.

The location of the borough is still uncertain. There is ample room on top of the hill within the outer defences but there is a church in the meadows by the bridge. Since the hill has a long broad back on the north-east side, it would not be as difficult to reach the hilltop as at some of the isolated hilltops where boroughs were attempted and failed, despite the castle's protection. The traditional place for the borough courts is at the farm *Neuadd*, just below the castle on this north eastern side, from which a track leads to the hill-top. On the fortified hill-top there is a flat central area in which the foundations of rectangular buildings can be discerned. Only excavation of these will show whether these are burgages or military buildings. The whole site has affinities with Bere, Dolforwyn, Deganwy and Painscastle, *q.v.*

KNIGHTON   Radnorshire   sheet 129   32/285724
by 1260

Knighton has only slight claims to be considered a planted town; the evidence from Domesday Book shows a waste manor of five hides. Bryn y Castell, a quarter of a mile east of the town, is a Norman motte which has been superseded by a more elaborate castle which stands at the opposite end of the town to the church. The earthworks of Offa's Dyke lie only a few hundred yards to the west of the castle site.

The church and castle and town seem to be all of a piece, but not—due to uneven ground—a completely formal and rectangular piece. This town had 126 burgesses holding 162½ burgages in 1304 (C133/114/8 m. 13); seventy-one taxpayers were recorded in 1292 (E179/242/57) and later accounts of 1361 and 1383 (SC6/1209/4 and 14) confirm that the town was a borough, although no charter has survived. There was a murage grant in 1260 (*Cal. Pat. Rolls, 1258–66*, p. 67).

Development of the same kind but on a much less successful scale may also have occurred at Knucklas castle (250745) (also built in the 1240's) which had burgages recorded in 1649 (*Arch. Camb.*, 5th ser., xvii (1900), p. 17) although only called a *vill* in medieval documents. Norton (305674) was separately assessed for taxation purposes in the same way as Knighton in 1292 (E179/242/57) when forty-seven paid. A separate jury was sworn for Norton (E179/242/48), a distinction usually reserved for castle-towns and boroughs; there was a castle there in 1191 (*R.C.H.M.W. Radnors.*, p. 132).

PAINSCASTLE   Radnorshire   sheet 141   32/167464
1231

In 1191 William de Braose rebuilt the early twelfth-century castle of Pain fitz John (d. 1137). This castle was defended by his wife Matilda in a siege of 1195 and was often known as *Castrum Matildae* (*Lloyd*, ii, p. 586).

The early name of the town was also *Castrum Matildae*. Henry III was here in July, August and September 1231 with the army while the great earthworks of a larger, stone castle were being thrown up at this strategic point in Llanbedr parish (*Cal. Chart. Rolls*, i, pp. 138–140). The foundation of the town, if it accompanied Henry III's work on the castle, is of the same period as the town of New Montgomery and of the borough of Deganwy. Nothing now remains above ground of the stone-work of the castle, but the building is well documented in royal letters of the period. A civil settlement here is suggested by an order of 1233 concerning "houses" in the vill of Castrum Matildae and by 1264 (C132/31) there were tolls from markets and fairs here. Burgesses are not specifically mentioned until 1309 (C134/15/3) when there were fifty, each paying 1s., as well as 146 free tenants (who need not all have been living by the castle). Similar figures were given in 1337 (C135/50/23) when it was stated that these tenants held 4,040 acres of land.

Its streets are quite shapeless, and burgage plots cannot be detected in modern hedge-lines. It is possible that the borough lay within the castle but the numbers recorded above make it unlikely.

RADNOR, NEW   Radnorshire   sheet 128   32/212609
1257

The "New" in its name and its grid-plan both witness to the origin of this town. Speed's plan of 1610 shows it as already considerably shrunken with many empty building plots within the area of the walled town. "The ruines of the old wall", which Speed saw, can still be discerned in the fields to the south and west of the town. There were gates on the west, south and east. The hill slopes to the north of the town carried the parish church and the castle, which the walls linked to the town in the fashion of Montgomery or Ludlow.

Old Radnor, like Old Montgomery, had much less substantial defences. The motte of *Castle Nimble* (248595) is probably the castle of Old Radnor, now simply a small group of houses near the church on the hillside above the motte. (The so-called "Castle" adjoining the church is in an improbable position for defence and seems to be the moated site of a domestic building, perhaps the Rectory.)

It is not certain when the move from Old Radnor to New Radnor took place; the new town had its church by 1291; it obtained a charter for a fair in 1306 (*Cal. Chart. Rolls.*, iii, p. 68) and the church is said to have been thirteenth-century work before its rebuilding in 1862 (*R.C.H.M.W., Radnors.*, pp. 129–134).

There is no surviving medieval borough charter: the original was said to have been destroyed in 1401 during Owen Glendower's rebellion, and a new charter was issued in 1562. Mr. E. J. Cole has kindly drawn attention to a document (no. 1513) in the capitular archives at Hereford cited below under *Radnor, Old.* In 1235 when the earl of Pembroke was granted custody of the de Breos lands they included the castle of Radnor and "the town of the castle" (*Cal. Chart. Rolls*, i, p. 192). It may not seem likely that such a phrase could have been used of Old Radnor.

The earliest known grant of murage, however, is 1257 when Roger Mortimer was allowed to take tolls to help to finance the enclosing of the town, and it is probably this document which has caused historians to place the foundation of New Radnor in the mid-thirteenth century.

The earliest information about the number of burgesses is in a 1301 survey (C133/101/6) when there were ninety-seven burgesses each paying 2s. a year rent; another of 1304 (C133/114/8) counted 262½ burgages, held by 189 tenants, but the total may include those 182 tenants in the out-parish (Radnor Foreign) who were separately counted in 1301. The total sum of 1304 (£14 2s. 7d.) is insufficient to give 262½ two-shilling rents. Some of these "foreigners" may have been burgesses of the wind (see p. 65) such as existed at Radnor in 1334 (SC6/1209/4). A long tax list of 1292 has 220 names under *Radnor* but it is very likely that this included the foreignry (E179/242/57) since the list of taxors (E179/242/48) has one group for the "Vill" and another for the "Valley". The tax list itself is broken up by paragraph signs and incidental arithmetical sums, which may indicate the different areas reckoned as "Radnor".

The foreignry, the rural area dependent on Old Radnor, was as valuable to the lord as the new town in 1336 (C135/45/21).

In 1360 and 1361 (C135/154; SC6/1236/3) the burgage rents and the tolls of fairs and markets were worth just over £13 to the lord.

RADNOR, OLD   Radnorshire   sheet 128   32/249590
1095–1100

Philip de Breos (Braose) succeeded his father as lord of Radnor in 1094 or 1095 and with only a short intermission held these lands until at least 1135 (*Lloyd*, ii, pp. 402–403 and 436). This Philip is usually thought to be the Philip who granted a burgage in Radnor to Gloucester abbey (*Cart. Glouc.* (Rolls Series) i, p. 110, and ii, p. 103; also Dean and Chapter archives, Hereford, no. 1513). Mr. E. J. Cole, to whom I owe the Hereford reference, tells me that this document is there ascribed to the late twelfth century. The Gloucester cartulary has merely a note of the grant: the Hereford document states that the grant was witnessed in the presence of Philip's wife, his knights and "many burgesses of that town", thirteen of whom are named; others were too numerous to name: *pluribus aliis quos enumerare longum est*. Whatever the date of this grant, it shows that Radnor was then a substantial place, but there is, of course, no reason why it should not refer to New Radnor and bring that borough forward from the vague mid-thirteenth century date usually ascribed to it. Mr. F. Noble, to whom I am indebted for discussion of mid-Welsh boroughs, takes the view that the minor earthworks at Old Radnor (like those at Old Montgomery) are too small to encompass baronial castles such as the contemporary works at Chepstow, Monmouth, Ludlow and Clun would lead one to expect. It follows from this view that "New" Radnor and "New" Montgomery were thirteenth-century rebuildings and extensions of Norman sites.

RHAYADER   Radnorshire   sheet 128   22/970680
?1304–60

The little town of Rhayader has every appearance of being planted. Its four streets cross at right angles and the burgage plots have an outer boundary which looks very much like a town ditch or wall.

The town is on the east bank of the Wye and adjoining what the survey of 1304 (C133/114/8) described as "the site of the ancient castle", possibly that begun in 1178. Until 1735 the town lay in the parish of Nantmel whose church is 5 miles to the east; the borough area is a small enclave in this parish; the town church of St. Clement is modern. On the opposite bank of the river is the much older church of St. Bridget at Cwmdeuddwr, a grange of Strata Florida abbey, given to it in 1184. In 1304 Rhayader was called simply a "vill" and the same word is used in the survey of 1360 (C135/154), but the accounts of 1360–61 and 1371–72 (SC6/1209/4 and 12) show that the rents came *de burgo*; there were markets and a fair here also in 1360 (SC6/1236/3); see also *Mont. Coll.*, xxx (1898), p. 211.

APPENDIX

In Gascony the English crown acquired and gave further privileges to towns that had been already founded by French kings and French seigneurs. The habit of town foundation among the Welsh princes and lords was less well developed, but Carnarvon, Welshpool and Beaumaris show that burghal institutions did exist independently of the English although there seems to have been no continuity of institutions in these particular cases. At Nevin and Pwllheli (Carnarvonshire) the Black Prince granted borough charters in 1355, but there was already a Welsh *burgus* in each place in 1284: there were twenty burgages in Welsh Pwllheli and about fifty in Nevin where there was a market, a port and a herring fishery (E. A. Lewis, *Medieval Boroughs of Snowdonia* (1912), pp. 9 and 56–57). There is little or no evidence to show whether these native Welsh boroughs were planted in any sense. It would be natural to expect their burgesses to be enfranchised tenantry of the *maenor* living near the lord's *llys* (that is, Hall) and the *maerdref* vill, in the same way that burgesses appeared in places like Abergele, Llanrwst and the Welsh predecessor of Denbigh. A grid plan of streets would be some evidence for a plantation.

There is another view: that town life was so alien to the traditional pattern of Welsh rural economy that every town must have been consciously contrived, rather as the lords of Powys imitated Henry III and Edward I in their boroughs of Machynlleth, Llanidloes and Caersws. If this view were accepted, one would need to add other places in medieval Wales where burgages appear. These include, besides Old Carnarvon (and perhaps Aberconway):

Abergele	(Denbighshire)
Cilgerran	(Pembrokeshire)
Hope	(Flintshire)
Llanrwst	(Denbighshire)
Presteign	(Radnorshire)
St. Clears	(Carmarthenshire)
Towyn	(Merionethshire)
Trevilan	(Cardiganshire)

For further information about these towns (and also Dinas Mawddwy, Fishguard and Machynlleth) see William Rees' bibliography in *Bull. B.C.S.*, ii (1925), pp. 321–382. H. Carter, *The Towns of Wales* (1965) should also be consulted.

CHAPTER SEVENTEEN

Gazetteer: Gascony

Note

THE entries in this Gazetteer are arranged alphabetically within modern Departments: a single alphabetical index of names giving cross-references to Departments will be found below.

For each place the figures on the right-hand side of the first line give the sheets of the Michelin Map (M) and the Carte Majeure (C) on which the town (or its site) appears. The reference to *Gouron* is to the number of an entry, not to the page. The date on the left-hand side is that of the foundation. References in the last line for each place are to the air photographs (A.P.) in the French national collection. All other abbreviations are identical with those employed in footnotes and listed on pp. xvii to xx. Topographical description and comments are on the basis of visits to Gascony during 1956, 1957, 1958, 1960 and 1962. Acts of foundation and charters can be located by the source-references, *Gouron, Testut, Vigié, G.C., R.F., R.G.* etc.

Alphabetical Index to Gascon Gazetteer

Name	*Department*
BETBEZER	Landes
BONNEGARDE EN CHALOSSE	Landes
BOULOGNE (St. Pé-St. Simon)	Lot et Garonne
BREUIL (Brolium Balengarii) (See Le Temple)	
BURGUS REGINAE	Gironde
CADILLAC	Gironde
CAMPARIAN	Gironde
CASTELNAU SUR GUPIE	Lot et Garonne
CASTELRÉAL	Dordogne
CASTELSAGRAT	Tarn et Garonne
CASTETCRABE	Landes
CASTILLONNÈS	Lot et Garonne
CAZALS	Lot
CORNEILLAS	Tarn et Garonne
CRÉON I	Gironde
CRÉON II	Landes
CUSSAC	Gironde
DAMAZAN	Lot et Garonne
DOMME	Dordogne
DONZAC	Tarn et Garonne
DUIRE	Gironde
DUNES	Tarn et Garonne
DURANCE	Lot et Garonne
FLEURANCE	Gers
FONFRÈDE	Landes
FONROQUE	Dordogne
FOURCÈS	Gers
FOURQUES	Lot et Garonne
GEAUNE EN TURSAN	Landes
GRANGES SUR LOT	Lot et Garonne
HASTINGUES	Landes
LA BASTIDE CASTELAMOUROUX	Lot et Garonne
LA BASTIDE CHALOSSE	Landes
LA BASTIDE D'ARMAGNAC	Landes
LA BASTIDE MONESTIER (Villefranche)	Dordogne
LA BASTIDE (MONPAZIER)	Landes
LA BASTIDE MURAT	Lot

Name	Department
LABOUHEYRE (near)	Landes
LACENNE	Lot et Garonne
LADOS	Gironde
LAGRUÈRE	Lot et Garonne
LALINDE	Dordogne
LA MONTJOIE ST. LOUIS	Lot et Garonne
LA PARADE	Lot et Garonne
LARÉE	Gers
LARROQUE	Gers
LE TEMPLE DE BREUIL (FELTON)	Lot et Garonne
LEVIGNAC	Lot et Garonne
LIAS	Gers
LIBOS	Lot et Garonne
LIBOURNE	Gironde
LONDRES (ST. ETIENNE)	Lot et Garonne
MARMANDE	Lot et Garonne
MAUVEZIN D'ARMAGNAC	Landes
MAUVEZIN SUR GUPIE (or d'Agenais) (near)	Lot et Garonne
MIRAMONT	Lot et Garonne
MOLIÈRES	Dordogne
MONCLAR	Gers
MONCLAR D'AGENAIS	Lot et Garonne
MONFLANQUIN	Lot et Garonne
MONGUILHEM	Gers
MONPAZIER	Dordogne
MONSÉGUR	Gironde
MONTBRUN	Gironde
MONTEGUT	Landes
MONTFAUCON DU LOT	Lot
MONTJOI	Tarn et Garonne
MONTPOUILLON	Lot et Garonne
MONTRÉAL	Lot et Garonne
MONTRÉAL DU GERS	Gers
NERBIS	Landes
NICOLE	Lot et Garonne
OZOURT	Landes
PELLEGRUE	Gironde

Name	*Department*
PIMBO	Landes
POLINGES	Landes
PORT DE LANNE	Landes
POURIET (Arbanats)	Gironde
PUGPITO	Dordogne
PUYMIROL	Lot et Garonne
REGALIS MONS (RIVES)	Lot et Garonne
REJAUMONT	Gers
RONDEBOEUF	Landes
ROQUEPINE	Dordogne
ROVIGNA	Lot et Garonne
ST. BARTÉLEMY DE BELLE-GARDE	Dordogne
ST. CLAR	Gers
ST. EDOUARD (BAIGTS)	Landes
STE. EULALIE (PUYGUILHEM)	Dordogne
STE. FOY LA GRANDE	Gironde
ST. GEIN EN MARSAN	Landes
STE. GEMME	Lot et Garonne
ST. JEAN DE CARIET	Lot et Garonne
ST. JULIEN DE COLORBISSE	Lot et Garonne
ST. JUSTIN	Landes
STE. MAURE DE PEYRIAC	Lot et Garonne
ST. MAURICE	Landes
ST. OSBERT	Gironde
ST. PASTOUR	Lot et Garonne
STE. QUITTERIE (Mas d'Aire)	Landes
ST. SARDOS	Lot et Garonne
ST. SAUVEUR DE MEILHAN	Lot et Garonne
SALESPISSE	Landes
SARRON	Landes
SAUVETERRE DE GUYENNE	Gironde
SORDE L'ABBAYE	Landes
SOUPROSSE	Landes
TOULOUZETTE	Landes
VACCA FERRA	?Dordogne
VALENCE D'AGEN	Tarn et Garonne
VALENCE SUR BAÏSE	Gers

Name	*Department*
VIANNE	Lot et Garonne
VILLEFRANCHE DE LONGCHAPT	Dordogne
(LOUCHAPT)	
VILLEFRANCHE DE QUEYRAN	Lot et Garonne
VILLEFRANCHE DU PÉRIGORD	Dordogne
(or DE BELVÈS)	
VILLENAVE	Landes
VILLENEUVE SUR LOT	Lot et Garonne
VILLERÉAL	Lot et Garonne

DEPARTMENT OF DORDOGNE

This modern Department corresponds almost exactly with the former county of Périgord. The progress of bastides within it has been discussed in detail by Testut and Vigié. The whole of Périgord was not reunited to English Gascony after the treaty of 1259 and the "process of Périgueux" occupied the Parlement of Paris in 1310–11. French bastides are found within southern Périgord at Domme and Vergt, in addition to Alphonsian bastides near the border of the Agenais. In north-western Périgord there were French plantations at Lisle, Bénévent, Montignac and Villefranche St. Louis (*Testut*, pp. 33–60). Eymet, founded on the frontier of the Agenais by Alphonse de Poitiers in 1270 did not form part of the transfer of 1279, being then reckoned in Périgord; the connection with the English is not well documented (*G.C.* 1274; *Testut*, p. 38) and its privileges were confirmed by the king of France when the English were driven from this part of Gascony in 1295.

BEAULIEU (Pertus)   M:79   C:193NW
by 1284   Not in *Gouron*, but see *R.G.*, ii, 802;
                          Testut, pp. 32–33; *Vigié*, p. 153

This bastide, together with five others, was farmed out by the king in July 1284 to Henry le Waleys for ten years. The site was in the honour of the castle of Puyguilhem, which eliminates Beaulieu-Annesse as a possible site. Vigié assigns *Bellus Locus* to the parish of Pertus or Perthus near Sigoulès (G.R. 44702736); and places near Sigoulès occur in *R.G.*, ii, 1719, which concerns a bastide of *Bellus Locus* alias *Novus Locus*.

This small and scattered village has no signs of regular streets nor of adjoining earthworks. No villager had heard of any field or hill-name which resembled Beaulieu, etc. The site shows no particular value for strategic purposes.

BEAUMONT DU PÉRIGORD   M:79   C:193NE
1272

A full account of the origins of this town is given above, pp. 30–34. Its grid within the walls is complete and the town is fully described in L. Testut, *La Bastide de Beaumont en Périgord, 1272–1789* (1920).

A. P. Mission Podensac/Belvès, 1950, no. 437.

BEAUREGARD   M:75   C:182NW
1286   Not in *Gouron*, but see *Testut*, p. 34,
                                      and *R.G.*, ii, 1557 and 1664; *G.C.*, 1779

The bastide was founded by Jean de Grilly as seneschal (*Vigié*, p. 65) and the king granted customs to the town in November 1286. Three years later Edward was receiving complaints from the lord of Grignols, 15 kilometres to the north-west, that his liegemen had absconded to the new bastide, and in the same year the lord of Montclar, to the south of Beauregard, complained that the bastides of Beauregard and Molières had been taking in his villeins and asked for help in expelling them from the new towns.

There is a plan of the town in *Lavedan*, fig. 198; *Testut*, p. 34, says that it could never have been very large. *Deffontaines*, p. 156, classes it as "scarcely existing", but this is a little severe. The village has a church, a chateau (now a children's holiday centre), a shop and perhaps a dozen houses. The Halle, retaining its original stone pillars, has been re-roofed and houses the machinery of one farmer. The place is grass-grown, but most striking are the rectilinear hollow ways to the east and south-east of the church. These may be the ruins called "Las Bastides" mentioned in A. de Gourgues, *Dictionnaire Topographique du Département de Dordogne* (1861), p. 16. The town must have been about twice the length of the present village, extending along a narrow ridge and falling to the north and south. On the west the ground also falls rather steeply, and down the slope runs a track which is worn down to the bare rock. This lane is still known as the Rue des Anglais. There is still a good deal of uncleared forest on three sides of the village, and the bastide marked the limit of English bastide building between the Dordogne and Périgueux.

A.P. Mission Ste. Foy la Grande/Le Bugue, 1950, no. 41.

CASTELRÉAL   M:75   C:182SE
1267   Not in *Gouron*; Testut, p. 35; *Vigié*,
                                       pp. 338–340.

In 1268 the king of France ordered the English to cease the work they had begun on this bastide. The abbot of Sarlat had complained of the injury to his interests. A plea of 1280 calls it a *castrum* only, but suggests that the English were still building. Shortly after, it was abandoned—probably at the time when resources were diverted to the building of Beaumont (1272).

The choice of site is similar to that of Domme, the bastide founded 12 miles up-river by Philippe le Hardi: there is a cliff-like descent to the floor of the Dordogne on the north side, and the steep-sided valley of a small tributary gives almost as steep descents on the short western end of the plateau and on the long south flank (49042815). There are ruins of a considerable tower and supporting walls at the west, and clear signs that the hill-top has been levelled and the defensive faces steepened. Terrace-roads give access, and there is a well near the centre of the site. The hill-top is still locally known as Castelréal and the local peasants had heard the legend of the English town. The narrowness of the plateau suggests that the scale of building would have had to be more modest than at Domme: perhaps one street wide, terminating at the castle and about 300 yards in length.

DOMME   M:75   C:194NW

1281   *Testut*: pp. 35–37

The higher ground on the south of the Dordogne is dissected by the deep valleys of minor streams, and between these Nature has often provided ideal sites for bastides, with steep slopes on three, and sometimes four, sides of level hill-tops. Such a magnificent site is Domme. In 1280–81 the king of France's seneschal was engaged in buying out for £200 sterling the local seigneur who had a few houses and land at Mont-de-Domme, the east end of the present town. The new foundation on the frontier of Quercy was something of a riposte to the local English foundations and the cession to Edward of the Alphonsian bastides by the Treaty of Amiens in 1279. The site was slow to be peopled, and in 1308 Philippe le Bel fined the plot-holders for their tardiness. Two years later the town was seized by Edward II in whose eyes the sale of 1280–81 was a breach of the treaty of 1259. In subsequent campaigns the town changed hands several times, and became permanently French only in 1438. (*Congrès Archéologique*, xc (1927), pp. 250–260.) There is a plan of the town in *Lavedan*, fig. 262.

Domme is equalled only by Beaumont in having walls, gates and streets virtually unaltered, and it surpasses Beaumont in the magnificent views in all directions, especially from the ramparts above the Dordogne. In a prophetic footnote (p. 37) Testut hoped that a little tourism might restore the fortunes of the isolated town, and there are signs that the quality of the town is being more widely appreciated.

The architects of the town had to cope with a site which narrowed considerably towards the west, and here—almost vertically above the riverside village of Cénac—the castle was built. It is now in ruins, but (by trespassing) it is possible to pass up through the concentric rings of walls, along terraces and up slipways until the summit is reached. There are a number of cave cellars and a well, all of it much over-grown.

The castle is enclosed within the same ramparts as the town, but gardens and or-chards separate the two. The bastide consists of a level portion to the north, with the church and Place, continuing downhill southwards to a second, less regular, Place (*de la Rode*) and to the three gates. The rectangular grid is preserved as far as possible in the descent but has to make occasional concessions. An inner road links the gates by following the foot of the wall.

The three gates (*del Bos, de la Caube* and *des Tours*) are well preserved, and from them the approach roads wind their way down to the valley. Inside the town, the *Halle* has been reconstructed over the entrances to the limestone grottoes. Opposite it are the church and the Governor's House; there are no *cornières*. Other buildings dating from the early days of the town are the Moneyer's House and the former *Hotel de Ville*.

The streets are of varying width. A broad street approaches the Place from the main gate but the grid is divided by much smaller passages, one of which has been blocked and converted into a private garage, another bridged over by an extension to a house, and another roofed over with vines. The inner road between the gates is grass-grown, and even when the coaches have unloaded their tourists it is isolated and private.

A.P. Mission Gourdon/La Capelle, 1948, no. 417.

FONROQUE   M:75   C:193NW
by 1284   *Testut*, p. 38: *Vigié*, p. 342

The bastide's early documentation is poor: a letter of 1284 records that the town had been let to farm for ten years to Henry le Waleys; and it is mentioned again in a survey of Périgord in 1364.

The town plan is shown in *Lavedan*, fig. 168 (c. 1830). It lies on the main road from Mont de Marsan to Périgueux and has lost any historical character.

A.P. Mission Podensac/Belvès, 1950, no. 303.

LA BASTIDE MONESTIER (Villefranche)   M:79   C:193NW
by 1284   *Testut*: pp. 53–54

The bastide of Villefranche is mentioned in the same document (of 1284) as the bastides of Ste. Eulalie, Fonroque and Beaulieu. In the hearth-tax of 1365 (*Vigié* pp. 342–343) is the entry: "43½ hearths in the bastide of Villefranche in Lenvila parish". Lenville is shown on maps of 1624 and 1740 as in Monestier, on the Lestignac (44562758) side. There is a small village called La Bastide, a mile west of Monestier and this probably represents the remains of the bastide. It has a central grass square and a decayed grid-pattern of paths and lanes. On the south-east of the square is a small parish church. There is one surviving *cornière*. There are considerably fewer than 43 hearths today.

LALINDE   M:75   C:182SE
1267   *Testut*, pp. 38–9

This early bastide stands on the north bank of the Dordogne and is now flanked by the Dordogne canal. The town was named after the royal officer, Jean de la Linde, who negotiated the foundation. Henry's charter of June 1267 was confirmed by Edward I in 1286.

Further public works were carried out here in 1289 when Bertrand Panissals contracted to build a bridge and a stone dam behind which there would be a fishery, and the waters of which would drive two mills.

The town has a well-preserved grid-plan, although some of the plots occupied in 1824, when the plan in *Lavedan* (Fig. 226) was drawn, are now empty. There do not seem to have been walls: there was a ditch on the east side of the town, and during the Hundred Years War a fortified brick gateway was built and still remains. The church is exterior to the town near the bridge-head, and this may indicate that there was an older settlement which was removed when the town was founded. A document of 1293 (*R.G.*, iii, 2135) shows that the rector was one of those who provided land for the town. See also L'Abbé Goustat, *Histoire de Lalinde*.

A.P. Mission Ste. Foy La Grande/Le Bugue, 1950, no. 327.

LE FLEIX   M:75   C:181SE
by 1315

R.G., iv, 1319 (March 1315) has reference to the defences of Gurçon (a castle near Villefranche de Longchapt) and a bastide, *Deu Fleys*, belonging to the widow of Jordain de L'Isle; see also *R.G.*, iv, 1800, of May 1317. La Fleix is a village on the north bank of the Dordogne, near Ste. Foy la Grande, that does not have any significant shape. The archivist of the Dordogne tells me that there is no other tradition of a bastide here. *R.F.*, 242 (1274), mentions the parish but no bastide.

A.P. Mission Libourne/Le Bugue, 1959, no. 104.

MOLIÈRES   M:75   C:182SE, 193NW
1278–84   *Vigié*, p. 321; *Testut*, pp. 40–42

The town was founded by Jean de Grilly, but there was probably already a small village. The church of St. John was parochial in 1115, and the bastide was sometimes known as "St. Jean de Molières". The charter of privileges dates from 1286, and in 1289 there were complaints to Edward I that the villeins of Montclar, north of Lalinde, were fleeing to the new town and being accepted there.

The bastide is one of the few to incorporate a castle, but it may post-date the foundation: work on it probably dates from 1316–20. In July 1320 it is described in the Gascon Roll as "lately begun", two years earlier the townspeople were concerned about the effect of the new tower on the fees of the custodian of the "old tower", probably the gateway which still stands over the south entrance to the village, (C61/32 mm. 10 and 14d).

The sadly decayed town is full of character: there is only one *cornière*, that of a house on the south-east side of the grass-grown square; the church is impressively towered, with a briar and weeds growing out of the bell-tower; the castle has gone, but its railed and padlocked site can be seen on the north where the gardens merge imperceptibly into the vineyards. Yet in 1365, after war and plague, there were still 172 houses.

There is a plan in *Lavedan*, Fig. 241, dated 1841: but several plots have lost their houses since then, and the plan makes the church only half its correct size. It omits the gate-tower on the south side of the bastide.

A.P. Mission Ste. Foy-la-Grande/Le Bugue, 1950, no. 360.

583

MONPAZIER   M:79   C:193NE

1285   *Testut*: pp. 42–45

This remarkable bastide is perhaps the best known of all in France to English readers
through the many reproductions of its street-plan, so geometrical as at first to mock
credulity (*Lavedan*, Fig. 119).   Now that the walls have been pulled down, the town
does not show the visitor the harshest rectangularity as he approaches, but once inside
(through one of three gates) the street pattern and the position of the houses within
the plots display the acme of geometrical planning.   The market place has a full
complement of *cornières*, through whose arches all through-traffic must pass, and to the
north-east of the Place is half an *ilôt* given over to the magnificent church and its
graveyard (formerly on the north side).

In view of the rigidity of the plan it is interesting to see that there was some difficulty in persuading settlers to take up their pigeon holes.   In 1289 Edward I threatened burgesses who had not occupied their plots with a penalty of £10, the fines to be
used for two public works of rather contrasting character: "for the fortification of the
said bastide or for the construction of a church at the said place" (*R.G.*, ii, no. 1403).
The church had in fact been commenced in 1286.

Jean de Grilly was again the king's agent in negotiating the *paréage* with Pierre
de Gontaud, lord of Biron.   The site was an empty hill-top overlooking the upper
Dropt, here only a small stream.   Apart from the military value of a fortified town
so far east, the project envisaged colonisation of the surrounding forest by the townspeople (see also *Pugpito*, below).   A good deal of woodland has been cleared but there
is sufficient forest along all the approaching roads still to give the town its medieval
setting.   It is one of the half-dozen bastides most worth seeing, but visitors should be
warned that the hotel accommodation does not match the town's fame, and when the
few available beds are full the next town is 10 miles away and no evening transport.
Teste me ipso.

A.P. Mission Podensac/Belvès, 1950, no. 274.

PUGPITO   M:75   C:193NE

1274   *Testut*: pp. 45–50

Our knowledge of this bastide derives from a claim of 1289 made by one of the parties
to an earlier *paréage* with Edward I.   The project had been abandoned because the
need had been met by the establishment of Monpazier.   The claim was made by
Peter de Machmon, who said that he had given a hill-top between Monpazier and
Rives to the reeve of Beaumont *ad faciendam bastidam*.   The seneschal of Périgord was
now ordered by Edward to return the land if enquiry truly found that the land had
been given on this condition and that no bastide was now projected.   The hill-top
was named *Pugpito* (*R.G.*, ii, 1643) and it has been suggested by M. G. Lavergne
(*Bull. de la Soc. Hist. et Arch. de Périgord*, liv (1927), pp. 265–267) that this is a scribe's
error for *Pugpico*, the "t" and "c" being very similarly formed.   In *Pugpico* M.
Lavergne saw the vernacular for the Latin *Podium de pico* (hill of Pico), and then
recalled that an earlier document (*R.F.*, 474) had dealt with an abortive bastide at
lo puoch apelat vulgarement lo puoch de Pico.   He concluded that the two documents, one

of 1274 and one of 1289, dealt with the same place, and the case is strengthened by noting that the *paréage* of 1274 was concluded by Peter de Machinon and his brother. The *Machinon* of 1274 is probably the *Machmon* of 1289.

The *paréage*, which is written in Gascon, is an interesting document. The two brothers made over to the king the hill-top "between the river Dropt and the frontier, in the diocese of Périgueux to make a bastide and an enpeoplement (*bastida e poblacio*)". Within it they were to have two building plots for themselves. The contract was witnessed by officials from Beaumont, Naussanes and Ste. Croix and drawn up by Hugo de Agia, notary of Beaumont, a town then only two years old.

The site has not previously been identified but I believe that it lay at G.R.:48112648 near the farm called Pey Picou. The *paréage* of 1274 and the claim of 1289 impose four conditions. The site must be (a) between the Dropt and the frontier; the frontier (the present Department boundary) passes along the stream at the foot of the scarp on which the farm stands; (b) between Monpazier and Rives; the site lies exactly on a straight line joining the two places; (c) in the diocese of Périgueux; the site is in the Department of Dordogne and before the creation of the bishopric of Sarlat in 1318 it lay in the correct diocese; (d) in the parish of "St. Sevi". The last condition presents the only difficulty, for there is no modern parish of that name. Ste. Sabine is too far to the west for Bémont's suggestion to be acceptable. The suggested site lies in St. Cassien parish: might not the *S. Sevi* of 1274 be a scribe's misreading of the second half of (*Cas*)*siani*?

There is a considerable flat area above the scarp near the farm which would have been available for the town, and the curving scarp gives protection on two sides. No sign of buildings or earthworks could be found in the cultivated clearings, but in the thick woods N.W. of the farm are the overgrown remains of a circular tower and accompanying buildings which give support to the military strength of this frontier site.

M. Lavergne's suggestion of Pépicou (48072628) fulfils some of the conditions but is in Parraquet parish; Bémont's Peybeton at 47572688 is too far away and Vigié's Pebeton at 47702634 is not a commanding site. Testut placed the site at Le Pic, a small hamlet at 47132725 (M:75, C:193NW). No earthworks were seen there and the hamlet has no bastide-like appearance; the site is very far from the frontier.

ROQUEPINE   M:79 C:193NW

1283   *Testut*: pp. 50–51

As early as 1274 (*R.F.*, 257, 258 and 260) there was a castle and honour of *Racopina* held of the king of England within the parish of *Beanghas* (?=Born-les-Champs (Dordogne)). In 1283 as part of the settlement of a dispute with Margaret de Turenne, lady of Bergerac, Edward I accorded her full rights *in bastida de Rocapina* (*R.G.*, ii, 713–714), a site which lay on the southern edge of Périgord, a little west of Edward's bastide of Beaumont. It is not certain that Edward abandoned all claims in the town, for the dispute was still in progress in 1289 (*R.G.*, ii, 1239). The place certainly existed in 1305 (*R.G.*, iii, 4710), and it was asked for a contribution towards the cost of Edward II's Scottish war in 1316 (*R.G.*, iv, 1610).

The site is not a commanding one, although it stands within a mile of the southern border of Dordogne. Testut stated that there was no sign of the bastide, but in fact there are clear traces of grass-grown hollow-ways very similar to those which Testut reports Prunis as having seen earlier. The present main road seems to follow the axial street of the bastide, with two parallel streets equidistant from it, one to the north east and one to the south west. The cross-roads in the small village is probably the central point. There is a small bridge just before the houses begin on the south-east of the village, and closer inspection showed that the ditch which it bridged is not a watercourse but a hollow-way joining others to form the polygonal perimeter of the bastide. It is best preserved in the north-west corner of the town. No traces of house foundations could be discovered.

A.P. Mission Podensac/Belvès, 1950, no. 287.

ST. BARTHÉLEMY DE BELLEGARDE
1316   *Testut*: p. 52   M:75   C:181NE

Edward II confirmed the customs of this new bastide which had been founded by his seneschal of Gascony, Amaury de Créon, and his seneschal of Périgord, William de Toulouse. Amaury was the founder of the bastide of Créon (1316), and William of Toulouzette in 1321 and probably of Cazals (Mons Tholosa) (*q.v.*). The new town was given the liberties enjoyed by Ste. Foy la Grande. It occupies a commanding hill-top and is the junction of many roads; the grid-pattern is only visible near the church. This bastide should not be confused with the St. Barthélemy of *Gouron* 1680–82: Edward II's confirmation (C61/32 m. 13) clearly has *bastida sancti Barthelemei de Goyrans . . . in senescalcia petragoricense*.

The small village has ceased to have a market, but the feast of St. Bartholomew still brings the travelling caravans of the *forains* to set up the fair-booths in the grass square outside the church. This is a good hill-top position with a long commanding view southwards over the Isle valley to the high ground on the Dordogne watershed. Within 200 yards of the church the ground also falls steeply in the other directions. There is little rectangularity in the remaining street. There would be room for more of the town on the hill-top although no earthworks suggest that there were ever more buildings. There are no walls, gates or *cornières*. The forest edge is still very near the town. From the wall of the churchyard one can look southwards down the slope to the edge of the cleared ground no more than 400 yards away; and one can walk through continuous woodland right down to the Isle meadows.

STE. EULALIE (Puyguilhem)
1265   *Testut*: p. 50   M:79   C:193NW

This early foundation was never very large: in 1365 it numbered only 24 hearths. In 1265 a number of local landowners joined together to offer land to the English if a bastide could be built outside the castle of Puyguilhem, (*a far una bastida clausa en marcadil fora lo casted de Pugh W.*) and the seneschal Jean de Grilly accepted. The new town was to be given the privileges of Ste. Foy la Grande, then only a decade old

(*R.F.*, 472). Puyguilhem is a finely placed hill-town which had burgesses (*R.F.*, 261) but with very little room left on the summit for a bastide, and the new town was placed 4 miles to the south where the church of St. Eulalie d'Eymet now stands. Most of the surviving buildings are on the west of the road where tracks mark out the faint remains of a street-grid. The position is a good one, for the river runs below a steep cliff. (N.B. the plan in *Lavedan*, fig. 136 is of Puyguilhem itself and not its bastide). (It is just possible that the petition of c. 1274–75 (SC8/272/13558) refers to this place as the bastide of *Vacca Ferra* sponsored by Jean de Grilly.) See J.-P. Trabut-Cussac, *Bull. Philol. et Hist.*, année 1962 (1965), p. 76.

VACCA FERRA   M:79   C:193NW
c. 1274–75
The evidence for this bastide is a petition (SC8/272/13558) in which it is stated that Bernard de Bordelia (Bourdeille) holds the castle of Puyguilhem *et bastidam de vacca ferra*. I owe this reference to M. Trabut-Cussac who has briefly mentioned the bastide (*Le Moyen Age*, lx, (1954), p. 99) as "an abortive creation of Jean de Grilly". It is just possible that *Vacca Ferra* is identical with St. Eulalie d'Eymet (or de Puyguilhem). M. Trabut-Cussac tentatively suggests La Bastide Villefranche (Monestier), *infra*.

VILLEFRANCHE DE LONGCHAT (Lonchapt)   M:75   C:181SE
by 1287   *Gouron*: 1616; *Testut*, pp. 54–55
This Villefranche is sometimes distinguished from the other bastides of the same name by the suffix "in the honour of Puynormand". The castle of Puynormand (Gironde) is 3 miles to the north-east. In a document of 1318 (C61/32 m. 10), this bastide was identified as lying between Puynormand and Gurçon (Dordogne), a royal castle which still stands, 2 miles to the south-east of Villefranche, and the town was reckoned a royal bastide in 1329–30 (E101/166/1 f. 5). Testut was only able to date the foundation within the broad limits of the reign of Philippe le Bel (1285–1314); *G.C.*, 1044 and 1045, date the *paréage* as 1310; *Gouron*, 1616, has the limits 1316–18, with reference to C61/32 m. 11: but the document need not bear that construction, and the town existed from 1287 (L. Gardeau, *Bull. Soc. Hist. et Arch. du Périgord*, lxxvi (1949), pp. 190–214, and lxxviii (1951), pp. 88–92).

   The town has a full and regular grid-pattern in its streets. It is a fine hill-top site falling away steeply to the south-east; but there are no *cornières*, gates or ramparts. The church is unusually sited on one side of the Place. The Halle shown in *Lavedan* (fig. 166 (1832)) has been pulled down. The Place is cobbled, with shops on two sides.

A.P. Mission Ste. Foy la Grande/Le Bugue, 1950, no. 137.

VILLEFRANCHE DU PÉRIGORD   M:75   C:193SE
1261   *Testut*: pp. 55–56
The bastide was established in the parish of Ste. Marie de Viel-Siorac and may have included part of Loubejac parish. As Testut showed (p. 56), this area of Périgord near the borders of the Agenais and Quercy was sometimes regarded as part of the

former and the bastide was sometimes called Villefranche d'Agenais or de Belvès. Its founder was the Alphonsian seneschal of Agenais and Quercy (*Albe*, p. 57). It was assigned to Edward I in 1287. The plan (*Lavedan* p. 338) shows five parallel streets running north-south with four others at right angles. It is one of the dwindling number of bastides to which it is possible to buy a railway ticket. It lies in the south-east corner of Périgord within 5 miles of the old frontier. The main road from Bergerac to Cahors passes through it. Not all the building plots seem to have been taken up (*Deffontaines* p. 156). In the hearth-tax of 1365 there were 270½ hearths here (*Vigié* p. 287). There are very few thirteenth-century remains in the town, which stands on the north side of a small valley. The slope gives a natural defence to the south side of the town, where there are signs of a wall.

DEPARTMENT OF GERS

There are many bastides in this Department but the majority were French foundations, the English influence being confined to the northern quarter of the Department.

FLEURANCE   M:82   C:217SW

1274   *Gouron*: 946–968

After the Agenais was ceded to Edward I in 1279 he confirmed the majority of the privileges of Fleurance (*R.G.*, ii, 1452, and *G.C.*, 1061, 1728 and 1733). In 1292 he ordered his officers to help in enclosing the town (C61/20, m. 9). *R.G.*, 1469 (of 1289), refers to the property owned at this site before the bastide was built for the king of France. In 1313 Edward II intended to give the bastide to the count of Foix but was deterred by strong letters of protest from the town and from his seneschal, Amaury de Créon. They said that the town was surrounded by land belonging to the count of Armagnac, an old enemy of Gaston de Foix, and they feared that they would be involved in any quarrel between them. Edward withdrew his plan (Trabut-Cussac, *Le Moyen Age*, lx (1954), pp. 111–112, citing SC1/33/115 and C61/28, m. 10).

The town occupies a low situation and its principal defences must always have been ditches; the irregular shape of the town, with an eastern bulge, may be dictated by the course of streams. The grid is large and well preserved. The Place has *cornières* and a high broad arcaded market hall of more recent date. The church occupies a whole chequer and is a most impressive building with a good deal of medieval brick. The town seems still to be prosperous although not so much as in 1313 when the seneschal told Edward II that its rents were worth £1,500 a year, more than those of Bayonne, Dax, Bazas and Condom put together, but C46/26/10 shows that this was an exaggeration. In a survey (?1284) Fleurance was stated to have 2,000 *placeae*, each rented at 1s., of which 1,155 had been taken up (*mensurantur et recipiuntur*). 1,100 of 2,000 *casalia* had also been taken up. (B.M. Cott. Julius E.I., f. 105d.) There are many houses of brick and wood, and some of mud and wood.

A.P. Mission Nogaro/Beaumont de Lomagne, 1950, no. 252.

FOURCÈS   M:79   C:216NE

1279–86   *Gouron*: 970

The early history of the town is obscure. From the word "parcioniers" in *R.G.*, 2141, Gouron believed there must have been a *paréage*. When a list of Gascon documents was drawn up in 1317 (C47/27/14 f. 2v) it included a roll containing *inter alia* "3rd. a similar instrument concerning the *paréage* at Fourcès (fforcesii)". In 1324 the inhabitants requested, and were granted, the assurance that they would always remain annexed to the English crown (SC8/10600 and 10891; C61/35 m. 2).

In appearance this is the most delightful of the bastides of the plain. On the west the slender river Lauzoue separates the little town from the traffic of the Nérac to Montréal road. The physical isolation has preserved the unique character of the town's lay-out which a single main road would have shattered. The plan is the simplest in France. Once across the little bridge the street enters the market place; around the market place stand the forty-one houses which make up Fourcès. Each house is set at a slight angle to its neighbour so that the market place is a 41-sided polygon. The forty-one houses are in seven groups and between each group there is a gap, giving access to a back lane which makes the complete circuit of the town. There are no walls and only partial remains of the moat which must have protected the town on the outside of this back-lane. The lane leading on to the meadows passes under a substantial gate and clock-tower. Outside the bastide, on the south-east corner is a small but attractive chateau. Alongside it, and occupying the space of perhaps half a dozen medieval houses, is a cinema. All the houses facing on to the market place have *cornières*, some arched and of stone, others with square gables and of wood.

Gouron dated the *paréage* 1289–93 but among the feudal obligations listed in 1283–86, after the cession of the Agenais to the English crown, were payments from the castle of Fourcès and from "the men of Fourcès and Larroque". *Item li home de Fources e de la Roqua devo 102 s. e 4 d. e 1 poges de morlans*: Ms. Bodley 917 f. 15 in Cuttino, *Le Livre d'Agenais* (1956), p. 12. The document does not specifically mention a bastide. A petition of 1270 from the lord of Fourcès castle mentions the bastide of Montréal founded within his territory but has nothing to say of Fourcès (*A.P.E.A.*, p. 349).

A.P. Mission Montréal/Montauban, 1950, no. 168.

LARÉE   M:82   C:216NE

1289   *Gouron*: 1146

The name was probably given as a tribute to Jean de Reda, a royal clerk who was concerned with other bastides (*Gouron*: 84) lying in the county of Juliac. There is only a small chateau, a church and a farm today. The site is quite level and has no advantageous position. No earthworks could be seen. The field roads and the main road make something of a chequer pattern, but this is not uncommon elsewhere.

A.P. Mission Nogaro/Beaumont de Lomagne, 1950, no. 149.

39   589

LARROQUE   M:79   C:216NE

1289–93   *Gouron*: 970 and 1151

I was not at first convinced that there was a separate bastide here. Gouron's references (C47/27/14 and E36/187 f. 166) concern Fourcès only, and I cannot find mention of *Rupes Forsesii* in these documents. Cuttino's edition of E36/187 (*G.C.*, 1732) confuses things further by having *Porfesio* for *Forsesio*. The document cited by Trabut-Cussac (*Le Moyen Age*, lx (1954), p. 113) is also innocent of mention of *Rupes Forsesii* (C61/35 m. 2). But the two other petitions (SC8/10060 (not 10600 as in *Trabut-Cussac*) and 10891) which he cites in further support do mention both places: *voz gentz liges de fforceis et de la Roke de fforceis pres de Condom*, but not as bastides. *R.G.*, 1033 (1289), also has "the castle and honour of Fourcès and Larroque-Fourcès" but no mention of a bastide. See also the entry in Ms. Bodley 917, f. 15, cited under *Fourcès* above for "the men of Larroque and Fourcès" in 1279. The village, which stands on the saddle of a small hill, has something of rectangularity in its simple lay-out.

LIAS   M:82   C:216SW

1308   *Gouron*: 1197

Gouron refers to a foundation a little before May 1313, but the bastides of Juliac and Lias (*de Leaco*) are mentioned in two documents of April 1308 (*R.G.*, iv, 96–97) when they were associated with the *baillie* of St. Sever. The Gouron reference is to a town in the *baillie* of St. Gein.

There are now only six farms and a church that lie down a by-road which forms the main axis of a grid. The site has no commanding views. The town was enclosed in 1316 but there are no signs of walls; the enclosure could well have been mere ditches.

A.P. Mission Toulouse O. et E., 1954, no. 508.

MONCLAR   M:82   C:216NW

c. 1304   *Gouron*: 1398–9

Bernard VI, count of Armagnac, was also responsible for the nearby bastides of Marguestau and La Bastide d'Armagnac. In 1314 a royal commission was set to enquire how much damage had come to Edward II from the establishment of Monclar, ten years or so earlier.

The little village of one street occupies a hill-top position adjoining the old frontier of Armagnac. It has very little in it to suggest a bastide, apart from a slender grid of a single main street and two back lanes. It must have been more substantial. The Black Prince narrowly escaped death in October 1355 when the town was fired by the French during the night after he had captured it. (H. J. Hewitt, *The Black Prince's Expedition 1355–7* (1958), p. 52.)

MONGUILHEM   M:82   C:216SW

1319   *Gouron*: 1423–24

This foundation was one of a pair (see *Montégut*) founded within a year of each other, one on each side of the frontier of Marsan and Armagnac (the modern departments of Landes and Gers). Like similar pairs (see *Hastingues*) the first foundation felt that it had a grievance and successfully attempted to prevent the second (C61/36 m. 8). Both foundations had the approval of the seneschal of Gascony, William de Montaigu, who showed a fine impartiality by incorporating his Christian name (Guillaume) into Monguilhem and his surname in Montégut (1320).

There was already a parish church, and presumably a village near; it was St. Peter of Berobie (*de Beonia*). The *paréage* is printed in full in L'Abbé Cazauran, *Monguilhem et Toujouse* (1890), pp. 383–386, from the archives of Villeneuve de Marsan.

The present town is rather characterless. It is near enough to the Landes to have had wooden buildings in the Middle Ages, which have been replaced by nondescript modern houses. The grid and Place remain. There are no *cornières*.

A.P. Mission Nogaro/Beaumont de Lomagne, 1950, no. 178.

MONTRÉAL DU GERS   M:79   C:216NE

1255   *Gouron*: 1483–87

None of the documents cited in *Gouron* give any indication of English interest in this bastide, but *G.C.*, 1035, shows that the archives had a copy of Alphonse's charter; there is a reference to the town in *R.F.*, 466 and 516 (placing it in the district of Sos). Domengie thought that the work in the town was not begun before 1289, but it became English soon after 1279. Petitions of February 1318 to Edward II protested that the count of Armagnac and others had entered the town, killed a number of people, taken booty off to Castelnau d'Auzan and led away thirteen men of the town to Lagruelet. (J. P. Trabut-Cussac (*Le Moyen Age*, lx (1954), p. 93, citing SC8/13424 and 14444; and C61/33 mm. 9 and 15d) suggests that the raid was to reclaim villeins of Armagnac who had fled to the bastide. *G.C.*, 1667 and 1694, assigned by Dr. Cuttino to this Montréal, cannot deal with Gers, since the disputes were with distant Villeréal.) *A.P.E.A.*, p. 349 (1270), shows that the town was planted within the territory of Fourcès castle.

This is a bastide of first quality, with a fine elevated situation, a steep rock rampart to the south, a well-preserved grid of streets, an impressive Place with *cornières* and a church which towers above the ramparts. There is evidence on the ground that the bastide once extended further west than at present. *Lavedan* fig. 247 is based on a plan of 1834.

The history of the town is to be found in L'Abbé Breuils, "Montréal" (*Bull. Soc. Arch. du Gers*, xi (1910), pp. 43–55 and 243–57).

A.P. Mission Montréal/Montaubon, 1950, no. 1.

RÉJAUMONT   M:82   C:217SW

1292   *Gouron*: 1619–27

The long series of charters from 1292 to 1553 testifies that this bastide was not abortive, but the present appearance of the village would give no indication of its medieval status. It occupies an ill-defined, grass hill-top position but has nothing of the conventional bastide in its plan. The church seems modern and there is virtually no Place and certainly no *cornière*. Such vagueness might be expected in the timber-buildings of the Landes, but the bastides which neighbour Réjaumont are four-square, stone-built towns. *Lavedan*, p. 291, cites the *paréage* as one of those with initial pessimism: unless twenty houses were built, the contract was to be void.

A.P. Mission Nogaro/Beaumont de Lomagne, 1950, no. 309.

ST. CLAR   M:82   C:217SE
1289   *Gouron*: 1682 and *G.C.*, no. 1048

There is a plan in *Lavedan*, p. 324, which shows a fairly regular lay-out of streets. The bastide, which is quite extensive, has a hill-top position on the west bank of the river Arrats, a site very like the bishop of Lectoure's own town. The Lavedan plan is dated 1833 and there have been extensive clearances near the church, with the result that the town now has more of a regular grid: the impression from Lavedan's plan is of an older nucleus near the church, rather shapeless in street-plan, with the recti-linear bastide adjoining it on the north. There are no walls or gates to be seen, although there is a tower to the south-east of the church. On the north and east the slope is very steep and there are ramparts.

The most striking feature of the town is the proliferation of *cornières* (*cf.* La Bastide d'Armagnac). Apart from the usual full set around the four sides of the Place, there is half a side of arches in the next chequer north, a full length in the chequer south, and three lengths in the (now open) space east of the church: all seem to be equally old. The Route Nationale skirts the town on the south but has left it undisturbed. There are few shops, but the town is said to be well known in the Lectourais for its prosperous artisans.

A.P. Mission Nogaro/Beaumont de Lomagne, 1950, no. 21.

VALENCE SUR BAÏSE   M:82   C:217SW
1274   *Gouron*: 2108–09

This was a foundation shared by the count of Armagnac and the abbot of Flaran. The abbey stands on a level site north of the river, and an extensive precinct wall and gatehouse survive. High on a hill to the south of the river was the place known as *Castella* where the founders decided to set out the bastide in 1274–76. Gouron did not notice the annexation of this bastide to the English crown in 1318 (C61/32 m. 13): in this document it is distinguished from Valence d'Agen, which is also mentioned, by being called "Valence beyond the river Garonne". It was also referred to in the Gascon Roll of 1293 as a bastide (*R.G.*, iii, 2095).

The town has *cornières*, and although the main road has civilised and renovated some parts, the hill-top situation gives it something of the character of bastides further north.

DEPARTMENT OF GIRONDE

This Department is made up of the Bordelais, the original hinterland of Bordeaux. The customs duties of Bordeaux gave preference to the wines of the Bordelais, and in all the wars with the French kings this area remained most loyal to the king-duke. It contains the first of Edward's bastides as well as the last, abortive foundation of his grandson; and also the bastide that has prospered most in modern times: Libourne. The intensity of plantation must have been limited by the prior existence of many old-established market towns, especially along the banks of the Garonne.

BAA   M:78   C:191NE and XV, 37

1287   *Gouron*: 282

The site was purchased for the king in the winter of 1286–87 (E36/201, f. 33) and there is good evidence that the bastide was actually commenced, for accounts survive from the period February–September 1287 (E36/201, ff. 11–61), and in 1289 a tailor of Bordeaux had a charter "like the other burgesses of the bastide of Baa": (*R.G.*, ii, 1550). Edward I was there on March 13 or 14, 1287 (E36/201/55) when he stood the men 8*s.* worth of drinks: *hominibus de nova bastida que vocatur Baa de dono regis ad potum quando visitavit predictam bastidam, viii s.* (The king was moving south from Bordeaux.)

The actual site has yet to be definitely located, although several hints of the locality are given in documents. In 1329 the forest belonging to Baa was reckoned to be in the administrative area of Camparian, another decayed bastide (*infra*) (E101/166/1). The close conjunction of Baa and Camparian is shown also by the payment recorded in B.M. Cott. Julius, F.I.i, f. 110, "*de Prepositura de Compriano cum Terra Comitali et Foresta de Baa*". The two bastides were clearly adjoining when a document of 1291 (*R.G.*, ii, 1971) has Edward I saying "the district of our bastide (*sic*) of Baa and Camparian". The singular "bastide" made me once suspect that perhaps there was only one bastide, with two names; that of the French settlement near which it was planned, and that of the English bishop and Chancellor after whom it was to be named. (Baa = Bath, *sc.* Robert Burnell, bishop of Bath). Other documents (*R.G.*, ii, 1081, 1524, 1532 and 1568) indicate that roads led to the bastide from Gargon, Léognan, Gradignan and Sarcignan. There is nothing significant in the air photograph: M. Trabut-Cussac has recently proposed that the site lay at the lost hamlet of La Forêt to the north of the chateau of Thouars (1 km. south of Talence, *G.R.*: 368281), ("*Date, fondation et identification de la bastide de Baa*", *Rev. Hist. de Bordeaux*, x (n.s.) (1961), pp. 133–144).

A.P. Mission Blaye/Pessac, 1956, no. 111.

BURGUS REGINAE   M:71   C:180NE

by 1288   *Gouron*: 652

Trabut-Cussac (*B.I.H.R.*, xxv (1952), pp. 161 and 187) has shown that there were not two bastides of this name. His suggestion for the site is the small group of houses at La Bastide near Labarde (36643066) on the west bank of the estuary exactly opposite the junction of the Garonne and the Dordogne. The farm bearing this name stands on the edge of dry ground and a little above the reclaimed marshes. To the north of the farm are a few houses but insufficient to determine finally whether the town lay here. No satisfactory alternative has been proposed.

Edward I stayed at this place between February 5 and May 8, 1288, as his letters attest. (SC1/45/59–62; SC1/10/131; SC1/12/148.) The bastide was named as a compliment to the Queen, who had been with Edward in the Médoc for most of the second half of February 1287. (Trabut-Cussac, *art. cit.*, p. 175.) In 1291 the town was developed enough to have a *portus* (*R.G.*, ii, 1977), and it cannot have been abortive, for it appears in a list of bastides drawn up in 1326 (C61/38 m. 3d). The air photograph is unhelpful. (Mission Blaye/Pessac, 1956, no. 81.) A large-scale plan of the Médoc by Claude Masse (1723–24) shows the area of (La)barde with a mill at La Baride (*sic*) but no sign of a grid plan. (Plan reprinted 1895–96 by Imprimerie Nationale, Paris, from originals in Municipal Library, Bordeaux.)

CADILLAC
1280   *Gouron*: 657–666   M:79   C:192NW

The town was founded by Jean de Grilly, seneschal of Edward I, acting on his own account as seigneur of Benauge. This bastide seems never to have concerned Edward I or II but in view of the intimate connection of its founder with other bastides it has been included.

The ramparts remain on the south and east sides, and there are gates on two sides, one crowned by a clock. There are *cornières* in two sides of the square. The church was built into the north gate, suggesting that the church (as at Vianne) antedated the bastide. The north-west quarter of the town is now occupied by the chateau of the Épernons which brings a touch of the Loire to the valley of the Garonne. A good plan of 1853 forms Fig. 238 of *Lavedan*.

The bastide was originally called St. Jean after the name-saint of de Grilly; later Caput Evilliacum ("head of the river Euille") and thence Cadillac.

A native of the town, Jean de Lamothe-Cadillac, went to America and continued Jean de Grilly's tradition by founding Detroit. Hence, by logical stages, came the Cadillac car.

CAMPARIAN
1287   *Gouron*: 668   M:78   C:191NE

There is a ruined church of Camparian on the west side of the N.132 on the fringe of the forests of the Landes (36322763). A modern farm to the north of the ruins bears the name Camparian and has clearly used some of the stones from the church in its outbuildings. A church bell is also in use there. Undergrowth covers the church which is in a small copse. The best preserved part of the church is the east with the remains of a window and two other windows nearby on the south side. The foundations of the chancel and two divisions of the nave are well preserved among the grass and trees. To the east of the church is another group of trees which also cover some stone foundations of a building and there are less well-marked earthworks of buildings in the open grassland between the church and the farm. In this open area there is also a well. There is no village of Camparian and the site is a part of the half-dozen fields cleared from the woodland. A convalescent home has recently been built on the other side of the road from the farm.

The document of 1291 mentioned *supra* under Baa has "the bastide of Baa and

594

Camparian" and another of 1289 (*R.G.*, ii, 1505) has "the reeve of Baa and Camparian", rather suggesting a single bastide at that date. In 1310 (*G.C.*, 2042, wrongly located by ed.) the king ordered an enquiry into the mischiefs done to "the royal bastide of Camparian" between 1294 and 1303. The document cited by Gouron (C61/115 m. 3) is an inspection by Henry V in 1414 of a charter issued in 1355 by Edward III but it does not refer to a bastide but merely to a "court", a "lord" and a "forest" from which it was permitted to take wood for the defences of Bordeaux in time of emergency. I would not be convinced that there was a bastide of Camparian distinct from that of Baa were it not that Edward I was here in June 1287 and again in June 1288 (SC1/12/142 and C202/C/2, no. 118, cited by J. P. Trabut-Cussac, *B.I.H.R.*, xxv (1952), pp. 179 and 190); see also B.M. Cott. Ms. Julius E.I., i, ff. 185–220, for Camparian rents.

A.P. Mission Blaye/Pessac, 1956, no. 44.

CRÉON I   M:75   C:192NW

1315   *Gouron*: 847–852

The bastide was named after the seneschal Amaury de Créon, although its foundation was questioned by the abbot of Sauve-Majeur before the parlement of Paris. (*Chaplais*, pp. 39 and 179.) In 1322 Edward renewed his grant of liberties first accorded at the foundation, but the town was damaged in the subsequent wars. Edward III confirmed the town's privileges in 1342. A later confirmation, long after the English expulsion, suggests that it had been damaged again and was being re-peopled (1487) by settlers coming from Poitou, Saintonge and Limousin (*Gouron*: 852.) The text of the liberties is printed by G. Loirette in *Annales du Midi*, lxiv (1952), pp. 290–295, and in *R.G.*, iv, 1626.

The site is level and the town small. The regular grid is focused on the market place which has *cornières* on three sides; the charter assigned building plots of 66 feet by 22 feet. The church, not aligned east-west, conforms to the grid. No defences are to be seen; the circumference of the town is nine-sided. A plan is given in *Lavedan* (Fig. 237). Trabut-Cussac ("Créon, bastide administrative", *Annales du Midi*, lxvi (1954), pp. 343–350) has shown that the bastide was planted as a centre for the provost of Entre-deux-mers previously located at La Sauve Majeure, a town which was considered to be too much under the control of its abbot. Créon was given the same market-day as La Sauve Majeure in 1320, to add insult to injury. Despite Edward II's promise to provide the town with gates there were none when it was pillaged in 1337–38 and it is not certain whether the money raised by the ten-year subsidies of 1342 and 1351 was spent on more than defensive ditches. (SC8/262/13083; C61/54 mm. 6, 8 and 12; C61/63 m. 1)

A.P. Mission Podensac/Belvès, 1950, no. 3.

CUSSAC   M:71   C:180NE or 181NW

1289

The principal reference to this bastide is an entry in the accounts of the keeper of the Wardrobe (E36/201 m. 19) of 1s. 3d. sterling for a journey *ultra Gerondam ad super-*

595

videndum bastidam de Cussak. Tout identified this bastide "over the Garonne" as Cassac in Grayan, in the north of the Médoc peninsula. Grayan but not Cassac is shown on the Michelin map. Cussac, on the west bank of the Gironde opposite Blaye (35873175), is another possibility. Neither of these sites has any striking features which suggest a bastide; it is even possible that the *Burgus Reginae* founded in 1288 (*q.v.*) may be the same bastide as Cussac. If *ultra* means "beyond" and not just "along" the Garonne there is much to commend M. Trabut-Cussac's suggestion of Cubzac-les-Ponts (*Rev. Hist. de Bordeaux*, x (n.s.), 1961, p. 133, fn. 1) where the N.10 and the railway now cross the Dordogne 10 miles north-north-east of Bordeaux. The present village of Cubzac consists of a decayed quarter on the disused road down to the former ferry (superseded by a suspension bridge of 1839) and a few more houses and shops on the Route Nationale. But just above the ferry there is a flat-topped river cliff which would suggest itself for a semi military site as well as commanding the important commercial traffic. Beginning here were the coastal roads to the hinterlands of Charente and Saintonge. It is on this cliff-top that the gate-way and part of the walls of the Chateau des Quatre Fils Aymon still remain. No remains of streets could be discerned among the vines and fruit trees, but on balance this seems to me to be the best contender for the title: see C47/24/2/17 for the port in 1289.

Masse's plan of 1723–24 (see Burgus Reginae *supra*) is unhelpful. There is a drawing of the castle at Cubzac in 1646 in *Arch. Hist. de la Gironde* (1904), plate 31.

DUIRE (Hure)   M:79 C:192SE
by 1315

In the appendix to vol. iv of *R.G.*, Y. Renouard publishes a tax assessment that dates from the end of 1315 or the beginning of 1316. One of the smallest sums from the Bazadais (*R.G.*, iv, p. 570) was the £30 *bordelais* from *universitas bastide Duire*. The editor equates Duire with Hure, a village on the south bank of the Garonne 5 kilometres from La Réole. No other references to this place as a bastide have yet been noted; the place is not indexed in *Gouron* or *G.C.*

A.P. Mission FR.122/250, no. 1341.

LADOS (Gironde)   M:79 C:192SW
1281   *Gouron*: 1112

The document of 1281 is an order to the abbot of Saint-Ferme and a royal clerk to repair to Lados and construct a bastide in a suitable place, whether on royal land or on the land of vassals, and to grant a charter for those who came to the new town. In 1287 (*G.C.*, 1821) there is a record of the king buying one-quarter of Lados from Raymond Guillaume de la Dos: this probably marks the moment of the *paréage*. There was a castle here in 1289 (*R.G.*, ii, 1675) but in 1279 (*R.G.*, ii, 340) Lados was called merely a "place" (*locus*).

The site is a hill-top one, but without any great defensive potential. The ground slopes gently to the south. The church dates from the period of the foundation of the new town. The houses are scattered and only fragments of a new grid can be discerned.

A.P. Mission Hostens/Langon, 1956, no. 8.

LIBOURNE   M:75   C:181SW

1270   *Gouron*: 1200–40

This has proved to be the most enduring and prosperous of all the English bastides in France. There had been a riverside agglomeration known as *Fozera* long before the bastide, and the town plan (*Lavedan*, Fig. 260) shows an irregular pattern of streets around the church of St. John in the south-west corner of the town. On the north side and now conjoined, is the much larger extent of the regular grid pattern of Sir Roger de Leybourne's bastide, projected in 1268 and chartered by the Lord Edward in the autumn of 1270 when he and Sir Roger were on their way to the Crusade. The Kentish nobleman was an old companion of the king: he had been in Gascony with Henry III in 1253, and the foundation of the town came near the end of his life, for he died in 1271. In 1281 the king gave the townspeople a grant of tolls towards the construction of a causeway across the marsh towards Bordeaux, but nothing was done to carry out the grant of 1281 and 1286 for the enclosing of the town. It was badly damaged in 1294 and not rebuilt before 1297. The town petitioned for stronger works in 1305 and again in 1311, but without much help from the king.

Edward I was here himself in May 1289, and the Black Prince's son, Richard II, was born here according to some authorities, although he is usually known as "of Bordeaux". Roger de Leybourne came from Leybourne (Kent) and not, as is sometimes said, Leyburn, Yorks. In Leybourne church there is a window of 1948 showing the Kentish castle and the gate tower of the Gascon town; the window is the gift of the Laybourn (*sic*) family and the citizens of Libourne. For the origins of the town and name see also two articles in *Rev. Hist. de Bordeaux*, viii, n.s. (1959), pp. 183–212; and J. P. Trabut-Cussac in *Annales du Midi*, lxxv (1963), pp. 7–30.

The town is placed at the junction of the rivers Isle and Dordogne: the great fortified river gate still stands. Libourne was intended as a fortress to face Fronsac, and stood on land confiscated from the Vicomte de Fronsac after the revolt of 1256–54. It was also intended as a port for the collection of customs on wine that came from Périgord down the Dordogne. Despite the continuing prosperity of the town, the grid plan has been very little altered, and the market place, although sophisticated in its shops, still shelters them under *cornières*. On the north side of the town there are fragments of the town wall built into modern houses. The town ditch has been levelled and forms the exterior boulevard. These boulevards and the position of the station outside the old town have pulled the social centre of gravity away from the Place. See also J.-P. Trabut-Cussac, "La Construction des Remparts de Libourne", *Rev. Hist. de Bordeaux*, iii, n.s. (1954), pp. 179–199.

A.P. Mission Le Porge/Libourne, 1950, no. 194.

MONSÉGUR   M:79   C:192NE

1263   *Gouron*: 1425–28

The site is an impressive one, as the name (*Mons Securus*) indicates, making use of a rocky hill-top overlooking the river Dropt; the bare rock and the walls are imperceptibly merged on the southern side. The grid of streets, shown in *Lavedan*, Fig. 259, has been adapted to fit the tapering shape of the hill-top. Its situation gives the town an attractive character, and the walk around the outside of the walls should not be missed. The bastide was named in 1263 (*R.F.*, 488) although the charter was not issued until 1265 (*Gouron*, 1425). The parish in which the town was planted was called Nuron (*R.F.*, 357, 489–494)—*parochiam de Nuron in qua est bastida*—and there may have been some fortification near the river (*Testut*, p. 64). The site belonged to Bertrand de Beauville.

The building plots were intended to be 72 feet by 24 feet, the proportion commonly found in bastides hereabouts. The town was one of those which had some fortification from the beginning, as befits its commanding position. In 1305 the community reminded the king of this and asked him to build four stone gates and to protect the castle with walls (SC8/125/6241 and 161/8050). The town promised to enclose the rest. The commercial side of the town's purpose appears from the foundation of the harbour on the Dropt in 1289.

A.P. Mission Podensac/Belvès, 1950, no. 197.

MONTBRUN
1285   *Gouron*: 60   M:79   C:192NW

The order of June 1285 (*R.G.*, ii, 901) was for the building of a bastide at, among other places—"the motte of Montbrun near the church of Portets".

Portets lies just off the main road from Bordeaux on the south bank of the Garonne. The name Montbrun does not appear on C:192NW, but there is a place called *la Motte* 1 km S.E. of Portets (GR: 38172696); no other documentation has yet been noted. The local post office had never heard of a place-name Montbrun in or near Portets, which is a prosperous village of medium size, without any features to suggest a bastide.

A.P. Mission Blaye/Pessac, 1956, no. 233.

PELLEGRUE
1272   *Gouron*: 1548   M:45   C:192NE

There was already a castle of Pellegrue in 1243 (*R.G.*, 1229) and part of the church may also antedate the town. The porch, chancel and apse all seem to be original thirteenth-century work; the transepts may be an addition.

In February 1272 Henry III made three agreements with local landowners with the object of founding a bastide (J. P. Trabut-Cussac, *Restitution du second livre noir de la Connétablie de Bordeaux*, nos. 510–512). In 1316, when Edward II was considering whether to retain the town in his own hands, the enquiry speaks of *castrum et bastida de Pelagraa* (Trabut-Cussac, *Le Moyen Age*, lx (1954), p. 114, citing C47/25/2/15).

The town, although elevated, has no self-fortified site such as Monségur or Puymirol. There is a slight fall on all sides. The grid is preserved, but not strikingly as the Route Nationale traverses the town. There are no longer any *cornières*, but the Place has its Halle. The church is on the southern edge of the town. There are no walls or gates surviving.

A.P. Mission Podensac/Belvès, 1950, no. 110.

POURIET (ARBANATS)   M:75   C:192NW

1348   *Gouron*: 185

The site cannot be definitely identified, for the grant of 3 August 1348 (C61/60, m. 13) signified Edward III's favourable answer to the petition of Elias de Pomeris and his wife, Regina, but left the siting of the new town undefined: *unam bastidam apud Pouriet vel alibi in districtu Varbenatus in solo suo proprio construere et constructam tenere.* Gouron mistakenly reads "Pomiers": this was the surname of the founder, but the Roll has clearly "Pouriet". Arbanats (sc. Varbenatus) is a small village just off the main road south-west from Bordeaux along the south bank of the Garonne. There is a slight grid in the plan. The narrow parish extends from the river to the edge of the forest. The site is too low to possess any defensive value and must have been de-signed as a river-side commercial bastide. Chronologically this is one of the last bastides, coming on the eve of the Black Death, like New Eagle, Lincolnshire. D. Petit and A. d'Anglade, *La Seigneurie de Portets, Castres et Arbanats* (1934), has nothing concerning the problem.

A.P. Mission Blaye/Pessac, 1956, no. 240.

STE FOY LA GRANDE   M:75   C:181SE

1255   *Gouron*: 1695–97

In July 1255 Alphonse de Poitiers made a *paréage* with the abbot of Ste. Foy de Conques and the seigneurs of Pineuil. Edward's confirmation of the charter of 1256 dates from 1292, but as early as 1276 the customs of Ste. Foy were being taken as a model for the new foundations of St. Osbert and Sauveterre de Guyenne. In 1326 the town was back in French hands; (see also SC8/4777 and 4785).

The bastide is large and still prosperous. There is a small extension beyond the line of the old walls in the direction of the railway station. The original street-plan is well preserved, although the fortifications have gone. The town seems to have been largely rebuilt in the last 200 years, although here and there timber-framed buildings peep from under stone or plaster facades. In August 1956 some *cornières* were being reconstructed in ferro-concrete. The town is still a small river port, and it has a fine riverside terrace. The plan in *Lavedan*, Fig. 254, confuses the church with a cross-pattern of streets.

A.P. Mission Ste. Foy la Grande/Bugue, 1950, no. 289.

ST. OSBERT   M:79   C:192SE

1276   *Gouron*: 1817

It is curious that this well-documented bastide "Sancti Oseberti" with its long charter of privileges (*R.G.*, ii, 55; C61/7 m. 5) has never been identified. It has been variously suggested as lying near La Réole, Langon and Lados. The same privileges were awarded at the same time to Castelnau-sur-Gupie, Miramont and Castetcrabe but these sites are too scattered to help to localise St. Osbert near them. (*R.G.*, ii, 13).

The building plots of the town were to be of the common dimensions, 72 feet by 24 feet. A document of 1277 (*R.F.*, 369) records the appointment of a provost (*perbost*)

599

of the bastide of "Sent Ausberg", which is probably this town. It has been suggested that St. Osbert was another name for Castelnau-sur-Gupie (*q.v.*) also founded in 1246 on the same day (Léo Drouyn, *La Guienne Militaire*, ii (1865), p. 399). But the difficulty is that the foundation charter of St. Osbert gave the new town the customs of three *other* places, one of which was Castelnau itself. J. de Font-Réaulx (*Annales du Midi*, lxxii (1960), pp. 413–414) has suggested that the town was really called "St. Albert", and that the site is at St. Albert de la Motte 5 km. from La Réole on the Marmande road (R.N. 127). The actual distance is about 7 km. (C: 192SE, GR: 418254). A witness to *R.F.*, 369, came from Jusix, 2 m. to the south of St. Albert, but two others from near Auros. The area adjoins a busy Route Nationale and is extensively worked as vineyards. Nothing suggestive of town earthworks could be seen. The site has no natural defences.

SAUVETERRE DE GUYENNE

1281

M:79 C:192NE

Gouron: 1917–34

The fullest account of the foundation is given by J. P. Trabut-Cussac, *Rev. Hist. de Bordeaux*, ii (1953), pp. 181–217, and some features of the disputes and delays that accompanied the foundation have been described above, pp. 243–44. (See also C47/25/1/13; C47/26/3; SC8/14112, 14142–3 and 14149).

The site of the bastide lies outside and a little below a hill-top castle. The initial agreements were made in the spring of 1281 but it was November 1283 before the charter of customs was sealed by Edward I. It gave the town the liberties of St. Osbert and Ste. Foy-la-Grande (*R.G.*, ii, 746).

Neighbouring towns of Castelmoron and Monségur disputed the limits of Sauveterre's jurisdiction (*R.G.*, ii, 1378, 1412 and 1619) and Sallebruneau used violence against the heralds when it was announced that Sauveterre was to have six fairs a year.

There is still a large market (actually known locally as *foire* and not *marché*) on alternate Tuesdays, and we were fortunate enough to visit Sauveterre when its market place, *cornières* and adjoining streets were packed with stalls and vans. The walls dating from 1288 have been thrown down and the ditch was filled in to make an encircling road in 1812. The four gates erected in 1283 have been left standing.

The *cornières* are complete, though probably rebuilt from time to time. A well-preserved timber house stands on the left of the road from the south gate to the Place. The church, with its modern steeple, has a building plot to itself north-east of the market. The walls were diamond shaped, with a gate at each corner, and roads leading diagonally. In a plan of 1829, kindly shown to us by the hospitable mayor, M. Sabourin, there was a market hall in the middle of the central Place. This plan marks the bounds of the rural communes, which came right up to the edge of the town, showing how the new town had been set down in a countryside where parish bounds of existing villages were already firmly established. One of these encircling communes was that of Puch, whence came Jordan, co-founder of the bastide. M. Sabourin pointed out to us that there were two types of medieval house in the town: a group surrounding the market place, of more elaborate design with inner courtyards, and the plainer houses with street-frontage and garden only. He suggested that the first group may be those built before Edward I ordered a standstill, and the second those of the resumed activity after the complaints had been dismissed.

A plan of the town is given in *Lavedan*, Fig. 251, but with north at the bottom.

A.P. Mission Podensac/Belvès, 1950, no. 334.

DEPARTMENT OF LANDES

This coastal fringe of Gascony, like the Gironde, remained loyal to the English in the wars with France. When the sands and marshes that covered so much of the area are taken into account, the density of the bastides is remarkable.

AROUILLE
M:79   C:216NW

1289   *Gouron*: 187–188 and 1320

Arouille was founded by *paréage* with Arnaud Guillaume of Mauvezin (*R.G.*, ii, 1033). A parish of this name (Arhulla) existed in 1270 (*R.G.*, 73), and the bastide was sometimes called *Rulha*.

The site consists of scattered farms set back from the road, with a good deal of common grassland between. On the east of the road is a large grass field with indented hollow-ways, some of which form a rectilinear plan. Further north there are similar hollow-ways in fields now under vines. There is a deeply-cut wooded valley at the eastern edge, crossed by a rough track on a causeway across what seems to be an old dam. There is no local tradition of a town site nor of English occupation.

The Black Prince's raiding force of October 1355 on its way from Bordeaux to Armagnac made Arouille the object of a 25 mile march from Castelnau and regained the town (H. J. Hewitt, *The Black Prince's Expedition* (1958), pp. 50–52.) Judging from the open nature of the plateau here the town cannot have been difficult to capture.

(Note: The Michelin plan has "Aronille" in error).

A.P. Mission Lit et Mixe/Cazaubon 1950 no. 422; Brocas/Cazaubon, 1960, no. 94.

BETBEZER
M:79   C:216NW

1308   *Gouron*: 439

There is only a single row of cottages and a church on the east side of the main road just north of a T-junction. No sign of any other road system could be seen in the fields; to the north-west is the chateau of Juliac. A kilometre away on the other bank of the Douze is the much more successful Bastide d'Armagnac, also founded by Arnaud-Guillaume de Mauvezin (c. 1291). East of Betbezer the field boundaries are remarkably rectilinear.

Gouron, 84 records a promise of liberties in general terms to the inhabitants of the viscounty of Juliac. A footnote refers to three bastides covered—Mauvezin, Arouille and Juliac (*ibid.* p. 33, fn.)—but no further mention of the latter is made, despite a *vide infra*. The place is, however, mentioned as having a bastide in 1308 (*R.G.*, iv, 96–97). Since Betbezer (a bastide) is practically outside Juliac castle, I equate these.

A.P. Mission Lit et Mixe/Cazaubon, 1956, no. 271; Brocas/Cazaubon, 1960, no. 43.

BONNEGARDE EN CHALOSSE   M:78 C:227NE
1283   *Gouron*: 479–480, but see *R.G.*, ii, 654,
                                       for earlier date

The site of the town stands above the river, Le Luy de Béarn, and less than 2 kilometres from the boundary between Basses Pyrénées and Landes, once the frontier of English Gascony.   Edward I stayed here in October 1287, again in the winter of 1288 (including Christmas) and on two occasions in the following spring (J. P. Trabut-Cussac in *B.I.H.R.*, xxv (1952), p. 183).

In 1283 Edward gave his consent to the purchase of land for Bonnegarde from Bernard of Arricou; in 1287 the new town was granted liberties based on those of Dax.   In 1291 there was a serious fire in the town and the king made an allowance of £50 to it.   A castle was then built outside the town (B. M. Cott. Julius, E.1, f. 180) but as late as 1340 the townspeople were asking for walls and a fortified bridge to defend the town itself.   (C61/52 m. 8 and SC8/14226.)

The modern village of Bonnegarde, with a nondescript church, looks a poor site for Edward to build a castle and to visit, for although there are steep slopes nearby—as the arrows on the Michelin plan show—there are none near the village.

The search for the castle site led to a neck of higher ground made by two streams which join near a mill, south-west of the village.   The hilltop is wooded but can be approached by the grass track to the empty house (seventeenth-century in part) known as the Chateau.   To the east of the Chateau are the tremendous tree-covered earthworks of Edward's castle, a great mound and ditch curved like a boomerang and cut on its northern edge by a hollow way in a deep cutting where the stones of a gatehouse still hang from the sand and tree-roots.   It would seem from the documents cited above that the bastide of Bonnegarde lay on the level or levelled ground where the chateau and the fields now are.   The sole inhabitant, a peasant of eighty-three years, told us that she had heard that there had been a town here destroyed by the English; and that local people said that the burial place for Bonnegarde used to be up here on the hill and not near the present church.

The former main street extends past the castle as a grass track before descending the hill and becoming a modern road.

A.P. Mission St. Vincent de Tyrosse/Gimont, no. 606; Hasparren/Arthez, 1948, no. 23.

CASTETCRABE (Castrum de Caprae)   M:82   C:216SW-NW
1276   *Gouron*: 706–707

The bastide was founded by Luke de Thanney, the king's seneschal of Gascony, and given the same liberties as St. Osbert (1276) and Castelnau sur Gupie (1276): basically those of Sainte-Foy-la-Grande (1255).   There appears to have been local opposition and then delay. A letter from Edward I at Rhuddlan in 1283 appointed three commissioners to recommence the work on the bastide, and two years later Constance de Béarn was complaining that the foundation injured her interests. (*R.G.*, ii, 643.)

The site is in the commune of Bougou (GR: 18003813) where a farm and mill bear the name. The soil is light and bears no traces of a town; there is much timber near by and stone buildings need not have been planned. No local tradition of a site could be discovered. The farm overlooks a small stream in the shallow valley and no military potential for the site appears.

A.P. Soustons/Mont de Marsan, 1950, no. 405.

CRÉON II   M:79   C:216NW
1285   *Gouron*: 847, fn., and 980

The identification is Gouron's, the grounds not stated. The document of 1285 (*R.G.*, ii, 881) records that Jean de Grilly, Edward's seneschal, had founded a bastide at an unnamed place within the baronry of Gabardan, *i.e.* the cantons of Gavarret, Cazaubon and Montréal du Gers. At the request of Gaston de Béarn, Edward, then in London, ordered his seneschal to revoke the charter of liberties.

The small and decaying village has a large grass-covered square in front of the church. Including the present main road, there is a simple street-grid and the grass field to the north has earthworks which may represent a third street.

FONFRÈDE   site unknown
by 1320   *Gouron*: 969

Edward II ordered his seneschal in Gascony to investigate whether it was proper to found a bastide at "Fonfrède". An agreement to set up a town had been made between two local landowners with the assent of the seneschal's lieutenant, Amanieu de Fossat.

GEAUNE EN TURSAN   M:82   C:228NW
1318   *Gouron*: 995–1007

Pierre II, lord of Castelnau-Tursan, was seigneur of territory in the adjoining parish of St. Jean de Pantagnan. As a military position Castelnau itself was greatly superior to the site chosen for the new bastide which lies in a wide-bottomed side valley of the Riveau du Bas; the new bastide was not on the frontier, like its neighbours Pimbo and Sarron, but lay on a road going south-west from Aire sur l'Adour. Its founders' motives would seem to be commerce and colonisation. The new town was to be called *Janua*, probably after Genoa, the home town of the seneschal Antonio de Passagno. The town has a very good grid system of streets dividing the town into 25 *îlots*, and on the east side may have been larger than now. A plan is given in *Lavedan*, Fig. 230. The church is unimpressive but the market place is as large as any bastide except Libourne; it has *cornières* on three sides. Until 1888 there was a market hall in the centre. Three of the four gates have now disappeared. In the north-west section of the town was the Augustinian church, of which only the tower and gateway remain. The *paréage*, the customal (based on Sarron) and an account of local topography are printed by B. Saint-Jours, *La Bastide de Geaune en Tursan* (1910).

A.P. Mission St. Vincent de Tyrosse/Hagetmau, 1948, no. 136.

HASTINGUES   M:85   C:227NW

1289–c. 1303   *Gouron*: 1047–61

Like Granges, Hastingues was the product of an agreement between the king and a monastic house possessing land at a place which seemed to have urban potentials. The abbey property on this hill-top was called Auriamala and this was probably the first name of the bastide. The Anglo-French war of 1294–1303 retarded work on the new town, and it was probably not undertaken until after 1303 (J. P. Trabut-Cussac in *Bibliothèque de l'Ecole des Chartes*, cxi (1953), pp. 241–242.) The liberties of the town were granted by Edward II in 1321, when the bastide was known as Haurihastinggs (*sic*). The first two syllables are clearly from the original *Auriamala* but the "Hastinggs" has come from John Hastings, lord of Abergavenny, who was seneschal of Gascony from 1302–04 and 1309–10 and described in a document of 1321 (C61/35 m. 18) as the town's founder. The liberties of 1321 were modelled on those of Bonnegarde (1283–89), the bastide where Edward I had been staying when he made the first agreement with the abbey.

At the time of the grant of 1321 the town was also given a ten-year grant of tolls to assist the enclosing of the town with walls and the building of a bridge across the moat (SC8/14482; C61/35, m. 18). Edward III licensed it to be a river port for the ships of Bayonne since it occupied an important position on the frontier of Navarre. The river is the broad Gave de Pau, and it is interesting to see how the departmental boundary between Landes and Basses Pyrénées (following the old frontier) here crosses the river to take in a small bit of territory on the south bank. In this enclave is Hastingues, placed where the river sweeps back against the higher ground. On the opposite bank is the bastide of Sorde l'Abbaye founded for the king of France in 1290 and re-founded by agreement between Edward II and the abbot in 1314. Another rival bastide had been built on the south bank by the countess of Béarn at Villefranche de Béarn in 1292, and some time before 1330 the English planned a bastide on the north bank of the river, at the junction with the Adour at Port de Lanne. In an account of 1302–04 (E101/159/4) Hastingues is appropriately called *Ripariae Fluminis*.

The commercial prosperity of Hastingues has now ebbed: perhaps a severe price to pay for the remarkable medieval atmosphere of this quiet town. The market place is grassy, the *cornières* are used for drying washing instead of selling wares; a wooden footbridge over the moat is largely for the convenience of the geese; the cellars of the jurat's house are empty; at the town's café the tables are set under the filled-in arches of the *cornières*; the south gate is ivy-grown and shows jagged teeth of stone where the town walls have been pulled down from around it.

Altogether, Hastingues is full of the character which the foreign visitor looks for in a bastide, and its nearness to the Biarritz coast and the Route des Pyrénées makes it easily accessible to tourists. (It is a pleasure to acknowledge the assistance of M. and Mme. Récart during visits to Hastingues.)

A.P. Mission Bayonne/Hasparren, 1954, no. 130.

LA BASTIDE CHALOSSE   M:78 C:227NE
by 1327–29   *Gouron*: 1085

In 1327–29 the bastide was let out at farm to two burgesses of St. Sever together with the revenues from the bastide of Toulouzette (E101/166/1). It was then called Pons Regin(a)e, a name difficult to explain, since La Bastide stands on a ridge nearly two miles from the river. A later document (C61/54 m. 25: June 1342) refers to "the bastide of Pons Reginae *in terra de Silhossa*", possibly Serreslous, 5 miles to the north-west; or Chalosse?

The village stretches along a single street, the little-used course of the former main road south from Hagetmau which must have used the Queen's bridge; the modern road takes the slope more gently by a more westerly course. The Place is empty and there are no *cornières*; there is a church.

A.P. Mission St. Vincent de Tyrosse/Gimont, no. 377.

LA BASTIDE D'ARMAGNAC   M:79 C:216NW
c. 1283–1291   *Gouron*: 1086–88

In 1283 Jean de Grilly, Edward I's lieutenant, gave a charter to the inhabitants, the bastide then being called *Bolonia*. One of its French founders had been Bernard VI, count of Armagnac. Lodge, p. 183, dates the foundation to before 1283.

There is a plan in *Lavedan*, p. 343; the grid is still well preserved. The Route Nationale runs outside the south wall of the town and has left the centre of the bastide in an excellent state of preservation. The large Place is unpaved, with trodden sand. On its north-eastern side is the magnificent west doorway of the church, and narrow streets leave in all four directions. The *cornières* extend past the Place into four of these streets and are of all periods and materials: wood, stone, brick and cast-iron can be seen side by side. There are crumbling remains of the south gate, in brick and stone. On the north and west sides the ground falls fairly steeply to the river, but on the east the approach is perfectly level.

A.P. Mission Lit et Mixe/Cazaubon, 1950, no. 271.

LA BASTIDE (MONPAZIER)   M:78 C:215NE
c. 1319   *Gouron*: 309 and 2039, fn.

The accounts for 1327–29 (E101/166/1) refer to two bastides, Monpazier and Montaigut, founded near Brassens. Gouron identifies the former with La Bastide.

The wooden houses of the village are characteristic of the Landes; they are scattered and there is no church. No grid pattern could be seen, and the only feature to suggest a bastide is the unusually long vista from the site over the country to the south

40   605

and south-west. Distant views are not often encountered in the level forest thereabouts.

A.P. Mission Lit et Mixe/Cazaubon, 1950, no. 310.

LABOUHEYRE (near)   M:78   C:?203
1307–15   *Gouron*: 1094

In a document of 1318 "the town of Labouheyre and its bastides" were annexed to the English crown (C61/32 m. 10). The names of the bastides were not given. No other references occur which would help to identify bastides within 12 miles of Labouheyre.

MAUVEZIN D'ARMAGNAC   M:79   C:216NW
1289   *Gouron*: 1320

The small village has a thirteenth-century church, and the main street together with the side-alleys may possibly be the remnants of the original grid. The site has no defensive potential, and it is not certain whether there was ever a bastide here. Gouron's only reference is to the document in *R.G.*, 1033, which deals with the shared rights of the parties in "a place called Mauvezin (Malo Vicino)" and in Puy de Juliac. It agrees that if bastides are founded within the territory of the vicomte de Juliac he and Edward should share jurisdiction, but the names of these bastides are not given. Since Arouille is mentioned in the charter, and had a foundation of its own on the very same day, it is possible that Arouille was in mind. Two years later La Bastide d'Armagnac was founded, almost within sight of the Juliac seat.

A.P. Mission Lit et Mixe/Cazaubon, 1950, nos. 248 and 266.

MONTÉGUT   M:82   C:216SW
1320   *Gouron*: 1459–60

This bastide was the partner and rival of Monguilhem, founded a year earlier. By 1329 (E101/166/1 ff. 20d. and 49d) the two were farmed out by the Crown for £90 a year (see also L'Abbé Cauzaran, *Monguihem et Toujouse* (1890), pp. 2 and 283).

Despite a good church of brick, there are few traces of the middle ages in the surviving buildings of the village. Hardly anything of the grid remains, although the outer enclosure of the town is recalled by a steep change of slope which is marked on the map. The roads are cut deep in the soft sandstone.

A.P. Mission Nigaro/Beaumont de Lomagne, no. 177.

NERBIS   M:78   C:215SE
1314   *Gouron*: 1505

The only reference to this bastide is as a project reported to Edward II's commissioners in 1314: but for the war in Gascony, the abbot of St. Sever would have concluded a *paréage* with the king for a bastide at Nerbe-Castet.

The little village of Nerbis occupies a commanding hill-top position overlooking the river Adour. Its street-plan has only the faintest suggestion of rectangularity.

It is, of course, possible that the project was for a bastide somewhere else in the parish. "Castet" does not appear on the map, but there is a *Cassiet* at 35151665 just below Mugron and alongside the river. The neighbouring bastide of Toulouzette, founded in 1321, is on the river bank.

A.P. Mission Soustons/Mont de Marsan, 1950, no. 379.

OZOURT   M:78   C:227NW

c. 1305

In two petitions addressed to Edward I, Arnaud-Loup of Estibeaux complained that the seigneur of Navailles and his men had committed many outrages in the country-side near Castelnau. Arnaud-Loup asked the king to ally with him: the form the alliance would take would be a bastide of protection. Two thousand men and more could be expected to come and settle there: *que vous voillez fare alliaunce avesque lui en tele manere que vous voillez fere novele bastie (sic) en le dit lieu (la quel est appelee Hosord)* . . . *et purra bien aver en la dite bastie asses de terres et de bois et ij.m homes* (SC8/2943 has *m.m. poblantiz) et plus.* The petitions, which are virtually identical, come from the time when Jean de Havering was seneschal (SC8/2943 and 14543).

There is a village of Ozourt between Estibeaux and Castelnau-Chalosse. The village is a straggling collection of farms, but at the southern extremity of the parish is a farm called La Bastide. No earthworks were to be seen; and the project may have been abortive.

PIMBO   M:82   C:228NW

1268   *Gouron*: 1561

The *paréage* between Edward's seneschal and the abbot of Pimbo (*R.F.*, 397) makes it clear that there were already some houses near the church, and the west end of the church must also be older than 1268. The abbot reserved the right to take certain dues from "the old and new inhabitants". The prince was to choose a site for a castle or stronghold and to lay out the bastide wherever he thought fit. The bastide is also described in the document simply as *novam populationem*.

The hill-top situation, looking southwards towards the nearby frontier, is delightful. At the east end of the village is the church, and at the west a farm which is probably the descendant of Edward's *domum fortem*. The single street is all that the hill-top has room for, and it has not the straightness of the planned town: it is probably the unaltered village street. In a list of bastides in 1342 (C61/54 m. 25) Pimbo is described only as a "place" (*locum*) and the bastide project may have been abortive.

The driver of a travelling grocer's van, encountered in the street in September 1957, had heard a tradition that the place had once been English. The customer whom he was serving, learning that we were English, reproached us with the damage done by the English to the church tower in the Hundred Years War. Several of the houses were separated by androynes, down which—like an arrowslit in a castle-wall—we could see across the old frontier into a country that had never known the English king as overlord.

A.P. Mission Hasparren/Arthez, 1948, no. 2.

POLINGES   site unknown

1281   *Gouron*: 1569

The only reference to the bastide is a document in *R.G.*, 446. In this, seneschal Jean
de Grilly appears as a partner in the foundation of a bastide within the diocese of
Dax, but no one has offered an identification of the place.

PORT DE LANNE   M:78 C:227NW

1331   *Gouron*: 1571–72

A petition of 1330–31 from Isarn de Lanne Plane to Edward III recalled that at
some point in the past the seneschal of Gascony and the men of Bayonne had agreed
to create a bastide at Lanne for the mutual profit of the king and his subjects: *un
bastie la quele serroit mult profetable au Roi nostre seignure a son comune poeple* (SC8/14359:
text in Trabut-Cussac, *Le Moyen Age*, lx (1954), pp. 127–128.) The war had intervened and delayed execution of the project. Isarn now asked for further action and a
paréage. In November 1331 this was granted. (C61/43 m. 6.)

The village of Lanne stands on the east bank of the Adour just north of the low-
lying ground where the Adour joins the Gave de Pau. The main road from Bayonne
to Pau and Tarbès crosses the Adour by a modern bridge which involves a substantial
détour, but the line of the old road, passing straight through Lanne and Port de
Lanne, is clear. It was probably the utility of the river-port as a place of intermediate
transhipment which explains the interest of the burgesses of the sea-port of Bayonne
in the bastide project.

I cannot decide whether the bastide was at Lanne. The document of 1331 merely
says "in the territory of Lanne". The village of Lanne has a broad, open green with
side roads making up a simple grid, but there is also rectangularity in the few lanes at
Port de Lanne.

A.P. Mission Hasparren/Arthez, 1948, no. 43.

RONDEBOEUF   M:82   C:216SW

1315   *Gouron*: p. 621, fn.

Geoffrey Front-de-Bœuf was seneschal of the Landes, mayor of Bayonne, and lieutenant to the seneschal of Gascony in 1315. In that year the foundation of a bastide
bearing his name gave rise to a dispute between the inhabitants of the new bastide and
those of two older foundations in the same district, St. Gein (1284) and Lias (1308):
pasture rights, probably in the forest of Aveyron, were being claimed by the newcomers over lands which the older towns had been accustomed to enjoying (C61/30
m. 20).

The three bastides stood on the frontier of Armagnac whose count was frequently
accused of violence against them. Edward II gave these three bastides the same
royal Keeper, who was much engaged in obtaining permission from the king to
spend money on the defences of the towns but who, in the end, had to use his own
money (C1/30 m. 11, and 41 m. 9).

After the documentation one would have hoped that Rondeboeuf would be a good hill-top bastide with the full equipment of buildings and streets. In fact it has about a dozen farms spread over a slightly elevated piece of ground. There is no marked street-grid, and no Place or *cornières*.

ST. EDOUARD (Baigts)   M:78   C:227NE
1316–17   *Gouron*: 284–285

Amaury de Créon, a seneschal of Gascony, who was concerned with the foundation of a number of bastides for Edward II, exchanged lands at Sort (near Dax) with the seigneur of Baigts so that a bastide could be built. In 1326 Reynaud complained that the bastide was founded but that he had not yet received the land at Sort: (C61/38 m. 3v (not 1v as *Gouron*, 285)). The bastide was also known as St. Edward. In 1317 the English seneschal of Saintonge, in the course of a diplomatic report to Edward II, recommended the confirmation of the act of Gilbert Pecche, seneschal of Gascony, in founding a bastide called St. Edward in Bazadais (*R.G.*, iv, p. 580; see also C61/60 m. 30).

It is not clear whether the bastide was at Baigts or within the parish. No place-name of St. Edouard appears on the map. Baigts is a small hill-top village, just the position for a bastide. It has a small Place near the church but there is no grid and the remaining houses are scattered.

ST. GEIN EN MARSAN   M:82   C:216SW
1284   *Gouron*: 1759

In September 1284 there was a *paréage* between the Constable of Bordeaux and the lord of Castandet. This bastide is the earliest foundation in the Lias-Rondeboeuf group, and from a grant of revenues and cash by Edward I in 1289 it would appear that a promise had been made to the newcomers that the town would be enclosed with ditches. The village stands on a busy main road but is small with few signs of a bastide in its present buildings or street plan. The main road probably follows the axial street of the bastide, with the church on the west (see also *R.G.*, ii, 1011 and 1352; C61/30 mm. 11 and 13; C61/42 m. 5; C61/53 m. 31).

ST. JUSTIN   M:79   C:216NW
1280   *Gouron*: 1778–80

A commission of enquiry from Edward II was sent (c. 1311–14) to see why the countess of Béarn had built the bastide within his jurisdiction but without his permission. The *paréage* of May 1289 was with the prior of St. Gilles; new customs were accorded by the countess in 1309.

This is a small hill-top bastide. The towers at or near the north and south gates survive, and between them there is a single street. The church lies to the north-east of the Place which has remains of *cornières*, although all commerce (except a hotel) has left the Place des Tilleuls for the Route Nationale which runs round the outside of the town on the west and south.

A.P. Mission Lit et Mixe/Cazaubon, 1950, no. 274.

ST. MAURICE   M:82 C:215SE

c. 1326   *Gouron*: 1814

The town was described as a bastide in 1340 (C61/52 m. 11) and had been given a foundation charter by the royal seneschal towards the end of the previous reign.   Like Toulouzette on its west, it stood on the bank of the Adour at the head of a large meander.   The river has now left this course and St. Maurice is high and dry, the nearest French equivalent to Winchelsea, although never as large.   There are no *cornières* and no Place.   The church may date from the fourteenth century.   The buildings of the village are almost wholly of river pebbles.   A small grid-plan can be discerned, some of it in grassy back-lanes.

A.P. Missions Soustons/Mont de Marsan 1950, no. 276.

STE. QUITTERIE (Aire sur l'Adour)   M:82 C:228NW

1289   *Gouron*: 1755–58

The town of Mas (d'Aire) or *Mansus Sanctae Quiteriae* had been burned in 1289, and local people petitioned for a bastide to be built for protection (*R.G.*, ii, 1042).   The king joined with bishop Peter III and the chapter of Ste. Quitterie in a *paréage* (*R.G.*, ii, 2180).   The town continued to have an unquiet history.   In 1316 the count of Armagnac built his own bastide immediately over the river at Barcelonne (*Cosset*) and in 1321 Edward II heard complaints that the count had burned Mas (C61/35 m. 13d).

The perfect grid of streets in the lower town (Aire sur l'Adour) suggests that the bastide was built at the bridge-head.   On the hill-top there are houses near the shrine of Ste. Quitterie, probably the site of the town before 1289.   The main road through the town is still confined by the grid of the bastide, although the narrowness has enforced a one-way street system for traffic.   Except for the two churches, one in the bastide, there is no atmosphere recalling the medieval town.   (See L. Sorbets, *L'Histoire d'Aire sur l'Adour* (3 vols., 1895).)

SALESPISSE   M:78 C:?227NE

c. 1306–13   *Rouron*: 1871

An enquiry of 1319 (B.M. Cott. Julius, E.I, f. 179v) reported that the king's seneschal, Amanieu de Fossat, and William Bernard, a seigneur of "Salis", had made a paréage which had proved abortive.   The commission of enquiry reported that the bastide would be "a tower and barbican (*turris et barbacana*) for all the king's lands and on the very frontier of Béarn, whence came so much loss and damage".

Gouron places "Salis" near Bonnut: if it is to be in the modern department of Landes it would need to be several miles north of Bonnut; but 3 miles further into Béarn is the village and castle of Sallespisse.   *Dictionnaire Topographique de Basses Pyrénées* (ed. P. Raymond, 1861), p. 156, gives 1304 as the earliest documented reference to Salespisse.   A river-name to the west and north is "Le Pas de Salles" (*ibid.*, p. 155).

The whole ridge from Bonnut to Salespisse commands the frontier on the north-east and also has extensive views to the south-west.   Bonnut itself now has nothing which suggests a bastide: the main street of Salepisse, on the other hand, terminates at the chateau, alongside which is the church; and there are one or two side-lanes which may represent the decayed grid-plan.

A.P. Mission St. Vincent/Gimont, no. 609, and Orthez/Lembeye, 1957, nos. 16–17.

SARRON   M:82   C:228NW

by 1318   *Gouron*: 1887–88

The original charter is not known, but when Geaune was founded in August 1318 the customs of Sarron were taken as a model. In September 1321 Edward II ordered the seneschal of Gascony to search the archives at Bordeaux and re-issue the charter of Sarron since the original had been destroyed when the town was burned by the count of Armagnac (C61/35 m. 13d). The bastide is here called "de Serrafronte", and Gouron suggested that Geoffrey Front-de-Bœuf, seneschal of the Landes (see Rondebœuf *supra*), may have had a part in the original foundation.

The town stood on the very frontier of the Landes. The main road from Aire to Bayonne passes through the modern village, probably along the central axis of the bastide of which there are few characteristic remains. There are no *cornières* and no Place. Two minor roads on the east and two on the west may represent part of the former grid, but the clearest remains are in hollow ways on the eastern side of the main road immediately to the south of the village. These are of the quality of Roquepine.

A.P. Mission Aire sur Adour/Gimont, 1948, no. 379.

SORDE L'ABBAYE   M:85   C:227NW

1290 and 1314   *Gouron*: 1958–59

In 1314 Edward II received an offer of a *paréage* from the abbot of Sorde and authorised his seneschal of Gascony, Amaury de Créon, to proceed with its preparation. The document does not actually mention a bastide, and may have been only intended to confer general privileges on an existing town. A *paréage* had been drawn up in 1290 between the abbot of that day and the seneschal of Toulouse acting in the name of the king of France. This offer by Eustace de Beaumarchais is a curious intervention, for there was no open war, and in 1280 (*R.G.*, ii, 364), Edward I had actually assisted with the expense of town walls at Sorde. It looks as though there was an old nucleus near the abbey to which a bastide was added.

The abbey occupies a fine riverside site, with its ivy-grown cloisters overlooking the former mill-dam which now holds back water for the small hydro-electric station. To the west of the abbey the streets assume a crude grid-pattern, and there is a gate; remnants of walls can be seen along the edge of the gardens which overhang the river.

SOUPROSSE   M:78   C:215SE

1289   *Gouron*: 1963–64

In 1314 Edward II's commissioners reported that the abbey of St. Sever had joined with the king before the war in order to found a bastide at Souprosse. In April

1289 Edward I had given his officials power to share the profits of justice at Souprosse with the prior of St. Sever, and although the document does not mention a bastide specifically, this was probably the purpose of the agreement.

The village is traversed by the main road and has lost all character. It has no defensive potentialities at all.

A.P. Mission Souston/Mont de Marsan, 1950, no. 291.

TOULOUZETTE

M:78 C:215SE

1321   *Gouron*: 1987–88

The bastide was named in honour of William of Toulouse, the king's seneschal of the Landes, who, together with Amaury de Créon, seneschal of Agenais, founded it. The formal act of foundation is described, possibly because it was on "foreign" soil (*in solo alieno*): William had made firm and planted the *palum* or pole, and granted to those who wanted to people the new town the right of building houses and possessing the liberties and customs of Geaune, a bastide then three years old (C61/35 m. 15).

The village is on the south bank of a small river which joins the Adour a mile further west. The grid pattern is elementary, with one main street, the thoroughfare. There is a grass-grown Place but no *cornières*.

A.P. Mission Soustons/Mont de Marsan, 1950, no. 381.

VILLENAVE

M:78 C:215NE

c. 1319   *Gouron*: 2039

This bastide derives its identification from the same document (E101/166/1) as La Bastide (Montpazier) *supra*, where William de Montaigut, seneschal of Gascony, is said to have founded the bastide of "Montaigut in the jurisdiction of Brassens". The suggestion of Gouron is that this bastide was Villenave. The barony of Brassens lay in the Grandes Landes near Morcenx, Arjuzanx and Arengosse (Gouron 38–39), which would seem to prevent the identification of this bastide with Montégut, *supra*, where the same seneschal was co-founder of a bastide in 1320.

At their best, the Landes bastides have very few medieval remains, and there is nothing in the topography of Villenave to support or to refute the suggestion of a site except that it has been chosen for one of the few fire-control look-out towers, suggesting that before afforestation there might have been commanding views at ground level.

A.P. Mission Lit et Mixe/Cazaubon, 1950, no. 312.

DEPARTMENT OF LOT

Quercy, or the diocese of Cahors, affected the king of France more than the king-duke. After the treaty of 1259 the majority of its seigneurs opted for allegiance to Paris and the English influence was confined to the areas handed over in compensation in 1286. Within this area two English bastides were founded, and in 1293

Edward purchased further land for a third. The bare and rock-strewn soils retarded colonisation by either party, and the only French bastides are found in the south-west, near to Montauban.

CAZALS   M:75   C:194NW
c. 1316–27

It would seem that this bastide was built on to or alongside the castle-town of Cazals by the seneschal of Périgord and Quercy, William of Toulouse, and apparently without the agreement of the seigneur of Cazals (SC8/274/13662 (not dated)) but with the king's authority: *bastidam vocatam de Montolza . . . auctoritate regia de novo erexit*. William de Tholosa had been a partner in founding Toulouzette in 1322 and St. Barthélemy de Bellegarde (by 1316) (*q.v.*). Some notes on the town in *Albe*, pp. 60 and 408, suggest the double topography. Cazal appears, not specifically as a bastide, in a list of "towns bastides and places" of January 1318 (C61/32 m. 13).

The site is slightly elevated on the north bank of a stream; it is crossed in its short axis by the road from Gourdon to Villeneuve-sur-Lot. To the north-east of the town is the walled chateau with an old church between it and the town; the church at the south-west is modern. The rectilinear street plan runs westward from the church and includes an open square, probably the original Place. There are no *cornières*.

A.P. Mission Gourdon/Grammat 1957, no. 157.

LA BASTIDE MURAT   M:79   C:194NE
c. 1290–1304

There is an entry—*Bastida Fortanerii de Gordonio restituta erat Regi Anglie*—in *Comptes Royaux 1285–1314*, ed. Fawtier, iii (1956), p. 45. The date of this document is 1304. Fortaner was lord of Gouron in 1290 (*G.C.*, 1086) and he had financial dealings with Edward I in the same year (*R.G.*, ii, 1807). The bastide is now known as Murat. It was planted in the parish of Soyriès of which the only remains is the belltower of the church half a mile south of the town. (*Albe*, p. 399.) There is a plan in *Lavedan*, p. 322. The town plan is now confused by the transfer of its centre of gravity to a large open Place at the north end of the town, leaving the old Place by the church deserted. In 1960 even the church seemed in disrepair. Beneath more recent alterations a long, narrow grid, with the church near the south end, could be discerned. On the west side (and eventually on the north) the ground falls steeply but the other sides are more level. There is no sign of walls, gates, or *cornières*. Like its neighbour a few miles to the north, Montfaucon, the town is placed on a spur of high ground in the midst of a dissected high plateau from which very extensive views towards the Garonne, Dordogne and Lot can be obtained, as well as north-eastwards into territory that was always French.

MONTFAUCON DU LOT   M:75   C:194NE
1292–93

This bastide, so far east, would be difficult to credit to the English were not the three documents on the Gascon Roll (*R.G.* 2148, 2168 and 2172) explicitly concerned with an agreement with the lord of the castle of Séniergues in 1293, and then with the expenses of making the bastide. It also appears in SC8/274/13662 and in a list of 1318 (C61/32 m. 12: Montis Falconis in Caturcinio) and in *G.C.*, 1723, where its customs are dated 1292. Its foundation followed the settlement of 1286 when Edward was given six parishes in Quercy in part settlement of the old dispute covering Joan of Castile's dowry (*Albe*, p. 483).

The plan in *Lavedan*, p. 345, is deceptive; the air photograph shows a well-defined grid which extends southwards into the fields. The town is well placed on a spur of land at the north end of which there is a chateau, now a P.T.T. sanatorium. This building and its courtyards have clearly encroached on the grid of the bastide to the west of the church, and the market-place is much diminished although two houses on the south side (and possibly a third which was being demolished in 1960) are medieval. The church has a thirteenth-century tower and porch. There are no *cornières* remaining. Roads come up the slopes from the valley to entrances in the middle of the east and west sides of the grid, obviously former gates. No walls remain, although there is some sign of artificial steepening on the east side. The streets, some of which are now grass-grown, were about 6½ yards wide; the grid pattern extends into the field-roads and fields.

A.P. Mission Condom/Gramont, 1957, no. 122.

DEPARTMENT OF LOT ET GARONNE

This Department corresponds roughly to the area of the Agenais, the seat of the first Gascon plantations by Alphonse de Poitiers. Its political history and the circumstances of acquisition by Edward in 1279 have been outlined above, p. 355. The Alphonsian bastides and their Edwardian successors give it a very high density of plantations. See also J-P. Poussou, "Introduction à l'Étude des chartes . . . de l'Agenais", *Rev. de l'Agenais*, xc (1964), pp. 115–126 and 207–225, which appeared after this gazetteer was compiled.

AIGUILLON   M:79   C:205NW

1296   *Gouron*: 164–171

The history of Aiguillon is confused. There seem to have been two adjoining towns, each associated with adjoining, and rival, castles, those of Lunac and Fossat. Even today, the town is on two different levels. The upper town is a regular grid-pattern of streets on the east of the chateau, which is poised on the edge of a steep cliff overlooking the Garonne. The lower town, also with a grid, focuses on the bridge carrying the R.N. 127 over the Lot. The two rivers join a mile north-west of Aiguillon, and the command of the junction and the river-crossing gave the bastides both commercial and military importance. Just across the river was a third bastide, Nicole (*q.v.*)

There were two seigneurial castles here before the coming of the bastide. At the request of the lord of Lunac, Edward I's officers planned a bastide at the entrance of the faubourg of Muneau, just under the walls of the castle of Fossat. (*Gouron*, 164 (1296); see also *R.G.*, iv, nos. 565 (1311) and 1709 (1316)). The lord of Fossat complained and the work may have halted. But in 1315 the consuls of Lunac asked Edward II for permission to rebuild the bastide which Arnaud-Garcias de Fossat had destroyed in the recent war, and in 1316 Edward II ordered his seneschal to investigate the continuing complaints of the lords of Fossat against the bastide of Lunac. In 1348 Edward III confirmed the privileges of "the town, royal castle and bastide of Lunac". The name St. Edward, sometimes given to this bastide during the reign of Edward II, was probably a tribute to the name-saint of Edward I, the original founder. The mention in the same document of 1348 (C61/60 m. 6) of *burgo seu castro de Fossato dicti loci de Aculeo* suggests that the Fossat part of the town (the lower) was not reckoned a bastide. The document freed the wine grown within a league of Aiguillon from the dues levied at Bordeaux; other wines handled in the town were to pay the full custom.

The dual topography is set out in a petition from Lunac to Edward II in 1320: "there are in Aiguillon two *castra*, that is one called Lunac belonging to us and the other called Fossat which is not ours; the inhabitants of Fossat enjoy freedom from the custom (wine dues) of Bordeaux and the inhabitants of Lunac wish to have a privilege of this sort such as Edward I of blessed memory promised them when he said that he would give them such liberties as one of his bastides of Agenais possessed".

In the same year Fossat was granted an annual eight-day fair. (See also *Recueil des ordonnances des rois de France de la troisième race* (1732–1849), vol. xii, pp. 397–403; R. L. Alis, *Histoire de la Ville d'Aiguillon* (1895).)

A.P. Mission Tonneins/Penne d'Agenais, 1950, no. 295.

ARTUS   M:79   C:192SE

1288   *Gouron*: 193

The settlement consists of four farms on or near a by-road leading up from the valley to a plateau (*G.R.* 42822553). There are faint signs of terraces and one hollow-way which might once have been a road, but no significant pattern. The church was demolished during the last century (*R.G.*, p. 339 fn. 4). The plateau-top site would not be out of character with local bastides.

The correction made to Bémont's date of the foundation charter has in turn been corrected by J. P. Trabut-Cussac, *B.I.H.R.*, xxv (1952), p. 189 fn.

The customs given the new town by Edward I were those of Castelnau-sur-Gupie, 4 kilometres to the south-west, founded twelve years earlier: *R.G.*, 56 and 1097. The existing inhabitants of the parish were to build their houses in the new bastide within two years, newcomers within three. Although Gouron treats *R.G.*, 1097, as a foundation charter for Artus, its language could mean that the parishioners of Artus were being allowed the opportunity of residing in Castelnau: *Habeant domos sufficientes in dicta bastida.*

BOULOGNE (St. Pé-St. Simon)   M:79   C:216NE
1289   *Gouron*: 1820–21

The dean of Paravis gave land for the bastide on the plateau of Lannegrasse (*Landagrassa*) where an earth motte had already been raised.   In Jean de Grilly's charter of customs (*R.G.*, 2128) the bastide was called *Bolonia Grasse*.   In *R.G.*, 1414 the bastide was in association with Cazaubon and Larée, which makes Bémont's assignment of the charter to Boulogne-sur-Gesse unlikely (*R.G.*, iii, p. cxii).   From *R.G.*, iv, 5136, it will be seen that Gaston de Béarn claimed rights in the bastide (June 1289).

The site suggested by Gouron is in the west of St. Pé and within a mile of the junction of the boundaries of the departments of Landes, Gers and Lot-et-Garonne.   The documentary reference to a motte suggests a strategical situation, and relative to the level terrain of the Landes, this requirement is met by the ground near the farm of Petit-Boulogne (*G.R.* 41811917).   There are man-made earthworks in the grass fields near the farm and the hill-top seems to have been levelled on the west, whence the ground drops about 120 feet to the river (and departmental boundary) on which the mill of Boulogne stands.   This plateau drops quite steeply to a minor valley on the north and the site is not unlike many chosen for a bastide.   The local countryside uses timber rather than stone for its buildings, and there are no signs of buried foundations.   There is the suggestion of a small moated site.   No local tradition could be discovered.   The soil is light and sandy, and it is fortunate that the ground near the farm has remained under grass and thus preserved something of the bastide project.

CASTELNAU SUR GUPIE   M:79   C:192SE
1276   *Gouron*: 696–698

The privileges granted in the charter of 1276 (*R.G.*, ii, 56) were those of Sainte-Foy-la-Grande, founded twenty-one years earlier.   There was a dispute with the town of Marmande over the boundaries of the bastide's jurisdiction, especially in Beaupuy parish.   (*R.G.*, ii, 256; C61/30 m. 21 (1315); see also C47/25/2 (1316).)   The size of the plot assigned in the charter was 72 feet by 24 feet.

The site is a good hill-top position similar to that of its neighbour Mauvezin. Despite the commanding position the town has lost the character which has clung to such towns as Domme and Beaumont du Périgord.

A.P. Mission La Teste de Buch/Marmande, 1950, 287.

CASTILLONNÈS   M:79   C:193NW
1259   *Gouron*: 719–730

The bastide was founded in 1259 by a *paréage* between the abbey of Cadouin and two local landowners on the one part and Alphonse de Poitiers' seneschal on the other. When the Agenais was restored to Edward I in 1279, half the town was expressly reserved to the king of France (G. P. Cuttino, ed., *Le Livre d'Agenais* (Toulouse, 1956)).

A document in *A.P.E.A.*, pp. 210–211 (1266), suggests that the bastide might have been founded in Raymond VII's time (*i.e.* before Alphonse).

616

The town was burned in 1272, and was then the object of partition between Edward I and the king of France: the latter took half the town and eighteen neighbouring parishes, the former the other half of the town and five or six parishes (SC8/4188–89). It became wholly English after 1303, but it was not until 1319 that the townspeople petitioned Edward II to provide the town with four gates if they bore the remaining cost of building walls. They described their position as being at the very edge of Agenais and near to the king of France's territory. (C61/33 m. 15, printed in Trabut-Cussac, *Le Moyen Age*, lxx (1954), p. 97.)

The town plan can be seen in *Lavedan*, p. 336. The bastide occupies a characteristic position on the edge of a small plateau, overlooking a small tributary of the Dropt.

A.P. Mission Podensac/Belvès, 1950, no. 229.

DAMAZAN   M:79   C:204NE
1250–69   *Gouron*: 853–858

This bastide was also known as *Castrum Comitale*; it was accorded its customs by Alphonse, c. 1269, and these were confirmed by Edward I (? in 1287). In 1289 its fair-days were altered so as not to clash with those of Tonneins, and in 1290 Edward called it "our bastide". (*R.G.*, ii, 1625, 1725, 1776; *G.C.*, 1050). It is listed among Alphonse's creations in C47/29/1/9–10, but as English in such lists as C61/32 m. 12 and 35, m. 6 (1318 and 1324).

The town has a well-preserved grid of streets, with the central Place and *cornières*. The site is on top of a cliff-like descent to the plain of Garonne; the Garonne canal now flows beneath its walls.

A.P. Mission Tonneins/Penne d'Agenais, 1950, no. 291.

DURANCE   M:79   C:204SE
1320   *Gouron*: 926

The only English reference found to this bastide was the gall-stained membrane of the Gascon Roll for 1324 (C61/35 m. 19v): *dictis novis bastidis videlicet novae bastidae Duran (. .) parochiam . . .*; but after M. Trabut-Cussac had suggested the reading "Durance", reference to *Gouron* gave the *paréage* of 1320 in the departmental archives of Basses-Pyrénées. Edward's *paréage* with the abbot of St. Jean de la Castelle suggests a grange site, and indeed the church of the grange and a possible part of the grange buildings can be found in the woodland about half a mile to the north of the town. Like the gatehouses and walls of the bastide the grange is sadly ruined but retains many of its interior architectural features; the irregular clearing in the forest and the farm-house nearby are very much in character with the original colonisation from this monastic outpost.

The bastide has one street from north to south, and a Place opposite the east end of the church (where three stalls were to be seen on a September Sunday morning in 1958). The west and south gates remain, the latter in the care of the Society of Science, Letters and Arts of Agen. In the north-east quarter is a large building known as the chateau of Henry IV.   Fragments of town wall can be seen in the south-west quadrant, and ditches follow its course along the east and west sides.   The site is quite flat and unprotected by nature.   It is very near the eastern extremity of the Landes, and woodland comes within fifty yards of the north gate of the town.

FOURQUES   M:79   C:192SE
1285   *Gouron*: 60 and 971

This was one of two bastides specifically named in a generally permissive order to make *paréages* for the founding of bastides in Gascony and the Agenais which Edward I issued from London in June 1285.

The site is very similar to that of Damazan, Lagruère and Monheurt, all on the left bank of the Garonne and placed where the valley floor meets the higher ground of the surrounding plateau.   Across the river is Marmande.   The Garonne canal passes by the northern edge of the village giving it a moated appearance: but there are no signs of any defences for the bastide which is a pure riverside *bastide du commerce*.   The church is well kept, but the village is small, with one shop and a café.   The Place has a new Halle, and is a sports field.   Caravans and a working tinker were the only sign of economic life when the village was visited.

A.P. Mission La Teste de Buche/Marmande, no. 523.

GRANGES SUR LOT   M:79   C:205NW
1291   *Gouron*: 1038–39

The bastide was to be called St. Damien; a monastic grange of the abbey of Clairac must have already existed here, on the south bank of the river Lot.   The grid plan of streets is laid out along the very edge of the river, with one street going down to the water's edge, perhaps to a ford.   The main road from Villeneuve to Bordeaux takes the outermost street of the grid, leaving the market place quietly on the north and the fabric of the buildings untouched by modern prosperity.   The buildings are of the characteristic flat brick together with timbering and half-timbering.   The riverside streets are very pleasant.

A.P. Mission Tonneins/Penne d'Agenais, 1950, no. 109.

LA BASTIDE CASTELAMOUROUX   M:79   C204NE
c. 1269   *Gouron*: 1082–84

Alphonse de Poitiers negotiated agreements for the foundation of this bastide c. 1269, two years before his death, but its charter seems to be no earlier than Edward I's grant of 1286 when the bastide was given privileges based on those of Valence d'Agenais.   Two years later the charter of Castelamouroux was in its turn taken as the model for the new bastide of St. Pastour (*q.v.*).   The customs are printed by H. Rébouis in *Nouv. Rev. Hist de Droit*, xii (1888), pp. 80 sqq. (the date is given as 1286 in *G.C.*, 1039, citing B.M. Cott. Julius, E.1, f. 132).

The characteristic plateau-edge situation is not inferior to any of the more successful bastides of the neighbourhood, but Castelamouroux has now only two farms and a ruined church. The farm roads and some of the field boundaries preserve part of the rectangular grid (see also *Lavedan*, Fig. 125) and the occupant of one farm said in 1957 that ploughing often revealed road foundations and boundary walls in line with this decayed grid. The church is surrounded with undergrowth and lacks a roof. The internal walls are almost complete and the south-west tower still has its staircase.

A.P. Mission Tonneins/Penne d'Agenais, 1950, no. 149.

LACENNE   M:79   C:205NW

1283   *Gouron*: 1102–09

This, like Hastingues, is an example of a bastide with a considerable delay between the original *paréage* and the erection of the town, although the delaying factor here seems to have been not war but a conflict with local privileges. In 1311 two commissioners heard complaints from the people of Agen against the proposals to have a bastide at *Apenchavila* and in 1318 Edward II ordered an inquiry to see why the consuls of Agen had stopped the work on the bastide. The order describes the bastide as *novam populationem seu bastidam ibidem factam*; and a *paréage* is reported between the abbot and a royal seneschal, Ralph Savage; there may have been an earlier *paréage* when William de Cohardon was seneschal of Agenais. In 1319 the abbot petitioned the king for a grant of privileges for the town, and in August 1320 the bastide "lately commenced" was given the liberties of Villeneuve and Monflanquin. (See also SC8/14118.)

The church of *Cena* (Lacenne) stands in isolation half a mile from the hamlet of Coulbau in Sembas (46442274). It was not possible to gain admission when visited in September 1957. The surrounding field-roads have something of a rectangular lay-out but this may be fortuitous; no earthworks or foundations could be seen.

A.P. Mission Tonneins/Penne d'Agenais, 1950, no. 236.

LAGRUÈRE   M:79   C:204NE

by 1289   *Gouron*: 1116

There is a plan of this bastide in *Lavedan* p. 331. The bounds of the jurisdiction of the new town were determined in 1291 (*R.G.*, ii, 1529, and iii, 1931) and its charter of privileges confirmed in 1310 by Edward I (*G.C.*, 1725).

The town stands on the edge of the Garonne; the plan in *Lavedan* is misleading, for there are only four farms and their gardens alongside the church. There are no shops, *cornières*, walls, gates nor a Place. There is a single street forming a long axis parallel to the river but it serves only as a farm road; the modern motor road passes along what must have been the edge of the town.

A.P. Mission Tonneins/Penne d'Agenais, 1950, no. 123.

LA MONTJOIE ST. LOUIS   M:79   C:205SW and 217NW

1299   *Gouron*: 1126–30

This bastide was in English hands by 1308 when Edward II confirmed the charter of Philippe le Bel's seneschal; it had been founded during the war near Ligardes castle

(*R.G.*, iv, 171). In 1318 it was annexed to the crown of England. The original foundation was one of those designed to pacify the local countryside.

It occupies a good hill-top position, but the centre of commercial activity has moved from the old Place, where the only shop is a grocer's, to an open square on the ramparts. There are no *cornières* in the old Place but the style has influenced the houses. Domengie thought this was the only bastide of the Agenais to lack them. *Deffontaines* (p. 154) states that the chequer pattern of the streets is continued into the field land of the bastide.

A.P. Mission Montréal/Montaubon, 1950, no. 363.

LA PARADE   M:79   C:205NW

1267   *Gouron*: 1136–42

This bastide occupies a magnificent site high above the Lot with a steep rampart on the south, walls on the west, and a moat to the north. The town well is 30 metres deep. The plan of the town is long and narrow with a perfect grid pattern but sadly decayed. The half-timbered houses are picturesque even in semi-ruin; the touristic possibilities have been neglected, and it is probably too late now. A visit is strongly recommended. The rather flat-sounding modern name is less characterful than the original and bold *Castrum Senioris*.

Between 1290 and 1320 the English kings were several times involved in disputes between the townspeople and the abbey of Clairac (*R.G.*, ii, 1771; C61/31 m. 2; 34 m. 2; and 34 m. 1).

A.P. Mission Tonneins/Penne d'Agenais, 1950, no. 111.

LE TEMPLE DE BREUIL (alias FELTON)   M:79   C:205NW

1320   *Gouron*: 1968–69

Gouron, 1968, cites a *paréage* of 1320 giving the bastide the customs which Nomdieu had acquired between 1305–08; and in 1348 Edward III ratified this agreement. The bastide was also known as Felton (*Inventaire sommaire des archives du Lot et Garonne*, Gi.) in 1363–66. John Felton was seneschal of the Agenais in 1319 (*G.C.*, 1025).

A document of 1348 (C61/60 m. 8) mentions "Felton" in association with two other parishes: *in parochiis de Sancto Michaele de Bas et de Sancto Calvario de Reda ut ante constructionem bastitae* (sic) *de Feltona legitime fieri censuentur*. Ranfroy de Montpezat occurs in this document as well as in those of 1320 and 1348. The identification of *Reda* and *Bas* proved impossible locally but M. Burias of the Archives of Lot et Garonne kindly suggested that they should read *Sancto Michaele de Lam* (or Lans) and *Sancto Caprasio de Lede*. The former church lay in Domayrac commune (M:79; C:205NW) and the latter in Monflanquin (M:79; C:193SE). St. Caprais du Temple (GR: 455238) may be a better suggestion since St. Caprais de Lede is remote from Le Temple de Breuil.

A further complication is that a bastide of Breuil (*Brolium Balengarii*) was projected in 1267 by Alphonse de Poitiers (*A.P.* i, p. 305; the editor was unable to locate the site and thought the project abortive.)

The bastide, like its neighbours Granges and St. Sardos, was badly injured in war between 1367 and 1372. An account of the town in *Rev. Agenais*, xxi (1898), p. 175, mentions a fifteenth-century rebuilding on an older plan. The present parish church was the church of the chateau (perhaps of the commandery of the Templars?). The town is very small, just off the Route Nationale, with a good deal of old building in the flat Toulousian brick, but without any clear grid plan.

LÉVIGNAC   M:79   C:192NE
1305   *Gouron*: 1196

The town lies just to the west of the main road and has remained unaffected by modern developments. There is no record of the actual foundation, only Edward I's order to his seneschal to examine the project.

A.P. Mission La Teste de Buch/Marmande, 1950, no. 90.

LIBOS   M:79   C:193SE
c. 1320   *Gouron*: 1198–99

The project is known only from a letter of c. 1320 informing the bishop of Agen that Pope John XXII approved of it, provided an enquiry showed that a bastide would be of some use here. The mover had been the prior of Monsempron whose priory owned the land at *Aribos* on the north bank of the Lot, 200 or 300 feet lower than Monsempron which was a hill-top town. The flat situation makes it a typical bastide of commerce, on a river bank and at a bridge head. There is a small east-west grid parallel to the river, with three streets, and a Place near the church on the north of the grid. The eastern limit of the town is set by the river Lemance which joins the Lot here. Modern building has left the town with little character, and it is almost continuous with Fumel.

A.P. Mission Cancon/Fumel, 1950, no. 58.

LONDRES (ST. ETIENNE)   M:79   C:192SE
? after 1327   *Gouron*: 1245

Apart from the characteristic adoptive name the only evidence of a bastide here is a source cited by Domengie and followed by *Lavedan*, pp. 285–286. The place appears in a list of *baillies* in 1363–66, derived from an Exchequer account in *Inventaire sommaire des archives du Lot et Garonne*, Gi. Gouron's tentative dating derives from the absence of any record in the rolls of Edward I or II.

The site is a hill-top plateau where there is still a small church. Opposite is a farm, and a little further away the tower of a windmill or dovecote. It has a carved fleur-de-lis coat of arms and an old nail-studded door. In the surrounding orchards and fields the lanes are sunken hollow-ways not unlike the abortive streets of Roque-pine. More documentation would be useful.

A.P. Mission FR. 122/250, 1950, no. 1353.

MARMANDE   M:79 C:192SE

1182   *Gouron*: 1277–94

This very early foundation antedates the main group of bastides, both English and French, by nearly a century, and its nearest parallels are Richard I's other creations at Petit Andelys and Portsmouth. The evidence for a bastide at Marmande rests on documents: Alphonse de Poitiers wrote *ad Mermandam seu in aliis bastidis nostris* (*A.P.*, ii, p. 265). In 1270 a petition from the town spoke of its rights *a principio fondationis dicte bastide* (*A.P.E.A.*, p. 307) and in another paragraph of the same petition (p. 308) *sub eis conditionibus quas recipiunt alie bastide*. Again, when the charter of Richard I was confirmed in 1340 it was recited in the language of bastides: "as the said place of Marmande, being new, has need of being peopled and made large, men of any place who come to live there will be welcomed by the men of the seigneur and of the town, and if the newcomer wishes to become a burgess he and his goods shall be safe." (P. Tamizey de Larroque, *Notice sur la Ville de Marmande* (1872), pp. 4–5, from Bibl. Nat., Coll. Baluzes, Les Armoires, xxv; (for a dissenting view of Marmande as a bastide see, C. Higounet, *Rev. de l'Agenais*, lxxxviii (1952), p. 4); in 1243 a list of 240 burgesses occurs, *ibid.*, pp. 24–26.

There were four gates to the old town which in the last two centuries has been absorbed into a prosperous provincial market town. An air-photograph in P. Deffontaines and M. J.-B. Delamarre, *Atlas Aérien*, iii (1958), no. 169, shows the rectilinear pattern of the bastides in the church quarter of the town alongside the market place (now covered) and the south wall of the town above the river. In their note the authors draw attention to the bastide but state that there was an older town to which it was attached. Tamizey de Larroque mentions no earlier town. In the Albigensian Crusade Marmande was besieged and sacked: Z. Oldenbourg, *Massacre at Montségur* (1959), p. 202.

A.P. Mission La Teste de Buch/Marmande, 1950, no. 497; FR. 122/250, 1950, no. 1313.

(near) MAUVEZIN SUR GUPIE (d'Agenais)   M:79 C:192SE

1278   *Gouron*: 1321–23

In 1355–59 there was an enquiry as to whether the foundation of a bastide within the jurisdiction of Mauvezin in 1278 had harmed the interests of the local seigneur. The bastide was not named; Mauvezin itself has not the clear grid plan of a bastide (*Lavedan*, Fig. 204) and I think it possible that the foundation referred to was Artus (*q.v.*) founded in 1288 a mile to the north. R. L. Alis, *Notice sur . . . Mauvezin* (1887), adds nothing relevant.

MIRAMONT   M:79 C:193SW

1278–86   *Gouron*: 1366–70

There was probably some delay in the execution of the agreement to found a town here, for in April 1289 Edward ordered the seneschal of Agenais to carry out the terms of the *paréage* which had been made when Jean de Grilly was seneschal. The customs were enrolled in 1294 (*G.C.*, 1714). It was not until 1324 that Edward II in response to a petition from the townspeople promised to provide four stone gates if the town would provide the stone walls. An undated petition (SC8/14215) from the town claimed that the lord of Lancaster "formerly Lieutenant in Gascony" had granted the town funds for the enclosure and fortification of its walls. Six years had elapsed and the townspeople had no means to accomplish the work. This "lord of Lancaster" was Henry of Lancaster, earl of Derby, Lieutenant in Aquitaine, 1345–47, and the petition dates from 1351–52.

The town occupies a small but not very striking hill-top position. The walls have now gone, and are replaced by an exterior boulevard, ambitious but now dilapidated. The main road enters the town at the site of the south gate and leaves by the west. An older road, now disused, can be traced from the north gate leading towards Eymet, which the modern road approaches more circumspectly. The *cornières* on the south side of the Place may be original, and are an interesting mixture of wood and stone. Old postcards show that there has been refurbishing of them this century. The grid is very well preserved, with androynes and narrow minor streets. There is a plan in *Lavedan*, p. 360; the foundation charter prescribed building plots of 72 feet by 24 feet. Despite its position on a main road the town is not without character.

A.P. Mission Cancon/Fumel, 1950, no. 258.

MONCLAR D'AGENAIS
M:79   C:193SW

1256   *Gouron*: 1400–3

In 1289 Edward I was concerned with a revision of the town government and referred to an earlier confirmation which he had made (?1279).

There is a plan of the town in *Lavedan*, p. 339; it occupies a hill-top with commanding views. Bare rock is exposed at several points in the streets and house-floors of the town. There are a number of good medieval houses in brick and wattle. There are ramparts on the north side, embracing the town well. The church is in the chequer south-east of the Place which has two of its sides arched with *cornières*.

MONFLANQUIN
M:79   C:193SE

1256   *Gouron*: 1408–19

The Alphonsian grant was confirmed by Edward I in 1284. In 1282 (Trabut-Cussac, *Le Moyen Age* lxx (1954), p. 98, citing SC1/55/17–8) Jean de Grilly resolved a dispute about responsibility for making the walls which had arisen between the bastide and the out-villages: the 1,772 houses in the area dependent on the bastide were to contribute £1,000 towards the fortifications, and in return were to share all the privileges of the bastide. (See also *A.P.*, 1895; and H. Rébouis in *Nouv. Rev. Hist. de Droit*, xiv (1890)). The town's charter was modelled on Ste. Foy and Monclar.

The town is still extensive, on a fine hill-top site (*Lavedan*, pp. 356–358), visible for many miles around. It is a prosperous place, and the whole hill-top is packed with houses except for a small open clearing (probably recent) in the north-east corner. The shape of the hill-top has given a circular perimeter to the bastide but the streets preserve a strict north-south and east/west alinement. The Place has *cornières* on all sides, but no Halle. The church is on the north-east of the Place, in the same relative position as at Villeneuve sur Lot, one of whose gates is named after this bastide. A fine three-storey stone house with *cornières* at the N.E. corner of the Place may well be contemporary with the foundation. There are several other houses in the Place with stone *cornières* and Gothic arches. There are no gates. There is only one entrance from the countryside, that on the south of the town, the remainder of the perimeter being ramparts of up to 20 feet in height. The church, which is of stone, is a great fortified building.

A.P. Mission Cancon/Fumel, 1950, no. 113.

MONTPOUILLAN   M:79   C:192SE
1265   *Gouron*: 1478–79

This is another early foundation. The charter was given by Eleanor of Provence in 1265, conferring the privileges of Monségur. These were confirmed by the Lord Edward in 1267. Its situation on the edge of a small river-cliff on the south bank of the Garonne is very similar to Fourques and Damazan, but it has prospered less. There is really nothing left of the bastide except the church; there are a few scattered farms and some of the lanes cross at right angles.

A.P. Mission La Teste de Buch/Marmande, no. 526.

MONTRÉAL   M:79   C:216NE
c. 1272–94   *Gouron*: 1488–89

This bastide, which had the name of *Pecharomas*, was planned to stand on the flat top of a steep hill overlooking the Garonne just north of Agen. The *paréage* was confirmed by Philippe le Bel (1294–99) when French authority was recognised in the Agenais, and again by Edward II in 1308 but there are no traces of the town on the hill-top, although the magnificent position must be acknowledged. There is a farm house, uninhabited, and two stone towers. The approach road is little more than a track.

NICOLE   M:79   C:204NE, 205NW
1291   *Gouron*: 1506–11

The bastide was founded in the parish of St. Symphorien *de Bruyera* (C47/25/2/5 and SC8/273/13607) by agreement between the king's seneschal and treasurer on the one part and the abbot of Clairac on the other. The site was also known as Cangio (*R.G.*, 1935, 2079, and 2086–87: C47/7/24/21). The high spur of ground on the north of the junction of Lot and Garonne is still called Pech de Berre, and according to *Deffontaines*, p. 79, the church on the heights was still used by the people of Nicole until the seventeenth century. There is now a more recent church down in the village.

Nicole faces Aiguillon across the Lot and occupies a similar position to the Low Town there. It is now a straggling village along a very busy main road. It is possible that a parallel terrace lane on the hill-side was once a second street of the bastide. In the early fourteenth century there was considerable damage done to the town by the lord of Tonneins (SC8/273/13607) and by 1348 the consuls of Aiguillon seem to have obtained jurisdiction over Nicole (C61/33 m. 8 and 60 m. 6).

M. Trabut-Cussac has suggested that Nicole, a common French form of "Lincoln", may indicate Hugh de Lacy, earl of Lincoln.

A.P. Mission Tonneins/Penne d'Agenais, 1950, no. 254.

PUYMIROL   M:79   C:205SE

1246   *Gouron*: 1603–15

Already in 1100 there were inhabitants at Grand-Castre (*Gouron*, 1603) but the *paréage* with the bishop of Agen in 1246 and Alphonse de Poitiers' charter (of ?1269) both refer explicitly to a new bastide of Grande Castrum on the hill of Puymirol. There may have been a migration from the plain to the hill-site (*Lavedan*, pp. 337–338 with plan) but "Grande-Castre" is unlikely to have been anywhere except on this very striking hill-top. *Deffontaines*, p. 155, describes recruitment for the bastide from the monks of St. Maurin (8 km. N.E.), their abbey ruined in the Albigensian war.

Edward I confirmed the charter of ?1269 in 1286, and made certain additions. According to Domengie, Edward I also began walling the town in 1283. After a period in French hands, the town was confirmed in its privileges by Edward III in 1368 (*Gouron*: 1610).

The ramparts are of sheer rock, and the west gateway (now decayed) commanded a deeply cut entrance road from the plain below; from it there are fine views of the Garonne valley up to Agen. Five parallel streets form the grid, converging to a pair of streets at the east and west gates. The whole street-plan conforms to the shape of the hill-top. There are many timber houses with wattle-and-daub infill, lacking the mixed wattle-and-brick infill so common in this locality. The church adjoins the Place to the north-east. The porch, in the main street, is on the south side, not at the usual west door, but it is ornate. The *cornières* are almost complete in the Place but most of the shops have been converted to houses. There is no Halle, but the town well in the Place, still used, has water at about 35 feet depth. The town seems quite prosperous still. Like other bastides in the area, its commanding position is emphasised by the choice of site for the modern water-towers, each of which serves 30 or 40 square miles of country (*cp.* Castelsagrat).

REGALIS MONS (Rives)   M:79   C:193NE/SE

1291   *Gouron*: 1674–75

This bastide was founded by the king of France in 1291 but soon came into conflict with the adjoining bastide of Villeréal. Its existence is attested by entries for *bastida de Rippis* in the French royal accounts between 1293 and 1299 (R. Fawtier, ed., *Comptes Royaux*, i, pp. 427, 518, 521 and 544; iii, pp. 23 and 438) and by the sale of the bastide to Edward I, c. 1304, when the *consuls* appealed to the parlement of Paris complaining that the king of England refused to acknowledge their customs. In April 1305 Edward I put the bastide under the same bailiff and consuls as Villeréal, its old rival, and its decay may date from this union. It will be noted that five years later (*R.G.*, iv, 898) the king remembered that he granted Oliver of Bordeaux part of the arrears owed by the consuls and community of Villeréal *pro coadunacione loci Regalis Montis dicte bastide facienda*. This seems to make plain that Villeréal and Regalis Montis were not different names for the same place.

The site is not known but the *Rippis* of the *comptes royaux* is certainly the little village of Rives which stands on a hill, facing Villeréal across the river Dropt. The bastide was also known as *Regalis Mons*, perhaps in deliberate opposition to Villa Regalis (Villeréal). The dispute between Villeréal and *Regalis Mons* has left its traces in *G.C.*, 1667 and 1694, with their *gravamina* and *controversia*.

A petition of 1305 (SC8/114/5695) from a Peter Gerbaldi of Villeréal asked for a post in a registry for his services in opposing the foundation of *bastida regalis montis incepta in parochiis de Ripis prope villam regalem*. Two documents from the Gascon Rolls (*R.G.*, 4741 and 4775) concern this petition and show that the place had recently been handed over to Edward I by the French and assigned to the seneschal of the Agenais. Gerbaldi's petition said, *illud negocium est destructum*, but whether it was the town that had come to an end, or only his advocacy, is not made clear. No local tradition of a site is reported. There is a group of farms called La Bastide but they lie to the south-east of Villeréal (47542593). The "Le Royet" of *Gouron*, 2074, suggests Rayet (47682627) to the east. Another piece of evidence for *Regalis Mons* as a distinct place is a list of parishes (B.M. Cott. Julius E. I., f. 99) assigned to *villa seu bastida vocata de Regali Monte*. These included Mazières, Rives, Doudrac, Naresse, Lolme, Ste. Sabin, Tourliac and St. Cassien. All these lay north of the Dropt: and Villeréal is south of it. M. Trabut-Cussac has attempted to convince me that *Regalis Mons* was the name given by Phillip III to the resumed work at Alphonse de Poitiers' foundation of Villeréal, and cannot be a separate place. *Mons Regalis* was already in use by Alphonse's own officials in 1269 as synonymous with Villeréal (*A.P.E.A.*, pp. 289, fn. 2, and 292; *A.P.*, 1487).

In 1299 a bastide, which seems to be this one, was reported to be held by the French: *Bastida nova que vocatur bastida Montis Regalis aut Regalis Montis, quam in preiudicium domini de Biron et domini Regis Anglie tenet Rex Francie* (Aberdeen Univ. Mss. 218 lines 121–124; transcript kindly loaned by Professor Rothwell).

ROVIGNA   M:79   C:?204SE/205SW

c. 1307–27   *Gouron*: 1673

Our knowledge of the proposed foundation comes from a complaint from a Bertrand de Rovignan that Edward II had begun to build a bastide within his jurisdiction; Bertrand appealed to the king of France (C47/3/29/1, no. 16). The site is uncertain: Gouron would place it within the commune of Buzet (G.R. 43702196) where a Bertrand de Rovignan was co-seigneur. Buzet overlooks the Baïse, between Vianne and Damazan. But Gouron also notes a castle of Révignan in Moncaut (G.R. 45252056) between Nérac and Agen. Buzet has no bastide features. The castle site could not be visited in 1958.

STE. GEMME   M:79   C:205SW

1305   *Gouron*: 1712

In March 1305 the king ordered his seneschals to examine the utility of a project for
a bastide offered by Rainfroy de Durfort. The town was to be in the parish of Ste.
Gemme near Bajamont. There is still a farm called Ste. Gemme two miles north west
of Bajamont (G.R. 46922197). The country hereabouts is very dissected with a
number of sugar-loaf hill-tops. The farm of Ste. Gemme is on the lower slopes of the
hill. The farm of La Belette is much older and may have been fortified. Owing
to the weather conditions in September 1957 it was possible to make only a cursory
examination of the ground, and nothing was seen of earthworks etc. (N.B. This is not
the Ste. Gemme of *R.G.*, ii, 1026 and 1458, which was in Gironde.) M. l'Abbé
Dupré, curé of Pont-du-Casée, kindly tells me that local farmers have heard the tradition of a church at Ste. Gemme, but that no stone is visible and no particular site
known.

A.P. Mission Tonneins/Penne D'Agenais, 1950, no. 350, and Nérac/Valence d'Agen,
1950, no. 45.

ST. JEAN DE CARIET   M:79   C:205SW

c. 1271–82   *Gouron*: 1766–67

The seigneurs concerned in the *paréage* with the count of Périgord were of Paravis
which lies across the river from Porte Ste. Marie (44442172), and in a document of
1313 the place is associated with Vianne (C61/27 m. 3.) Gouron, without specifically identifying the site, places it in Feugarolles. I note *Cadiet* on the map nearby
(44122138), but there is a *Carrié* near Paravis itself (44552164). *Deffontaines*, p. 156,
says that the site is unknown to anyone. *R.G.*, 1494 (1289), locates Cariet near
Vianne.

Visits to the sites support the suggestion of Cadiet in Feugarolles. It is on a
plateau on the opposite side of the Baïse from Vianne, and there is a roofless church
which stands alone in a field, presumably that of St. Jean. Carrié, on the other hand,
is a farm on low ground in the flood-plain of the Garonne, an unlikely site for a town.

ST. JULIEN DE COLORBISSE   M:79   C:204SE

1300   *Gouron*: 1775–77

The original *paréage* was between the seneschal of the king of France and Jourdain de
l'Isle; in 1305 Jourdain petitioned Edward I claiming that the *paréage* he had made
when the king of France held the Agenais was of great benefit to the lord of Agen,
and asking whether the king would confirm the *paréage* (SC8/5860). Edward
ordered his seneschal to make local enquiries and to confirm or suppress the agreement according to what he found (*R.G.*, 4826). *G.C.* has a *paréage* dated 1310 which
may be the favourable result of the seneschal's investigations.

The present village is a scattered woodland settlement with only the vestiges of a
Place, and houses scattered along several roads (42802174). According to *De-*
ffontaines, p. 156, the bastide was never peopled.

STE. MAURE DE PEYRIAC

c. 1324   M:79   C:216NE

Gouron: 1340

A single document, much stained with ink-gall and only partially legible even with the aid of the ultra-violet lamp, witnesses that there was a bastide at Ste. Maure within the jurisdiction of Mezin, from which there had come a petition of protest (C61/35 m. 19v (*olim* 2v): June 9 1324). It is there described as a "new bastide", and "linked to the parish of *deux peyrres*". "Peyre" and "Peyriac" appear on the map (42501925) today near Ste. Maure but the woodland village is scattered and no sign of the characteristic bastide works could be seen. The church, however, stands some distance from the houses.

A.P. Mission Montréal/Montaubon, 1950, no. 419.

ST. PASTOUR

c. 1250–59   M:79   C:193SW

Gouron: 1818–19

In 1289 Edward I granted to this Alphonsian bastide a charter similar to those of Villeréal, La Bastide Castelamouroux and Valence d'Agen. This charter is printed by Rébouis in *Nouv. Rev. Hist. de Droit*, xii (1888), and by Bémont in *R.G.*, ii, 1297.

There is a plan in *Lavedan*, p. 333. *Deffontaines*, p. 156, says that the building plots were finally occupied only during the sixteenth and seventeenth centuries. The western half of the shaded area in Lavedan's plan consists of gardens and fields, but the siting of the west gate and the chateau half way along the plan make it likely that only the eastern half of the area shown was ever occupied. The site is on a hill-top with sharply defined slopes on all sides except the west where there is a saddle-like continuation of the hill. There are ramparts to the north and south; the church, like those of Beaumont and Montréal du Gers, is on the edge of the hill with its south wall incorporated in the defences.

A.P. Mission Cancon/Fumel, 1950, no. 79.

ST. SARDOS

1323   M:79   C:205NW

Gouron: 1828–32

This bastide has the distinction, if it be one, of having an Anglo-French war (1323–25) named after it (see pp. 237–39 above). It is not absolutely clear what lay settlement was already here when the bastide project was formulated. *In dicto loco Sancti Sacerdotis non poterant fieri quinquaginta hospicia ultra illa que erant* (? 1324): (*The War of St. Sardos*, ed. P. Chaplais (Camden Soc., 3rd ser., lxxxvii (1954)), p. 255). *Gouron* gives indirect references to a *paréage* of 1289, but it is difficult to say why there should have been such a fuss in 1322 if a bastide had been agreed a generation earlier. After the war the little town was certainly reckoned a bastide (*Gouron*, 1831–32; dated 1328–29).

It is now a hill-top village with the streets in no marked rectangular pattern. The pattern is a concentric ring with the focus point at the priory (now parish) church. The street-plan is further complicated by the former presence of the priory precinct.

No walls could be seen, but the natural fall of the hillside is sufficient to give protection with only a little artificial steepening.   There is a plan in *Lavedan*, p. 328.

A.P. Mission Tonneins/Penne d'Agenais, 1950, no. 246.

ST. SAUVEUR DE MEILHAN M:79   C:192SE

1318–23 *Gouron*: 1833

The bastide is simply called St. Sauveur (*Sanctus Salvator*) in the first two entries on the Gascon Roll (C61/35, m. 6), but in the second (C61/54 m. 15) the bastide is called St. Sauveur in the diocese of Bazas.   This accords with the suggestion of Marboutin (noted by Gouron) that the bastide was at St. Sauveur de Meilhan.   The street-plan, however, has very little of a grid in it.   There is a church; and perhaps ten rather scattered farms.   The ground is fairly high but not commanding.

A.P. Mission Hostens/Langdon, 1956, no. 65.

VIANNE M:79   C:204SE

1284 *Gouron*: 2021–23

The *paréage* was between Jourdain de l'Isle, lord of Mongaillard, where the agreement was drawn up, and Jean de Grilly acting for the king.   Some hold that the name derives from Jourdain's uncle, Vianne de Gontaud-Biron, others that it is from the town of Viana in Pampelune.

Mongaillard itself is on higher ground to the north-west of the riverside site of the bastide.   There may have already been a village near Vianne, for the bastide was reckoned to be in the parish of St. Mary Villelongue.   The town's fine Romanesque church has a remarkable position for a bastide, being very near the gate, and askew to the streets and building line, suggesting that the new settlement had been laid out with the minimum disturbance to an older church.   The blocked Romanesque south porch was probably replaced at the building of the bastide by the Gothic west front and door.

Only a slender bridge connects with the main road from Porte Ste. Marie to Lavardac, and Vianne has been given an isolation which has preserved much of its character, particularly the walls and gates that are the best of any bastide which has been visited.

As at Libourne and other bastides of the Dordogne, the new town's foundation was followed by public works, partly at the king's expense.   Mills were built in 1289, and in 1291 the town petitioned for a new road towards Nérac, the old road being dangerous.   I suspect that the danger may have been from passing below the castle of Lavardac whose men were often in dispute with the bastide (*R.G.*, ii, 1287, 1411 and 1513).   The request for the new road was granted by the king (C61/19 m. 4; see also J. de B. la Laffore, *Rev. Agenais*, vii (1880), p. 4.)

Although raised above the Baïse on a small cliff, the town was vulnerable to attack from the higher ground immediately above it to the west, and it was therefore walled for defence.   Each corner has a roofed angle tower, and there are fine gates where the three landward roads leave the town. The churchyard was cleared of scrub in 1958 and there is access to the rampart and the interior of the north gatehouse.

A.P. Mission Nérac/Valence d'Agen, 1950, no. 160.

VILLEFRANCHE DE QUEYRAN   M:79   C:204NE
by 1281   *Gouron*: 2036–38

The first reference of 1281 (*R.G.*, ii, 516) is to a bastide that had already been in existence for several years; in 1291 the bounds of the new town were being disputed by her neighbours, Lagruère and La Bastide Castelamouroux.

The older church of St. Sabin stands in semi-ruin to the south-west of the town; the place chosen for the bastide was on slightly lower ground near the little river Ourbise. There is a regular grid plan in *Lavedan*, fig. 187. If a petition of 1305 refers to this bastide, the inhabitants were then seeking means to erect a chapel, enclose the town with walls and build a town hall. The petition is partly printed in Trabut-Cussac, *Le Moyen Age*, lx (1954), pp. 103–104; the dating is his: original is SC8/145/7213, but SC8/291/14544 which is the head of the same petition, refers to Villefranche as in the diocese of Périgueux, which would seem to rule out this bastide and make the document refer to Villefranche de Longchapt or Villefranche du Périgord.

A.P. Mission Tonneins/Penne d'Agenais, 1950, no. 287.

VILLENEUVE SUR LOT   M:79   C:205NW
1264   *Gouron*: 2041–63

The Alphonsian *paréage* of June 1264 involved the village of Gajac and its lands, part of which were to be incorporated in the new town, possibly to provide for the inhabitants of the hill-top town of Pujols that had been badly affected by the Albigensian war. The new town, in contrast, was placed on level ground on the north bank of the river Lot on land provided by the abbey of Eysses which lay 2 kilometres to the north-east, but now within the suburbs of Villeneuve.

Alphonse's charter (probably of June 1270) is known only from a copy made in 1680 which was printed by Cassany-Mazet in 1846. In November 1286 Robert Burnell, bishop of Bath, issued a charter in Edward I's name which took the form, not of a confirmation of the Alphonsian charter, but of a fresh charter in virtually identical terms; it mentioned the count of Toulouse only as the founder of the town and not as the author of its liberties. This charter was traced by M. Trabut-Cussac to the David Smith Mathematical Library, Columbia University, New York ("Les Archives de la Gascogne Anglaise", *Rev. Hist. de Bordeaux*, v, n.s. (1956), p. 75) and the text subsequently published in "La Charte Anglaise des Coutumes de Villeneuve sur Lot", *Rev. de l'Agenais*, lxxxviii (1962), pp. 151–176.

In 1287 the English built the new stone bridge (*A.P.E.A.*, p. 312) which connects with the parish of St. Etienne, an extension of Villeneuve on the south bank. The street-plan here is not quite so rectilinear but the church seems to be late thirteenth century also, and a second *paréage* of 1264 between Alphonse and the seigneur of

Pujols (*Gouron*: 2042) may refer to this territory on the Pujols side of the river. In 1269 and 1271 documents refer to Villeneuve as *villa nova de Pojoliis* (*A.P.E.A.*, p. cv, fn. 3).

The defences of Villeneuve are not so old as the bastide. As late as 1313 the consuls of the town were protesting to Edward II that their town was in need of gates, and a document of 1323 shows that king was tardy in providing them (Trabut-Cussac, *Le Moyen Age*, lx (1954), p. 98, citing C61/27 m. 1).

The town has been one of the most successful of bastides from the point of view of commercial success, and after the walls were abandoned by Louis XVI the town spread out beyond the set square grid of the bastide. The north gate has been preserved (appropriately named Porte Monflanquin, since it leads to another Alphonsian bastide), and is a fine stone and brick structure. Brick is the principal building material in the town, where many timber-framed houses have brick used as infill. The great church of St. Catherine occupies a chequer to the north-east of the Place and is completely of brick.

In 1321 Amaury de Créon as seneschal granted the town land on which to build a common hall. The old commercial centre of the Place has well-preserved buildings but is no longer the hub of affairs. The broad exterior boulevard outside the north gate has the larger shops and the markets; the *cornières* at the Place are continuous to the four corners, so that there is no diagonal entry for traffic: all must go under the arches. On the south of the river are the railway station and the principal hotels, but the former has been closed since 1939 and is now a farmers' cooperative. Despite its modern prosperity the town has retained a strong historical flavour and is visually one of the most attractive of all the Gascon bastides.

A.P. Mission/Tonniens/Penne d'Agenais, 1950, no. 94.

VILLERÉAL

M:75   C:193NE

1265   *Gouron*: 2064–75

Alphonse de Poitiers made a *paréage* with Gaston de Gontaud and the convent of Aurillac in 1265 (*A.P.E.A.*, p. lxxvi fn., and *Gouron*, p. 772 fn.) for the foundation of a bastide in the forest of Montlabour.

Edward I confirmed the charter in 1289. *R.G.*, 1108, records the original marginal note of the Roll: *Alphonsus quondam comes Pictavenis fecit istam bastidam*. I have noted under Rives above that *G.C.*, 1667 and 1694, properly belong to this bastide. SC8/5695 (c. 1305) also suggests that there was considerable friction between Villeréal and Le Royet until the latter became English in 1303. In the early years of Henry V of England the town of Villeréal asked to have Rives reunited to it and also to have a confirmation of the old charters. *Gouron*, 2074, does not give the number of the Ancient Petition cited.

There is a complete street-grid but the walls are set at 45 degrees to the axis of the bastide, producing a diamond shape enclosing a square. In the Place there is a very well-preserved wooden *cornière* with exterior stairs leading to an upper storey. The church stands eccentric to the axis of the plan, and has a magnificent west front and tower. Although only on a slight eminence, the slope of the approaching roads is sufficient to give the site the impression of command; the view from the west, with the *cornière* arches framing the road, is particularly impressive. There is a plan in *Lavedan*, Fig. 233.

A.P. Mission Cancon/Fumel, 1950, no. 174.

DEPARTMENT OF TARN ET GARONNE

Most of the modern Department lay in the county of Toulouse, and it contains, in St. Nicholas de la Grave and Montauban, two of the earliest bastides of that county. The western edge of the Department, where the English acquired two Alphonsian bastides and built two others, once lay within the Agenais. Castelsagrat and Montjoi were acquired from Quercy in the settlement of 1286 and then incorporated in the Agenais.

CASTELSAGRAT   M:79   C:205SE
1255–62   *Gouron*: 700–702

The customs of this Alphonsian bastide (*A.P.E.A.*, p. 312) were confirmed by Edward I, probably after the settlement of 1286. (*R.G.*, 1015–16 and 4822; *G.C.*, 1721, *Albe*, pp. 488–489; B.M. Julius, E.1, f. 217, pencil numeration.) In 1289 the bastide was annexed to the Agenais, from whose border it is about 5 miles distant (*ibid*, f. 158). The bastide church was for a long time subordinate to the mother church of St. Michel d'Ursaud, a small village 2 km. to the south-east, the parish within which the bastide had been founded. The foundation was opposed by Montjoi, its nearest neighbour (*A.P.E.A.*, p. 324).

Despite its name, the town is not outstandingly situated. It is on a hill-top but without any sudden changes of slope. The Place has a full complement of *cornières* and a well, with the church taking up the adjacent chequer to the south-east. There are four parallel streets in the long axis of the grid; on the short side the west end of the town has reverted to gardens. Gates and walls have gone.

CORNEILLAS   M:79   C:205SE
1280

This project is documented in the *Livre d'Agenais* (Bodley Ms. 917: edited by G. P. Cuttino, pp. 20–26, 33–35 and 38). In 1280 Jean de Grilly, Edward I's seneschal, bought out a half-interest which the priory of St. Caprais at Lerm had in the village; the other half-interest had already come to the king from the count of Toulouse with the cession of the Agenais. The purpose of the bargain with the prior was declared to be the construction of a bastide, in which the priory was promised a *placea*. The foundation of the town was then delayed by negotiations to buy out a sub-interest possessed by a family of Agen, the Lamarques, and the discovery that the original agreement had not allowed for enough land. Further land in *Bordas* was therefore acquired in February 1283.

Bordas is probably the land to the north east of Valence (G.R.: 48542026) and Corneillas itself is at 48502040; the Ste. Foi de Mauquer also mentioned in the agreements may be the Ste. Foix of 48402001.

Corneillas consists of the church of St. Caprais, a mill and a few farms, and the project seems to have been abortive. A likely explanation is the proximity of Valence d'Agen (*infra*) founded in 1279 and given its formal customs in 1283, the year of the Corneillas charter. Corneillas lies at the foot of the hills which rise steeply on the north side of the Garonne valley and there is a chateau on the hill-slopes above it. But as a bastide site Corneillas had neither military potential, being at the foot of a hill, nor commercial potential, being 2 miles from the river.

It must be noted that Cuttino's placing of *Cornelhanus* (*G.C.*, 1717) in Mirande is both impossible and unnecessary. The purchase of Corneillas for Edward I made the compiler of the *Livre d'Agenais* note that sums (*acaptes*) due to the king from the village were no longer paid as the king was now himself the owner (J. P. Trabut-Cussac, *Bibl. de l'École des Chartes*, cxv (1957), pp. 179–89) . . . *lo rei l'a comprat.*

DONZAC
M:79   C:205SE

1270
Gouron: 920–922

The *paréage* was between the seneschal of Quercy and the Cistercian house of Belle-perche; the site was a wood near the abbey's grange of Donzac. In 1279 the consuls of the town rendered homage to Edward I and recited the privileges which they had been given. The *paréage* is mentioned in an English list (after 1317: C47/27/14) and a *vidimus* in *G.C.*, 1776, is dated 1311. See also *A.P.*, 875 and 1268; *A.P.E.A.*, p. lxxvi, fn.).

The town stands on a low bluff, an old river bank of the Garonne, a little west of Valence d'Agen. Only the skeleton of an original grid remains. Some modern houses in the main street have continued the *cornière* motif; one arch in an old house north of the church suggests that the Place may once have been there. There are no gates or walls.

A.P. Mission Nérac/Valence d'Agen, 1950, no. 352.

DUNES
M:79   C:205SE, 217NE

1263–66
Gouron: 925

This town was acknowledged as Alphonsian in C47/29/1/9 but was one of those ceded to the count of Lomagne by Edward II. Other evidence of an English interest is its appearance in a list of *paréages* preserved in the English archives (C47/27/14). In *G.C.*, 1777, a *paréage* is dated 1311 (see also *A.P.E.A.*, pp. 329, and lxxvi, fn.; *A.P.*, 476 and 1434).

Dunes, with a well-preserved grid, occupies a site with a hill-top slope on one side and a stream on the other. Its long axis has four parallel streets and its short axis probably had seven, but there are vacant chequers on the north side of the town. There is a stone Halle and a Place with an almost complete set of *cornières*, at least four of which are wooden. The exterior boulevard clearly marks the former limits of the town and it is significant that the church stands outside this limit.

A.P. Mission Nérac/Valence d'Agen, 1950, no. 355.

MONTJOI   M:79   C:205SE

1255   *Gouron*: 1473–74

The bastide was planted in the parish of St. Martin Posicastels whose church was
below the walls of the town and about 50 yards outside (*Albe*, p. 54).   The Alphonsian customs (*A.P.E.A.*, p. 324, fn.) were confirmed by Edward I in 1289.   The
decaying village is on a hill-top, but small, with a long east-west axis and a pair of
parallel back lanes.   The western end of the village is much decayed and the two
former town-streets emerge into a green.   There may have been a gate here, but the
fall of ground is severe.   What seems to be an old track, worn down to bare rock,
climbs this hill and may have made for a north gate.   The east gate survives.   It is
significant that the church is outside this gate; it looks modern but its site does not
correspond to the position described by Albe.   Montjoi opposed the founding of the
bastide of Castelsagrat (1255–62) two years later (*A.P.E.A.*, pp. 324–325).   The
count replied firmly and curtly: *non intendit amovere bastidam.*

A.P. Mission Nérac/Valence d'Agen, 1950, no. 195.

VALENCE D'AGEN   M:79   C:205SE

1279   *Gouron*: 2014–17

William de Valence, earl of Pembroke, Edward I's uncle, was in the Agenais during
the second half of 1279 and the *paréage* is probably that described (*G.C.*, 1717) as
Valencie in territorio de Cornelhana, for Corneillas is a village 2 miles north of the present
town of Valence d'Agen: the date of the *paréage*—1289—looks like an error for 1279
since the full grant of customs to the new town by Edward I is clearly dated 1283.
(Rymer, *Foedera* (ed. 1727), ii, pp. 260–263; E36/275, fo. 236–237 and 363–365;
G.C., 1043 and 1719).   If a document in the *Livre d'Agenais* (ed. Cuttino, p. 19) is
correctly dated as 1279 it also witnesses the existence of Valence by the words *homines
Valencie*.   M. Trabut-Cussac has also drawn my attention to an extract from Liber
D of the Constable of Bordeaux, 1311, preserved in a note in Bibl. Nat. Ms.
Duchesne 106, fol. 325 v: *bastidam de Valentia in Agenesio populavit Guillelmus de Valentia
nomine domini nostri regis, du temps de Johannes de Grilly ou environ.*

Between 1280 and 1283 negotiations were also in progress for sufficient land on
which to build a bastide at Corneillas (*supra, q.v.*) but this seems to have been abortive.   Bastides could be planted as close to each other as this (*cf.* Montjoi and
Castelsagrat nearby) but not with comfort.

Valence is now situated on a main road, the N.133.   Post-medieval prosperity has
played havoc with the facades of many buildings although good timber-framed houses
can be seen in the side street.   The grid-plan is well preserved, but there has been
clearance of houses at the east end of the church to make room for a second market
place.   The main Place has *cornières* on three sides but the Route Nationale has
claimed the other.   The town is on level ground with a river cliff on the south side,
above the Garonne canal.

A.P. Mission Nérac/Valence d'Agen, 1950, no. 347.

APPENDIX

PLANTATIONS BY ENGLISH KINGS WITHIN THE ANGEVIN DOMINION, BUT OUTSIDE GASCONY

Short notes are given on three planted towns that have been noted in the area north of Gascony during the brief period between the union of Anjou with the English crown in 1154 and the loss of Poitou, Maine and Touraine in 1224. It is also possible that Henry I founded Nonancourt (Eure) after 1112, and Pont Orson (Manche).

ANDELYS, PETIT (Eure)   M:55   C:31SW

1197

The town of Old Andelys and the surrounding parishes were the most valuable estate which the archbishops of Rouen possessed.

In 1196 both Richard I of England and the king of France had designs upon it, since it lay on the frontier of Normandy. The treaty of Louviers in that year provided for its neutrality but after a quarrel Richard seized an island in the Seine opposite the old town, fortified it, and then began to erect on the high chalk cliffs his great castle of Château Gaillard, "the saucy castle", where he was able to apply the lessons of military architecture and massive defence which he had observed in Syria. In October 1197 the archbishop agreed to exchange the whole manor of Andelys for other lands, including the port of Dieppe.

Richard took personal interest in the building works and was constantly at the castle between February 1198 and January 1199. It was of considerable importance in this part of Normandy that the frontiers should be strengthened with castles since the frontier ran along rivers and across plains, with few forests and no mountains to make natural and permanent divisions.

To the castle he added the new town of Petit Andelys. "A new town was laid out by the riverside to serve the needs of the elaborate system of defences that bound together rock and water" (F. M. Powicke, *The Loss of Normandy* (1961), p. 191). Old Andelys was not on the bank of the Seine but about half a mile up a small tributary, the Gambon. Where the Gambon joins the Seine the cliffs fall away for a few hundred yards, and there is an island opposite. The site chosen for the town was this narrow stretch of river bank dominated by the castle above. The Gambon was diverted to flow into the town moats and a pool was created between Petit Andelys and Old Andelys. These water defences were augmented by fortified bridges and towers of wood and stone (Powicke, *op. cit.*, pp. 115–116; 190–196, and endpaper plan).

The town was given the privileges of Rouen by a charter of 1200 (*Rot. Cart.*, i, p. 65). Its plan is a simple rectilinear grid culminating in a small Place at the southeast end which is closed by the church. The long axis is parallel to the river.

635

BEAUVOIR (Sarthe)   M:60

The chronicler Robert de Torigny recorded: *rex Henricus fecit castrum munitissimum et burgum pergrande iuxta haiam de Malaffre quod vocatum est Bealveer* (R. Howlett, ed., *Chronicles of the reigns of Stephen, Henry II and Richard I* (Rolls Series, lxxxii), pt. 4, p. 243). A place of this name near the border of Maine and Normandy (arr. Mamers) has a commanding hill-top occupied only by a farm. However, Delisle and Berger, *Recueil des Actes de Henri II*, i (1916), pp. 522, 547 and 578, place Bealveer at Bourg le Roi in the nearby commune of St. Paterne. This village has the remains of gates and walls.

ST. RÉMY (Vienne)   M:68   C:132NE
c. 1184

This town, together with Marmande and Petit Andelys, form the trio of foundations undertaken by Richard I. The little village stands on the river Creuse near La Haye Descartes. In a law-suit a witness recalled that the town had been created by the king: *ex parte regis fuit ibi libera villa creata*; in isolation this might imply nothing more than the creation of a free community from an existing village, but another witness recalled seeing Richard's clerks giving over plots of land to any who would rent them and build houses thereon (F. M. Powicke, *The Loss of Normandy* (1961), pp. 191–192). The burgage rents were 5s. per year, and newcomers were promised protection against the jealousy of the lord of the nearest town, Châtellerault. As at Andelys, Richard acquired the site from the church: in this case the abbey of Maillezais (A. Teulet, ed., *Layette du Trésor des Chartes* (1863), p. 142). The site lay on the lands of an abbey grange and its attractiveness was in its frontier position: the river Creuse divided Poitou, Richard's county, from Touraine. In *Archives Historiques de Poitou*, viii (1879), pp. 39–50, Bardonnet printed eye-witness accounts of the construction of the town from a thirteenth-century law-suit.

Chronological List of Plantations:

ENGLAND

ST. ALBANS	c.	950
ROMNEY, NEW	by	960
DURHAM		995–1006
RICHARD'S CASTLE		1066–86
SKIPSEA		1066–1102
HASTINGS	c.	1069
BATTLE		1070–71
MARAZION		1070–1215
ARUNDEL	c.	1071
SARUM, OLD		1075–86
BELVOIR		1076–1100
NEWCASTLE UPON TYNE		1080–1130
CORFE		1080–1215
HYTHE	by	1086
PONTEFRACT	by	1086
RYE	by	1086
TICKHILL	by	1086
LAUNCESTON	c.	1086
OKEHAMPTON	c.	1086
TREMATON	c.	1086
LUDLOW		1086–94
LYNN, KING'S		1086–95
BRIDGNORTH		1086–1101
CLITHEROE		1086–1102
BOSTON		1086–1113
BROUGH, CHURCH	c.	1092–1100
SHOREHAM		1096–1103
OSWESTRY	c.	1100
NEWBOROUGH		1100–39
MITFORD		?1100–57
WYMONDHAM	c.	1107
WINDSOR, NEW		1107–31
RICHMOND (Yorks., N.R.)		1109–14
APPLEBY	c.	1110

ST. IVES	c.	1110
BARNARD CASTLE	c.	1112
ST. NEOTS		1113–22
DUNSTABLE	c.	1119
WATFORD		1119–46
EGREMONT	c.	1125
SLEAFORD, NEW		1123–47
BISHOP'S CASTLE	by	1127
NEWPORT (Salop.)		1129–35
HUNGERFORD	by	1131
DEVIZES		1135–39
THIRSK, NEW		1135–45
HEDON		1138–48
UXBRIDGE	by	1145
BOROUGHBRIDGE	c.	1145
WOKINGHAM	by	1146
BUCKENHAM, NEW		1146–56
ALNMOUTH	by	1147
MOUNTSORREL	by	1148
BALDOCK		1148–85
TRURO	c.	1153
NEWCASTLE UNDER LYME		1154–62
MALTON, NEW		1154–73
WOODSTOCK, NEW		1154–74
CAPUT MONTIS (DOWNEND)	by	1159
WYKE UPON HULL		1160–93
HARTLEPOOL		1162–83
HOLME	by	1167
HARBOROUGH, MARKET		1167–77
YARMOUTH (I.O.W.)	c.	1170
POOLE	c.	1170–80
BRACKLEY, NEW	by	1173
NEWPORT (I.O.W.)		1177–84
HENLEY ON THAMES	by	1179
RADECLIVE		1179–89
PLESHEY	c.	1180
PETERSFIELD		1182–83
BRIGG	by	1183
MIDHURST	by	1184
LYMINGTON, NEW		1184–1216
HENLEY IN ARDEN		1185–1220
ROYSTON	c.	1189
LOSTWITHIEL	by	1190
PLYMPTON ERLE (ST. MAURICE)		1194

PORTSMOUTH		1194
HONITON	c.	1194–1217
WEARE, NETHER		1195–1225
BROUGH, MARKET	by	1196
STRATFORD UPON AVON		1196
CASTLETON		?1196
NEWTON ABBOT		1196–1200
TREGONEY	?by	1197
BRETFORD	by	1199
BARNET	c.	1199
CHELMSFORD		1199–1201
BAWTRY		1199–1213
MORPETH		1199–1239
CAUS	by	1200
ALRESFORD, NEW		1200
FELTON	?c.	1200
STOCKBRIDGE	c.	1200
LOOE, EAST	by	1201
LOOE, WEST	by	1201
SALTASH	by	1201
STRATFORD, STONY	by	1202
STRATFORD, FENNY		1202–04
BOSCASTLE		?1204
BEAULIEU		1204–27
LEEDS		1207
LIVERPOOL		1207
PEVENSEY (NEAR)		1207
DOWNTON		1208–09
WULVESFORD IN WITHAM		1212
COGGES, (NEWLAND)		1212–13
EYNSHAM, (NEWLAND)		1215
OVERTON		1217–18
NEWMARKET		1217–23
SODBURY, CHIPPING		1218
NEWTOWN (IN BURGHCLERE)		1218
SALISBURY, NEW		1219
KINGSBRIDGE	c.	1219
HINDON		1219–20
NEW THAME		1219–21
HASLEMERE		1221
NEWBOROUGH		1221
SHIELDS, NORTH		1225
COLYFORD		1225–38
NEWTON POPPLEFORD		?1226

BASCHURCH	by	1227
NORTHLEACH		1227
SHERBORNE NEWLAND		1227–28
MORETON IN MARSH		1228–46
HARWICH	by	1229
LONGTOWN	by	1234
SHIELDS, SOUTH	by	1235
PENRYN		1236
BROUGH ON HUMBER		1239
MITCHELL		?1239
RAVENSERODD		1240–50
WEYMOUTH		1244
NEWTON BUSHEL		1246
FLOOKBURGH	?c.	1246
WARENMOUTH		1247
NEWTON IN WARKWORTH	by	1249
FORD, NORTH	?by	1250
BRIDGETOWN POMEROY	c.	1250
AIRMYN	by	1253
NEWTOWN (FRANCHEVILLE)		1255–56
BOW		1259–1326
CAMELFORD	by	1260
WARDOUR		1262–67
ZEAL, SOUTH		?1264
KINGTON	by	1267
MOUSEHOLE	by	1267
MELCOMBE REGIS		1268
MAIDENHEAD	by c.	1270
STOFORD	by	1273
NEWTON (DORSET)		1286
NOSS MAYO		?1286
NEW WINCHELSEA		1288
BUNTINGFORD	c.	1288
NEWPORT (IN BISHOP'S TAWTON)		1291
KNUTSFORD, NETHER	?c.	1292
POLRUAN	c.	1292
KINGSTON UPON HULL		1293
BERE ALSTON		1295–1305
GRAMPOUND	by	1296
KENNFORD	c.	1298
WAVERMOUTH		1300
SKINBURGH		1301
RUYTON, NEW		1304–10
NEWTON ARLOSH		1305

WADEBRIDGE		?1312
HAYDON BRIDGE	?c.	1323
TOTNES, LITTLE	by	1326
PENZANCE	by	1327
EAGLE, NEW		1345
QUEENBOROUGH		1368
FALMOUTH		1613

Chronological List of Plantations:

WALES

Period I: before 1066

RHUDDLAN I	921

Period II: 1066–1135

MONMOUTH	1070–72
CHEPSTOW	1072–75
RHUDDLAN II	1073
CARDIFF	1081–93
ABERGAVENNY	1087–1100
BRECON	1087–1100
COWBRIDGE	1090–1262
RADNOR, OLD	1095–1100
BUILTH	1095–1102
TENBY	early 12th century
LOUGHOR	after 1100
NEATH	1100–30
KIDWELLY (OLD TOWN)	1106–15
CARMARTHEN	1109
PEMBROKE	1110
HAVERFORD WEST	1110–17
SWANSEA	1116
KIDWELLY (NEW TOWN)	c. 1130
USK	by 1131
WISTON	1135

Period III: 1136–1274

KENFIG	1147–54
ABERAVON	?1147–83
NARBERTH	c. 1150
TRELLECH	c. 1150
GROSMONT	1154–89

642

CARDIGAN	c.	1165
	perhaps c.	1110–15
NEWPORT (Mon.)	by	1191
WHITECASTLE	after	1185
SKENFRITH	after	1190
NEWPORT (Pem.)	c.	1197
BRIDGEND	by	1197
NEW MOAT	by	1219
MONTGOMERY, NEW		1223
PAINSCASTLE		1231
HAY		?1237
CEFNLLYS		1240–46
WELSHPOOL		1247–52
DEGANWY		1248
DYSERTH		1248
RADNOR, NEW		?1257
KNIGHTON	by	1260
LLANTRISSANT	by	1262
CAERPHILLY		1271
LAMPETER		1271–77
DRYSLWYN		?1271–89
DOLFORWYN		1273

Period IV : after 1274

DYNEVOR, OLD		1276–80
LLANDOVERY		?1276–1316
FLINT		1277
ABERYSTWYTH		1277
LAUGHARNE	before	1278–82
RHUDDLAN III		1278
TREFNANT		1278
NEWTOWN (Mont.)		1280–1321
LLANIDLOES		1280–93
RUTHIN		1282
HOLT		1282–1311
TEMPLETON	by	1283
CARNARVON		1283
CONWAY		1283
HARLECH		1283
DENBIGH		1283–90
NEVIN	by	1284
PWLLHELI	by	1284
CRICCIETH		1284

BERE		1284
CAERWYS		1290
LLAWHADEN		1290–92
MOSTYN, NEW	by	1292
OVERTON		1292
? LLANFYLLIN		?1293
BEAUMARIS		1295
NEWTOWN (Dynevor)	c.	1298
NEWCASTLE EMLYN		1303
NEWBOROUGH		1303
RHAYADER		?1304–60
TALGARTH	by	1309
BALA	c.	1310
LLANDILO	by	1326
ADPAR	by	1326
ABERGWILI	by	1326
LLANELLY		n.d.
CAERSWS		n.d.

Note: The chronological list for Gascony appears in Chapter 13, pp. 353 and 357–58.

APPENDIX III

Select Bibliography:

MEDIEVAL TOWN PLANTATION IN GASCONY

This survey of the literature comprises a brief account of the development of the subject, followed by a list of articles and books discussed, arranged alphabetically by authors' names. In general, titles of histories of single towns are not given here: reference will be found in the main Gazetteer entries. A full list of town histories published before 1935 will be found in *Gouron*, pp. xxvii–lix. For articles in local periodicals up to 1940 see R. Gandilhon and C. Samaran, *Bibliographie Générale des Travaux Historiques et Archéologiques* (Paris, 1944, and in progress); and for books, International Committee of Historical Sciences, *International Bibliography of Historical Sciences* (i, 1926; in progress).

Even if the Gascon bastides can no longer be claimed as the pioneers in medieval town plantation, the serious study of town plantation was certainly pioneered in Gascony. As in England, the early nineteenth century saw much interest in local history, which in small towns took the form of a study of municipal constitutions, customs and liberties. In 1842 J-F. Samazeuilh published his chronological table of Gascon customs in the *Bulletin de la Société Scientifique de Pau*; meanwhile A. Cassaney-Mazet had published his *History of Villeneuve sur Lot* in 1837; and R. Guinodie his *History of Libourne* in 1845. These important towns happened to be *villes neuves*, and in 1850–51 F. Verneilh-Puyrazeau singled out the characteristic buildings of the *villes neuves* for a paper in architectural history published in three successive volumes of the *Annuaire de l'Archéologue français*. In 1862 he presented a list of bastides in the southwest to the 28th Session of the Congrès Archéologique de France, meeting at Bordeaux, and in the same year the abbé Larroque published his note on the bastide of Marciac, supplementing his previous note on the bastide of Beaumarchés and its founder, Eustache de Beaumarchés: both were printed in the *Bulletin du comité d'histoire d'Auch*. In 1865 Léo Drouyn published a two-volume study of military architecture in Gascony that inevitably brought him to the surviving gates and walls of bastides.

All this, it will be noted, had been achieved twelve years before Alceste Curie-Siembres published the first version of what is usually taken to be the classic statement of the bastide theme. This essay appeared in *Mémoires de la Société Archéologique du Midi de France* in 1874, and appeared as a book in 1880. In 1875 G. Tholin had initiated closer regional studies with his paper on the bastides of the Department of Lot et Garonne, comprising mainly the Agenais, and in 1879 Anthyme St. Paul had reported 225 bastides. Curie-Seimbres's essay was a general survey of origins of bastides, drawing examples from 261 places in all parts of the south-west. He himself lived at Trie, in the Department of Hautes Pyrénées, a bastide with a full grid-plan. In the French provinces they honour their local historians, and his house in the Place at Trie is now marked out with a commemorative plaque.

Further study could go no faster than the publication of documents permitted. Histories of single towns continued to appear, but the identification of bastides was greatly aided when the Gascon Rolls in the Public Record Office began to be published in 1885. Previously, those working remote from London had to rely on the selective calendar in the *Catalogue* of Carte and Palmeuse, published in 1743, or on transcripts made by antiquaries and historians in London and deposited in the Bibliothèque Nationale, Paris. By 1906 Charles Bémont had published the Gascon Rolls from 1273 to 1307, thus covering the most active period of town plantation in Gascony, and between 1894 and 1900 Auguste Molinier published documents emanating from the administration of Alphonse de Poitiers which showed the parallel creation of bastides in the county of Toulouse. This era may be said to have ended with Bémont's edition of the *Recogniciones Feodorum* in 1914, for it was fifty years before another volume of the *Rôles* appeared.

Meanwhile the collation of charters in municipal and Department archives continued on a regional basis. Canon Pottier had published a survey of the customs of towns in Tarn-et-Garonne at Montauban in 1889; in 1908–09, Lavergne and Mastron produced their list of the charters of Gers; and in 1915 Laval published a similar list for Bas-Quercy.

These efforts facilitated further regional studies of bastides, taking further the general principles set out by Curie-Seimbres and aiming at a complete identification of bastides within an area, similar to that of Tholin. Such was Tauzin's study of the Landes (1901), and Vigié's of Périgord (1907). The latter was the most thorough of the regional studies to appear, and in 1920 it was given a worthy partner in Testut's great study of Beaumont du Périgord, the most detailed and most loving treatment that any single bastide is ever likely to receive. In the same year Domengie's first papers on the bastides of the Agenais appeared, the last of the regional studies before the revival of interest in the subject in the late 1930's. Only the bastides of the Bordelais lacked their historian.

The most recent wave of interest in the subject may truly be said to begin with Marcel Gouron's catalogue of the charters of liberties of Gascony (1935). This was a painstaking assembly of information from local, national and foreign sources, comprising 2,075 items.

The work of the last twenty years has taken the form of a number of important articles which have placed the bastides deeper into their historical context, both political and economic. A vigorous and combative fore-runner was M. Z. Baqué, whose two papers published on the eve of the Second World War brought a realistic if cynical and Marxist eye to an activity of seigneurs which had previously been clouded with grateful local pride. Baqué's articles embodied no original research, but they were designed to place the bastides in History.

Professor Charles Higounet now has a wide array of articles on the general settlement history of the south-west, particularly of the French county of Toulouse, and of Comminges, the subject of his book. A book on the bastides in general is said to be appearing.

Another large-scale regional study that inevitably includes material on town plantation is Tucoo-Chala's book on Béarn, and there is other information about this area in Dr. Jean Ellis Rosenthal's Oxford thesis on Gaston de Béarn: not, alas, published.

M. Trabut-Cussac's *forte* has been his familiarity with the archives of Gascon administration that remain unpublished in the Public Record Office. This close scrutiny places his work in a class quite apart from those who know only the records that happen to have been published. In the course of his work in the Public Record Office for his dissertation, he was able to explore the misty areas of the Ancient Petitions, the Ancient Correspondence and the Chancery Diplomatic Documents, poorly indexed or not indexed at all and—although his main subject was Edward I in Gascony and not bastides—he managed to identify bastides previously unidentified, give dates to bastides that were undated, and unmask the errors of others with ruthlessness and charm. One indication of the importance of this by-product of his main exercise is that the *Gascon Calendar of 1322*, published by the Royal Historical Society only in 1949, now needs complete revision.

Dr. Cuttino's edition of this *Calendar*, begun before the war, is the first work in English to be mentioned here. The English contribution to Anglo-Gascon studies has not been very bulky. Eleanor Lodge's *English Rule in Gascony* is a general survey, well grounded on the materials at Bordeaux that she had used for her earlier monograph, and on the printed sources then available. It is greatly superior to F. B. Marsh's shorter study with a similar title. The whole of Anglo-Gascon relations to 1307 form an important part of Sir Maurice Powicke's great two-volume study of *Henry III and the Lord Edward* (1947) and of his volume *The Thirteenth Century* in the Oxford History of England (1953). Edward I is portrayed as a hero, *rex et bastidor*, and the detailed narrative rests on a lifetime's knowledge of the source-materials.

Trade as well as Angevin blood linked medieval England with Gascony, and English economic historians have contributed to Gascon studies. Following on the early study by George Unwin's pupil, F. Sargeant, Dr. M. K. James and Professor Carus-Wilson have used the customs accounts for two studies of the wine-trade that possess not only precision and quantification, but also considerable feeling for the totality of relations between London and Bordeaux. It is to be regretted that Dr. James's thesis has not been published. Recently the economic history of viticulture and the trade in wine has been the subject of an excellent book by R. Dion, and of a review and an article by Y. Renouard, who as the editor of the fourth volume of *Rôles Gascons* was well placed to see the importance of the trade in Anglo-Gascon relations.

Histories of town-planning have inevitably included some account of the bastides, although with a conservative affection for confining their journeys to an Inner Circle from Monpazier to Montauban and back again, via a few other well-known stations. There are three exceptions, two of them English. One is G. H. R. Heritage's R.I.B.A. thesis, with excellent plans drawn in the field, and it is a great pity that the thesis was never published, although a few of the plans have had wider circulation through F. R. Hiorns' study, an exceptionally wide-ranging survey of urbanism with many original examples and illustrative materials. The third contribution from historians of town-planning is Pierre Lavedan's tremendous survey, published in two volumes in 1926. The towns of the south-west of France occupy nearly one hundred pages of his first volume, and his argument is accompanied by a very generous selection of town-plans, mostly taken from the local cadastral maps of the second quarter of the nineteenth century.

In 1932 Pierre Deffontaines published his study of what would now be called the historical geography of the middle Garonne basin, using a technique of working backward from the present landscape. This study has some perceptive things to say about the relation of the bastides to other forms of medieval settlement in the area, and there are some interesting photographs of bastides before the age of the motor car had begun to despoil them, though viewed through the mist which seems to afflict so many reproductions of photographs in French historical works.

At the Phototèque at Saint-Mandé the Institut Géographique makes air photographs easily available for public inspection, study and purchase. Both existing and abortive bastides lend themselves well to study from the air. There is a selection of bastide photographs in P. Deffontaines and M. J-B. Delamarre, *Atlas Aérien* (5 vols., 1955–64), especially in vol. iii (1958). Air photographs have also begun to infiltrate local periodicals in France, even the most erudite, and there are signs that fear of *basse vulgarisation* through photographic illustrations is being assuaged. Soon, perhaps, the English national historical periodicals will be alone in guarding their long chastity.

BIBLIOGRAPHY

ALBE, E. "Les Suites du traité de Paris de 1259 pour Quercy", *Annales du Midi*, xxiii (1911), pp. 472–491; xxiv (1912), pp. 59–78; 218–231 and 396–410.

BAQUÉ, M. Z. "Des Bordes aux Bastides", *Bull. de la Soc. Arch. Hist. Lit. et Scien. du Gers*, xl (1939), pp. 55–74 and 131–150.

BÉMONT, C. *Recogniciones Feodorum in Aquitania* (Paris, 1914).

Id. See also Michel, F. and Bémont, C.

BOUTRUCHE, R. *La Crise d'une Société: seigneurs et paysans du Bordelais* (Paris, 1947).

CARTE, T. and PALMEUSE, D. *Catalogue des rolles gascons*, 2 vols. (London, 1743).

CARUS-WILSON, E. M. "The Effects of the Acquisition and of the Loss of Gascony on the English Wine Trade", *B.I.H.R.*, xxi (1948), pp. 145–154.

CHAPLAIS, P. "Le Duché-pairie de Guyenne", *Annales du Midi*, lxix (1957), pp. 5–38; lxx (1958), pp. 135–160.

Id. "The Chancery of Guyenne, 1289–1453", in J. C. Davies, ed., *Studies presented to Sir Hilary Jenkinson* (1957), pp. 61–96.

Id. *The War of St. Sardos, 1323–5* (Camden Soc. 3rd ser., lxxxvii (1954).

CURIE-SEIMBRES, M. A. *Essai sur les Villes fondées dans le sud-ouest de la France aux xiiie. et xive. siècles sous le nom générique de bastides* (Toulouse, 1880).

CUTTINO, G. P. *Le Livre d'Agenais, Bodley Ms. no. 917* (Toulouse, 1956).

Id. *The Gascon Calendar of 1322* (Camden Soc., 3rd ser., lxx (1949)).

DEFFONTAINES, P. *Les hommes et leurs Travaux dans le pays de la Moyenne Garonne* (Lille, 1932).

DION, R. *Histoire de la Vigne et du Vin en France* (Paris, 1959).

DOMENGIE, Y. "Les bastides de l'Agenais", *Rev. de l'Agenais*, xlvii (1920), pp. 260–279 and 360–368; xlviii (1921), 25–42, 111–122, 183–198 and 244–271.

DROUYN, L. *La Guienne Militaire* (Bordeaux, 2 vols., 1865).

ELLIS, JEAN See Rosenthal, J. E.

FAWTIER, R. and MAILLARD, F. *Comptes Royaux, 1285–1314* (Paris, 3 vols., 1953–56).

FOURNIER, P-F. and GUÉBIN, P. *Enquêtes Administratives d'Alphonse de Poitiers, 1249–71* (Paris, 1959).

GARDELLES, J. "Les châteaux des rois d'Angleterre en Agenais," *Rev. de l'Agenais*, lxxxviii (1962), pp. 83–96).

GOURON, M. *Les Chartes de Franchises de Guienne et Gascogne* (Paris, 1935).

HERITAGE, G. H. R. *The Bastides of Guienne* (R.I.B.A. thesis, 1937: R.I.B.A. Library, London, unpublished.)

HIGOUNET, C. "Bastides et Frontières", *Le Moyen Age*, liv (1948), pp. 113–121.

Id. "Cisterciens et Bastides", *Le Moyen Age*, lvi (1950), pp. 69–84.

Id. "La Frange Orientale des Bastides", *Annales du Midi*, lxi (1948–49), pp. 359–367.

Id. "L'arrière-pays de Bordeaux au xiiie. siècle", *Rev. Hist. de Bordeaux*, n.s., iv (1955), pp. 201–210.

Id. *Le Comté de Comminges* (2 vols., Toulouse, 1949).

Id. "Les Alaman Seigneurs, Bastidors et Péagers du xiiie. siècle", *Annales du Midi*, lxviii (1956), pp. 227–253.

Id. "Les Sauvetés de Moissac", *Annales du Midi*, lxxv (1964), pp. 505–512.

Id. "L'occupation du sol du Pays entre Tarn et Garonne au Moyen Age", *Annales du Midi*, lxv (1953), pp. 301–330.

Id. "Villeneuves et bastides désertées" in *Villages Désertés* (Paris, 1965)

JAMES, M. K. "Les Activités Commerciales des Négociants en vin Gascons en Angleterre", *Annales du Midi*, lxv (1953), pp. 35–48.

Id. "The Fluctuations of the Anglo-Gascon Wine Trade since the 14th Century", *Ec.H.R.*, 2nd ser., iv (1951), pp. 170–196.

LAVAL, E. "Les chartes de coutumes du Bas Quercy", *Bull. Phil. et Hist.*, *1914*, pp. 82–110.

LAVEDAN, P. *L'Histoire de l'Urbanisme* (Paris, 2 vols., 1926).

LAVERGNE, A. and MASTRON P. "Liste des chartes de coutumes du Gers", *Bull. Soc. Arch. du Gers*, ix (1908), pp. 171 and 297; x (1909), pp. 175, 256 and 321.

LODGE, E. C. *Gascony Under English Rule* (1926).

MAILLARD F. and FAWTIER, R. *Comptes Royaux, 1314–28* (2 vols., Paris, 1961).

MARSH, F. B. *English Rule in Gascony, 1199–1259* (1912).

MICHEL, F. and BÉMONT C. *Rôles Gascons*, vol. 1, and Supplement (2 vols, Paris, 1885–96); continued by C. Bémont, *Rôles Gascons*, vols. 2 and 3; and by Y. Renouard, *Rôles Gascons*, vol. 4.

MOLINIER, A. M. E. *Correspondence Administrative d'Alphonse de Poitiers* (2 vols., Paris, 1894–1900).

OULIAC, P. "Les Villages de la Région Toulousaine", *Annales*, iv (1949), pp. 268–277.

POUSSOU, J. P. "Introduction à l'Étude des chartes de franchises de l'Agenais et du Brulhois," *Rev. de l'Agenais*, xc (1964), pp. 115–26 and 207–25.

RENOUARD, Y, ed. *La Guyenne sous les rois d'Angleterre, 1154–1453* (Bordeaux, 1952).

Id. "Le Grand Commerce des Vins de Gascogne au Moyen Age", *Rev. Hist.*, ccxxi (1959), pp. 261–304.

Id. "Les Consequences de la Conquête de la Guienne", *Annales du Midi*, lxi (1948), pp. 15–31.

Id. "Vignobles, Vignes et Vin de France au Moyen Age", *Le Moyen Age*, lxvi (1960), pp. 337–351.

Id. See also Michel, F., *above*.

ROSENTHAL, J. E. *Gaston de Béarn* (D. Phil. thesis, Oxford, 1952, unpublished).

ST. BLANQUAT, O. de "Comment se sont créés les Bastides du Sud-Ouest de la France?", *Annales*, iv (1949), pp. 278–289.

ST. PAUL, A. "Liste de bastides", in *Annuaire de l'Archéologue Français, 1879*.

SARGEANT, F. "The Trade with Gascony" in G. Unwin, ed., *Studies in Finance and Trade under Edward III* (1918), pp. 257–311.

TAUZIN, J-J-C. "Les bastilles landaises", *Rev. des Questions Historiques*, lxix (1901), pp. 456–517.

TESTUT, L. *La Bastide de Beaumont en Périgord, 1272–1789* (Bordeaux, 2 vols., 1920).

THOLIN, G. "Bastides du Lot-et-Garonne", *Congrès Arch. de France*, xli (1875), pp. 179–203.

TRABUT-CUSSAC, J-P. "Actes gascons dispersés émanant d'Edouard Ier d'Angleterre... 1286–89", *Bull. Phil. et Hist. 1962* (1965), pp. 63–139.

Id. "Bastides ou Forteresses?", *Le Moyen Age*, lx (1954), pp. 81–135.

Id. "Créon, bastide administrative", *Annales du Midi*, lxvi (1954), pp. 343–350.

Id. "Date, fondation et identification de la bastide de Baa", *Rev. Hist. de Bordeaux*, n.s., x (1961), pp. 133–144.

Id. "La Charte Anglaise des Coutumes de Villeneuve sur Lot", *Rev. de l'Agenais*, lxxxviii (1962), pp. 151–76.

Id. "La fondation de Sauveterre de Guyenne", *Rev. Hist. de Bordeaux*, n.s., ii (1953) pp. 181–217.

Id. "Le Livre d'Agenais à propos d'une édition récente", *Bibl. de l'École des Chartes*, cxv (1957), pp. 179–189.

Id. "Les archives de la Gascogne Anglaises", *Rev. Hist. de Bordeaux*, n.s., v (1956), pp. 69–82.

Id. "Les cartulaires gascons", *Bibl. de l'École des Chartes*, cxi (1953), pp. 65–106.

Id. "Les Coutumes ou droits de douane perçus à Bordeaux sur les vins . . . 1252–1307", *Annales du Midi*, lxii (1950), pp. 135–150.

Id. "L'Itinéraire d'Edouard I en France, 1286–9", *B.I.H.R.* xxv (1952), pp. 160–203.

TUCOO-CHALA, P. *Gaston Fébus et le Vicomte de Béarn, 1343–91* (Bordeaux, 1959).

VIGIÉ, A. "Les bastides du Périgord", *Acad. des Scs. et Lettres de Montpellier*, 2nd ser., iii (1907), pp. 279–473.

Id. "Les bastides du Périgord et les Rôles Gascons", *Bull. Soc. Hist. et Arch. du Périgord*, xlvii (1920), pp. 143–154.

A Note on Medieval Town Plantation Outside England, Wales and Gascony

These brief notes serve to indicate some evidence, mainly in printed sources, that has been noticed in the course of collecting material for the present book. It does not claim to be exhaustive. The arrangement is by modern territorial divisions.

SCOTLAND

W. M. Mackenzie, *The Scottish Burghs* (1949), Chapter IV, is wholly concerned with New Towns. See also G. S. Pryde, *The Burghs of Scotland* (1965).

IRELAND

There is no basic study of Irish towns before the Ulster plantations. The raw materials for an examination of the royal and seigneurial foundations of the medieval period lie partly in the Public Record Office, London, and partly in the field-study of local topographies. E. Curtis, *Medieval Ireland* (1938), pp. 408–416, is a short essay on "The Towns of Ireland". The Norman families who invaded Ireland after 1166 were already experienced as town-planters in South Wales and the Marches, and occasional references to a *novus burgus* occur among the surveys of their Irish lands (e.g. C133/32/7, 127 burgages in *Nova Villa* in Leys; C133/130, *nova villa Jeripontis*; C133/127, New Ross).

FRANCE

South-west (outside Gascony): see p. 373, above.
North-west: for the Norman foundation problems, see p. 332, above, and appendix to Chapter XVII; also M. Dillay, *Les Chartes du Poitou* (Paris, 1927), p. 67, for Villeneuve la Comtesse. For Brittany see the discussion in H. Bourde de la Rogerie, "Les fondations de villes et de bourgs en Bretagne", *Mems. de la Soc. d'Hist. et d'Arch. de Bretagne*, ix (1928), pp. 69–106.
Paris Basin and central France: the title of F. L. Ganshof, *Étude sur le developpement des villes entre Loire et Rhin au Moyen Age* (Brussels, 1943), arouses unfulfilled hopes; his fig. 14 (Étampes) derives from the discussion by Prou in *Mélanges d'Histoire Offerts à Henri Pirenne* (1926), where Louis VI's *novum forum* between *vetus vicus* and *novum*

castrum is called "en réalité la fondation d'une ville neuve". For its typical thirteenth-century planned town the *Atlas de France* takes Villeneuve le Comte (Seine et Marne). J. Garnier, *Chartes de Communes . . . en Bourgogne* (Dijon, 1918), i, pp. 261–4, hints at town plantations. F. Bouquelot, "Études sur les Foires de Campagne", *Mémoires présentées par divers savants à l'Acad. des Inscrip. et Belles-Lettres,* 2nd ser., v (Paris, 1865), pp. 55–59, was fully aware of the importance of planted towns in that area, and gives many names and references.

North-east: two plantations have been studied in some detail. G. Robert, "La ville neuve de Florent", *Trav. de L'Acad. de Rheims,* cxliii (1930), pp. 98–154; and P. Pietresson St. Aubin, "Une ville neuve inconnue, Catillon sur Sambre", *Rev. du Nord,* 1937, pp. 186–194. Some of the more general studies mentioned under Belgium also deal with the area now within France but once part of the county of Flanders. Calais itself, acquired by Edward III in 1347, has a planned shape, possibly the work of an early thirteenth-century count of Boulogne (F. Lennel, *Histoire de Calais,* i (Calais, 1908), pp. 1–9; and *Hist. King's Works,* i, p. 423); an unidentified place near Guisnes that was burned in 1355 was then described as *bastide* (Rymer, *Foedera* (ed. 1727), v, p. 822).

South-east: medieval Savoy, at its height, included territory now in France as well as that discussed below in Switzerland. Blondel's book (see below) has historical details and plans of the planted bourgs in the Department of Savoy, including some now deserted and others semi-deserted. Mr. A. J. Taylor has pointed out the positional and scenic parallels between the bourgs in the foot-hills of the Alps, south of Geneva, and the work of the Savoyard masons in the towns of North Wales. Allowing for a scale where Snowdon becomes Mont Blanc, the views are, indeed, strikingly similar. Between Geneva and Lyon are the plantations of St. Georges d'Espéranche and St. André la Côte; and in the Alps, Barcelonnette.

General: *Lavedan* drew on examples in France beyond Gascony in his discussion of medieval towns but did not range widely until his treatment of the sixteenth to eighteenth centuries in vol. ii, pp. 71–276. J. Flach, *Les Origines de l'Ancienne France* (Paris, 2 vols., 1886–93) has a useful discussion of plantations, with references (ii, pp. 139–157; 177–186; 343–347); and L. Verriest, *Institutions Mediévales* (Mons, 1946), has wide-ranging references to French town plantation in i, pp. 126–168 and 217.

SPAIN

See E. Hinojosa, *El Régimen Señorial* (Madrid, 1905), pp. 9–11 for list of plantations and pp. 62–63 for quotations from founding charters of *el poblador.*

ITALY

Professor Higounet has recently extended his studies to an area north and west of Florence, where five new foundations were executed between 1299 and 1332: C. Higounet, 'Les *terre nuove* florentines du xive. siècle", *Studi in Onore di Amintore Fanfani* (Milan, 1962), iii, pp. 31–37, and plates 1–8; he refers to reports on town plantation in southern Italy by E. Sestan.

BELGIUM

L. A. Warnkönig, *Histoire de la Flandre*, trans. A. E. Gheldorf (Brussels, 1835–64, 5 vols.) has a list of Flemish towns in v, pp. 231–234, with indications that they were planted rather than organic; see also *ibid.*, p. 366. Some of this evidence is used by B. Lyon, "Medieval Real Estate Developments and Freedom", *Amer. Hist. Rev.*, lxiii (1957–58), pp. 47–61. The studies of Henri Pirenne were largely focused on urban developments at old-established Roman and episcopal sites, but there are a few references to plantations: e.g. *Medieval Cities*, trans. F. D. Halsey (Princeton, 1925), p. 156. L. Verriest, *Le Régime Seigneurial dans le Comté de Hainaut* (Louvain, 1956), pp. 48–72, has an account of plantations, with plans. C-J. Joset, *Les Villes au Pays de Luxembourg* (Univ. de Louvain Recueil de Travaux d'Hist. de Philol., 3rd ser., v (1940)), has references to plantations at pp. 70, 74, 78, 111 and 164. A. de Smet, "L'origine des ports du Zwin", in F. L. Ganshof, ed., *Études d'Histoire dédiées à la mémoire de Henri Pirenne* (Brussels, 1937), pp. 125–142, brings together information on Damme-by-Bruges and other projects nearby; see also J. Dhondt, "Développement Urbain et Initiative Comtale" *Rev. du Nord*, xxx (1948), pp. 133–156.

SWITZERLAND

There were extensive town plantations in both the German- and the French-speaking parts of modern Switzerland. The former, broadly speaking, has towns similar to those of the Rhine valley and southern Germany, with Zahringian affiliations: the latter has towns built under the influence of the counts of Savoy. The Savoyan tradition has already been discussed above, pp. 93–95, since it reached as far as Edward I's towns in north Wales, and references to Mr. A. J. Taylor's work will be found in the footnotes. The charters of the *villes neuves* are printed in F. Forel, ed., *Les Chartes Communales du Pays de Vaud dès l'an 1214 à l'an 1527* (Méms. et Docs. pub. par la Soc. d'Hist. de la Suisse Romande, xxvii (1872)). See also J. Bugnion, *Les villes de franchises au Pays de Vaud, 1144–1350* (1952); H. Amman and K. Schib, *Atlas Historique de la Suisse* (Aarau, 1958), plate 17. A monograph is Roger Deglon, *Yverdon au Moyen Age* (Lausanne, 1949). Plans of planted towns (including many now deserted) are given in L. Blondel, *Châteaux de l'Ancien Diocèse de Genève* (Méms. et Docs. pub. par la Soc. d'Hist. et d'Arch. de Genève, sér. in 4, vii (1956)). There are very informed accounts of towns in M. Godet, H. Turler and V. Attinger, *Dictionnaire Historique et Bibliographique de la Suisse* (Lausanne, 1921–24, 8 vols.).

A recent volume of air photographs is prefaced by a number of long essays, in the course of which the extent of town plantation in both French- and German-speaking Switzerland is clearly exposed, with distribution maps, and with plans to match the aerial views. This analysis also shows that all except three of the Swiss plantations date from before 1344, and that the last plantation was in 1384, a similar chronology to that for England, Wales and Gascony (Paul Hofer in Hans Boesch and Paul Hofer, *Flugbild der Schweizer Stadt* (Bern, 1963), pp. 85–144). Hans Bernouilli, *Die Stadt und Ihr Boden* (Zurich, 1946), is concerned not only with Switzerland but with the Germanic towns in general.

Although most of the bourgs lie in the lowlands of Switzerland where there is a good deal of industry, the preservation of the town plan and many of its medieval buildings has been most generously supported by the local authorities. As an education for Englishmen brought up in modern towns, the Swiss bourgs rank with the bastides of Gascony. The deserted sites, to which the plans in Blondel are the best introduction, are well worth visiting. A Land Rover and thorn-proof clothing are of assistance.

HOLLAND

G. L. Burke, *The Making of Dutch Towns* (1956), is an excellent introduction to the process of urbanisation that accompanied the reclamation of land from the waters. Chapter III is specifically devoted to planted towns, but all the chapters have first-rate plans and photographs. For more plans see H. Brugmans and C. H. Peters, *Oud Nederlandsche Steden* (Leiden, 1909), i, pp. 194–203.

GERMANY

The massive eastward colonisation of the twelfth and thirteenth centuries produced urban plantations on a scale unsurpassed in Europe. German scholars have produced a substantial amount of work on this process and on the biographies and plans of individual towns. A useful approach in English is offered by Professor R. E. Dickinson, in "The Development and Distribution of the Medieval German Town", *Geography*, xxvii (1942), pp. 9–21 and 47–53, especially the distribution map (p. 49, after Kötzschke and Ebert) and the 59-item bibliography. Individual plans are given in his "Morphology of the Medieval German Town", *Geog. Rev.*, xxxv (1945), pp. 74–97. More plans and bibliographies will be found in *West European City* (1951). The basic works in German are E. J. Siedler, *Märkischer Städtebau im Mittelalter* (Berlin, 1914); E. Hamm, *Die Städtegrundungen der Herzöge von Zähringen in südwest-deutschland* (Freibourg, 1932); E. Hamm, *Die Deutsche Stadt im Mittelalter* (Stuttgart, 1935); R. Kötzschke and W. Ebert, *Geschichte der ostdeutschen Kolonisation* (Leipzig, 1937); H. Bernouilli, *Die Stadt und Ihr Boden* (Zurich, 1946); H. Planitz, *Die Deutsche Stadt im Mittelalter* (Graz-Cologne, 1954).

POLAND

A collection of studies from a Paris symposium has been edited by Pierre Francastel, *Les Origines des Villes Polonaises* (Paris, 1960); see also A. Gieysztor "Le Origini delle città nella Polonia medioevale", *Studi in Onore di Armando Sapori* (Milan, 1957), i, pp. 129–145.

SCANDINAVIA

See J. Leighley, *The Towns of Malardalen in Sweden* (Univ. of California Publns. in Geog., iii (1928)); and R. E. Dickinson, *West European City* (1951), pp. 13–28 and 398–411; *Camb. Econ. Hist. of Europe*, ii (1952), pp. 188–189 and 223.

CENTRAL EUROPE

E. A. Gutkind, *Urban Development in Central Europe* (New York, 1964), has some relevant material.

General Index

by JOAN NEWISS, B.A., A.L.A.

Note: The Gazetteers for England, Wales and Gascony have separate alphabetical indexes to their place-names on pp. 387–93 (England), pp. 532–34 (Wales), and pp. 575–79 (Gascony). These entries are not indexed again below, but places mentioned in Appendices III and IV do appear. The subject-matter of the Gazetteers is not usually indexed.

Page numbers in italics indicate references to Figures, Plates and Tables; those in **bold type** indicate the more important passages.

LP/I/69